INTRODUCTION

 S0-BOL-396

This study is designed to aid persons preparing for the following FAA written exams:

Instrument Rating — Airplane

Instrument Rating — Rotorcraft-Helicopter

Instrument Rating — Airplane Additional

Instrument Rating — Rotorcraft-Helicopter Additional

Flight Instructor — Instrument — Airplane

Flight Instructor — Instrument — Rotorcraft-Helicopter

Flight Instructor — Instrument — Airplane Additional

Flight Instructor — Instrument — Rotorcraft-Helicopter Additional

Ground Instructor — Instrument

Instrument Rating — Foreign Pilot

The questions in this book are a reproduction of the Instrument Rating Question Book (FAA-T-8080-7) published by the FAA in early 1984. This book is to be the instrument test book by fall of 1984. Except for pen and ink changes that may be made, questions in the guide will be *exact duplicates* of those in the FAA test book.

USING THIS BOOK

Sixteen years of experience have shown us that there is *no substitute* for competent ground school instruction and dedicated study on the part of the applicant. Rote memorization can never replace an in-depth knowledge of the subject matter. This book should be used primarily to review the effectiveness of one's ground training.

Many of the questions in the book apply only to helicopter or airplane operations. Appendix 3 lists the question categories and the FAA's reference source for each question. Answer those questions relevant to your test (airplane or helicopter). We have found certain questions which have no correct answer choice. These are deleted from Appendix 3.

It is possible that you will be asked one or more of the deleted questions on your test. If this happens, just mark any of the four choices and you will receive credit for a correct answer. Make sure that you do answer the question, because no response will be graded as an incorrect answer choice. As new question selection sheets are issued to examiners, invalid questions will cease to appear on the test.

The correct answer to all questions, references and short explanations are contained in Appendix A.

We at ASA hope you find this publication to be a useful training aid. Good luck in your flying endeavors.

TABLE OF CONTENTS

7001. What minimum flight hours in the past 6 months are required to maintain instrument currency in an airplane?

1—3 hours of actual or simulated instrument time in the same class airplane.
2—3 hours of actual or simulated instrument time in an airplane.
3—3 hours of actual instrument time.
4—3 hours of instrument time in IFR conditions in the same category aircraft.

7002. What minimum conditions are necessary for the instrument approaches required for IFR currency?

1—The approaches may be made in an aircraft, approved instrument ground trainer, or any combination of these.
2—At least three approaches must be made in an aircraft.
3—At least three approaches must be made in the same category of aircraft to be flown.
4—At least three approaches must be made in the same category and class of aircraft to be flown.

7003. What additional approaches, if any, must you perform to maintain IFR currency in a helicopter? Within the past 6 months you have accomplished:

one approach in a helicopter
two approaches in an airplane
two approaches in an approved simulator

1—None.
2—One approach in an airplane, helicopter, or approved simulator.
3—Two approaches in a helicopter and one approach in an approved simulator.
4—Five approaches in a helicopter.

7004. A pilot's recent IFR experience expires on July 1 of this year. What is the latest date the pilot can meet the IFR experience requirement without having to take an instrument competency check?

1—December 31, this year.
2—June 30, next year.
3—July 31, this year.
4—September 30, this year.

7005. What additional approaches, if any, must you perform to maintain IFR currency in a helicopter? Within the past 6 months you have accomplished:

two approaches in a helicopter
two approaches in an airplane
two approaches in a simulator

1—None.
2—One in a helicopter.
3—One in either a helicopter or an airplane.
4—One in a helicopter and one in an airplane.

7006. An instrument rated pilot who has not logged any instrument time in 1 year or more, cannot serve as pilot in command under IFR, unless he/she

1—completes the required 6 hours of instrument time under actual or simulated conditions, and six instrument approaches of any kind.
2—completes the required 6 hours and six approaches, followed by an instrument competency check given by an FAA designated examiner.
3—passes an instrument competency check in the category of aircraft involved, given by an approved FAA examiner, instrument instructor, or FAA inspector.
4—passes an instrument competency check in the category of aircraft involved followed by 6 hours and six instrument approaches, 3 of those hours in the category of aircraft involved.

7007. How long does a pilot remain current for IFR flight after successfully completing an instrument competency check if no further IFR flights are made?

1—90 days.
2—2 years.
3—6 months.
4—12 months.

7008. To satisfy the IFR recency of experience requirement regarding instrument approaches, the pilot must have made at least

1—six instrument approaches within the past 6 months, three of which must have been in the category of aircraft to be flown.
2—six instrument approaches within the past 6 months in an aircraft or approved instrument ground trainer.
3—three instrument approaches within the past 90 days in the same category and class aircraft to be flown.
4—six instrument approaches within the past 6 months, three of which must have been in actual or simulated instrument flight in an airplane.

7009. After your recent IFR experience lapses, how much time do you have before you must pass an instrument competency check to act as pilot in command under IFR?

1—6 months.
2—90 days.
3—12 months.
4—24 months.

7010. To meet the minimum required instrument experience to remain current for IFR operations, you must accomplish during the past 6 months at least

1—six instrument approaches and 6 hours of instrument time; 3 of the 6 hours in flight in the category of aircraft to be flown.
2—six instrument approaches and 6 hours of instrument time in any aircraft.
3—six instrument approaches, three of which must be in the same category and class of aircraft to be flown, and 6 hours of instrument time in any aircraft.
4—six instrument approaches, three of which must be in the same category of aircraft to be flown; and 6 hours of instrument time, 3 hours of which must be in the same category of aircraft to be flown.

7011. What minimum instrument time is required within the last 6 months in order to be current for IFR?

1—6 hours; at least 3 of the 6 hours in the category of aircraft to be flown.
2—6 hours; at least 3 of the 6 hours in actual instrument conditions.
3—6 hours in the same category aircraft.
4—6 hours in the same category aircraft, and at least 3 of the 6 hours in actual conditions.

7012. What minimum conditions are necessary for the instrument approaches required for IFR currency in an airplane or helicopter?

1—A minimum of six in any approved instrument ground trainer or aircraft within the past 6 months.
2—A minimum of six, at least three of which must be in an aircraft within the past 6 months.
3—A minimum of six in an aircraft within the past 6 months.
4—A minimum of six in an aircraft, at least three of which must be in the same category within the past 6 months.

7013. How may a pilot satisfy the recent instrument experience requirement necessary to act as pilot in command in IFR weather conditions?

1—Log 6 hours instrument time under actual or simulated IFR conditions within the last 6 months, including six instrument approaches of any kind. Three of the 6 hours must be in–flight in the category of aircraft involved.
2—Log 6 hours instrument time under actual or simulated IFR conditions within the last 6 months, including at least three instrument approaches of any kind. Three of the 6 hours must be in–flight in the category of aircraft involved.
3—Log 6 hours instrument time under actual or simulated IFR conditions within the last 3 months, including at least six instrument approaches of any kind. Three of the 6 hours must be in–flight in any category aircraft.
4—Log 6 hours instrument time under actual or simulated IFR conditions within the last 6 months, including six instrument approaches of any kind. All 6 hours must be in the category of aircraft involved.

7014. What additional instrument time, if any, must you acquire to maintain IFR currency in a helicopter? Within the past 6 months you have accomplished:

1 hour actual IFR and 1 hour simulated IFR in a helicopter
2 hours actual IFR in an airplane
1 hour in an approved simulator

1—None.
2—1 hour actual or simulated IFR in a helicopter.
3—1 hour actual or simulated IFR in an aircraft.
4—1 hour actual or simulated IFR in a helicopter and 2 hours in a simulator.

7015. Which additional IFR experience allows you to meet the recent IFR experience requirements to act as pilot in command of a helicopter under IFR? Your present instrument experience within the past 6 months is:

2 hours and one instrument approach in an approved simulator
4 hours simulated IFR and one instrument approach in an airplane

1—3 hours of simulated instrument flight time in a helicopter and four instrument approaches in a simulator.
2—1 hour of simulated instrument flight time and four instrument approaches in a helicopter.
3—Three instrument approaches in a helicopter.
4—Four instrument approaches in an airplane or helicopter.

7016. Which additional IFR experience allows you to meet the recent IFR experience requirements to act as pilot in command of a helicopter under IFR? Your present instrument experience within the past 6 months:

1 hour and one instrument approach in an approved simulator.
2 hours and two instrument approaches in an airplane

1—Three instrument approaches in an approved simulator and 3 hours of simulated instrument flight time in a helicopter.
2—3 hours of actual instrument flight time and three instrument approaches in any aircraft.
3—3 hours of simulated or actual instrument flight time in any aircraft.
4—Three instrument approaches in a helicopter.

7017. What additional approaches, if any, must you perform to maintain IFR currency in a helicopter? Within the past 6 months you have accomplished:

two approaches in a helicopter
two approaches in an airplane
one approach in an approved simulator

1—None.
2—One approach in an airplane, helicopter, or approved simulator.
3—One approach in a helicopter and two approaches in an approved simulator.
4—Four approaches in a helicopter.

7018. Which additional IFR experience allows you to meet the recent IFR experience requirements to act as pilot in command of a helicopter under IFR? Your present instrument experience within the past 6 months:

1 hour and two instrument approaches in an approved simulator
1 hour and three instrument approaches in an airplane

1—One instrument approach and 4 hours of simulated instrument flight time in a helicopter.
2—Three instrument approaches in a helicopter.
3—Three instrument approaches and 3 hours of simulated instrument flight time in a helicopter.
4—4 hours of simulated instrument flight time in a helicopter.

7019. Which additional IFR experience allows you to meet the recent IFR experience requirements to act as pilot in command of a helicopter under IFR? Your present instrument experience within the past 6 months:

1 hour simulated IFR and two instrument approaches in a helicopter
1 hour actual IFR and three instrument approaches in an airplane

1—1 hour of simulated instrument flight time in a helicopter and three instrument approaches in a simulator.
2—2 hours of simulated instrument flight time in a helicopter and one instrument approach in an airplane.
3—One instrument approach in an approved simulator, 2 hours of simulated instrument flight time in a helicopter, and 2 hours actual IFR in an airplane.
4—Three instrument approaches in a helicopter and 4 hours of simulated instrument flight time in any aircraft.

7020. What additional instrument time, if any, must you acquire to maintain IFR currency in a helicopter? Within the past 6 months you have accomplished:

1 hour actual IFR conditions and 2 hours simulated IFR conditions in a helicopter
1 hour actual instrument time in an airplane
1 hour IFR in an approved simulator

1—None.
2—2 hours in a helicopter or approved simulator.
3—1 hour in an airplane, approved simulator, or helicopter.
4—3 hours in a helicopter.

7021. Which additional IFR experience allows you to meet the recent IFR experience requirements to act as pilot in command of a helicopter under IFR? Your present instrument experience within the past 6 months:

2 hours simulated IFR and one instrument approach in a helicopter
1 hour and two instrument approaches in an approved simulator
1 hour actual IFR and two instrument approaches in an airplane

1—One instrument approach in a helicopter and 1 hour of simulated instrument flight time in a helicopter.
2—1 hour of simulated instrument flight time in each, a helicopter and an airplane, and one instrument approach in a simulator.
3—Three instrument approaches and 2 hours of simulated instrument flight time in either a helicopter or a simulator.
4—Two instrument approaches in a helicopter and 2 hours of simulated instrument flight time in any aircraft.

7022. What additional flight hours within the past 6 months are required to maintain IFR currency in a helicopter if you already have 3 hours in an instrument simulator?

1—3 hours of actual or simulated instrument time in the same type helicopter.
2—3 hours of actual or simulated instrument time in a helicopter.
3—3 hours of actual instrument time in any rotorcraft class.
4—3 hours of simulated instrument time in any aircraft.

7023. Which additional IFR experience allows you to meet the recent IFR experience requirements to act as pilot in command of a helicopter under IFR? Your present instrument experience within the past 6 months:

3 hours and one instrument approach in a simulator
3 hours and one instrument approach in an airplane

1—Four instrument approaches in an approved simulator and 3 hours of simulated instrument flight time in any aircraft.
2—3 hours of simulated or actual instrument flight time in a helicopter and four instrument approaches in an airplane or helicopter.
3—Three instrument approaches in a helicopter.
4—Two instrument approaches in an airplane and three instrument approaches in a helicopter.

7024. Which additional IFR experience allows you to meet the recent IFR experience requirements to act as pilot in command of a helicopter under IFR? Your present instrument experience within the past 6 months:

4 hours and one instrument approach in a simulator
1 hour and two instrument approaches in an airplane

1—2 hours of simulated or actual instrument flight time and two instrument approaches in a helicopter.
2—1 hour of simulated instrument flight time in a helicopter and three instrument approaches in a helicopter.
3—1 hour of simulated instrument flight time and three instrument approaches in any aircraft.
4—3 hours of simulated instrument flight time in a helicopter and three instrument approaches in a simulator.

7025. Which additional IFR experience allows you to meet the recent IFR experience requirements to act as pilot in command of a helicopter under IFR? Your present instrument experience within the past 6 months:

2 hours and three instrument approaches in an approved simulator
2 hours and one instrument approach in an airplane

1—3 hours of simulated or actual instrument flight time in a helicopter.
2—2 hours of simulated instrument flight time and two instrument approaches in a helicopter.
3—3 hours of simulated or actual instrument flight time in a helicopter and two instrument approaches in an approved simulator.
4—2 hours of simulated instrument flight time and two instrument approaches in any aircraft or approved simulator.

7026. What additional instrument time, if any, must you acquire to maintain IFR currency in a helicopter? Within the past 6 months you have accomplished:

2 hours simulated IFR in a helicopter
2 hours actual IFR in an airplane
4 hours in an approved simulator

1—None.
2—1 hour in a helicopter.
3—1 hour in either a helicopter or an airplane.
4—1 hour in each, a helicopter and an airplane.

7027. What minimum instrument time in the past 6 months meet the requirement to maintain IFR currency in a helicopter?

1—3 hours of actual or simulated instrument time in the same type helicopter.
2—3 hours of actual or simulated IFR in a helicopter.
3—3 hours of actual or simulated IFR in a helicopter and 3 hours in an approved simulator.
4—6 hours in an approved simulator.

7028. What minimum conditions are necessary for the instrument approaches required for IFR currency in a helicopter?

1—Three must be made in a helicopter.
2—Three must be made in a rotorcraft category.
3—Three must be made in an aircraft.
4—All may be made in an airplane, helicopter, or approved simulator.

7029. How long does a helicopter rated pilot remain current for IFR after successfully completing an instrument competency check if no further IFR flights are made?

1—90 days.
2—120 days.
3—6 months.
4—12 months.

7030. An instrument competency check must be passed prior to acting as pilot in command under IFR, if that pilot has not met the recent experience requirements of FAR Part 61, within the past

1—3 months.
2—6 months.
3—9 months.
4—12 months.

7031. Which operation requires an instrument-rated pilot in command?

1—Special VFR in Group I TCA's.
2—VFR in a restricted area.
3—VFR On Top.
4—DVFR and Oceanic Routes.

7032. Under which condition must the pilot in command of a civil aircraft have at least an instrument rating?

1—When operating in the continental control area.
2—For a flight in VFR conditions while on an IFR flight plan.
3—For any flight above an altitude of 1,200 ft. AGL, when the visibility is less than 3 mi.
4—When operating above a solid overcast.

7033. FAA Deletion.

7034. The pilot in command of a civil aircraft must have an instrument rating only when operating

1—an aircraft which is controlled solely by reference to flight instruments, regardless of weather conditions.
2—under instrument flight rules in controlled airspace and in a positive control area or positive control route segment.
3—under instrument flight rules, in weather conditions less than the minimum for VFR flight, and in a positive control area or route segment.
4—in weather conditions less than the minimum prescribed for VFR flight.

7035. Under which condition are you required to have an instrument rating for flight in VFR weather conditions?

1—Flight through a military operations area.
2—VFR in a TCA.
3—Flight into an ADIZ.
4—Flight in a positive control area.

7036. Under which condition may you act as pilot in command of a helicopter under IFR?

Your certificates and ratings: Private Pilot Certificate with ASEL and airplane instrument, rotorcraft category, and helicopter class rating.

1—Meet the recent helicopter IFR experience requirements.
2—Acquire a helicopter ATP certificate with VFR restrictions.
3—Acquire a helicopter instrument rating and meet IFR currency requirements.
4—Be accompanied by a second in command who is instrument rated.

7037. To carry passengers for hire in an airplane on cross-country flights of more than 50 nautical miles from the departure airport the pilot in command is required to hold at least a Commercial Pilot Certificate and

1—a Category A pilot authorization.
2—a Category II pilot authorization.
3—a First-Class Medical Certificate.
4—an instrument pilot rating.

7038. Which limitation is imposed on the holder of a commercial pilot certificate if that person does not hold an instrument rating?

1—That person is limited to private pilot privileges at night.
2—The carrying of passengers or property for hire on cross-country flights at night is limited to a radius of 50 nautical miles.
3—The carrying of passengers for hire on cross-country flights is limited to 50 nautical miles and the carrying of passengers for hire at night is prohibited.
4—The carrying of passengers for hire on cross-country flights is limited to 50 nautical miles for night flights, but not limited for day flights.

7039. You intend to carry passengers for hire on a night VFR flight in a single-engine airplane within a 25-mile radius of the departure airport. You are required to possess at least which rating(s)?

1—An Airline Transport Pilot Certificate with a single-engine land rating.
2—A Commercial Pilot Certificate with a single-engine land rating.
3—A Commercial Pilot Certificate with a single-engine and instrument (airplane) rating.
4—A Private Pilot Certificate with a single-engine land and instrument airplane rating.

7040. A certificated commercial pilot who carries passengers for hire in an airplane at night is required to have at least

1—a Third-Class Medical Certificate that was issued within the preceding 12 calendar months.
2—a type rating if the airplane is of the multiengine class.
3—a First-Class Medical Certificate.
4—an airplane instrument pilot rating.

7041. Under which condition may you act as pilot in command of a helicopter in IFR conditions?

Your certificates and ratings: Private Pilot Certificate with AMEL and airplane instrument, rotorcraft category rating, and helicopter class rating.

1—If a certificated helicopter instrument flight instructor is on board.
2—If you meet the recent helicopter IFR experience requirements.
3—If you acquire an Airline Transport Pilot—Airplane Certificate.
4—If you acquire a helicopter instrument rating and meet IFR currency requirements.

7042. Do regulations permit you to act as pilot in command of a helicopter in IFR conditions if you hold a Private Pilot Certificate with ASEL, airplane instrument rating, rotorcraft category, and helicopter class rating?

1—Yes; if you comply with the recent IFR experience requirements for a helicopter.
2—No; you must hold either an unrestricted Airline Transport Pilot—Helicopter Certificate or a helicopter instrument rating.
3—No; however, you may do so if you hold an Airline Transport Pilot—Helicopter Certificate, limited to VFR.
4—Yes; if the second in command holds an airplane or helicopter instrument rating.

7043. Before beginning any flight under IFR, the pilot in command must become familiar with all available information concerning that flight. In addition, the pilot must

1—list an alternate airport on the flight plan and become familiar with the instrument approaches to that airport.
2—list an alternate airport on the flight plan and confirm adequate takeoff and landing performance at the destination airport.
3—be familiar with all instrument approaches at the destination airport.
4—be familiar with the runway lengths at airports of intended use, and the alternatives available if the flight cannot be completed.

7044. What are the minimum fuel requirements for a flight in IFR conditions, if the first airport of intended landing is forecast to have a 1,500-foot ceiling and 3 mi. visibility at flight planned ETA? Fuel to fly to the first airport of intended landing,

1—and fly thereafter for 30 min. at normal cruising speed.
2—and fly thereafter for 45 min. at normal cruising speed.
3—fly to the alternate, and fly thereafter for 45 min. at normal cruising speed.
4—fly to the alternate, and fly thereafter for 30 min. at normal cruising speed.

7045. When an alternate airport is required on the flight plan, you must have sufficient fuel to complete the flight to the first airport of intended landing, fly to the alternate, and thereafter fly for at least

1—30 min. at normal cruising speed.
2—45 min. at holding speed; then make a normal instrument approach.
3—45 min. at normal cruising speed.
4—30 min. at normal cruising speed; then make a normal instrument approach.

7046. What are the fuel requirements for an IFR flight in a helicopter when an alternate airport is not required?

1—Enough fuel to complete the flight to the first airport of intended landing.
2—Enough fuel to complete the flight to the first airport of intended landing and fly after that for 30 min.
3—Enough fuel to complete the flight to the first airport of intended landing and fly after that for 45 min. at cruising speed.
4—Enough fuel to complete the flight to the first airport of intended landing, make an approach, and fly thereafter for 45 minutes at cruising speed.

7047. Who is responsible for determining that the altimeter system has been checked and found to meet FAR requirements for a particular instrument flight?

1—Owner.
2—Operator.
3—A certificated mechanic.
4—Pilot in command.

7048. A coded transponder equipped with altitude reporting capability is required in all controlled airspace

1—except control zones.
2—above 12,500 ft. MSL, excluding at and below 2,500 ft. AGL.
3—above 2,500 ft. above the surface.
4—below 10,000 ft. MSL, excluding at and below 2,500 ft. AGL.

7049. In the 48 contiguous states, excluding the airspace at or below 2,500 ft. AGL, an operable coded transponder equipped with Mode C capability is required in all controlled airspace above

1—12,500 ft. MSL.
2—14,500 ft. MSL.
3—FL180.
4—FL240.

7050. When must an operational check on the aircraft VOR equipment be accomplished to operate under IFR?

1—Within the preceding 30 days.
2—Within the preceding 10 days or 10 hours flight time.
3—Within the preceding 30 days or 30 hours flight time.
4—Within the preceding 60 days.

7051. What record shall be made in the aircraft log or other permanent record by the pilot making the VOR operational check?

1—The date, frequency and bearing reading of VOR or VOT, tach reading, and signature.
2—The date, place, bearing error, and signature.
3—The date, frequency of VOR or VOT, number of flight hours since last check, and signature.
4—The date, place, satisfactory or unsatisfactory, and signature.

7052. Which entry, in addition to date and signature, shall be recorded by the person performing a VOR operational check?

1—Approval or disapproval of the VOR receiver and the frequency used.
2—Frequency, radial and facility used, and bearing error.
3—Flight hours and number of days since last check and bearing error.
4—Place and bearing error.

7053. Which of the following data must be recorded in the aircraft log or other appropriate log by a pilot making a VOR operational check for IFR operations?

1—VOR name or identification, date of check, amount of bearing error, and signature.
2—Place of operational check, amount of bearing error, date of check, and signature.
3—Date of check, VOR name or identification, place of operational check, and amount of bearing error.
4—Date of check, location of check, amount of bearing error, and model type VOR receiver.

7054. When making an airborne VOR check, what is the maximum allowable tolerance between the two indicators of a dual VOR system (units independent of each other except the antenna)?

1—4° between the two indicated bearings to a VOR.
2—Plus or minus 4° when set to identical radials of a VOR.
3—6° between the two indicated radials of a VOR.
4—4° when set to identical radials of a VOR.

7055. What is the oxygen requirement for an unpressurized airplane at 15,000 ft.?

1—All occupants must use oxygen for the entire time at this altitude.
2—Crew must start using oxygen at 12,000 ft. and passengers at 15,000 ft.
3—Crew must use oxygen for the entire time above 14,000 ft. and passengers must be provided supplemental oxygen only above 15,000 ft.
4—Crew must start using oxygen at 12,500 ft. and passengers must be provided supplemental oxygen at 14,000 ft.

7056. What is the maximum cabin pressure altitude at which a pilot can fly for longer than 30 min. without using supplemental oxygen?

1—10,000 ft.
2—10,500 ft.
3—12,000 ft.
4—12,500 ft.

7057. What is the maximum IFR altitude you may fly in an unpressurized airplane without providing passengers with supplemental oxygen?

1—12,500 ft.
2—14,000 ft.
3—15,000 ft.
4—18,000 ft.

7058. If an unpressurized aircraft is operated above 12,500 ft. MSL, but not more than 14,000 ft. MSL, for a period of 2 hr. 20 min., how long during that time is the minimum flightcrew required to use supplemental oxygen?

1—2 hr. 20 min.
2—1 hr. 20 min.
3—1 hr. 50 min.
4—Supplemental oxygen is not required.

7059. During a stabilized climbing turn at constant rate, the instruments which indicate the correct pitch and bank are the

1—airspeed indicator and directional gyro.
2—vertical speed indicator and turn–and–slip indicator.
3—altimeter and turn–and–slip indicator.
4—flight indicator and turn–and–slip indicator.

7060. You check your flight instruments while taxiing to the runup area and find that the VSI (vertical speed indicator) indicates a descent of 100 ft./min. In this case, you

1—must return to the parking area and have the instrument corrected by an authorized instrument repairman.
2—may take off and use 100 ft. descent as the zero indication.
3—may not take off until the instrument is corrected by either the pilot or a mechanic.
4—may take off without any correction because this instrument is used very little during instrument flight.

7061. What minimum navigation equipment is required for IFR flight?

1—NAV equipment compatible with ground facilities en route.
2—VOR/LOC receiver, transponder, and DME.
3—VOR receiver and, if in ARTS III environment, a coded transponder equipped for altitude reporting.
4—Navigation equipment appropriate to the ground facilities to be used.

7062. To meet the requirements for flight under IFR, a helicopter must be equipped with certain operable instruments and equipment. One of those required is

1—DME (distance measuring equipment).
2—a clock with sweep–second pointer or digital presentation.
3—a radar altimeter.
4—an ELT (emergency locator transmitter).

7063. A helicopter being operated under IFR is required to have, in addition to the equipment required for VFR and night, at least

1—a radar altimeter.
2—distance measuring equipment.
3—dual VOR receivers.
4—a slip–skid indicator.

7064. A helicopter operated under IFR is required to have which of the following?

1—Radar altimeter.
2—Dual VOR system.
3—Gyroscopic direction indicator.
4—Flight director system.

7065. Where is DME required for instrument flight?

1—At or above 24,000 ft. MSL if VOR navigational equipment is required.
2—In positive control areas.
3—Above 18,000 ft. MSL.
4—In the continental control area if VOR navigational equipment is used.

7066. An aircraft altimeter system test and inspection must be accomplished within

1—12 calendar months.
2—18 calendar months.
3—24 calendar months.
4—48 calendar months.

7067. Which checks and inspections of flight instruments or instrument systems must be accomplished before an airplane can be flown under IFR?

1—VOR within 30 days, altimeter systems within 24 calendar months, and transponder within 24 calendar months.
2—ELT test within 30 days, altimeter systems within 12 calendar months, and transponder within 24 calendar months.
3—VOR within 24 calendar months, transponder within 24 calendar months, and altimeter system within 12 calendar months.
4—Airspeed indicator within 24 calendar months, altimeter system within 24 calendar months, and transponder within 12 calendar months.

7068. Your airplane had the static pressure system and altimeter tested and inspected on January 5, of this year, and was found to comply with FAA standards. These systems must be reinspected and approved for use in controlled airspace under IFR by

1—January 5, next year.
2—January 5, 2 years hence.
3—January 31, 2 years hence.
4—January 31, next year.

7069. If you depart from an airport located outside controlled airspace during IFR conditions, you must file an IFR flight plan and receive a clearance before

1—takeoff.
2—entering IFR conditions.
3—entering controlled airspace.
4—arriving at the en route portion of the flight.

7070. Operation in which airspace requires filing an IFR flight plan?

1—Any airspace when the visibility is less than 1 mi.
2—Any airspace above 700 ft. AGL, or 1,200 ft. AGL where designated, if the visibility is less than 1 mi.
3—Controlled airspace with IFR weather conditions and positive control area.
4—Positive control area, continental control area, and all other airspace, if the visibility is less than 1 mi.

7071. When is an IFR clearance required during VFR weather conditions?

1—When operating in the continental control area and a positive control area.
2—When operating in a positive control area.
3—When operating in airspace above 14,500 ft.
4—When practicing instrument approaches.

7072. To operate an aircraft under IFR, a flight plan must have been filed and an ATC clearance received prior to

1—takeoff.
2—controlling the aircraft solely by use of instruments.
3—entering weather conditions in any airspace.
4—entering controlled airspace.

7073. To operate under IFR below 18,000 ft., a pilot must file an IFR flight plan and receive an appropriate ATC clearance prior to

1—entering controlled airspace.
2—entering weather conditions below VFR minimums.
3—takeoff.
4—flying by reference to instruments in controlled airspace.

7074. Prior to which operation must an IFR flight plan be filed and an appropriate ATC clearance received?

1—Flying by reference to instruments in controlled airspace.
2—Entering controlled airspace when IFR weather conditions exist.
3—Takeoff when IFR weather conditions exist.
4—Entering weather conditions below VFR minimums.

7075. When is an IFR flight plan required?

1—When the visibility is less than 1 mi. in uncontrolled airspace and less than 3 mi. in controlled airspace.
2—When less than VFR conditions exist in either controlled or uncontrolled airspace and in positive controlled airspace.
3—In all controlled airspace when conditions are below VFR, in positive control airspace, and in defense zone airspace.
4—In controlled airspace when IFR conditions exist and in positive control areas or positive control route segments.

7076. What minimum conditions must exist at your destination to avoid listing an alternate airport on an IFR flight plan when a standard instrument approach procedure is available?

1—From 2 hours before to 2 hours after ETA, forecast ceiling 2,000, and visibility 2-1/2 mi.
2—From 2 hours before to 2 hours after ETA, forecast ceiling 3,000, and visibility 3 mi.
3—From 1 hour before to 1 hour after ETA, forecast ceiling 3,000, and visibility 2-1/2 mi.
4—From 1 hour before to 1 hour after ETA, forecast ceiling 2,000, and visibility 3 mi.

7077. Under what condition are you not required to list an alternate airport on an IFR flight plan for an IFR flight in a helicopter?

1—When the ceiling is forecast to be at least 1,000 ft. above the lowest of the MEA, MOCA, or initial approach altitude within 2 hours of your ETA at the destination airport.
2—When the weather reports or forecasts indicate the ceiling and visibility will be at least 2,000 ft. and 3 mi. for 1 hour before to 1 hour after your ETA at the destination airport.
3—When the ceiling is forecast to be at least 1,000 ft. above the lowest of the MEA, MOCA, or initial approach altitude and the visibility is 2 mi. more than the minimum landing visibility within 2 hours of your ETA at the destination airport.
4—When the weather forecast indicates a ceiling of at least 1,000 ft. and a visibility of 3 mi. or more within 2 hours of your ETA at the destination airport.

7078. Is an alternate airport required for an IFR flight from RIC (Richmond) to ATL (Atlanta Hartsfield) if the proposed ETA is 1930Z?

GIVEN: FT (Terminal Forecast) for ATL (Atlanta Hartsfield International Airport).

ATL FT AMD 1 161615 1630Z C20 BKN 6RW– VRBL 20 SCT C40 BKN OCNL 4RW– 3315. 18Z 40 SCT C100 BKN 3110 OCNL C20 BKN 6RW– CHC C10 OVC 3TRW 3310G20 AFT 21Z. 09Z MVFR CIG R..

1—An alternate is required because the ceiling could fall below 2,000 ft. within 2 hours before to 2 hours after the ETA.
2—An alternate is not required because the ceiling and visibility are forecast to remain at or above 1,000 ft. and 3 mi., respectively.
3—An alternate is required because the ceiling could fall below 3,000 ft. within 1 hour of the ETA.
4—An alternate is not required because the ceiling and visibility are forecast to be at or above 2,000 ft. and 3 mi. within 1 hour before to 1 hour after the ETA.

7079. What minimum weather conditions must be forecast for your ETA at an airport that has only a VOR approach with standard alternate minimums, for the airport to be listed as an alternate on your IFR flight plan?

1—800–foot ceiling and 1 statute mile visibility.
2—800–foot ceiling and 2 statute miles visibility.
3—1,000–foot ceiling and visibility to allow descent from MEA, approach, and landing under basic VFR.
4—600–foot ceiling and 3 statute miles visibility.

7080. What minimum weather conditions must be forecast for your ETA at an airport that has a precision approach procedure, with standard alternate minimums, in order to list it as an alternate for your IFR flight?

1—600–foot ceiling and 2 statute miles visibility at your ETA.
2—600–foot ceiling and 2 statute miles visibility from 2 hours before to 2 hours after your ETA.
3—600–foot ceiling and 3 statute miles visibility from 2 hours before to 2 hours after your ETA.
4—800–foot ceiling and 2 statute miles visibility at your ETA.

7081. What are the minimum weather conditions that must be forecast to list an airport as an alternate when the airport has no approved instrument approach procedure?

1—The ceiling and visibility at ETA, 2,000 ft. and 3 mi., respectively.
2—The ceiling and visibility from 2 hours before until 2 hours after ETA, 2,000 ft. and 3 mi., respectively.
3—The ceiling and visibility from 2 hours before until 2 hours after ETA, 1,000 ft. above the highest obstacle, and 3 mi., respectively.
4—The ceiling and visibility at ETA must allow descent from MEA, approach, and landing, under basic VFR.

7082. What standard minimums are required to list an airport as an alternate on an IFR flight plan if the airport has a VOR approach only?

1—Ceiling and visibility at ETA, 800 ft. and 2 mi., respectively.
2—Ceiling and visibility from 2 hours before until 2 hours after ETA, 800 ft. and 2 mi., respectively.
3—Ceiling and visibility at ETA, 600 ft. and 2 mi., respectively.
4—Ceiling and visibility from 2 hours before until 2 hours after ETA, 1,000 ft. and 3 mi., respectively.

7083. What is the recommended procedure for transitioning from VFR to IFR on a composite flight plan?

1—Prior to transitioning to IFR, contact the nearest FSS, close the VFR portion, and request ATC clearance.
2—Upon reaching the proposed point for change to IFR, contact the nearest FSS and cancel your VFR flight plan, then contact ARTCC and request an IFR clearance.
3—Upon reaching the proposed point for change to IFR, contact ARTCC, request your IFR clearance, and instruct them to cancel the VFR flight plan.
4—Upon reaching the proposed point for change to IFR, contact ARTCC, give a position report, and request your IFR clearance.

7084. When filing a composite flight plan where the first portion of the flight is IFR, which fix(es) should be indicated on the flight plan form?

1—All points of transition from one airway to another, fixes defining direct route segments, and the clearance limit fix.
2—Only the fix where you plan to terminate the IFR portion of the flight.
3—Only those compulsory reporting points on the IFR route segment.
4—All NAVAIDS and intersections along the route of flight.

7085. When may a pilot file a composite flight plan?

1—When requested or advised by ATC.
2—Any time a portion of the flight will be VFR.
3—Any time a landing is planned at an intermediate airport.
4—Only if the entire flight is in controlled airspace.

7086. How is your flight plan closed when your destination airport has IFR conditions and there is no control tower or FSS on the field?

1—The ARTCC controller will close your flight plan upon clearing you for the approach.
2—The ARTCC controller will close your flight plan when you report the runway in sight.
3—You may close your flight plan any time after starting the approach by contacting any FSS or ATC facility.
4—Upon landing, you must close your flight plan by radio or by telephone to any FSS or ATC facility.

7087. When may a pilot cancel the IFR flight plan prior to completing the flight?

1—Any time.
2—Any time an emergency occurs.
3—Any time a clearance may cause a deviation from FAR.
4—Only in VFR conditions outside positive control airspace.

7088. FAA Deletion.

7089. What information should be entered in block 7 of an IFR flight plan if the flight has 3 legs, each at a different altitude? (See Figure 1.)

1—Altitude for first leg.
2—Altitude for first leg and highest altitude.
3—Highest altitude.
4—All three altitudes.

7090. The time entered in block 12 (see Figure 1) for an IFR flight should be based on which fuel quantity?

1—Total fuel required for the flight.
2—Total usable fuel on board.
3—The amount of fuel required to fly to the destination airport, then to the alternate, plus a 45 min. reserve.
4—The required fuel plus enough to hold for 30 min.

7091. Which item(s) should be checked in block 1 (see Figure 1) for a composite flight plan?

1—VFR with an explanation in block 11.
2—IFR with an explanation in block 11.
3—DVFR.
4—VFR and IFR.

7092. For which speed variation should you notify ATC?

1—When the groundspeed changes more than 5 knots.
2—When the true airspeed changes more than 5 knots.
3—When the true airspeed changes 5 percent or 10 knots, whichever is greater.
4—Any time the groundspeed changes 10 MPH.

7093. Preferred IFR routes beginning with a fix indicate that departing aircraft will normally be routed to the fix via

1—the established airway(s) between the departure airport and the fix.
2—a SID, radar vectors, or direct routing.
3—direct route only.
4—any routing which the pilot considers most appropriate.

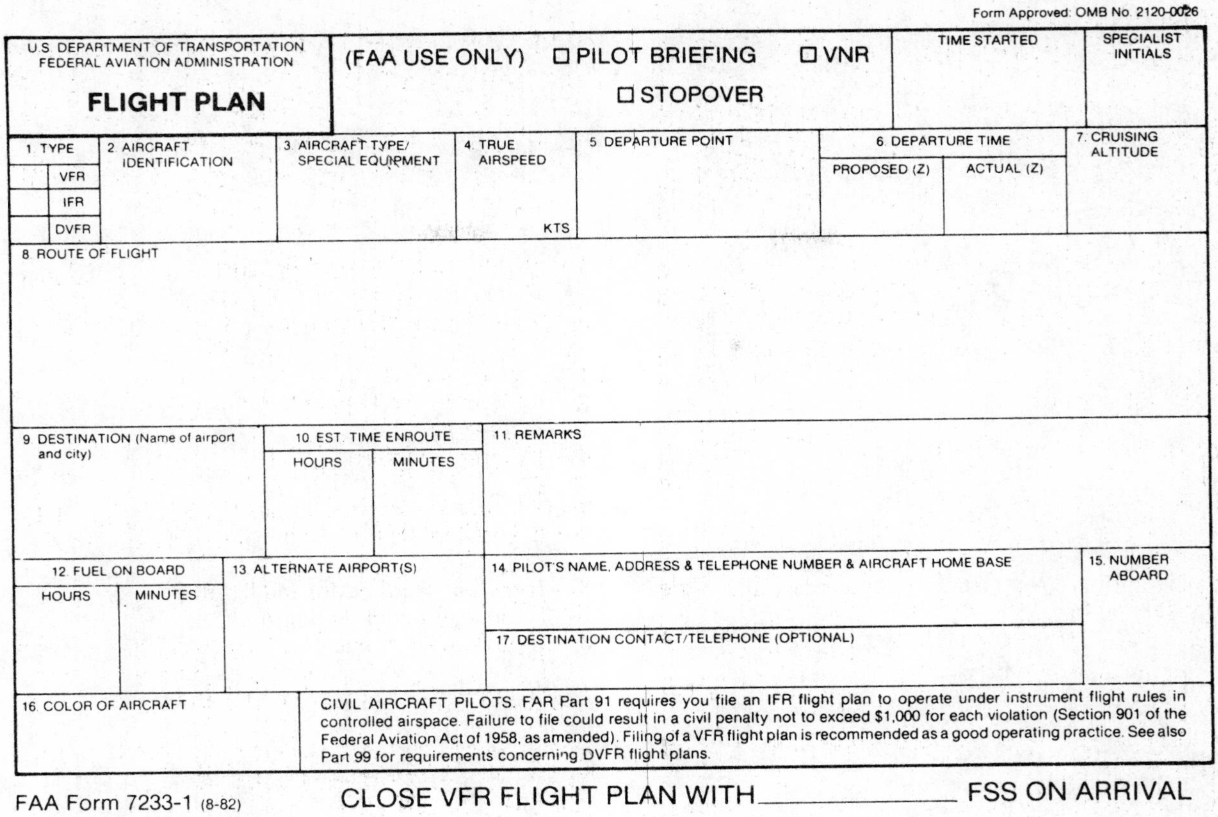

Form Approved: OMB No. 2120-0026

U.S. DEPARTMENT OF TRANSPORTATION FEDERAL AVIATION ADMINISTRATION **FLIGHT PLAN**	(FAA USE ONLY) ☐ PILOT BRIEFING ☐ VNR ☐ STOPOVER		TIME STARTED	SPECIALIST INITIALS

1. TYPE	2. AIRCRAFT IDENTIFICATION	3. AIRCRAFT TYPE/ SPECIAL EQUIPMENT	4. TRUE AIRSPEED	5. DEPARTURE POINT	6. DEPARTURE TIME		7. CRUISING ALTITUDE
VFR IFR DVFR			KTS		PROPOSED (Z)	ACTUAL (Z)	

8. ROUTE OF FLIGHT

9. DESTINATION (Name of airport and city)	10. EST. TIME ENROUTE		11. REMARKS
	HOURS	MINUTES	

12. FUEL ON BOARD		13. ALTERNATE AIRPORT(S)	14. PILOT'S NAME, ADDRESS & TELEPHONE NUMBER & AIRCRAFT HOME BASE	15. NUMBER ABOARD
HOURS	MINUTES			
			17. DESTINATION CONTACT/TELEPHONE (OPTIONAL)	

16. COLOR OF AIRCRAFT	CIVIL AIRCRAFT PILOTS. FAR Part 91 requires you file an IFR flight plan to operate under instrument flight rules in controlled airspace. Failure to file could result in a civil penalty not to exceed $1,000 for each violation (Section 901 of the Federal Aviation Act of 1958, as amended). Filing of a VFR flight plan is recommended as a good operating practice. See also Part 99 for requirements concerning DVFR flight plans.

FAA Form 7233-1 (8-82)   CLOSE VFR FLIGHT PLAN WITH_____ FSS ON ARRIVAL

Figure 1

7094. What is the recommended procedure for filing an IFR flight plan while airborne?

1—Contact ARTCC on the appropriate sector frequency and remain VFR until receipt of the clearance.
2—Contact the nearest departure control and remain VFR until receipt of the clearance.
3—Contact ARTCC on the appropriate sector frequency and request radar vectors to the destination.
4—Contact the nearest FSS and remain VFR until receipt of the clearance.

7095. Which sources of aeronautical information, when used collectively, provide the latest status of airport conditions (e.g., runway closures, runway lighting, snow conditions)?

1—Airman's Information Manual, Aeronautical Charts, and Distant (D) NOTAMS.
2—Airport Facility Directory, FDC NOTAMS, and Local (L) NOTAMS.
3—Airport Facility Directory, Distant (D) NOTAMS, and Local (L) NOTAMS.
4—Standard Instrument Approach Procedures, FDC NOTAMS, and the Airman's Information Manual.

7096. What is the purpose of FDC NOTAMS?

1—To provide the latest information on the status of navigation facilities to all FSS facilities for scheduled broadcasts.
2—To issue notices for all airports and navigation facilities in the shortest possible time.
3—To provide all information considered essential to flight safety in one publication.
4—To advise of changes in flight data which affect instrument approach procedures, aeronautical charts, and flight restrictions prior to normal publication.

7097. Which airspaces are depicted on the En Route Low Altitude Chart?

1—Control zones, victor airways, and special use airspace.
2—Airport traffic areas, victor airways, and special use airspace.
3—Positive control areas, special use airspace, control zones, and transition areas.
4—Special use airspace, transition areas, airport traffic areas, terminal control areas, and air defense identification zones.

11

7098. Under what condition, if any, could DME signals be used for navigation when approaching El Paso International Airport from the west beyond 30 nautical miles? (See Figure 2.)

1—None, the DME is unusable beyond 25 nautical miles.
2—By maintaining an altitude no lower than 2,500 ft. AGL.
3—By maintaining an altitude of 12,500 ft. MSL or above.
4—By using the TACAN channel with the DME receiver.

7099. On what frequency and during what time period can you receive the complete TWEB (Transcribed Weather Broadcast) at Snohomish Co (Paine Field)? (See Figure 2.)

1—On 114.2 MHz from 1300Z to 0600Z.
2—On 396 kHz continuously.
3—On 114.2 MHz from 0600Z to 1300Z.
4—On 396 kHz from 6 a.m. to 10 p.m. local standard time.

7100. Under what condition, if any, will the approach lights be available at Hot Springs Memorial Field if you arrive at approximately 9:00 p.m. local standard time? (See Figure 2.)

1—The approach lights will be available only when IFR conditions prevail.
2—By keying 120.3 seven times in 5 sec.
3—The approach lights will be on at the time of arrival.
4—You must make arrangements prior to arrival.

7101. How can you determine that Orange County Airport has one or more published FAA instrument approach procedures? (See Figure 2.)

1—By noting the shape of the airport symbol on the en route chart.
2—By noting that Montgomery has both an (H) VORTAC and an NDB facility listed in the Airport/Facility Directory.
3—By noting that Poughkeepsie FSS has an LRCO at Huguenot VORTAC.
4—By noting the symbol IAP in the Airport/Facility Directory.

7102. IFR conditions exist at Orange County Airport. How should you close your IFR flight plan upon arrival? (See Figure 2.)

1—By calling Poughkeepsie FSS on the toll-free telephone number.
2—By using Huguenot LRCO when cleared for the approach.
3—By calling UNICOM on 122.7 when the landing is completed.
4—You need not close the flight plan because ATC will close it when you are cleared for the approach.

7103. What is the procedure for receiving your IFR clearance on Snohomish County–Paine Field between 1500 – 0700Z? (See Figure 2.)

1—Make a local phone call to Seattle FSS prior to startup.
2—Contact Seattle center departure control on 128.5 MHz prior to taxi.
3—Contact clearance delivery on ground control (120.2 MHz) prior to taxi.
4—Contact ground control on 121.8 MHz prior to taxi.

7104. From what facility should you obtain the latest FDC NOTAMS prior to an IFR flight from Hot Springs Memorial Field? (See Figure 2.)

1—From Hot Springs FSS on the field.
2—From Little Rock FSS by phone or through the Hot Springs LRCO.
3—From the tower or ground control on the airport.
4—From Memphis Center or Hot Springs Departure Control, whichever is appropriate for the time.

7105. On which frequency is Transcribed Weather Broadcast provided for El Paso International Airport? (See Figure 2.)

1—120.0 MHz.
2—115.0 MHz.
3—125.0 MHz.
4—242 kHz.

7106. On which frequency should you contact El Paso International for Stage III services when inbound to the airport and north of V–16? (See Figure 2.)

1—118.7 MHz.
2—119.7 MHz.
3—119.1 MHz.
4—118.3 MHz.

7107. FAA Deletion.

EVERETT

§ SNOHOMISH CO (PAINE FLD) (PAE) 6.1 SW GMT−8(−7DT) SEATTLE H-1A, L-1D
47°54'29"N 122°16'57"W IAP
603 B S4 FUEL 80, 100, JET A, LRA CFR Index A
RWY 16-34: H9010X200 (ASPH) S-85, D-110, DT-230 HIRL
RWY 16: MALSR. Trees.
RWY 11-29: H4948X75 (ASPH) S-60, D-119, DT-143 MIRL
RWY 11: Thld dsplcd 809'. Trees. RWY 29: Trees.
RWY 03-21: H3726X150 (ASPH) S-30, D-44, DT-68
RWY 03: Thld dsplcd 1094'. Trees. RWY 21: Building.
AIRPORT REMARKS: Attended 1500-0500Z‡, other hours call (206) 355-6600 for svc, fee. Rwy 11-29 used only during tower opr 1500-0700Z‡, Rwy 16-34 closed to air carrier 0700-1500Z‡ except with prior permission and aircraft using rwy announce intentions on 121.3 prior to takeoff or landing. Aircraft in the Control Zone 0700-1500Z‡ monitor 121.3. Rwy 03-21 light aircraft only. Control Zone effective 1500-0700Z‡.
COMMUNICATIONS: ATIS 128.65 opr 1500-0700Z‡ UNICOM 122.95
® SEATTLE FSS (SEA) LC 259-6844 NOTAM FILE PAE
® SEATTLE CENTER APP CON 128.5
® PAINE TOWER 121.3 120.2 opr 1500-0700Z‡ GND CON 128.5
® SEATTLE CENTER DEP CON 128.5
RADIO AIDS TO NAVIGATION:
SEATTLE (H) ABVORTAC 340'/28.4 NM
PAINE (L) ABVOR 114.2 ■PAE 47°54'11"N 122°17'12"W on fld.
General outlook on TWEB 0600-1300Z‡.
VOR unusable 200'-235' beyond 12 NM below 2600'.
320'-335' beyond 32 NM below 4500'.
RITTS NDB (LOM) 396 PA 48°03'11"N 122°17'15"W 157° 7.8 NM to fld.
ILS 109.3 I-PAE Rwy 16 LOM RITTS NDB ILS unmonitored when tower closed.

HOT SPRINGS

§ MEMORIAL FLD (HOT) 2.6 SW GMT−6(−5DT) MEMPHIS H-4F, L-14E
34°28'41"N 93°05'46"W IAP
540 B S4 FUEL 100 JET A CFR Index A
RWY 05-23: H6595X150 (ASPH-GRVD) S-80, D-110, DT-190 HIRL .57% up NE
RWY 05: Tree RWY 23: Thld dsplcd 500'. Pole.
RWY 13-31: H4099X150 (ASPH) S-28 MIRL .37% up SE
RWY 13: Road. RWY 31: Trees.
AIRPORT REMARKS: Attended 1200-0400Z‡. For MALSR 0400-1200Z‡ key 120.3 7 times in 5 sec high, 5 times in 5 sec med, 3 times in 5 sec low. Last 500' Rwy 05 closed to takeoffs. Control Zone effective 1300-0500Z‡.
COMMUNICATIONS:
LITTLE ROCK FSS (LIT) NOTAM FILE HOT
HOT SPRINGS LRCO 122.1R 110.0T (Little Rock FSS)
HOT SPRINGS APP CON 118.85 (1200-0400Z‡)
MEMPHIS CENTER APP CON 132.3 (0400-1200Z‡)
HOT SPRINGS TOWER 120.3 (1200-0400Z‡) GND CON 121.7
HOT SPRINGS DEP CON 118.85 (1200-0400Z‡)
MEMPHIS CENTER DEP CON 132.3 (0400-1200Z‡)
RADIO AIDS TO NAVIGATION:
LITTLE ROCK (H) VORTAC 250'/47.0 NM
HOT SPRINGS (L) VOR 110.0 HOT 34°28'43"N 93°05'26"W at fld
HOT SPRINGS 346'-055' beyond 20 NM below 3500'
056'-140' beyond 20 NM below 6500'
141'-227' beyond 26 NM below 3500'
228'-311' beyond 20 NM below 3500'
312'-345' beyond 15 NM below 5500'
312'-345' beyond 32 NM below 9500'
HOT SPRINGS NDB (HW/LOM) 385 HO 34°25'21"N 93°11'22"W 048° 4.2 NM to fld.
ILS 111.5 I-HOT Rwy 05 Unmonitored when tower closed.

MONTGOMERY

§ ORANGE CO (MGJ) 0.9 SW GMT−5(−4DT) JET A NEW YORK H-3D, L-25B, L-28H
41°30'41"N 74°15'51"W IAP
365 B S4 FUEL 80, 100, JET A
RWY 03-21: H5000X100 (CONC) S-25E HIRL
RWY 03: REIL. Thld dsplcd 300'. Trees.
RWY 08-26: H4000X100 (CONC) S-25E
RWY 08: Thld dsplcd 300'. Trees. RWY 26: REIL. Thld dsplcd 550'. Trees.
RWY 11-29: H2800X50 (CONC) S-25E
RWY 11: Thld dsplcd 250'. Trees. RWY 29: Thld dsplcd 250'. Trees.
AIRPORT REMARKS: Attended May 1 to Oct 30 1200-0200Z‡. Other times 1200-2400Z‡. Fee for aircraft over 12,500 pounds except when fuel purchased. Extensive glider activity.
COMMUNICATIONS: UNICOM 122.7
POUGHKEEPSIE FSS (POU) Toll free call dial 1-800-942-8220.
HUGUENOT LRCO 122.1R 116.1T (POUGHKEEPSIE FSS)
RADIO AIDS TO NAVIGATION:
HUGUENOT (H) VORTAC 116.1 HUO Chan 108 41°24'35"N 74°35'31"W 080° 15.7 NM to fld.1300/11W
VOR unusable 029°-034' all altitudes
035'-040' beyond 10 NM below 3000', beyond 30 NM below 5000'
210'-230' beyond 20 NM below 6500'
OTIMS NDB (LOM) 353 MG 41°26'42"N 74°17'33"W 027° 4.1 NM to fld.
ILS 111.7 I-MGJ Rwy 03 LOM OTIMS NDB

EL PASO

§ EL PASO INTERNATIONAL (ELP) 4.3 NE GMT−7(−6DT) EL PASO H-2G, L-4G
31°48'23"N 106°22'58"W IAP
3956 B S4 FUEL 80, 100, 100LL, JET A1 +, JET B + OX 2, 4 AOE
CFR Index C
RWY 04-22: H11012X150 (ASPH) S-100, D-180, DT-350 HIRL
RWY 04: VASI—GA 3.0° TCH 55'. Rgt tfc. RWY 22: SSALR.
RWY 08-26: H9008X150 (ASPH) S-100, D-180, DT-350 HIRL .37% up E.
RWY 08: Rgt tfc. RWY 26: REIL. VASI—Upper GA 3.0° TCH 81'. Lower GA 2.50° TCH 49'.
AIRPORT REMARKS: 1082' stopway/taxiway SW end of rwy 04-22; available for takeoffs rwy 04 with prior permission only. Rwy 08-26 has 3004'X75' stopway/taxiway West end; lighted and marked as taxiway.
COMMUNICATIONS: ATIS 120.0 UNICOM 122.95
FSS (ELP) on arpt 122.55, 122.4, 122.2, 122.1R (915) 778-6448.
APP CON 118.7 (N. of V-16), 119.7 (S. of V-16), 119.1, 115.2T
TOWER 118.3 GND CON 121.9 CLNC DEL 125.0
DEP CON 119.7 APP CON
STAGE III SVC ctc
ASR
RADIO AIDS TO NAVIGATION: VHF/DF ctc EL PASO FSS
(H) BVORTAC 115.2 ELP Chan 99 31°48'56.9"N 106°16'52.9"W 243° 4.3 NM to fld.
4020/12E
VOR unusable 290-070° beyond 25 NM below 12,000' MSL
140-160° beyond 20 NM
220-225° beyond 20 NM
250-255° beyond 20 NM
DME unusable 260-290° beyond 30 NM below 12,500'
VALTR NDB (H-SAB/LOM) 242 EL 31°51'36.8"N 106°19'01.9"W 218° 3.7 NM to fld.
ILS 111.5 I-ELP Rwy 22 LOM VALTR NDB
COMM/NAVAID REMARKS: ATIS ops 1200-0500Z‡. STAGE III restricted 200-320° blo 9200' MSL 1200-1200Z‡.
NM TWEB avbl. Route forecast only 0500-1200Z‡.

Figure 2

7108. Under which weather conditions may you select Nampa Municipal as an alternate airport on an IFR flight plan? (See Figure 3.)

1—If the ceiling and visibility is forecast to be 600 ft. and 2 statute miles, respectively, within 1 hour of ETA.
2—If the ceiling and visibility is forecast to be 800 ft. and 2 statute miles, respectively, within 1 hour of ETA.
3—If the forecast weather at ETA will allow descent from cruising altitude and landing under special VFR conditions.
4—If the forecast weather at ETA will allow descent from MEA, approach, and landing under basic VFR.

7109. Which information in the Airport/Facility Directory indicates that Rexburg–Madison County Airport has one or more published FAA Instrument Approach Procedures? (See Figure 3.)

1—Runway 17–35 is equipped with lighting for instrument approaches.
2—One VORTAC and one VOR are within range for instrument approaches.
3—Salt Lake City Center provides approach and departure control for the airport.
4—The symbol IAP denotes FAA instrument approach procedures.

7110. How should you obtain the latest FDC NOTAMS for an IFR flight departing Pocatello Municipal Airport? (See Figure 3.)

1—From the tower or ground control.
2—By a local call to Burley FSS.
3—From Salt Lake City Center on the approach control frequency.
4—From an instrument approach procedure book.

7111. How should you obtain the latest FDC NOTAMS for an IFR flight departing Rexburg–Madison County Airport? (See Figure 3.)

1—From Salt Lake City Center on the departure control frequency.
2—By toll–free call to Idaho Falls FSS.
3—From an instrument approach procedure book.
4—Call the airport manager's office on UNICOM.

7112. On what frequency(ies) can you get the TWEB (Transcribed Weather Broadcast) at Boise Air Terminal? (See Figure 3.)

1—123.9 MHz only.
2—123.9 and 113.3 MHz only.
3—113.3 MHz and 359 kHz only.
4—123.9 MHz, 113.3 MHz, and 359 kHz.

7113. How should you perform the VOR receiver accuracy check at Pocatello Municipal? (See Figure 3.)

1—Align the aircraft to a magnetic heading of 035°, select 112.6 MHz, and determine if the CDI centers between OBS settings of 356 and 004 with a FROM indication.
2—Taxi to the checkpoint on the parking ramp south of the terminal, select 112.6 MHz and determine if the CDI centers between OBS settings of 031 and 039 with a FROM indication.
3—Align the aircraft to a magnetic heading of 035° at the checkpoint on the parking ramp south of the terminal, select 112.6 MHz and determine if the CDI centers between OBS settings of 031 and 039 with a TO indication.
4—Taxi to the checkpoint on the parking ramp south of the terminal, select 112.6 MHz and determine if the CDI centers between OBS settings of 176 and 184 with a FROM indication.

7114. How should you perform the VOR receiver accuracy check prior to an IFR departure from Boise Air Terminal? (See Figure 3.)

1—Fly over the dam outlet on the south end of Lucky Peak Reservoir at 5,000 ft. with the Omni tuned to 113.3 MHz and determine if the CDI centers between OBS settings of 082 and 094 with a FROM indication.
2—Taxi to the center N/S taxiway between Rwys 28L–10R and 28R–10L. With the Omni tuned to 113.3 MHz, determine if the CDI centers between OBS settings of 080 and 088 with a FROM indication.
3—Fly over the dam outlet on the south end of Lucky Peak Reservoir at 5,000 ft. with the Omni tuned to 113.3 MHz. The CDI should center if the MH is between 080° and 088° and the OBS is set to north.
4—Taxi to the center N/S taxiway between Rwys 28L–10R and 28R–10L. With the Omni tuned to 113.3 MHz and an MH of 084°, determine if the CDI centers between OBS settings of 356 and 004 with a FROM indication.

7115. Where are the compulsory reporting points, if any, on a direct flight not flown on radials or courses of established airways or routes?

1—Fixes selected to define the route.
2—The points where the direct course crosses an airway.
3—There are no compulsory reporting points unless advised by ATC.
4—At the COP (changeover points).

7116. What is a waypoint when used for an IFR flight?

1—A predetermined geographical position used for an RNAV route or an RNAV instrument approach.
2—A reporting point defined by the intersection of two VOR radials.
3—A holding fix when used in conjunction with an en route flight.
4—A location on a victor airway which can only be identified by VOR and DME signals.

VOR RECEIVER CHECK POINTS

Facility Name (Arpt Name)	Freq/Ident	Type Check Pt. Gnd. AB/ALT	Azimuth from Fac. Mag	Dist. from Fac. N.M.	Check Point Description
Boise	113.3/BOI	A/5000	088	8.5	Over dam outlet S end Lucky Peak Reservoir
Boise (Boise Air Terminal/Gowen Fld)	113.3/BOI	G	084	0.9	On center N/S twy between rwys 28L-10R and 28R-10L.
Coeur D'Alene	108.8/COE	A/3500	233	5.8	Over Post Falls NDB
Idaho Falls (Fanning Field)	109.0/IDA	G	009		At junction of N/S twy and Rwy 16-34 at NE corner of arpt.
Lewiston (Lewiston-Nez Perce County) ..	108.2/LWS	A/3000	247	7	Over tetrahedron on arpt.
Pocatello (Pocatello Muni)	112.6/PIH	G	035	3.2	On parking ramp S of terminal.
Twin Falls (Twin Falls City-Co, Joslin Fld)	115.8/TWF	G	243		On tic in area at apch end rwy 25.

BOISE

§ **BOISE AIR TERMINAL-GOWEN FLD**   (BOI)   3.5 S   GMT−7(−6DT)   **SALT LAKE CITY**
                                                                                                    H-1B, L 9A
43°33'54"N 116°13'27"W   **IAP**
2858   B   S4   FUEL 80, 100, JET A1+   OX 2, 4   CFR Index C
RWY 10L-28R: H9763X190 (ASPH)   S-150, D-200, DT-315   HIRL   .4% up SE
RWY 10R: MALSR, VASI—GA 3.0° TCH 46'. Arrest Device.
RWY 28L: VASI—GA 3.0° TCH 46'.
RWY 10L-28R: H7400X150 (ASPH)   S-60, D-170, DT-295   HIRL   .4% up SE
RWY 10L: VASI—GA 3.0° TCH 53.2'.
RWY 28R: VASI—GA 3.0° TCH 55'. Rgt tfc.
AIRPORT REMARKS: Attended continuously. Rwys 10L-28R, 10R-28L porous friction course full lgth and
width. Extensive copter opr surface to 3500' within 1 mi E and W and 3 mi S of Rwy 10R-28L. Clsd
to F100 tkofs permanently. Security requires prior request with fixed base operator due to locked
gates and fencing between hrs 0500-1400Z‡ for ingress/egress to arpt. In emerg ctc tower, can
expect short delay. Potential bird activity at sewage lagoon ½ mile SW of arpt.
COMMUNICATIONS: ATIS 123.9   UNICOM 122.95
BOISE FSS (BOI) on arpt 122.6, 122.2, 122.1R, 113.3T (208) 343-2525
® APP CON 126.9(277°-097°)118.9(098°-276°) 125.5 (Rwy 10L/28R)   GND CON 121.7   CLNC DEL 125.9
TOWER 118.1 (Rwy 10R/28L) 125.5 (Rwy 10L/28R)
® DEP CON 126.9(277°-097°)118.9(098°-276°)
STAGE III SVC ctc APP CON
RADIO AIDS TO NAVIGATION: VHF/DF ctc Boise FSS
(H) ABVORTAC 113.3   ▪BOI   Chan 80   43°34'06"N 116°14'34"W   at fld. 2800/19E
    VORTAC unusable 360°-030° beyond 22 NM below 9700'
                           030°-050° beyond 25 NM below 9700'
                           350°-360° beyond 25 NM below 9700'
USTIK NDB (H-SAB/LOM) 359   ▪BO   43°35'49"N 116°18'51"W   098° 3.5 NM to fld
ILS 108.5 I-BOI Rwy 10R LOM USTIK NDB

§ **NAMPA MUNI**   (S67)   1.7 E   GMT−7(−6DT)   **SALT LAKE CITY**
                                                                                  L-9A
2535   B   S4   FUEL 80, 100   TPA—3535(1000)   MIRL
RWY 11-29: H4050X75 (ASPH)   S-12.5   MIRL
RWY 11: VASI—GA 3.0° TCH 30.1'. Smokestack.   RWY 29: VASI—GA 3.0° TCH 29.5'. Tree.
AIRPORT REMARKS: Attended dawn-dusk. For VASI key 122.8 5 times for on, 7 times for off; remains on
10 minutes.
COMMUNICATIONS: UNICOM 122.8
BOISE FSS (BOI) LC 466-0786
RADIO AIDS TO NAVIGATION:
BOISE (H) ABVORTAC 255°/12.5 NM

§ **POCATELLO MUNI**   (PIH)   7.8 NW   GMT−7(−6DT)   42°54'48"N 112°35'39"W   **SALT LAKE CITY**
                                                                                                                H-1B, L7D
4448   B   S4   FUEL 80, 100, JET A1 +   OX 1, 3   CFR Index B   **IAP**
RWY 03-21: H9046X150 (ASPH)   S-80, D-110, DT-160   HIRL
RWY 03: VASI—GA 3.0° TCH 53'.   RWY 21: SSALR
RWY 16-34: H8347X300 (ASPH)   S-30, D-45   HIRL
RWY 34: VASI—GA 3.0° TCH 55'.   RWY 16: S-30, D-45
RWY 07-25: H8249X300 (ASPH)   S-30, D-45   HIRL
AIRPORT REMARKS: Attended continuously. Arpt clsd to Civil Aeronautics Board cert non-sked air carrier
0600-1400Z‡ without prior permission. Arpt clsd to air carrier call 208-233-1313. Flocks of waterfowl in vcnty arpt
Nov-May. Rwys 07-25 and 16-34 closed to aircraft over 12,500 lbs.Control Zone effective
continuously.
COMMUNICATIONS: UNICOM 122.95
BURLEY FSS (BYI) LC 233-3532 NOTAM FILE PIH
POCATELLO LRCO 122.1R 112.6T (BURLEY FSS)
® SALT LAKE CITY CENTER APP CON 134.5
TOWER 119.1 opr 1300-0500Z‡   GND CON 121.9
® SALT LAKE CITY CENTER DEP CON 134.5
RADIO AIDS TO NAVIGATION:
(H) ABVORTAC 112.6   ▪PIH   Chan 73   42°52'14"N 112°39'05"W   033° 2.9 NM to fld
    4430/17E
    TWEB available 1200-0500Z‡
    VOR unusable 085°-120° beyond 40 NM below 14000'
                           085°-120° beyond 40 NM below 14000'
TYHEE NDB (LOM) 383   PI   42°57'50"N 112°30'56"W   208° 3.8 NM to fld
ILS 110.3 I-PIH Rwy 21 LOM TYHEE NDB
COMM/NAVAID REMARKS: Freq 121.5 not avbl.

§ **REXBURG-MADISON CO**   (U11)   0.9 NW   GMT−7(−6DT)   43°49'30"N 111°49'00"W   **SALT LAKE CITY**
                                                                                                                L-98
4859   B   S4   FUEL 80, 100, JET A   OX 1   **IAP**
RWY 17-35: H4205X75 (ASPH)   S-17   MRRL   RWY 35: Tree.
RWY 17: VASI—GA 3.0° TCH 50'.
AIRPORT REMARKS: Attended 1500-0100Z‡
COMMUNICATIONS: UNICOM 122.8
IDAHO FALLS FSS (IDA) Toll free call, dial 1-800-632-4810.
® SALT LAKE CITY CENTER APP/DEP CON 134.5
RADIO AIDS TO NAVIGATION:
DUBOIS (H) ABVORTAC 115°/23.2 NM
IDAHO FALLS (L) ABVOR 109.0   ▪IDA   43°31'09"N 112°03'47"W   014° 21.9 NM to fld.

Figure 3

15

7117. What frequency provides the Transcribed Weather Broadcast in the Oklahoma City area? (See Figure 4.)

1—125.6 MHz.
2—350 kHz.
3—115.0 MHz.
4—113.4 MHz.

7118. With whom should you file an IFR flight plan while at Will Rogers World Airport? (See Figure 4.)

1—Pre–taxi clearance delivery on 123.7 MHz.
2—Rogers Tower on 118.3 MHz.
3—Oklahoma City FSS by local telephone.
4—Oklahoma City FSS on the airport.

7119. Which En Route Low Altitude Chart(s) cover routes for flights which terminate at Oklahoma City? (See Figure 4.)

1—H–21 and H–4E.
2—L–21 and L–4E.
3—L–6 and L–13.
4—L–6 only.

7120. For which airports in the Oklahoma City area is NOTAM D information disseminated? (See Figure 4.)

1—All airports in the OKC FSS area.
2—Only Will Rogers World Airport.
3—Only those airports having control towers.
4—Only those airports annotated with the NOTAM service symbol in the AFD.

7121. On which frequency should you request your IFR clearance when departing Wiley Post Airport at 0600Z? (See Figure 4.)

1—124.6 MHz.
2—119.7 MHz.
3—118.3 MHz.
4—123.0 MHz.

7122. What is the procedure for closing an IFR flight plan at Clarence E. Page Municipal Airport under IFR conditions? (See Figure 4.)

1—Approach control will automatically close the flight plan upon issuing a clearance for an approach.
2—Approach control will automatically close the flight plan when the pilot reports the final approach fix.
3—The pilot should close the flight plan with OKC FSS upon receiving the clearance for an approach.
4—The pilot should close the flight plan with OKC FSS by phone after landing.

7123. What instrument approach lighting is installed at Will Rogers World Airport for Rwy 35R? (See Figure 4.)

1—High–intensity approach lighting, Category II configuration.
2—Medium–intensity approach lighting with sequenced flashing lights.
3—Simplified short approach lighting.
4—Omnidirectional high–intensity approach lights with sequenced flashing.

7124. What is a proper procedure to check the accuracy of your VOR receiver prior to an IFR flight from Will Rogers World Airport? (See Figure 4.)

1—Select 115.0 MHz, turn aircraft to 096°, center the CDI and check for desired indication between 092° and 100° with FROM.
2—Select 115.0 MHz, center the CDI and check for desired indication between 356° and 004° with FROM.
3—Select 108.8 MHz, turn aircraft to 360°, center the CDI and check for desired indication between 356° and 004° with TO.
4—Select 108.8 MHz, center the CDI and check for desired indication between 176° and 184° with TO.

OKLAHOMA

VOR RECEIVER CHECK POINTS

Facility Name (Arpt Name)	Freq/Ident	Type Check Pt. Gnd. AB/ALT	Azimuth from Fac. Mag	Dist. from Fac N.M.	Check Point Description
Oklahoma City (Clarence E. Page Muni)	115.0/OKC	G	313	3.8	On runup pad to rwy 17L.
	115.0/OKC	G	307	3.4	On runup pad to rwy 35R.
Okmulgee (Okmulgee Muni)	112.2/OKM	G	241	4.8	At intersection of perimeter twy and twy to gas pumps.
Pioneer (Ponca City Muni)	113.2/PER	G	101	3.0	On twy at junction of terminal ramp.
Sayre (Sayre Muni)	115.2/SYO	A/3000	175	8	Over rotating beacon.
Stillwater (Searcy Field)	108.4/SWO	G	173	4	At intersection of NW ramp and twy.
Wiley Post (Wiley Post)	113.4/PWA	G	155		On runup pad to rwy 35R.

VOR TEST FACILITIES (VOT)

Facility Name (Airport Name)	Freq.	Type VOT Facility	Remarks
Oklahoma City (Will Rogers World)	108.8	G	
Tulsa International	109.0	G	

OKLAHOMA

OKLAHOMA CITY FSS (OKC) on Wiley Post — **DALLAS-FT. WORTH**
122.65, 122.4, 122.2, 122.1R 115.0T (405) 787-9323 — **H-2I, 3A, 4E, L-6G, 13C**

OKLAHOMA CITY 35°26'33"N 97°46'21"W — **DALLAS-FT. WORTH**
(H) VORTAC 115.0 OKC Chan 97 096° 8.0 NM to Will Rogers World. 040° 8.1 NM to Wiley Post. 1360/09E

OKLAHOMA CITY

§ **CLARENCE E PAGE MUNI** (F29) 3.5 SW GMT–6(–5DT) 35°29'15"N 97°49'00"W
1353 B S4 **FUEL** 100LL, JET A OX 3 — **DALLAS-FT. WORTH** **L-6G, 13C** **IAP**
RWY 17R-35L: 3700X200 (TURF) Marked 17-35
RWY 17R: Trees. Rgt tfc. **RWY 35L:** Brush.
RWY 17L-35R: H3500X75 (ASPH) S-17 MIRL
RWY 17L: Trees. **RWY 35R:** Trees. Rgt tfc.
RWY 16-34: 2000X200 (TURF)
RWY 16: Trees. Rgt tfc. **RWY 34:** Trees.
RWY 01-19: 2000X200 (TURF)
RWY 01: P-line. **RWY 19:** Windsock. Rgt tfc.
AIRPORT REMARKS: Attended 1400-2330Z‡. Svc after hours call 354-6270. Rwy 17L-35R marked 17-35.
COMMUNICATIONS: UNICOM 122.8
OKLAHOMA CITY FSS (OKC)
Ⓡ **OKE CITY APP/DEP CON** 124.6 opr 1200-0500Z‡, 118.3 opr 0500-1200Z‡
STAGE III SVC ctc **APP CON**
RADIO AIDS TO NAVIGATION:
OKLAHOMA CITY (H) VORTAC 115.0 OKC Chan 97 35°26'33"N 97°46'21"W 309° 3.4 NM to fld. 1360/09E

EXPRESSWAY AIRPARK (2EJ) 5.2 NE GMT–6(–5DT) 35°32'24"N 97°27'14"W
1070 B S4 **FUEL** 80, 100LL — **DALLAS-FT. WORTH** **L-6G, 13C**
RWY 02-20: H3000X63 (ASPH) S-12.5 LIRL
RWY 02: Tree. **RWY 20:** Trees.
AIRPORT REMARKS: Attended continuously.
COMMUNICATIONS: UNICOM 122.8
OKLAHOMA CITY FSS (OKC)
RADIO AIDS TO NAVIGATION:
OKLAHOMA CITY (H) VORTAC 060°/16.7 NM

§ **WILEY POST** (PWA) 7 NW GMT–6(–5DT) 35°32'03"N 97°38'48"W — **DALLAS-FT. WORTH**
1299 B S4 **FUEL** 100, JET A OX 1, 2, 3, 4 — **H-2I, 3A, 4E, L-6G, 13C** **IAP**
RWY 17L-35R: H7198X150 (CONC) S-35, D-50, DT-80 HIRL
RWY 17L: MALSR. VASI—GA 3.0° TCH 54'. Trees. Rgt tfc.
RWY 35R: VASI—GA 3.0° TCH 31'. Bldg.
RWY 12-30: H4563X100 (CONC) S-35, D-50, DT-90 MIRL .61%(up NW)
RWY 12: VASI—GA 3.0° TCH 31'. Road. Rgt tfc.
RWY 30: VASI—GA 4.0° TCH 55'. Thld dsplcd 360'. Tree.
RWY 03-21: H3409X75 (ASPH) S-12.5 .56% (up SW)
RWY 03: VASI—GA 3.0° TCH 34'. Trees. **RWY 21:** VASI—GA 3.0° TCH 25'. Trees. Rgt tfc
RWY 17R-35L: H3232X75 (ASPH) S-12.5
RWY 17R: VASI—GA 3.5° TCH 31'. Trees. Rgt tfc **RWY 35L:** VASI—GA 3.5° TCH 31'. Ground.
AIRPORT REMARKS: Attended continuously. Rwy 12-30 closed daily 0400-1200Z‡. Rwy 17L OKC FSS will have control of MALSR when ATCT closed. Arpt closed to acft over 54,000 lbs gross weight. Rwy 12-30 closed to jets. Rwy 12 closed to tkof & Rwy 30 closed to lndg for acft over 12,500 lbs. gross weight. Touch & go or stop & go lndgs not authorized rwy 12-30. Helicopter lndg area not marked.
COMMUNICATIONS: ATIS 113.4 **UNICOM** 123.0
OKLAHOMA CITY FSS (OKC) on arpt. 122.65, 122.4, 122.2, 119.7 (405) 787-9323
Ⓡ **OKE CITY APP CON** 124.6 118.45 opr 1200-0500Z‡, 118.3 opr 0500-1200Z‡
TOWER 119.7 Opr 1200-0400Z‡ FSS provides AAS on 119.7 when twr closed **GND CON** 121.7
Ⓡ **OKE CITY DEP CON** 124.6 opr 1200-0500Z‡, 118.3 opr 0500-1200Z‡
STAGE III SVC ctc **APP CON**
RADIO AIDS TO NAVIGATION:
OKLAHOMA CITY (H) VORTAC 040°/8.2 NM
(T) VOR 113.4 PWA 35°31'58.4"N 97°38'48.7"W at fld
ILS 108.7 I-PWA Rwy 17L

§ **WILL ROGERS WORLD** (OKC) 6.1 SW GMT–6(–5DT) 35°23'37"N 97°35'59"W — **DALLAS-FT. WORTH**
1295 B S4 **FUEL** 80, 100, JET A, JET B + OX 1, 2, 3, 4 LRA — **H-21, 4E, L-6G, 13C** **IAP**
CFR Index C
RWY 17L-35R: H9801X50 (ASPH-CONC) S-50, D-103, DT-168 HIRL, CL
RWY 17L: VASI—GA 3.0° TCH 55'. P-lines. Trees.
RWY 35R: ALSF2, TDZ, Rgt tfc.
RWY 17R-35L: H9800X150 (CONC) S-50, DT-400 HIRL
RWY 17R: MALSR, Rgt tfc. **RWY 35L:** VASI—GA 3.0° TCH 52'.
RWY 12-30: H6528X150 (ASPH-CONC) S-34, D-42, DT-77 MIRL
RWY 12: REIL. VASI—GA 3.0° TCH 52'. Rgt tfc.
RWY 30: VASI—GA 3.0° TCH 52'. P-lines. Trees.
RWY 18-36: H2975X75 (ASPH) S-50, D-150, DT-240
RWY 18: Rgt tfc
AIRPORT REMARKS: Attended continuously. LLWSAS. Rwy 17R-35L has 35' paved shoulders each side of rwy and plastic grooving full length and width. Rwy 12-30 weights permitted S-50, D-200, DT-350. Rwy 17L-35R weights permitted D-200, DT-350. Acft 350,000 lbs permitted Rwy 12-30. Southeast 1200' Rwy 12-30 closed until approximately Jan 1981. Prior permission required for parking on FSS AERONAUTICAL CENTER ramp. Rwy 18-30 600' W of rwy 17R-35L on existing taxiway. VFR dalgt operations only. Used as taxiway when not used as rwy. Lgtd as taxiway. Rwy 17L VASI out of service until further notice. Rwy 17L-35R has sawed cut grooving. Flight Notification Service (ADCUS) available.
COMMUNICATIONS: ATIS 125.6 (1300-0600Z‡) **UNICOM** 122.95
OKLAHOMA CITY FSS (OKC)
Ⓡ **OKE CITY APP CON** 126.65 (171°-260°) 124.6 (261°-360°) 124.2 (081°-170°) 121.05 (001°-080°) 119.3 opr 1200-0500Z‡, 118.3 opr 0500-1200Z‡
ROGERS TOWER 118.3 **GND CON** 121.9 **CLNC DEL** 123.7 **PRE-TAXI CLNC** 123.7
Ⓡ **OKE CITY DEP CON** 126.65 (171°-260°) 124.6 (261°-360°) 124.2 (081°-170°) 121.05 (001°-080°) opr 1200-0500Z‡, 118.3 opr 0500-1200Z‡
STAGE III SVC ctc **APP CON**
RADIO AIDS TO NAVIGATION:
OKLAHOMA CITY (H) VORTAC 115.0 OKC Chan 97 35°26'32.7"N 97°46'20.6"W 096° 5.0 NM to fld. 1360/09E
TULOO NDB (MHW/LOM) 406 OK 35°28'17.2"N 97°36'18.2"W 171° 4.0 NM to fld
GALLY NDB (H-SAB/LOM) 350 ■ RG 35°17'42"N 97°35'18"W 352° 5.0 NM to fld.
ILS/DME 110.9 I-RGR Chan 46 Rwy 35R LOM GALLY NDB.
ILS/DME 110.7 I-OKC Chan 44 Rwy 17R LOM TULOO NDB.
ASR

Figure 4

7125. You are departing from a high altitude heliport on a helicopter instrument flight under hot day conditions. At what altitude will this helicopter's rate of climb be reduced to 150 ft./min.? (See Figure 5.)

1—9,500 ft.
2—8,200 ft.
3—7,000 ft.
4—6,300 ft.

7126. You are departing on an instrument flight from a high altitude airport under standard day conditions. At what altitude will this helicopter's rate of climb be reduced to 400 ft./min.? (See Figure 5.)

1—8,400 ft.
2—10,500 ft.
3—12,100 ft.
4—17,000 ft.

7127. You are departing on an instrument flight from a high altitude heliport. Determine the altitude at which this helicopter's rate of climb will be reduced to 300 ft./min. (See Figure 5.)

Temperature..−5° C

1—11,300 ft.
2—10,100 ft.
3— 9,200 ft.
4— 8,400 ft.

7128. What is the maximum rate of climb you can expect in this helicopter during a departure on an instrument flight? (See Figure 5.)

Altitude...6,200 ft.
Temperature...+22° C

1—190 ft./min.
2—240 ft./min.
3—300 ft./min.
4—350 ft./min.

7129. What is the maximum rate of climb you can expect in this helicopter during a departure on an instrument flight? (See Figure 5.)

Altitude...7,500 ft.
Temperature...+5° C

1—250 ft./min.
2—350 ft./min.
3—450 ft./min.
4—650 ft./min.

7130. What is the maximum rate of climb you can expect in this helicopter during a departure on an instrument flight? (See Figure 5.)

Altitude...7,500 ft.
Temperature..−5° C

1—650 ft./min.
2—700 ft./min.
3—825 ft./min.
4—975 ft./min.

7131. What is the maximum rate of climb you can expect in this helicopter during a departure on an instrument flight? (See Figure 5.)

Altitude...9,000 ft.
Temperature...Standard

1—250 ft./min.
2—350 ft./min.
3—425 ft./min.
4—475 ft./min.

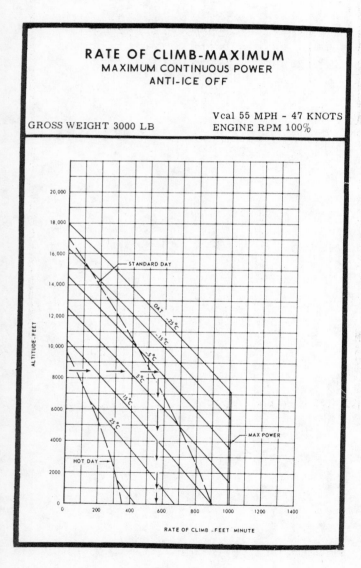

Figure 5

7132. Prior to departure on an instrument flight, ATC issues you a clearance with this climb restriction:

CROSS ALPHA VORTAC AT ONE THOUSAND...CROSS BRAVO INTERSECTION AT EIGHT THOUSAND....

Determine the average rate of climb you can expect in this helicopter between 1,000 and 8,000 ft. (See Figure 6.)

Temperature at 1,000 ft. ....0° C
Temperature at 8,000 ft. .... –15° C

1—430 ft./min.
2—560 ft./min.
3—620 ft./min.
4—715 ft./min.

7133. Prior to departure on an instrument flight, ATC issues you a clearance with this climb restriction:

CROSS ALPHA VORTAC AT THREE THOUSAND...CROSS BRAVO INTERSECTION AT TEN THOUSAND....

Determine the average rate of climb you can expect in this helicopter between 3,000 and 10,000 ft. (See Figure 6.)

Temperature ....Standard

1—150 ft./min.
2—275 ft./min.
3—325 ft./min.
4—425 ft./min.

7134. Prior to departure on an instrument flight, ATC issues you a clearance with this climb restriction:

...CROSS ALPHA VORTAC AT THREE THOUSAND...CROSS BRAVO INTERSECTION AT NINE THOUSAND....

Determine the average rate of climb you can expect in this helicopter between 3,000 and 9,000 ft. (See Figure 6.)

Temperature at 3,000 ft. ....+5° C
Temperature at 9,000 ft. .... –25° C

1—520 ft./min.
2—610 ft./min.
3—750 ft./min.
4—810 ft./min.

7135. Prior to departure on an instrument flight, ATC issues you a clearance with this climb restriction:

...CROSS ALPHA VORTAC AT TWO THOUSAND...CROSS BRAVO INTERSECTION AT SIX THOUSAND....

Determine the average rate of climb you can expect in this helicopter between 2,000 and 6,000 ft. (See Figure 6.)

Temperature at 2,000 ft. .... –5° C
Temperature at 6,000 ft. ....+7° C

1—550 ft./min.
2—600 ft./min.
3—650 ft./min.
4—700 ft./min.

7136. The performance of an aircraft for takeoff and climb is based upon

1—pressure altitude.
2—density altitude.
3—true altitude.
4—density altitude corrected for temperature.

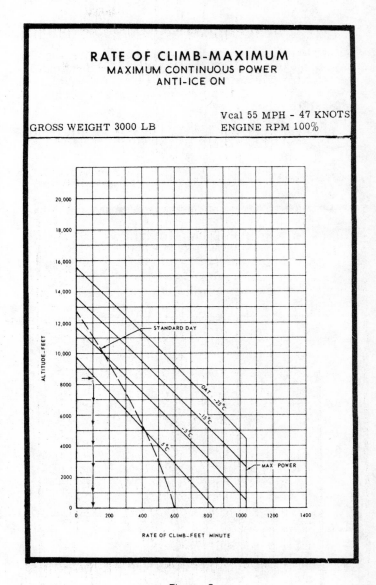

Figure 6

19

7137. An instrument flight is planned from a heliport where the pressure altitude is 6,500 ft. and the ATIS reported temperature is +73° F (+23°C). Determine the maximum gross weight at which you can hover in ground effect. (See Figure 7.)

1—2,650 lb.
2—2,730 lb.
3—2,900 lb.
4—3,000 lb.

7138. An instrument flight is planned from a heliport where the pressure altitude is 8,000 ft. and the ATIS reported temperature is +58° F (+14° C). Determine the maximum gross weight at which you can hover in ground effect. (See Figure 7.)

1—2,650 lb.
2—2,760 lb.
3—2,850 lb.
4—2,950 lb.

7139. An instrument flight is planned from a heliport where the pressure altitude is 9,500 ft. and the ATIS reported temperature is +55° F (+13° C). Determine the maximum gross weight at which you can hover in ground effect. (See Figure 7.)

1—2,600 lb.
2—2,750 lb.
3—2,850 lb.
4—2,950 lb.

7140. An instrument flight is planned from a heliport where the pressure altitude is 3,000 ft. and the ATIS reported temperature is +95° F (+35° C). Determine the maximum gross weight at which you can hover in ground effect. (See Figure 7.)

1—2,550 lb.
2—2,700 lb.
3—2,850 lb.
4—2,900 lb.

7141. An instrument flight is planned from a heliport where the pressure altitude is 10,500 ft. and the ATIS reported temperature is +68° F (+20° C). Determine the maximum gross weight at which you can hover in ground effect. (See Figure 7.)

1—2,350 lb.
2—2,500 lb.
3—2,650 lb.
4—2,800 lb.

7142. An instrument flight is planned from a heliport where the pressure altitude is 4,500 ft. and the ATIS reported temperature is +104° F (+40° C). Determine the maximum gross weight at which you can hover in ground effect. (See Figure 7.)

1—2,350 lb.
2—2,550 lb.
3—2,700 lb.
4—2,800 lb.

7143. An instrument flight is planned from a heliport where the pressure altitude is 5,500 ft. and the ATIS reported temperature is +82° F (+28° C). Determine the maximum gross weight at which you can hover in ground effect. (See Figure 7.)

1—2,675 lb.
2—2,725 lb.
3—2,850 lb.
4—3,000 lb.

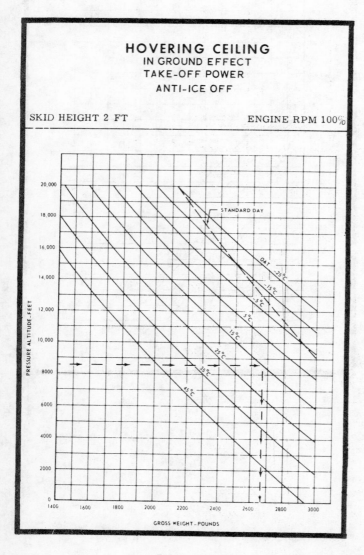

Figure 7

7144. Prior to departure on an instrument flight, you determine that the gross weight of your helicopter is 2,750 lb. What is its forward CG limit? (See Figure 8.)

1—112.8.
2—106.0.
3—105.0.
4—104.0.

7145. You are preparing to depart on an instrument flight in a helicopter that has a gross weight of 2,450 lb. What is its aft CG limit? (See Figure 8.)

1—113.0.
2—113.7.
3—114.2.
4—112.0.

7146. Prior to departure on an instrument flight, you determine that the gross weight of your helicopter is 2,250 lb. What is its aft CG limit? (See Figure 8.)

1—112.8.
2—113.3.
3—113.8.
4—114.2.

7147. Prior to departure on an instrument flight, you determine that the gross weight of your helicopter is 2,400 lb. What is its aft CG limit? (See Figure 8.)

1—113.2.
2—113.8.
3—114.0.
4—114.2.

7148. Prior to departure on an instrument flight, you determine that the gross weight of your helicopter is 2,600 lb. What is its aft CG limit? (See Figure 8.)

1—112.2.
2—112.8.
3—113.4.
4—113.8.

7149. Prior to departure on an instrument flight, you determine that the gross weight of your helicopter is 2,850 lb. What is its aft CG limit? (See Figure 8.)

1—112.0.
2—112.6.
3—113.0.
4—114.2.

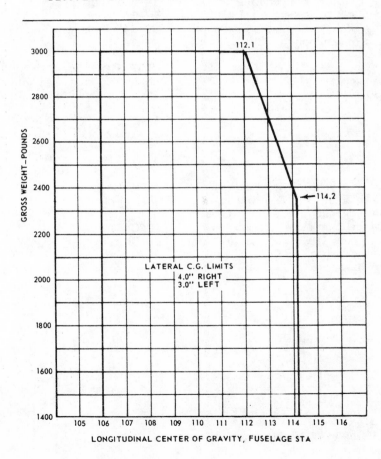

CENTER OF GRAVITY vs GROSS WEIGHT

Figure 8

7150. Prior to departure on an instrument flight, you determine that your helicopter's gross weight is 2,400 lb. and its CG is 107.5″ aft of datum. What is the amount and direction of CG movement resulting from the in–flight fuel burn outlined below?

Fuel tank centroid —— fuselage station 86.9
Fuel burn —— 1.2 hr. at 110 lb./hr.

1—1.2″ aft.
2—1.9″ forward.
3—2.7″ aft.
4—3.4″ forward.

7151. Prior to departure on an instrument flight, you determine that your helicopter's gross weight is 2,350 lb. and its total moment is 277,680.0 lb.-in. What is the amount and direction of CG movement resulting from the in–flight fuel burn outlined below?

Fuel tank centroid — fuselage station 149.2
Fuel burn — 1.3 hr. at 180 lb./hr.

1—3.4″ forward.
2—2.9″ forward.
3—1.5″ aft.
4—.3″ aft.

7152. Prior to departure on an instrument flight, you determine that your helicopter's gross weight is 2,450 lb. and its CG is 112.5″ aft of datum. What is the amount and direction of CG movement resulting from the in–flight fuel burn outlined below?

Fuel tank centroid — fuselage station 122.3
Fuel burn — 1.5 hr. at 180 lb./hr.

1—3.4″ forward.
2—1.2″ forward.
3—2.2″ aft.
4—1.6″ aft.

7153. You determine that your helicopter's gross weight is 2,420 lb. and its total moment is 278,720.0 lb.-in. What is the amount and direction of CG movement resulting from the in–flight fuel burn outlined below?

Fuel tank centroid — fuselage station 148.0
Fuel burn — 1.2 hr. at 155 lb./hr.

1—1.6″ aft.
2—2.8″ aft.
3—4.1″ forward.
4—2.7″ forward.

7154. A pilot determines that a helicopter's gross weight is 2,450 lb. and its total moment is 275,650.0 lb.-in. What is the amount and direction of CG movement resulting from the in–flight fuel burn outlined below?

Fuel tank centroid — fuselage station 142.0
Fuel burn — 1.5 hr. at 170 lb./hr.

1—1.6″ aft.
2—2.8″ aft.
3—4.1″ forward.
4—3.4″ forward.

7155. At speeds below 200 knots (where compressibility is not a factor), true airspeed can be found by correcting

1—calibrated airspeed for pressure altitude and temperature.
2—calibrated airspeed for atmospheric pressure and temperature.
3—indicated airspeed for indicated altitude and temperature.
4—indicated airspeed for true altitude and temperature.

7156. What calibrated airspeed is required to obtain 170 knots TAS with a pressure altitude of 11,500 ft. and a temperature of − 16° C?

1—151 knots.
2—148 knots.
3—145 knots.
4—143 knots.

7157. Determine the approximate CAS you should use to obtain 180 knots TAS with a pressure altitude of 8,000 ft. and a temperature of − 2° C.

1—158 knots.
2—160 knots.
3—162 knots.
4—164 knots.

7158. Under which condition is a forward CG most critical in an airplane?

1—On landing.
2—On takeoff.
3—During a spin.
4—When in an unusual attitude.

INTENTIONALLY LEFT BLANK

Table 1

WEIGHT & BALANCE

OPERATING CONDITIONS				A-1		A-2		A-3		A-4		A-5		A-6	
Seats	1	2	Arm = 37"	170	165	170	160	160	175	165	175	160	150	200	205
Seats	3	4	Arm = 68"			100	120			170	160			175	30
Seats	3	4	Arm = 71"	100	50			80	90			200			
Seats	5	6	Arm = 102"							85	90			65	105
Baggage	Nose Compartment			100				50		155		150		155	
Baggage	Wing Locker					50		50						50	
Baggage	Arm - 96"							50				100			
Baggage	Arm - 124"							50				105			
Baggage	Arm - 126"					65				50				65	
Fuel	Main Wing Tanks			100		100		100		100		100		100	
Fuel	Aux. Wing Tanks			63		63		63		63		63		63	
Fuel	Wing Locker Tanks			40		20		40				20			

NOTE: All operating conditions are stated in pounds except fuel, which is given in gallons.

7159. FAA Deletion.

7160. What is the CG in inches aft of datum for operating conditions A–2? (See Tables 1 and 2.)

1—40.03".
2—39.93".
3—39.22".
4—3.92".

7161. What is the CG in inches aft of datum for operating conditions A–3? (See Tables 1 and 2.)

1—3.89".
2—3.92".
3—38.87".
4—39.16".

7162. What is the CG in inches aft of datum for operating conditions A–4? (See Tables 1 and 2.)

1—40.02".
2—39.14".
3—4.00".
4—3.91".

7163. What is the CG in inches aft of datum for operating conditions A–5? (See Tables 1 and 2.)

1—41.20".
2—40.92".
3—39.56".
4—38.71".

7164. What is the CG in inches aft of datum for operating conditions A–6? (See Tables 1 and 2.)

1—38.84".
2—39.71".
3—40.01".
4—41.13".

Table 2

WEIGHT AND MOMENT TABLES

BAGGAGE

WEIGHT (POUNDS)	NOSE COMPARTMENT ARM = -31"	WING LOCKER ARM = 63"	CABIN COMPARTMENTS		
			ARM = 96"	ARM = 124"	ARM = 126"
		MOMENT/100			
10	-3	6	10	12	13
20	-6	13	19	25	25
30	-9	19	29	37	38
40	-12	25	38	50	50
50	-16	32	48	62	63
60	-19	38	58	74	76
70	-22	44	67	87	88
80	-25	50	77	99	101
90	-28	57	86	112	113
100	-31	63	96	124	126
110	-34	69	106	136	139
120	-37	76	115	149	151
130	-40	82	125	161	164
140	-43	88	134	174	176
150	-46	94	144	186	189
160	-50	101	154	198	202
170	-53	107	163		
180	-56	113	173		
190	-59	120	182		
200	-62	126	192		
210	-65	132			
220	-68	139			
230	-71	145			
240	-74	151			
250	-78				
260	-81				
270	-84				
280	-87				
290	-90				
300	-93				
310	-96				
320	-99				
330	-102				
340	-105				
350	-108				

CREW AND PASSENGERS

WEIGHT (POUNDS)	1ST OR 2ND SEATS ARM = 37"	3RD OR 4TH SEATS		5TH OR 6TH SEAT ARM = 102"
		BENCH SEAT ARM = 71"	INDIVIDUAL SEAT ARM = 68"	
		MOMENT/100		
10	4	7	7	10
20	7	14	14	20
30	11	21	20	31
40	15	28	27	41
50	18	36	34	51
60	22	43	41	61
70	26	50	48	71
80	30	57	54	82
90	33	64	61	92
100	37	71	68	102
110	41	78	75	112
120	44	85	82	122
130	48	92	88	133
140	52	99	95	143
150	56	106	102	153
160	59	114	109	163
170	63	121	116	173
180	67	128	122	184
190	70	135	129	194
200	74	142	136	204
210	78	149	143	214
220	81	156	150	224
230	85	163	156	235
240	89	170	163	245
250	92	178	170	255
260	96	185	177	265
270	100	192	184	275
280	104	199	190	286
290	107	206	197	296
300	111	213	204	306

FUEL

GALLONS	WEIGHT (POUNDS)	MAIN WING TANKS ARM = 35"	AUXILIARY WING TANKS ARM = 47"	WING LOCKER TANKS ARM = 49"
		MOMENT/100		
5	30	10	14	15
10	60	21	28	29
15	90	32	42	44
20	120	42	56	59
25	150	52	70	74
30	180	63	85	88
35	210	74	99	103
40	240	84	113	118
45	270	94	127	
50	300	105	141	
55	330	116	155	
60	360	126	169	
63	378	132	178	
65	390	136		
70	420	147		
75	450	158		
80	480	168		
85	510	178		
90	540	189		
95	570	200		
100	600	210		

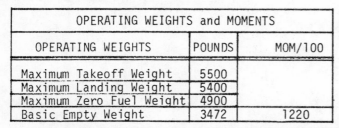

OPERATING WEIGHTS and MOMENTS		
OPERATING WEIGHTS	POUNDS	MOM/100
Maximum Takeoff Weight	5500	
Maximum Landing Weight	5400	
Maximum Zero Fuel Weight	4900	
Basic Empty Weight	3472	1220

CENTER of GRAVITY LIMITS (Reference = 0.00 Inches)			
C.G. LIMIT @ WEIGHT		INCHES AFT DATUM	%MAC
FORWARD	5500	38.67 Inches	26.69
	4500 or less	32.00 Inches	15.84
AFT	5500	43.10 Inches	33.90
	5100 or less	43.60 Inches	34.71

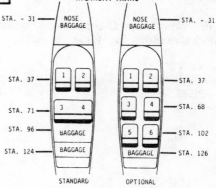

PASSENGER SEAT AND BAGGAGE MOMENT ARMS

Table 3

WEIGHT & BALANCE

OPERATING CONDITIONS				B-1		B-2		B-3		B-4		B-5		B-6	
Seats	1	2	Arm = 37"	170	160	180	130	165	150	150	165	175	170	200	180
Seats	3	4	Arm = 68"			50	30	170	180					120	
Seats	3	4	Arm = 71"							180	200				
Seats	5	6	Arm = 102"			40	30								
Baggage		Nose Compartment		110		50		50		40				30	
		Wing Locker				30		60		10					
		Arm - 96"													
		Arm - 124"								50					
		Arm - 126"						30				60		50	
Fuel		Main Wing Tanks		100		100		100		100		85		100	
		Aux. Wing Tanks		63		63		63		50		50		60	
		Wing Locker Tanks		-		40		20		-		-		20	

NOTE: All operating conditions are stated in pounds except fuel, which is given in gallons.

7165. What is the CG in inches aft of datum for operating conditions B–1? (See Tables 2 and 3.)

1—33.91".
2—34.68".
3—35.38".
4—36.01".

7166. What is the CG in inches aft of datum for operating conditions B–2? (See Tables 2 and 3.)

1—37.03".
2—37.67".
3—38.00".
4—38.99".

7167. What is the CG in inches aft of datum for operating conditions B–3? (See Tables 2 and 3.)

1—38.73".
2—39.03".
3—39.23".
4—39.89".

7168. FAA Deletion.

7169. What is the CG in inches aft of datum for operating conditions B–5? (See Tables 2 and 3.)

1—37.19".
2—37.99".
3—38.76".
4—39.01".

7170.
FAA Deletion.

Table 4

WEIGHT & BALANCE

OPERATING CONDITIONS				C-1		C-2		C-3		C-4		C-5		C-6	
Seats	1	2	Arm = 37"	160	170	130	180	150	165	165	150	180	205	170	170
Seats	3	4	Arm = 68"			150	150			75	190			170	175
Seats	3	4	Arm = 71"	80	60			80	90			155	160		
Seats	5	6	Arm = 102"			130	140			120	15				170
Baggage		Nose Compartment		130				80		120				70	
		Wing Locker								40					
		Arm - 96"		40				30				70			
		Arm - 124"						60				70			
		Arm - 126"		40		50				60				60	
Fuel		Main Wing Tanks		90		100		85		100		100		90	
		Aux. Wing Tanks		63		63		63		63		63		63	
		Wing Locker Tanks		40		20		20		-		-		20	

NOTE: All operating conditions are stated in pounds except fuel, which is given in gallons.

7171. What is the CG in inches aft of datum for operating conditions C–1? (See Tables 2 and 4.)

1—3.71″.
2—37.19″.
3—37.96″.
4—38.23″.

7172. What is the CG in inches aft of datum for operating conditions C–2? (See Tables 2 and 4.)

1—26.65″.
2—34.37″.
3—40.09″.
4—42.27″.

7173. What is the CG in inches aft of datum for operating conditions C–3? (See Tables 2 and 4.)

1—3.88″.
2—38.48″.
3—3.80″.
4—37.99″.

7174. What is the CG in inches aft of datum for operating conditions C–4? (See Tables 2 and 4.)

1—35.14″.
2—37.43″.
3—39.11″.
4—39.98″.

7175. What is the CG in inches aft of datum for operating conditions C–5? (See Tables 2 and 4.)

1—24.15″.
2—25.14″.
3—35.13″.
4—40.25″.

7176. What is the CG in inches aft of datum for operating conditions C–6? (See Tables 2 and 4.)

1—34.56″.
2—35.13″.
3—40.66″.
4—41.05″.

Table 5

NORMAL TAKEOFF DISTANCE

OPERATING CONDITIONS	D-1	D-2	D-3	D-4	D-5	D-6
Weight (lb.)	5,500	5,300	4,900	4,500	4,300	5,100
Runway	36	18	3	27R	30	26
Runway Surface Level, Hard/Firm, Dry	Concrete	Asphalt	Sod	Sod	Concrete	Asphalt
Wind Direction/Speed	055°/18	280°/10	120°/20	010°/10	015°/20	360°/10
Temperature	23°F	50°F	10°C	41°F	-10°C	5°F
Pressure Altitude (ft.)	3,000	1,500	6,000	1,000	8,500	6,000

7177. What is the normal takeoff distance for operating conditions D–1? (See Tables 5 and 6 and Figure 9.)

1—1,980 ft.
2—2,205 ft.
3—2,278 ft.
4—2,695 ft.

7178. What is the normal takeoff distance for operating conditions D–2? (See Tables 5 and 6 and Figure 9.)

1—1,950 ft.
2—2,153 ft.
3—2,261 ft.
4—2,355 ft.

7179. What is the normal takeoff distance for operating conditions D–3? (See Tables 5 and 6 and Figure 9.)

1—3,043 ft.
2—2,820 ft.
3—2,597 ft.
4—2,463 ft.

7180. What is the normal takeoff distance for operating conditions D–4? (See Tables 5 and 6 and Figure 9.)

1—1,296 ft.
2—1,340 ft.
3—1,407 ft.
4—1,518 ft.

7181. What is the ground roll distance for operating conditions D–5? (See Tables 5 and 6 and Figure 9.)

1—1,910 ft.
2—1,815 ft.
3—1,751 ft.
4—1,696 ft.

7182. What is the ground roll distance for operating conditions D–6? (See Tables 5 and 6 and Figure 9.)

1—2,174 ft.
2—2,070 ft.
3—1,990 ft.
4—1,966 ft.

Table 6

NORMAL TAKEOFF DISTANCE

CONDITIONS:
1. Power - FULL THROTTLE and 2700 RPM Before Brake Release
2. Mixtures - LEAN For Field Elevation
3. Wing Flaps - UP
4. Cowl Flaps - OPEN
5. Level, Hard Surface, Dry Runway

NOTE:
1. If full power is applied without brakes set, distances apply from point where full power is applied.
2. Decrease all distances 7% for each 10 knots headwind.
3. Increase all distances 5% for each 2 knots tailwind.
4. Increase all distances 7.9% for operation on firm dry sod runway.

WEIGHT-POUNDS	TAKEOFF TO 50-FOOT OBSTACLE SPEED-KIAS	PRESSURE ALTITUDE-FEET	-20°C (-4°F)		-10°C (14°F)		0°C (32°F)		10°C (50°F)	
			GROUND ROLL - FEET	TOTAL DISTANCE TO CLEAR 50 FEET	GROUND ROLL - FEET	TOTAL DISTANCE TO CLEAR 50 FEET	GROUND ROLL - FEET	TOTAL DISTANCE TO CLEAR 50 FEET	GROUND ROLL - FEET	TOTAL DISTANCE TO CLEAR 50 FEET
5500	92	Sea Level	1330	1650	1440	1760	1550	1890	1660	2020
		1000	1470	1810	1580	1940	1700	2080	1830	2240
		2000	1610	1990	1740	2140	1880	2300	2020	2470
		3000	1780	2200	1920	2360	2070	2540	2300	2800
		4000	1970	2430	2130	2620	2370	2900	2550	3120
		5000	2180	2700	2430	2980	2620	3220	2820	3470
		6000	2490	3080	2690	3320	2900	3590	3130	3880
		7000	2770	3440	2990	3730	3240	4040	3500	4380
		8000	3090	3880	3350	4220	3620	4590	3920	5000
		9000	3470	4420	3760	4830	4080	5290	4420	5800
		10,000	3880	5050	4220	5550	4580	6130	4980	6810
5100	88	Sea Level	1110	1380	1200	1480	1290	1580	1380	1690
		1000	1220	1510	1320	1620	1420	1740	1520	1860
		2000	1340	1660	1450	1780	1560	1910	1680	2040
		3000	1480	1820	1600	1960	1720	2100	1850	2250
		4000	1630	2010	1760	2160	1900	2330	2050	2500
		5000	1800	2220	1940	2390	2100	2570	2330	2840
		6000	1990	2460	2150	2650	2400	2930	2580	3160
		7000	2210	2730	2470	3030	2660	3270	2870	3530
		8000	2540	3140	2750	3400	2970	3680	3210	3980
		9000	2840	3540	3080	3840	3330	4170	3610	4530
		10,000	3170	3990	3440	4340	3730	4730	4040	5160
4700	85	Sea Level	920	1140	990	1220	1060	1300	1140	1390
		1000	1010	1250	1080	1340	1170	1430	1250	1530
		2000	1100	1360	1190	1460	1280	1570	1370	1670
		3000	1210	1500	1310	1600	1410	1720	1510	1840
		4000	1340	1650	1440	1770	1550	1900	1670	2030
		5000	1470	1810	1590	1940	1710	2090	1840	2240
		6000	1620	2000	1750	2150	1890	2310	2030	2480
		7000	1800	2210	1940	2380	2090	2560	2260	2760
		8000	1990	2460	2160	2650	2330	2860	2600	3170
		9000	2230	2750	2490	3060	2690	3300	2900	3560
		10,000	2560	3160	2770	3420	3000	3700	3240	4010
4300	81	Sea Level	750	930	800	1000	860	1060	920	1130
		1000	820	1020	880	1090	940	1160	1010	1240
		2000	890	1110	960	1190	1030	1270	1110	1360
		3000	980	1210	1050	1300	1130	1390	1220	1490
		4000	1080	1330	1160	1430	1250	1530	1340	1630
		5000	1180	1460	1270	1560	1370	1680	1470	1790
		6000	1300	1600	1400	1720	1510	1840	1620	1980
		7000	1440	1770	1550	1900	1670	2040	1800	2190
		8000	1590	1960	1720	2100	1850	2260	2000	2430
		9000	1770	2180	1910	2340	2060	2530	2230	2720
		10,000	1960	2420	2120	2610	2290	2810	2560	3120

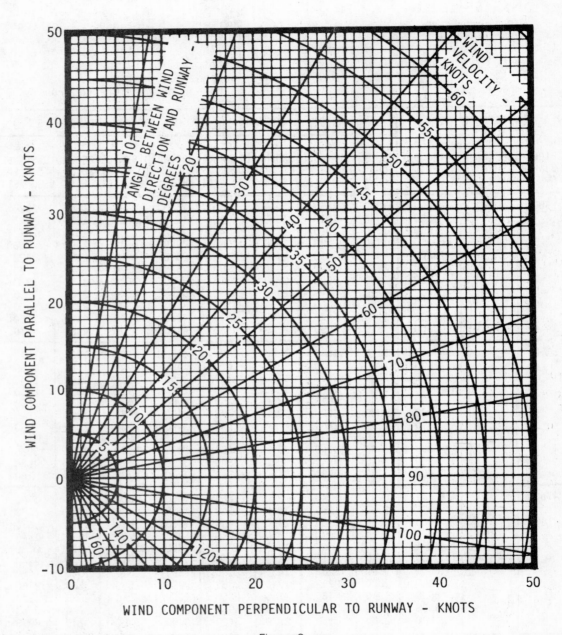

Figure 9

30

Table 7

NORMAL TAKEOFF DISTANCE

OPERATING CONDITIONS	E-1	E-2	E-3	E-4	E-5	E-6
Weight (lb.)	5,100	4,700	4,500	5,500	4,300	5,300
Runway	21	9L	1	15	34	26C
Runway Surface Level, Hard/Firm, Dry	Concrete	Asphalt	Sod	Asphalt	Sod	Concrete
Wind Direction/Speed	210°/20	180°/20	120°/12	Calm	050°/30	Calm
Temperature	25°C	40°C	86°F	104°F	95°F	77°F
Pressure Altitude (ft.)	4,000	3,500	1,000	9,500	8,000	S/L

7183. FAA Deletion.

7186. FAA Deletion.

7184. FAA Deletion.

7187. FAA Deletion.

7185. FAA Deletion.

7188. FAA Deletion.

Table 8

NORMAL TAKEOFF DISTANCE

CONDITIONS:
1. Power - FULL THROTTLE and 2700 RPM Before Brake Release
2. Mixtures - LEAN For Field Elevation
3. Wing Flaps - UP
4. Cowl Flaps - OPEN
5. Level, Hard Surface, Dry Runway

NOTE:
1. If full power is applied without brakes set, distances apply from point where full power is applied.
2. Decrease all distances by 7% for each 10 knots tailwind.
3. Increase all distances 5% for each 2 knots tailwind.
4. Increase all distances 7.9% for operation on firm dry sod runway.

WEIGHT-POUNDS	TAKEOFF TO 50-FOOT OBSTACLE SPEED-KIAS	PRESSURE ALTITUDE-FEET	20°C (68°F)		30°C (86°F)		40°C (104°F)	
			GROUND ROLL - FEET	TOTAL DISTANCE TO CLEAR 50 FEET	GROUND ROLL - FEET	TOTAL DISTANCE TO CLEAR 50 FEET	GROUND ROLL - FEET	TOTAL DISTANCE TO CLEAR 50 FEET
5500	92	Sea Level	1780	2170	1910	2320	2050	2480
		1000	1970	2400	2110	2570	2330	2820
		2000	2240	2710	2400	2910	2570	3120
		3000	2470	3010	2650	3230	2850	3470
		4000	2740	3360	2950	3610	3170	3890
		5000	3040	3740	3270	4040	3520	4360
		6000	3380	4200	3650	4550	3930	4940
		7000	3780	4760	4080	5180	4410	5650
		8000	4240	5470	4590	5990	4970	6600
		9000	4790	6400	5200	7110	5640	7990
		10,000	5410	7640	5880	8720	6390	10,270
5100	88	Sea Level	1480	1800	1590	1930	1700	2060
		1000	1640	1990	1750	2130	1880	2270
		2000	1800	2190	1930	2340	2070	2510
		3000	1990	2420	2130	2590	2360	2850
		4000	2270	2750	2440	2950	2620	3170
		5000	2510	3050	2700	3280	2900	3530
		6000	2780	3400	2990	3660	3220	3950
		7000	3100	3810	3340	4120	3600	4450
		8000	3470	4310	3740	4670	4040	5080
		9000	3900	4930	4220	5370	4560	5880
		10,000	4380	5650	4750	6210	5140	6870
4700	85	Sea Level	1220	1490	1310	1590	1400	1690
		1000	1340	1630	1440	1740	1540	1860
		2000	1470	1790	1580	1910	1690	2040
		3000	1620	1970	1740	2110	1870	2260
		4000	1790	2180	1920	2330	2070	2500
		5000	1980	2400	2130	2580	2350	2840
		6000	2190	2670	2430	2940	2610	3150
		7000	2510	3050	2700	3280	2900	3530
		8000	2800	3410	3010	3680	3240	3970
		9000	3130	3850	3380	4170	3650	4510
		10,000	3500	4350	3780	4720	4090	5130
4300	81	Sea Level	990	1210	1060	1290	1130	1370
		1000	1080	1320	1160	1410	1240	1500
		2000	1190	1450	1270	1540	1360	1650
		3000	1300	1590	1400	1700	1500	1810
		4000	1440	1750	1540	1870	1650	2000
		5000	1580	1920	1700	2060	1820	2200
		6000	1750	2120	1880	2270	2010	2430
		7000	1930	2350	2080	2520	2300	2770
		8000	2150	2620	2390	2880	2560	3100
		9000	2480	3010	2670	3240	2870	3480
		10,000	2760	3360	2970	3620	3200	3910

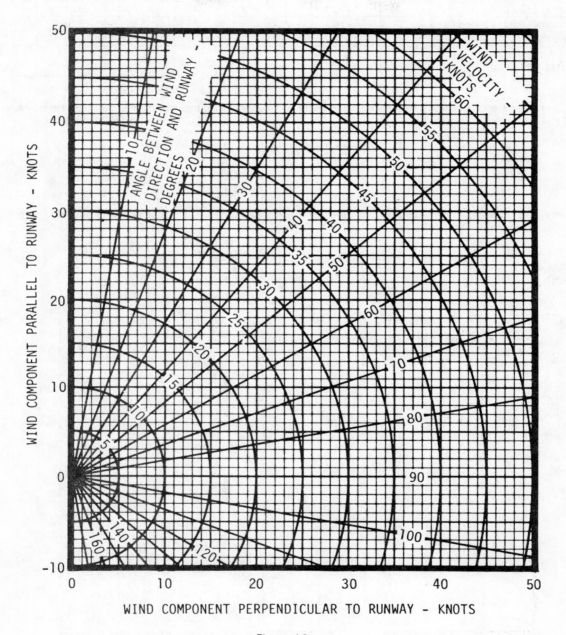

Figure 10

33

Table 9

ACCELERATE-STOP DISTANCE

OPERATING CONDITIONS	F-1	F-2	F-3	F-4	F-5	F-6
Weight (lb.)	5,500	5,300	5,100	4,700	5,500	4,500
Pressure Altitude (ft.)	5,500	2,000	8,000	S/L	9,000	6,000
Temperature	10°C	59°F	40°C	5°F	35°C	68°F
Wind Components - knots (+)=HW (-)=TW	-4	Calm	+16	+20	-2	Calm

7189. What is the accelerate/stop distance for operating conditions F–1? (See Tables 9 and 11.)

1—4,761 ft.
2—5,290 ft.
3—5,545 ft.
4—5,819 ft.

7190. What is the accelerate/stop distance for operating conditions F–2? (See Tables 9 and 11.)

1—3,600 ft.
2—3,720 ft.
3—3,840 ft.
4—3,960 ft.

7191. What is the accelerate/stop distance for operating conditions F–3? (See Tables 9 and 11.)

1—5,120 ft.
2—5,650 ft.
3—6,420 ft.
4—7,190 ft.

7192. What is the accelerate/stop distance for operating conditions F–4? (See Tables 9 and 11.)

1—1,795 ft.
2—1,844 ft.
3—2,170 ft.
4—2,496 ft.

7193. What is the accelerate/stop distance for operating conditions F–5? (See Tables 9 and 11.)

1—7,875 ft.
2—8,290 ft.
3—8,705 ft.
4—9,115 ft.

7194. What is the accelerate/stop distance for operating conditions F–6? (See Tables 9 and 11.)

1—2,785 ft.
2—2,970 ft.
3—3,315 ft.
4—3,535 ft.

Table 10

ACCELERATE-STOP DISTANCE

OPERATING CONDITIONS	G-1	G-2	G-3	G-4	G-5	G-6
Weight (lb.)	4,300	4,500	4,700	4,900	5,100	5,500
Pressure Altitude (ft.)	7,500	4,000	3,000	1,000	2,500	8,500
Temperature	104°F	86°F	59°F	41°F	5°F	40°C
Wind Components - knots (+)=HW (-)=TW	+8	-2	+4	-4	Calm	+8

7195. What is the accelerate/stop distance for operating conditions G–1? (See Tables 10 and 11.)

1—3,798 ft.
2—4,040 ft.
3—4,122 ft.
4—4,282 ft.

7196. What is the accelerate/stop distance for operating conditions G–2? (See Tables 10 and 11.)

1—3,078 ft.
2—3,240 ft.
3—3,375 ft.
4—3,402 ft.

7197. What is the accelerate/stop distance for operating conditions G–3? (See Tables 10 and 11.)

1—2,988 ft.
2—3,080 ft.
3—3,160 ft.
4—3,260 ft.

7198. What is the accelerate/stop distance for operating conditions G–4? (See Tables 10 and 11.)

1—2,550 ft.
2—2,835 ft.
3—2,980 ft.
4—3,119 ft.

7199. What is the accelerate/stop distance for operating conditions G–5? (See Tables 10 and 11.)

1—3,063 ft.
2—3,160 ft.
3—2,965 ft.
4—2,875 ft.

7200. What is the accelerate/stop distance for operating conditions G–6? (See Tables 10 and 11.)

1—7,680 ft.
2—8,170 ft.
3—8,378 ft.
4—8,660 ft.

INTENTIONALLY LEFT BLANK

Table 11

ACCELERATE STOP DISTANCE

CONDITIONS:
1. Power - FULL THROTTLE and 2700 RPM Before Brake Release.
2. Mixtures - LEAN for field elevation
3. Wing Flaps - UP.
4. Cowl Flaps - OPEN.
5. Level, Hard Surface, Dry Runway.
6. Engine Failure at Engine Failure Speed.
7. Idle Power and Heavy Braking After Engine Failure.

NOTE:
1. If full power is applied without brakes set, distances apply from point where full power is applied.
2. Decrease distance 3% for each 4 knots headwind.
3. Increase distance 5% for each 2 knots tailwind.

WEIGHT - POUNDS	ENGINE FAILURE SPEED - KIAS	PRESSURE ALTITUDE - FEET	TOTAL DISTANCE - FEET						
			-20°C -4°F	-10°C +14°F	0°C 32°F	+10°C +50°F	+20°C +68°F	+30°C +86°F	+40°C +104°F
5500	92	Sea Level	3020	3190	3370	3550	3740	3930	4120
		1000	3220	3400	3590	3790	3990	4210	4490
		2000	3430	3630	3830	4050	4340	4570	4820
		3000	3660	3880	4100	4400	4650	4910	5180
		4000	3920	4160	4480	4730	5000	5290	5590
		5000	4200	4530	4810	5090	5390	5700	6030
		6000	4590	4880	5180	5490	5820	6170	6530
		7000	4950	5270	5600	5940	6310	6700	7110
		8000	5360	5710	6070	6460	6870	7310	7780
		9000	5830	6210	6630	7060	7530	8020	8560
		10,000	6330	6770	7230	7720	8250	8810	9420
5100	88	Sea Level	2540	2680	2830	2980	3140	3300	3470
		1000	2710	2860	3020	3180	3350	3530	3710
		2000	2880	3050	3220	3390	3580	3770	3970
		3000	3070	3250	3440	3630	3830	4040	4330
		4000	3290	3480	3680	3900	4190	4420	4660
		5000	3520	3730	3950	4250	4500	4750	5020
		6000	3770	4010	4320	4580	4850	5130	5430
		7000	4060	4390	4660	4950	5240	5560	5890
		8000	4470	4750	5050	5360	5690	6050	6420
		9000	4840	5160	5490	5840	6220	6610	7030
		10,000	5250	5600	5970	6370	6790	7230	7710
4700	85	Sea Level	2110	2230	2350	2470	2600	2740	2870
		1000	2250	2370	2500	2640	2770	2920	3070
		2000	2390	2520	2660	2810	2960	3120	3280
		3000	2540	2690	2840	3000	3160	3340	3510
		4000	2720	2880	3040	3210	3390	3580	3780
		5000	2900	3080	3260	3440	3640	3840	4130
		6000	3110	3300	3500	3700	3910	4210	4450
		7000	3340	3550	3760	3990	4300	4550	4820
		8000	3600	3830	4070	4390	4660	4940	5230
		9000	3900	4230	4490	4770	5070	5380	5710
		10,000	4300	4580	4870	5180	5510	5860	6240
4300	81	Sea Level	1730	1820	1920	2020	2120	2230	2340
		1000	1830	1940	2040	2150	2260	2380	2500
		2000	1950	2060	2170	2290	2410	2530	2660
		3000	2070	2190	2310	2440	2570	2710	2850
		4000	2210	2340	2470	2610	2750	2900	3060
		5000	2360	2500	2640	2790	2950	3110	3280
		6000	2520	2680	2830	2990	3160	3340	3530
		7000	2710	2870	3040	3220	3410	3600	3880
		8000	2910	3090	3280	3470	3680	3970	4200
		9000	3140	3340	3550	3760	4070	4310	4570
		10,000	3390	3610	3830	4150	4410	4680	4970

Table 12

ACCELERATE-GO DISTANCE

OPERATING CONDITIONS	H-1	H-2	H-3	H-4	H-5	H-6
Weight (lb.)	5,500	5,100	4,700	5,300	5,300	4,300
Pressure Altitude (ft.)	4,500	4,000	S/L	2,000	1,000	3,000
Temperature	-10°C	104°F	104°F	5°F	10°C	23°F
Wind Components - knots (+)=HW (-)=TW	-5	Calm	+30	-5	Calm	+15

7201. What is the accelerate/go distance for operating conditions H–1? (See Tables 12 and 14.)

1—8,576 ft.
2—9,013 ft.
3—10,015 ft.
4—11,017 ft.

7202. What is the accelerate/go distance for operating conditions H–2? (See Tables 12 and 14.)

1—9,673 ft.
2—10,430 ft.
3—11,005 ft.
4—11,645 ft.

7203. What is the accelerate/go distance for operating conditions H–3? (See Tables 12 and 14.)

1—2,017 ft.
2—2,276 ft.
3—2,460 ft.
4—2,904 ft.

7204. FAA Deletion.

7205. What is the accelerate/go distance for operating conditions H–5? (See Tables 12 and 14.

1—2,940 ft.
2—3,325 ft.
3—3,550 ft.
4—4,105 ft.

7206. What is the accelerate/go distance for operating conditions H–6? (See Tables 12 and 14.)

1—1,720 ft.
2—1,890 ft.
3—2,060 ft.
4—2,130 ft.

7207. FAA Deletion.

7208. What is the accelerate/go distance for operating conditions I–2? (See Tables 13 and 14.)

1—2,280 ft.
2—2,375 ft.
3—2,480 ft.
4—2,678 ft.

Table 13

ACCELERATE-GO DISTANCE

OPERATING CONDITIONS	I-1	I-2	I-3	I-4	I-5	I-6
Weight (lb.)	4,300	4,500	4,700	4,900	5,100	5,300
Pressure Altitude (ft.)	500	5,000	5,500	2,500	6,000	1,000
Temperature	9°F	-4°F	104°F	32°F	41°F	23°F
Wind Components - knots (+)=HW (-)=TW	Calm	-4	+15	Calm	-6	+30

Table 14

ACCELERATE GO DISTANCE

CONDITIONS:
1. Power - FULL THROTTLE and 2700 RPM Before Brake Release.
2. Mixtures - Lean for field elevation
3. Wing Flaps - UP.
4. Cowl Flaps - OPEN.
5. Level Hard Surface Dry Funway.
6. Engine Failure At Engine Failure Speed.
7. Propeller Feathered and Landing Gear Retracted During Climb.
8. Maintain Engine Failure Speed Until Clear of Obstacle.

NOTE:
1. If full power is applied without brakes set, distances apply from point where full power is applied.
2. Decrease distance 6% for each 10 knots headwind.
3. Increase distance 2% for each knot of tailwind.
4. Distance in boxes represent rates of climb less than 50 ft/min.

WEIGHT - POUNDS	ENGINE FAILURE - SPEED - KIAS	PRESSURE ALTITUDE - FEET	TOTAL DISTANCE TO CLEAR 50-FOOT OBSTACLE						
			-20°C -4°F	-10°C +14°F	0°C 32°F	+10°C +50°F	+20°C +68°F	+30°C +86°F	+40°C +104°F
5500	92	Sea Level	2600	2850	3120	3450	3840	4320	4950
		1000	3010	3330	3700	4160	4760	5560	6810
		2000	3530	3970	4520	5250	6370	8080	11,540
		3000	4310	4990	5950	[7520]	10,350	------	------
		4000	5650	7020	9550	[15,790]	------	------	------
		5000	8470	[13,010]	------	------	------	------	------
		6000	------	------	------	------	------	------	------
		7000	------	------	------	------	------	------	------
		8000	------	------	------	------	------	------	------
		9000	------	------	------	------	------	------	------
		10,000	------	------	------	------	------	------	------
5100	88	Sea Level	2030	2190	2360	2560	2780	3030	3320
		1000	2280	2470	2690	2940	3220	3540	3940
		2000	2580	2820	3090	3400	3770	4230	4810
		3000	2960	3270	3630	4060	4600	5330	6430
		4000	3490	3910	4430	5110	6130	7620	10,430
		5000	4200	4820	5680	7030	9280	[14,630]	------
		6000	5350	6500	8480	12,550	------	------	------
		7000	7800	11,240	------	------	------	------	------
		8000	------	------	------	------	------	------	------
		9000	------	------	------	------	------	------	------
		10,000	------	------	------	------	------	------	------
4700	85	Sea Level	1600	1720	1840	1980	2130	2290	2460
		1000	1780	1910	2060	2210	2390	2580	2800
		2000	1980	2130	2300	2490	2700	2930	3200
		3000	2210	2400	2600	2830	3090	3390	3740
		4000	2510	2730	2990	3280	3620	4030	4540
		5000	2860	3140	3460	3850	4320	4930	5820
		6000	3320	3690	4130	4700	5450	6610	8370
		7000	3960	4500	5200	6190	7820	10,780	------
		8000	4990	5920	7350	10,020	[16,800]	------	------
		9000	7040	9510	[15,370]	------	------	------	------
		10,000	[13,110]	------	------	------	------	------	------
4300	81	Sea Level	1270	1360	1450	1550	1650	1760	1890
		1000	1400	1500	1600	1710	1830	1960	2100
		2000	1540	1650	1760	1890	2030	2180	2340
		3000	1700	1820	1960	2110	2270	2440	2640
		4000	1890	2040	2190	2370	2560	2770	3020
		5000	2100	2270	2460	2670	2900	3170	3470
		6000	2360	2570	2790	3050	3340	3690	4100
		7000	2690	2940	3220	3550	3950	4430	5110
		8000	3110	3430	3810	4280	4860	5720	6850
		9000	3690	4150	4710	5460	6610	8330	11,760
		10,000	4490	5190	6160	7730	10,510	------	------

7209. FAA Deletion.

7210. What is the accelerate/go distance for operating conditions I-4? (See Tables 13 and 14.)

1—2,450 ft.
2—2,640 ft.
3—2,905 ft.
4—3,360 ft.

7211. What is the accelerate/go distance for operating conditions I-5? (See Tables 13 and 14.)

1—10,010 ft.
2—10,515 ft.
3—11,777 ft.
4—12,620 ft.

7212. What is the accelerate/go distance for operating conditions I-6? (See Tables 13 and 14.)

1—2,135 ft.
2—2,499 ft.
3—3,048 ft.
4—3,597 ft.

7213. What is the maximum rate-of-climb for operating conditions J-1? (See Table 15 and Figure 11.)

1—1,400 ft./min.
2—1,550 ft./min.
3—1,700 ft./min.
4—1,900 ft./min.

7214. What is the maximum rate-of-climb for operating conditions J-2? (See Table 15 and Figure 11.)

1—1,500 ft./min.
2—1,625 ft./min.
3—1,700 ft./min.
4—1,750 ft./min.

7215. What is the maximum rate-of-climb for operating conditions J-3? (See Table 15 and Figure 11.)

1—1,200 ft./min.
2—1,350 ft./min.
3—1,450 ft./min.
4—1,550 ft./min.

7216. What is the maximum rate-of-climb for operating conditions J-4? (See Table 15 and Figure 11.)

1—500 ft./min.
2—600 ft./min.
3—725 ft./min.
4—850 ft./min.

7217. What is the maximum rate-of-climb for operating conditions J-5? (See Table 15 and Figure 11.)

1—1,550 ft./min.
2—2,150 ft./min.
3—2,200 ft./min.
4—2,500 ft./min.

7218. What is the maximum rate-of-climb for operating conditions J-6? (See Table 15 and Figure 11.)

1—1,100 ft./min.
2—1,250 ft./min.
3—1,400 ft./min.
4—1,525 ft./min.

Table 15

RATE-OF-CLIMB - MAXIMUM CLIMB

OPERATING CONDITIONS	J-1	J-2	J-3	J-4	J-5	J-6
Weight (lb.)	4,700	5,300	5,150	5,100	5,500	4,900
Pressure Altitude (ft.)	5,000	5,000	7,500	12,500	S/L	10,000
OAT	32°F	-10°C	0°F	50°F	80°F	ISA +5°C

RATE-OF-CLIMB - MAXIMUM CLIMB

WEIGHT	CLIMB SPEED - KIAS				
Pounds	Sea Level	5000 Feet	10,000 Feet	15,000 Feet	20,000 Feet
5500	107	103	99	95	91
5100	103	99	96	92	88
4700	99	95	92	88	85

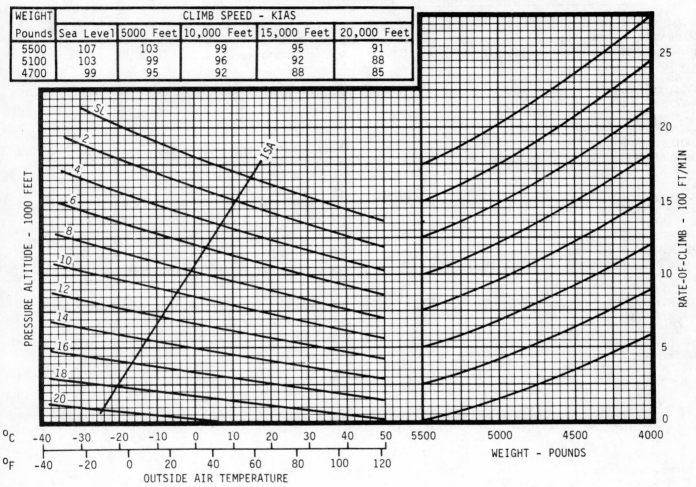

Figure 11

41

Table 16

RATE-OF-CLIMB - SINGLE ENGINE

OPERATING CONDITIONS	K-1	K-2	K-3	K-4	K-5	K-6
Weight (lb.)	5,500	5,300	4,700	5,450	4,250	5,300
Pressure Altitude (ft.)	S/L	1,000	2,500	8,000	10,000	9,000
OAT	15°C	80°F	ISA -5°C	90°F	40°F	10°C

7219. What is the rate-of-climb, single-engine, for operating conditions K-1? (See Table 16 and Figure 12.)

1—450 ft./min.
2—410 ft./min.
3—375 ft./min.
4—325 ft./min.

7220. What is the rate-of-climb, single-engine, for operating conditions K-2? (See Table 16 and Figure 12.)

1—315 ft./min.
2—330 ft./min.
3—365 ft./min.
4—390 ft./min.

7221. What is the rate-of-climb, single-engine, for operating conditions K-3? (See Table 16 and Figure 12.)

1—350 ft./min.
2—390 ft./min.
3—430 ft./min.
4—465 ft./min.

7222. What is the rate-of-climb, single-engine, for operating conditions K-4? (See Table 16 and Figure 12.)

1—35 ft./min.
2—20 ft./min.
3—0 ft./min.
4— – 20 ft./min.

7223. What is the rate-of-climb, single-engine, for operating conditions K-5? (See Table 16 and Figure 12.)

1—170 ft./min.
2—190 ft./min.
3—210 ft./min.
4—275 ft./min.

7224. What is the rate-of-climb, single-engine, for operating conditions K-6? (See Table 16 and Figure 12.)

1—0 ft./min.
2—40 ft./min.
3—65 ft./min.
4—80 ft./min.

RATE OF CLIMB ·· SINGLE ENGINE

WEIGHT	CLIMB SPEED - KIAS				
Pounds	Sea Level	2500 Feet	5000 Feet	7500 Feet	10,000 Feet
5500	106	103	100	97	94
5100	102	99	96	93	90
4700	98	95	92	89	86

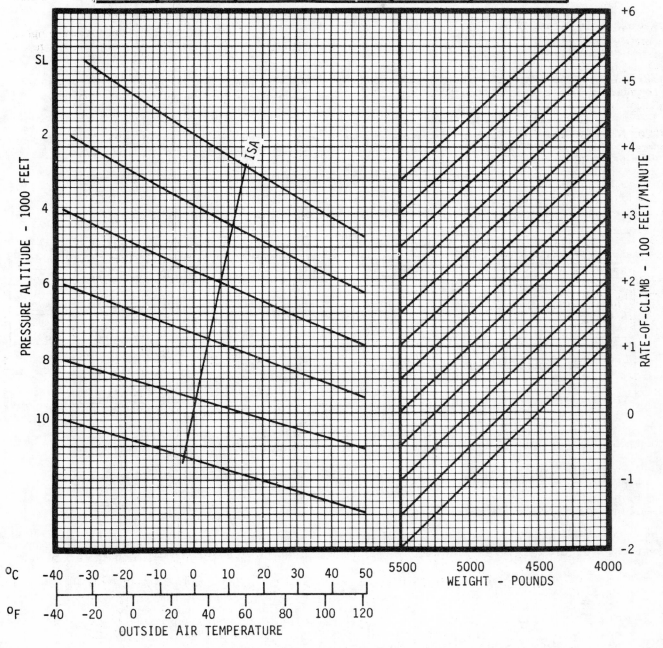

Figure 12

43

7225. What is the time, fuel, and distance for operating conditions L–1? (See Table 17 and Figure 13.)

1—8 min., 34 lb., and 14 NM.
2—7 min., 29 lb., and 12 NM.
3—6 min., 24 lb., and 10 NM.
4—5 min., 21 lb., and 8 NM.

7226. What is the time, fuel, and distance for operating conditions L–2? (See Table 17 and Figure 13.)

1—5 min., 22 lb., and 10 NM.
2—6 min., 24 lb., and 11 NM.
3—7 min., 26 lb., and 14 NM.
4—9 min., 36 lb., and 17 NM.

7227. What is the time, fuel, and distance for operating conditions L–3? (See Table 17 and Figure 13.)

1—8 min., 30 lb., and 12 NM.
2—9 min., 38 lb., and 18 NM.
3—11 min., 48 lb., and 21 NM.
4—12 min., 51 lb., and 22 NM.

7228. What is the time, fuel, and distance for operating conditions L–4? (See Table 17 and Figure 13.)

1—6 min., 21 lb., and 12 NM.
2—7 min., 26 lb., and 14 NM.
3—8 min., 27 lb., and 15 NM.
4—10 min., 40 lb., and 19 NM.

7229. What is the time, fuel, and distance for operating conditions L–5? (See Table 17 and Figure 13.)

1—8 min., 30 lb., and 15 NM.
2—9.5 min., 36 lb., and 17 NM.
3—11 min., 39 lb., and 19 NM.
4—14 min., 50 lb., and 26 NM.

7230. What is the time, fuel, and distance for operating conditions L–6? (See Table 17 and Figure 13.)

1—3 min., 13 lb., and 5 NM.
2—4 min., 18 lb., and 6 NM.
3—5 min., 22 lb., and 8 NM.
4—6 min., 26 lb., and 9 NM.

Table 17

TIME, FUEL, AND DISTANCE TO CLIMB - MAXIMUM CLIMB

OPERATING CONDITIONS		L-1	L-2	L-3	L-4	L-5	L-6
Weight (lb.)		5,500	5,100	4,700	4,900	5,300	5,500
Departure Airport	Pressure Altitude (ft.)	2,000	3,000	S/L	6,000	1,000	S/L
	OAT	20°F	10°C	89°F	60°F	40°F	80°F
Cruise	Pressure Altitude (ft.)	8,500	11,000	12,500	14,000	11,500	6,000
	OAT	ISA	0°C	ISA+10°C	ISA -7°C	32°F	59°F

7231. What is the time, fuel, and distance for operating conditions M–1? (See Table 18 and Figure 13.)

1—7.5 min., 30 lb., and 14 NM.
2—9 min., 38 lb., and 17 NM.
3—10 min., 39 lb., and 19 NM.
4—11 min., 41 lb., and 20 NM.

7232. What is the time, fuel, and distance for operating conditions M–2? (See Table 18 and Figure 13.)

1—6 min., 28 lb., and 13 NM.
2—8 min., 33 lb., and 15 NM.
3—10 min., 38 lb., and 17 NM.
4—11 min., 40 lb., and 19 NM.

7233. What is the time, fuel, and distance for operating conditions M–3? (See Table 18 and Figure 13.)

1—4 min., 17 lb., and 7 NM.
2—5 min., 21 lb., and 9 NM.
3—6 min., 25 lb., and 11 NM.
4—7 min., 29 lb., and 13 NM.

7234. What is the time, fuel, and distance for operating conditions M–4? (See Table 18 and Figure 13.)

1—13 min., 34 lb., and 14 NM.
2—8 min., 30 lb., and 13 NM.
3—6 min., 25 lb., and 11 NM.
4—4 min., 16 lb., and 8 NM.

7235. What is the time, fuel, and distance for operating conditions M–5? (See Table 18 and Figure 13.)

1—7 min., 27 lb., and 14 NM.
2—9 min., 36 lb., and 17 NM.
3—11 min., 45 lb., and 20 NM.
4—12 min., 47 lb., and 21 NM.

7236. What is the time, fuel, and distance for operating conditions M–6? (See Table 18 and Figure 13.)

1—18 min., 70 lb., and 34 NM.
2—14 min., 52 lb., and 27 NM.
3—12 min., 46 lb., and 23 NM.
4—10 min., 34 lb., and 20 NM.

Table 18

TIME, FUEL, AND DISTANCE TO CLIMB - MAXIMUM CLIMB

OPERATING CONDITIONS		M-1	M-2	M-3	M-4	M-5	M-6
Weight (lb.)		5,500	5,300	5,100	4,900	4,700	5,500
Departure Airport	Pressure Altitude (ft.)	1,000	1,500	2,000	3,000	4,000	5,000
	OAT	95°F	80°F	60°F	90°F	32°F	50°F
Cruise	Pressure Altitude (ft.)	9,000	10,500	8,000	9,000	12,000	14,000
	OAT	50°F	ISA	ISA+11°C	40°F	ISA+10°C	ISA

TIME, FUEL AND DISTANCE TO CLIMB - MAXIMUM CLIMB

NOTE:

1. Time, fuel and distance for the climb are determined by taking the difference between the departure airport and cruise altitude conditions.

2. For total fuel used, add 25 pounds for start, taxi and takeoff.

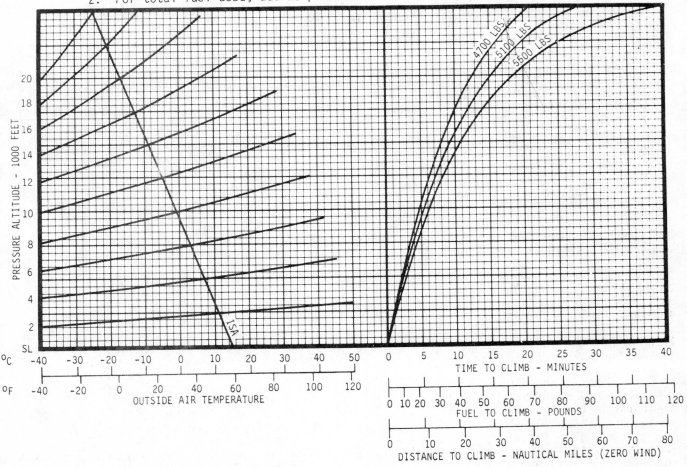

Figure 13

45

7237. FAA Deletion.

7238. FAA Deletion.

7239. FAA Deletion.

7240. FAA Deletion.

7241. FAA Deletion.

7242. FAA Deletion.

Table 19

TIME, FUEL, AND DISTANCE TO CLIMB - CRUISE CLIMB

OPERATING CONDITIONS		N-1	N-2	N-3	N-4	N-5	N-6
Weight (lb.)		5,500	5,300	5,100	4,900	4,700	5,500
Departure Airport	Pressure Altitude (ft.)	1,000	1,500	2,000	3,000	4,000	500
	OAT	95°F	80°F	60°F	90°F	32°F	100°F
Cruise	Pressure Altitude (ft.)	9,000	10,500	8,000	9,000	12,000	7,000
	OAT	50°F	ISA	ISA+11°C	40°F	ISA +2°C	50°F

7243. FAA Deletion.

7244. FAA Deletion.

7245. FAA Deletion.

7246. FAA Deletion.

7247. FAA Deletion.

7248. FAA Deletion.

Table 20

TIME, FUEL, AND DISTANCE TO CLIMB - CRUISE CLIMB

OPERATING CONDITIONS		0-1	0-2	0-3	0-4	0-5	0-6
Weight (lb.)		5,500	5,100	4,700	4,900	5,300	5,500
Departure Airport	Pressure Altitude (ft.)	2,000	3,000	S/L	6,000	1,000	S/L
	OAT	20°F	10°C	89°F	60°F	40°F	80°F
Cruise	Pressure Altitude (ft.)	8,500	11,000	12,500	14,000	11,500	6,000
	OAT	ISA	0°C	ISA+10°C	ISA -7°C	32°F	59°F

TIME, FUEL AND DISTANCE TO CLIMB - CRUISE CLIMB

NOTE:

1. Time, fuel and distance for the climb are determined by taking the difference between the departure airport and cruise altitude conditions.

2. For total fuel used, add 25 pounds for start, taxi and takeoff.

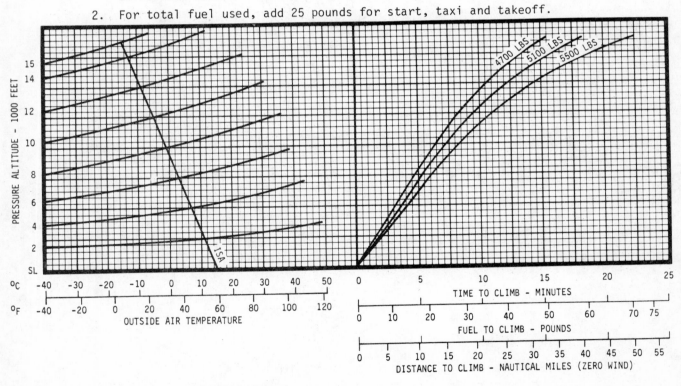

Figure 14

47

Table 21

SINGLE-ENGINE SERVICE CEILING

OPERATING CONDITIONS	P-1	P-2	P-3	P-4	P-5	P-6
OAT	0°C	50°F	23°F	104°F	6°C	30°C
Weight (lb.)	5,500	5,300	4,900	5,500	5,500	5,250
Altimeter Setting	30.02	29.82	29.97	29.87	29.97	29.92

7249. What is the single-engine service ceiling for operating conditions P-1? (See Table 21 and Figure 15.)

1—7,500 ft.
2—7,600 ft.
3—8,100 ft.
4—8,200 ft.

7250. What is the single-engine service ceiling for operating conditions P-2? (See Table 21 and Figure 15.)

1—7,900 ft.
2—8,000 ft.
3—8,100 ft.
4—8,300 ft.

7251. What is the single-engine service ceiling for operating conditions P-3? (See Table 21 and Figure 15.)

1—9,950 ft.
2—10,050 ft.
3—10,100 ft.
4—10,200 ft.

7252. What is the single-engine service ceiling for operating conditions P-4? (See Table 21 and Figure 15.)

1—5,400 ft.
2—5,650 ft.
3—5,750 ft.
4—5,900 ft.

7253. What is the single-engine service ceiling for operating conditions P-5? (See Table 21 and Figure 15.)

1—7,175 ft.
2—7,350 ft.
3—8,000 ft.
4—8,075 ft.

7254. What is the single-engine service ceiling for operating conditions P-6? (See Table 21 and Figure 15.)

1—8,600 ft.
2—8,400 ft.
3—7,400 ft.
4—7,200 ft.

7255. What is the single-engine service ceiling for operating conditions Q-1? (See Table 22 and Figure 15.)

1—9,400 ft.
2—9,600 ft.
3—10,000 ft.
4—10,200 ft.

7256. What is the single-engine service ceiling for operating conditions Q-2? (See Table 22 and Figure 15.)

1—8,050 ft.
2—8,200 ft.
3—8,350 ft.
4—8,400 ft.

7257. What is the single-engine service ceiling for operating conditions Q-3? (See Table 22 and Figure 15.)

1—8,250 ft.
2—8,400 ft.
3—8,550 ft.
4—8,625 ft.

7258. What is the single-engine service ceiling for operating conditions Q-4? (See Table 22 and Figure 15.)

1—8,780 ft.
2—8,820 ft.
3—9,000 ft.
4—9,020 ft.

7259. What is the single-engine service ceiling for operating conditions Q-5? (See Table 22 and Figure 15.)

1—8,380 ft.
2—8,420 ft.
3—8,780 ft.
4—8,820 ft.

7260. What is the single-engine service ceiling for operating conditions Q-6? (See Table 22 and Figure 15.)

1—5,860 ft.
2—6,050 ft.
3—7,330 ft.
4—7,690 ft.

Table 22

SINGLE-ENGINE SERVICE CEILING

OPERATING CONDITIONS	Q-1	Q-2	Q-3	Q-4	Q-5	Q-6
OAT	-10°C	-20°C	60°F	80°F	-15°C	32°F
Weight (lb.)	4,950	5,500	5,100	4,900	5,300	5,500
Altimeter Setting	30.12	30.07	29.77	29.94	29.90	29.73

SINGLE-ENGINE SERVICE CEILING

CONDITIONS:
1. Single-Engine Climb Configuration.

NOTE:
1. Single-engine service ceiling is the maximum altitude where the airplane has the capability of climbing 50 feet per minute with one engine inoperative and feathered.
2. Increase indicated service ceiling 100 feet for each 0.10 inches Hg. altimeter setting greater than 29.92.
3. Decrease indicated service ceiling 100 feet for each 0.10 inches Hg. altimeter setting less than 29.92.

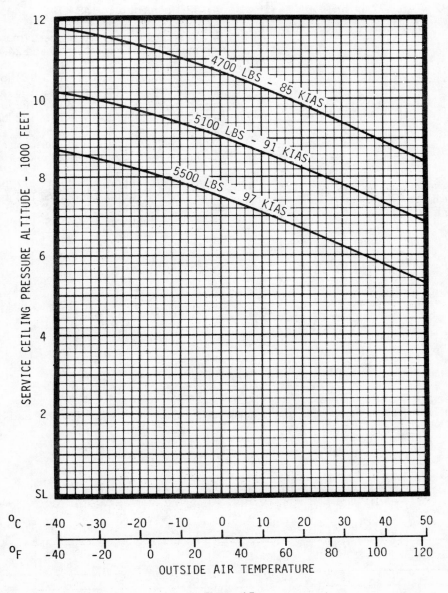

Figure 15

49

Table 23

CRUISE PERFORMANCE - RECOMMENDED LEAN MIXTURE

OPERATING CONDITIONS	R-1	R-2	R-3	R-4	R-5	R-6
Pressure Altitude (ft.)	5,000	5,000	2,500	5,000	2,500	2,500
RPM/MP	2300/24.5	2400/23	2200/23	2100/20	2100/22	2100/21
OAT	ISA	ISA+10°C	32°F	77°F	ISA -10°C	ISA+10°C
Weight (lb.)	5,100	4,200	5,100	4,900	4,700	4,900

7261. What is the cruise performance for operating conditions R–1? (See Tables 23 and 24.)

1—68.9 percent bhp, 180 KTAS, 173 lb./hr.
2—70.9 percent bhp, 182 KTAS, 175 lb./hr.
3—68.9 percent bhp, 184 KTAS, 173 lb./hr.
4—68.3 percent bhp, 182 KTAS, 177 lb./hr.

7262. FAA Deletion.

7263. FAA Deletion.

7264. What is the cruise performance for operating conditions R–4? (See Tables 23 and 24.)

1—40.9 percent bhp, 138 KTAS, 108 lb./hr.
2—41.3 percent bhp, 141 KTAS, 111 lb./hr.
3—41.3 percent bhp, 145 KTAS, 114 lb./hr.
4—43.1 percent bhp, 148 KTAS, 114 lb./hr.

7265. What is the cruise performance for operating conditions R–5? (See Tables 23 and 24.)

1—50.6 percent bhp, 152 KTAS, 131 lb./hr.
2—50.6 percent bhp, 155 KTAS, 133 lb./hr.
3—49.7 percent bhp, 157 KTAS, 129 lb./hr.
4—48.8 percent bhp, 159 KTAS, 133 lb./hr.

7266. What is the cruise performance for operating conditions R–6? (See Tables 23 and 24.)

1—44.7 percent bhp, 148 KTAS, 117 lb./hr.
2—43.9 percent bhp, 145 KTAS, 115 lb./hr.
3—43.7 percent bhp, 144 KTAS, 113 lb./hr.
4—43.2 percent bhp, 143 KTAS, 111 lb./hr.

Table 24

CRUISE PERFORMANCE
WITH RECOMMENDED LEAN MIXTURE

NOTE:
1. At 2500 feet, increase speed by 2 KTAS for each 400 pounds below 5500 pounds.
2. At 5000 feet, increase speed by 2 KTAS for each 400 pounds below 5500 pounds.
3. Operations at peak EGT may be utilized with power settings within the boxes if the airplane is equipped with the optional EGT system.

ALTITUDE	RPM	MP	-10°C (14°F) PERCENT BHP	KTAS	TOTAL LB/HR	10°C (STD TEMP) (50°F) PERCENT BHP	KTAS	TOTAL LB/HR	30°C (86°F) PERCENT BHP	KTAS	TOTAL LB/HR
2500 FEET	2500	24.5	76.5	181	191	73.8	182	185	71.1	184	179
	2500	23.0	69.9	175	176	67.4	176	170	65.0	177	164
	2500	22.0	65.8	171	166	63.5	172	161	61.1	172	156
	2500	21.0	61.5	166	156	59.3	167	152	57.2	167	147
	2400	24.5	73.3	178	184	70.7	179	178	68.1	180	171
	2400	23.0	67.1	172	169	64.8	173	164	62.4	174	158
	2400	22.0	63.1	168	160	60.9	169	155	58.7	169	150
	2400	21.0	59.2	163	151	57.1	164	147	55.0	164	142
	2300	24.5	68.3	173	172	65.9	174	166	63.5	175	161
	2300	23.0	62.7	167	159	60.5	168	154	58.3	169	149
	2300	22.0	59.1	163	151	57.0	164	146	54.9	164	142
	2300	21.0	55.3	158	143	53.4	159	138	51.4	159	133
	2200	24.5	63.9	169	162	61.7	170	157	59.4	170	152
	2200	23.0	58.7	163	150	56.7	163	146	54.6	163	141
	2200	22.0	55.4	158	143	53.4	159	138	51.5	159	134
	2200	21.0	51.9	154	135	50.1	154	130	48.2	153	126
	2200	20.0	48.4	149	126	46.7	148	122	45.0	147	118
	2100	24.5	58.7	163	150	56.7	163	146	54.6	163	141
	2100	23.0	53.8	156	139	51.9	157	135	50.0	156	130
	2100	22.0	50.6	152	131	48.8	152	127	47.0	151	123
	2100	21.0	47.2	146	123	45.5	146	119	43.9	144	115
	2100	20.0	44.0	141	116	42.4	140	112	40.9	138	108
	2100	19.0	40.8	134	108	39.4	133	105	37.9	130	101

ALTITUDE	RPM	MP	-15°C (5°F) PERCENT BHP	KTAS	TOTAL LB/HR	5°C (STD TEMP) (41°F) PERCENT BHP	KTAS	TOTAL LB/HR	25°C (77°F) PERCENT BHP	KTAS	TOTAL LB/HR
5000 FEET	2500	24.5	80.7	188	201	77.8	190	194	75.0	192	188
	2500	23.0	73.5	182	185	70.9	184	178	68.4	185	172
	2500	22.0	69.1	178	174	66.7	179	168	64.2	180	162
	2500	21.0	64.5	173	163	62.3	174	158	60.0	174	153
	2400	24.5	76.9	185	192	74.2	187	186	71.5	188	180
	2400	23.0	70.4	179	177	67.9	181	171	65.4	181	165
	2400	22.0	66.1	175	167	63.8	176	161	61.5	176	156
	2400	21.0	62.0	170	157	59.8	171	153	57.7	171	148
	2300	24.5	71.4	180	179	68.9	182	173	66.4	182	167
	2300	23.0	65.5	174	165	63.2	175	160	60.9	176	155
	2300	22.0	61.9	170	157	59.7	171	152	57.5	171	147
	2300	21.0	57.8	165	148	55.8	165	144	53.7	165	139
	2200	24.5	66.5	175	168	64.2	176	162	61.8	177	157
	2200	23.0	61.2	169	156	59.0	170	151	56.9	170	146
	2200	22.0	57.8	165	148	55.8	165	144	53.7	165	139
	2200	21.0	54.3	160	140	52.4	160	136	50.5	160	131
	2200	20.0	50.7	155	132	48.9	154	127	47.2	153	123
	2100	24.5	61.0	169	155	58.8	170	150	56.7	170	146
	2100	23.0	56.2	163	145	54.2	163	140	52.2	163	135
	2100	22.0	53.0	158	137	51.1	158	133	49.2	157	128
	2100	21.0	49.7	153	129	47.9	153	125	46.2	151	121
	2100	20.0	46.4	147	121	44.8	146	117	43.1	145	114
	2100	19.0	43.1	141	113	41.6	139	110	40.0	136	106
	2100	18.0	39.9	134	106	38.5	131	102	37.1	126	99

Table 25

CRUISE PERFORMANCE - RECOMMENDED LEAN MIXTURE

OPERATING CONDITIONS	S-1	S-2	S-3	S-4	S-5	S-6
Pressure Altitude (ft.)	7,500	10,000	7,500	10,000	7,500	10,000
RPM/MP	2200/20	2500/18	2500/22	2500/17	2100/18	2200/19
OAT	50°F	5°F	-10°C	50°F	ISA	41°F
Weight (lb.)	4,700	5,300	5,100	5,300	5,490	4,800

7267. What is the cruise performance for operating conditions S–1? (See Tables 25 and 26.)

1—49 percent bhp, 154 KTAS, 130 lb./hr.
2—49 percent bhp, 160 KTAS, 132 lb./hr.
3—50 percent bhp, 166 KTAS, 130 lb./hr.
4—51 percent bhp, 167 KTAS, 132 lb./hr.

7268. What is the cruise performance for operating conditions S–2? (See Tables 25 and 26.)

1—54.8 percent bhp, 168 KTAS, 142 lb./hr.
2—55.8 percent bhp, 170 KTAS, 143 lb./hr.
3—55.8 percent bhp, 172 KTAS, 144 lb./hr.
4—57.8 percent bhp, 174 KTAS, 146 lb./hr.

7269. What is the cruise performance for operating conditions S–3? (See Tables 25 and 26.)

1—69.7 percent bhp, 182 KTAS, 178 lb./hr.
2—79.9 percent bhp, 185 KTAS, 178 lb./hr.
3—70.9 percent bhp, 188 KTAS, 178 lb./hr.
4—71.3 percent bhp, 189 KTAS, 182 lb./hr.

7270. What is the cruise performance for operating conditions S–4? (See Tables 25 and 26.)

1—47.8 percent bhp, 161 KTAS, 125 lb./hr.
2—48.3 percent bhp, 163 KTAS, 127 lb./hr.
3—49.1 percent bhp, 163 KTAS, 128 lb./hr.
4—49.6 percent bhp, 164 KTAS, 129 lb./hr.

7271. What is the cruise performance for operating conditions S–5? (See Tables 25 and 26.)

1—39.1 percent bhp, 133 KTAS, 104 lb./hr.
2—40.5 percent bhp, 138 KTAS, 107 lb./hr.
3—40.5 percent bhp, 140 KTAS, 110 lb./hr.
4—42.0 percent bhp, 141 KTAS, 113 lb./hr.

7272. What is the cruise performance for operating conditions S–6? (See Tables 25 and 26.)

1—49.3 percent bhp, 160 KTAS, 128 lb./hr.
2—48.4 percent bhp, 165 KTAS, 126 lb./hr.
3—47.5 percent bhp, 158 KTAS, 124 lb./hr.
4—47.5 percent bhp, 159 KTAS, 126 lb./hr.

Table 26

CRUISE PERFORMANCE
WITH RECOMMENDED LEAN MIXTURE

NOTE:
1. At 7500 Feet, increase speed by 3 KTAS for each 400 pounds below 5500 pounds.
2. At 10,000 Feet, increase speed by 4 KIAS for each 400 pounds below 5500 pounds.
3. Operations at peak EGT may be utilized with power settings within the boxes if the airplane is equipped with the optional EGT system.

ALTITUDE	RPM	MP	-20°C (-4°F)			0°C (STD TEMP) (32°F)			20°C (68°F)		
			PERCENT BHP	KTAS	TOTAL LB/HR	PERCENT BHP	KTAS	TOTAL LB/HR	PERCENT BHP	KTAS	TOTAL LB/HR
7500 FEET	2500	23.2	77.9	190	194	75.2	192	188	72.4	194	182
	2500	22.0	72.2	185	181	69.7	187	175	67.1	187	169
	2500	21.0	67.3	180	170	64.9	181	164	62.6	181	159
	2500	20.0	63.0	175	160	60.8	176	155	58.5	176	150
	2400	23.0	73.4	186	184	70.8	188	178	68.2	189	172
	2400	22.0	68.9	182	173	66.5	183	168	64.0	183	162
	2400	21.0	64.7	177	163	62.4	178	158	60.1	178	153
	2400	20.0	60.6	172	154	58.4	172	150	56.3	172	145
	2300	23.0	68.2	181	172	65.8	182	166	63.4	183	160
	2300	22.0	64.4	176	163	62.1	177	158	59.8	178	153
	2300	21.0	60.2	171	153	58.1	172	149	56.0	172	144
	2300	20.0	56.5	166	145	54.5	167	141	52.5	166	136
	2200	23.0	63.4	175	161	61.2	176	156	58.9	176	151
	2200	22.0	60.1	171	153	57.9	172	148	55.8	172	144
	2200	21.0	56.5	166	145	54.5	167	141	52.5	166	136
	2200	20.0	52.8	161	137	50.9	161	132	49.0	159	128
	2200	19.0	49.3	155	128	47.6	154	124	45.9	153	120
	2200	18.0	45.7	148	120	44.1	147	116	42.5	144	112
	2100	22.0	55.3	165	143	53.4	165	138	51.4	164	133
	2100	21.0	52.0	160	135	50.2	159	130	48.3	158	126
	2100	20.0	48.7	154	127	47.0	153	123	45.3	151	119
	2100	19.0	45.3	148	119	43.7	146	115	42.1	143	111
	2100	18.0	42.0	141	111	40.5	138	107	39.0	133	104

ALTITUDE	RPM	MP	-25°C (-13°F)			-5°C (STD TEMP) (23°F)			15°C (59°F)		
10,000 FEET	2500	21.0	69.9	187	176	67.5	188	170	65.0	189	164
	2500	20.0	65.5	182	165	63.2	183	160	60.9	183	155
	2500	19.0	61.1	176	156	59.0	177	151	56.8	176	146
	2500	18.0	56.8	170	146	54.8	170	142	52.8	169	137
	2500	17.0	52.4	163	136	50.5	163	131	48.7	161	127
	2400	21.0	67.0	184	169	64.7	185	163	62.3	185	158
	2400	20.0	62.9	179	159	60.7	179	155	58.5	179	150
	2400	19.0	58.7	173	150	56.6	173	146	54.6	172	141
	2400	18.0	54.5	167	141	52.5	166	136	50.6	165	131
	2400	17.0	50.2	159	131	48.5	158	126	46.7	157	122
	2300	21.0	62.5	178	158	60.3	179	154	58.1	179	149
	2300	20.0	58.7	173	150	56.7	173	146	54.6	173	141
	2300	19.0	55.0	168	142	53.0	167	137	51.1	166	133
	2300	18.0	51.1	161	133	49.3	160	128	47.5	158	124
	2300	17.0	47.2	153	123	45.5	152	119	43.8	149	115
	2200	21.0	58.4	172	150	56.4	173	145	54.3	172	140
	2200	20.0	54.7	167	141	52.8	167	137	50.8	165	132
	2200	19.0	51.1	161	133	49.3	160	128	47.5	158	124
	2200	18.0	47.5	154	124	45.8	153	120	44.2	150	116
	2200	17.0	43.9	147	115	42.4	144	112	40.8	139	108
	2100	21.0	54.3	166	140	52.4	166	136	50.4	165	131
	2100	20.0	50.9	161	132	49.1	160	128	47.3	158	124
	2100	19.0	47.4	154	124	45.7	153	120	44.0	149	116
	2100	18.0	44.0	147	116	42.4	144	112	40.9	140	108
	2100	17.0	40.5	138	107	39.1	133	104	37.6	123	100

Table 27

TIME, FUEL, AND DISTANCE TO DESCEND

OPERATING CONDITIONS	T-1	T-2	T-3	T-4	T-5	T-6
Cruise Pressure Altitude (ft.)	8,500	11,000	12,500	14,000	11,500	9,500
Destination Airport Pressure Altitude (ft.)	2,000	3,000	S/L	6,000	1,500	3,250

7273. What is the time, fuel, and distance for operating conditions T–1? (See Table 27 and Figure 16.)

1—13 min., 33 lb., 40 NM.
2—15 min., 39 lb., 43 NM.
3—17 min., 43 lb., 49 NM.
4—21 min., 53 lb., 60 NM.

7274. What is the time, fuel, and distance for operating conditions T–2? (See Table 27 and Figure 16.)

1—21 min., 53 lb., 63 NM.
2—18 min., 46 lb., 54 NM.
3—15 min., 38 lb., 46 NM.
4—13 min., 30 lb., 43 NM.

7275. What is the time, fuel, and distance for operating conditions T–3? (See Table 27 and Figure 16.)

1—21 min., 50 lb., 65 NM.
2—22.5 min., 57 lb., 68 NM.
3—23.5 min., 63 lb., 70 NM.
4—24 min., 67 lb., 72 NM.

7276. What is the time, fuel, and distance for operating conditions T–4? (See Table 27 and Figure 16.)

1—12 min., 29 lb., 39 NM.
2—13 min., 34 lb., 42 NM.
3—14.5 min., 39 lb., 45 NM.
4—16 min., 44 lb., 49 NM.

7277. What is the time, fuel, and distance for operating conditions T–5? (See Table 27 and Figure 16.)

1—24.5 min, 61 lb., 73 NM.
2—23 min., 58 lb., 68 NM.
3—21.5 min., 54 lb., 65 NM.
4—18.5 min., 47 lb., 57 NM.

7278. What is the time, fuel, and distance for operating conditions T–6? (See Table 27 and Figure 16.)

1—12.5 min., 32 lb., 39 NM.
2—15 min., 38 lb., 43 NM.
3—17.5 min., 43 lb., 51 NM.
4—19 min., 48 lb., 57 NM.

7279. What is the time, fuel, and distance for operating conditions U–1? (See Table 28 and Figure 16.)

1—16.5 min., 42 lb., 49 NM.
2—18 min., 46 lb., 54 NM.
3—19.5 min., 50 lb., 59 NM.
4—20.5 min., 54 lb., 61 NM.

7280. What is the time, fuel, and distance for operating conditions U–2? (See Table 28 and Figure 16.)

1—23.5 min., 59 lb., 70 NM.
2—20.5 min., 52 lb., 62 NM.
3—17.5 min., 45 lb., 54 NM.
4—15.5 min., 41 lb., 50 NM.

7281. What is the time, fuel, and distance for operating conditions U–3? (See Table 28 and Figure 16.)

1—20 min., 50 lb., 55 NM.
2—16 min., 41 lb., 47 NM.
3—14 min., 38 lb., 43 NM.
4—12 min., 31 lb., 35 NM.

7282. What is the time, fuel, and distance for operating conditions U–4? (See Table 28 and Figure 16.)

1—12 min., 31 lb., 36 NM.
2—14 min., 37 lb., 39 NM.
3—18 min., 46 lb., 50 NM.
4—20 min., 50 lb., 53 NM.

7283. What is the time, fuel, and distance for operating conditions U–5? (See Table 28 and Figure 16.)

1—12 min., 25 lb., 32 NM.
2—14 min., 36 lb., 43 NM.
3—16 min., 45 lb., 49 NM.
4—17 min., 50 lb., 51 NM.

7284. What is the time, fuel, and distance for operating conditions U–6? (See Table 28 and Figure 16.)

1—13 min., 34 lb., 40 NM.
2—14 min., 38 lb., 43 NM.
3—16 min., 48 lb., 47 NM.
4—17 min., 54 lb., 51 NM.

Table 28

TIME, FUEL, AND DISTANCE TO DESCEND

OPERATING CONDITIONS	U-1	U-2	U-3	U-4	U-5	U-6
Cruise Pressure Altitude (ft.)	9,000	10,500	8,000	9,000	12,000	7,000
Destination Airport Pressure Altitude (ft.)	1,000	1,500	2,000	3,000	4,000	500

TIME, FUEL AND DISTANCE TO DESCEND

CONDITIONS:
1. Power - As Required.
2. Above 10,000 Feet, Descend at 1000 Feet Per Minute.
3. Below 10,000 Feet, Descend at 500 Feet Per Minute.
4. Landing Gear - UP.
5. Wing Flaps - UP.
6. Airspeed - 170 KIAS.

NOTE:
1. Time, fuel and distance for the descent are determined by taking the difference between the cruise altitude and the destination airport conditions.

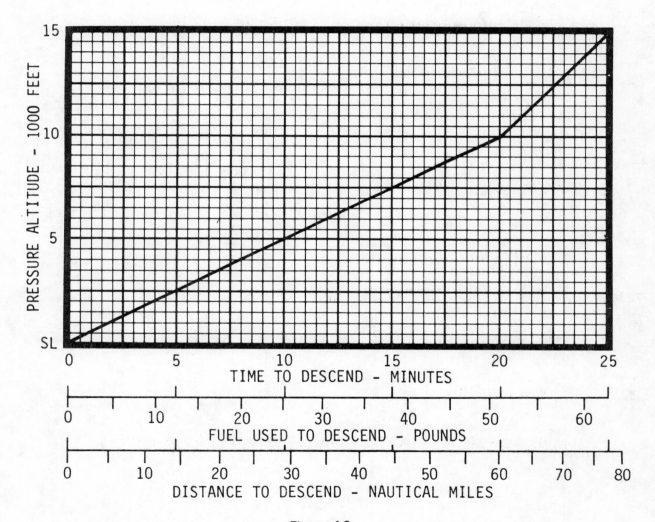

Figure 16

Table 29

NORMAL LANDING DISTANCE

OPERATING CONDITIONS	V-1	V-2	V-3	V-4	V-5	V-6
Weight (lb.)	4,600	5,000	5,000	5,400	4,400	4,200
Pressure Altitude (ft.)	1,500	S/L	S/L	1,000	8,000	6,000
Runway	36	18	9	27R	30	26
Runway Surface Level, Hard/Firm, Dry	Concrete	Asphalt	Sod	Sod	Concrete	Asphalt
Wind Direction/Speed	030°/23	280°/10	150°/16	010°/10	Calm	360°/10
Temperature	32°F	5°F	50°F	41°F	-10°C	5°F
Wing Flap Setting	35°	35°	UP	35°	UP	35°

7285. What is the ground roll distance for operating conditions V–1? (See Tables 29 and 30 and Figure 17.)

1—602 ft.
2—523 ft.
3—455 ft.
4—387 ft.

7286. FAA Deletion.

7287. FAA Deletion.

7288. FAA Deletion.

7289. What is the total distance to clear a 50–foot obstacle for operating conditions V–5? (See Tables 29 and 30 and Figure 17.)

1—688 ft.
2—1,079 ft.
3—1,660 ft.
4—2,241 ft.

7290. What is the total distance to clear a 50–foot obstacle for operating conditions V–6? (See Tables 29 and 30 and Figure 17.)

1—1,487 ft.
2—1,565 ft.
3—1,643 ft.
4—1,711 ft.

7291. What is the total distance to clear a 50–foot obstacle for operating conditions W–1? (See Figure 17 and Tables 31 and 32.)

1—1,061 ft.
2—1,632 ft.
—1,920 ft.
—2,203 ft.

7292. What is the ground roll distance for operating condtions W–2? (See Figure 17 and Tables 31 and 32.)

1—510 ft.
2—550 ft.
3—605 ft.
4—696 ft.

7293. FAA Deletion.

7294. FAA Deletion.

Table 30

NORMAL LANDING DISTANCE

CONDITIONS:
1. Throttles - IDLE
2. Landing Gear - DOWN
3. Wing Flaps - 35%
4. Cowl Flaps - CLOSE
5. Level, Hard Surface Runway
6. Maximum Braking Effort

NOTE:
1. Increase all distances by 25% of ground run for operation on firm sod runway.
2. When landing with flaps UP, increase the normal approach speed by 12 knots. Expect total landing distance to increase by 35%.
3. Decrease all distances by 3% for each 4 knots headwind. For operations with tailwinds up to 10 knots, increase all distances by 5% for each 2 knots of wind.

WEIGHT-POUNDS	SPEED AT 50-FOOT OBSTACLE KIAS	PRESSURE ALTITUDE - FEET	-20°C (-4°F)		-10°C (14°F)		0°C (32°F)		10°C (50°F)	
			GROUND ROLL - FEET	TOTAL DISTANCE TO CLEAR 50-FOOT OBSTACLE	GROUND ROLL - FEET	TOTAL DISTANCE TO CLEAR 50-FOOT OBSTACLE	GROUND ROLL - FEET	TOTAL DISTANCE TO CLEAR 50-FOOT OBSTACLE	GROUND ROLL - FEET	TOTAL DISTANCE TO CLEAR 50-FOOT OBSTACLE
5400	93	Sea Level	570	1720	590	1740	610	1760	630	1780
		1000	590	1740	610	1760	630	1780	660	1810
		2000	610	1760	630	1780	660	1810	680	1830
		3000	630	1780	660	1810	680	1830	710	1860
		4000	660	1810	680	1830	710	1860	730	1880
		5000	680	1830	710	1860	730	1880	760	1910
		6000	710	1860	730	1880	760	1910	790	1940
		7000	730	1880	760	1910	790	1940	820	1970
		8000	760	1910	790	1940	820	1970	850	2000
		9000	790	1940	820	1970	850	2000	880	2030
		10,000	820	1970	850	2000	890	2040	920	2070
5000	89	Sea Level	480	1630	500	1650	520	1670	540	1690
		1000	500	1650	520	1670	540	1690	560	1710
		2000	520	1670	540	1690	560	1710	580	1730
		3000	530	1680	560	1710	580	1730	600	1750
		4000	550	1700	580	1730	600	1750	620	1770
		5000	580	1730	600	1750	620	1770	640	1790
		6000	600	1750	620	1770	640	1790	670	1820
		7000	620	1770	640	1790	670	1820	690	1840
		8000	640	1790	670	1820	690	1840	720	1870
		9000	670	1820	700	1850	720	1870	750	1900
		10,000	700	1850	720	1870	750	1900	780	1930
4600	86	Sea Level	400	1550	420	1570	430	1580	450	1600
		1000	410	1560	430	1580	450	1600	460	1610
		2000	430	1580	450	1600	460	1610	480	1630
		3000	450	1600	460	1610	480	1630	500	1650
		4000	460	1610	480	1630	500	1650	520	1670
		5000	480	1630	500	1650	520	1670	540	1690
		6000	500	1650	520	1670	540	1690	560	1710
		7000	520	1670	540	1690	560	1710	580	1730
		8000	540	1690	560	1710	580	1730	600	1750
		9000	560	1710	580	1730	600	1750	620	1770
		10,000	580	1730	600	1750	620	1770	650	1800
4200	82	Sea Level	330	1480	340	1490	350	1500	370	1520
		1000	340	1490	350	1500	370	1520	380	1530
		2000	350	1500	370	1520	380	1530	390	1540
		3000	370	1520	380	1530	390	1540	410	1560
		4000	380	1530	390	1540	410	1560	420	1570
		5000	390	1540	410	1560	420	1570	440	1590
		6000	410	1560	420	1570	440	1590	460	1610
		7000	420	1570	440	1590	460	1610	470	1620
		8000	440	1590	460	1610	470	1620	490	1640
		9000	460	1610	480	1630	490	1640	510	1660
		10,000	480	1630	490	1640	510	1660	530	1680

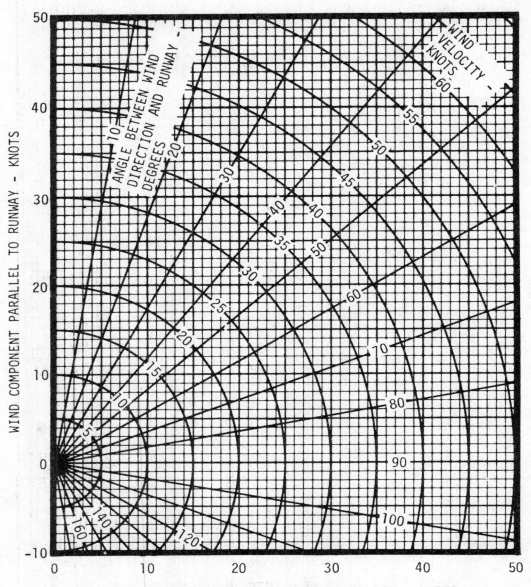

Figure 17

Table 31

NORMAL LANDING DISTANCE

OPERATING CONDITIONS	W-1	W-2	W-3	W-4	W-5	W-6
Weight (lb.)	5,400	4,800	4,600	5,200	4,600	4,200
Pressure Altitude (ft.)	4,000	3,000	1,000	9,000	8,000	S/L
Runway	21	9L	1	15	34	26C
Runway Surface Level, Hard/Firm, Dry	Concrete	Asphalt	Sod	Asphalt	Sod	Concrete
Wind Direction/Speed	210°/20	180°/20	120°/12	Calm	050°/24	340°/23
Temperature	25°C	40°C	77°F	104°F	95°F	77°F
Wing Flap Setting	UP	35°	35°	UP	35°	

58

Table 32

NORMAL LANDING DISTANCE

CONDITIONS:
1. Throttles - IDLE
2. Landing Gear - DOWN
3. Wing Flaps - 35%
4. Cowl Flaps - CLOSE
5. Level, Hard Surface Runway
6. Maximum Braking Effort

NOTE:
1. Increase all distances by 25% of ground run for operation on firm sod runway.
2. When landing with flaps UP, increase the normal approach speed by 12 knots. Expect total landing distance to increase by 35%.
3. Decrease all distances by 3% for each 4 knots headwind. For operations with tailwinds up to 10 knots, increase all distances by 5% for each 2 knots of wind.

WEIGHT-POUNDS	SPEED AT 50-FOOT OBSTACLE KIAS	PRESSURE ALTITUDE - FEET	20°C (68°F)		30°C (86°F)		40°C (104°F)	
			GROUND ROLL - FEET	TOTAL DISTANCE TO CLEAR 50-FOOT OBSTACLE	GROUND ROLL - FEET	TOTAL DISTANCE TO CLEAR 50-FOOT OBSTACLE	GROUND ROLL - FEET	TOTAL DISTANCE TO CLEAR 50-FOOT OBSTACLE
5400	93	Sea Level	660	1810	680	1830	700	1850
		1000	680	1830	700	1850	730	1880
		2000	710	1860	730	1880	750	1900
		3000	730	1880	760	1910	780	1930
		4000	760	1910	780	1930	810	1960
		5000	790	1940	810	1960	840	1990
		6000	820	1970	850	2000	870	2020
		7000	850	2000	880	2030	910	2060
		8000	880	2030	910	2060	940	2090
		9000	920	2070	950	2100	980	2130
		10,000	950	2100	980	2130	1020	2170
5000	89	Sea Level	550	1700	570	1720	590	1740
		1000	570	1720	590	1740	610	1760
		2000	600	1750	620	1770	640	1790
		3000	620	1770	640	1790	660	1810
		4000	640	1790	660	1810	680	1830
		5000	670	1820	690	1840	710	1860
		6000	690	1840	710	1860	740	1890
		7000	720	1870	740	1890	770	1920
		8000	750	1900	770	1920	800	1950
		9000	770	1920	800	1950	830	1980
		10,000	800	1950	830	1980	860	2010
4600	86	Sea Level	460	1610	480	1630	490	1640
		1000	480	1630	500	1650	510	1660
		2000	500	1650	510	1660	530	1680
		3000	520	1670	530	1680	550	1700
		4000	530	1680	550	1700	570	1720
		5000	550	1700	570	1720	590	1740
		6000	580	1730	600	1750	610	1760
		7000	600	1750	620	1770	640	1790
		8000	620	1770	640	1790	660	1810
		9000	650	1800	670	1820	690	1840
		10,000	670	1820	690	1840	720	1870
4200	82	Sea Level	380	1530	390	1540	410	1560
		1000	390	1540	410	1560	420	1570
		2000	410	1560	420	1570	440	1590
		3000	420	1570	440	1590	450	1600
		4000	440	1590	450	1600	470	1620
		5000	460	1610	470	1620	490	1640
		6000	470	1620	490	1640	500	1650
		7000	490	1640	510	1660	520	1670
		8000	510	1660	530	1680	540	1690
		9000	530	1680	550	1700	560	1710
		10,000	550	1700	570	1720	590	1740

7295. FAA Deletion.

7296. What is the ground roll distance for operating conditions W–6? (See Figure 17 and Tables 31 and 32.)

1—362 ft.
2—385 ft.
3—408 ft.
4—436 ft.

7297. The primary cause of all changes in the Earth's weather is

1—variation of solar energy received by the Earth's regions.
2—changes in air pressure over the Earth's surface.
3—changes in air moisture content.
4—movement of the air masses.

7298. How much colder is the actual temperature at 9,000 ft., as indicated in the following excerpt from the Winds and Temperture Aloft Forecast, than standard temperature?

| | FT.......6000 | 9000....... |
| | 0737–04 | 1043–10 |

1—3° C.
2—10° C.
3—1° C.
4—7° C.

7299. A common type of ground– or surface–based temperature inversion is that produced by

1—warm air being lifted rapidly aloft in the vicinity of mountainous terrain.
2—the movement of colder air over warm air, or the movement of warm air under cold air.
3—widespread sinking of air within a thick layer aloft resulting in heating by compression.
4—ground radiation on clear, cool nights when the wind is light.

7300. If a pilot changes the altimeter setting from 30.11 to 29.96, what is the approximate change in indication?

1—Altimeter will indicate 15 ft. higher.
2—Altimeter will indicate 15 ft. lower.
3—Altimeter will indicate 150 ft. lower.
4—Altimeter will indicate 150 ft. higher.

7301. Which condition would cause the altimeter to indicate a lower altitude than actually flown (true altitude)?

1—Air temperature lower than standard.
2—Atmospheric pressure lower than standard.
3—Pressure altitude the same as indicated altitude.
4—Air temperature warmer than standard.

7302. Under what condition(s) will pressure altitude be equal to true altitude?

1—When the OAT (outside air temperature) is standard for that altitude.
2—When the atmospheric pressure is 29.92″ of Hg.
3—When standard atmospheric conditions exist.
4—When indicated altitude is equal to the pressure altitude.

7303. Under what condition is pressure altitude and density altitude the same value?

1—At standard temperature.
2—When the altimeter setting is 29.92.
3—When indicated and pressure altitudes are the same value on the altimeter.
4—At sea level, when the temperature is 0° C.

7304. Altimeter setting is the value to which the scale of the pressure altimeter is set so the altimeter indicates

1—true altitude at field elevation.
2—pressure altitude at field elevation.
3—density altitude at field elevation.
4—pressure altitude at sea level.

7305. What type altitude does a pilot maintain at FL210?

1—Indicated.
2—Pressure.
3—Calibrated.
4—Corrected (approximately true).

7306. Under what condition will true altitude be lower than indicated altitude with an altimeter setting of 29.92?

1—In warmer than standard air temperature.
2—In colder than standard air temperature.
3—When density altitude is higher than indicated altitude.
4—Under higher than standard pressure at standard air temperature.

7307. Which force, in the northern hemisphere, acts at a right angle to the wind and deflects it to the right until parallel to the isobars?

1—Centrifugal.
2—Pressure gradient.
3—Coriolis.
4—Advective.

7308. What relationship exists between the winds at 2,000 ft. above the surface and the surface winds?

1—The winds at 2,000 ft. and the surface winds flow in the same direction, but the surface winds are weaker due to friction.
2—The winds at 2,000 ft. and the surface winds are approximately the same except when eddies form due to obstructions.
3—The winds at 2,000 ft. tend to parallel the isobars while the surface winds cross the isobars at an angle toward lower pressure and are weaker.
4—The surface winds tend to veer to the right of the winds at 2,000 ft. and are usually weaker.

7309. Winds at 5,000 ft. AGL on a particular flight are southwesterly while most of the surface winds are southerly. This difference in direction is primarily due to

1—a stronger pressure gradient at higher altitudes.
2—friction between the wind and the surface.
3—stronger Coriolis force at the surface.
4—the influence of pressure systems at the lower altitudes.

7310. What causes surface winds to flow across the isobars at an angle rather than parallel to the isobars?

1—Coriolis force.
2—Surface friction.
3—The greater density of the air at the surface.
4—The greater atmospheric pressure at the surface.

7311. Clouds, fog, or dew will always form when

1—water vapor condenses.
2—water vapor is present.
3—relative humidity reaches or exceeds 100 percent.
4—the temperature and dew point are equal.

7312. The amount of water vapor which air can hold largely depends on

1—relative humidity.
2—air temperature.
3—stability of air.
4—the dew point.

7313. What temperature condition is indicated if you encounter wet snow?

1—The temperature is above freezing at your altitude.
2—The temperature is above freezing at higher altitudes.
3—You are flying from a warm air mass into a cold air mass.
4—You are in an "inversion" with colder air below.

7314. What is meant by the term dew point?

1—The temperature to which air must be cooled to become saturated.
2—The temperature at which condensation and evaporation are equal.
3—The temperature at which dew will always form.
4—The spread between actual temperature and the temperature during evaporation.

7315. Which conditions result in the formation of frost?

1—The temperature of the collecting surface is at or below freezing and small droplets of moisture are falling.
2—When dew forms and the temperature is below freezing.
3—Temperature of the collecting surface is below the dew point of surrounding air and the dew point is colder than freezing.
4—Small drops of moisture falling on the collecting surface when the surrounding air temperature is at or below freezing.

7316. The presence of ice pellets at the surface is evidence that

1—there are thunderstorms in the area.
2—a cold front has passed.
3—there is freezing rain at a higher altitude.
4—you can climb to a higher altitude without encountering more than light icing.

7317. What is indicated if you encounter ice pellets at 8,000 ft.?

1—You are approaching an area of thunderstorms.
2—Freezing rain at higher altitude.
3—You will encounter hail if you continue your flight.
4—High altitude cold front or upper trough.

7318. From which measurement of the atmosphere can stability be determined?

1—Surface temperature.
2—The dry adiabatic lapse rate.
3—The ambient lapse rate.
4—Atmospheric pressure.

7319. At approximately what altitude above the surface would you expect the base of cumuliform clouds if the surface air temperature is 82° F and the dew point is 55° F?

1—5,000 ft.
2—6,000 ft.
3—8,000 ft.
4—9,000 ft.

7320. A temperature inversion will form only

1—in stable air.
2—in unstable air.
3—when a stratiform layer merges with a cumuliform mass.
4—when stratus clouds form.

7321. Unsaturated air flowing upslope will cool at the rate of about

1—3° C per 1,000 ft.
2—2° C per 1,000 ft.
3—2.5° C per 1,000 ft.
4—4.4° C per 1,000 ft.

7322. Which of the following combinations of weather producing variables would likely result in cumuliform type clouds, good visibility, showery rain, and possible clear type icing in clouds?

1—Stable, moist air and orographic lifting.
2—Unstable, moist air and no lifting mechanism.
3—Stable, dry air and orographic lifting.
4—Unstable, moist air and orographic lifting.

7323. What determines the structure or type of clouds which form as a result of air being forced to ascend?

1—The method by which the air is lifted.
2—The relative humidity of the air after being lifted.
3—The stability of the air before lifting occurs.
4—The amount of condensation nuclei present after lifting occurs.

7324. Stability can be determined from which measurement of the atmosphere?

1—Low-level winds.
2—Ambient lapse rate.
3—Atmospheric pressure.
4—Difference between standard temperature and surface temperature.

7325. What are some characteristics of unstable air?

1—Nimbostratus clouds and poor surface visibility.
2—Nimbostratus clouds and good surface visibility.
3—Turbulence and poor surface visibility.
4—Turbulence and good surface visibility.

7326. What feature is associated with a temperature inversion?

1—A stable layer of air.
2—An unstable layer of air.
3—Chinook winds on mountain slopes.
4—Air mass thunderstorms.

7327. What are the characteristics of stable air?

1—Good visibility, showery precipitation, and cumulus type clouds.
2—Good visibility, steady precipitation, and stratus type clouds.
3—Poor vsibility, intermittent precipitation, and cumulus type clouds.
4—Poor visibility, steady precipitation, and stratus type clouds.

7328. Moist, stable air flowing upslope can be expected to

1—produce stratus type clouds.
2—produce a temperature inversion.
3—cause showers and thunderstorms.
4—develop convective turbulence.

7329. What type clouds can be expected when an unstable air mass is forced to ascend a mountain slope?

1—Stratified clouds with intermittent showers.
2—Layered clouds with little vertical development.
3—Stratified clouds with considerable associated turbulence.
4—Clouds with extensive vertical development.

7330. Which is a characteristic of stable air?

1—Fair weather cumulus clouds.
2—Stratiform clouds.
3—Unlimited visibility.
4—Rapid temperature decrease with altitude.

7331. The general characteristics of unstable air are:

1—Good visibility, showery precipitation, and cumuliform type clouds.
2—Good visibility, steady precipitation, and stratiform type clouds.
3—Poor visibility, intermittent precipitation, and cumuliform type clouds.
4—Poor visibility, steady precipitation, and stratiform type clouds.

7332. What type of clouds will be formed if very stable moist air is forced upslope?

1—First stratified clouds and then vertical clouds.
2—First vertical clouds and then stratified clouds.
3—Vertical clouds with increasing height.
4—Stratified clouds with little vertical development.

7333. What are the four families of clouds?

1—Stratus, cumulus, nimbus, and cirrus.
2—Nimbus, layered, lumpy, and vertical.
3—Clouds formed by: updrafts, fronts, cooling layers of air, and precipitation into warm air.
4—High, middle, low, and those with extensive vertical development.

7334. Which family of clouds is least likely to contribute to structural icing on an aircraft?

1—Low clouds.
2—Middle clouds.
3—High clouds.
4—Clouds with extensive vertical development.

7335. The presence of standing lenticular altocumulus clouds is a good indication of

1—a jet stream.
2—very strong turbulence.
3—heavy icing conditions.
4—an approaching storm.

7336. The suffix nimbus, used in naming clouds, means a

1—cloud with extensive vertical development.
2—raincloud.
3—dark massive, towering cloud.
4—cloud with an anvil shaped top.

7337. ACSL (standing lenticular clouds), in mountainous areas, indicate

1—an inversion.
2—unstable air.
3—turbulence.
4—light variable winds.

7338. Which clouds have the greatest turbulence?

1—Towering cumulus.
2—Cumulonimbus.
3—Nimbostratus.
4—Altocumulus castellanus.

7339. Which are characteristics of a cold air mass moving over a warm surface?

1—Cumuliform clouds, turbulence, and poor visibility.
2—Cumuliform clouds, turbulence, and good visibility.
3—Stratiform clouds, smooth air, and poor visibility.
4—Stratiform clouds, turbulence, and good visibility.

7340. Frontal waves normally form on

1—slow moving cold fronts or stationary fronts.
2—slow moving warm fronts and strong occluded fronts.
3—rapidly moving cold fronts or warm fronts.
4—occluded fronts.

7341. Which weather phenomenon is always associated with the passage of a frontal system?

1—A wind change.
2—An abrupt decrease in pressure.
3—Clouds, either ahead or behind the front.
4—An abrupt decrease in temperature.

7342. Which statement about low–level wind shear, as it relates to frontal activity, is correct?

1—The amount of wind shear in cold fronts is much greater than found in warm fronts.
2—With a warm front, the most critical period is before the front passes the airport.
3—With a cold front, the most critical period is just before the front passes the airport.
4—With a cold front, the problem ceases to exist after the front passes the airport.

7343. What is an important characteristic of wind shear?

1—It occurs exclusively at lower levels and is associated with strong horizontal temperature variations.
2—It is primarily associated with the lateral vortices generated by thunderstorms.
3—It usually exists only in the vicinity of thunderstorms, but may be found near a strong temperature inversion.
4—It may be associated with either a wind shift or a windspeed gradient at any level in the atmosphere.

7344. Where can wind shear associated with a thunderstorm be found? (Choose the most complete answer.)

1—In front of the thunderstorm cell (anvil side) and on the right side of the cell.
2—Ahead of the roll clouds or gust front and on the left side of the thunderstorm cell.
3—In front of the thunderstorm cell and directly under the cell.
4—On all sides of the thunderstorm cell and directly under the cell.

7345. Where does wind shear occur?

1—Primarily in the lower altitudes in mountainous areas.
2—Exclusively in thunderstorms.
3—Wherever there is an abrupt decrease in pressure and/or temperature.
4—With either a wind shift or a windspeed gradient at any level in the atmosphere.

7346. When flying in stratiform clouds where ice is forming on the aircraft, the pilot can likely alleviate the icing by changing to a flight level where the temperatures are not within which minimum range?

1— $-2°$ C to $-15°$ C.
2— $0°$ C to $-15°$ C.
3— $-2°$ C to $-10°$ C.
4— $0°$ C to $-10°$ C.

7347. What is an operational consideration if you fly into rain which freezes on impact?

1—You have flown into an area of thunderstorms.
2—Temperatures are above freezing at some higher altitude.
3—You have flown through a cold front.
4—If you descend, you will fly out of the icing condition.

7348. In which environment is aircraft structural icing most likely to have the highest rate of accumulation?

1—Cumulonimbus clouds.
2—High humidity and freezing temperature.
3—Heavy wet snow.
4—Freezing rain.

7349. Why is frost considered hazardous to flight operation?

1—The increased weight requires a greater takeoff distance.
2—Frost changes the basic aerodynamic shape of the airfoil.
3—Frost decreases control effectiveness.
4—Frost causes early airflow separation resulting in a loss of lift.

7350. Which procedure is recommended when operating in an area of suspected or known icing?

1—A deice system should always be engaged as soon as a light accumulation of ice has formed on the leading edges.
2—If unable to maintain airspeed above the pre–stall buffet due to ice accumulation, altitude should be traded for airspeed.
3—Anti–ice equipment should not be actuated in anticipation of suspected icing.
4—As airframe ice builds up and adds weight, the angle of attack should be increased and the power reduced if level flight is to be maintained.

7351. Tornadoes and destructive winds are generally associated with which thunderstorms?

1—Thunderstorms with bases near the surface.
2—Large air mass thunderstorms developing in areas where the ground temperature is warmer than the air above.
3—Steady–state thunderstorms associated with cold fronts or squall lines.
4—Thunderstorms associated with any type front which produces considerable rain.

7352. What are the requirements for the formation of a thunderstorm?

1—Sufficient water vapor and a lifting action.
2—A cumulus cloud with sufficient moisture.
3—A cumulus cloud with sufficient moisture and an inverted lapse rate.
4—Sufficient moisture, an unstable lapse rate, and a lifting action.

7353. What is an indication that downdrafts have developed and the thunderstorm cell has entered the mature stage?

1—The anvil top has completed its development.
2—Precipitation begins to fall from the cloud base.
3—A gust front forms.
4—Gusty surface winds have increased in intensity.

7354. Which procedure is recommended if a pilot should unintentionally penetrate embedded thunderstorm activity?

1—The pilot should reverse aircraft heading or proceed toward an area of known VFR conditions.
2—Reduce airspeed to maneuvering speed and maintain a constant altitude.
3—Set power for recommended turbulence penetration airspeed and attempt to maintain a level flight attitude.
4—Reduce airspeed to maneuvering speed and thereafter maintain a constant airspeed.

7355. Which thunderstorms generally produce the most severe conditions, such as heavy hail and destructive winds?

1—Warm front.
2—Squall line.
3—Air mass.
4—Cold front.

7356. Which weather phenomenon is always associated with a thunderstorm?

1—Lightning.
2—Heavy rain showers.
3—Supercooled raindrops.
4—Hail.

7357. During the life cycle of a thunderstorm, which stage is characterized predominately by downdrafts?

1—Cumulus.
2—Dissipating.
3—Mature.
4—Anvil.

7358. What conditions are necessary for the formation of a thunderstorm?

1—Frontal activity, cumulus clouds, and sufficient moisture.
2—Cumulus clouds, unbalance of static electricity, and turbulence.
3—Sufficient heat, moisture, and electricity.
4—Lifting action, unstable air, and sufficient moisture.

7359. What is indicated by the term "embedded thunderstorms"?

1—Thunderstorms have been visually sighted.
2—Severe thunderstorms are embedded within a squall line.
3—Thunderstorms are predicted to develop in a stable air mass.
4—Thunderstorms are obscured by massive cloud layers and cannot be seen.

7360. If you fly into severe turbulence, which condition should you attempt to maintain?

1—Constant altitude.
2—Constant airspeed (V_A).
3—Level flight attitude.
4—Constant altitude and constant airspeed.

7361. What precautions, in addition to controlling the airplane, should you take if you cannot avoid thunderstorm penetration?

1—Tighten safety belts, turn on autopilot to altitude hold mode, turn on cockpit lights and pitot heat.
2—Adjust altitude to below the freezing level; turn on autopilot to altitude hold mode, and turn on pitot heat.
3—Turn on pitot heat, carburetor heat or alternate air, deicing and anti–icing equipment, and turn cockpit lights to highest intensity.
4—Tighten safety belts, turn on pitot heat, turn on carburetor heat or alternate air, and turn cockpit lights to highest intensity.

7362. What is the best procedure for controlling an airplane in a thunderstorm, if thunderstorm penetration is unavoidable?

1—Maintain altitude and maneuvering speed—don't turn back.
2—Maintain a constant attitude and safe operating range power setting—don't turn back.
3—Maintain airspeed in safe operating range—don't turn back.
4—Reduce airspeed to maneuvering speed—turn 180° as soon as possible.

7363. Which is the most common hazard of lightning strikes on airplanes?

1—Igniting fuel in the tanks.
2—Temporary blindness of the pilot.
3—Failure of entire electrical system.
4—Structural damage of major components of the airplane.

7364. Under which condition does advection fog usually form?

1—Moist air moving over colder ground or water.
2—Warm, moist air settling over a cool surface under no–wind conditions.
3—A light breeze blowing colder air out to sea.
4—A land breeze blowing a cold air mass over a warm water current.

7365. Which are characteristics of advection fog, radiation fog, and steam fogs?

1—Advection fog deepens as windspeed increases up to 20 knots; steam fog requires calm or very light wind; radiation fog forms when the ground or water cools the air by radiation.
2—Radiation fog is restricted to land areas; advection fog is most common along coastal areas; steam fog forms over a water surface.
3—Steam fog forms from moist air moving over a colder surface; advection fog requires cold air over a warmer surface; radiation fog is produced by radiational cooling of the ground.
4—Radiation fog results from cooling the air to its dew point, while steam and advection fog require the addition of moisture to the air near the surface, through evaporation.

7366. Which conditions are favorable for the formation of radiation fog?

1—Relatively warm rain or drizzle falling through cool air.
2—Moist air moving over colder ground or water.
3—Cloudy sky and a light wind moving saturated warm air over a cool surface.
4—Clear sky, little or no wind, small temperature/dew point spread, and over a land surface.

7367. What situation is most conducive to the formation of radiation fog?

1—Warm, moist air over low, flatland areas on clear, calm nights.
2—Moist, tropical air moving over cold, offshore water.
3—The movement of cold air over much warmer water.
4—Light wind moving warm, moist air upslope during the night.

7368. What types of fog depend upon a wind in order to exist?

1—Radiation fog and ice fog.
2—Steam fog and downslope fog.
3—Precipitation–induced fog and ground fog.
4—Advection fog and upslope fog.

7369. In what localities is advection fog most likely to occur?

1—Coastal areas.
2—Mountain slopes.
3—Level inland areas.
4—Mountain valleys.

7370. In which situation is advection fog most likely to form?

1—A warm, moist air mass on the windward side of mountains.
2—An air mass moving inland from the coast in winter.
3—A light breeze blowing colder air out to sea.
4—Warm, moist air settling over a warmer surface under no–wind conditions.

7371. At times, fog is prevalent in industrial areas because of

1—atmospheric stabilization around cities.
2—an abundance of condensation nuclei from combustion products.
3—increased temperatures due to industrial heating.
4—a high concentration of steam from industrial plants.

7372. Which weather condition can be expected when moist air flows from a relatively warm surface to a colder surface?

1—Stratocumulus clouds.
2—Increased visibility.
3—Convective turbulence due to surface heating.
4—Fog.

7373. The strength and location of the jet stream is normally

1—stronger and farther north in the winter.
2—weaker and farther north in the summer.
3—stronger and farther north in the summer.
4—weaker and farther south in the winter.

7374. The Severe Weather Outlook Chart depicts

1—areas of probable severe thunderstorms by the use of hatching on the chart.
2—general direction of thunderstorm movement as indicated by the arrow.
3—areas of forecast severe or extreme turbulence and areas of severe icing for the next 24 hours.
4—areas of general (excluding severe) thunderstorm activity by the use of hatching on the chart.

7375. What is meant by the entry in the remarks section of this Surface Aviation Weather Report for BOI?

BOI SA 1854 – X M7 OVC 1 1/2R+F
990/63/61/3205/ 980/RF2 RB12

1—Runway fog, visibility 2 mi.; runway braking reduced 12 percent.
2—Runway fog, visibility 2 mi.; base of the rain clouds 1,200 ft.
3—Rain and fog obscuring 2/10 of the sky; rain began 12 min. before the hour.
4—Rain and fog obscuring 2/10 of the sky; rain began 12 min. after the hour.

7376. What is the significance of the "F2" in the remarks portion of this Surface Aviation Weather Report for CLE?

CLE SP 1350 – X E80 BKN 150 OVC 1GF
169/67/67/2105/003/R23LVV11/2 F2

1—The restriction to visibility is caused by fog and the prevailing visibility is 2 statute miles.
2—The partial obscuration is caused by fog and the visibility value is variable, 1–1/2 to 2 statute miles.
3—Fog is obscuring 2/10 of the sky.
4—The surface based obscuration is caused by fog and is 200 ft. thick.

7377. The reporting station originating this Surface Aviation Weather Report has a field elevation of 1,000 ft. If the reported sky cover is one continuous layer, what is its thickness?

MDW RS 1856 M7 OVC 11/2R+F 990/63/61/
3205/ 980/... UA.../SK OVC 65

1—4,800 ft.
2—5,000 ft.
3—5,800 ft.
4—6,500 ft.

7378. A ceiling is defined as the height of the

1—highest layer of clouds or obscuring phenomena aloft that covers over 6/10 of the sky.
2—lowest layer of clouds that contributed to the overall overcast.
3—lowest layer of clouds which is at least thin overcast.
4—lowest layer of clouds or obscuring phenomena aloft that is reported as broken or overcast.

7379. How often are terminal forecasts issued, and what is the valid time period of each?

1—Three times daily; valid for 8 hours.
2—Two times daily; valid for 12 hours.
3—Every 6 hours; valid for 12 hours.
4—Three times daily; valid for 24 hours.

7380. A pilot reporting turbulence that momentarily causes slight, erratic changes in altitude and/or attitude should report it as

1—light turbulence.
2—moderate turbulence.
3—light chop.
4—moderate chop.

7381. The Surface Analysis Chart depicts

1—actual pressure systems, frontal locations, cloud tops, and precipitation as the time shown on the chart.
2—frontal locations and expected movement, pressure centers, cloud coverage, and obstructions to vision at the time of chart transmission.
3—actual frontal positions, pressure patterns, temperature, dew point, wind, weather, and obstructions to vision at the valid time of the chart.
4—actual pressure distribution, frontal systems, cloud heights and coverage, temperature, dew point, and wind at the time shown on the chart.

7382. The Weather Depiction Chart in Figure 18 indicates that the costal sections of Texas and Louisiana are reporting

1—ceilings of 250 ft. with patchy ground fog.
2—all ceilings at or above 20,000 ft. with visibilities of 20 mi. or more.
3—marginal VFR conditions due to broken ceilings of 2,000 ft.
4—VFR conditions with scattered clouds at 2,000 ft. and higher cirroform.

7383. The Weather Depiction Chart in Figure 18 indicates the heaviest precipitation along the front is occurring in

1—Oklahoma.
2—Missouri.
3—Illinois.
4—Kansas.

7384. The Weather Depiction Chart in Figure 18 indicates that northern Illinois and southern Wisconsin is reporting

1—marginal VFR conditions due to reduced visibility in drizzle and fog.
2—low IFR conditions due to ceilings below 500 ft. with drizzle.
3—IFR conditions due to overcast ceilings less than 1,000 ft. with reduced visibilities in rain and rain showers.
4—VFR ceilings but reduced visibilities due to fog and haze.

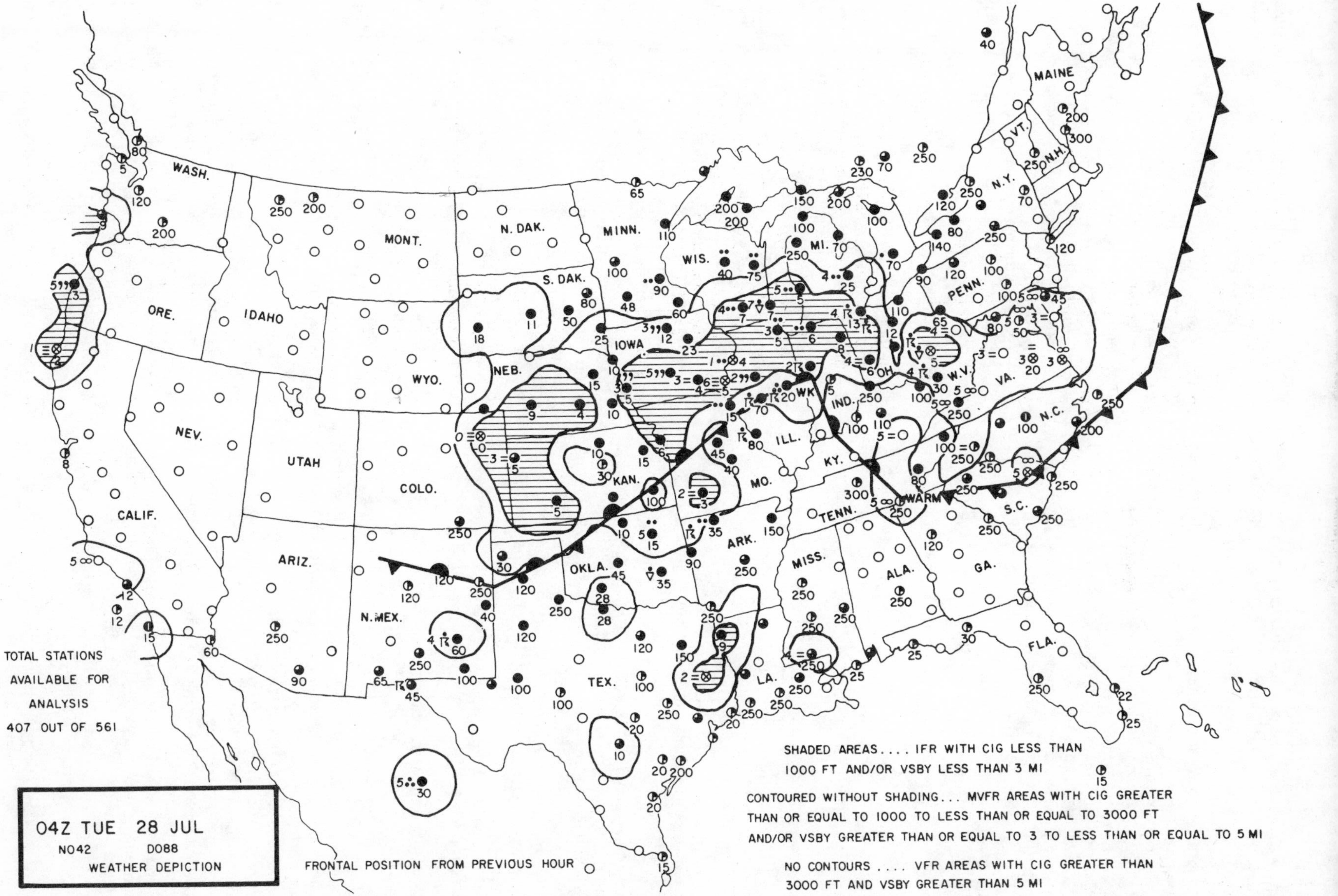
04Z TUE 28 JUL
N042 D088
WEATHER DEPICTION
TOTAL STATIONS
AVAILABLE FOR
ANALYSIS
407 OUT OF 561
FRONTAL POSITION FROM PREVIOUS HOUR
SHADED AREAS.... IFR WITH CIG LESS THAN
1000 FT AND/OR VSBY LESS THAN 3 MI
CONTOURED WITHOUT SHADING... MVFR AREAS WITH CIG GREATER
THAN OR EQUAL TO 1000 TO LESS THAN OR EQUAL TO 3000 FT
AND/OR VSBY GREATER THAN OR EQUAL TO 3 TO LESS THAN OR EQUAL TO 5 MI
NO CONTOURS .... VFR AREAS WITH CIG GREATER THAN
3000 FT AND VSBY GREATER THAN 5 MI
WASH.
ORE.
CALIF.
NEV.
IDAHO
MONT.
WYO.
UTAH
ARIZ.
COLO.
N. MEX.
N. DAK.
S. DAK.
NEB.
KAN.
OKLA.
TEX.
MINN.
IOWA
MO.
ARK.
LA.
WIS.
ILL.
MI.
IND.
OH
KY.
TENN.
MISS.
ALA.
GA.
FLA.
S.C.
N.C.
VA.
W.V.
PENN.
N.Y.
VT.
N.H.
MAINE
WARM
WK

Figure 18

7385. What weather conditions are depicted in the area indicated by arrow A on the Radar Summary Chart? (See Figure 19.)

1—Moderate to strong echoes; echo tops 30,000 ft. MSL; line movement toward the northwest.
2—Weak to moderate echoes; average echo bases 30,000 ft. MSL; cell movement toward the southeast; rain showers with thunder.
3—Moderate echoes; echo bases 3,000 ft. MSL; limited cell movement; rain showers.
4—Strong to very strong echoes; echo tops 30,000 ft. MSL; thundershowers and rain showers.

7386. FAA Deletion.

7387. What weather conditions are depicted in the area indicated by arrow C on the Radar Summary Chart? (See Figure 19.)

1—Average echo bases 2,800 ft. MSL; thundershowers; intense to extreme echo intensity.
2—Cell movement toward the northwest at 20 knots; intense echoes; echo bases 28,000 ft. MSL.
3—Area movement toward the northeast at 20 knots; strong to very strong echoes; echo tops 28,000 ft. MSL.
4—Echo tops 2,800 ft. MSL; very heavy thunderstorms; area movement toward the northwest at 20 knots.

7388. What weather conditions are depicted in the area indicated by arrow D on the Radar Summary Chart? (See Figure 19.)

1—Echo tops 2,900 ft. MSL; intense to extreme echoes within the smallest contour; area movement toward the northeast at 50 knots.
2—Echo tops 4,100 ft. MSL; strong to very strong echoes within the smallest contour; area movement toward the northeast at 50 knots.
3—Intense to extreme echoes within the smallest contour; echo tops 29,000 ft. MSL; cell movement toward the northeast at 50 knots.
4—Strong to very strong echoes within the smallest contour; echo bases 29,000 ft. MSL; cell in northeast Nebraska moving northeast at 50 knots.

7389. What weather conditions are depicted in the area indicated by arrow E on the Radar Summary Chart? (See Figure 19.)

1—Highest echo tops 30,000 ft. MSL; weak to moderate echoes; thundershowers; cell movement toward northwest at 15 knots.
2—Echo bases 29,000 to 30,000 ft. MSL; strong echoes; rain showers increasing in intensity; area movement toward northwest at 15 knots.
3—Thundershowers decreasing in intensity; area movement toward northwest at 15 knots; echo bases 30,000 ft. MSL.
4—Thunderstorms with no change in intensity; echo tops 30,000 ft. MSL; area movement northwest at 15 knots.

7390. What weather conditions are depicted in the area indicated by arrow F on the Radar Summary Chart? (See Figure 19.)

1—Extreme echoes along solid line; area movement toward northeast at 44 to 45 knots; thunderstorms increasing in intensity.
2—Line of echoes; thunderstorms; highest echo tops 46,000 ft. MSL; no line movement indicated.
3—Echo bases vary from 15,000 ft. to 46,000 ft. MSL; thunderstorms increasing in intensity; line of echoes moving rapidly toward the north.
4—Line of severe thunderstorms moving from south to north; echo bases vary from 4,400 ft. to 4,600 ft. MSL; extreme echoes.

7391. What weather conditions are depicted in the area indicated by arrow G on the Radar Summary Chart? (See Figure 19.)

1—Echo bases 10,000 ft. MSL; cell movement toward northeast at 15 knots; weak to moderate echoes; rain.
2—Area movement toward northeast at 15 knots; rain decreasing in intensity; echo bases 1,000 ft. MSL; strong echoes.
3—Strong to very strong echoes; area movement toward northeast at 15 knots; echo tops 10,000 ft. MSL; light rain.
4—Echo bases 1,000 ft. MSL; rain decreasing in intensity; cell movement toward northeast at 15 knots; moderate intensity echoes.

7392. For most effective use of the Radar Summary Chart during preflight planning, a pilot should

1—consult the chart to determine more accurate measurements of freezing levels, cloud cover, and wind conditions between reporting stations.
2—compare it with the Weather Depiction Chart to get a three-dimensional picture of clouds and precipitation.
3—utilize the chart as the only source of information regarding storms and hazardous conditions existing between reporting stations.
4—utilize the chart as the best source of information for ceilings, cloud tops, and cloud coverage between reporting stations.

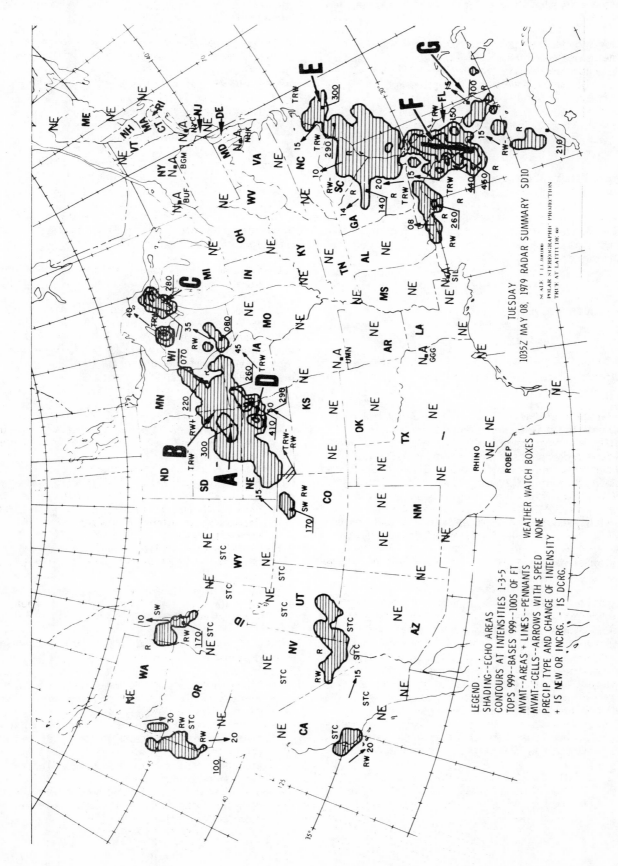

Figure 19

7393. What important information is provided by the Radar Summary Chart that is not shown on other weather charts?

1—Lines and cells of hazardous thunderstorms.
2—Ceilings and precipitation between reporting stations.
3—Types of precipitation between reporting stations.
4—Areas of cloud cover and icing levels within the clouds.

7394. What conclusion(s) can be drawn from a 500–millibar Constant Pressure Chart for a planned flight at FL180?

1—Winds aloft at FL180 generally flow across the height contours.
2—Station circles that are shaded indicate the degree of cloud coverage present at that altitude.
3—Observed temperature, wind, and temperature/dew point spread along the proposed route can be approximated.
4—Upper highs, lows, troughs, and ridges will be depicted by the use of lines of equal pressure.

7395. FAA Deletion.

7396. What is specifically implied by the omission of visibility and wind entries in the Terminal Forecast?

1—Visilibity more than 3 mi.; wind less than 15 knots.
2—Visibility more than 6 mi.; wind less than 10 knots.
3—Visibility more than 10 mi.; wind less than 7 knots.
4—Visibility more than 15 mi.; wind less than 3 knots.

7397. The absence of a visibility entry in a Terminal Forecast specifically implies that the surface visibility is

1—5 mi. or more.
2—more than 6 mi.
3—at least 5 mi. more than the landing requirement.
4—forecast to be at least 5 mi. in all directions.

7398. The body of an FT (Terminal Forecast) covers a geographical area within

1—a 5–mile radius of the center of a runway complex.
2—25 mi. of the center of an airport.
3—10 mi. of the station originating the FT.
4—a 10–mile radius of the center of the airport.

7399. What expected windspeed is specifically implied at 2200Z by this Terminal Forecast for Memphis?

MEM 251010 C5 X 1/2F 1710 OCNL CO X 1/2F.
16Z C25 BKN 11/2F 1720. 22Z 20 SCT. 00Z CLR.

1—Less than 3 knots.
2—Less than 5 knots.
3—Less than 10 knots.
4—Calm and variable.

7400. The word WIND in the 6–hour categorical outlook in the Terminal Forecast means that the wind during that period is forecast to be

1—10 to 15 knots.
2—10 knots or stronger.
3—less than 25 knots.
4—25 knots or stronger.

7401. The absence of a visibility entry in a Terminal Forecast specifically implies that the surface visibility

1—exceeds basic VFR minimums.
2—exceeds 10 mi.
3—exceeds 6 mi.
4—is at least 15 mi. in all directions from the center of the runway complex.

7402. Omission of a wind entry in a Terminal Forecast specifically implies that the wind is expected to be less than

1—5 knots.
2—6 knots.
3—8 knots.
4—10 knots.

7403. Which primary source should be used to obtain forecast weather information at your destination for the planned ETA?

1—Area Forecast.
2—Weather Depiction Chart.
3—Radar Summary and Weather Depiction Charts.
4—Terminal Forecast.

7404. The absence of a visibility entry in a Terminal Forecast specifically implies that the surface visibility is expected to be more than

1—3 mi.
2—6 mi.
3—10 mi.
4—15 mi.

7405. The section of the Area Forecast entitled SIG CLDS AND WX contains a

1—summary of cloudiness and weather significant to flight operations broken down by states or other geographical areas.
2—summary of forecast sky cover, cloud tops, visibility, and obstructions to vision along specific routes.
3—statement of AIRMETs and SIGMETs still in effect at the time of issue.
4—summary of only those clouds and weather considered adverse to safe flight operations.

7406. The section of the Area Forecast entitled FLT PRCTN contains

1—a summary of the expected hazardous weather.
2—a statement listing those AIRMET's still in effect.
3—a summary of general weather conditions over several states.
4—the statement TSTMS IMPLY PSBL SVR OR GTR TURBC, SVR ICG, AND LOW–LVL WIND SHEAR.

7407. Which forecast provides specific information concerning expected sky cover, cloud tops, visibility, weather and obstructions to vision in a route format?

1—DFW FA 131240.
2—MEM FT 132222.
3—249 TWEB 252317.
4—CHI WA 300300.

7408. A pilot planning to depart at 1100Z on an IFR flight is particularly concerned about the hazard of icing. What sources reflect the most accurate information on icing conditions (current and forecast) at the time of departure?

1—Convective SIGMETS (WST), Freezing Level Chart, and RADATS.
2—Low Level Sig Weather Prog Chart, RADATS, and the Area Forecast.
3—The Area Forecast, and the Freezing Level Chart.
4—PIREPS, AIRMETS, and SIGMETS.

7409. Which of the following meteorological conditions is issued in the form of a SIGMET (WS)?

1—Widespread sandstorm lowering visibility to less than 3 mi.
2—Moderate icing.
3—Widespread areas of visibility less than 3 mi. and/or ceilings less than 1,000 ft.
4—Sustained winds of 30 knots or greater at the surface.

7410. What significant cloud coverage is reported by a pilot in this SA?

MOB...M9 OVC 2LF 131/44/43/3212/991/UA/OV 15NW
MOB 1355/SK OVC 025/045 OVC 090

1—Three separate overcast layers exist with tops at 2,500, 7,500, and 13,500 ft.
2—Three separate overcast layers exist with bases at 2,500, 7,500, and 13,500 ft.
3—The top of lower overcast is 2,500 ft.; base and top of second overcast layer is 4,500 and 9,000 ft., respectively.
4—The base of second overcast layer is 2,500 ft.; top of second overcast layer is 7,500 ft.; base of third layer is 13,500 ft.

7411. SIGMET's are issued as a warning of weather conditions potentially hazardous

1—particularly to light aircraft.
2—to all aircraft.
3—only to light aircraft operations.
4—particularly to heavy aircraft.

7412. At what time are current AIRMET's broadcast in their entirety by FSS?

1—15 minutes after the hour only.
2—Every 15 minutes until the AIRMET is canceled.
3—15 and 45 minutes after the hour during the first hour after issuance.
4—On the hour and each 15 minutes thereafter for 1 hour after issuance.

7413. When is the wind-group at one of the forecast altitudes omitted at a specific location or station in the Winds and FD (Temperatures Aloft Forecast)? When the wind

1—at the altitude is within 2,500 ft. of the station elevation.
2—is less than 5 knots.
3—is less than 10 knots.
4—at the altitude is within 1,500 ft. of the station elevation.

7414. When is the temperature at one of the forecast altitudes omitted at a specific location or station in the Winds and FD (Temperatures Aloft Forecast)?

1—When the temperature is standard for that altitude.
2—For the 3,000-foot altitude (level) or when the level is within 2,500 ft. of station elevation.
3—Only when the winds are omitted for that altitude (level).
4—Only when a reporting station fails to submit a report.

7415. What wind direction and speed is represented by the entry 9900+00, for 9,000 ft., on a Winds and FD (Temperatures Aloft Forecast)?

1—090° and calm.
2—Light and variable; less than 5 knots.
3—VORTEX winds exceeding 200 knots.
4—Light and variable; less than 10 knots.

7416. Decode the excerpt from the Winds and Temperature Aloft Forecast (FD) for OKC at 39,000 ft.

FT	3000	6000 ... 39000
OKC		830558

1—Wind 110° at 50 knots, temperature −58° C.
2—Wind 130° at 50 knots, temperature −58° C.
3—Wind 330° at 105 knots, temperature −58° C.
4—Wind 330° at 205 knots, temperature −58° C.

7417. What values are used for winds aloft forecasts?

1—Magnetic direction and knots.
2—Magnetic direction and MPH.
3—True direction and knots.
4—True direction and MPH.

7418. Which weather forecast describes prospects for an area coverage of both severe and general thunderstorms during the following 24 hours?

1—Terminal Forecast.
2—Convective Outlook.
3—Severe Weather Watch Bulletin.
4—Special Flight Forecast.

7419. What information is provided by an AC (Convective Outlook)?

1—It provides a narrative description of ceiling and visibility conditions for the next 24 hours.
2—It describes areas of probable severe icing and severe or extreme turbulence during the next 24 hours.
3—It provides prospects of both general and severe thunderstorm activity during the following 24 hours.
4—It indicates areas of probable convective turbulence and the extent of instability in the upper atmosphere (above 500 mb).

7420. A prognostic chart depicts the conditions

1—existing at the surface during the past 6 hours.
2—which presently exist from the 1,000–millibar through the 700–millibar level.
3—forecast to exist at a specific time in the future.
4—representing the trend of the weather at the time of observation.

7421. Figure 20, an excerpt from a U.S. High Level Significant Prognostic Chart, indicates

1—continuous dense cirriform clouds covering five-eighths of the sky with bases and tops 24,000 ft. and 30,000 ft., respectively.
2—five layers of clouds with bases and tops 24,000 ft. and 30,000 ft., respectively.
3—five-tenths of the sky covered by layered clouds with cumulonimbus tops 30,000 ft.
4—50 percent probability of layered cirriform clouds with tops ranging between 24,000 ft. and 30,000 ft.

Figure 20

7422. Which meteorological conditions do a prognostic chart depict?

1—Conditions existing at the time of the observation.
2—Interpretation of weather conditions for geographical areas between reporting stations.
3—Conditions forecast to exist at a specific time shown on the chart.
4—Representation of a past weather trend.

7423. The Low Level Significant Weather Prog Chart depicts weather conditions

1—that are forecast to exist at a valid time shown on the chart.
2—as they existed at the time the chart was prepared.
3—that existed at the time shown on the chart which is about 3 hours before the chart is received.
4—that are forecast to exist 6 hours after the chart was prepared.

7424. Interpret the PIREP (Pilot Weather Report).

UA/OVR MRB FL060/SK INTMTLY BL/TB MDT/RM R TURBC INCRS WWD.

1—Ceiling 6,000 intermittently below moderate thundershowers; turbulence increasing westward.
2—Flight level 60,000, intermittently below clouds; moderate rain, turbulence increasing with the wind.
3—At 6,000 ft.; intermittently between layers; moderate turbulence; moderate rain; turbulence increasing westward.
4—At 6,000 ft.; intermittently between layers; thunderstorms moderate; rain and turbulence increasing with wind.

7425. The chart symbols over southern California on the 12–hour Sig Weather Prog (Figure 21) indicate

1—expected top of moderate turbulent layer to be 12,000 ft. MSL.
2—expected base of moderate turbulent layer to be 12,000 ft. MSL.
3—light turbulence expected above 12,000 ft. MSL.
4—light turbulence expected below 12,000 ft. MSL.

7426. The 12–hour Sig Weather Prog chart (Figure 21) indicates that eastern Kentucky and eastern Tennessee can expect probable ceilings

1—1,000–3,000 ft. inclusive and/or visibility 3–5 mi. inclusive.
2—less than 1,000 ft. and/or visibility less than 3 mi.
3—less than 1,000 ft. and/or visibility less than 3 mi., and moderate turbulence below 10,000 ft. MSL.
4—less than 1,000 ft. and/or visibility less than 3 mi., and moderate turbulence above 10,000 ft. MSL.

7427. The 12–Hour Surface Prog Chart (Figure 21) indicates that West Virginia will likely experience

1—scattered showers and thunderstorms covering less than half of the area.
2—continuous or showery precipitation covering half or more of the area.
3—thunderstorms and rain showers covering half or more of the area.
4—continuous rain covering less than half of the area.

7428. A planned low altitude flight from central Oklahoma to western Tennessee at 1200Z (Figure 21) is likely to encounter

1—continuous or intermittent rain or rain showers, moderate turbulence, and freezing temperatures below 8,000 ft.
2—continuous rain with little change in precipitation intensity, severe turbulence, and freezing temperatures lower to the east.
3—continuous or showery rain over half or more of the area, moderate turbulence, and freezing temperatures above 10,000 ft.
4—showery precipitation covering less than half the area, no turbulence below 18,000 ft., and freezing temperatures above 12,000 ft.

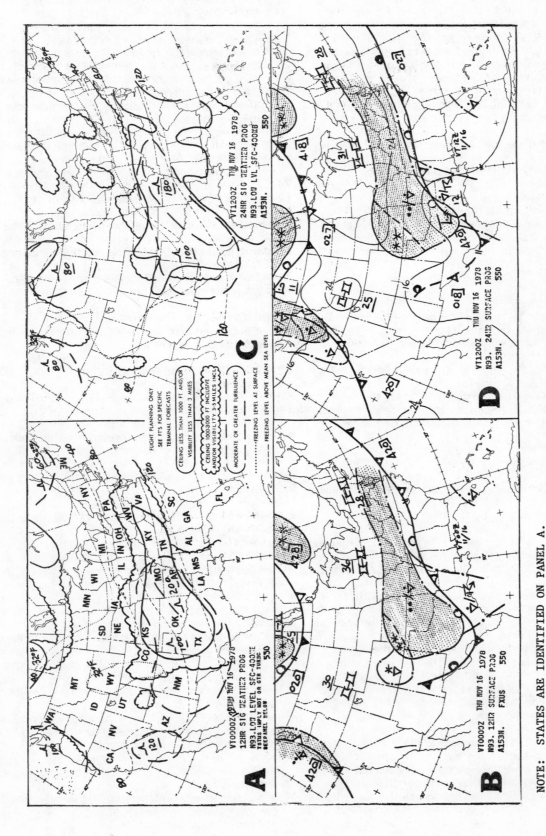

Figure 21

NOTE: STATES ARE IDENTIFIED ON PANEL A.

7429. What should be the indication on the magnetic compass as you roll into a standard rate turn to the left from a west heading in the Northern Hemisphere?

1—The compass will indicate a turn to the left, but at a slower rate than is actually occurring.
2—The compass will initially indicate a turn to the right.
3—The compass will remain on west for a short time, then gradually catch up to the magnetic heading of the airplane.
4—The compass will indicate the approximate correct magnetic heading if the roll into the turn is smooth.

7430. What should be the indication on the magnetic compass as you roll into a standard rate turn to the left from a north heading in the Northern Hemisphere?

1—The compass will indicate a turn to the left, but at a faster rate than is actually occurring.
2—The compass will intially indicate a turn to the right.
3—The compass will remain on north for a short time, then gradually catch up to the magnetic heading of the airplane.
4—The compass will lead the correct heading approximately 30°.

7431. What should be the indication on the magnetic compass as you roll into a standard rate turn to the left from an east heading in the northern hemisphere?

1—The compass will indicate a turn to the left, but at a slower rate than is actually occurring.
2—The compass will initially indicate a turn to the right.
3—The compass will remain on east for a short time, then gradually catch up to the magnetic heading of the airplane.
4—The compass will indicate the approximate correct magnetic heading if the roll into the turn is smooth.

7432. What should be the indication on the magnetic compass as you roll into a standard rate turn to the right from a westerly heading in the Northern Hemisphere?

1—The compass will indicate a turn to the right, but at a faster rate than is actually occurring.
2—The compass will initially show a turn in the opposite direction, then turn to a northerly indication but lagging behind the actual heading of the aircraft.
3—The compass will remain on a westerly heading for a short time, then gradually catch up to the actual heading of the aircraft.
4—The compass will indicate the approximate correct magnetic heading if the roll into the turn is smooth.

7433. What should be the indication on the magnetic compass as you roll into a standard rate turn to the right from a northerly heading in the Northern Hemisphere?

1—The compass will indicate a turn to the right, but at a faster rate than is actually occurring.
2—The compass will initially indicate a turn to the left.
3—The compass will remain on north for a short time, then gradually catch up to the magnetic heading of the airplane.
4—The compass will lead the correct magnetic heading approximately 30°.

7434. What should be the indication on the magnetic compass as you roll into a standard rate turn to the right from an easterly heading in the Northern Hemisphere?

1—The compass will indicate a turn to the right, but at a slower rate than is actually occurring.
2—The compass will initially indicate a turn to the left.
3—The compass will remain on east for a short time, then gradually catch up to the magnetic heading of the airplane.
4—The compass will indicate the approximate correct magnetic heading if the roll into the turn is smooth.

7435. What should be the indication on the magnetic compass as you roll into a standard rate turn to the right from a south heading in the Northern Hemisphere?

1—The compass will indicate a turn to the right, but at a faster rate than is actually occurring.
2—The compass will initially indicate a turn to the left.
3—The compass will remain on south for a short time, then gradually catch up to the magnetic heading of the airplane.
4—The compass will indicate the approximate correct magnetic heading if the roll into the turn is smooth.

7436. On what headings will the magnetic compass read most accurately during a level 360° turn, with a bank of approximately 15°?

1—45°, 135°, 225°, and 315°.
2—135° through 225°.
3—90° and 270°.
4—180° and 0°.

7437. What causes the northerly turning error in a magnetic compass?

1—Oversensitivity when nearer one of the magnetic poles.
2—Coriolis force at the mid–latitudes.
3—Centrifugal force acting on the compass card.
4—The magnetic dip characteristic.

7438. What should be the indication on the magnetic compass when you roll into a standard rate turn to the left from a south heading in the northern hemisphere?

1—The compass will indicate a turn to the left, but at a faster rate than is actually occurring.
2—The compass will initially indicate a turn to the right.
3—The compass will remain on south for a short time, then gradually catch up to the magnetic heading of the airplane.
4—The compass will lag the correct magnetic heading approximately 30°.

7439. Without visual aid, postural sense often interprets centrifugal force as a sensation of

1—rising or falling.
2—turning.
3—motion reversal.
4—acceleration or deceleration.

7440. When may ATC request a detailed report of an emergency even though a rule has not been violated?

1—When priority has been given.
2—Anytime an emergency occurs.
3—When the emergency occurs in controlled airspace.
4—When the pilot deviates from a clearance.

7441. The most current en route and destination flight information for an instrument flight should be obtained from

1—the ATIS broadcast.
2—the FSS.
3—ARTCC.
4—Notices to Airmen (Class II).

7442. From what source can you obtain the latest FDC NOTAMS?

1—In Notices to Airmen (Class II NOTAMS).
2—At an FAA Flight Service Station.
3—In the Airport/Facility Directory.
4—In Graphic Notices and Supplemental Data.

7443. Pilots using the fast file flight plan system are urged to

1—listen to the appropriate recorded weather briefing before speaking, and not pause longer than 30 sec. when reading flight plan elements.
2—call at least 1 hour before the proposed departure time, and use the FSS briefer number to confirm that the flight plan has been entered into the ARTCC computer.
3—call at least 30 min. in advance of the proposed departure time and speak at a normal speech rate without lengthy pauses.
4—speak at a normal level when entering flight plan elements, and wait until the briefer comes on the line before asking questions.

7444. If a control tower and an FSS are located on the same airport, which tower function is assumed by the FSS during those periods when the tower is closed?

1—Automatic closing of the IFR flight plan.
2—Clearance to start approach.
3—Airport Advisory Service.
4—All functions of the tower.

7445. Which service is provided for IFR arrivals by a Flight Service Station located on an airport without a control tower?

1—Automatic closing of the IFR flight plan.
2—Airport advisories.
3—Clearance to start instrument approach.
4—All functions of approach control.

7446. When are you required to utilize the Category II holding lines on airport taxiways?

1—When IFR conditions exist and landings are in progress.
2—When the ceiling is less than 200 ft.
3—At all times on an airport that is approved for Category II operations.
4—Anytime Category II operations are in progress at that airport.

7447. Which safety hazard will be prevented if the pilot remains behind the Category II holding line before receiving takeoff clearance during Category II operations?

1—Interference with the radar altimeter.
2—Interference with ILS guidance signals.
3—Clutter on the PAR scope.
4—Distortion of the inner marker signal.

7448. In the following illustration what is the distance from the end of the precision instrument runway to the fixed distance marker?

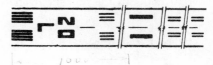

1—500 ft.
2—750 ft.
3—1,000 ft.
4—1,500 ft.

7449. In the following illustration which marking designates the touchdown zone marker for the precision instrument runway?

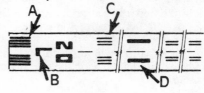

1—A.
2—B.
3—C.
4—D.

7450. In the following illustration what distance is the touchdown zone marker from the end of the runway?

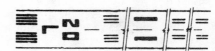

1—300 ft.
2—1,500 ft.
3—1,000 ft.
4—500 ft.

7451. In the following illustration what night operations, if any, are authorized between the displaced threshold and the approach end of the runway?

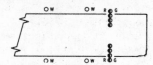

1—Only taxi operations are permitted.
2—Neither taxi, takeoff, nor landing operations are permitted.
3—All operations are permitted, provided the pilot is aware of the overrun condition and weight bearing limitations.
4—Taxi and takeoff operations are permitted.

7452. Which runway marking indicates a displaced threshold on an instrument runway?

1—Cross mark in the nonlanding portion of the runway.
2—Arrows leading to the threshold mark.
3—Centerline dashes starting at the threshold.
4—Red chevron marks in the nonlanding portion of the runway.

7453. The following radio transmission by the tower controller indicates that

CENTRAL TWO TWENTY FIVE, CENTERFIELD WIND ZERO TWO ZERO AT ONE FIVE, WEST BOUNDARY WIND THREE FOUR ZERO AT THREE FIVE.

1—a pilot west of the airport reported winds at 35 knots.
2—an apparent discrepancy in wind velocities exists and pilots should exercise caution.
3—wake turbulence exists to the west side of the active runway and the departing aircraft should use caution.
4—there is a possible hazardous wind shear.

7454. Which type of runway lighting consists of a pair of synchronized flashing lights, one on each side of the runway threshold?

1—RAIL.
2—HIRL.
3—REIL.
4—TDZL.

7455. The primary purpose of runway end identifier lights, installed at many airfields, is to provide

1—an outline of the touchdown zone on runways with a displaced threshold.
2—rapid identification of the approach end of the runway during reduced visibility.
3—a warning of the final 3,000 ft. of runway remaining as viewed from the takeoff or approach position.
4—rapid identification of proper runway alignment during reduced visibility.

7456. The operation of an airport rotating beacon during daylight hours may indicate that

1—the in-flight visibility is less than 3 mi. and the ceiling is less than 1,500 ft. within the control zone.
2—the ground visibiity is less than 3 mi. and/or the ceiling is less than 1,000 ft. in the control zone.
3—an IFR clearance is required to operate within the airport traffic area.
4—a special VFR clearance is required to operate within the airport traffic area.

7457. When are ATIS broadcasts updated?

1—Upon receipt of any official weather, regardless of content change and reported values.
2—Every 30 min. if weather conditions are below basic VFR; otherwise, hourly.
3—Only when the ceiling varies more than 100 ft., the altimeter setting is changed, visibility varies more than 1/4 mi., or the runway is changed.
4—Each 30 min. or when conditions change enough to require a change in the active runway or instrument approach.

7458. When are ATIS broadcasts updated?

1—Every 30 min. if weather conditions are below basic VFR; otherwise, hourly.
2—Upon receipt of any official weather, regardless of content change or reported values.
3—Only when conditions change enough to require a change in the active runway or instrument approach in use.
4—Only when the ceiling and/or visibility changes by a reportable value.

7459. Absence of the sky condition and visibility on an ATIS broadcast specifically implies that

1—the ceiling is at least 5,000 ft. and visibility is 5 mi. or more.
2—the sky condition is clear and visibility is unrestricted.
3—weather conditions are at or above VFR minimums.
4—the ceiling is at lest 3,000 ft. and visibility is 5 mi. or more.

7460. What procedure should a pilot use prior to an IFR departure when ATIS (Automatic Terminal Information Service) is available?

1—Contact ground control for any changes in ATIS just prior to takeoff.
2—Receive ATIS information and advise ATC you "have the numbers."
3—Receive ATIS information and advise ATC "information (alphabetical code) received."
4—Contact clearance delivery prior to taxi for ATIS IFR information.

7461. Which instrument indicates the quality of a turn?

1—Miniature aircraft of a turn coordinator.
2—Attitude indicator.
3—Heading indicator or magnetic compass.
4—Ball of the turn coordinator.

7462. When airspeed is increased in a turn, what must be done to maintain level flight?

1—Decrease the angle of bank.
2—Increase the angle of bank and/or decrease the angle of attack.
3—Decrease the angle of attack.
4—Decrease the angle of bank and/or the angle of attack.

7463. When should you contact ground control on landing at a controlled airport?

1—Prior to turning off the runway.
2—After clearing the active runway.
3—After crossing the runway holding lines.
4—When the tower instructs you to do so.

7464. Upon landing at a controlled airport, you should switch to ground control only

1—if you wish to proceed to the parking area.
2—upon crossing the runway-taxiway boundary.
3—if the tower hands you off to ground control.
4—upon crossing the runway holding lines.

7465. What does the RVR (Runway Visual Range) value depicted on certain straight-in Instrument Approach Procedure Charts represent?

1—The slant visual range which a pilot should see during the final approach segment.
2—The horizontal distance a pilot will see down the runway from the approach end, based on sighting HIRL or visual contrast of other targets.
3—The greatest horizontal visibility equaled or exceeded throughout at least half the horizon circle.
4—The distance which an instrument can detect a light source located along the runway.

7466. If the RVR is not reported, what meteorological value should you substitute for 2,400 RVR?

1—A ground visibility of 1/2 nautical mile.
2—A slant range visibility of 2,400 ft. for the final approach segment of the published approach procedure.
3—A ground visibility of 1/2 statute mile.
4—A ground visibility of 5/8 statute mile.

7467. What does the RVR (Runway Visual Range) value, depicted on certain straight-in Instrument Approach Procedure Charts, represent?

1—The slant range distance the pilot can see down the runway while crossing the threshold on glide slope.
2—The horizontal distance a pilot should see down the runway from the approach end of the runway.
3—The slant visual range a pilot should see down the final approach and during landing.
4—The greatest distance that can be seen in all directions around the horizon circle.

7468. How should you pre-flight check the altimeter prior to an IFR flight?

1—Set the altimeter to 29.92. With current temperature and the altimeter indication, determine the true altitude to compare with the field elevation.
2—Set the altimeter to the current temperature. With current temperature and the altimeter indication determine the calibrated altitude to compare with the field elevation.
3—Set the altimeter first with 29.92 and then the current altimeter setting. The change in altitude should correspond to the change in setting.
4—Set the altimeter to the current altimeter setting. The indication should be within 75 ft. of the actual elevation for acceptable accuracy.

7469. What practical test should be made on the electric gyro instruments prior to starting an engine?

1—Check that the electrical connections are secure on the back of the instruments.
2—Check that the attitude of the miniature aircraft is wings level before turning on electrical power.
3—Turn on the electrical power and listen for any unusual or irregular mechanical noise.
4—Reset the heading indicator to be sure setting knobs are operative.

7470. Prior to starting an engine, you should check the turn-and-slip indicator to determine if the

1—needle indication properly corresponds to the angle of the wings or rotors with the horizon.
2—needle is approximately centered and the tube is full of fluid.
3—ball will move freely from one end of the tube to the other when the aircraft is rocked.
4—needle and ball are resting on the same side of the instrument.

7471. What indications should you get from the turn-and-slip indicator during taxi?

1—The needle and ball should move freely in the direction of the turn.
2—The ball moves freely opposite the turn, and the needle deflects in the direction of the turn.
3—The needle deflects in the direction of the turn, but the ball remains centered.
4—The ball deflects opposite the turn, but the needle remains centered.

7472. What is the maximum tolerance allowed for an operational check of the aircraft VOR equipment when using a VOT?

1—Plus or minus 2° from 360.
2—Plus or minus 2° from 180.
3—Plus or minus 4°.
4—Plus or minus 4° for a check on the ground and 6° while airborne.

7473. What is the maximum allowable range of the OBS (CDI centered) when checking a VOR receiver by use of a VOT?

1—178° to 182° FROM.
2—176° to 184° TO.
3—356° to 004° TO.
4—358° to 002° FROM.

7474. Which is the correct indication and acceptable tolerance when performing a ground check of the aircraft VOR equipment using a VOT frequency?

1—CDI centered; OBS within 6° of 180°; TO indication.
2—CDI centered; OBS within 4° of 000°; FROM indication.
3—CDI centered; OBS within 4° of 000°; TO indication.
4—CDI centered; OBS within 4° of 180°; FROM indication.

7475. Which is the correct indication and maximum permissible error when performing a ground check of the aircraft VOR equipment using a VOT?

1—CDI centered; TO indication; OBS within 4° of 180°.
2—CDI centered; FROM indication; OBS within 4° of 180°.
3—CDI centered; TO indication; OBS within 2° of 000°.
4—CDI centered; FROM indication; OBS within 2° of 000°.

7476. When an airplane is located on the designated ground checkpoint at an airport, a VOR receiver check can be made by tuning the receiver to the VOR frequency and setting the OBS to

1—000°. The CDI should center within plus or minus 4° with a FROM indication.
2—180°. The CDI should center within plus or minus 4° with a TO indication.
3—the designated radial and centering the CDI with the OBS if necessary. The OBS must read within plus or minus 4° of the designated radial with a FROM indication.
4—the designated radial and centering the CDI with the OBS if necessary. The OBS must read within plus or minus 4°of the designated radial with a TO indication.

7477. What is the maximum permissible variation between the two indicated bearings when checking the dual VOR system, each unit independent of the other except for the antenna?

1—Ground check 4° or airborne check 6°.
2—Ground or airborne check 4°.
3—Ground check 6° or airborne check 4°.
4—Ground or airborne check 6°.

7478. When making an airborne VOR check, what is the maximum allowable tolerance between the two indicators of a dual VOR system (units independent of each other except the antenna)?

1—4° between the two indicated bearings to a VOR.
2—Plus or minus 4° when set to identical radials of a VOR.
3—6° between the two indicated radials of a VOR.
4—4° when set to identical radials of a VOR.

7479. Which indications are acceptable tolerances when checking both of your VOR receivers by use of the VOT?

1—175° TO and 178° TO, respectively.
2—360° TO and 003° TO, respectively.
3—001° FROM and 005° FROM, respectively.
4—176° TO and 003° FROM, respectively.

7480. When checking your VOR receiver by use of a VOT, which is a correct setting with the CDI (Course Deviation Indicator) centered?

1—The OBS is 0 with a FROM indication.
2—The OBS is 180 with a FROM indication.
3—The OBS is 180 with either a TO or FROM indication.
4—The OBS is from 356 thru 004 with a TO indication.

7481. In which publication can the VOR receiver ground checkpoint(s) for a particular airport be found?

1—Airman's Information Manual.
2—En route Low Altitude Chart.
3—Airport/Facility Directory.
4—Graphic Notices and Supplemental Data publication.

7482. Which is the maximum tolerance for the VOR indication when the CDI is centered and the airplane is directly over the airborne checkpoint?

1—Plus or minus 6° of the designated radial – FROM.
2—Plus or minus 4° of the designated radial – TO.
3—Plus or minus 4° of the designated radial – FROM.
4—Plus or minus 6° of the designated radial – TO.

7483. Which transponder codes should you take caution not to switch through while changing codes?

1—0700, 7700, 7600.
2—7700, 7600, 7500.
3—0000, 3100, 7700.
4—3333, 7600, 7700.

7484. When should your transponder be on Mode C while on an IFR flight?

1—Only when ATC requests Mode C.
2—At all times if the equipment has been calibrated, unless requested otherwise by ATC.
3—When passing 12,500 ft. MSL.
4—Only when operating in TCA's, control zones, and on airways.

7485. Which condition during taxi is an indication that an attitude indicator is unreliable?

1—The horizon bar tilts more than 5° while making taxi turns.
2—The horizon bar vibrates during warmup.
3—The horizon bar does not align itself with the miniature airplane after warmup.
4—The miniature airplane does not tilt sufficiently to indicate a turn while taxiing.

7486. What pre–takeoff check should be made of the attitude indicator in preparation for an IFR flight?

1—The horizon bar does not vibrate during warmup.
2—The miniature airplane should deflect in the direction of taxi turns after a 5–minute warmup.
3—The miniature airplane should erect and become stable within 5 min.
4—The horizon bar should erect and become stable within 5 min.

7487. What pre–takeoff check should be made of a vacuum–driven heading indicator in preparation for an IFR flight?

1—The heading indicator card should not rotate during the first 5 min. of engine operation.
2—After 5 min., set the indicator to the magnetic heading of the aircraft and check for proper alignment after taxi turns.
3—After 5 min., check that the heading indicator card aligns itself with the magnetic heading of the aircraft.
4—Determine that the heading indicator does not precess more than 2° in 5 min. of ground operation.

7488. On the taxi check, the magnetic compass should

1—be checked for proper deviation and fluid level.
2—swing opposite to the direction of turn when turning from north.
3—exhibit the same number of degrees of dip as the latitude.
4—swing freely and indicate known headings.

7489. What is the recommended climb procedure when a nonradar departure control instructs a flight to climb to the assigned altitude?

1—Maintain a continuous optimum climb until reaching assigned altitude and report passing each 1,000–foot level.
2—Climb at a maximum angle of climb to within 1,000 ft. of the assigned altitude, then 500 ft./min. the last 1,000 ft.
3—Climb to within 1,000 ft. of the assigned altitude on the right side of the airway, then join the airway.
4—Maintain an optimum climb on the centerline of the airway without intermediate level–offs until 1,000 ft. below assigned altitude, then 500 ft./min.

7490. What service is provided by departure control to an IFR flight when operating from an airport with a terminal radar service area (Stage III)?

1—Separation from all aircraft operating in the TRSA.
2—Position and altitude of all traffic within 2 mi. of the IFR pilot's line of flight and altitude.
3—Position of all participating VFR aircraft within the airport traffic area.
4—Separation from all IFR aircraft and participating VFR aircraft.

7491. What indication should a pilot receive when a VOR station is undergoing maintenance and may be considered unreliable?

1—No coded identification, but possible navigation indications.
2—Coded identification, but no navigation indications.
3—Navigation and coded signals, but an intermittent "OFF" flag.
4—A voice recording on the VOR frequency announcing that the VOR is out of service for maintenance.

7492. A particular VOR station is undergoing routine maintenance. This is evidenced by

1—removal of the navigational feature.
2—broadcasting a maintenance alert signal on the voice channel.
3—removal of the identification feature.
4—transmitting a series of "dots" after each identification signal.

7493. What is the meaning of a single coded identification received only once approximately every 30 seconds from a VORTAC?

1—The VOR and DME components are operative.
2—VOR and DME components are both operative, but voice identification is out of service.
3—VOR and DME components are both inoperative.
4—The DME component is operative and the VOR component is inoperative.

7494. Which DME indication should you receive when you are directly over a VORTAC site at approximately 6,000 ft. AGL?

1—0.
2—1.
3—1.3.
4—6.

7495. Which information is always given in an abbreviated clearance?

1—SID or transition name and altitude to maintain.
2—Name of the first compulsory reporting point when not in radar environment, and altitude to maintain.
3—Name of destination airport or specific fix and altitude.
4—Altitude to maintain and code to squawk.

7496. On the run–up pad, you receive the following clearance from ground control:

CLEARED TO DALLAS–LOVE AIRPORT AS FILED— MAINTAIN SIX THOUSAND—SQUAWK ZERO SEVEN ZERO FOUR JUST BEFORE DEPARTURE—DEPARTURE CONTROL WILL BE ONE TWO FOUR POINT NINER.

An abbreviated clearance, such as this, will always contain the

1—departure control frequency.
2—transponder code.
3—assigned altitude.
4—time or place to activate transponder.

7497. When departing from an airport not served by a control tower, the issuance of a clearance containing a void time indicates that

1—ATC will assume the pilot has not departed if no transmission is received before the void time.
2—the pilot must advise ATC as soon as possible, but no later than 30 min., of his intentions if not off by the void time.
3—ATC will protect the airspace only to the void time.
4—the pilot must contact FSS and file a flight plan not later than the void time specified in the clearance.

7498. What response is expected when ATC issues an IFR clearance to a pilot?

1—Read back the entire clearance as required by regulation.
2—Read back those parts containing altitude assignments or vectors and any part requiring verification.
3—Read–back should be unsolicited and spontaneous to confirm that the pilot understands all instructions.
4—Read back the initial route clearance, altitude assignments, and transponder codes.

7499. Which clearance items are always given in an abbreviated IFR departure clearance? (Assume radar environment.)

1—Altitude, destination airport, and one or more fixes which identify the initial route of flight.
2—Destination airport, altitude, and SID Name–Number–Transition, if appropriate.
3—Altitude, one or more en route fixes, SID, STAR, and delay information, if appropriate.
4—Clearance limit, and SID Name–Number–Transition, if appropriate.

7500. Which distance is displayed by the DME indicator?

1—Slant range distance in nautical miles.
2—Slant range distance in statute miles.
3—The distance from the aircraft to a point at the same altitude directly above the VORTAC.
4—Line of sight direct distance from aircraft to VORTAC in statute miles.

7501. Where does the DME indicator have the greatest error between ground distance to the VORTAC and displayed distance?

1—High altitudes far from the VORTAC.
2—High altitudes close to the VORTAC.
3—Low altitudes far from the VORTAC.
4—Low altitudes close to the VORTAC.

7502. For operations off established airways at 17,000 ft. MSL in the contiguous United States, (H) Class VORTAC facilities used to define a direct route of flight should be no farther apart than

1—40 NM.
2—75 NM.
3—100 NM.
4—200 NM.

7503. The course selector of each aircraft shown in (Figure 22) is set on 360°. Which aircraft would have a FROM indication on the ambiguity meter and the CDI pointing left of center?

1—A.
2—B.
3—C.
4—D.

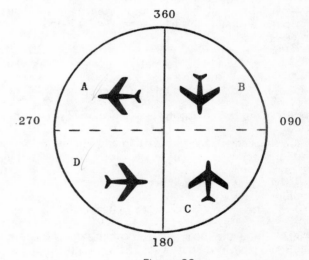

Figure 22

7504. Refer to the instruments in Figure 23. On the basis of this information, the magnetic bearing FROM the station would be

1—085°.
2—175°.
3—255°.
4—355°.

7505. Refer to instruments in Figure 23. On the basis of this information, the magnetic bearing TO the station would be

1—085°.
2—175°.
3—255°.
4—355°.

Figure 23

Figure 24

7506. Refer to instruments in Figure 24. On the basis of this information, the magnetic bearing FROM the station would be

1—030°.
2—060°.
3—240°.
4—270°.

7507. Refer to instruments in Figure 24. On the basis of this information, the magnetic bearing TO the station would be

1—030°.
2—060°.
3—240°.
4—270°.

7508. Refer to Figure 25. If the radio magnetic indicator is tuned to a VOR, which illustration indicates the aircraft is on the 335 radial?

1—A.
2—B.
3—C.
4—D.

7509. Refer to Figure 25. If the radio magnetic indicator is tuned to a VOR, which illustration indicates the aircraft is on the 115 radial?

1—A.
2—B.
3—C.
4—D.

7510. Refer to Figure 25. If the radio magnetic indicator is tuned to a VOR, which illustration indicates the aircraft is on the 315 radial?

1—A.
2—B.
3—C.
4—D.

7511. Refer to Figure 25. If the radio magnetic indicator is tuned to a VOR, which illustration indicates the aircraft is on the 010 radial?

1—A.
2—B.
3—C.
4—D.

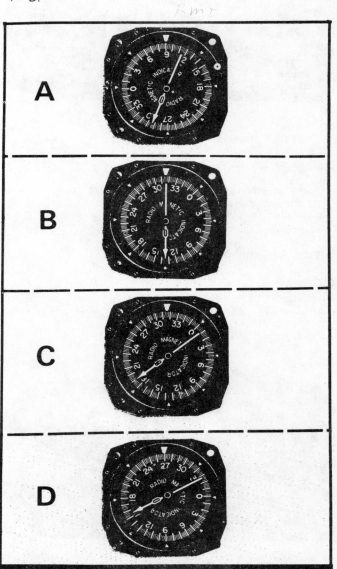

Figure 25

7512. FAA Deletion.

7513. FAA Deletion.

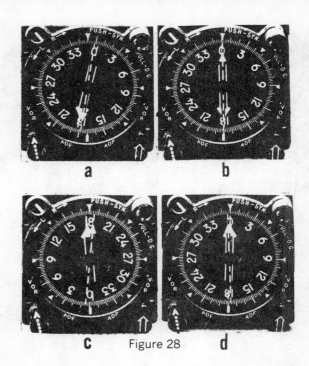

Figure 28

Figure 26

7514. FAA Deletion.

7516. When checking a dual VOR system by use of a VOT, which illustration indicates the VOR's are satisfactory? (See Figure 28.)

1—a.
2—b.
3—c.
4—d.

7517. When checking your VOR receiver by use of a VOT, which is a correct setting with the Course Deviation Indicator (CDI) centered?

1—OBS 180; TO indication.
2—OBS 0; TO indication.
3—OBS 0; either TO or FROM indication.
4—OBS from 176 through 184; FROM indication.

7518. Where can the VOT frequency for a particular airport be found?

1—On the Instrument Approach Procedure Chart and in the Airport/Facility Directory.
2—In the Graphic Notices and Supplemental Data publication and on the Instrument Approach Procedure Chart.
3—Only in the Airport/Facility Directory.
4—In the Airport/Facility Directory and on the A/G Voice Communication Panel of the En Route Low Altitude Chart.

7515. FAA Deletion.

Figure 27

7519. Which is an acceptable range of accuracy when performing an operational check of dual VOR's using one system against the other? (See Figure 29.)

1—a.
2—b.
3—c.
4—d.

7520. While airborne, what is the maximum permissible variation between the two indicated bearings when checking one VOR system against the other?

1—Plus or minus 4° when set to identical radials of a VOR.
2—4° between the two indicated bearings to a VOR.
3—Plus or minus 6° when set to identical radials of a VOR.
4—6° between the two indicated bearings to a VOR.

7521. How should the pilot make a VOR receiver check when the airplane is located on the designated checkpoint on the airport surface?

1—With the aircraft headed directly toward the VOR and the OBS set to 000° the CDI should center within plus or minus 4° of that radial with a TO indication.
2—Set the OBS on the designated radial. The CDI must center within plus or minus 4° of that radial with a FROM indication.
3—Set the OBS on 180° plus or minus 4°; the CDI should center with a FROM indication.
4—With the aircraft headed directly away from the VOR and the OBS set to 180°, the CDI should center within plus or minus 4° of 180° with a FROM indication.

INTENTIONALLY LEFT BLANK

Figure 29

7522. What is the minimum rate climb per nautical mile to 9,000 ft. required for the Reno Six Departure? (See Figure 30.)

1—300 ft.
2—350 ft.
3—765 ft.
4—875 ft.

7523. What is the minimum rate of climb (ft./min.) to 9,000 ft. on the Reno Six Departure at a GS of 150 knots? (See Figure 30.)

1—350 ft./min.
2—500 ft./min.
3—765 ft./min.
4—875 ft./min.

7524. What procedure should be followed if communications are lost before reaching 9,000 ft.? (See Figure 30.)

1—At 9000, turn left direct to RNO VORTAC, then via assigned route if at proper altitude; if not, climb in holding pattern until reaching the proper altitude.
2—Continue climb to WAGGE INT, turn left direct to RNO VORTAC, then if at or above MCA, proceed on assigned route; if not, continue climb in holding pattern until a proper altitude.
3—Continue climb on LOC course to cross WAGGE INT at or above 9000, turn left direct to RNO VORTAC to cross at 10000 or above, and continue on assigned course.
4—Turn left direct to RNO VORTAC and enter the depicted holding pattern. Climb to 10000 in the holding pattern and continue climb while proceeding on assigned route.

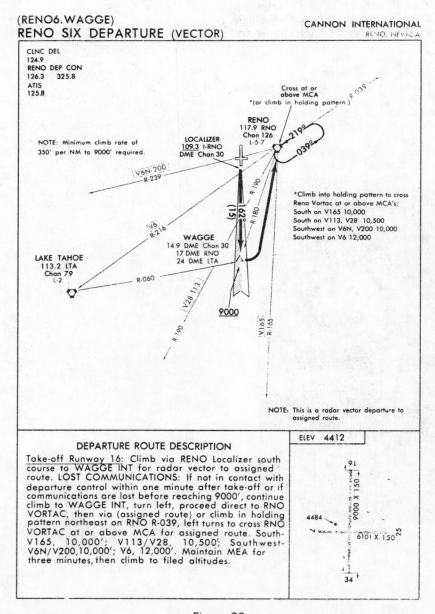

Figure 30

7525. What route should you take if cleared for the Reno Six Departure and your assigned route is V6N? (See Figure 30.)

1—Climb on the LOC south course to WAGGE where you will be vectored to V6N.
2—Climb on the LOC south course to cross WAGGE at 9000, turn left and fly direct to RNO VORTAC and cross at or above 10000, and proceed on RNO R–239.
3—Climb on the LOC south course to WAGGE, turn left and fly direct to RNO VORTAC. If at 10000 turn left and proceed on RNO R–239, if not at 10000, enter depicted holding pattern and climb to 10000 before proceeding on RNO R–239.
4—Climb on the LOC south course to WAGGE, if able to cross direct to RNO VORTAC, if not at 9000, climb in circular holding pattern to 9000 and proceed to RNO to cross at 10000 before proceeding on course.

7526. Which combination of indications confirm that you are approaching WAGGE Intersection slightly to the right of the LOC centerline on departure? (See Figures 30 and 31.)

1—a and c.
2—a and d.
3—b and c.
4—b and d.

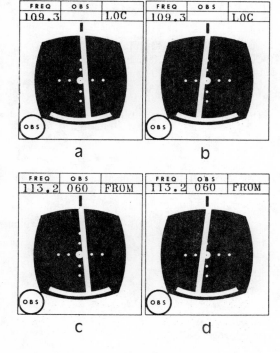

Figure 31

7527. What action is recommended if a pilot does not wish to use a SID?

1—Advise clearance delivery or ground control before departure.
2—Advise departure control upon initial contact.
3—Enter "No SID" in the REMARKS section of the IFR flight plan.
4—No action is necessary. ATC will not assign a SID unless specifically requested by the pilot.

7528. A particular SID (Standard Instrument Departure) requires a minimum climb rate of 210 ft. per nautical mile to 8,000 ft. If you climb with a groundspeed of 140 knots, what is the rate of climb required in ft./min.?

1—210.
2—300.
3—450.
4—490.

7529. Which procedure applies to SID's (Standard Instrument Departures)?

1—SID clearances will not be issued unless requested by the pilot.
2—The pilot in command must accept a SID when issued by ATC.
3—If a SID is accepted, the pilot must possess at least a textual description.
4—ATC will issue a SID whenever it is necessary to amend a departure clearance.

7530. During a take–off into IFR conditions with low ceilings, when should the pilot contact departure control?

1—Before penetrating the clouds.
2—When advised by the tower.
3—Upon completing the first turn after takeoff or upon establishing cruise climb on a straight–out departure.
4—When clear of the airport and established on the heading given in the clearance.

7531. You receive the following clearance from ATC:

CLEARED TO DALLAS–LOVE AIRPORT AS FILED MAINTAIN FIVE THOUSAND, TURN RIGHT TO ZERO SIX ZERO AFTER TAKEOFF—SQUAWK FOUR TWO ONE FOUR JUST BEFORE DEPARTURE AND DEPARTURE CONTROL ONE TWO FOUR POINT SIX...

When should you contact departure control?

1—Upon arriving at 5,000 ft.
2—When established on a heading of 060.
3—Prior to penetrating the clouds.
4—When instructed by the tower.

NOTE: Refer to Figure 32 and the following information for questions 7532 through 7535.

Var. 21°E; Avg. wind 320° at 30 knots; TAS 180 knots; Alt. setting 29.92.
Temperature at 5,000 ft. 10° C; at 12,000 ft. – 3° C.
Fuel burn: 30 gal./hr. or 180 lb./hr. Determine ETA as follows: Use cruise airspeed for entire distance, then add 1 min. for each 2,000 ft. of climb. An alternate is required.

7532. (See NOTE.) What is your ETE for a round–robin flight from Seattle–Tacoma International (a) via V23 MCKEN (e), V204 YKM (d), V25 EAT (b), V2N SEA?

1—1 hr. 30 min.
2—1 hr. 33 min.
3—1 hr. 36 min.
4—1 hr. 39 min.

7533. (See NOTE.) What is the required fuel for an instrument flight if your ETE is 1 hr. 40 min., and your ETE to alternate is 24 min.? Add 22 lb. of additional fuel for taxi, takeoff, and climb.

1—395 lb.
2—415 lb.
3—505 lb.
4—529 lb.

7534. (See NOTE.) What CAS is necessary to obtain a TAS of 180 knots at 5,000 ft.?

1—166.
2—169.
3—171.
4—173.

7535. (See NOTE.) What CAS is necessary to obtain a TAS of 180 knots at 12,000 ft.?

1—146.
2—148.
3—150.
4—152.

7536. You lose two–way communications at YKM (d). Which procedure, regarding altitude, should you use if your last assigned altitude is 7000 and your route from YKM is V25 EAT (b), V2N SEA (a)? (See Figure 32.)

1—7000 to ELN (c), 8600 to EAT, and 12000 to SEA or IAF.
2—7000 until necessary to start climb to cross ELN at 8600, 8600 until necessary to start climb to cross EAT at 12000, 12000 to SEA or IAF.
3—7000 to ELN, 9000 to EAT, 12000 to TAGOR, 5000 to SEA or IAF.
4—7000 to ELN, 8600 to EAT, 12000 to TAGOR, 7000 SEA or IAF.

7537. What are the MEAs, and MCAs if higher, from SEA (a) via V4 YKM (d), V25 EAT (b), V2N back to SEA? (See Figure 32.)

1—6000 to BLAKO, 10000 to CHINS, 7000 to TITON, 5500 to ELN, with MCA of 6800, 8600 to EAT, 12000 to TAGOR, and 5000 to SEA.
2—4000 to BLAKO with 7500 MCA, 10000 to CHINS, 7000 to TITON, 5500 to GLEED, 5000 to YKM, 5600 to ELN with MCA of 6800, 8600 to EAT, 12000 to TAGOR, and 8500 to SEA.
3—4000 to BLAKO, 10000 to CHINS, 7000 to TITON, 5500 to GLEED, 5000 to YKM, 5600 to ELN with MCA of 6800, 8600 to EAT, 12000 to TAGOR, and 5000 to SEA.
4—6000 to BLAKO with 7500 MCA, 10000 to CHINS, 7000 to TITON, 5500 to GLEED, 5000 YKM, 5600 to ELN with MCA of 6800, 8600 to EAT, 12000 to TAGOR, and 5000 to SEA.

7538. Where is the VOR changeover point when flying from SEA (a) to YKM (d) on V4? (See Figure 32.)

1—Upon passing RADDY Intersection.
2—At the mid–point between RADDY and CHINS.
3—At the mid–point between SEA and YKM.
4—CHINS Intersection.

7539. What are the minimum altitudes you may fly from YKM (d) to EAT (b) via V25 with a "VFR On Top" clearance if the top of the overcast is 7000 ft. MSL? (See Figure 32.)

1—8500 to ELN and 9500 to EAT.
2—8000 to ELN and 9000 to EAT.
3—8500 to ELN and 7500 to EAT.
4—7500 to ELN and 9000 to EAT.

7540. After passing a VORTAC, the CDI shows 1/2 scale deflection to the right. What is indicated if the deflection remains constant for a period of time?

1—The VORTAC is undergoing maintenance.
2—The airplane is getting closer to the radial.
3—The OBS is erroneously set on the reciprocal heading.
4—The airplane is flying away from the radial.

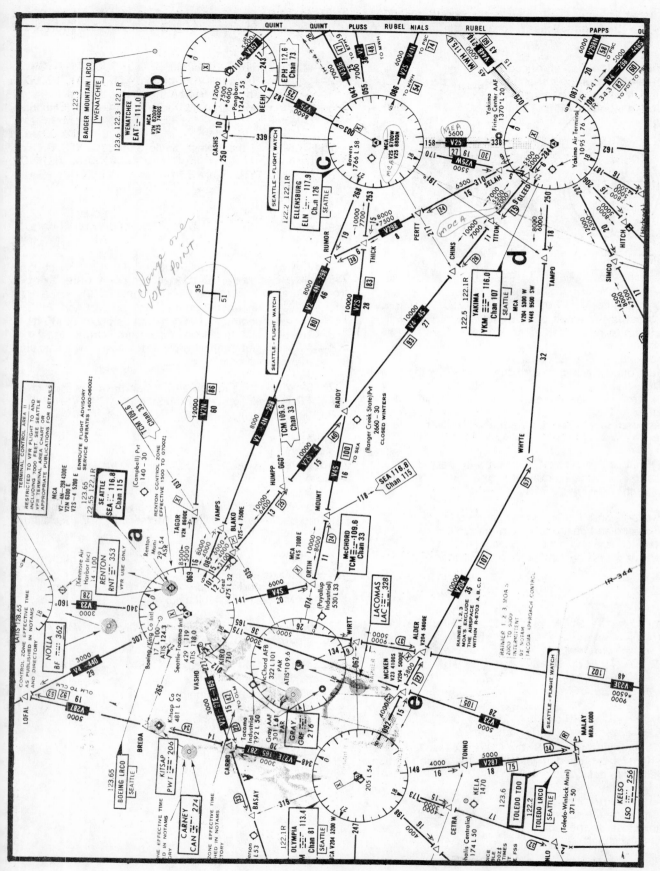

Figure 32

7541. What is your position with respect to the 060° bearing to the nondirectional beacon as indicated in Figure 33?

1—You are outbound, left of course.
2—You are outbound, right of course.
3—You are inbound, on course.
4—You are inbound, right of course.

Figure 33

7542. What is the result of flying toward an NDB with a 0° relative bearing in a left crosswind?

1—The heading remains constant.
2—The ground track curves to the downwind side of the NDB.
3—The ground track curves to the upwind side of the NDB.
4—The airplane makes a slow but continuous turn to the right.

7543. What is the aircraft position with respect to the 190° course and the beacon while making an NDB RWY 19 approach? (See Figure 34.)

1—On course and outbound from the beacon.
2—On course and past the beacon inbound.
3—Left of course and past the beacon inbound.
4—Right of course and inbound to the beacon.

Figure 34

7544. While flying to a VOR, the CDI indicates 1/4 scale to the right of center. If it remains in the same position for several minutes, you are

1—flying away from the radial.
2—maintaining the same distance from the radial.
3—flying closer to the radial.
4—gradually changing heading.

7545. When the VOR ambiguity meter indicates TO and the deviation indicator (CDI) is centered, the aircraft will always be

1—inbound to the VOR station.
2—outbound from the VOR station.
3—on the radial identified on the course selector.
4—on the reciprocal of the radial identified on the course selector.

7546. What is the lowest single altitude a VFR On Top flight could maintain from OLM VORTAC (b) to AST VOR (h) on V27E? (See Figure 35.)

1—4,000 ft.
2—5,000 ft.
3—5,500 ft.
4—6,500 ft.

7547. What is the procedure for an IFR flight penetrating the airway restriction on V23 (c)? (See Figure 35.)

1—The pilot should get permission from McChord AFB.
2—The pilot should request an altitude above 5,000 ft.
3—The pilot should get clearance from Seattle Center.
4—ATC will automatically clear the flight when issuing the route clearance.

7548. What is the lowest altitude an IFR flight may cross ALDER Intersection (f) northbound on V23E? (See Figure 35.)

1—4,100 ft.
2—5,000 ft.
3—5,800 ft.
4—9,000 ft.

7549. What is the MEA, if any, between CETRA Intersection (e) and WINLO Intersection (g)? (See Figure 35.)

1—4,000 ft.
2—5,000 ft.
3—3,000 ft. northbound and 4,000 ft. southbound.
4—An MEA is not established.

7550. Where is the COP from Olympia VORTAC (b) southward on V165? (See Figure 35.)

1—At 49–1/2 mi.
2—WINLO Intersection.
3—Mileage breakdown point.
4—At 32 DME mi.

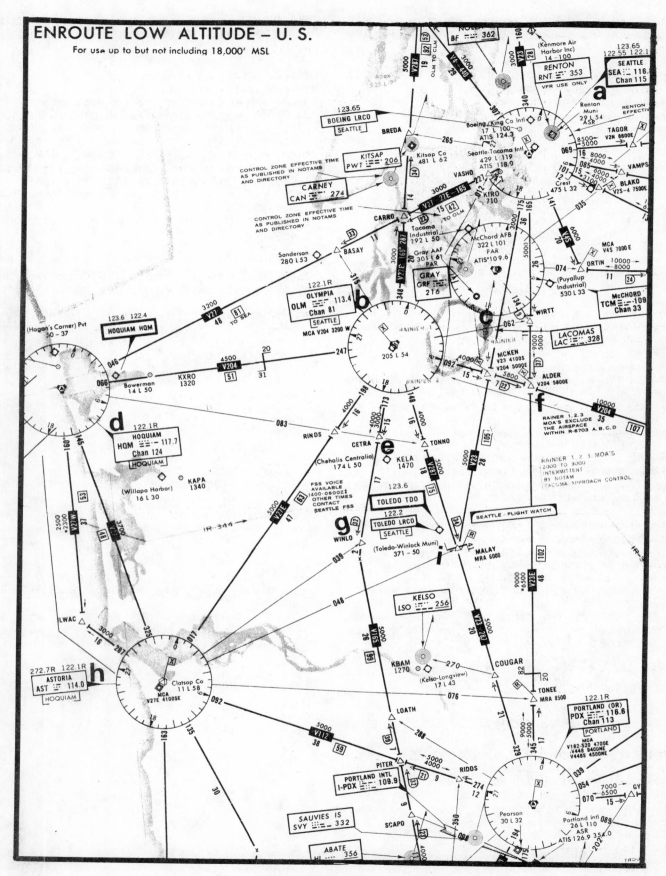

Figure 35

7551. What is the aircraft position with respect to the 180° bearing to the beacon while making an NDB RWY 18 approach? (See Figure 36.)

1—Right of course and outbound.
2—Right of course and inbound.
3—Left of course and outbound.
4—On course outbound.

Figure 36

7552. What is the designation for a geographical location used for route definition on an RNAV flight?

1—A TACAN installation.
2—A waypoint.
3—A DME fix.
4—A VDP fix.

7553. What minimum equipment is required for IFR flights in the TCA identified by the box at (d)? (See Figure 37.)

1—VOR and DME.
2—VOR, DME, and transponder.
3—VOR, DME, appropriate communications equipment, and an altitude reporting transponder.
4—VOR, appropriate communications equipment, and an altitude reporting transponder.

7554. What services are available through the San Francisco NAVAIDs (b)? (See Figure 37.)

1—Navigation signals only.
2—Navigation signals and flight plan service only.
3—Navigation signals, flight plan service, and weather information only.
4—Navigation signals, flight plan service, weather information, and airport advisories when the tower is not in operation.

7555. How can a pilot identify OLYMM Intersection (a)? (See Figure 37.)

1—SFO R–281 and SAU R–204 only.
2—SFO R–281 and SAU R–204 or SFO R–281 and SFO DME only.
3—SFO localizer 281° course and SAU R–281 and ISFO DME.
4—SFO localizer 281° course and SAU R–204 only.

7556. What frequency should you use for the EFAS at Oakland (c) below FL180? (See Figure 37.)

1—Transmit 122.1 and receive 116.8 MHz.
2—122.5 MHz.
3—122.2 MHz.
4—122.0 MHz.

7557. What is the maximum speed limit for an IFR flight cleared into the San Francisco TCA (b)? (See Figure 37.)

1—For whatever speed ATC clears the flight.
2—250 knots from 10,000 ft. to the airport.
3—250 knots from 10,000 ft. to the airport traffic area, then 156 knots.
4—250 knots from 10,000 ft. to the TCA, then 200 knots.

7558. Which radio call and frequency should the pilot use to obtain En Route Flight Advisory Service in the Oakland area? (See Figure 37.)

1—"OAKLAND Center En Route Advisory" on 122.0 MHz.
2—"OAKLAND Flight Watch" on 122.0 MHz.
3—"OAKLAND En Route Flight Advisory" on 123.0 MHz.
4—"OAKLAND Flight Service En Route Advisory" on 123.6 MHz.

7559. During the en route phase of an IFR flight, the pilot is advised "Radar service terminated." What action is appropriate?

1—Set transponder to code 1200.
2—Resume normal position reporting.
3—Activate the IDENT feature of the transponder to re-establish radar contact.
4—Select STANDBY or OFF on the transponder.

7560. Which report should be made to ATC without a specific request only when not in radar contact?

1—When leaving any assigned holding fix or point.
2—When leaving final approach fix inbound on final approach.
3—The time and altitude or flight level upon reaching a holding fix or point to which cleared.
4—When an altitude change will be made if operating on a clearance specifying VFR On Top.

7561. FAA Deletion.

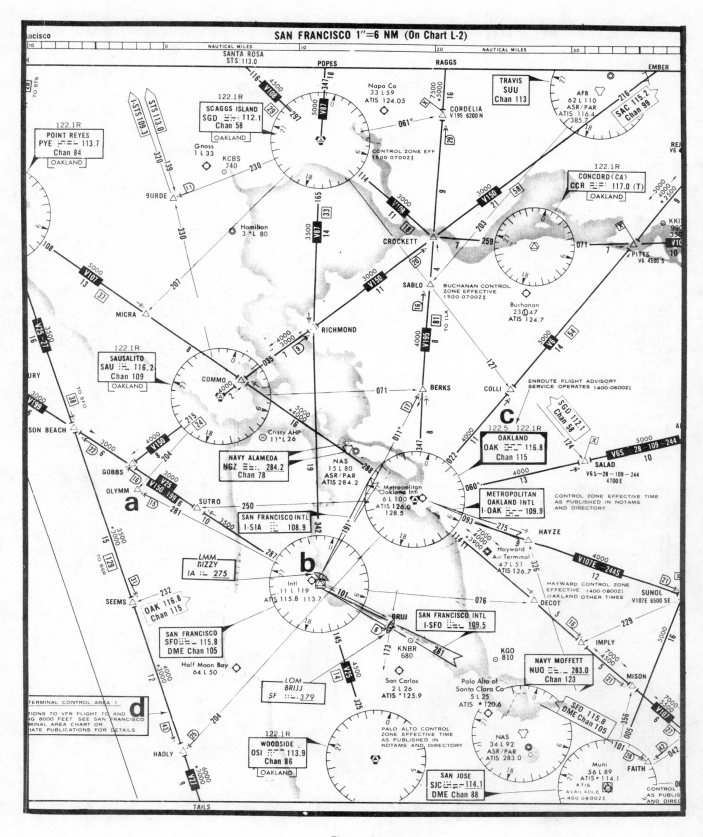

Figure 37

7562. Which RMI illustration in Figure 38 indicates the aircraft is located on the 055° radial of the station and heading away from the station?

1—A.
2—B.
3—C.
4—D.

7563. Which RMI illustration in Figure 38 indicates the aircraft is southwest of the station and moving closer to the station?

1—A.
2—B.
3—C.
4—D.

7564. Which RMI illustration in Figure 38 indicates the aircraft to be flying outbound on the magnetic bearing of 235° from the station? (Wind 050° at 20 knots.)

1—A.
2—B.
3—C.
4—D.

7565. What is the magnetic bearing to the station as indicated by illustration D of Figure 38?

1—285°.
2—055°.
3—235°.
4—330°.

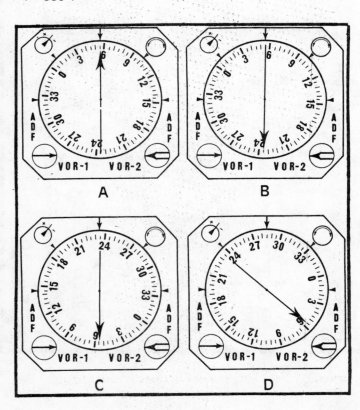

A

B

C

D

Figure 38

7566. Which phraseology is recommended for contacting a designated ATC facility when operating IFR in a radar environment?

1—"Ft. Worth Center, Traveler 1234 Victor, Over."
2—"Ft. Worth Center, Traveler 34 Victor, at 10,000 estimating Dallas at 35, Over."
3—"Ft. Worth Center, Traveler 1234 Victor, at 10,000 ft., Over."
4—"Dallas Approach Control, Traveler 1234 Victor, 10,000 ft., squawking 1200, Over."

7567. Where is the VOR COP (changeover point) southeastbound from Ukiah VORTAC (b) on V199? (See Figure 39.)

1—FROST Intersection.
2—BOARS Intersection.
3—52-1/2 nautical miles from UKI VORTAC (halfway).
4—MOLEN Intersection.

7568. What is the lowest cruising altitude permissible with a VFR On Top clearance from SGD (Scaggs Island) VORTAC (d) to Maxwell VORTAC (a) via V87? (See Figure 39.)

1—1,000 ft. above the highest obstacle along the route.
2—5,000 ft.
3—5,500 ft.
4—6,500 ft.

7569. The purpose of the 7,000-foot MRA at GETER Intersection (c) is to provide (See Figure 39.)

1—an adequate altitude to navigate on all the airways forming the fix.
2—the minimum altitude to receive R-226 from ILA VORTAC.
3—the minimum altitude to receive R-335 from PYE VORTAC.
4—the minimum altitude to receive R-335 and DME signals from PYE VORTAC and R-129 and DME signals from UKI VORTAC.

7570. Where is the VOR changeover point when en route from Maxwell VORTAC (a) to Scaggs Island VORTAC (d) on V87? (See Figure 39.)

1—RUMSY Intersection.
2—Mileage breakdown point.
3—At 34-1/2 nautical miles (halfway).
4—LAKE Intersection.

7571. What FSS frequencies, if any, are available for communications through POINT REYES VORTAC (e)? (See Figure 39.)

1—None.
2—The pilot can receive on 113.7 only.
3—The pilot can receive on 122.1 only.
4—113.7, 121.5, 122.0, and 122.2.

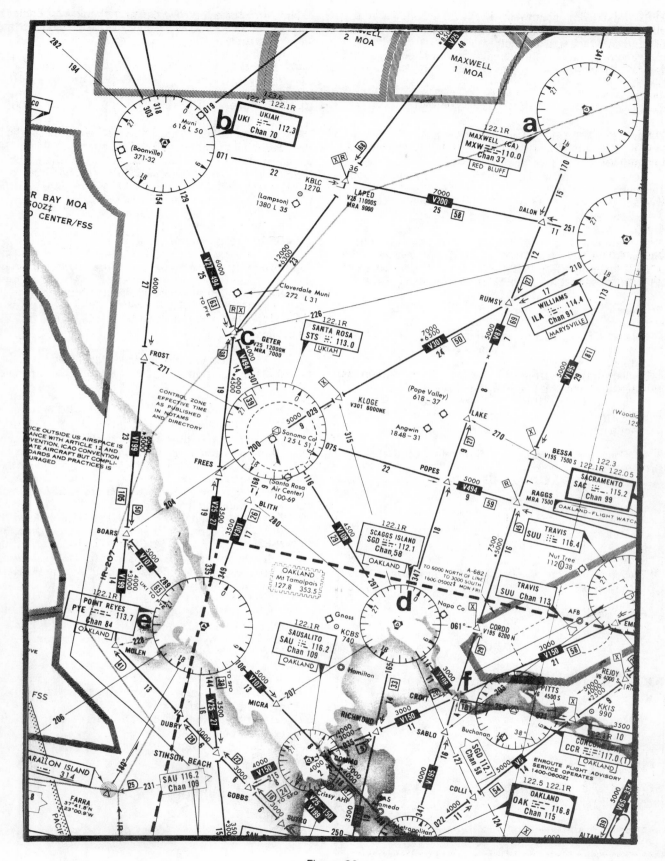

Figure 39

7572. While flying southwest on V102 at an assigned altitude of 6,000 ft., you are advised to expect 12000 at Carlsbad (b). Just after passing Hobbs (a) you have two – way communications failure. What altitudes should you fly from DYETT Intersection (c) to Salt Flat (d)? (See Figure 40.)

1—Descend to and maintain 5,600 ft. to Carlsbad, then climb to 10,800 ft.
2—Maintain 6,000 ft. to Carlsbad, then climb to 12,000 ft.
3—Maintain 6,000 ft. to near Carlsbad, climb to at least 7,000 ft. to cross Carlsbad, and then climb and maintain 12,000 ft.
4—Maintain 6,000 ft. to near Carlsbad, climb to 10,800 ft. to cross Carlsbad, and then climb to 12,000 ft.

7573. What effect does MTR (Military Training Route) IR–144 (north of FT STOCKTON VORTAC (h) have on IFR civilian flights en route between FT STOCKTON VORTAC and MIDLAND VORTAC on V81? (See Figure 40.)

1—Civilian IFR flights are restricted from entering or crossing the MTR when it is in use.
2—Civilian IFR flights are not affected because military aircraft are flown at high speeds above 1,500 ft. AGL but less than the MEA.
3—Civilian IFR aircraft must remain above 10,000 ft. MSL when crossing the MTR if it is active.
4—Civilian IFR aircraft are not prohibited from flying within the MTR, active or not, but vigilance should be maintained.

7574. Which facility controls IFR flights over Carlsbad VORTAC (b)? (See Figure 40.)

1—Carlsbad FSS.
2—Carlsbad Center.
3—Ft. Worth Center.
4—Albuquerque Center.

7575. At what maximum distance from FT STOCKTON VORTAC (h) are you assured an acceptable navigation signal to maintain V198 westbound? (See Figure 40.)

1—64.5 NM.
2—40 NM.
3—62 NM.
4—100 NM.

7576. What type navigation facility is at Pecos (g)? (See Figure 40.)

1—VOR only.
2—VOR/DME.
3—TACAN.
4—TACAN and VORTAC combination.

7577. On what VHF frequencies can Wink FSS (f) transmit? (See Figure 40.)

1—112.1, 122.05, and 123.6 MHz only.
2—112.1, 122.1, 122.05, and 123.6 only.
3—112.1, 121.5, 122.05, 122.2, and 123.6 MHz only.
4—112.1, 121.5, 122.05, 122.1, 122.2, and 123.6 MHz.

7578. What discrete VHF frequency should you expect to be assigned by ARTCC between Carlsbad VORTAC (b) and Salt Flat VORTAC (d)? (See Figure 40.)

1—122.35 MHz.
2—122.2 MHz.
3—133.1 MHz.
4—127.1 MHz.

7579. During a flight, the controller advises "traffic 2 o'clock 5 miles southbound." The pilot is holding 20° correction for a crosswind from the right. Where should the pilot look for the traffic?

1—40° to the right of the airplane's nose.
2—20° to the right of the airplane's nose.
3—Straight ahead.
4—40° to the right of the airplane's direction of travel.

7580. What is meant when departure control instructs you to "resume own navigation" after you have been vectored to a Victor airway?

1—You should maintain the airway by use of your navigation equipment.
2—Radar service is terminated.
3—Advisories will no longer be issued by ATC.
4—You are still in radar contact, but must make position reports.

7581. What does the ATC term "Radar Contact" signify?

1—Your aircraft has been identified and you will receive separation from all aircraft while in contact with this radar facility.
2—Your aircraft has been identified on the radar display and radar flight following will be provided until radar identification is terminated.
3—You will be given traffic advisories until advised the service has been terminated or that radar contact has been lost.
4—ATC is receiving your transponder and will furnish vectors and traffic advisories until you are advised that contact has been lost.

7582. Upon intercepting the assigned radial, the controller advises you that you are on the airway and to "RESUME OWN NAVIGATION." This phrase means that

1—you are still in radar contact, but must make position reports.
2—radar services are terminated and you will be responsible for position reports.
3—you are to contact the center at the next compulsory reporting point.
4—you are to assume responsibility for your own navigation.

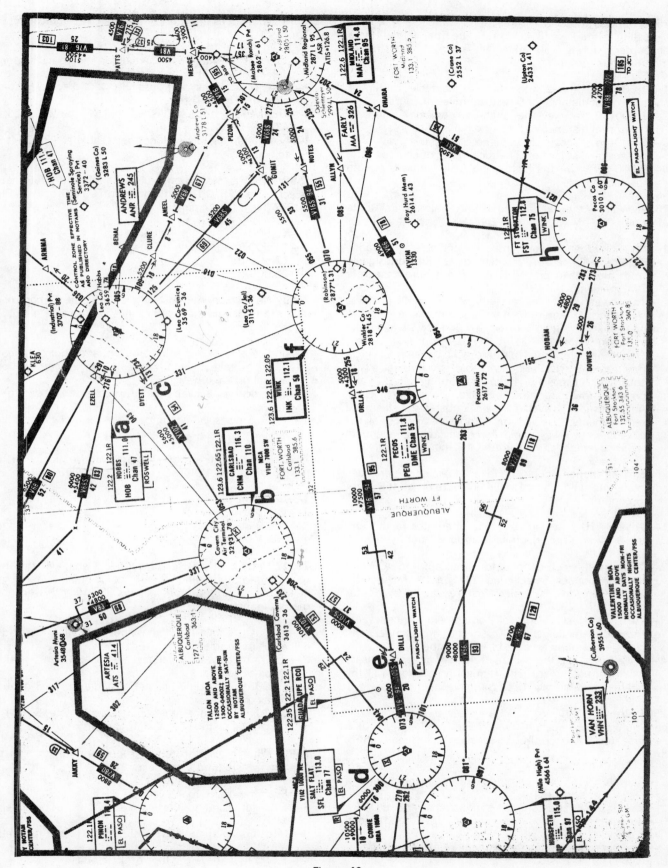

Figure 40

95

7583. Unless otherwise prescribed, what is the rule regarding altitude and course to be maintained by a helicopter during an IFR off—airways flight over mountainous terrain?

1—1,000 ft. above the highest obstacle within a horizontal distance of 5 nautical miles of course.
2—1,000 ft. above the highest obstacle within a horizontal distance of 5 statute miles of course.
3—7,500 ft. above the highest obstacle within a horizontal distance of 3 nautical miles of course.
4—2,000 ft. above the highest obstacle within 5 statute miles of course.

7584. What is the definition of MEA (Minimum En Route Altitude)?

1—An altitude which meets obstacle clearance requirements, assures acceptable navigation signals from more than one VORTAC, and assures accurate DME mileage.
2—The lowest published altitude which meets obstacle clearance requirements, assures acceptable navigational signal coverage, and two—way radio communications.
3—The lowest published altitude which meets obstacle requirements, assures acceptable navigational signal coverage, two—way radio communications, and provides adequate radar coverage.
4—An altitude which meets obstacle clearance requirements, assures acceptable navigation signal coverage, two—way radio communications, adequate radar coverage, and accurate DME mileage.

7585. What action should be taken if a pilot experiences complete alternator failure while en route on an IFR flight in IFR conditions?

1—Advise ATC that you have had alternator failure and are turning off all electrical equipment until your ETA is up.
2—Turn off all electrical equipment except one VOR and the transponder. Select code 7600 on the transponder and listen on the voice feature of the VOR for instructions.
3—Turn off all electrical equipment except the transponder. Select 7700 on the transponder and change course to an area of VFR weather.
4—Advise ATC of the failure, turn off all unnecessary electrical equipment, and request an approach at the nearest suitable facility en route.

7586. In addition to a VOR receiver and two—way communications capability, which additional equipment is required for IFR operation in a Group I terminal control area?

1—Another VOR and communications receiver and a coded transponder.
2—Standby VOR and communications receiver and DME.
3—Standby communications receiver, DME, and coded transponder.
4—An operable coded transponder having Mode C capability.

7587. What does the note, MEA GAP (e), indicate? (See Figure 41.)

1—There is no MEA established for the route segment depicted.
2—The MEA does not provide 2,000—foot obstacle clearance in this area.
3—The MEA is not established, but will be assigned by ATC.
4—Navigation signals may not be reliable at 12,000 ft. in this area.

7588. What is the lowest cruising altitude a pilot should select for a VFR On Top flight from FLG VOR (a) to PHX VORTAC (d)? (See Figure 41.)

1—10,500 ft.
2—11,500 ft.
3—12,500 ft.
4—13,500 ft.

7589. No person may operate an aircraft in controlled airspace under IFR unless he/she files a flight plan (See Figure 41.)

1—and receives a clearance by telephone prior to takeoff.
2—prior to takeoff and requests the clearance upon arrival on an airway.
3—and receives a clearance prior to entering controlled airspace.
4—and receives a clearance upon entering controlled airspace.

7590. What is the ARTCC discrete VHF frequency for IFR flights in the INW VORTAC (c) area? (See Figure 41.)

1—122.6 MHz.
2—122.15 MHz.
3—126.9 MHz.
4—263.1 MHz.

7591. Unless otherwise prescribed, what is the rule regarding altitude and course to be maintained by a helicopter during an off—airways IFR flight over non—mountainous terrain?

1—1,000 ft. above the highest obstacle within 5 statute miles of course.
2—2,000 ft. above the highest obstacle within 5 statute miles of course.
3—1,000 ft. above the highest obstacle within 3 nautical miles of course.
4—1,500 ft. above the highest obstacle within a horizontal distance of 3 statute miles of course.

7592. What cruising altitude is appropriate for VFR On Top on a westbound flight below 18,000 ft.?

1—Even thousand—foot levels.
2—Even thousand—foot levels plus 500 ft., but not below MEA.
3—Odd thousand—foot levels plus 500 ft., but not below MEA.
4—1,000 feet above the tops of the clouds.

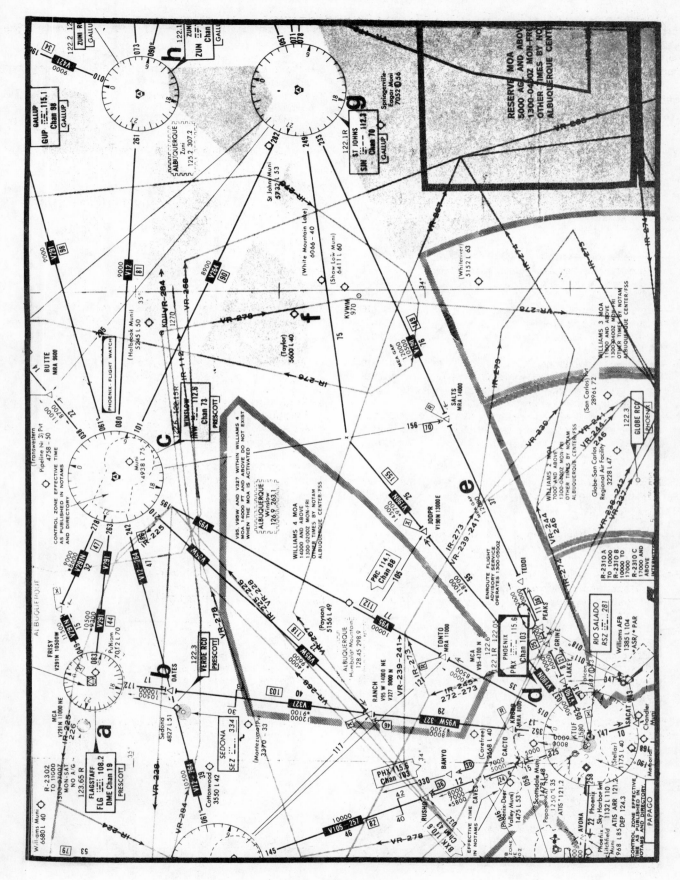

Figure 41

97

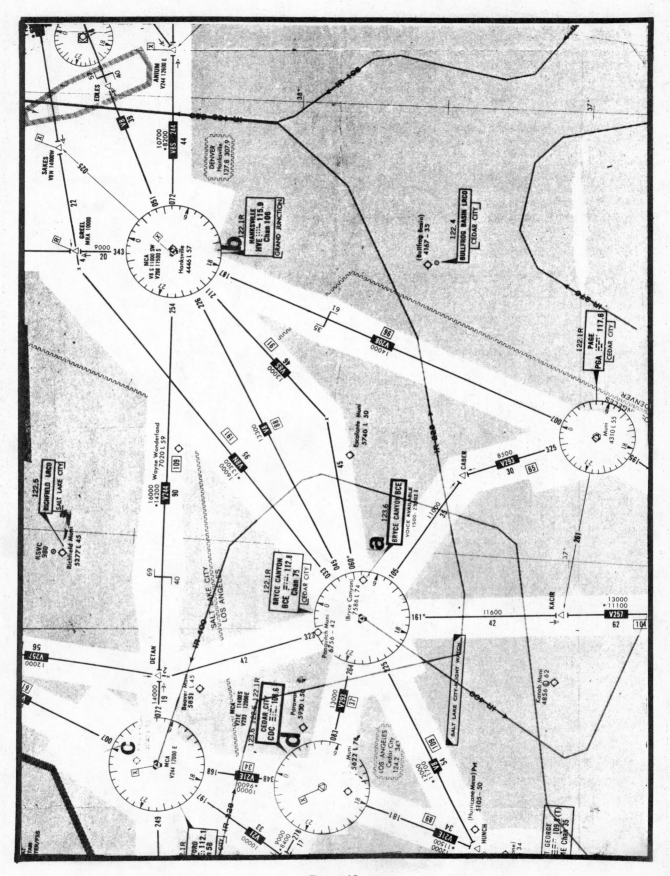

Figure 42

98

7593. When flying from Milford Muni (c) to Bryce Canyon (a) via V21E and V293, what minimum altitude should you have when you cross Cedar City VOR (d)? (See Figure 42.)

1—10,000 ft.
2—11,400 ft.
3—12,000 ft.
4—13,000 ft.

7594. What VHF frequencies are available for communications with Bryce Canyon FSS (a)? (See Figure 42.)

1—123.6 MHz only.
2—122.2, 121.5, and 123.6 MHz only.
3—122.2, 121.5, 122.0, and 123.6 MHz only.
4—122.2, 121.5, 122.0, 123.6, and 122.1R/112.8T MHz.

7595. What are the oxygen requirements for an IFR flight northeastbound on V8N at cruising altitude from Bryce Canyon (a) in an unpressurized aircraft? (See Figure 42.)

1—The required minimum crew must be provided and use supplemental oxygen for that part of the flight of more than 30 min.
2—The required minimum crew must be provided and use supplemental oxygen for that part of the flight of more than 30 min., and the passengers must be provided supplemental oxygen.
3—The required minimum crew must be provided and use supplemental oxygen, and all occupants must be provided supplemental oxygen for the entire flight upon reaching your assigned altitude.
4—Each occupant must be provided and use supplemental oxygen for the entire flight at these altitudes.

7596. On what frequency should you obtain En Route Flight Advisory Service below FL180? (See Figure 42.)

1—122.1T/112.8R MHz.
2—123.6 MHz.
3—123.0 MHz.
4—122.0 MHz.

7597. In the event of two–way radio communications failure while operating on an IFR clearance in VFR conditions over HVE (b), the pilot should

1—continue by the route assigned in the last ATC clearance received.
2—continue the flight under VFR and land as soon as practical.
3—continue the flight by the most direct route to the fix specified in the last clearance.
4—continue the flight by the route filed in the flight plan.

7598. What type airspace exists above Bryce Canyon Airport (a) from the surface to 700 ft. AGL? (See Figure 42.)

1—Transition area.
2—Part–time control zone.
3—Control area.
4—Uncontrolled.

7599. What is the ARTCC discrete frequency from the COP on V8S to Bryce Canyon VORTAC (a)? (See Figure 42.)

1—127.8 MHz.
2—123.6 MHz.
3—124.2 MHz.
4—122.4 MHz.

7600. What is your relationship to the mileage breakdown point while en route from BCE VORTAC (a) to HVE VORTAC (b) on V8S? (See Figure 42 and 43.)

1—Right of course approaching the point.
2—Left of course approaching the point.
3—Right of course and past the point.
4—Left of course and past the point.

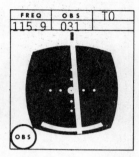

Figure 43

7601. What altitude may a pilot select upon receiving a VFR On Top clearance?

1—Any altitude at least 1,000 ft. above the meteorological condition.
2—Any appropriate VFR altitude at or above the MEA in VFR weather conditions.
3—Any VFR altitude appropriate for the direction of flight at least 1,000 ft. above the meteorological condition.
4—Any VFR or IFR altitude above 3,000 ft. AGL, above the MEA, and at least 1,000 ft. above the meteorological condition.

7602. When must a pilot fly at a cardinal altitude plus 500 ft. on an IFR flight plan?

1—When flying above 18,000 ft. in VFR conditions.
2—When flying in VFR conditions above clouds.
3—When assigned a VFR On Top clearance.
4—Anytime VFR conditions exist and the pilot has requested a VFR On Top clearance.

7603. The MEA (Minimum En Route Altitude) assures acceptable navigational signal coverage and

1—intersection identification.
2—DME response.
3—radar coverage.
4—meets obstacle clearance requirements.

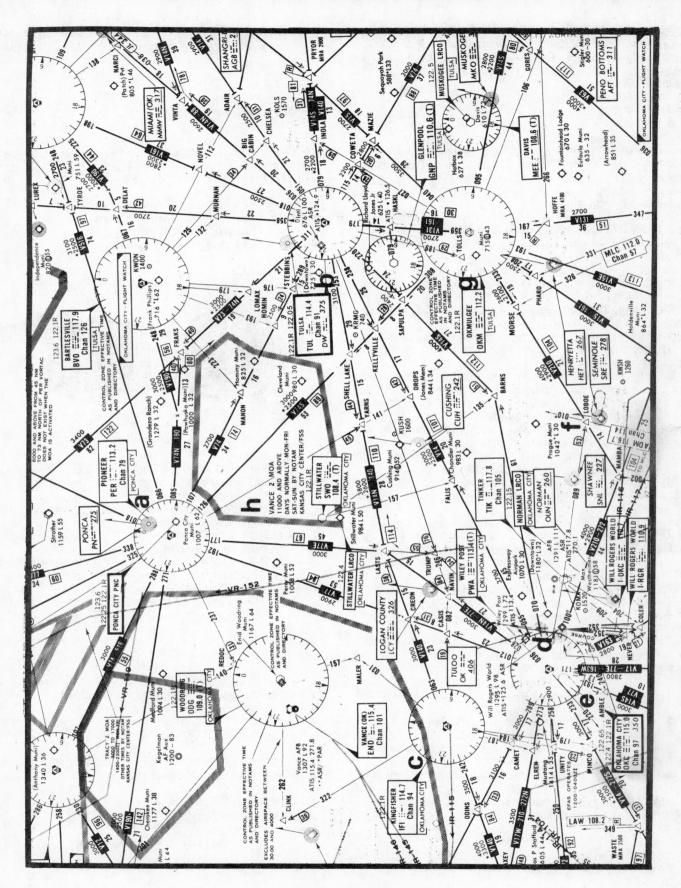

Figure 44

7604. You have filed an IFR flight plan with a VFR On Top clearance in lieu of an assigned altitude. If you receive this clearance and fly a course of 180°, at what altitude should you fly? (Assume VFR conditions.)

1—An altitude assigned by ATC.
2—Any IFR altitude which will enable you to remain in VFR conditions.
3—An odd thousand–foot MSL altitude plus 500 ft.
4—An even thousand–foot MSL altitude plus 500 ft.

7605. Which service is limited at Will Rogers World Airport (d) as indicated by the star in the airport information? (See Figure 44.)

1—The tower frequency is remoted to a collocated FSS for use when the tower is closed.
2—ATIS operates less than continuous or part time.
3—ASR approaches are available on prior request only.
4—125.6 MHz is the primary frequency for the tower.

7606. What is the lowest cruising altitude for a VFR On Top flight for the entire distance on V210 from OKC VORTAC (e) to OKM VORTAC (g)? (See Figure 44.)

1—2,900 ft.
2—4,000 ft.
3—4,500 ft.
4—5,500 ft.

7607. Military operations areas, such as the Vance 2 MOA (h), are established to (see Figure 44)

1—prohibit all civil aircraft because of hazardous or secret activities.
2—separate certain military training activities from IFR traffic.
3—restrict civil aircraft during periods of high–density training activities.
4—separate civil IFR and VFR traffic from hazardous or dangerous military activities.

7608. You receive a clearance to Okmulgee Municipal (g), "cruise 3,000" while passing PER VORTAC (a) on V74S. Where is the first point you may start a descent to 2,500 ft.? (See Figure 44.)

1—Over OKM VOR.
2—22 NM from OKM VOR.
3—Halfway between PER VOR and OKM VOR.
4—Upon accepting the clearance.

7609. Identify the changeover point on V140 for a flight from TUL VORTAC (b) to IFI VORTAC (c). (See Figure 44.)

1—YARNS Intersection.
2—At 55 mi.
3—At 57 mi.
4—LASTS Intersection.

7610. Which illustration(s) indicate when the turn outbound should be initiated while holding in the depicted holding pattern at LOBOE Intersection (f)? (See Figure 44 and 45.)

1—a and b.
2—a and c.
3—b and c.
4—d.

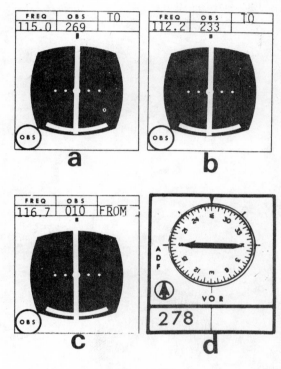

Figure 45

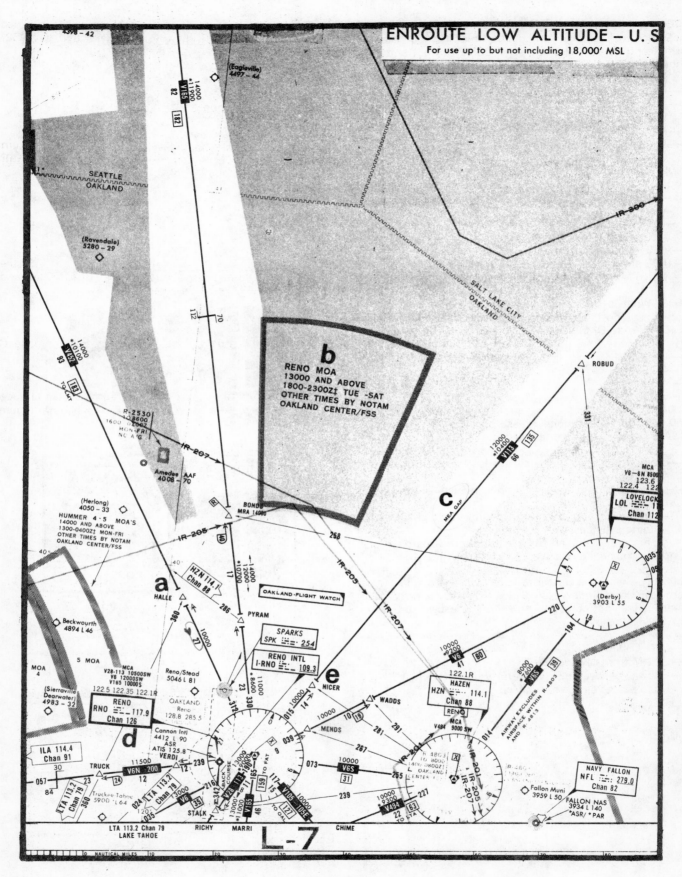

Figure 46

7611. What is the minimum crossing altitude at Reno VORTAC (d) for a southbound IFR flight making a transition from V6 to V165? (See Figure 46.)

1—10,000 ft.
2—11,000 ft.
3—12,000 ft.
4—13,000 ft.

7612. What is the lowest VFR On Top cruising altitude along V113 when flying from NICER (e) to ROBUD Intersections? (See Figure 46.)

1—10,400 ft.
2—11,500 ft.
3—12,000 ft.
4—13,500 ft.

7613. What does the MEA GAP (c) indicate? (See Figure 46.)

1—The MEA has not been established in this area.
2—The MEA does not afford obstacle clearance in this area.
3—The navigation signal is unreliable when at the MEA in this area.
4—The MEA will not be assigned by ATC but IFR flight at MOCA is permitted.

7614. MOA (military operations areas), such as the Reno MOA (b), are established to (see Figure 46.)

1—prohibit all civil aircraft because of hazardous or secret activities.
2—separate certain military activities from IFR traffic.
3—restrict civil aircraft during periods of high–density training activities.
4—separate civil IFR and VFR traffic from hazardous or dangerous military activities.

NOTE: Refer to Figure 46 and the following information for questions 7615 through 7617.

At 1815, you receive the following instructions:

"NOVEMBER EIGHT TWO PAPA CHARLIE—HOLD SOUTH OF HALLE INTERSECTION ON VICTOR FOUR FIFTY TWO —TEN MILE LEG—LEFT TURNS—EXPECT FURTHER CLEARANCE AT FOUR ZERO."

7615. FAA Deletion.

7616. What type entry is recommended for the assigned holding pattern (a) if you are southeastbound on V452? (Heading 137) (See Figure 46 and Note.)

1—Direct only.
2—Teardrop only.
3—Parallel only.
4—Teardrop or parallel.

7617. Which instrument indicates when it is time to turn to the inbound leg in the assigned holding pattern (a)? (See Figures 46 and 47 and NOTE.)

1—a.
2—b.
3—c.
4—d.

7618. Which condition is guaranteed for all of the following altitude limits: MAA, MCA, MRA, MOCA, and MEA? (Non–mountainous area.)

1—Adequate navigation signals.
2—Adequate communications.
3—Adequate radar coverage if equipped with Mode C transponder.
4—1,000–foot obstacle clearance.

7619. If no MCA is specified, what is the lowest altitude for crossing a radio fix, beyond which a higher minimum applies?

1—The MEA at which the fix is approached.
2—The MRA at which the fix is approached.
3—The MAA for the route segment beyond the fix.
4—The MOCA for the route segment beyond the fix.

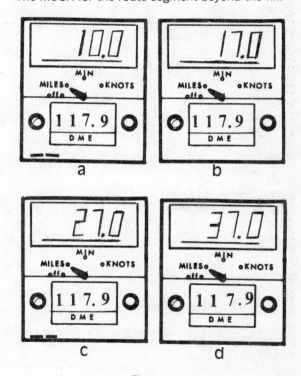

Figure 47

7620. Reception of signals from an off–airway radio facility may be inadequate to identify the fix at the designated MEA. In this case, which altitude is designated for the fix?

1—MRA.
2—MAA.
3—MCA.
4—MOCA.

7621. What should be the approximate elapsed time from BZN VOR (b) to DBS VORTAC (c), if the wind is 24 knots from 260° and your intended TAS is 185 knots? (VAR – 17°E.) (See Figure 48.)

1—33 min.
2—35 min.
3—37 min.
4—39 min.

7622. What lighting is indicated on the chart for Jackson Hole Airport (h)? (See Figure 48.)

1—Lights on prior request.
2—Lights temporarily out of service.
3—Pilot controlled lighting.
4—Heliport lighting.

7623. What is the function of the Yellowstone RCO (e)? (See Figure 48.)

1—Long range communications outlet for Idaho Falls Center.
2—Remote communications outlet for Idaho Falls FSS.
3—Satellite FSS controlled by Idaho Falls FSS with limited service.
4—Long range radar control outlet for Idaho Falls Center.

7624. What is the minimum crossing altitude at SABAT Intersection (d) when eastbound on V298? (See Figure 48.)

1—8,500 ft.
2—9,800 ft.
3—11,100 ft.
4—13,000 ft.

7625. What is the minimum crossing altitude at DBS VORTAC (c) for a northbound IFR flight on V257? (See Figure 48.

1—7,500 ft.
2—8,600 ft.
3—11,100 ft.
4—12,000 ft.

7626. What are the two limiting cruising altitudes usable for a VFR On Top flight from BZN VOR (b) to DBS VORTAC (c)? (See Figure 48.)

1—13,200 and 18,000 ft.
2—14,000 and 18,000 ft.
3—14,500 and 18,500 ft.
4—14,500 and 16,500 ft.

7627. What are the oxygen requirements for an IFR flight eastbound on V520 from DBS VORTAC (c) in an unpressurized aircraft at the MEA? (See Figure 48.)

1—The required minimum crew must be provided and use supplemental oxygen for that part of the flight of more than 30 min.
2—The required minimum crew must be provided and use supplemental oxygen for that part of the flight of more than 30 min., and the passengers must be provided supplemental oxygen.
3—The required minimum crew must be provided and use supplemental oxygen.
4—Each occupant must be provided and use supplemental oxygen for the entire flight at these altitudes.

7628. At what time should you arrive at DBS VORTAC (c) if you crossed over Butte VORTAC (a) at 0850 and over DIVID Intersection at 0854? (See Figure 48.)

1—0939.
2—0943.
3—0947.
4—0911.

7629. Where should you change over VOR frequencies when en route from DBS VORTAC (c) to DNW VORTAC (g) on V298? (See Figure 48.)

1—LAMON Intersection.
2—41–1/2 mi. (halfway).
3—68 mi. from DBS VORTAC.
4—QUIRT Intersection.

7630. Which of the following is a transponder requirement for helicopter operations?

1—Helicopters with a certificated gross weight of more than 12,500 lb. that are engaged in commercial operations are required to be equipped with operable ATC transponders.
2—Under the terms of a letter of agreement, helicopters may be operated at or below 1,000 ft. AGL within Group I and Group II TCA's without an operable ATC transponder.
3—Operable ATC transponders are required when operating helicopters within control zones at night under special VFR.
4—Helicopters are required to be equipped with operable ATC transponders during all commercial operations above 3,000 ft. AGL.

7631. FAA Deletion.

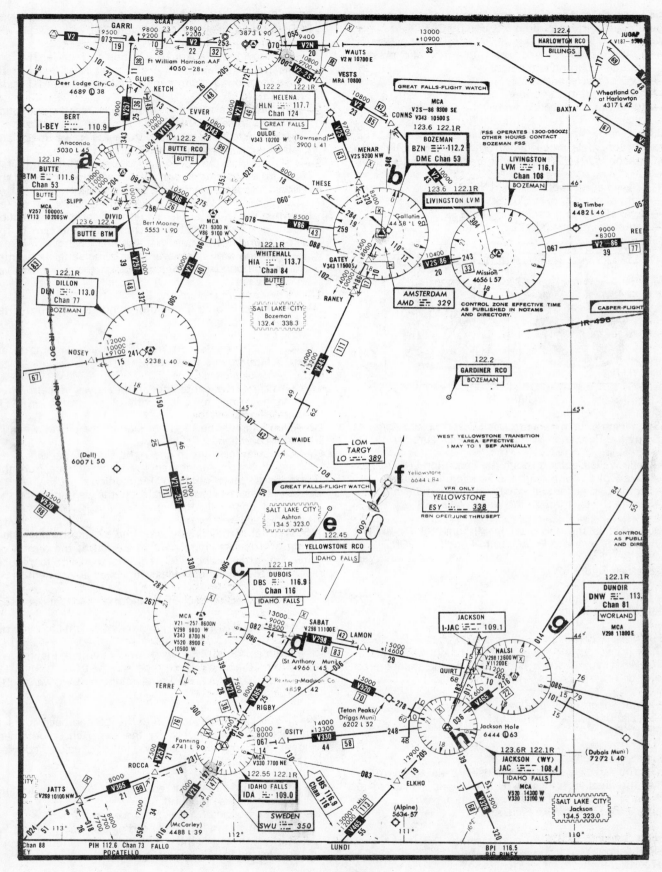

Figure 48

7632. Which of the following is required equipment for operating an airplane within a Group II TCA?

1—A 4096 code transponder with automatic pressure altitude reporting equipment.
2—A VOR receiver with DME.
3—A 4096 code transponder.
4—An automatic direction finder.

7633. What is your position relative to V112 and LYLES Intersection while proceeding from Pendleton VORTAC (i) to Spokane VORTAC (b)? (See Figures 49 and 50.)

1—Left of course, approaching LYLES.
2—Right of course, past LYLES.
3—Right of course, approaching LYLES.
4—Left of course, past LYLES.

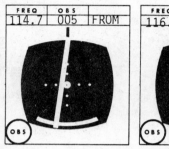

Figure 49

7634. Which facility controls IFR en route aircraft crossing the Pendleton VORTAC (i)? (See Figure 50.)

1—Walla Walla Center through the Pendleton LRCO.
2—Walla Walla FSS through the Pendleton LRCO.
3—Seattle Center through the Pendleton remote site.
4—Seattle Center through the Walla Walla FSS.

7635. What is the approximate MH and GS for an IFR flight from Spokane VORTAC (b) to Pendleton VORTAC (i) via V112? (Wind, 270° at 30 knots; TAS, 180 knots; Var. 20°E.) (See Figure 50.)

1—194° – 165 knots.
2—193° – 195 knots.
3—198° – 175 knots.
4—176° – 190 knots.

7636. What type airspace is depicted by the shaded area (brown on original charts) (j)? (See Figure 50.)

1—Military operations area.
2—Special use (wilderness area).
3—Restricted.
4—Uncontrolled.

7637. You are cleared from Moses Lake VOR (d) to WIPES Intersection (c) via MWH R–014 and instructed to hold in the depicted holding pattern. What is the recommended entry? (See Figure 50.)

1—Direct only.
2—Parallel only.
3—Teardrop only.
4—Direct or teardrop.

7638. What is the purpose of the 6,000–foot MRA at RODNA Intersection (e)? (See Figure 50.)

1—To provide an adequate altitude to receive GEG and PDT VORTAC's.
2—To provide a high enough altitude for ATC radar coverage.
3—To provide a minimum altitude to receive navigation signals from EPH VORTAC.
4—To provide an adequate altitude to receive R–185 and DME signals from GEG VORTAC.

7639. When holding at an NDB, at what point should the timing begin for the second leg outbound?

1—When the wings are level and the wind drift correction angle is established after completing the turn to the outbound heading.
2—When the wings are level after completing the turn to the outbound heading, or abeam the fix, whichever occurs first.
3—When abeam the holding fix.
4—At the end of a 1 minute standard rate turn after station passage.

7640. Which procedure is required while climbing to an assigned altitude on the airway?

1—Climb on the centerline of the airway except when maneuvering to avoid other air traffic in VFR conditions.
2—Climb slightly on the right side of the airway when in VFR conditions.
3—Climb far enough to the right side of the airway to avoid climbing or descending traffic coming from the opposite direction if in VFR conditions.
4—Climb as near as possible on the centerline of the airway under all conditions.

7641. What is the pilot in command's responsibility when flying a propeller aircraft within 20 mi. of the airport of intended landing and ATC requests the pilot to reduce speed to 160? (Pilot complies with speed adjustment.)

1—Reduce TAS to 160 knots and maintain until advised by ATC.
2—Reduce IAS to 160 MPH and maintain until advised by ATC.
3—Reduce IAS to 160 knots and maintain that speed within 10 knots.
4—Reduce TAS to 160 knots and maintain within 10 knots.

7642. You are being vectored to the ILS approach course, but have not been cleared for the approach. It becomes evident that you will pass through the localizer course. What action should be taken?

1—Start a turn that will enable you to return to the localizer course inbound.
2—Turn outbound and make a procedure turn.
3—Continue on the assigned heading and query ATC.
4—Start a turn to the inbound heading and inquire if you are cleared for the approach.

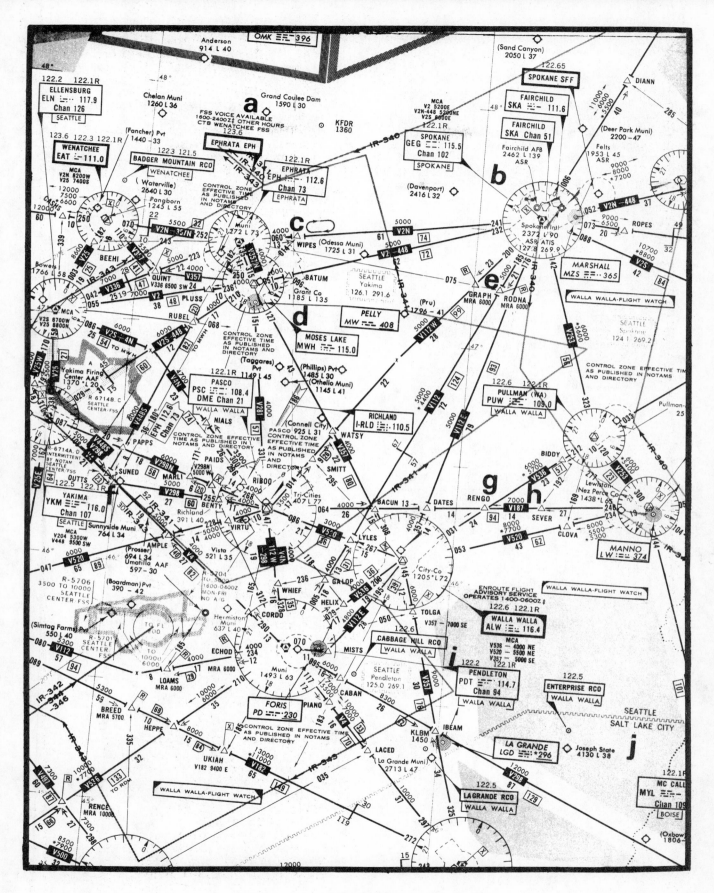

Figure 50

107

7643. How is ATC radar used for instrument approaches when the facility is approved for approach control service?

1—Precision approaches, weather surveillance, and as a substitute for any inoperative component of a navigation aid used for approaches.
2—ASR approaches in emergencies and to eliminate the need for position reports on nonradar approaches.
3—ASR approaches, weather surveillance, and course guidance by approach control.
4—Course guidance to the final approach course, ASR and PAR approaches, and the monitoring of nonradar approaches.

7644. Which clearance procedures may be issued by ATC without prior pilot request?

1—SID's, STAR's, and contact approaches.
2—Contact and visual approaches.
3—SID's, STAR's, contact approaches, and visual approaches.
4—SID's, STAR's, and visual approaches.

7645. What is the significance of an ATC clearance which reads ". . . CRUISE SIX THOUSAND . . . ."?

1—The pilot may climb at any rate to 6,000.
2—The pilot must maintain 6,000 until reaching the IAF serving the destination airport, then execute the published approach procedure.
3—It authorizes a pilot to conduct flight at any altitude from minimum IFR altitude up to and including 6,000.
4—The pilot is authorized to conduct flight at any altitude from minimum IFR altitude up to and including 6,000, but each change in altitude must be reported to ATC.

7646. What is expected of you as pilot on an IFR flight plan if you are descending or climbing in VFR conditions?

1—If on an airway, maintain the centerline at all times; if being vectored, maintain a constant heading.
2—If on an airway, climb or descend to the right of the centerline.
3—Advise ATC you are in visual conditions and will remain a short distance to the right of the centerline while climbing.
4—You should execute gentle banks, left and right, at a frequency which permits continuous visual scanning of the airspace about you.

7647. Thrust is managed to maintain IAS, and glide slope is being flown. What characteristics should be observed when a headwind shears to be a constant tailwind?

1—PITCH ATTITUDE: Decreases;
 REQUIRED THRUST: Reduced, then increased;
 VERTICAL SPEED: Increases;
 IAS: Decreases.
2—PITCH ATTITUDE: Increases;
 REQUIRED THRUST: Increased, then reduced;
 VERTICAL SPEED: Increases;
 IAS: Increases, then decreases to approach speed.
3—PITCH ATTITUDE: Decreases;
 REQUIRED THRUST: Increased, then reduced;
 VERTICAL SPEED: Increases;
 IAS: Decreases, then increases to approach speed.
4—PITCH ATTITUDE: Increases;
 REQUIRED THRUST: Reduced, then increased;
 VERTICAL SPEED: Decreases;
 IAS: Decreases, then increases to approach speed.

7648. When cleared to execute a published side-step maneuver for a specific approach and landing on the parallel runway, at what point is the pilot expected to commence this maneuver?

1—At the MDA for the localizer approach and on the glide slope.
2—At the published minimum altitude for a circling approach.
3—As soon as possible after the runway or runway environment is in sight.
4—At the localizer MDA minimum and when the runway is in sight.

7649. Which altimeter depicts 12,000 ft.? (See Figure 51.)

1—A.
2—B.
3—C.
4—D.

Figure 51

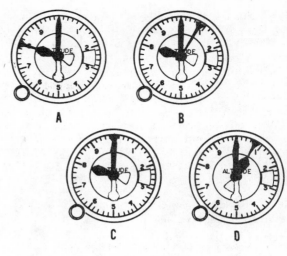

Figure 52

7650. How does a pilot normally obtain the current altimeter setting during an IFR flight in controlled airspace below 18,000 ft.?

1—The pilot should contact the nearest FSS at least every 100 nautical miles and request the altimeter setting.
2—The pilot should contact ARTCC at least every 100 nautical miles and request the altimeter setting.
3—Flight Service Stations along the route broadcast the weather information at 15 minutes past the hour.
4—ATC periodically advises the pilot of the proper altimeter setting.

7651. En route at FL290, your altimeter is set correctly but you fail to reset it to the local altimeter setting of 30.26 during descent. If the field elevation is 134 ft. and your altimeter is functioning properly, what will it indicate after landing?

1—100 ft. MSL.
2—474 ft. MSL.
3—206 ft. below MSL.
4—Sea level.

7652. Which altimeter depicts 8,000 ft.? (See Figure 52.)

1—A.
2—B.
3—C.
4—D.

7653. What is the procedure for setting the altimeter when assigned an IFR altitude of 18,000 ft. or higher on a direct flight off airways?

1—Set the altimeter to the current reported setting of a station within 100 nautical miles of the aircraft.
2—Set the altimeter to 29.92 before takeoff.
3—Set the altimeter to the current altimeter setting until reaching the assigned altitude, then set to 29.92.
4—Set the altimeter to the current reported setting for climbout and 29.92 upon reaching 18,000 ft.

7654. En route at FL290, the altimeter is set correctly, but not reset to the local altimeter setting of 30.57 during descent. If the field elevation is 650 ft. and the altimeter is functioning properly, what is the approximate indication upon landing?

1—585 ft.
2—715 ft.
3—1,300 ft.
4—Sea level.

7655. While you are flying at FL250, you hear ATC give an altimeter setting of 28.92" Hg in your area. At what pressure altitude are you flying?

1 —24,000 ft.
2—25,000 ft.
3—25,500 ft.
4—26,000 ft.

7656. In which airspace are "VFR On Top" operations prohibited?

1—On airways that penetrate a MOA (military operations area).
2—In a positive control area.
3—During off-airway direct flights.
4—When flying through a TCA.

7657. What is your position from ALENS Intersection (e) during an eastbound flight on V6? (VOR receivers indicate as shown in Figure 53.) (See Figure 54.)

1—Southwest.
2—Southeast.
3—Northeast.
4—Northwest.

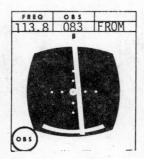 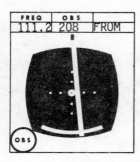

Figure 53

7658. FAA Deletion.

7659. Which combination of radials form WAPEL Intersection (g)? (See Figure 54.)

1—OTM R–071 and BRL R–322.
2—OTM R–071 and IOW R–142.
3—MZV R–253 and BRL R–322.
4—MZV R–253 and IOW R–142.

7660. Which facility controls IFR en route traffic in the Bradford, IL area (h)? (See Figure 54.)

1—Chicago Center through the Bradford remote site.
2—Chicago Center through the Chicago remote FSS communications.
3—Bradford ATC remoted from the Chicago FSS.
4—Bradford ARTCC.

7661. What action should you take if your DME fails at FL240?

1—Request an altitude below FL240 and continue to your destination.
2—Advise ATC of the failure and land at the nearest available airport where repairs can be made.
3—Notify ATC that it will be necessary for you to go to a lower altitude, since your DME has failed.
4—Notify ATC of the failure and continue to the next airport of intended landing where repairs can be made.

7662. Which rules apply to the pilot in command when operating on a VFR On Top clearance?

1—VFR only.
2—IFR only.
3—VFR and IFR.
4—VFR when "in the clear" and IFR when "in the clouds."

7663. When can a "VFR On Top" clearance be assigned by ATC?

1—Anytime IFR conditions exist at the departure point, but not at the destination.
2—Only upon request of the pilot when conditions are indicated to be suitable.
3—Anytime suitable conditions exist and ATC wishes to expedite traffic flow.
4—When VFR conditions exist, but there is a layer of clouds below the MEA.

7664. Which ATC clearance should instrument–rated pilots request in order to climb through a cloud layer or an area of reduced visibility and then continue the flight VFR?

1—Special VFR with radar vectors.
2—To VFR On Top.
3—Special VFR to VFR Over–The–Top.
4—VFR Over–The–Top.

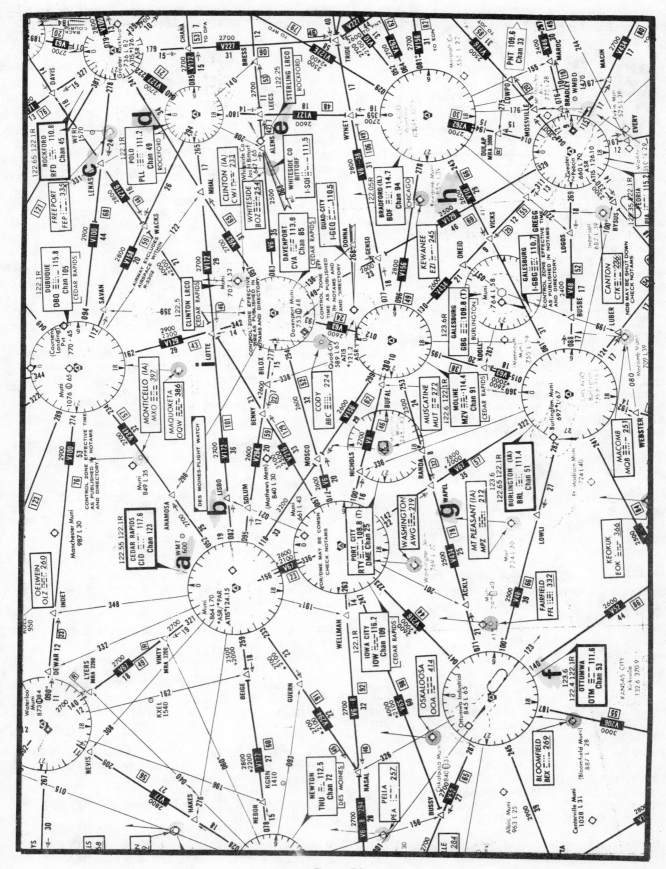

Figure 54

111

FREQ	OBS	
114.4	032	FROM

414

Figure 55

7665. What is your position with relation to ALBER Intersection (f) while northwest–bound on V321? (See Figures 55 and 56.)

1—Past ALBER and right of course.
2—Past ALBER and on course.
3—Approaching ALBER and left of course.
4—Approaching ALBER and on course.

7666. Which facility assumes control of an IFR flight from VUZ VORTAC (d) on V7E after passing FOLSO Intersection? (See Figure 56.)

1—Memphis Center through the Huntsville remote site.
2—Memphis Center direct from the Memphis site.
3—Muscle Shoals FSS through Decatur Radio.
4—Memphis Center through Muscle Shoals FSS.

7667. Which combination of indications confirms ARBEE Intersection (e)? (See Figure 56.)

1—VUZ R–046 and GAD R–316.
2—VUZ R–046 and DCU R–131.
3—VUZ R–046 and DWY magnetic bearing 136° (TO).
4—DWY magnetic bearing 136° (TO) and GAD DME 14 nautical miles.

7668. What should be the approximate ETA at MSL VORTAC (a) if you cross over HOKES Intersection (g) at 1843 and GAD VORTAC (h) at 1845? (See Figure 56.)

1—1916.
2—1918.
3—1920.
4—1922.

7669. What is the lowest altitude which assures acceptable navigation signal coverage at BOUNT and FOLSO Intersections for navigation outbound on V7E north of VULCAN VORTAC (d)? You are DME equipped. (See Figure 56.)

1—2,300 ft. at BOUNT; 3,000 ft. at FOLSO.
2—3,000 ft. at BOUNT; 3,000 ft. at FOLSO.
3—3,000 ft. at BOUNT; 7,000 ft. at FOLSO.
4—4,000 ft. at BOUNT; 7,000 ft. at FOLSO.

7670. Where is the COP (changeover point) for an IFR flight from DCU VOR (b) to GAD VORTAC (h)? (See Figure 56.)

1—59 nautical miles from DCU VOR.
2—24.5 nautical miles from DCU VOR.
3—Memphis/Atlanta Center border.
4—Mileage breakdown point.

7671. You have been cleared to hold south of WHEAL Intersection (c) on the Huntsville Localizer, left–hand turns. If you approach WHEAL from DCU VOR on R–131, what type entry is recommended? (No wind correction required.) (See Figure 56.)

1—Direct only.
2—Teardrop only.
3—Parallel only.
4—Teardrop or parallel.

7672. While operating on an IFR flight plan with a VFR restriction, a pilot should expect that ATC will

1—not apply IFR separation, outside of TCA's and TRSA's, during the "VFR restriction" portion of the flight.
2—cancel the IFR flight plan, thus if IFR conditions are encountered a new IFR flight plan must be filed.
3—continue to apply IFR separation until the pilot requests the IFR flight plan be cancelled.
4—not issue radar traffic advisories during the "VFR restriction" portion of the flight.

7673. Under which of the following circumstances may ATC issue a VFR restriction to an IFR flight?

1—When the pilot requests it.
2—Whenever a traffic conflict might otherwise occur.
3—Whenever the pilot reports the loss of any navigational aid.
4—When it is necessary to provide separation between IFR and special VFR traffic.

7674. What is the minimum flight visibility and distance from clouds for flight at 10,500 ft. with a "VFR On Top" clearance?

1—3 statute miles, 1,000 ft. above, 500 ft. below, and 2,000 ft. horizontal.
2—5 statute miles, 1,000 ft. above, 1,000 ft. below, and 1 mi. horizontal.
3—3 statute miles, 500 ft. above, 1,000 ft. below, and 2,000 ft. horizontal.
4—5 statute miles, 1,000 ft. above, 500 ft. below, and 1 mi. horizontal.

7675. What is the required flight visibility and distance from clouds if you are operating in controlled airspace at 9,500 ft. with a VFR On Top clearance?

1—3 statute miles, 1,000 ft. above, and 500 ft. below, and 2,000 ft. horizontal.
2—5 statute miles, 500 ft. above, 1,000 ft. below, and 2,000 ft. horizontal.
3—3 statute miles, 500 ft. above, 1,000 ft. below, and 2,000 ft. horizontal.
4—5 statute miles, 1,000 ft. above, 500 ft. below, and 1 mi. horizontal.

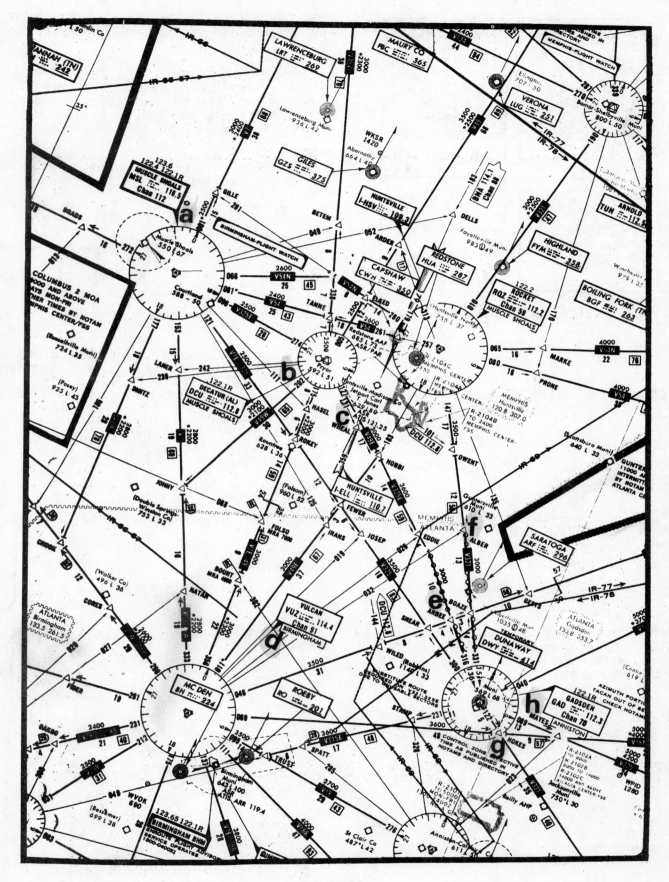

Figure 56

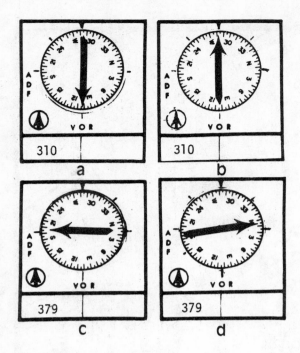

Figure 57

7676. Which combination of indications confirms that you are passing over CRABI Intersection (c)? (See Figures 57 and 58.)

1—a and c.
2—a and d.
3—b and c.
4—b and d.

7677. Which two-way VHF frequencies are available for normal communications at the New Orleans FSS (a)? (See Figure 58.)

1—122.6 and 122.1 only.
2—122.2, 122.6, and 122.1 only.
3—122.0, 122.2, 122.6, and 122.1 only.
4—122.0, 122.2, and 122.6.

7678. What should be the approximate elapsed time for an IFR flight from Grand Isle NDB (b) to Egmont Key NDB (d) on Gulf Route 26? (Wind, 210° at 25 knots; TAS, 185 knots.) (See Figure 58.)

1—2 hr. 5 min.
2—2 hr. 9 min.
3—2 hr. 12 min.
4—2 hr. 16 min.

7679. To which facility should an IFR flight report when passing CRABI Intersection (c)? (See Figure 58.)

1—Wakul Radio.
2—Gainesville FSS.
3—St. Petersburg FSS.
4—Miami Center.

7680. What reports are required of a flight operating on an IFR clearance specifying VFR On Top in a nonradar environment?

1—The same reports that are required for any IFR flight.
2—All normal IFR reports except vacating altitudes.
3—All normal IFR reports except vacating altitudes and en route position reports.
4—Only the reporting of any unforecast weather.

7681. What cloud clearance must a pilot observe when operating with a VFR On Top clearance above 1,200 ft. AGL and 10,000 ft. MSL?

1—Clear of clouds.
2—500 ft. below, 1,000 ft. above, and 2,000 ft. horizontally.
3—1,000 ft. below, 1,000 ft. above, and 1 mi. horizontally.
4—1,000 ft. below, 1,000 ft. above, and 2,000 ft. horizontally.

7682. What minimums must be considered in selecting an altitude when operating with a VFR On Top clearance?

1—At least 500 ft. above the lowest MEA, or appropriate MOCA, and at least 1,000 ft. above the existing meteorological condition.
2—At least 1,000 ft. above the lowest MEA, appropriate MOCA, or existing meteorological condition.
3—Minimum IFR altitude, minimum distance from clouds and visibility appropriate to altitude selected.
4—At least 3,000 ft. above the surface and 1,000 ft. above the existing meteorological condition.

7683. When on a VFR On Top clearance the cruising altitude is based on

1—true course.
2—true heading.
3—magnetic course.
4—magnetic heading.

7684. In which airspace is "VFR On Top" operation prohibited?

1—In a TCA.
2—All controlled airspace.
3—In positive controlled areas.
4—In a control zone.

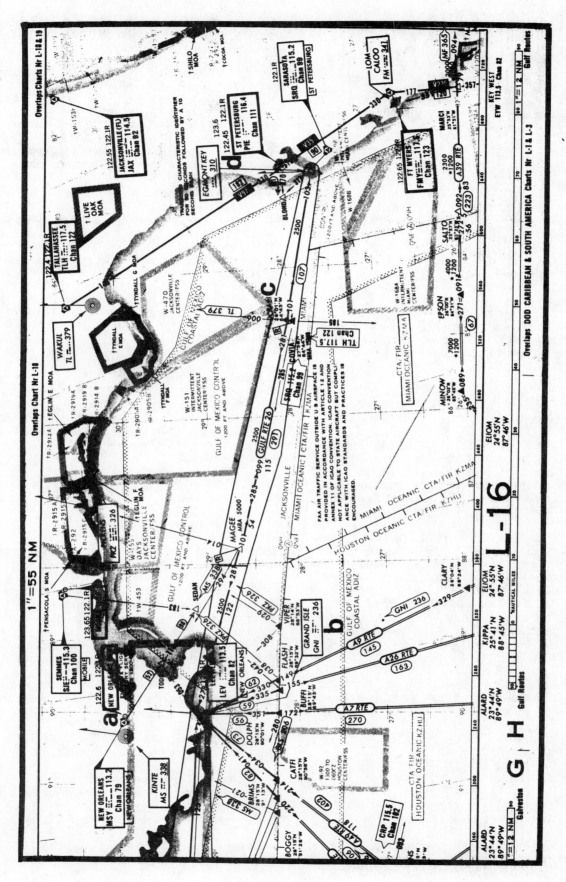

Figure 58

115

 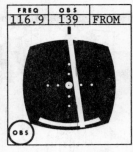

FREQ	OBS	
114.5	264	FROM

FREQ	OBS	
116.9	139	FROM

Figure 59

7685. What is your position with reference to False Intersection (g) if your VOR receivers indicate as shown? (See Figure 59 and 60.)

1—Southeast.
2—Northeast.
3—Northwest.
4—Southwest.

7686. At STRUT Intersection (b) ATC instructs you to proceed direct to the KEYLI LOM (c) and hold. What entry procedure is recommended? (See Figure 60.)

1—Parallel.
2—Teardrop.
3—Direct.
4—Direct or teardrop.

7687. While holding at KEYLI LOM (c) for an ILS approach to Rwy 15 at Lake Charles Muni. Airport, ATC advises you to expect clearance for the approach at 1015. At 1007 you experience two–way radio communications failure. Which procedure should be followed? (See Figure 60.)

1—Squawk 7700 for 1 min. then 7600. After 2 min. have elapsed start your approach.
2—Squawk 7600 and listen on the LOM frequency for instructions from ATC. If no instructions are received, start your approach at 1015.
3—Squawk 7700 for 1 min., then 7600. After 1 min., descend to the minimum final approach fix altitude. Start your approach at 1015.
4—Squawk 7700 for 1 min., then 7600. Begin your approach at 1015.

7688. Where is the VOR changeover point when flying east on V306 from Daisetta (a) to Lake Charles (d)? (See Figure 60.)

1—At the halfway point.
2—At OFERS Intersection.
3—At SILBE Intersection.
4—30 mi. east of Daisetta.

7689. What is indicated by the localizer course symbol at Scholes Field (i)? (See Figure 60.)

1—The airport has a Category II ILS approach procedure.
2—The airport has an LDA approach procedure.
3—An ILS localizer course with an ATC function.
4—An SDF localizer course with an ATC function.

7690. Which VHF frequencies, other than 121.5, can be used to receive Lake Charles FSS (d) during the day in the Lake Charles area? (See Figure 60.)

1—121.1, 122.3 only.
2—121.1, 122.3, 122.2 only.
3—122.2, 122.3, 113.4 only.
4—121.1, 122.2, 123.3, 113.4.

7691. Why are both the front and back ILS localizer courses at Jefferson County (e) depicted with large symbols? (See Figure 60.)

1—Both the front and back courses are not aligned with a runway.
2—Both the front and back courses have a glide slope.
3—The localizer on both the back and front courses have ATC functions.
4—The ILS and back course approaches are classified as "special".

7692. Where is the VOR changeover point between Jefferson County (e) and Hobby (i)? (See Figure 60.)

1—Halfway point.
2—Mocks Intersection.
3—Anahuac Beacon.
4—Fryed Intersection.

7693. Flying northeast on V70 you cross Scholes (j) at 0832 and 20 sec.; you cross Bolds (k) Intersection at 0839 and 02 sec. What is your ETA to nearest 10 sec. for Lake Charles (d) if you maintain the same groundspeed? (See Figure 60.)

1—0914 and 50 sec.
2—0921 and 30 sec.
3—0921 and 45 sec.
4—0928 and 10 sec.

7694. Prior to conducting timed approaches from a holding fix, which one of the following is required?

1—The airport where the approach is to be conducted must have a control tower in operation.
2—The pilot must execute a procedure turn when cleared for the approach.
3—The pilot must have established two–way communications with the tower before departing the holding fix.
4—The time required to fly from the primary facility to the field boundary must be determined by a reliable means.

7695. A "CRUISE FOUR THOUSAND FEET" clearance would mean that the pilot is authorized to

1—vacate 4,000 ft. without notifying ATC.
2—descend (under IMC conditions) below the applicable minimum IFR altitude.
3—climb to, but not descend from 4,000 ft., without further ATC clearance.
4—use any altitude from minimum IFR to 4,000 ft., but must report leaving each altitude.

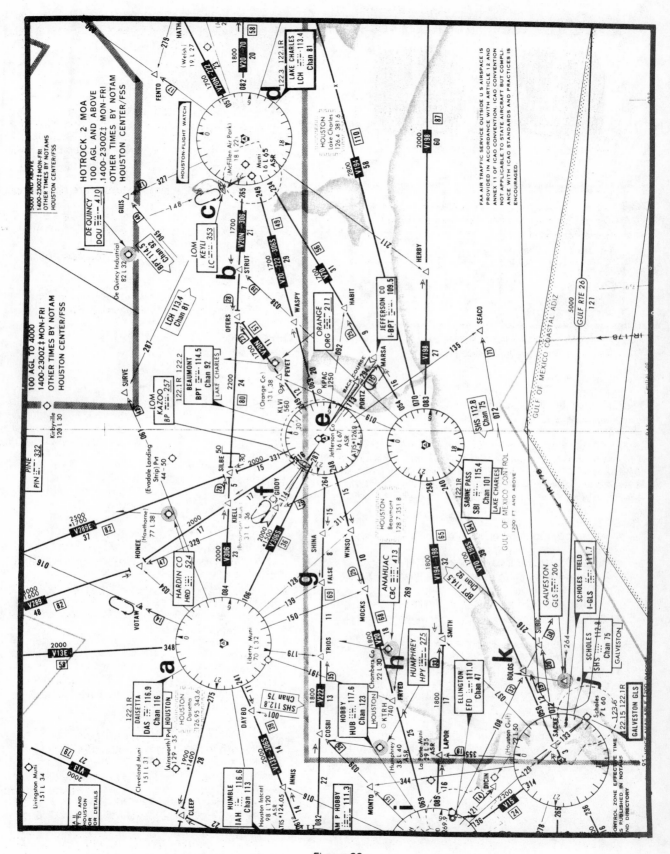

Figure 60

117

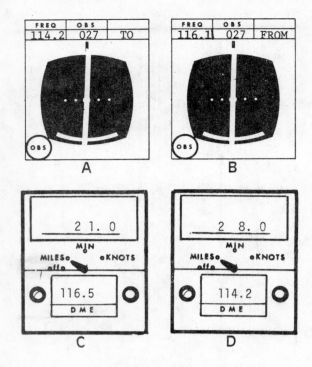

FREQ	OBS	
114.2	027	TO

FREQ	OBS	
116.1	027	FROM

A

B

C

D

Figure 61

7696. Which VOR and DME indications properly identify your position at FRAUD Intersection (d)? (See Figures 61 and 62.)

1—A and D.
2—B and C.
3—A and C.
4—B and D.

7697. What does the symbol ➤ at Columbus Metropolitan (a) indicate? (See Figure 62.)

1—A Category II ILS approach is available.
2—There is no back course procedure available.
3—An SDF approach is available.
4—A published ILS and/or localizer procedure is available.

7698. Which ARTCC(s) and frequency(ies) would you expect to use on a flight from Columbus (a) to Albany (g)? (See Figure 62.)

1—Atlanta Center on 134.7 for the entire flight.
2—Atlanta Center on 134.7 and Jacksonville Center on 127.2.
3—Atlanta Center and Jacksonville Center both on 134.7.
4—Jacksonville Center on 127.2 after leaving Columbus departure control.

7699. Determine the magnetic heading and groundspeed when flying southwest from Vienna (c) on V70 with the conditions listed. (See Figure 62.)

Wind...340° at 21 knots
Altitude...9,000 ft. (PA)
Temperature..– 10° C
Variation .... 1°W
CAS..128 knots

1—267° – 140 knots.
2—251° – 149 knots.
3—251° – 141 knots.
4—267° – 145 knots.

7700. Determine the fuel required for an IFR flight from Weedon Airport (e) to Perry–Fort Valley Airport (b). The approach starts at Vienna VORTAC (c). (See Figure 62.)

Route......................V70 VNA (No alternate required)
TAS...160 knots
Wind...190° at 20 knots
Altitude..5,000 ft.
Variation .... 1°W
Cruise fuel burn .... 78 lb./hr.
Add 20 lb. for taxi,
climb, and approach

1—88 lb.
2—99 lb.
3—105 lb.
4—118 lb.

7701. What is your responsibility, if any, as pilot in command with regard to the special use airspace southeast of Columbus (a), when on an IFR flight from Albany (g) via V321? (See Figure 62.)

1—Before entering the special use airspace, you should contact Columbus approach control and advise them that you are approaching the airway restriction.
2—Since you have been cleared via V321, you have no additional responsibility regarding flight through this airspace.
3—You should contact Columbus radio before reaching the restricted area to ensure that Lawson tower has been notified.
4—You should make a position report to ARTCC upon entering the restricted area with restrictions.

7702. On an instrument flight between Albany (g) and Eufaula (e) on V159, when are you required to be at or above an altitude of 2,800 ft.? (See Figure 62.)

1—Only when ATC is unable to approve a lower altitude.
2—Only when other traffic is flying at the MEA.
3—When you have not made a request to fly at the MEA's.
4—When you have been instructed to report at SHANY Intersection and do not have DME.

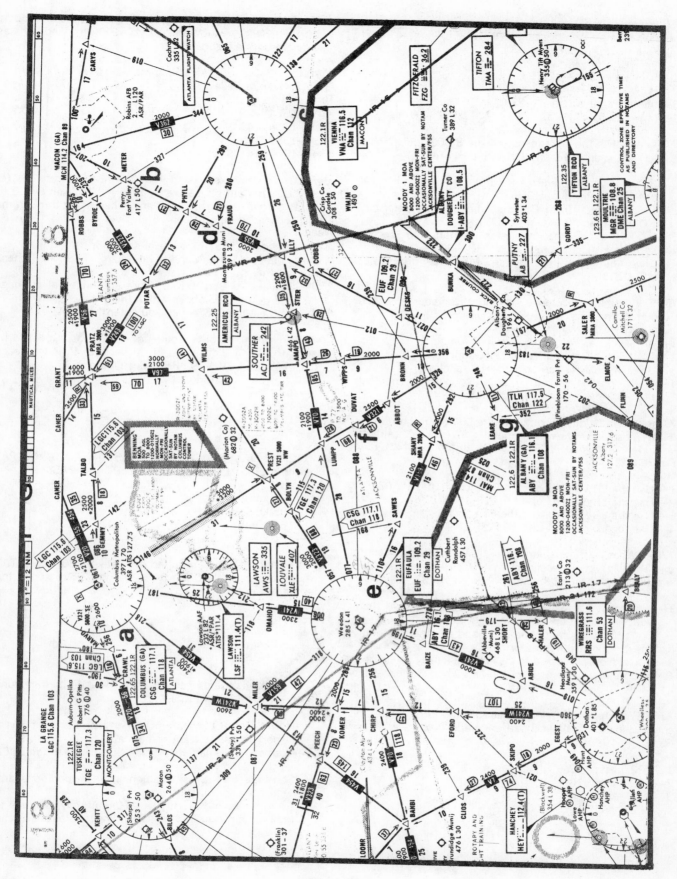

Figure 62

7703. Which radio call and frequency should you use to obtain en route weather advisories when flying in the Ft. Myers area (a)? (See Figure 63.)

1—Ft. Myers FSS – 122.65.
2—Ft. Myers FSS – 122.1.
3—Miami Flight Watch – 122.0.
4—Miami FSS – 122.3.

7704. What is the significance of the 3,000–foot MRA at HOMEY (f) when flying on V225? (See Figure 63.)

1—3,000 ft. is the minimum altitude when using R–298 of PBI to determine HOMEY.
2—DME distance from PBI must be used to determine HOMEY at an altitude of 3,000 ft.
3—3,000 ft. is the minimum altitude to receive satisfactory communication at HOMEY.
4—The minimum altitude to use DME to identify HOMEY is 3,000 ft.

7705. What is indicated by the localizer course symbol used at Palm Beach Intl. (d)? (See Figure 63.)

1—An SDF localizer course with ATC function.
2—An ILS localizer course with ATC function.
3—An LDA localizer course with ATC function.
4—The airport is served by a Category II ILS approach procedure as well as a normal ILS.

7706. When flying outbound on the LBV (e) R–161, which is the most accurate way to identify SWAGS (b)? (Aircraft equipped with one VOR receiver and one DME) (See Figure 63.)

1—Use the LBV R–161 and 44 DME mi from FMY (a).
2—Use the LBV R–161 and the PHK (f) R–217.
3—Use the LBV R–161 and the FMY R–120.
4—Use the LBV R–161 and 39 DME mi.

7707. What is your responsibility, if any, for entrance into the MOA (g) after receiving an IFR clearance via V267 which passes through the MOA? (See Figure 63.)

1—You must contact the Miami ARTCC and give them your estimated time of entering the area.
2—You should contact Miami FSS and ask them to notify the proper military authority.
3—You are only required to stay on the airway as cleared.
4—You need only to contact the FSS when you enter the MOA.

7708. Which VHF frequencies should be used for communication with Fort Meyers Radio (e)? (See Figure 63.)

1—122.1 and 123.6.
2—122.1 and 110.4.
3—122.1, 122.2, or 121.5.
4—122.1 or 122.2.

7709. What should be your ETA and magnetic heading from La Belle (e) to Miami (c) via V97 with conditions as indicated? (See Figure 63.)

Wind: 360 at 25 TAS 162 knots VAR 1°W
Time Over La Belle 1330

1—1354; 129°.
2—1354; 141°.
3—1359; 129°.
4—1359; 141°.

7710. You have requested V157 northbound from LBV (e) at 7,000 ft., but subsequently receive V157E at 8,000 ft. What is your responsibility, if any, when flying through the MOA? (See Figure 63.)

1—Stay on V157E at the assigned altitude.
2—Contact Miami Center or Miami FSS and check whether the MOA is activated.
3—Advise ATC that V157E is not authorized at altitudes of 7,000 ft. and above within the MOA.
4—Advise Miami FSS when you enter the MOA.

7711. Which en route frequency would you expect to be assigned for a flight from Ft. Meyers (a) to Palm Beach (d), via V225 LBV, V492 PBI? (See Figure 63.)

1—132.25.
2—128.5 and 132.25.
3—122.5 and 133.55.
4—133.55.

7712. What should be your TAS at 7,000 ft. (PA), temperature +15° C, if you use 150 knots CAS?

1—162 knots.
2—165 knots.
3—168 knots.
4—171 knots.

7713. What CAS is required to obtain 180 knots TAS when flying at 8,000 ft.? (PA is 7,500 and the temperature is 15° C.)

1—165 knots.
2—162 knots.
3—159 knots.
4—157.5 knots.

7714. What is the procedure when the DME malfunctions at or above 24,000 ft. MSL?

1—Notify ATC of the malfunction and land at the nearest airport where repairs can be made.
2—Notify ATC immediately and request an altitude below 24,000 ft.
3—Continue to your destination in VFR conditions and report the malfunction.
4—After immediately notifying ATC, you may continue to the next airport of intended landing where repairs can be made.

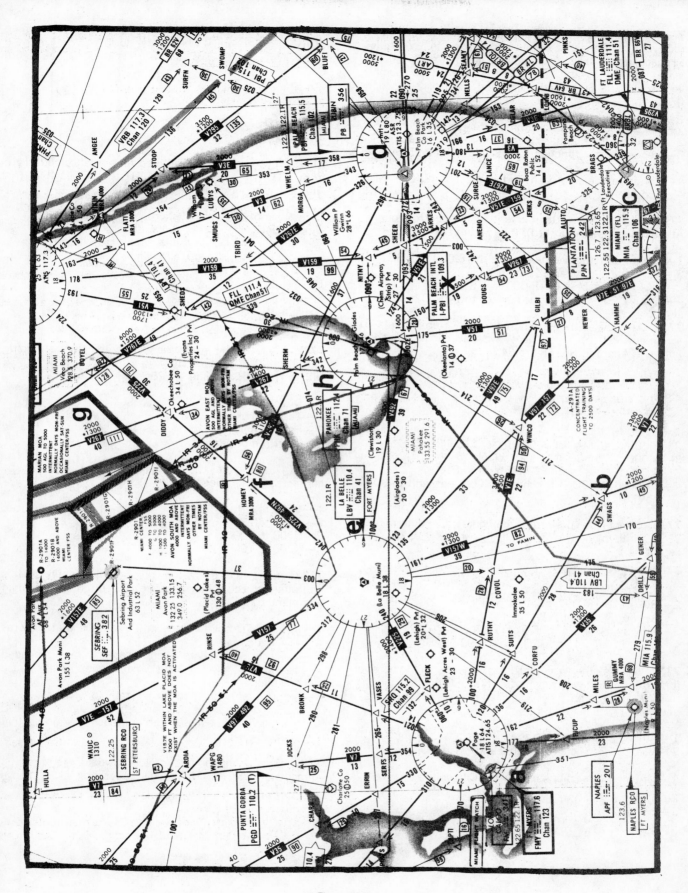

Figure 63

7715. What action, if any, should you take if your No. 1 receiver malfunctions while operating in controlled airspace under IFR? Your aircraft is equipped with two VOR receivers: the No. 1 receiver has Omni/Localizer/Glide Slope capability, and the No. 2 has only Omni.

1—Report the malfunction immediately to ATC.
2—Continue the flight as cleared; no report is required.
3—Report the malfunction to ATC if you do not have ADF for backup.
4—Continue the approach and request a VOR or NDB approach.

7716. What is the vertical extent of the control zone at Athens Municipal Airport (d)? (See Figure 64.)

1—From 700 ft. above the surface to 18,000 ft. MSL.
2—From the surface to 14,500 ft. MSL.
3—From 807 ft. MSL to 18,000 ft. MSL.
4—From 1,200 ft. above the surface to 14,500 ft. MSL.

7717. At what altitude(s) should you fly from Atlanta (i) to Greenwood (b) if you have two-way communications failure at Atlanta? (See Figure 64.)

Cleared to Greenwood County Airport via V18 MADDI, V454.
Maintain 3000 — IFR conditions entire route.

1—3,000 ft.
2—3,000 ft. to MADDI; 4,000 ft. to GRD.
3—3,000 ft. to CONNI; start climb to cross CONNI at 4,000 ft.; descend to 2,500 ft. at VESTO.
4—3,000 ft. to CONNI; climb to 4000; descend to 3000 at VESTO.

7718. Select the preferred method(s) for determining VESTO Intersection (c) when flying west on V325? (See Figure 64.)

1—Only by use of R–092 of AHN (d) and R–183 of ELW (a).
2—By use of R–092 of AHN and either 25 DME from AHN or R–183 of ELW.
3—Only by use of 25 DME from AHN and R–092 of AHN.
4—By use of R–241 of GRD and R–092 of AHN.

7719. Unless otherwise instructed, where should you give a position report when flying from GLOSS Intersection (h) to ELW (a)? (You have been advised that radar contact has been lost.) (See Figure 64.)

1—Athens and Electric City.
2—MADDI Intersection, Athens, and Electric City.
3—Electric City only.
4—MADDI Intersection and Electric City only.

7720. What is the minimum altitude for determining CORVI Intersection (f) when flying north on V5? (You have two VOR receivers, DME, and a transponder.) (See Figure 64.)

1—5,000 ft.
2—4,500 ft.
3—3,500 ft.
4—2,500 ft.

7721. How much fuel is required for an instrument flight from ATL (i) to GRD (b) via V18 MADDI, V454? (An alternate is required.) (See Figure 64.)

TAS 190 knots — Time to alternate from GRD 30 min.
Wind: 040° at 25 knots — Variation 1°W
Fuel burn: 144 lb./hr. (allow additional 8 lb. for
                    taxi, run–up, and climb)

1—294 lb.
2—284 lb.
3—195 lb.
4—185 lb.

7722. What is the recommended entry to the holding pattern at APIAN Intersection (g) when flying west on V18 with a magnetic heading of 275°? (See Figure 64.)

1—Direct only.
2—Teardrop only.
3—Parallel only.
4—Teardrop or parallel.

7723. During what hours can Anderson FSS (a) be contacted (EST)? (See Figure 64.)

1—0600 to 2200.
2—0700 to 2300.
3—0700 to 1900.
4—0800 to 1900.

7724. If the ADF navigation receiver malfunctions while operating in controlled airspace under IFR, the pilot in command must

1—advise ATC not to issue any clearance that requires ADF equipment.
2—continue as cleared and request an amended clearance only if the malfunction will cause deviations.
3—report the malfunction immediately to ATC.
4—continue the flight as planned; if assigned an NDB approach, request another approach explaining that your ADF is inoperative.

7725. Which equipment failure would require an immediate report to ATC when operating at or above 24,000 ft. MSL?

1—Transponder altitude encoding.
2—RNAV receiver capability.
3—DME.
4—One of two VOR receivers.

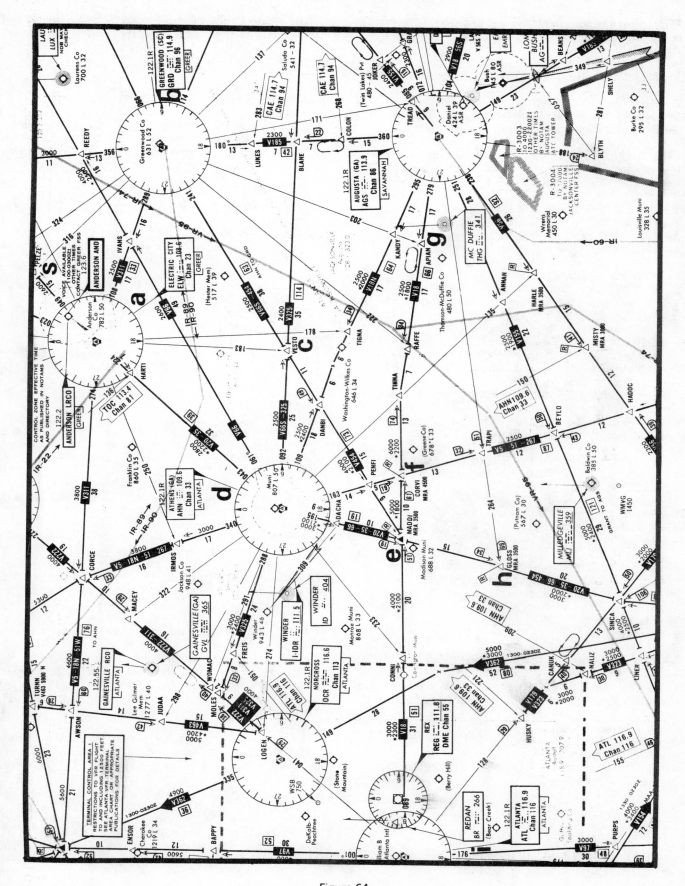

Figure 64

7726. How can you determine if the runway lights will be on at Barkley Airport (h), if arriving after dark? (See Figure 65.)

1—By reference to data on the En Route Low Altitude Chart.
2—By reference to the Airman's Information Manual.
3—By reference to the Airport/Facility Directory (SE US).
4—By determining if Barkley has a control zone.

7727. Paducah FSS (i) can be contacted on which VHF frequencies? (Choose answer with all available FSS frequencies.) (See Figure 65.)

1—121.5, 123.6, 122.5, 122.1.
2—121.5, 122.2, 122.5, 122.1.
3—122.5, 122.1.
4—122.2, 122.5.

7728. When south of Marion VOR (f), approaching BUNKO, you are instructed to contact Memphis Center on 128.05, but are unable. Which procedure should now be followed? (See Figure 65.)

1—Call Kansas City Center on 125.3 and inform them you are unable to contact Memphis Center on 128.05.
2—Call Memphis Center on 121.5, explain that you could not contact them on 128.05.
3—Call Paducah FSS and ask them to advise Memphis Center of your position.
4—Call Paducah Tower (Barkley) and advise that you are unable to contact Memphis Center.

7729. What type of instrument approach is indicated by the symbol shown at Barkley airport (h)? (See Figure 65.)

1—A back course localizer.
2—An ILS and/or localizer.
3—A localizer procedure only.
4—An SDF.

7730. Which is the recommended entry to the holding pattern at ARNOL Intersection (a) when southbound on V9 with a heading of 171°? (See Figure 65.)

1—Teardrop only.
2—Parallel only.
3—Direct or parallel.
4—Parallel or teardrop.

7731. Where is the VOR changeover point when flying from CNG (j) to FAM (e) via V178N? (See Figure 65.)

1—At the halfway point.
2—PAMPI Intersection.
3—ALING Intersection.
4—At the geographical point you are told to contact Kansas City Center.

7732. Where is the VOR changeover point when flying from CGI (g) to ENL (b) via V313? (See Figure 65.)

1—GENTS Intersection.
2—37 mi. from CGI.
3—DEVER Intersection.
4—Halfway between GENTS and DEVER.

7733. How can you determine from the Low Altitude En Route Chart whether Sparta Community Airport (c) has an approved instrument approach procedure? (See Figure 65.)

1—The NDB symbol will have a flag.
2—This information will be given under the airport symbol.
3—The airport symbol will be printed in blue.
4—A transition route will be shown giving a bearing or radial to the facility.

7734. What is your planned ETA at MAW (k) if you pass over ENL VORTAC (b) at 10:32 and 25 sec. and over ZORAL Intersection (d) at 10:43 and 7 sec.? (Assume constant groundspeed and give answer to the nearest minute.) (See Figure 65.)

1—11:17.
2—11:20.
3—11:23.
4—11:26.

7735. What action should a pilot take if the air/ground communications receiver malfunctions intermittently while operating in controlled airspace under IFR?

1—Squawk 7600 and proceed as cleared.
2—Descend immediately to MEA/MOCA and squawk 7700 for 1 min., then 7600 for 15 min.
3—Report the malfunction immediately to ATC.
4—Continue the flight as cleared and file a written report to the Administrator, if requested.

7736. What action is necessary when a partial loss of ILS receiver capability occurs while operating in controlled airspace under IFR?

1—Request radar monitoring if an ILS approach is attempted.
2—Inform ATC of the malfunction at once.
3—Continue as cleared, but file a malfunction report upon landing.
4—If the aircraft is equipped with other approach radio gear, no further action is necessary.

7737. While on an IFR flight, a pilot has an emergency which causes a deviation from an ATC clearance. What action must be taken?

1—Request an amended clearance or cancel the IFR flight plan.
2—Notify ATC of the deviation as soon as possible.
3—Squawk 7700 for the duration of the emergency.
4—Submit a detailed report to the chief of the ATC facility within 48 hours.

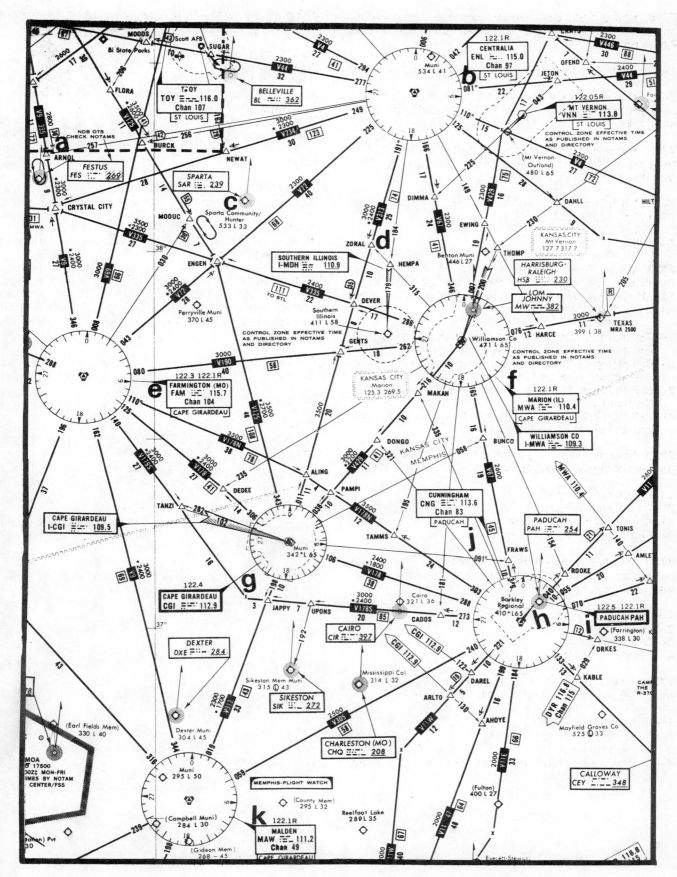

Figure 65

7738. FAA Deletion.

7739. Which frequencies are available at Huntington FSS (e)? (See Figure 66.)

1—121.5, 122.1R, 122.2, and 122.6.
2—121.5, 122.1R, and 122.6 only.
3—122.1R, and 122.6 only.
4—122.1R, 122.6, and 123.6 only.

7740. Between Lexington (h) and Newcombe (f), you are unable to contact Huntington FSS on 122.6. Which phraseology and frequency should now be used? (See Figure 66.)

1—"Huntington FSS, Comanche 6841 on 122.1, Over."
2—"Huntington Radio, Comanche 6841 on 121.5, Over."
3—"Huntington Radio, Comanche 6841, Over." (Transmit 123.6)
4—"Huntington Radio, Comanche 6841, receiving Newcombe VOR." (Transmit 122.1)

7741. FAA Deletion.

7742. FAA Deletion.

7743. FAA Deletion.

7744. FAA Deletion.

7745. FAA Deletion.

7746. FAA Deletion.

7747. Which transponder operation should you use to alert ATC if you experience two—way communication failure?

1—Squawk Mode A/3, code 7600.
2—Squawk code 7600 for 1 min., then code 7700 for 15 min.; repeat as practicable.
3—Squawk Mode A/3, code 7700.
4—Squawk code 7700 for 1 min., then code 7600 for 15 min.; repeat as practicable.

7748. What procedure should you use to alert ATC that you are unable to contact them on any of the voice channels?

1—Squawk 7600 for 1 min., then 7700 for 1 min. (repeat as necessary).
2—Squawk 7600 for 1 min., then 7700 for 15 min. (repeat as necessary).
3—Squawk 7700 for 1 min., then 7600 for 15 min. (repeat as necessary).
4—Squawk 7700 for 15 min., then 7600.

7749. While in IFR weather conditions, your communications and navigation receivers both fail. If your transponder is still operating, which code should you use?

1—0736 (code assigned by ATC).
2—7500.
3—7700.
4—7600.

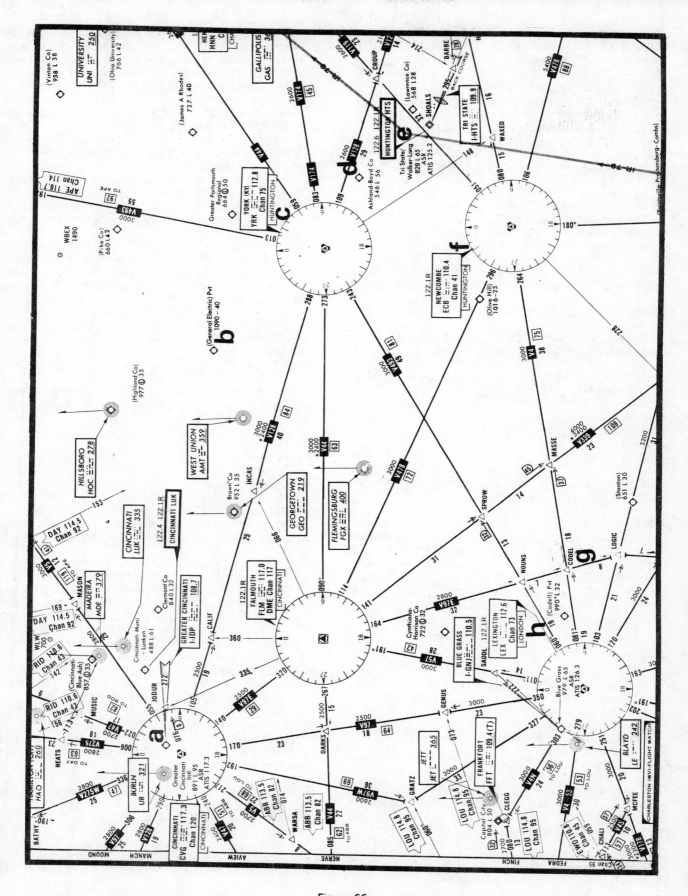

Figure 66

127

7750. Which frequency and radio call should you use to obtain the JXN (g) terminal forecast if you are over Fort Wayne (a)? (See Figure 67.)

1—122.1T, 109.6R; Jackson radio.
2—122.1T, 117.8R; Jackson flight watch.
3—122.45; Fort Wayne radio.
4—122.0; Indianapolis flight watch.

7751. Which ARTCC would you expect to be advised to contact shortly after passing MODEM Intersection (e) when northbound on V221? (See Figure 67.)

1—Chicago Center on 120.45.
2—Cleveland Center on 120.45.
3—Chicago Center on 120.6.
4—Indianapolis Center on 135.6.

7752. Where is the VOR changeover point when flying southbound from Salem (h) on V275? (See Figure 67.)

1—At the halfway point to KLINE.
2—74 mi. from Salem.
3—Upon intercepting the Ft. Wayne 071 radial.
4—At SONIL Intersection.

7753. Where is the VOR changeover point on V116 between Salem (h) and Jackson (g)? (See Figure 67.)

1—RASAK Intersection.
2—At the halfway point.
3—26 mi. from Salem.
4—21 mi. from Salem.

7754. Determine your ETA at Jackson (g) with the conditions listed. (See Figure 67.)

Over Findlay VORTAC (c) at 1021
TAS .... 150 knots
Route ....V8 GAREN V221 JXN
Wind ....330° at 25 knots
Avg. TC from GAREN to JXN .... 25°
Variation .... 2°W

1—1117.
2—1120.
3—1123.
4—1126.

7755. Where is the VOR changeover point when flying from Salem (h) to Ft. Wayne (a) on V11? (See Figure 67.)

1—EDGEE Intersection.
2—52 mi. from Ft. Wayne.
3—HIRED Intersection.
4—56 mi. from Salem.

7756. Where are you expected to give an en route position report on an IFR flight from Ft. Wayne Municipal (a) to Jackson County–Reynolds Field via V221? You are not in radar contact. (See Figure 67.)

1—At GAREN, MODEM, and LFD.
2—At LFD and JXN only.
3—At JXN only.
4—At GAREN and LFD.

7757. Which procedure should you use if your VOR navigation receivers become inoperative after passing WINES (b) when on an IFR flight to Ft. Wayne Municipal (a) flying in IFR conditions? Your communication radios are operative. (See Figure 67.)

1—Advise ATC that you must be vectored to an area forecast to have VFR conditions.
2—Immediately advise ATC of the equipment affected, and give the nature and extent of assistance desired.
3—Continue along the route assigned in the last ATC clearance, using dead reckoning, then contact Ft. Wayne approach for an ASR approach.
4—Advise Cleveland ARTCC that you are diverting south to Van Wert Municipal and will execute the NDB approach.

7758. What is the minimum altitude for identifying GRABI Intersection (d) when flying northeast on V11? (Aircraft is equipped with DME and two VOR receivers.) (See Figure 67.)

1—2,600 ft. MSL.
2—3,000 ft. MSL.
3—3,600 ft. MSL.
4—4,000 ft. MSL.

7759. What is the recommended entry procedure to the holding pattern at IRISH Intersection (f) when flying on V11 with a heading of 45°? (See Figure 67.)

1—Direct.
2—Parallel.
3—Teardrop.
4—Direct or parallel.

7760. You are in IFR weather conditions and have two–way radio communications failure. If you do not exercise emergency authority, what procedure are you expected to follow?

1—Set transponder to code 7700 for 1 min., then to 7600. Continue flight on assigned route and fly at the last assigned altitude or the MEA, whichever is higher.
2—Set transponder to code 7700 for 1 min., then to 7600, and fly to an area with VFR weather conditions.
3—Set transponder to 7600 and fly to an area where you can let down in VFR conditions.
4—Set transponder to code 7600 and continue the flight as planned. Fly at the last assigned altitude or requested altitude, whichever is higher.

7761. Which procedure should you follow if you experience two–way communications failure while holding at a holding fix with an EAC time? (The holding fix is not the same as the approach fix.)

1—Depart the holding fix to arrive at the approach fix as close as possible to the EAC time.
2—Depart the holding fix at the EAC time.
3—Depart the holding fix on the flight planned ETA.
4—Proceed immediately to the approach fix and hold until EAC.

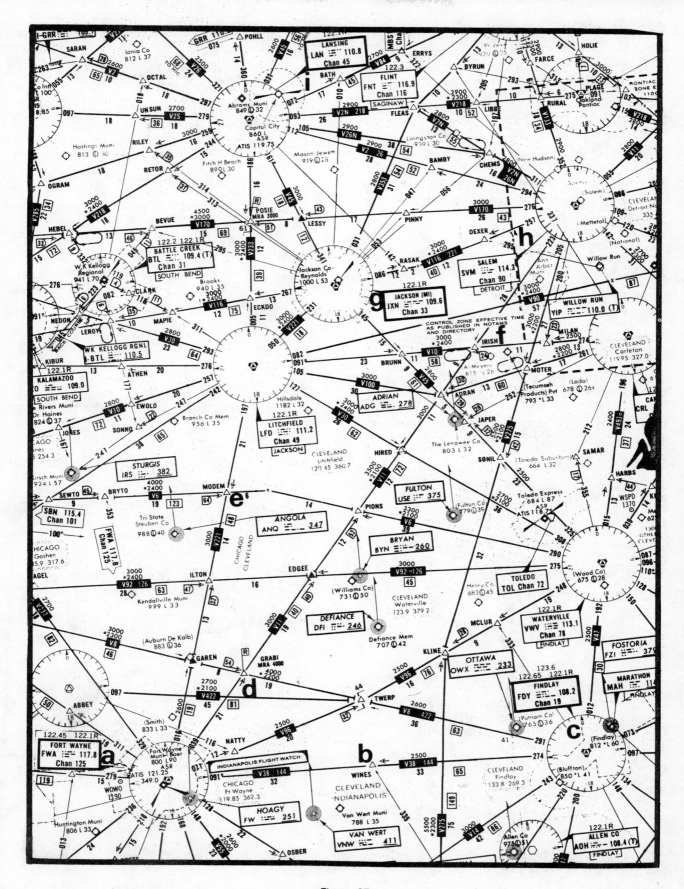

Figure 67

129

7762. Which low–altitude routing from LaGuardia Airport (K) to Bradley International Airport (c) is recommended to minimize route changes? (Proposed departure time 0000 GMT.) (See Figure 68 and Appendix 2.)

1—MARES V467 BDR014 JUDDS CMK058 BRISS.
2—V467 SEAMO V433 TERRY BDL.
3—V467 HFD BDL.
4—V123 CMK CMK058 BRISS.

7763. What is the ETA at MOLDS Intersection (a) on a flight from LGA (k) with the conditions listed? (See Figure 68.)

Route..V467 HFD V130 MOLDS
CAS...133
Altimeter Setting..29.92
Altitude..7000
Variation..13°W
Wind.............................355° at 30 knots
Temperature..................................Standard
Over LGA at..0840

1—0934.
2—0937.
3—0940.
4—0943.

7764. Where is the VOR changeover point when flying from HFD (g) to LGA (k) on V467? (See Figure 68.)

1—SEAMO Intersection.
2—Midway between facilities.
3—MARES Intersection.
4—44 mi. from HFD.

7765. What altitudes should you maintain from Duffy Intersection (l) to HFD (g) and when should you start your approach to Hartford–Brainard (f) assuming the conditions listed? (See Figure 68.)

CLEARED TO HARTFORD–BRAINARD AIRPORT VIA V229, MAINTAIN 2000. IFR conditions exist the entire route; you have two–way radio communications failure at DUFFY Intersection; the approach begins at HFD VORTAC.

1—2000 to HFD; start approach upon arrival at HFD VORTAC, but not before the expect approach clearance time or flight plan ETA.
2—2000 to MAD; then climb and maintain 2600 to HFD; start approach upon arrival at HFD VORTAC.
3—2000 until necessary to begin climb to cross MAD at 2300 or above; continue climb to 2600 and maintain to HFD; start approach when over the VORTAC.
4—2000 until necessary to begin climb to cross MAD at 2300 or above; continue climb to 2600 and maintain to HFD; start approach upon arrival at HFD, but not before the flight time ETA as amended with ATC.

7766. What is the recommended entry to the holding pattern at CMK VORTAC (i) when approaching the VOR on V123 with a heading of 010°? (See Figure 68.)

1—Direct.
2—Parallel.
3—Teardrop.
4—Either parallel or teardrop.

7767. What type of approaches are indicated by the chart symbols at Westchester Co. Airport (j)? (See Figure 68.)

1—LOC BC and ILS.
2—SDF and/or LDA.
3—ILS and/or LOC.
4—LDA and ILS.

7768. Which ATC frequency would you probably be assigned, a few miles past PWL (d) when flying northeastward on V93? (See Figure 68.)

1—134.0.
2—133.2.
3—124.2.
4—132.65.

7769. Barnes Control Zone (b) is effective during which hours (EDT)? (See Figure 68.)

1—1200 to 1600.
2—0800 to 2400.
3—0700 to 2300.
4—0700 to 2400.

7770. What approach procedures are available at Bradley Intl. Airport (c) as indicated by the symbols? (See Figure 68.)

1—One back course LOC and two ILS.
2—Three LOC and one ILS.
3—One ILS and two SDF.
4—Three ILS and/or localizer.

7771. Which procedure should you follow if, during an IFR flight in VFR conditions, you have two–way radio communications failure?

1—Continue the flight under VFR and land as soon as practicable.
2—Continue the flight at assigned altitude and route; start approach at your ETA; or, if late, start approach upon arrival.
3—Land at the neareast airport that has VFR conditions.
4—Continue the flight along assigned route at the highest of the following altitudes: assigned altitude, MEA, or altitude ATC may have advised you to expect.

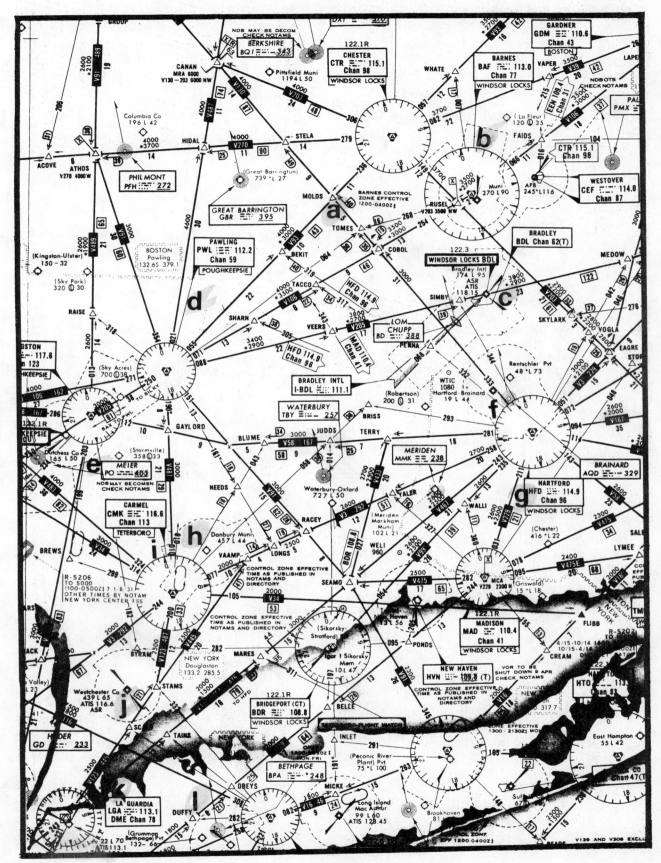

Figure 68

7772. What type navigation facility is located at Washington (c)? (See Figure 69.)

1—VOR only.
2—VOR/DME.
3—VORTAC.
4—TACAN.

7773. What frequency is established to communicate with Washington Flight Watch (b)? (See Figure 69.)

1—122.2 MHz.
2—122.1 MHz.
3—122.0 MHz.
4—123.0 MHz.

7774. The altitude restriction on V170–312 at (d) indicates that (see Figure 69)

1—no separation would be provided from traffic above 13,000.
2—communications and radar identification would be impaired above 13,000.
3—IFR flights above 13,000 are controlled by the Dept. of Defense.
4—flight above 13,000 is not authorized.

7775. You are holding in the pattern depicted at DEALE Intersection (e). When you cross the fix at 1803, ATC clears you to depart DEALE Intersection at 1810. How should you adjust the holding pattern to depart on time? (See Figure 69.)

1—Make three 2–minute 360° turns and one 1–minute 360° turn.
2—Make one pattern with 2–1/2–minute legs.
3—Make one normal pattern and one with 30–second legs.
4—Make one normal pattern and one with 30–second 180° turns.

7776. What equipment is specifically required for an IFR flight to operate within the TCA over Washington National Airport (c)? (See Figure 69.)

1—VOR and two–way communications only.
2—VOR, transponder, and two–way communications only.
3—VOR, DME, and two–way communications only.
4—VOR, DME, transponder, and two–way communications.

7777. At what point does the MEA change from 2600 to 2000 on V265 between EMI and KRANT Intersection? (See Figure 69.)

1—Approaching DATED Intersection.
2—DATED Intersection.
3—CLEAT Intersection.
4—BELTS Intersection.

7778. FAA Deletion.

7779. At what time are current AIRMETs broadcast by the FSS?

1—15 minutes after the hour only.
2—Every 15 minutes until the AIRMET is canceled.
3—15 and 45 minutes after the hour during the first hour after issuance.
4—On the hour and each 15 minutes thereafter for 1 hour after issuance.

7780. Pilots of IFR flights seeking ATC in–flight weather avoidance assistance should keep in mind that

1—ATC radar limitations and frequency congestion may limit the controllers capability to provide this service.
2—circumnavigating severe weather can only be accommodated in the en route areas away from terminals because of congestion.
3—ATC Narrow Band Radar does not provide the controller with weather intensity capability.
4—controllers must rely on weather radar repeater scopes or the Radar Summary Chart to identify precipitation intensity and movement.

7781. When are you required to establish communications with the tower, if you cancel your IFR flight plan 10 mi. from the destination?

1—Immediately after canceling the flight plan.
2—When advised by ARTCC.
3—At least 5 mi. from the center of the airport.
4—Immediately prior to entering the traffic pattern.

7782. What altitude and route should be used if you are flying in IFR weather conditions and have two–way radio communication failure?

1—Continue on the route specified in your clearance; fly at an altitude that is the highest of: last assigned altitude, altitude ATC has informed you to expect, or the MEA.
2—Fly direct to an area that has been forecast to have VFR conditions; fly at an altitude that is at least 1,000 ft. above the highest obstacles along the route.
3—Descend to MEA and, if clear of clouds, proceed to the nearest appropriate airport. If not clear of clouds, maintain the highest of the MEA's along the clearance route.
4—Fly the most direct route to your destination, maintaining the highest of last assigned altitude or MEA.

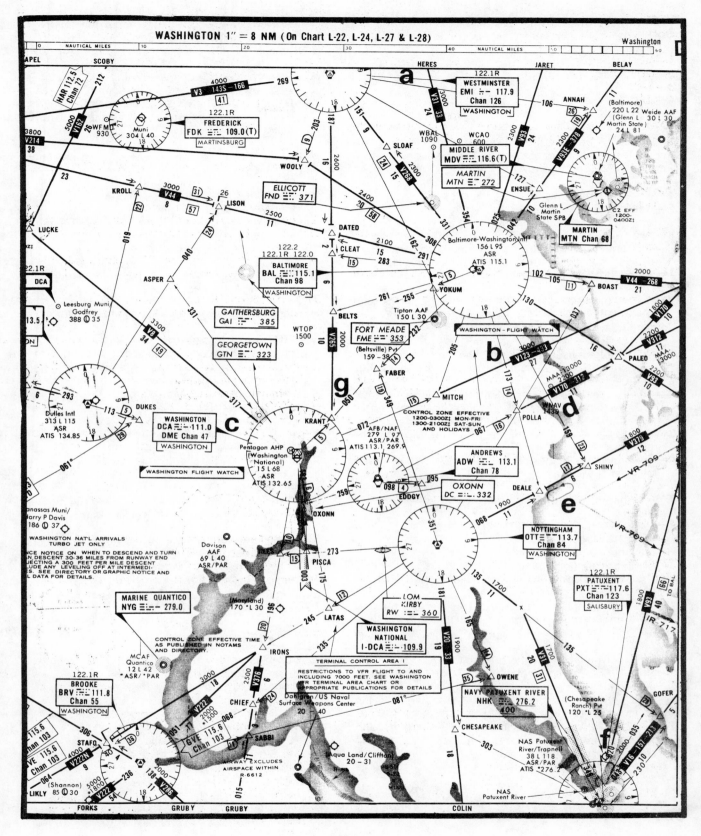

Figure 69

133

7783. What is the HAA for Category A aircraft during the VOR RWY 9R approach at Metropolitan Oakland International? (See Figure 70.)

1—494.
2—455
3—460.
4—500.

7784. What does the symbol ▼ in the minimums section indicate for Metropolitan Oakland International? (See Figure 70.)

1—Takeoff minimums are 800 ft. and 2 mi.
2—Takeoff minimums are 1 mi. for aircraft having two engines or less and 1/2 mi. for those with more than two engines.
3—Instrument takeoffs are not authorized on Rwy 9R.
4—Takeoff minimums are not standard and/or departure procedures are published.

7785. What is the purpose of the VDP (visual descent point) for the VOR RWY 9R approach at Metropolitan Oakland International? (See Figure 70.)

1—To provide a visual checkpoint for the pilot to initiate descent from MDA during straight–in or circling approaches.
2—To provide a point from which normal descent from MDA may be commenced, provided visual references are established.
3—To provide a visual confirmation of the MDA for the pilot.
4—To provide a point for the pilot to level off after descent to MDA.

7786. What type altitude is indicated at the FAF? (See Figure 70.)

1—Mandatory altitude.
2—Maximum altitude.
3—Minimum altitude.
4—Recommended altitude.

7787. Which information is provided in the AFD for Rwy 9R at Metropolitan Oakland International? (See Figure 70.)

1—HIRL only and threshold displaced 220 ft.
2—HIRL, VASI, threshold displaced 220 ft., and open to all aircraft.
3—HIRL, VASI, threshold displaced 220 ft., and landing restrictions for some aircraft.
4—TDZL, HIRL, VASI, threshold displaced 220 ft., and restricted to jet–type aircraft over 12,500 lb., and 4–engine (reciprocating) aircraft.

7788. How should you determine the MAP (missed approach point) on the S–9R VOR RWY 9R approach at Metropolitan Oakland International? (See Figure 70.)

1—Station passage at the VORTAC.
2—When at 460 ft. on the descent path.
3—Upon passing the visual descent point.
4—When time has expired for 1.4 nautical mile past the VDP.

7789. A contact approach is an approach procedure that may be used

1—when a pilot has filed to an airport with an approved instrument approach procedure and wishes to land at a nearby airport that does not have an authorized instrument approach procedure.
2—in lieu of conducting a standard instrument approach procedure.
3—if assigned by ATC and will facilitate the approach.
4—in lieu of a visual approach.

7790. Under which condition does ATC issue a STAR?

1—To all pilots wherever STARS are available.
2—To any pilot only upon request.
3—Only if the pilot requests a STAR in the "Remarks" section of the flight plan.
4—When ATC deems it appropriate, unless the pilot requests "No STAR."

7791. What timing procedure should be used when performing a holding pattern at a VOR?

1—Timing for the outbound leg begins over or abeam the VOR, whichever occurs later.
2—Timing should be adjusted by varying the rate of turn.
3—Timing for the inbound leg begins when initiating the turn inbound.
4—Adjustments in timing of each pattern should be made on the inbound leg.

7792. Which publication covers the procedures required for aircraft accident and incident reporting responsibilities for pilots?

1—FAR Part 61.
2—FAR Part 91.
3—FAR Part 23.
4—NTSB 830.

OAKLAND
§ METROPOLITAN OAKLAND INTL   (OAK)   4.3 S   GMT—8(—7DT)

SAN FRANCISCO
H-1A, 2E, L-2F, A
IAP

37°43'17"N 122°13'11"W

06   B   S4   FUEL 80, 100, 100LL, JET A   OX 1, 2, 3, 4   TPA—1006(1000)
LRA   CFR Index C
RWY 11-29: H10,000X150 (ASPH-GRVD)   S-200, D-200, DT-400, DDT-900   HIRL, CL
RWY 11: MALSR. Rgt tfc.   RWY 29: ALSF1, TDZ
RWY 09R-27L: H6212X150 (ASPH)   S-155, D-158, DT-253, DDT-525   HIRL
RWY 09R: VASI(V4L)—GA 3.0° TCH 46'. Thld dsplcd 220'. Fence.
RWY 27L: VASI(V4L)—GA 3.0° TCH 55'. Rgt tfc.
RWY 15-33: H3364X75 (ASPH-GRVD)   S-12.5, D-65, DT-100   HIRL
RWY 33: Control tower. Rgt tfc.
RWY 09L-27R: H5453X150 (ASPH)   S-100, D-115, DT-180   HIRL
RWY 09L: VASI(V4L)—GA 3.0° TCH 37.7'. Building.   RWY 27R: MALSR. Building. Rgt tfc.
AIRPORT REMARKS: Attended continuously. Fee rwy 11-29 and overnight tiedown. Flocks of birds feeding in nearby garbage dumps and along shoreline adjacent to arpt. Rwy 09L-27R closed to air carrier acft except taxiway 09L and 27R for taxiing. Turbo-jet/fan turbo-prop acft with certificated gross weight over 12,500 lbs & 4-engine reciprocating acft prohibited from takeoff 27R, 27L or landing 09L & 09R. This prohibition not applicable or effective in emergency or when rwy 11-29 is closed. Acft with experimental or limited certification having over 1000 h.p or 4000 lbs are restricted to rwy 11-29 for all ops due to maintenance, construction, or reasons of safety. Rwy 15-33 restricted to aircraft 12,500 lbs or less and is for 24 hour use. The pavement between rwy 27L and relocated thld rwy 33 is now a 50' wide unlighted lead-in taxiway limited to aircraft 30,000 lbs or less. Rwy 09R-27L FAA gross weight strength DC 10-10 350,000 pounds, DC 10-30 450,000 pounds, L-1011 350,000 pounds.Rwy 11-29 FAA gross weight strength DC 10-10 600,000 pounds, DC 10-30 700,000 pounds, L-1011 600,000 pounds. Flight Notification Service (ADCUS) available.
COMMUNICATIONS: ATIS 126.0 (N. Complex), 128.5 (415-635-5850) (S. Complex)   UNICOM 122.95
Ⓡ OAKLAND FSS (OAK) on arpt. LC 527-9980 122.5, 122.2, 122.1R, 122.0
Ⓡ BAY APP CON 124.4 (S. Complex), 135.4 (N. Complex), 134.5
OAKLAND TOWER 118.3 (N. Complex) (1600-0400Z‡) 127.2 (S. Complex) 124.9
GND CON 121.75 (S. Complex), 121.9 (N. Complex)   CLNC DEL 121.1
Ⓡ BAY DEP CON 120.9 (NW-E), 135.1 (SE-W)
STAGE III svc ctc APP CON 124.4
RADIO AIDS TO NAVIGATION:
OAKLAND (H) VORTAC 116.8   OAK   Chan 115   37°43'34"N 122°13'21"W   at fld. 10/17E
RORAY NDB (LMM) 341   AK   37°43'17"N 122°11'35"W   275° 0.5 NM to fld.
ILS 108.7 I-HNB Rwy 29
ILS 111.9 I-AAZ Rwy 11
ILS 109.9 I-OAK Rwy 27R LMM RORAY NDB
COMM/NAVAID REMARKS: FSS provides airport advisory svc on freq. 119.8 when tower closed.

SAN FRANCISCO
H-1A, 2E, L-2F, A

OAKLAND   37°43'34"N 122°13'21"W
(H) VORTAC 116.8   OAK   Chan 115   at Metropolitan Oakland Int'l. 10/17E
VOR unusable 307-323° beyond 10 NM below 5000'   307-323° beyond 17 NM below 12,500'
VOR unusable 307-323° beyond 17 NM below 12,500'   350-030° beyond 20 NM below 3500'
DME unusable:
307-323° beyond 30 NM below 1500'
040-065° beyond 30 NM below 4100'

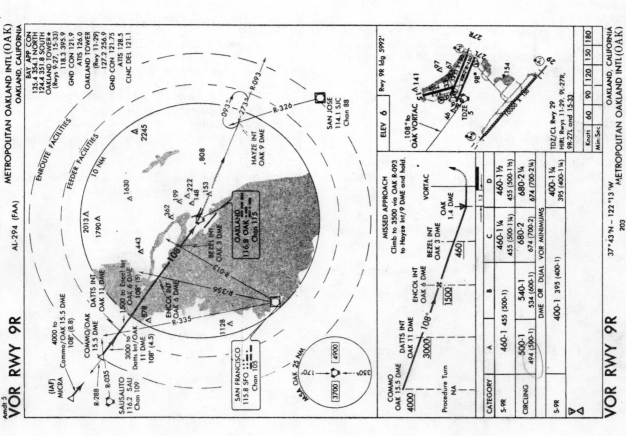

VOR RWY 9R   METROPOLITAN OAKLAND INTL(OAK)
OAKLAND, CALIFORNIA

Figure 70

7793. How should you identify the missed approach point for the S–LDA/GS 5 approach to Roanoke Municipal? (See Figure 71.)

1—Arrival at 1,540 ft. on the glide slope.
2—Arrival at 1.0 DME on the LDA course.
3—Time expired for distance from OM to MAP.
4—Time expired for distance from CLAMM Intersection to MAP.

7794. What are the procedure turn restrictions on the LDA RWY 5 approach at Roanoke Municipal? (See Figure 71.)

1—Remain within 10 nautical miles of CALLAHAN NDB and on the north side of the approach course.
2—Remain within 10 nautical miles of the airport on the north side of the approach course.
3—Remain within 10 nautical miles of the outer marker on the north side of the approach course.
4—It must be executed between DIXXY Intersection and the 10 nautical miles ring.

7795. At what minimum altitude should you cross CLAMM Intersection during the S–LDA 5 approach at Roanoke Municipal? (See Figure 71.)

1—4200.
2—4167.
3—2800.
4—5000.

7796. How does an LDA facility, such as the one at Roanoke Municipal, differ from a standard ILS approach facility? (See Figure 71.)

1—The LOC is wider.
2—The GS is 3° or steeper.
3—The LOC is offset from the runway.
4—The GS is unusable beyond the MM.

7797. What action should be taken if you are unable to identify SKIRT OM during an S–LDA 5 approach at Roanoke Municipal? (See Figure 71.)

1—Advise ATC, but continue the approach as depicted.
2—Advise ATC, and request the MM to be identified by radar.
3—Change the MDA to 2800.
4—Abandon the approach and request another attempt.

7798. Aircraft approach categories are based on

1—certificated approach speed at maximum gross weight.
2—1.3 times the stall speed in landing configuration at maximum gross landing weight.
3—the aircraft's normal circling approach speed.
4—1.3 times the stall speed at maximum gross weight.

7799. What is the landing minimum for a helicopter on the straight–in LDA/GS RWY 5 approach at Roanoke Municipal? (See Figure 71.)

1—1/2 mi.
2—1740 and 1 mi.
3—1540 and 1 mi.
4—365 and 1/2 mi.

7800. Between CLAMM Intersection and SKIRT OM, a pilot of a helicopter is advised that the visibility is 3/4 mi. If, upon arrival at the MDA and expiration of required time, the runway is in sight, what action is appropriate? (See Figure 71.)

1—A missed approach must be initiated because the landing minimum is 1 mi.
2—A landing may be made because the landing visibility minimum for helicopters is 1/2 mi.
3—The pilot may descend below the MDA but may not land since the visibility is below helicopter minimums.
4—The pilot may not land because the visibility is less than one–half the circling minimums.

7801. An airplane may use the COPTER VOR 241° Instrument Approach Procedure Chart (See Figure 72.)

1—under no circumstances.
2—by applying the listed MDA and increasing the listed visibility by 50 percent.
3—by increasing both the listed MDA and visibility by 50 percent.
4—if equipped with airborne radar.

7802. The procedure turn area for the COPTER VOR 241 approach is (see Figure 72)

1—10 nautical miles.
2—10 statute miles.
3—5 nautical miles.
4—5 statute miles.

7803. The instrument approach criteria for helicopters are based on airspeeds not exceeding

1—70 knots.
2—80 knots.
3—90 knots.
4—100 knots.

7804. FAA Deletion.

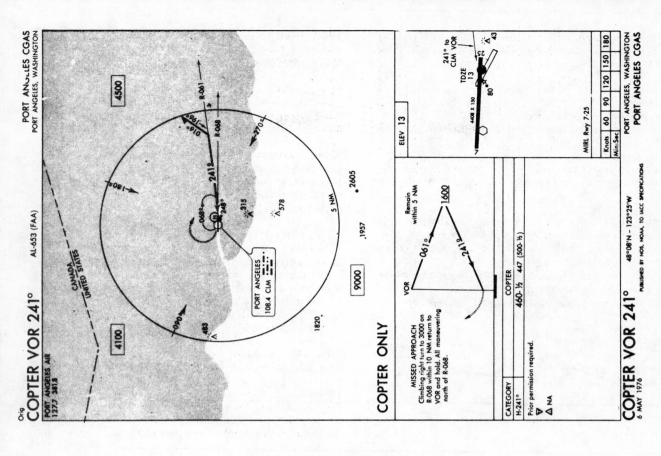

COPTER VOR 241°

Orig

PORT ANGELES CGAS
PORT ANGELES, WASHINGTON

AL-653 (FAA)

PORT ANGELES AIR
127.7 381.8

4500

4100

9000

CANADA
UNITED STATES

PORT ANGELES
108.4 CLM

5 NM

ELEV 13

241° to
CLM VOR

TDZE
13

4408 X 150

7

MIRL Rwy 7-25

Knots	60	90	120	150	180
Min-Sec					

COPTER ONLY

MISSED APPROACH
Climbing right turn to 3000 on
R-068 within 10 NM return to
VOR and hold. All maneuvering
north of R-068.

Remain
within 5 NM

1600

061°

241°

VOR

COPTER

CATEGORY		
H-241°	460-½	447 (500-½)
Prior permission required.		
△ NA		

COPTER VOR 241°

6 MAY 1976

48°08'N – 123°25'W
PUBLISHED BY NOS, NOAA, TO IACC SPECIFICATIONS

PORT ANGELES, WASHINGTON
PORT ANGELES CGAS

Figure 72

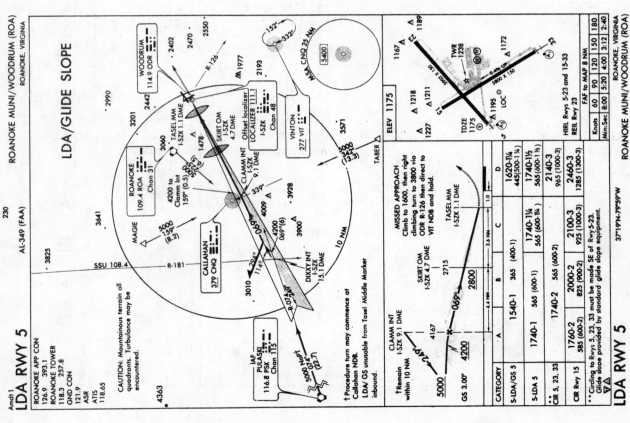

LDA RWY 5

Amdt 1

230

ROANOKE MUNI/WOODRUM (ROA)
ROANOKE, VIRGINIA

AL-349 (FAA)

ROANOKE APP CON
126.9   393.1
ROANOKE TOWER
118.3   257.8
GND CON
121.9
ASR
ATIS
118.65

LDA/GLIDE SLOPE

CAUTION: Mountainous terrain all
quadrants. Turbulence may be
encountered.

WOODRUM
114.9 ODR

R-126

SKIRT OM
I-SZK
4.7 DME

Offset localizer
LOCALIZER 111.1
I-SZK
Chan 48

VINTON
277 VIT

ROANOKE
109.4 ROA
Chan 31

TASEL MM
I-SZK 1.1 DME

CLAMM INT
I-SZK
9.1 DME

4200 to
Clamm Int
15° (0.5)

MAGIE

5000
15°
(8.2)

4200
069°(6)

CALLAHAN
379 CNQ

DIXXY INT
I-SZK
15.1 DME

R-181

SSU 108.4

R-071

IAF
PULASKI
116.8 PSK
Chan 115

5000 NoPT
071°
(22.7)

5000
071°

4167

114°

292°

CLAMM INT
I-SZK 9.1 DME

4200

069°

2800

SKIRT OM
I-SZK 4.7 DME

2715

TASEL MM
I-SZK 1.1 DME

MISSED APPROACH
Climb to 1600, then right
climbing turn to 3800 via
ODR R-126 then direct to
VIT NDB and hold.

ELEV 1175

1167

1218   1189

TWR
1238

1211   1172

TDZE
1175

LOC

Knots	60	90	120	150	180
Min-Sec	8:00	5:20	4:00	3:12	2:40

HIRL Rwys 5-23 and 15-33
REIL Rwy 23

FAF to MAP 8 NM

† Procedure turn may commence at
Callahan NDB.
LDA/GS unusable from Tasel Middle Marker
inbound.

† Remain
within 10 NM

GS 3.00°

CATEGORY	A	B	C	D
S-LDA/GS 5		1540-1 365 (400-1)		1620-1¼ 445 (500-1¼)
S-LDA 5	1740-1 565 (600-1)		1740-1¼ 565 (600-1¼)	1740-1½ 565 (600-1½)
CIR 5, 23, 33	1740-2 565 (600-2)		2140-3 965 (1000-3)	
CIR Rwy 15	1760-2 585 (600-2)	2000-2 825 (900-2)	2100-3 925 (1000-3)	2460-3 1285 (1300-3)

** Circling to Rwys 5, 23, 33 must be made SE of Rwy 5-23.
* Circling to Rwys 5-23, glide slope provided by standard glide slope equipment.

LDA RWY 5

37°19'N-79°59'W

ROANOKE, VIRGINIA
ROANOKE MUNI/WOODRUM (ROA)

Figure 71

137

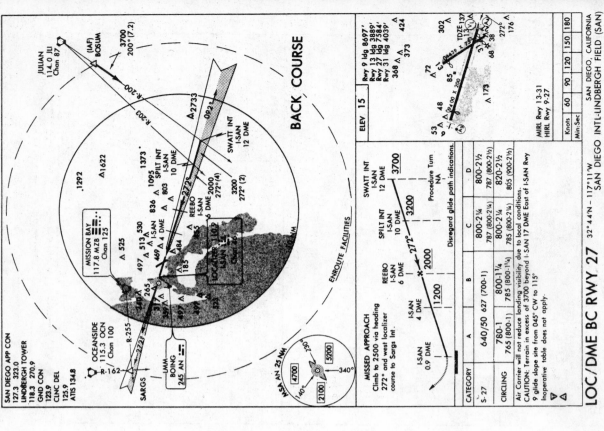

Amdt 5
LOC/DME BC RWY 27
AL-373 (FAA)   314   SAN DIEGO INTL-LINDBERGH FIELD (SAN)
SAN DIEGO, CALIFORNIA

SAN DIEGO APP CON
127.3   323.0
LINDBERGH TOWER
118.3   270.9
GND CON
123.9
CLNC DEL
125.9
ATIS 134.8

BACK COURSE

MISSED APPROACH
Climb to 2500 via heading 272° and west localizer course to Sargs Int.

Disregard glide path indications.

	SWATT INT I-SAN 12 DME			3700	
	SPILT INT I-SAN 10 DME		272°	3200	Procedure Turn NA
REEBO I-SAN 6 DME		X	2000		
	I-SAN 4 DME	1200			
I-SAN 0.9 DME					

CATEGORY	A	B	C	D
S-27	640/50 627 (700-1)		800-2¼ 787 (800-2¼)	800-2½ 787 (800-2½)
	780-1 765 (800-1)	800-1¼ 785 (800-1¼)	800-2¼ 785 (800-2¼)	820-2½ 805 (900-2½)
CIRCLING				

Air Carrier will not reduce landing visibility due to local conditions.
CAUTION: Terrain in excess of 3700 beyond I-SAN 17 DME East of I-SAN Rwy
9 glide slope site from 045° CW to 115°
Inoperative table does not apply.

ELEV 15

Rwy 9 ldg 8697'
Rwy 13 ldg 3889'
Rwy 27 ldg 7584'
Rwy 31 ldg 4039'

MIRL Rwy 13-31
HIRL Rwy 9-27

Knots	60	90	120	150	180
Min:Sec					

LOC/DME BC RWY 27
32°44'N – 117°11'W   SAN DIEGO, CALIFORNIA
SAN DIEGO INTL-LINDBERGH FIELD (SAN)

Figure 74

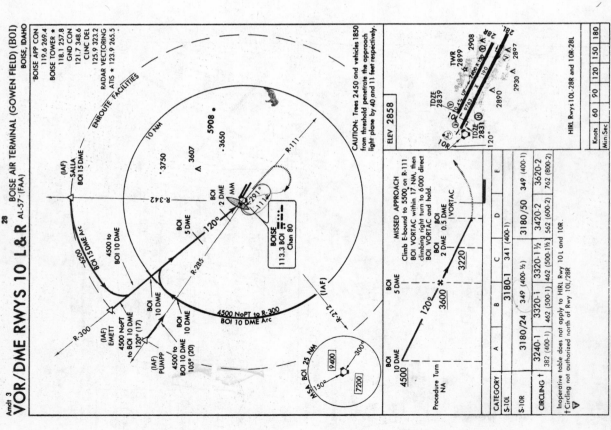

Amdt 3
VOR/DME RWYS 10 L & R
AL-57 (FAA)   28   BOISE AIR TERMINAL (GOWEN FIELD) (BOI)
BOISE, IDAHO

BOISE APP CON
119.6 269.4
BOISE TOWER ★
118.1 257.8
GND CON
121.7 348.6
CLNC DEL
125.9 323.2
RADAR VECTORING
ATIS ★ 123.9 265.5

ENROUTE FACILITIES

BOISE
113.3 BOI
Chan 80

CAUTION: Trees 2450 and vehicles 1850
from threshold penetrate the approach
light plane by 40 and 11 feet respectively.

MISSED APPROACH
Climb E-bound to 5500 on R-111
BOI VORTAC within 17 NM, then
climbing right turn to 6000 direct
BOI VORTAC and hold.

BOI 5 DME					3220	
	BOI 2 DME	BOI 0.5 DME I-VORTAC				
120°	X	3600				
BOI 10 DME					4500	Procedure Turn NA

ELEV 2858

CATEGORY	A	B	C	D	E
S-10L	3180-1		3320-1½ 341 (400-1)	3180-1	3620-1 349 (400-1)
S-10R	3180/24 349	3320-1 349	3320-1½ 462 (500-1½)	3420-2 562 (600-2)	3620-2 762 (800-2)
CIRCLING †	3240-1 382 (400-1)	3320-1 462 (500-1)	3320-1½ 462 (500-1½)		

Inoperative table does not apply to HIRL Rwy 10L and 10R.
† Circling not authorized north of Rwy 10L/28R.

VOR/DME RWYS 10 L & R
43°34'N-116°14'W   BOISE, IDAHO
BOISE AIR TERMINAL (GOWEN FIELD) (BOI)

Figure 73

138

7805. Between which radials from the VORTAC is the minimum safe altitude of 7200 established at Boise Air Terminal? (See Figure 73.)

1—212 to 342.
2—120 to 330.
3—150 to 300.
4—212 to 300.

7806. What is the HAT for the VOR/DME RWY 10R at Boise Air Terminal? (See Figure 73.)

1—341.
2—349.
3—382.
4—400.

7807. What is the MDA and landing minimum for a helicopter with a DME and one VOR receiver, if cleared for a straight–in approach, to Rwy 10R at Boise Air Terminal? (See Figure 73.)

1—3180 and 1 mi.
2—400 and 1/2 mi.
3—349 and RVR 24.
4—3180 and RVR 12.

7808. What type entry is recommended for the missed approach holding pattern at Boise Air Terminal? (See Figure 73.)

1—Direct only.
2—Teardrop only.
3—Parallel only.
4—Teardrop or parallel.

7809. How should the missed approach point be identified on the straight–in Rwy 10L approach at Boise Air Terminal? (See Figure 73.)

1—0.5 DME indication.
2—TO/FROM reversal on VOR indication.
3—Timing from FAF to MAP.
4—Arrival at 3180 on glidepath.

7810. What weather minimums must be forecast to list Boise Air Terminal as an alternate airport on an IFR flight plan if you intend to utilize the VOR/DME RWYS 10L and R approach? (See Figure 73.)

1—600 ft. and 2 mi.
2—800 ft. and 2 mi.
3—1,000 ft. and 1 mi.
4—Those shown in the IFR Alternate Minimums Section.

7811. When is radar service automatically terminated during the LOC/DME BC RWY 27 approach at Lindbergh Field? (See Figure 74.)

1—When the pilot is instructed to contact Lindbergh Tower.
2—Over the FAF (REEBO Intersection).
3—When the landing is completed or the tower controller has the aircraft in sight, whichever occurs first.
4—When established on the final approach leg at SWATT Intersection.

7812. Which descent procedures should be used when cleared for VOR/DME RWYS 10L and R circling approach, if you start the approach at SALLA Intersection? (See Figure 73.)

1—Descend to 6200 to cross SALLA, to 4500 in the turn to R–300, to 3600 after 10 DME, to 3220 after the FAF, and to 3180 after 2 DME to the MAP.
2—Descend to 6200 after crossing SALLA, to 4500 in the turn to R–300, to 3600 after 10 DME, to 3220 after the FAF, and to 3180 after 2 DME to the MAP.
3—Descend to 6200 to cross SALLA, to 4500 in the turn to R–300, to 3600 after 10 DME, and to 3240 after the FAF to the MAP.
4—Descend to 6200 after crossing SALLA, to 4500 after established on R–300, to 3600 after 10 DME, and to 3240 after the FAF to the MAP.

7813. At San Diego Intl.–Lindbergh Field, the reported weather is W7X1/2F. Do regulations permit you to make a straight–in LOC/DME BC RWY 27 approach and landing in a helicopter? (See Figure 74.)

1—Yes; you may reduce the visibility prescribed for Category A airplanes by 50 percent.
2—No; the reported ceiling meets the helicopter minimums but the visibility does not.
3—Yes; the only requirement for a helicopter is a 200–foot ceiling and sufficient forward visibility for a safe flight.
4—No; neither the ceiling nor visibility meet the required minimums.

7814. How should the pilot determine the MAP on a straight–in LOC/DME BC RWY 27 at Lindbergh Field? (See Figure 74.)

1—Calculate the time that should expire for 5.1 nautical miles from the FAF to MAP.
2—When arriving at 640 ft. on the LOC path.
3—Upon receiving a 0.9 nautical mile indication on I–SAN DME.
4—Upon receiving a TO/FROM reversal from I–SAN.

7815. You have been cleared for the LOC/DME BC RWY 27 approach at Lindbergh Field from BOSUM Intersection. What is your relationship to SWATT Intersection? (See Figures 74 and 75.)

1—West of JLI R–200 and north of LOC course.
2—East of JLI R–200 and north of LOC course.
3—West of JLI R–200 and south of LOC course.
4—East of JLI R–200 and south of LOC course.

 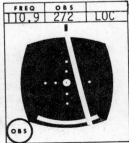

Figure 75

7816. Which indication is acceptable for an operational check of the VOR system at CANNON International? (See Figures 76 and 78.)

1—a.
2—b.
3—c.
4—d.

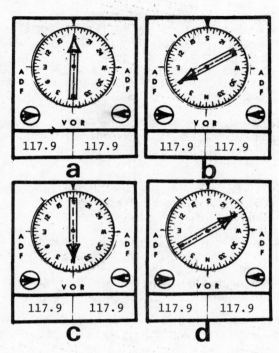

Figure 76

7817. What is your relationship to the ILS LOC, G/S, and SPARKS NDB? (See Figures 77 and 78.)

1—Left of course, above G/S, and approaching SPARKS.
2—Right of course, above G/S, and past SPARKS.
3—Left of course, below G/S, and past SPARKS.
4—Right of course, below G/S, and approaching SPARKS.

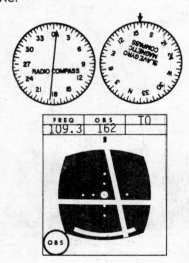

Figure 77

7818. What minimum altitudes are effective for the ILS–A approach at Cannon International if cleared for the approach over RNO VORTAC? (See Figure 78.)

1—Last assigned altitude to SPARKS NDB, 9000 to the start of the procedure turn, 8500 to G/S intercept, and then maintain G/S to 5400.
2—Last assigned altitude to SPARKS NDB, 9000 to LOC intercept inbound, 8500 to G/S intercept, and then maintain G/S to 5400.
3—9000 to SPARKS NDB, 8500 to G/S intercept via the procedure turn, and then maintain G/S to 5400.
4—9000 to completing the procedure turn and inbound on course, 8500 to G/S intercept, and then maintain G/S to 5400.

7819. How may a pilot receive the Transcribed Weather Broadcast at Reno? (See Figure 78.)

1—By telephone, (702) 785 – 3000.
2—By radio on 125.8 MHz.
3—By radio on 117.9 MHz or 254 kHz.
4—By radio on 122.0 MHz.

7820. When should the pilot intitiate the missed approach procedure when making the ILS–A approach at Cannon International? (See Figure 78.)

1—Upon arrival at the LMM if the required visual references have not been established.
2—When time has expired from the FAF to MAP.
3—Upon arrival at the MDA.
4—When over the runway threshold.

7821. What is the procedure for the ILS–A if cleared for the approach at PYRAM Intersection? (See Figure 78.)

1—Intercept the LOC course with a 180° heading and continue on the inbound course to the MDA.
2—Fly 180° heading to the point indicated and execute the procedure turn, then continue straight–in to the MDA.
3—Fly 180° heading to LOC/GS intercept and continue on the glide slope to the LMM.
4—Fly 180° heading to WARMM Intersection, LOC course to WAGGE Intersection for course reversal, LOC course to procedure turn, and then straight–in to the LMM.

7822. What action should you take if you complete the ILS–A approach to the LMM, have received clearance to land on Rwy 16, have the necessary visual references and flight visibility, and are in a position from which descent to a landing can be made at a normal rate of descent? (See Figure 78.)

1—You must circle to land because a straight–in approach and landing is not authorized in this procedure.
2—You should continue straight ahead and land without further clearance.
3—You should make a circling approach and land on Rwy 16.
4—You should inform the tower that you will turn right and land on Rwy 7.

VOR RECEIVER CHECK POINTS

Facility Name (Arpt Name)	Fred/Ident	Type Check Pt. Gnd. AB/ALT	Azimuth from Fac. Mag	Dist. from Fac. N.M.	Check Point Description
Elko (Elko Muni-J.C. Harris Fld)	114.5/EKO	A/6100	324	4.1	Over the center field taxiway intersection.
Ely (Ely Arpt/Yelland Fld)	110.6/ELY	G	060		On southside twy leading to passenger terminal area.
Las Vegas (McCarran Intl)	116.9/LAS	G	351	9	On taxiway W between rwy 19L and taxiway D.
Reno (Cannon Intl)	117.9/RNO	G	229	5.8	On A.S.I. ramp at taxiway
Reno (Reno/Stead)	117.9/RNO	A/7000	291	5.5	Northwest end taxiway A
Wells (Harriet Field)	114.2/LWL	A/6300	112	14.0	Over approach end rwy 08.

SAN FRANCISCO H-1A, L-5A, 7A IAP

RENO

§ **CANNON INTL** (RNO) 3.4 SE GMT—8(—7DT) 39°29'52"N 119°46'04"W **SAN FRANCISCO** H-1A, L-5A, 7A IAP
4412 B S4 FUEL 80, 100, 100LL, JET A1 + OX 1, 2, 3, 4
TPA—See Remarks LRA CFR Index C
RWY 16-34: H9000X150 (CONC-GRVD) S-75, D-185, DT-350 HIRL
RWY 16: ALSF1. VAS(V4L)—GA 3.0° TCH 61.84'. RWY 34: VAS(V4L)—GA 2.75° TCH 19'.
RWY 07-25: H6101X150 (ASPH) S-60, D-170, DT-260 MIRL
RWY 07: REIL. Pole. RWY 25: REIL.
AIRPORT REMARKS: Attended continuously. Migratory waterfowl concentrated N of rwy 25 and E of rwy 16. Runway 34 VASI not to be used beyond 6 NM due to high terrain. Rwy C and G maximum gross weight limit 12,500 lbs. Access to Butler Aviation shall be via taxiway D, prior permission required from Butler for aircraft over 12,500 lbs, traffic controlled by Butler signalman. TPA— 5212(800) single engine, 5412(1000) larger/high performance acft. Noise sensitive area all quadrants. Pilots of turbojet aircraft use recommended noise abatement procedures, available on request. Pilots of non-turbojet aircraft use best abatement procedures and settings. Avoid as much as feasible flying over populated areas. Practice approaches or landings by turbojet aircraft discouraged. Flight Notification Service (ADCUS) available.
COMMUNICATIONS: ATIS 125.8 UNICOM 122.95
® **RENO FSS** (RNO) on fld. 122.5 122.35 122.2 122.1R 117.9T (702) 785-3000
® **RENO APP CON** 119.2 (West) 120.8 (East) 128.2 **CLNC DEL** 124.9
RENO TOWER 118.7 **GND CON** 121.9
® **RENO DEP CON** 126.3
STAGE III SVC Acft monitor ATIS 25 NM out for frequency assignment
RADIO AIDS TO NAVIGATION:
RENO (H) ABVORTAC 117.9 **RNO** Chan 126 39°31'53"N 119°39'18"W 237° 5.5 NM to fld.
  5940/18E. Route forecast only 0600-1300Zt.
SPARKS NDB (H-SAB) 254 **SPK** 39°41'48"N 119°46'06"W 162° 11.2 NM to fld
  Route forecast only 0600-1300Zt.
ILS/DME 109.3 I-RNO Chan 30 Rwy 16 LMM 351 NO
ASR

INSTRUMENT APPROACH PROCEDURES (CHARTS)

⚠ IFR ALTERNATE MINIMUMS

AIRPORT NAME	ALTERNATE MINIMUMS
CANNON INTL Reno, Nevada	ILS-A, 1400-2
	LOC-C, 1200-2
	LOC/DME (BC)-B, 1400-2
	RADAR-1, 2000-2*
	VOR-D, 2000-2
	ILS DME Rwy 16, 1400-2
	NDB Rwy 16, 1700-3

*Category E, 2200-2

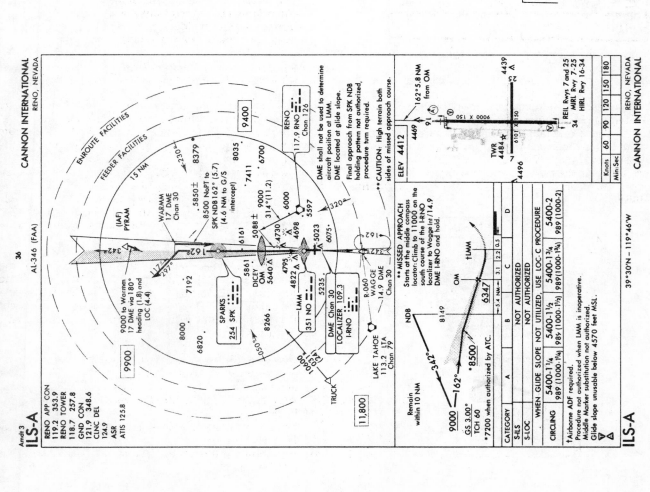

Amdt 3
ILS-A 36 AL-346 (FAA)

CANNON INTERNATIONAL
RENO, NEVADA

RENO APP CON 119.2 353.9
RENO TOWER 118.7 257.8
GND CON 121.9 348.6
CLNC DEL 124.9
ASR
ATIS 125.8

39°30'N - 119°46'W

CANNON INTERNATIONAL
RENO, NEVADA

ILS-A

Figure 78

141

7823. During an en route descent in a fixed thrust–and–pitch attitude conditions, both the ram air input and drain hole become completely blocked by ice. What airspeed indication can be expected?

1—Increase in indicated airspeed.
2—Indicated airspeed decreases to zero and remains at that value until the blockage is removed.
3—Decrease in indicated airspeed.
4—Indicated airspeed remains the same as it was prior to blockage.

7824. RVR minimums for takeoff or landing are prescribed in an instrument approach procedure, but RVR is inoperative and cannot be reported for the intended runway at the time. Which of the following would be correct?

1—RVR minimums which are specified in the procedures should be converted and applied as ground visibility.
2—RVR minimums may be disregarded, providing the runway has an operative HIRL system.
3—RVR minimums may be disregarded, providing all other components of the ILS system are operative.
4—RVR minimums may be disregarded, providing the pilot does not descend below the highest MDA listed for that approach procedure.

7825. When being radar vectored for an ILS approach, at what point may you start a descent from your last assigned altitude to a lower minimum altitude if cleared for the approach?

1—You may descend immediately to the procedure turn altitude.
2—When established on a segment of a published route or instrument approach procedure.
3—You may descend immediately to published glide slope interception altitude.
4—Only after you are established on the final approach unless informed otherwise by ATC.

7826. Which lighting aid, if inoperative, requires an increase in visibility on all instrument approaches?

1—Runway end identifier lights.
2—High–intensity runway lights.
3—Touchdown zone lights.
4—Approach light system.

7827. Which position is indicated by the instrument illustrations shown in Figure 79, when making the LOC/DME BC RWY 17R approach at Stapleton International? (See Figure 80.)

1—West of course and 12.0 mi. from DEN VORTAC.
2—West of course and 12.2 mi. from the runway threshold.
3—East of course and 11.2 mi. from the Middle Marker.
4—East of course and 12.2 mi. from the runway threshold.

7828. What are the minimum altitudes for the LOC/DME BC RWY 17R approach at Stapleton International if the approach is started at JASIN Intersection? (See Figure 80.)

1—10000 to lead radial; 9500 to localizer; 9000 to 13 DME fix; 7000 to 5.7 DME fix; MDA 5580.
2—10000 to DEN R–344; 9500 to localizer course; 9000 to 13 DME fix; 7000 to TOT fix; MDA 5580.
3—10000 to DEN R–338; 9500 to DEN R–344; 9000 to 13 DME fix; 7000 to 5.7 DME fix; MDA 5580.
4—10000 to DEN R–338; 9500 to DEN R–344; 9000 until on localizer; 7000 to Thornton NDB; MDA 5880.

7829. Which approach and tower frequencies are appropriate if you are approaching Stapleton International from the north and are cleared for the LOC/DME BC RWY 17R approach? (See Figure 80.)

1—120.8 and 118.3.
2—120.8 and 119.5.
3—120.5 and 118.3.
4—120.5 and 119.5.

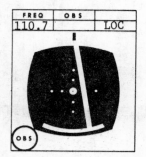

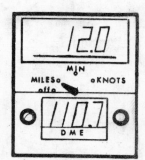

Figure 79

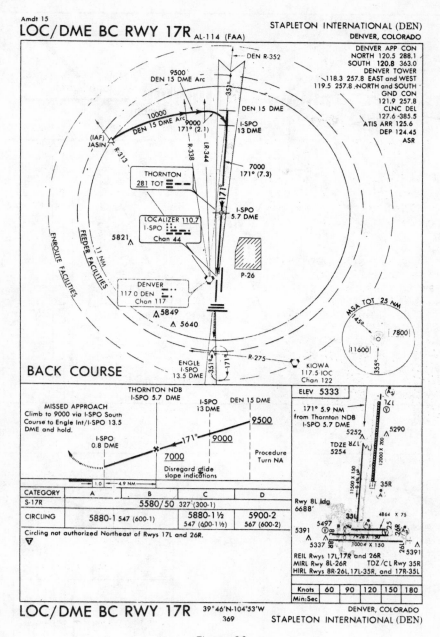

Figure 80

7830. What is the landing minimum if you are cleared for the S–17R LOC/DME BC approach at Stapleton International? (See Figure 80.)

1—5,000 RVR.
2—300–foot ceiling and 1 mi. visibility.
3—327–foot ceiling and 1 mi. visibility.
4—300–foot ceiling and 5,000 ft. visibility.

7831. What is the Category B HAA for the LOC/DME BC RWY 17R approach at Stapleton International? (See Figure 80.)

1—600.
2—626.
3—547.
4—327.

7832. What are the alternate minimums for the LOC/DME BC RWY 17R approach at Stapleton International? (See Figure 80.)

1—800–2.
2—600–2.
3—Nonstandard.
4—Not authorized.

7833. What minimum equipment, in addition to voice communications, is required to make the LOC/DME BC RWY 17R approach at Stapleton International? (Group II TCA) (See Figure 80.)

1—Transponder with no altitude, VOR/LOC, and DME.
2—VOR/LOC, ADF, and DME.
3—DME, transponder with altitude, VOR/LOC, and Marker Beacon.
4—VOR/LOC, ADF, DME, and transponder with altitude.

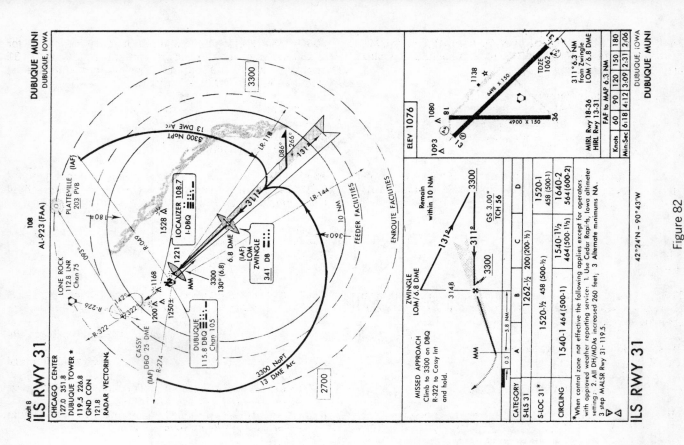

Amdt 8
ILS RWY 31

DUBUQUE MUNI
DUBUQUE, IOWA

108
AL-923 (FAA)

CHICAGO CENTER
127.0 351.7
DUBUQUE TOWER ★
119.5 226.8
GND CON
121.8
RADAR VECTORING

LONE ROCK
112.8 LNR
Chan 75

PLATTEVILLE (IAF)
203 PVB

3300

3300 NoPT
13 DME Arc

LOCALIZER 108.7
I-DBQ

1528 ∧

1221
6.8 DME

ZWINGLE
341 DB

(IAF)
LOM

1168 ∧
1200 ∧
1250 ±

3300
130° (6.8)

MM

DUBUQUE
115.8 DBQ
Chan 105

CASSY
(IAF) DBQ 25 DME

3300 NoPT
13 DME Arc

FEEDER FACILITIES

ENROUTE FACILITIES

10 NM

2700

MISSED APPROACH
Climb to 3300 on DBQ
R-322 to Cassy Int
and hold.

ZWINGLE
LOM / 6.8 DME

Remain
within 10 NM

3300

131°

311°

3300

GS 3.00°
TCH 56

3148

MM

5.8 NM

0.5

CATEGORY	A	B	C	D
S-ILS 31		1262-½ 200 (200-½)		1520-1 458 (500-1)
S-LOC 31*	1520-½ 458 (500-½)		1540-1½ 464 (500-1½)	1640-2 564 (600-2)
CIRCLING	1540-1 464 (500-1)		1540-1½ 464 (500-1½)	1640-2 564 (600-2)

*When control zone not effective the following applies except for operators
with approved weather reporting service: 1. Use Cedar Rapids, Iowa altimeter
setting; 2. All DH/MDAs increased 260 feet; 3 Alternate minimums NA.
3 step MALSR Rwy 31-119.5.

ELEV 1076

311°-6.3 NM
from Zwingle
LOM / 6.8 DME

TDZE
1062

1138 ☆

1080
∧ 81

1093
∧

4900 X 150

6498 X 150

	Knots	60	90	120	150	180
FAF to MAP 6.3 NM	Min:Sec	6:18	4:12	3:09	2:31	2:06

MIRL Rwy 18-36
HIRL Rwy 13-31

DUBUQUE, IOWA
DUBUQUE MUNI

ILS RWY 31   42°24'N – 90°43'W

Figure 82

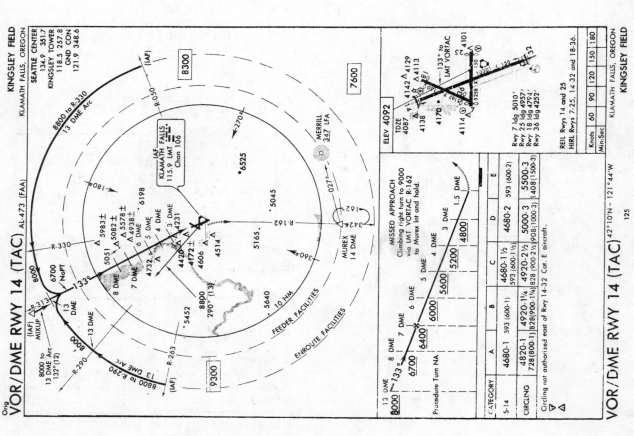

Orig
VOR/DME RWY 14 (TAC) AL-473 (FAA)

KINGSLEY FIELD
KLAMATH FALLS, OREGON

SEATTLE CENTER
134.9 351.7
KINGSLEY TOWER
118.5 257.8
GND CON
121.9 348.6

8300

8800 to R-330
13 DME Arc

(IAF)

R-050

KLAMATH
FALLS
115.9 LMT
Chan 106

IAF

7600

MERRILL
247 LFA

6525

6198

5045

5983±
5082±
5578±
4938±
4231
4514

6 DME
5 DME
4 DME
3 DME

R-162

5051

R-330

4732±
4420±
4606
4172±

6700
NoPT
133°

8 DME
7 DME

8890 (13)

290° (13)

MUREX
14 DME

342°

027°

180°

270°

360°

162°

5165.

5640

10 NM

FEEDER FACILITIES

ENROUTE FACILITIES

(IAF)
MIXUP
R-313

8000
6700

8000
13 DME

13 DME Arc

8800 to R-290
R-290

R-263

8800 to R-290
13 DME Arc
132° (12)

9300

8000
133°
6700

(IAF)

MISSED APPROACH
Climbing right turn to 9000
via LMT VORTAC R-162
to Murex Int and hold.

9000

1.5 DME

133° to
LMT VORTAC

4800

3 DME

4 DME

5200

5 DME

5600

6 DME

6000

7 DME

6400

8 DME

6700

13 DME

Procedure Turn NA

CATEGORY	A	B	C	D	E
S-14	4680-1 593 (600-1)		4680-1½ 593 (600-1½)	4680-2 593 (600-2)	5500-3 1408 (1500-3)
CIRCLING	4820-1 728 (800-1)	4920-1¼ 828 (900-1¼)	4920-2½ 828 (900-2½)	5000-3 908 (1000-3)	5500-3 1408 (1500-3)

Circling not authorized east of Rwy 14-32 Cat. E aircraft.

ELEV 4092

TDZE
4087

4092

4142 ∧ 4129
4113

4138

4170

4114

4101

133° to
LMT VORTAC

14

32

Rwy 7 ldg 5010'
Rwy 25 ldg 4957'
Rwy 18 ldg 4754'
Rwy 36 ldg 4252'

REIL Rwys 14 and 25
HIRL Rwys 7-25, 14-32 and 18-36.

	Knots	60	90	120	150	180
	Min:Sec					

KLAMATH FALLS, OREGON
KINGSLEY FIELD

VOR/DME RWY 14 (TAC) 42°10'N – 121°44'W

125

Figure 81

7834. What is the function of R–290 and R–330 of LMT VORTAC on the VOR/DME RWY 14 approach at Kingsley Field? (See Figure 81.)

1—Lead–in radials for either DME arc.
2—They form fixes for MEA changes.
3—Both radials are procedural tracks.
4—They outline protected airspace for the final approach course.

7835. What is the minimum visibility for a helicopter landing when making the VOR/DME RWY 14 approach? (See Figure 81.)

1—1/4 mi.
2—1/2 mi.
3—3/4 mi.
4—1 mi.

7836. Where is the missed approach point during a straight–in VOR/DME RWY 14 approach at Kingsley Field? (See Figure 81.)

1—At 4680 on the simulated glidepath.
2—At the 1.5 DME fix.
3—7 nautical miles from the FAF.
4—1.5 DME mi. from the runway threshold.

7837. What is the touchdown zone elevation for the VOR/DME RWY 14 approach at Kingsley Field? (See Figure 81.)

1—4087.
2—4092.
3—4133.
4—4142.

7838. What procedure should you use if you are cleared for another attempt of the VOR/DME RWY 14 approach from the missed approach holding pattern? (See Figure 81.)

1—Intercept the 13 DME arc and proceed to either IAF at or above the minimum sector altitude, then continue the approach as depicted.
2—Proceed inbound on the R–162 to the LMT VORTAC and fly outbound on the R–313 for a procedure turn between the 8 DME fix and the 13 DME fix.
3—Proceed inbound on the R–162 to the LMT VORTAC; fly outbound on the R–290 to intercept the 13 DME arc; then continue the approach as depicted.
4—There is no established procedure. ATC will furnish appropriate heading or instructions to initiate the approach.

7839. Where should a missed approach be initiated for the ILS RWY 31 at Dubuque Municipal? (See Figure 82.)

1—At 1262 on the glide slope.
2—At the MM.
3—At 6.3 nautical miles past the FAF.
4—Over the runway threshold.

7840. What are the approach and landing minimums for a Category A aircraft on a straight–in ILS RWY 31 approach when the control zone is not effective at Dubuque Municipal? (See Figure 82.)

1—DH 1262; visibility 1/2 mi.
2—DH 1262; visibility 1 mi.
3—DH 1522; visibility 1/2 mi.
4—DH 1522; visibility 1 mi.

7841. What are the DH and landing minimums for a helicopter when making the ILS RWY 31 approach at Dubuque Municipal? (See Figure 82.)

1—DH 1522; visibility 1/4 mi.
2—DH 1262; visibility 1/2 mi.
3—DH 1262; visibility 1/4 mi.
4—DH 1540; visibility 1/2 mi.

7842. What are the procedure turn restrictions for the ILS RWY 31 approach at Dubuque Municipal? (See Figure 82.)

1—Remain inside the 13 DME arc and east of the approach course.
2—Remain between the 13 DME arc and the 10 nautical miles inner ring.
3—Remain between ZWINGLE LOM and the 10 nautical miles ring on the east side of the approach course.
4—Remain within 10 nautical miles of ZWINGLE LOM on either side of the approach course.

7843. Which RMI indication shown in Figure 83 should you receive when at proper position to start the turn outbound in the missed approach holding pattern? (See Figure 82.)

1—W.
2—X.
3—Y.
4—Z.

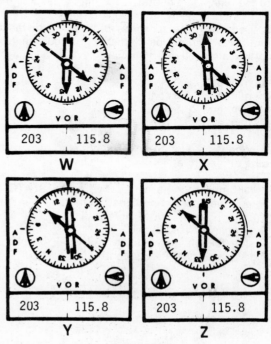

Figure 83

145

7844. While flying a 3° glide slope, a headwind shears to a tailwind. Which conditions should the pilot expect?

1—Airspeed and pitch attitude decrease and there is a tendency to go below glide slope.
2—Airspeed and pitch attitude increase and there is a tendency to go below glide slope.
3—Airspeed and pitch attitude increase and there is a tendency to go above glide slope.
4—Airspeed and pitch attitude decrease and there is a tendency to go above glide slope.

7845. If both the ram air input and drain hole of the pitot system are blocked, what airspeed indication can be expected?

1—No variation of indicated airspeed in level flight even if large power changes are made.
2—Decrease of indicated airspeed during a climb.
3—Constant indicated airspeed during a descent.
4—Zero indicated airspeed until blockage is removed.

7846. What wind condition prolongs the hazards of wake turbulence on a landing runway for the longest period of time?

1—Direct headwind.
2—Direct tailwind.
3—Light quartering tailwind.
4—Light quartering headwind.

7847. Wake turbulence is near maximum behind a jet transport just after takeoff because

1—of gear and flap configuration at slow airspeed and maximum thrust output.
2—the engines are at maximum thrust output at slow airspeed.
3—the gear and flap configuration increases the turbulence to maximum.
4—of the high angle of attack and high gross weight.

7848. Determine the approximate time and distance to a station if a 5° wingtip bearing change occurs in 1.5 min. with a true airspeed of 95 knots.

1—11 min. and 40.0 NM.
2—16 min. and 14.3 NM.
3—18 min. and 28.5 NM.
4—18 min. and 33.0 NM.

7849. When is a pilot on an IFR flight plan responsible for avoiding other aircraft?

1—At all times when not in radar contact with ATC.
2—When weather conditions permit, regardless of whether operating under IFR or VFR.
3—Only when advised by ATC.
4—During takeoff and landing and until established on the airway if not in radar control.

7850. Which altimeter shown in Figure 84 indicates the MDA for a straight-in NDB/VOR RWY 11 approach at Walker Field? (See Figure 86.)

1—E.
2—F.
3—G.
4—H.

E   F

G   H

Figure 84

7851. After a missed approach for the NDB RWY 11 approach at Walker Field, you are cleared for another approach. If your RMI indicates as shown in Figure 85, what is your position? (See Figure 86.)

1—Approaching FRU NDB and on the final approach course.
2—Past FRU NDB and inbound on the final approach course.
3—Approaching FRU NDB and north of the final approach course.
4—Past FRU NDB and north of the final approach course.

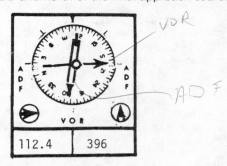

Figure 85

7852. What minimum weather conditions must exist at Walker Field for Category A or B aircraft to be cleared for a visual approach? (See Figure 86.)

1—1,000-foot ceiling and 3 mi. visibility.
2—700-foot ceiling and 3/4 mi. visibility.
3—1,000-foot ceiling and 1 mi. visibility.
4—1 mi. visibility and clear of clouds.

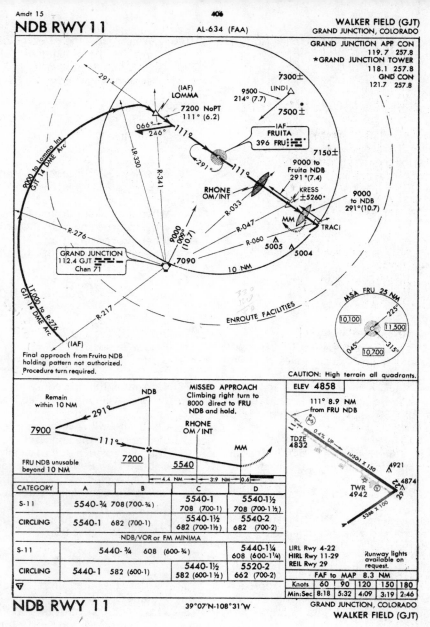

Figure 86

7853. What action should be taken if a pilot fails to identify RHONE OM/INT during the NDB RWY 11 approach at Walker Field? (See Figure 86.)

1—Advise Grand Junction Approach Control and initiate a missed approach procedure.
2—Continue the approach and use 5490 as the MDA.
3—Continue the approach and use 5540 as the MDA.
4—Continue the approach and use 5590 as the MDA.

7854. What is the function of the GJT LR–330 on the NDB RWY 11 approach at Walker Field? (See Figure 86.)

1—Limits length of the procedure turn.
2—Establishes an intermediate approach fix.
3—Serves as a lead radial to start the turn from the arc.
4—Denotes an MEA change from 9000 to 7200.

7855. FAA Deletion.

7856. What responsibility does the pilot in command of an IFR flight assume upon entering VFR conditions?

1—Advise ATC when entering VFR conditions.
2—Report VFR conditions to ARTCC so that an amended clearance may be issued.
3—Use VFR operating procedures.
4—To see and avoid other traffic.

7857. What is the position of LABER relative to the reference facility? (See Figure 87.)

1—316°; 24.3 NM.
2—177°; 5 NM.
3—177°; 10 NM.
4—198°; 8 NM.

7858. What type of entry is recommended to the missed approach holding pattern if the inbound heading is 050°? (See Figure 87.)

1—Direct only.
2—Parallel only.
3—Teardrop only.
4—Parallel or teardrop.

7859. How should the missed approach point be identified when executing the RNAV RWY 36 approach at Adams Field? (See Figure 87.)

1—When the DME indicates 1.5 mi.
2—When the TO–FROM indicator changes.
3—Upon arrival at 760 ft. on the glidepath.
4—When time has expired for 5 nautical miles past the FAF.

7860. What minimum airborne equipment is required to be operative for RNAV RWY 36 approach at Adams Field? (See Figure 87.)

1—An ADF, transponder, and approved RNAV receiver having the capability for storing at least two waypoints.
2—An approved RNAV receiver that provides both horizontal and vertical guidance.
3—A transponder and an approved RNAV receiver that provides both horizontal and vertical guidance.
4—Any approved RNAV receiver.

7861. As you approach LABER during a straight–in RNAV RWY 36 approach in a helicopter, Little Rock Approach Control advises that the ceiling is 400 ft. and the visibility is 1/4 mi. Do regulations permit you to continue the approach and land? (See Figure 87.)

1—Yes, you may disregard the reported ceiling and land if you find the visibility allows safe and proper control of the helicopter.
2—No, you may not reduce the visibility prescribed for Category A airplanes by more than 50 percent.
3—Yes, only a 1/4 mi. visibility or an RVR of 1,200 ft. is required for any approach, including RNAV.
4—No, neither the ceiling nor the visibility meet regulatory requirements.

7862. What indication should you get when it is time to turn inbound while in the procedure turn at LABER? (See Figure 87.)

1—4 min. elapsed time after completion of the turn outbound.
2—4 DME mi. from LABER.
3—10 DME mi. from the MAP.
4—12 DME mi. from LIT VORTAC.

7863. What are the helicopter MDA and visibility minimums for the straight–in SDF RWY 19 procedure at Pitt–Greenville Airport when Seymour Johnson AFB altimeter setting is used? (See Figure 88.)

1—680 and 1 mi.
2—680 and 1/2 mi.
3—540 and 1 mi.
4—540 and 1/2 mi.

7864. When is a procedure turn required for the SDF RWY 19 approach? (See Figure 88.)

1—When proceeding from TYI.
2—When proceeding from ISO only.
3—When proceeding from ZAGGY only.
4—When proceeding from either ISO or ZAGGY.

7865. What is the elapsed time from FAF to MAP if you maintain 75 knots groundspeed? (See Figure 88.)

1—3 min. 22 sec.
2—3 min. 31 sec.
3—3 min. 38 sec.
4—3 min. 46 sec.

7866. What is the procedure for closing an IFR flight plan at Pitt–Greenville Airport? (See Figure 88.)

1—Close it with approach control upon receiving clearance for the approach.
2—The flight plan is automatically closed upon landing.
3—Contact New Bern FSS after landing.
4—The flight plan will be closed automatically when ATC issues the approach clearance.

7867. What is the function of the LR–020 from ISO VORTAC? (See Figure 88.)

1—Mileage breakdown from TYI VORTAC to KENIR Intersection.
2—Divides the area into sectors with minimum safe altitudes.
3—Establishes an MRA of 1900 between its intersection with TYI R–114 and KENIR Intersection.
4—Establishes the position at which a pilot with only one VOR/LOC receiver should change from the VOR frequency to the SDF frequency.

7868. What is the MDA for a circling approach (Category C) at Pitt–Greenville when the local altimeter setting is not available? (See Figure 88.)

1—540.
2—590.
3—640.
4—680.

7869. How should a pilot indentify the MAP when making the SDF RWY 19 approach? (See Figure 88.)

1—Upon receiving Belvoir FM.
2—After 2 min. 56 sec. have elapsed with a TAS of 90 knots.
3—When 2 min. 12 sec. have elapsed after passing the FAF inbound with a GS of 120 knots.
4—When reaching 400 ft. MSL on the final approach.

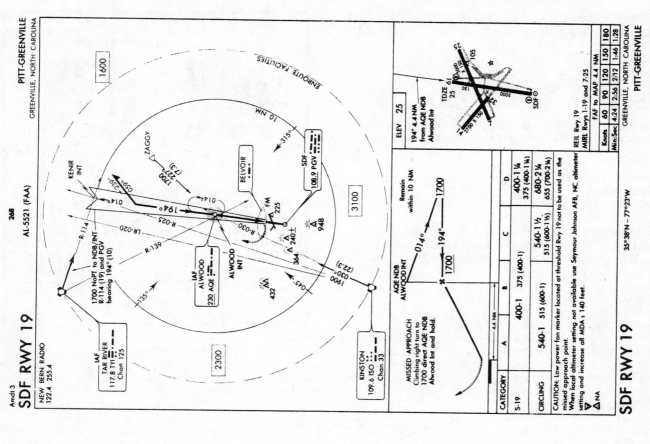

Figure 88

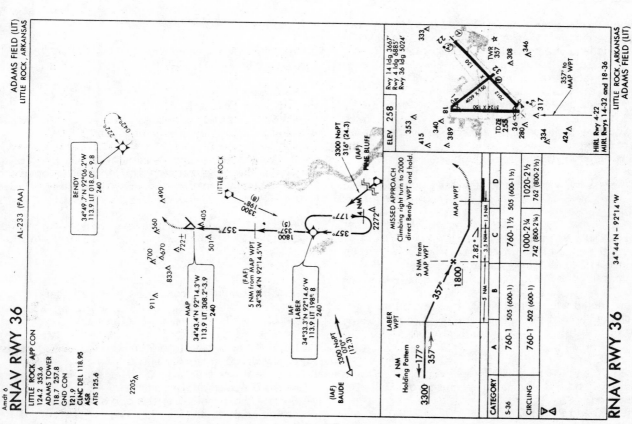

Figure 87

149

7870. Which illustrations shown in Figure 89 indicate that you are west of the localizer course and north of the LOM?

1—a and e.
2—b and e.
3—a and f.
4—b and f.

7871. Which illustrations shown in Figure 89 indicate that you are east of the localizer course and north of the LOM?

1—a and e.
2—a and f.
3—b and e.
4—b and f.

7872. Which illustrations shown in Figure 89 indicate that you are west of the localizer course and outbound from the LOM?

1—a and c.
2—b and c.
3—a and d.
4—b and d.

7873. Which illustrations shown in Figure 89 indicate that you are east of the localizer course and outbound from the LOM?

1—a and c.
2—a and d.
3—b and c.
4—b and d.

7874. When the reported RVR for Rwy 22 is 1,200 ft., do regulations permit you to make a straight–in ILS approach to Rwy 22 and land in a helicopter? (See Figure 90.)

1—No; the minimum requirements to perform this procedure are 1,800 ft. RVR and a ceiling of 1,718 ft.
2—Yes; you may use reduced visibility, but no lower than 1,200 ft. RVR.
3—Yes; you may make an approach and landing with an RVR of 900 ft.
4—No; the required visibility for helicopters is 1 mi.

7875. If necessary, when should a missed approach be initiated during a S–LOC 22 approach at Tri–City? (See Figure 90.)

1—When at 2,400 ft. on the glide slope.
2—When at the inner marker.
3—When the FAF to MAP time has expired.
4—When passing the MM.

7876. How should you identify KEIPY Intersection during the initial approach to Rwy 22 at Tri–City Airport? (See Figure 90.)

1—On the LOC and 9.7 DME mi. from LOC site.
2—On the LOC and R–351 of HMV VORTAC.
3—On the LOC and 6.8 nautical miles timed from ENDAL Intersection.
4—On the LOC and 9.7 DME mi. from MOCCA LOM.

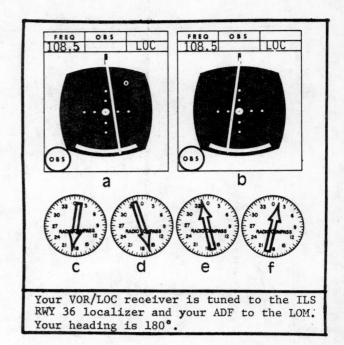

Your VOR/LOC receiver is tuned to the ILS RWY 36 localizer and your ADF to the LOM. Your heading is 180°.

Figure 89

7877. What is the minimum sector altitude in the sector encompassing the procedure turn at Tri–City? (See Figure 90.)

1—3600.
2—4000.
3—5500.
4—7400.

7878. What runway lighting is available on Rwy 22 at Tri–City Airport? (See Figure 90.)

1—HIRL only.
2—HIRL and TDZL only.
3—HIRL, TDZL, and centerline lighting.
4—HIRL, TDZL, centerline lighting, and MALSR.

7879. What is the landing minimum for Category B, at Tri–City if cleared for a straight–in localizer approach (dual VOR equipment) when the RVR is inoperative? (See Figure 90.)

1—1/2 mi.
2—3/8 mi.
3—5/8 mi.
4—3/4 mi.

7880. What minimum conditions must exist at Tri–City Airport, your destination, to avoid listing an alternate airport on the IFR flight plan? (See Figure 90.)

1—From 2 hours before to 2 hours after ETA, forecast ceiling 3,000 ft. and visibility 5 mi.
2—From 2 hours before to 2 hours after ETA, forecast ceiling 3,600 ft. and visibility 3 mi.
3—From 1 hour before to 1 hour after ETA, forecast ceiling 1,000 ft. and visibility 3 mi.
4—From 1 hour before to 1 hour after ETA, forecast ceiling 2,000 ft. and visibility 3 mi.

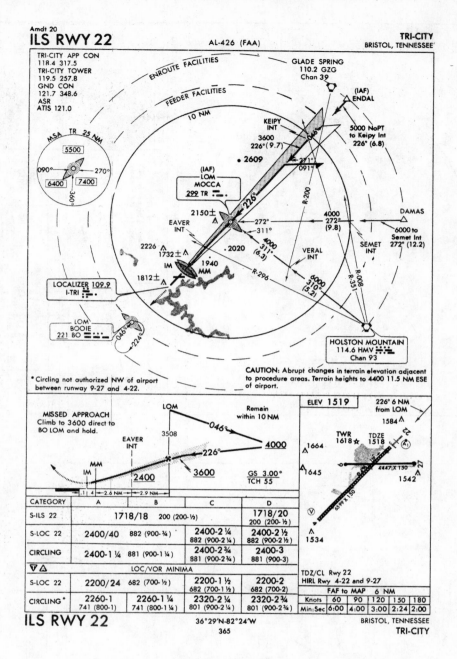

Figure 90

7881. Which substitution is appropriate during an ILS approach?

1—LOC minimums should be substituted for ILS minimums whenever the glide slope becomes inoperative.
2—DME, when located at the localizer antenna site, should be substituted for either the outer or middle marker.
3—ADF bearings crossing either the outer or middle marker sites may be substituted for these markers.
4—A VOR radial crossing the middle marker site may be substituted for the middle marker.

7882. Which substitution is permitted when an ILS component is inoperative?

1—A compass locator or precision radar may be substituted for the ILS outer or middle marker.
2—When the ILS glide slope is inoperative, the published circling minimums apply.
3—ADF or VOR bearings which cross either the outer or middle marker sites may be substituted for these markers.
4—DME, when located at the localizer antenna site, should be substituted for the outer or middle marker.

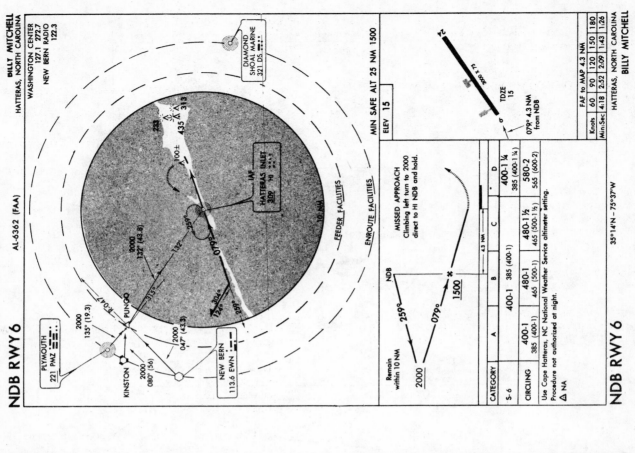

NDB RWY 6

BILLY MITCHELL
HATTERAS, NORTH CAROLINA

AL-6362 (FAA)

WASHINGTON CENTER 127.1 272.7
NEW BERN RADIO 122.3

PLYMOUTH 221 PMZ
2000 135° (19.3)
R-047
2000 047° (43.3)
KINSTON 2000 080° (56)
NEW BERN 113.6 EWN
315°
132°
124°
299°
259°
132° (43.8) 2000

IAF
HATTERAS INLET 389 HI

DIAMOND SHOAL MARINE 321 DS

FEEDER FACILITIES

ENROUTE FACILITIES

MIN SAFE ALT 25 NM 1500

ELEV 15

TDZE 15

079° 4.3 NM from NDB

MISSED APPROACH
Climbing left turn to 2000 direct to HI NDB and hold.

Remain within 10 NM
2000
259°
079°
NDB
1500
4.3 NM

CATEGORY	A	B	C	D
S-6	400-1 385 (400-1)	400-1 385 (400-1)	480-1½ 465 (500-1½)	400-1¼ 385 (400-1¼)
CIRCLING	400-1 385 (400-1)	480-1 465 (500-1)	480-1½ 465 (500-1½)	580-2 565 (600-2)

Use Cape Hatteras, NC National Weather Service altimeter setting.
Procedure not authorized at night.
△ NA

			FAF to MAP 4.3 NM			
Knots	60	90	120	150	180
Min:Sec	4:18	2:52	2:09	1:43	1:26

NDB RWY 6

35°14'N – 75°37'W

HATTERAS, NORTH CAROLINA
BILLY MITCHELL

Figure 92

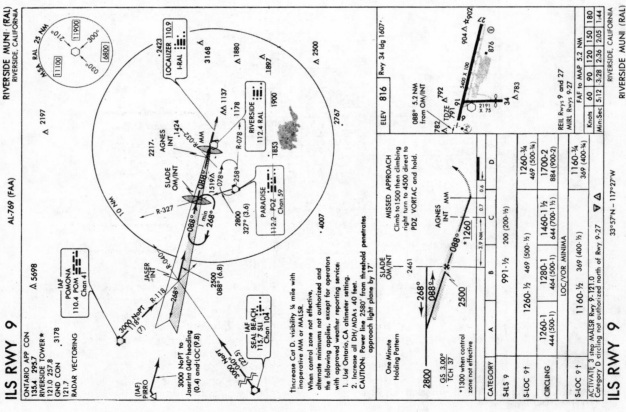

ILS RWY 9

RIVERSIDE MUNI (RAL)
RIVERSIDE, CALIFORNIA

AL-769 (FAA)

ONTARIO APP CON 135.4 295.7
RIVERSIDE TOWER * 121.0 257.8
GND CON 121.7 .3178
RADAR VECTORING

MSA RAL 25 NM

LOCALIZER 110.9 I-RAL

RIVERSIDE 112.4 RAL

PARADISE 112.2 PDZ Chan 59

AGNES INT
SLADE OM/INT
088° 268°

IAF POMONA 110.4 POM Chan 41

(IAF) PIRRO

3000 NoPT 180° heading (7) R-118

JASER INT 268°

IAF SEAL BEACH 115.7 SLI Chan 104

3000 NoPT to Jaser Int 040° heading (0.4) and I-LOC (9.8)

2000 NoPT

2500 088° (6.8)

†Increase Cat D visibility ¼ mile with inoperative MM or MALSR.
When control zone not effective, alternate minimums not authorized and the following applies, except for operators with approved weather reporting service:
1. Use Ontario,CA altimeter setting.
2. Increase all DH/MDAs 40 feet.
CAUTION: Power line 2580' from threshold penetrates approach light plane by 17'.

ELEV 816

Rwy 34 ldg 1607'

MISSED APPROACH
Climb to 1500 then climbing right turn to 4500 direct to PDZ VORTAC and hold.

One Minute Holding Pattern

2800

GS 3.00°
TCH 37

AGNES INT MM
*1260
SLADE OM/INT 2461
268° 088°
2500
3.9 NM 0.7 0.6

*1300 when control zone not effective

CATEGORY	A	B	C	D
S-ILS 9	991-½ 200 (200-½)			
S-LOC 9†	1260-1 444 (500-1)	1260-½ 469 (500-½)	1260-¾ 469 (500-¾)	1260-¾ 469 (500-¾)
CIRCLING	1260-1 464 (500-1)	1280-1 464 (500-1)	1460-1½ 644 (700-1½)	1700-2 884 (900-2)
S-LOC 9†	1160-½ 369 (400-½)		1160-¾ 369 (400-¾)	

LOC/VOR MINIMA

ACTIVATE 3 step MALSR Rwy 9-121.0
Category D circling not authorized north of Rwy 9-27

			FAF to MAP 5.2 NM			
Knots	60	90	120	150	180
Min:Sec	5:12	3:28	2:36	2:05	1:44

ILS RWY 9

33°57'N – 117°27'W

RIVERSIDE, CALIFORNIA
RIVERSIDE MUNI (RAL)

Figure 91

152

7883. What action should the pilot take if the marker beacon receiver becomes inoperative during the S–ILS 9 approach at Riverside Municipal? (See Figure 91.)

1—Request an LOC or other type of approach.
2—Raise the DH 100 ft. (50 ft. for the OM and 50 ft. for the MM).
3—Substitute SLADE INT. for the OM, and raise the DH 50 ft. due to the inability to identify the MM.
4—Substitute SLADE INT. for the OM and surveillance radar for the MM.

7884. Why are two (VOR/LOC) receivers necessary to obtain a MDA of 1160 when making a S–LOC 9 approach to Riverside Muni? (See Figure 91.)

1—In order to identify Jasper Intersection when on the localizer.
2—To obtain R–327 of PDZ when on the localizer course.
3—In order to identify Riverside VOR.
4—To utilize the published step–down fix.

7885. If the control zone is not effective, what is the LOC/VOR minima for a helicopter if cleared for the S–LOC 9 approach at Riverside Municipal? (See Figure 91.)

1—1160 and 1/2 mi.
2—1200 and 1/4 mi.
3—991 and RVR 24.
4—1300 and 1/4 mi.

7886. What type of entry is recommended for the missed approach holding pattern at Riverside Municipal? (See Figure 91.)

1—Direct only.
2—Parallel only.
3—Teardrop only.
4—Parallel or teardrop.

7887. What is the descent procedure (minimum altitudes) if cleared for the S–ILS 9 approach from Seal Beach VORTAC? (See Figure 91.)

1—Descend and maintain 3000 to JASER INT, descend to and maintain 2500 until crossing SLADE, descend and maintain 1260 until crossing AGNES, and to 991 (DH) after passing AGNES.
2—Descend and maintain 3000 to JASER INT, descend to 2800 when established on the LOC course, intercept and maintain the GS to 991 (DH).
3—Descend and maintain 3000 to JASER INT, descend to 2500 while established on the LOC course inbound, intercept and maintain the GS to 991 (DH).
4—Descend and maintain 3000 until intercepting the GS and maintain the GS to 991 (DH).

7888. How should a pilot reverse course to get established on the inbound course of the ILS RWY 9, if radar vectoring or the three IAF's are not utilized? (See Figure 91.)

1—Execute a standard 45° procedure turn on the side of the depicted holding pattern.
2—Execute a standard 45° procedure turn toward Seal Beach VORTAC or Pomona VORTAC.
3—Make an appropriate entry to the depicted holding pattern at SLADE OM/INT.
4—Use any type of procedure turn, but remain within 10 nautical miles of Riverside VOR.

7889. What is the landing minimum for a helicopter on an NDB RWY 6 approach at Billy Mitchell Airport? (See Figure 92.)

1—1 mi. visibility.
2—1,800 ft. RVR.
3—1/2 mi. visibility.
4—1,200 ft. RVR.

7890. What ATC facility controls the NDB RWY 6 approach at Billy Mitchell Airport? (See Figure 92.)

1—Washington Approach Control.
2—Billy Mitchell Tower.
3—New Bern FSS.
4—Washington Center.

7891. What is your position (as shown in Figure 93) with relation to the NDB RWY 6 FAF while on final approach at Billy Mitchell Airport? (See Figure 92.)

1—Approaching the FAF on course.
2—Approaching the FAF left of course.
3—Past the FAF and right of course.
4—Past the FAF and on course.

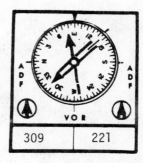

Figure 93

7892. When passing through an abrupt wind shear which involves a shift from a tailwind to a headwind, what power management would normally be required to maintain a constant indicated airspeed and ILS glide slope?

1—Higher than normal power initially, followed by a further increase as the wind shear is encountered, then a decrease.
2—Lower than normal power initially, followed by a further decrease as the wind shear is encountered, then an increase.
3—Higher than normal power initially, followed by a decrease as the shear is encountered, then an increase.
4—Lower than normal power initially, followed by an increase as the shear is encountered, then a decrease.

7893. What facilities may be substituted for an inoperative middle marker during an ILS approach without affecting the straight–in minimums?

1—PAR or ASR.
2—Compass locator or PAR.
3—Compass locator, PAR, or ASR.
4—Compass locator, PAR, ASR, or airborne radar.

7894. What is the helicopter landing minimum for the VOR RWY 36 approach at Carbon County Airport? (See Figure 94.)

1—500–foot ceiling and 1/2 mi. visibility.
2—1 mi. visibility.
3—6340 MDA and 1 mi. visibility.
4—1/2 mi. visibility.

7895. What is the helicopter MDA for a straight–in VOR RWY 36 approach at Carbon County Airport (VOR only)? (See Figure 94.)

1—250.
2—6090.
3—500.
4—6340.

7896. How should a pilot be able to determine when the DME at Carbon County Airport is inoperative? (See Figure 94.)

1—Salt Lake City Radio will announce the condition over PUC VOR at 15 minutes after each hour.
2—The airborne DME will always indicate "0" mileage.
3—The airborne DME will "search," but will not "lock on."
4—The airborne DME may appear normal, but there will be no code tone.

7897. What type entry is recommended for the missed approach holding pattern depicted on the VOR RWY 36 approach chart for Carbon County Airport? (See Figure 94.)

1—Direct only.
2—Teardrop only.
3—Parallel only.
4—Teardrop or parallel.

7898. How should you determine the MAP for the VOR RWY 36 approach? (See Figure 94.)

1—Zero indication on the DME.
2—Station passage on the VOR.
3—Arrival at 6340 on the descent path.
4—Expiration of time from the 4 DME fly to the airport.

7899. FAA Deletion.

7900. What is the purpose of the 10300 MSA on the Carbon County Airport Approach Chart? (See Figure 94.)

1—It is the minimum altitude for transition from the en route to the initial approach.
2—It provides safe clearance above the highest obstacle in the defined sector out to 25 nautical miles.
3—It provides an altitude above which navigational course guidance is assured.
4—It is the minimum vector altitude for radar vectors in the sector southeast of PUC between 020° and 290° magnetic bearing to PUC VOR.

7901. At which points may you initiate a descent to the next lower minimum altitude if you are cleared for the VOR RWY 36 approach, from the PUC R–026 IAF (DME operative)? (See Figure 94.)

1—Start descent from 11000 at PUC R–093, from 8000 when established on final, from 6500 at the 4 DME fix, and from 6220 when landing requirements are met.
2—Start descent from 11000 at PUC R–093, from 8000 upon starting turn to final, from 6500 at the 4 DME fix, and from 6220 when landing requirements are met.
3—Start descent from 11000 at PUC R–125, from 8000 upon starting turn to final, from 7500 when established on final, from 6340 at the 4 DME fix, and from 6220 at the VOR.
4—Start descent from 11000 at PUC R–093, from 8000 when established on final, from 6500 from the 10 DME fix, from 6340 at the 4 DME fix, and from 6220 at the VOR.

7902. Which indications will a pilot receive where an IM (inner marker) is installed on a front course ILS approach?

1—One dot per second and a steady amber light.
2—Six dots per second and a flashing white light.
3—Alternate dots and dashes and a purple light.
4—Alternate dashes and a blue light.

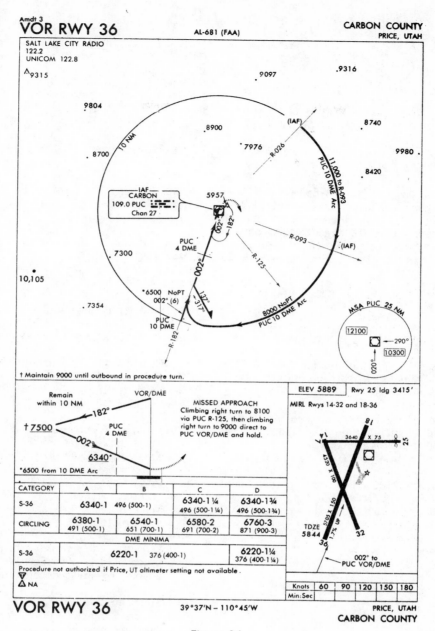

SALT LAKE CITY RADIO
122.2
UNICOM 122.8

△9315

.9316

.9097

9804

.8900

(IAF)

8740

.8700

10 NM

.7976

R-026

9980 .

8420

IAF
CARBON
109.0 PUC
Chan 27

5957

002°
182°

11,000 to R-093
PUC 10 DME Arc

.7300

002°

PUC
4 DME

R-093

(IAF)

R-125

10,105

*6500 NoPT
002° (6)

137°

317°

8000 NoPT
PUC 10 DME Arc

MSA PUC 25 NM

.7354

PUC
10 DME

R-182

12100

290°

10300

020°

† Maintain 9000 until outbound in procedure turn.

Remain
within 10 NM

VOR/DME

182°

† 7500

002°

PUC
4 DME

6340°

*6500 from 10 DME Arc

MISSED APPROACH
Climbing right turn to 8100
via PUC R-125, then climbing
right turn to 9000 direct to
PUC VOR/DME and hold.

ELEV 5889   Rwy 25 ldg 3415'

MIRL Rwys 14-32 and 18-36

18

3640   X 75

25

4520 X 150

5705 X 150

1.7% UP

TDZE
5844

32

36

002° to
PUC VOR/DME

CATEGORY	A	B	C	D
S-36	6340-1 496 (500-1)		6340-1¼ 496 (500-1¼)	6340-1¾ 496 (500-1¾)
CIRCLING	6380-1 491 (500-1)	6540-1 651 (700-1)	6580-2 691 (700-2)	6760-3 871 (900-3)
DME MINIMA				
S-36	6220-1 376 (400-1)			6220-1¼ 376 (400-1¼)

Procedure not authorized if Price, UT altimeter setting not available.

▽
△ NA

Knots	60	90	120	150	180
Min:Sec					

VOR RWY 36

39°37'N – 110°45'W

PRICE, UTAH
CARBON COUNTY

Figure 94

7903. Upon reaching the MDA during an instrument approach with the runway in sight, a pilot starts a circling approach. If the pilot loses sight of the runway or an identifiable part of the airport, which procedure should be followed? (ATC has given no alternate procedure.)

1—Maintain MDA, turn towards landing runway and if runway is in sight, land; if not, follow printed missed approach instructions.
2—Make 90° turn in the direction of the landing runway with an immediate 90° turn in the opposite direction. If runway is in sight, continue approach; if not, proceed with missed approach procedure.
3—Make an initial climbing turn towards the landing runway and continue the turn until in a safe position to intercept the missed approach course.
4—Turn in the direction of the missed approach course and follow the printed missed approach procedure.

7904. When may a pilot make a straight–in landing, if using an instrument approach procedure having only circling minimums?

1—A straight–in landing may not be made, but the pilot may continue to the runway at MDA and then circle to land on the runway.
2—The pilot may land straight–in if the runway is the active runway and he has been cleared to land.
3—A straight–in landing may be made if the pilot has the runway in sight in sufficient time to make a normal approach for landing, and has been cleared to land.
4—Only if the field does not have a tower, and ATC clears the pilot for the approach.

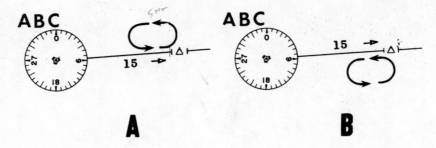

A   B

Figure 95

7905. Clearance is received to HOLD WEST OF THE ONE FIVE DME FIX ON THE ZERO EIGHT SIX RADIAL OF ABC VORTAC, FIVE MILE LEGS, LEFT TURNS. You arrive at the 15 DME fix on a heading of 350°. Which holding pattern shown in Figure 95 correctly complies with these instructions and what is the recommended entry procedure?

1—A – teardrop.
2—B – direct.
3—A – direct.
4—B – direct or parallel.

7906. What are the minimum altitudes for the VOR RWY 17 approach at Stillwater Municipal if you do not obtain the local altimeter setting? (See Figure 96.)

1—Assigned altitude to VOR; 3000 until in the holding pattern; 2400 until inbound on the final approach course; 2200 to VOR; MDA 1380.
2—Assigned altitude to VOR; 2400 until inbound; 2200 to VOR; MDA 1380.
3—3,000 ft. to VOR; 2400 in holding pattern until crossing the FAF inbound; MDA 1580.
4—3,000 ft. to VOR; 2400 until inbound on course; 2200 to VOR; MDA 1580.

7907. FAA Deletion.

7908. Which condition requires you to start a missed approach when making a VOR approach to Rwy 17 at Stillwater? (See Figure 96.)

1—Descent to the MDA, but without any visual references to the intended runway.
2—Flying 3.5 DME mi. from SWO with the runway not in sight.
3—Flying for 2 min. 20 sec. past SWO at an estimated groundspeed of 90 knots with no visual reference to the intended runway.
4—Reaching the MDA and not in position from which a normal landing could be made.

7909. What is the MDA for the VOR RWY 17 approach if landing on Rwy 35, using the Oklahoma City altimeter setting? (See Figure 96.)

1—1640.
2—1580.
3—1440.
4—1380.

7910. What is the landing minimum for the Stillwater VOR RWY 17 approach if the local altimeter setting is not available? (Category B.) (See Figure 96.)

1—Ceiling 1,440 ft.; visibility 1 mi.
2—Ceiling 1,380 ft.; visibility 1–1/4 mi.
3—Visibility 1 mi.
4—Visibility 1–1/4 mi.

7911. Which procedure should be followed if you execute a missed approach from the VOR RWY 17 approach at Stillwater? (See Figure 96.)

1—Inform ATC on 122.1 that you are making a missed approach and advise them of your intentions.
2—Make a 180° turn and fly direct to the VOR while climbing to 2400.
3—Climb to 2400, make a left turn and fly direct to SWO VOR and enter depicted holding pattern. As soon as practicable, contact Fort Worth Center on 128.3 and advise of missed approach, reason, and your intentions.
4—Start climbing turn to 2400 and proceed to SWO VOR direct. Contact OKC FSS on 122.4, advise you are making a missed approach and your intentions.

7912. What procedure should be used to close your flight plan at Stillwater? (Reported ceiling is 500 ft.) (See Figure 96.)

1—Close your flight plan with Fort Worth Center when starting the final approach.
2—Upon landing contact OKC FSS on 108.4T and receive on 122.1R.
3—Upon landing your flight plan will be closed automatically.
4—Upon landing contact OKC FSS on 122.4 or use toll-free telephone number.

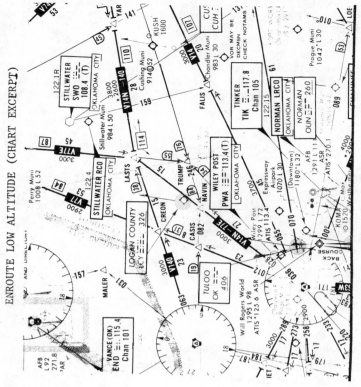

§ **STILLWATER MUNI** (SWO) 2.6 NW GMT −6(−5DT) 36°09′31″N 97°05′09″W WICHITA
984 B S4 FUEL 100, JET A OX 1, 2 CFR Index A H-2I, 3A, L-6H
RWY 04-22: H5002X75 (ASPH) S-12 .58% up S.W. IAP
RWY 04: Trees. RWY 22: Tree.
RWY 13-31: H5003X150 (CONC) S-12 .30% up N.W.
RWY 13: Tree. RWY 31: P-line.
RWY 17-35: H5002X150 (ASPH) S-19, D-46 MIRL .46% up S.
RWY 17: REIL. VASI(V4L)—GA 3.0° TCH 26′. Poles.
RWY 35: REIL. VASI(V4L)—GA 3.0° TCH 26′. Trees.
AIRPORT REMARKS: Attended dalgt hours. After hours on request. All jet acrft use Rwy 17-35. VASI on request only,
call (405) 372-7881.
COMMUNICATIONS: UNICOM 122.7
OKLAHOMA CITY FSS (OKC) Toll free call dial 1-800-522-3325.
LRCO 122.1R 108.4T (OKE CITY FSS)
RCO 122.4 (OKLAHOMA CITY FSS)
Ⓡ **FORT WORTH CENTER APP/DEP CON** 128.3
RADIO AIDS TO NAVIGATION:
PIONEER (H) VORTAC 113.2 PER Chan 79 36°44′47″N 97°09′35″W 165° 35.4 NM to fld.
1060/09E.
(T) VOR 108.4 SWO 36°13′27″N 97°04′51″W 177° 3.5 NM to fld.

ENROUTE LOW ALTITUDE (CHART EXCERPT)

NOTE: The questions based on Figure 95 pertain to an instrument flight from OKC to Stillwater (SWO). You are flying at an assigned altitude of 4,000 feet and upon arrival at LASTS intersection you are cleared for the approach. Fort Worth Center frequency is 128.3 and communication can be maintained at 2,400 feet. (Category A airplane)

Figure 96

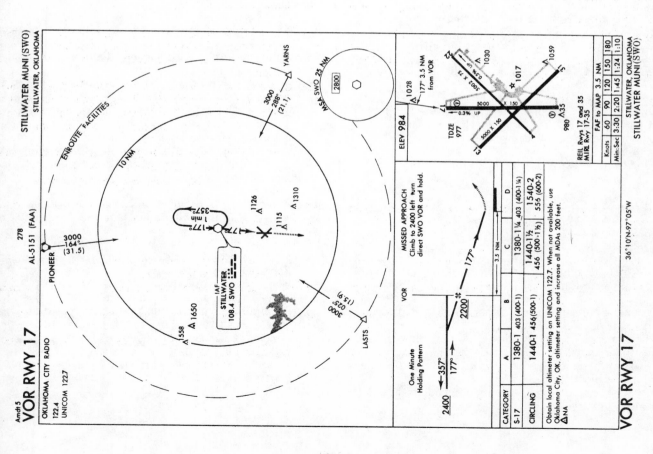

Amdt 5
VOR RWY 17
OKLAHOMA CITY RADIO
122.4
UNICOM 122.7

278
AL-5151 (FAA)

STILLWATER MUNI (SWO)
STILLWATER, OKLAHOMA

MISSED APPROACH
Climb to 2400 left turn direct SWO VOR and hold.

CATEGORY	A	B	C	D
S-17	1380-1	403 (400-1)	1440-1¼ 403 (400-1¼)	1540-2 556 (600-2)
CIRCLING	1440-1 456 (500-1)		1440-1½ 456 (500-1½)	1540-2 556 (600-2)

Obtain local altimeter setting on UNICOM 122.7. When not available, use
Oklahoma City, OK, altimeter setting and increase all MDAs 200 feet.
△NA

REIL Rwys 17 and 35
MIRL Rwy 17-35

Knots	60	90	120	150	180
FAF to MAP 3.5 NM					
Min:Sec	3:30	2:20	1:45	1:24	1:10

VOR RWY 17
36°10′N-97°05′W
STILLWATER, OKLAHOMA
STILLWATER MUNI (SWO)

157

7913. You are inbound for the SDF BC RWY 9 approach. From the instrument indications shown in Figure 97 determine your position with respect to the final approach fix and the SDF course centerline. (See Figure 98.)

1—North of the centerline and approaching the FAF.
2—South of the centerline and approaching the FAF.
3—North of the centerline and past the FAF.
4—South of the centerline and past the FAF.

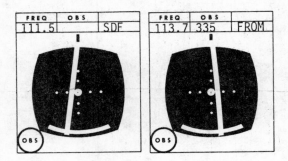

Figure 97

7914. What are the altitude minimums for the SDF BC RWY 9 approach to Elkhart Municipal with the conditions listed? (See Figure 98, NOTE.)

Last assigned altitude 3,000
Cleared for the approach at South Bend VORTAC

1—3000 until established on the localizer course; 2800 to the FAF; MDA 1240.
2—3000 until established on the localizer course; 2800 to the FAF; MDA 1280.
3—2800 on the SBN R–138 and on the localizer to the FAF; MDA 1240.
4—2800 on the SBN R–138 and on the localizer to the FAF; MDA 1280.

7915. What time should you reach the missed approach point for the SDF BC RWY 9 approach at Elkhart with the conditions given below? (See Figure 98.)

Inbound over CORVY at 1015 and 25 sec.
Wind: 100° at 15 knots; TAS 105 knots; VAR 1°W

1—1018 and 55 sec.
2—1019 and 12 sec.
3—1019 and 25 sec.
4—1020 and 00 sec.

7916. What lighting aids are available for the Rwy 9 approach? (See Figure 98.)

1—Medium–intensity runway lights, VASI, and medium–intensity approach lights.
2—High–intensity runway lights, and runway end identifier lights.
3—Medium–intensity approach lights, VASI, and runway end identifier lights.
4—Runway end identifier lights and medium–intensity runway lights.

7917. What is the recommended entry to the holding pattern at POLER Intersection after a missed approach to Rwy 9? (See Figure 98.) Wind calm.

1—Teardrop only.
2—Direct only.
3—Parallel only.
4—Parallel or teardrop.

7918. You are inbound to the holding fix after having entered the holding pattern at POLER Intersection. When should you start timing for the outbound leg? (See Figure 98.)

1—Upon crossing the R–030 of Goshen.
2—On completion of the turn to the outbound leg.
3—When abeam the fix.
4—1 minute after passing the fix.

7919. What procedure should be used to close the flight plan at Elkhart? (See Figure 98, NOTE.)

1—The flight plan is closed automatically when the landing is completed.
2—South Bend Approach Control will cancel the flight plan after clearing you for the approach.
3—Contact South Bend Approach Control while still airborne, weather permitting, or South Bend FSS after landing by telephone.
4—Contact South Bend FSS on 123.65 when established on the final approach course.

7920. When is radar service terminated during a visual approach?

1—Automatically when ATC instructs the pilot to contact the tower.
2—Immediately upon acceptance of the approach by the pilot.
3—When ATC advises, "Radar service terminated; resume own navigation."
4—When the pilot is on final approach for a landing.

7921. What are the requirements for a contact approach to an airport that has an approved instrument approach procedure, if the pilot is on an instrument flight plan and clear of clouds?

1—The controller must determine that the pilot can see the airport at the altitude flown and can remain clear of clouds.
2—The controller must be reasonably sure the pilot can remain clear of clouds and must give the pilot an alternative in case the visibility decreases or the ceiling lowers.
3—The pilot must agree to the approach when given by ATC and the controller must have determined that the visibility was at least 1 mi. and be reasonably sure the pilot can remain clear of clouds.
4—The pilot must request the approach, have at least 1 mi. visibility, and be reasonably sure of remaining clear of clouds.

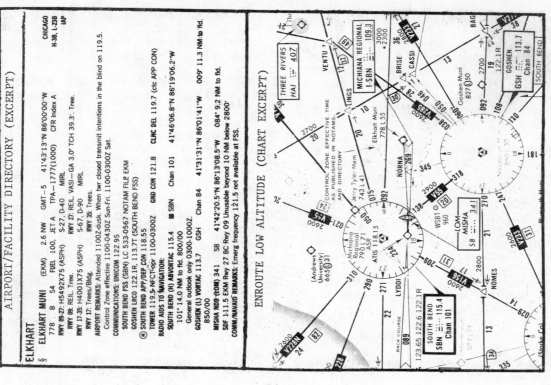

NOTE: IFR Flight from Chicago to Elkhart Municipal;
       ETA SBN 0515Z; Approach Category A.

Figure 98

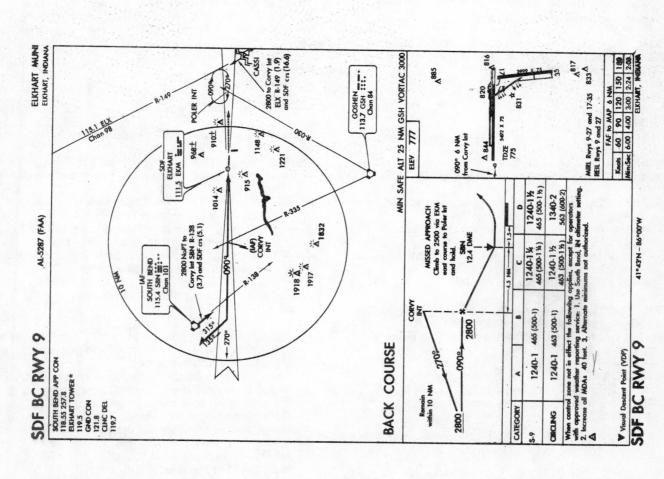

159

7922. What conditions are necessary before ATC can issue a visual approach?

1—The pilot must remain clear of clouds, surface visibility must be 1 mi., and ceiling at least 1,000 ft.
2—You must have the preceding aircraft in sight, and be able to remain in VFR weather conditions.
3—You must have the airport and the preceding aircraft in sight, or be able to proceed to, and land in VFR conditions.
4—You must have the airport in sight or a preceding aircraft to be followed and be able to proceed to the airport in VFR conditions.

7923. What are the main differences between a visual approach and a contact approach?

1—The pilot is assigned a contact approach; the pilot must request a visual approach and higher weather minimums must exist.
2—The pilot must request a contact approach; the pilot may be assigned a visual approach and higher weather minimums must exist.
3—The pilot must request a visual approach and report having the field in sight; ATC may assign a contact approach if VFR conditions exist.
4—Anytime the pilot reports the field in sight, ATC may clear the pilot for a contact approach; for a visual approach, the pilot must advise that the approach can be made under VFR conditions.

7924. What is the minimum altitude to be sure of receiving adequate signals when using the CEW R–345 at PICKS Intersection? (See Figure 99.)

1—2300.
2—3000.
3—3500.
4—4000.

7925. Which facility will control the remainder of your flight from PICKS Intersection? (See Figure 99, Note.)

1—Atlanta Center until starting your approach and then Jacksonville Center.
2—Atlanta Center to the final approach fix (BELLE), then Jacksonville Center.
3—Atlanta Center to Monroeville, then Mobile FSS upon entering the MOA.
4—Atlanta Center (approach control).

7926. If during the approach (VOR/DME RWY 9) there was a windshift and you decided to land on Rwy 18, what would be your MDA and landing minimums? (See Figure 99.)

1—920 – visibility 1–1/4 mi.
2—960 – visibility 1 mi.
3—960 – ceiling 800 ft. and visibility 1 mi.
4—920 – ceiling 700 ft. and visibility 1 mi.

7927. What are the minimum altitudes after being cleared for the VOR/DME RWY 9 approach to Middleton Field? You are cleared for the approach approximately 10 mi. from MVC. (See Figure 99, NOTE.)

1—3000 to depicted holding pattern; 2000 to final fix; 1300 to 13 DME fix; 920 until the runway is in sight.
2—2000 to final fix; 920 until the necessary visual references are established.
3—3000 until inbound on course; 2000 to final fix; 920 until runway is in sight.
4—2300 to MVC; 2000 to final fix; 1300 to 13 DME fix; 920 until the required visual references are established.

7928. Which procedure should be used to close your flight plan? (See Figure 99, NOTE.)

1—Request Mobile FSS to close your flight plan upon reaching the 11 DME fix.
2—Upon landing contact Monroeville LRCO and request Mobile FSS to close your flight plan; if unable, contact Mobile FSS by telephone.
3—Request Atlanta Center Approach Control to close your flight plan before starting the approach.
4—Your flight plan will be closed automatically when you are cleared for the approach.

7929. What is the recommended holding pattern entry if a missed approach is executed after making the VOR/DME RWY 9 approach? (Aircraft heading 285.) (See Figure 99, NOTE.)

1—Parallel.
2—Teardrop.
3—Direct.
4—Parallel or teardrop.

7930. When may you obtain a contact approach?

1—ATC may assign a contact approach if VFR conditions exist or you report the runway in sight and are clear of clouds.
2—ATC may assign a contact approach if you are below the clouds and the visibility is at least 1 mi.
3—ATC will only assign a contact approach if you have the runway in sight and VFR conditions exist.
4—ATC will assign a contact approach only upon request if the reported visibility is at least 1 mi.

7931. Under which conditions is hydroplaning most likely to occur?

1—During heavy precipitation of rain or wet snow and a landing is made at minimum landing speed and abrupt initial runway contact.
2—When rudder is used for directional control instead of allowing the nosewheel to contact the surface early in the landing roll on a wet runway.
3—During conditions of standing water, slush, high speed, and smooth runway texture.
4—During a landing on any wet runway when brake application is delayed until a wedge of water begins to build ahead of the tires.

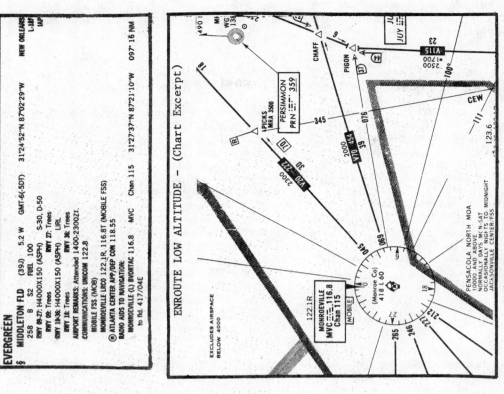

AIRPORT/FACILITY DIRECTORY (Excerpt)

EVERGREEN

§ **MIDDLETON FLD** (39J) 5.2 W GMT-6(-5DT) 31²24'52"N 87°02'29"W NEW ORLEANS
258 B S2 FUEL 100 S-30, D-50 L-18B
RWY 09-27: H4000X150 (ASPH) RWY 27: Trees IAP
RWY 09: Trees
RWY 18-36: H4000X150 (ASPH) LIRL
RWY 18: Trees RWY 36: Trees
AIRPORT REMARKS: Attended 1400-2300Z‡.
COMMUNICATIONS: UNICOM 122.8
MOBILE FSS (MOB)
MONROEVILLE LRCO 122.1R, 116.8T (MOBILE FSS)
® ATLANTA CENTER APP/DEP CON 118.55
RADIO AIDS TO NAVIGATION:
MONROEVILLE (L) BVORTAC 116.8 MVC Chan 115 31°27'37"N 87°21'10"W 097° 16 NM
to fld. 417/04E

ENROUTE LOW ALTITUDE – (Chart Excerpt)

NOTE:

You are on an IFR flight flying SW on V20 approaching Picks Intersection. Your destination is Middleton Field which has IFR weather conditions. You will make the VOR/DME RWY 9 approach. (Apch. Cat B)

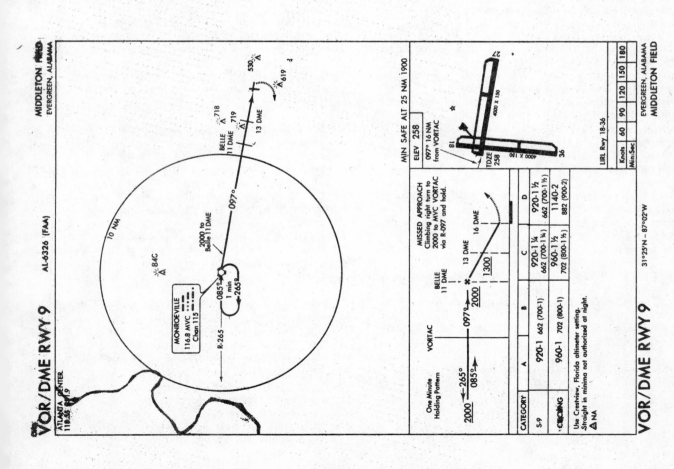

VOR/DME RWY 9 — MIDDLETON FIELD, EVERGREEN, ALABAMA

Figure 99

7932. What are the minimum altitudes for the VOR RWY 12 approach at Will Rogers World Airport, if you are cleared for the approach at NOCKS Intersection (a) while flying at your assigned altitude of 5000? (See Figure 100, En Route Chart Excerpt.)

1—5000 to the 10 DME circle; 3000 to the OKC VORTAC; 2000 to the FAF; 1700 to the MAP.
2—5000 to the 10 DME circle; 3000 to OKC VORTAC inbound; 2000 to SOONE Intersection; 1700 until the runway or visual references are in sight.
3—5000 to OKC VORTAC; 3000 for procedure turn and on course inbound; 2000 to final fix; MDA 1700.
4—3000 to OKC VORTAC and in procedure turn (holding pattern); 2000 to SOONE Intersection; MDA 1700.

7933. Where is the missed approach point for the straight-in VOR RWY 12 approach for Will Rogers World Airport? (See Figure 100.)

1—Upon reaching the MDA and the runway or other visual requirements not in sight.
2—1 min. 56 sec. from SOONE Intersection when flying at 90 knots IAS.
3—7.9 nautical miles from OKC VORTAC.
4—2.9 nautical miles from OKC.

7934. Which procedure should be followed if your navigation receivers fail while being vectored for a VOR RWY 12 approach to Will Rogers World Airport? (See Figure 100.) (Your communication receivers are working and the reported ceiling and visibility are 600 ft. and 1 mi.)

1—Contact approach control and ask for a vector to an area with VFR conditions.
2—Advise approach control of your equipment malfunction and request an ASR approach.
3—Advise approach control of your navigation receiver failure and that you will climb above the clouds and fly to an area where you can descend in VFR conditions.
4—Contact OKC FSS and request a DF steer for a DF landing.

7935. Which is the most accurate way of determining SOONE Intersection? (See Figure 100.)

1—Use OKC R–097 and PWA R–182.
2—Use 5 DME mi. from OKC VORTAC.
3—Use 5 DME mi. from OKC VORTAC and PWA R–182.
4—Use OKC R–097 and 5 DME mi. from OKC VORTAC.

7936. What is the MDA and landing minimum for the VOR RWY 12 approach at Will Rogers World Airport when landing on Rwy 35L? (See Figure 100, aircraft approach Category B.)

1—1700; 500–foot ceiling and 1 mi. visibility.
2—1740; 500–foot ceiling and 1 mi. visibility.
3—1740; 1 mi. visibility.
4—1760; 1 mi. visibility.

7937. Between which two OKC radials (clockwise) is the sector which indicates that the MSA within 25 nautical miles of the VORTAC is 3,100 ft.? (See Figure 100.)

1—R–277 and R–193.
2—R–075 and R–345.
3—R–255 and R–165.
4—R–097 and R–193.

7938. Which runways at Will Rogers World Airport have Visual Approach Slope Indicators? (See Figure 100.)

1—12, 17L, 30, and 35L.
2—12, 17L, and 18.
3—All runways except 18 and 36.
4—Only Rwys 17L and 35L.

7939. Which type of instrument approach lighting is provided on Rwy 35R at Will Rogers World? (See Figure 100.)

1—MALS with sequence flashers.
2—SSALR.
3—ALSF–2 with sequence flashers.
4—MALSR.

7940. You arrive at your destination airport on an IFR flight plan in a helicopter. Which is a prerequisite condition for the performance of a contact approach?

1—Clear of clouds and at least 1 statute mile flight visibility.
2—A ground visibility of at least 2 statute miles.
3—A flight visibility of at least 1/2 nautical mile.
4—Air traffic control assignment of the approach.

7941. During a precision instrument approach (using Category A minimums) a helicopter may not be operated below DH unless

1—the associated ground components and visual aids are all operative.
2—runway alignment indicator lights are clearly visible.
3—positioned such that a normal approach to the runway of intended landing can be made.
4—the visibility is reported to be at or above the landing minimums prescribed for that procedure.

7942. Which procedure should be followed by a pilot who is circling to land in a Category B airplane, but is maintaining a speed 5 knots faster than the maximum specified for that category?

1—Use the approach minimums appropriate for Category C.
2—Use Category B minimums.
3—Use Category A minimums since they apply to all circling approaches.
4—Use Category D minimums since they apply to all circling approaches.

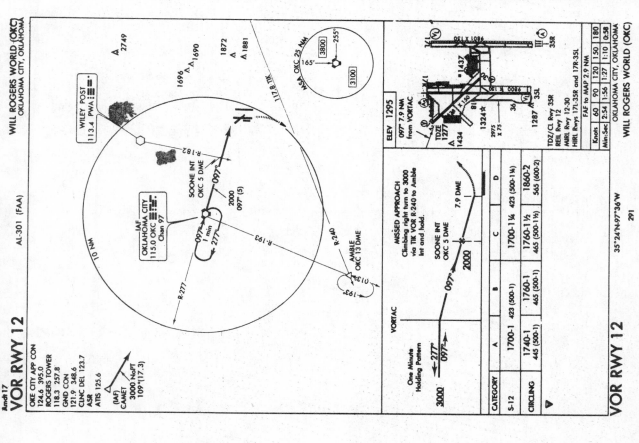

Figure 100

7943. While flying a 3° glide slope, a constant tailwind shears to a calm wind. Which conditions should the pilot expect?

1—Airspeed and pitch attitude decrease and there is a tendency to go below glide slope.
2—Airspeed and pitch attitude increase and there is a tendency to go below glide slope.
3—Airspeed and pitch attitude increase and there is a tendency to go above glide slope.
4—Airspeed and pitch attitude decrease and there is a tendency to go above glide slope.

7944. What is the MSA for the area within 25 nautical miles of the LOM for ILS RWY 8? (See Figure 101.)

1—3600.
2—5000.
3—3100.
4—2800.

7945. What is the minimum altitude ATC may approve before reaching CHINN Intersection for the ILS RWY 8 approach to the William B. Hartsfield Atlanta Intl. Airport? (See Figure 101.)

1—5000.
2—3100.
3—3700.
4—2800.

7946. Which Approach Lighting System is installed for Rwy 8 at the William B. Hartsfield Atlanta Intl. Airport? (See Figure 101.)

1—MALSR.
2—ALSF–1 with sequenced flashers.
3—MALS with sequenced flashers.
4—SSALSR.

7947. Upon landing at the William B. Hartsfield Atlanta Intl. Airport (see Figure 101), when should you change to ground control frequency?

1—As soon as you turn off the runway.
2—When reaching a marked taxiway.
3—Only after the tower directs you to contact ground control.
4—As soon as practicable after you are instructed to turn off at a particular intersection or you have left the runway.

7948. Which frequency should be used to contact Atlanta Flight Watch? (See Figure 101.)

1—122.45.
2—122.6.
3—122.2
4—122.0.

7949. At what altitude above the threshold of Rwy 8 does the electronic glide slope cross? (See Figure 101.)

1—200 ft.
2—156 ft.
3—56 ft.
4—35 ft.

7950. FAA Deletion.

7951. If all ILS components are operating and the required visual references are not established, the missed approach should be initiated upon

1—arrival at the DH on the glide slope.
2—arrival at the visual descent point.
3—arrival at the middle marker.
4—expiration of the time listed on the approach chart for missed approach.

7952. The rate of descent required to stay on the ILS glide slope

1—will be determined by true airspeed.
2—must be increased if the groundspeed is decreased.
3—will remain constant if the indicated airspeed remains constant.
4—must be decreased if the groundspeed is decreased.

7953. Which procedure should you follow to avoid wake turbulence if a large jet crosses your course from left to right approximately 1 mile ahead and at your altitude?

1—Slow your airspeed to V_A and maintain altitude and course.
2—Make sure you are slightly above the path of the jet.
3—Make sure you are slightly below the path of the jet and perpendicular to the course.
4—Descend 200 ft. and turn 20° left; return to course and altitude after passing the path of the jet.

7954. What effect would a light crosswind of approximately 7 knots have on vortex behavior?

1—The light crosswind would rapidly dissipate vortex strength.
2—The upwind vortex would tend to remain over the runway.
3—The downwind vortex would tend to remain over the runway.
4—Both vortices would move downwind at a greater rate than if the surface wind was aligned with the runway.

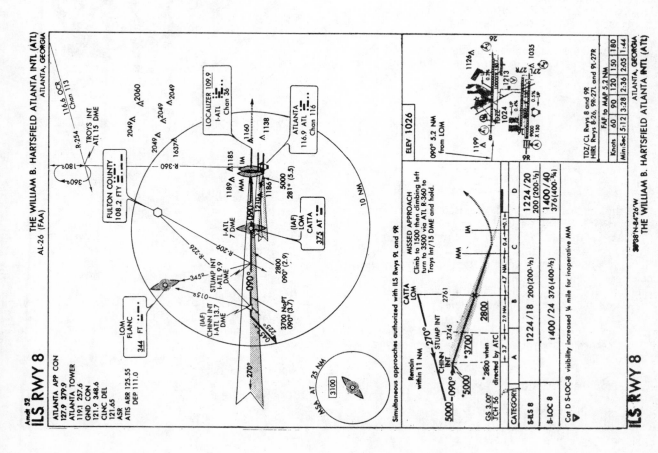

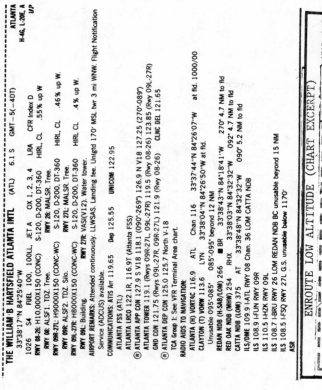

Figure 101

165

7955. The rate of descent on the glide slope is dependent upon

1—true airspeed.
2—calibrated airspeed.
3—groundspeed.
4—indicated airspeed.

7956. Approximately what height is the glide slope centerline at the MM of a typical ILS?

1—100 ft.
2—200 ft.
3—300 ft.
4—500 ft.

7957. When landing behind a large jet aircraft, at which point on the runway should you plan to land?

1—If any crosswind, land on the downwind side of the runway and prior to the jet's touchdown point.
2—If any crosswind, land on the windward side of the runway and prior to the jet's touchdown point.
3—At least 1,000 ft. beyond the jet's touchdown point.
4—Beyond the jet's touchdown point.

7958. What facilities may be substituted for an inoperative middle marker during an ILS approach without affecting the straight-in minimums?

1—ASR and PAR.
2—Compass locator and PAR.
3—Compass locator, PAR, and ASR.
4—Compass locator, PAR, ASR, and DME.

7959. Which of these facilities may be substituted for a MM (middle marker) during a complete ILS instrument approach procedure?

1—Surveillance and precision radar.
2—Compass locator and precision radar.
3—A VOR/DME fix.
4—DME and compass locator.

7960. Which pilot action is appropriate if more than one component of a ILS is unusable?

1—Use the highest minimum required by any single component that is unusable.
2—Request another approach appropriate to the equipment that is usable.
3—Raise the minimums a total of that required by each component that is unusable.
4—Raise the DH by 50 ft. and landing minimum by 1/4 mi. for each component that is unusable.

7961. Which information, in addition to headings, does the radar controller provide without request during an ASR approach?

1—The recommended altitude for each mile from the runway.
2—When reaching the MDA.
3—When to commence descent to MDA, the aircraft's position each mile on final from the runway, and arrival at the MAP.
4—Arrival at the end of the runway.

7962. Where may you use a surveillance approach?

1—At any airport that has an approach control.
2—At any airport which has radar service.
3—At airports for which civil radar instrument approach minimums have been published.
4—At any airport that has a DF facility.

7963. Which of the following causes an increase in V_{MCA}?

1—An increase in weight.
2—Forward movement of CG.
3—5° bank toward the inoperative engine.
4—An increase in altitude.

7964. The pressure altitude is set opposite the outside air temperature. What indications in the following illustration will the pointer present?

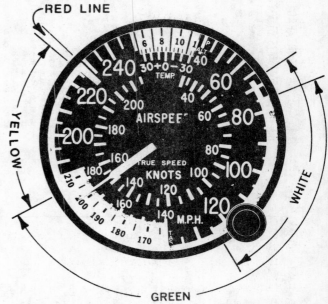

1—Indicated airspeed in knots and MPH and true airspeed in knots.
2—Indicated airspeed in knots and MPH and true airspeed in MPH.
3—True airspeed and indicated airspeed in knots.
4—True airspeed in MPH and equivalent airspeed in knots.

7965. What indication should be observed on a turn coordinator when making a left turn while taxiing?

1—The miniature aircraft will show a turn to the left and the ball remains centered.
2—The miniature aircraft will show a turn to the left and the ball moves to the right.
3—Both the miniature aircraft and the ball will remain centered.
4—The miniature aircraft will remain level and the ball will move to the left.

7966. FAA Deletion.

7967. To remain on the ILS glidepath, the rate of descent must be

1—increased if the airspeed is decreased.
2—decreased if the airspeed is increased.
3—decreased if the groundspeed is increased.
4—increased if the groundspeed is increased.

7968. What is the primary bank instrument during a standard rate turn?

1—Altitude indicator.
2—Turn coordinator.
3—Heading indicator.
4—Magnetic compass.

7969. What does the miniature aircraft of the turn coordinator directly display?

1—Angle of bank and rate of roll.
2—Rate of roll and rate of turn.
3—Angle of bank and rate of turn.
4—Angle of bank.

7970. What visual illusion creates the same effect as a narrower-than-usual runway?

1—An upsloping runway.
2—A wider-than-usual runway.
3—A down-sloping runway.
4—Ground lighting illusion.

7971. What is the correct sequence of the three skills used in instrument flying?

1—Aircraft control, cross-check, and instrument interpretation.
2—Instrument interpretation, cross-check, and aircraft control.
3—Cross-check, instrument interpretation, and aircraft control.
4—Cross-check, aircraft control, and instrument interpretation.

7972. Due to visual illusion, when landing on a narrower-than-usual runway, the aircraft will appear to be

1—higher than actual, leading to a lower-than-normal approach.
2—lower than actual, leading to a higher-than-normal approach.
3—higher than actual, leading to a higher-than-normal approach.
4—lower than actual, leading to a lower-than-normal approach.

7973. The gyroscopic heading indicator is inoperative. What is the primary bank instrument in unaccelerated straight and level flight?

1—Magnetic compass.
2—Attitude indicator.
3—Miniature aircraft of turn coordinator.
4—Inclinometer of the turn indicator.

7974. The rate of turn at any airspeed is dependent upon

1—the horizontal lift component.
2—the vertical lift component.
3—aircraft weight and center of gravity.
4—centrifugal force.

7975. As a rule of thumb, to minimize DME slant range error, how far from the facility should you be to consider the reading as accurate?

1—Two miles or more for each 1,000 ft. of altitude above the facility.
2—One or more miles for each 1,000 ft. of altitude above the facility.
3—No specific distance is specified since the reception is line-of-sight.
4—Two miles or more for each 2,000 ft. of altitude above the facility.

7976. During a skidding turn to the right, what is the relationship between the component of lift, centrifugal force, and load factor?

1—Centrifugal force is less than horizontal lift and the load factor is increased.
2—Centrifugal force is greater than horizontal lift and the load factor is increased.
3—Centrifugal force and horizontal lift are equal and the load factor is decreased.
4—Centrifugal force and horizontal lift are equal and the load factor is increased.

7977. As power is increased to enter a 500 ft./min. rate of climb in straight flight, which instruments are primary for pitch, bank, and power respectively?

1—Airspeed indicator, heading indicator, and manifold pressure guage or tachometer.
2—Vertical speed indicator, attitude indicator, and airspeed indicator.
3—Airspeed indicator, attitude indicator, and manifold pressure guage or tachometer.
4—Vertical speed indicator, heading indicator, and airspeed indicator.

7978. What instruments are considered supporting bank instruments during a straight, stabilized climb at a constant rate?

1—Attitude indicator and turn coordinator.
2—Heading indicator and attitude indicator.
3—Heading indicator and turn coordinator.
4—Turn coordinator and magnetic compass.

7979. What instruments are primary for pitch, bank, and power, respectively, when transitioning into a constant airspeed climb?

1—Attitude indicator, heading indicator, and manifold pressure guage or tachometer.
2—Attitude indicator for both pitch and bank; airspeed indicator for power.
3—Vertical speed, attitude indicator, and manifold pressure or tachometer.
4—Attitude indicator, heading indicator, and airspeed indicator.

7980. What instrument(s) is(are) supporting bank instrument when entering a constant airspeed climb?

1—Heading indicator.
2—Attidue indicator and turn coordinator.
3—Turn coordinator and heading indicator.
4—Attitude indicator.

7981. Which instruments are considered to be supporting instruments for pitch during change of airspeed in a turn?

1—Airspeed indicator and vertical speed indicator.
2—Altimeter and attitude indicator.
3—Attitude indicator and vertical speed indicator.
4—Airspeed indicator and attitude indicator.

7982. Which instrument is considered primary for power as the airspeed reaches the desired value during change of airspeed in a turn?

1—Airspeed indicator.
2—Attitude indicator.
3—Altimeter.
4—Tachometer or manifold pressure guage.

7983. Which instruments are considered primary and supporting for bank, respectively, when establishing a standard rate turn?

1—Turn coordinator and attitude indicator.
2—Attitude indicator and turn coordinator.
3—Turn coordinator and heading indicator.
4—Attitude indicator and heading indicator.

7984. What is the primary pitch instrument when establishing a standard rate turn?

1—Attitude indicator.
2—Altimeter.
3—Vertical speed indicator.
4—Airspeed indicator.

7985. What is the initial primary bank instrument when establishing a standard rate turn?

1—Turn coordinator.
2—Heading indicator.
3—Magnetic compass.
4—Attitude indicator.

7986. What indications are displayed by the miniature aircraft of a turn coordinator?

1—Rate of roll and rate of turn.
2—Direct indication of bank angle and pitch attitude.
3—Indirect indication of bank angle and pitch attitude.
4—Bank angle and rate of turn.

7987. What is the primary pitch instrument when making a climbing left turn at cruise climb airspeed?

1—Attitude indicator.
2—Vertical speed indicator.
3—Power instruments.
4—Airspeed indicator.

7988. Which initial pitch attitude change on the attitude indicator should be made to correct altitude while at normal cruise in a helicopter?

1—One-fourth bar width.
2—One-half bar width.
3—One bar width.
4—Two bar widths.

7989. What is the primary pitch instrument during a stabilized autorotation?

1—Attitude indicator.
2—Altimeter.
3—Airspeed indicator.
4—Vertical speed indicator.

7990. A stabilized descent during an autorotation, approximately what flight attitude should be established on the attitude indicator?

1—Two bar widths above the artificial horizon.
2—Two bar widths below the artificial horizon.
3—A pitch attitude that will give an established rate of descent of not more than 500 ft./min.
4—Level flight attitude.

7991. During the initial acceleration on an instrument takeoff in a helicopter, what flight attitude should be established on the attitude indicator?

1—Level flight attitude.
2—Two bar widths low.
3—One bar width high.
4—Two bar widths high.

7992. Upon what maximum airspeed is the instrument approach criteria for a helicopter based?

1—110 knots.
2—100 knots.
3—90 knots.
4—80 knots.

7993. All helicopters are considered to be in which approach category for a helicopter instrument approach procedure?

1—A.
2—A or B, depending upon weight.
3—B.
4—B or C, depending upon weight.

7994. What reduction, if any, to visibility requirements is authorized when using a fixed-wing instrument approach procedure for a helicopter instrument approach?

1—No reduction to visibility requirements is authorized.
2—All visibility requirements may be reduced by one-half.
3—All visibility requirements may be reduced by one-fourth.
4—The visibility requirements may be reduced by one-half, but in no case lower than 1200 RVR or one-fourth mile.

7995. Which fixes on the Instrument Approach Procedure Charts are initial approach fixes?

1—Only those on the en route facilities ring and those at the start of an arc approach.
2—Any fix on the en route facilities ring, the feeder facilities ring, and those at the start of arc approaches.
3—Only the fixes at the start of arc approaches and those on either the feeder facilities ring or en route facilities ring that have a transition course shown to the approach procedure.
4—Any fix that is identified by the letters IAF.

7996. When a pilot elects to proceed to the selected alternate airport, which minimums apply for landing at the alternate?

1—IFR alternate minimums.
2—600–1 if the airport has an ILS.
3—Ceiling 200 ft. above the published minimum; visibility 2 mi.
4—The landing minimums for the approach to be used.

7997. Lift produced by an airfoil is the net force generated perpendicular to the

1—Earth's surface.
2—chord.
3—relative wind.
4—longitudinal axis of the aircraft.

7998. While en route IFR, in level cruising flight in a helicopter, a pilot experiences low–frequency vibrations (100 to 400 cycles per minute). These vibrations are normally associated with the

1—engine.
2—cooling fan.
3—main rotor.
4—tail rotor.

7999. The purpose of the lead–lag (drag) hinge in a three–bladed, fully–articulated helicopter rotor system is to compensate for

1—lateral instability during autorotation.
2—Coriolis effect.
3—geometric unbalance.
4—dissymmetry of lift.

8000. During IFR flight, you inadvertently place your helicopter in an attitude and power condition that results in settling–with–power. You can recover with the least loss of altitude by

1—increasing forward speed and partially lowering collective pitch.
2—decreasing forward speed.
3—increasing forward speed and raising collective pitch.
4—decreasing forward speed and partially raising collective pitch.

8001. You are operating at high forward speed during an IFR helicopter flight. What is a major warning of retreating blade stall?

1—In a three–bladed rotor system, a lateral oscillation and pitchup.
2—In a two–bladed rotor system, an abnormal two–per–revolution vibration.
3—Tendency of the helicopter to roll away from the stalled side.
4—An intermittent low–frequency vertical vibration.

8002. During the en route phase of an IFR flight, what limits the high airspeed potential of a helicopter?

1—Harmonic resonance.
2—Retreating blade stall.
3—Rotor RPM limitations.
4—Tail rotor flutter.

8003. While en route IFR in a helicopter, the pilot should maintain the airspeed below V_{NE}. In most helicopters, this speed

1—decreases as altitude decreases.
2—remains the same at all altitudes.
3—decreases up to critical altitude and increases above critical altitude.
4—is lower at high altitude than at low altitude.

8004. When operating at high forward airspeeds during IFR flight in a helicopter, which condition is least likely to be associated with retreating blade stall?

1—Turbulence.
2—High density altitude.
3—High gross weight.
4—High rotor RPM.

8005. Which conditions could you expect to be associated with retreating blade stall during IFR flight in a heavily loaded helicopter?

1—High rotor RPM, smooth air, and lower than standard temperature.
2—Turbulent air, higher than standard temperature, and low rotor RPM.
3—Lower than standard temperature, low rotor RPM, and smooth air.
4—High rotor RPM, turbulent air, and lower than standard temperature.

8006. You are planning to depart IFR in a helicopter from a high altitude airport. Which condition would most adversely affect performance?

1—Lower than standard temperature and high relative humidity.
2—Higher than standard temperature and low relative humidity.
3—Lower than standard temperature and low relative humidity.
4—Higher than standard temperature and high relative humidity.

Figure 102

8007. Interpret the flight attitude. One system which transmits information to the instruments has malfunctioned. (See Figure 102.)

1—Climbing turn to left.
2—Climbing turn to right.
3—Level turn to left.
4—Level turn to right.

Figure 103

8008. Interpret the flight attitude. One system which transmits information to the instruments has malfunctioned. (See Figure 103.)

1—Climbing turn to the right.
2—Level turn to the right.
3—Level turn to the left.
4—Straight–and–level flight.

Figure 104

8009. Interpret the flight attitude. One instrument has malfunctioned. (See Figure 104.)

1—Climbing turn to the right.
2—Climbing turn to the left.
3—Descending turn to the right.
4—Descending turn to the left.

Figure 105

8010. Interpret the flight attitude. One instrument has malfunctioned. (See Figure 105.)

1—Climbing turn to the right.
2—Level turn to the right.
3—Climbing turn to the left.
4—Level turn to the left.

Figure 106

8011. Interpret the flight attitude. One system which transmits information to the instruments has failed. (See Figure 106.)

1—Climbing turn to right.
2—Level turn to left.
3—Descending turn to right.
4—Level turn to right.

Figure 107

8012. Which system that transmits information to the instruments has malfunctioned? (See Figure 107.)

1—Electrical.
2—Vacuum.
3—Pitot.
4—Static air.

8013. Which instrument provides the most pertinent information (primary) for pitch control in straight–and–level flight?

1—Attitude indicator.
2—Airspeed indicator.
3—Altimeter.
4—Vertical speed indicator.

8014. Which instrument provides the most pertinent information (primary) for bank control in straight–and–level flight?

1—Turn–and–slip indicator.
2—Attitude indicator.
3—Heading indicator.
4—Magnetic compass.

8015. Which instruments should be used to make a pitch correction when you have deviated from your assigned altitude?

1—Altimeter and vertical speed indicator.
2—Manifold pressure gauge and vertical speed indicator.
3—Manifold pressure gauge and airspeed indicator.
4—Attitude indicator, altimeter, and vertical speed indicator.

8016. Which instruments, in addition to the attitude indicator, are pitch instruments?

1—Altimeter and turn coordinator.
2—Altimeter and airspeed only.
3—Altimeter and vertical speed indicator only.
4—Altimeter, airspeed indicator, and vertical speed indicator.

8017. Which is the correct sequence for recovery from a spiraling, nose–low, increasing airspeed, unusual flight attitude?

1—Increase pitch attitude, reduce power and level wings.
2—Reduce power, correct the bank attitude, and raise the nose to a level attitude.
3—Reduce power, raise the nose to level attitude, and correct the bank attitude.
4—Correct the bank attitude, reduce power, and raise the nose until the altimeter has reversed direction of travel.

8018. If your airplane is in an unusual flight attitude and the attitude indicator has exceeded its limits, which instruments should you first rely on to determine pitch attitude before starting recovery?

1—Turn indicator and vertical speed indicator.
2—Airspeed and altimeter.
3—Vertical speed indicator and airspeed to detect approaching V_{S1} or V_{MO}.
4—Turn indicator and rate of climb.

8019. While recovering from an unusual flight attitude without the aid of the attitude indicator, approximate level pitch attitude is reached when the

1—airspeed and altimeter stop their movement and the vertical speed indicator reverses its trend.
2—airspeed arrives at cruising speed, the altimeter reverses its trend, and the vertical speed stops its movement.
3—altimeter and vertical speed reverse their trend and the airspeed stops its movement.
4—vertical speed stops its movement and the airspeed and altimeter reverse their trend.

8020. What changes in control displacement should be made so that "F" in Figure 108 would result in a coordinated standard rate turn?

1—Increase right rudder and decrease rate of turn.
2—Increase right rudder and increase rate of turn.
3—Decrease right rudder and increase angle of bank.
4—Center the ball and maintain the present rate of turn.

8021. What changes in control displacement should be made so that "E" in Figure 108 would result in a coordinated standard rate turn?

1—Increase left rudder and increase rate of turn.
2—Increase left rudder and decrease rate of turn.
3—Decrease left rudder and decrease angle of bank.
4—Center the ball and maintain the present rate of turn.

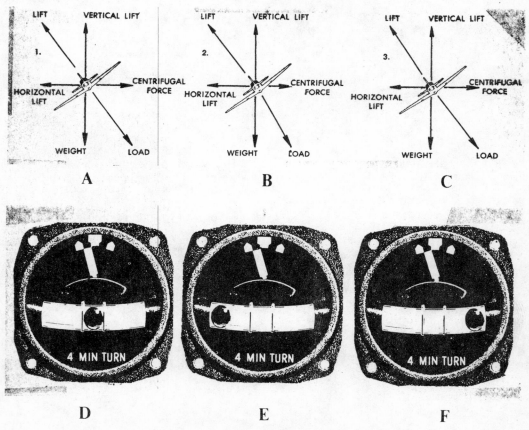

Figure 108

8022. Which combination in Figure 108 indicates a skidding turn to the left?

1—B and E.
2—A and F.
3—C and F.
4—B and F.

8023. Which combination in Figure 108 indicates a left slipping turn?

1—A and E.
2—B and E.
3—C and F.
4—C and E.

8024. Which combination in Figure 108 indicates a coordinated turn?

1—B and D.
2—C and D.
3—A and E.
4—A and D.

8025. What force causes an airplane to turn?

1—Rudder pressure or force around the vertical axis.
2—Vertical lift component.
3—Horizontal lift component.
4—Increased angle of attack.

8026. What is the relationship between centrifugal force and the horizontal lift component in a turn?

1—Horizontal lift exceeds centrifugal force.
2—Horizontal lift and centrifugal force are equal.
3—Centrifugal force exceeds horizontal lift.
4—Vertical lift exceeds horizontal lift.

8027. When the system in Figure 109 is in the free gyro mode, depressing the clockwise manual heading drive button (adjustment) will rotate the remote indicating compass card to the

1—right to eliminate left compass card error.
2—right to eliminate right compass card error.
3—left to eliminate left compass card error.
4—left to eliminate right compass card error.

8028. The heading on a remote indicating compass is 5° to the left of that desired. What action is required to move the desired heading under the heading reference? (See Figure 109.)

1—Select the free gyro mode and depress the clockwise heading drive button.
2—Select the slaved gyro mode and depress the clockwise heading drive button.
3—Select the free gyro mode and depress the counter-clockwise heading drive button.
4—Select the slaved gyro mode and depress the counter-clockwise heading drive button.

8029. The heading on a remote indicating compass is 120° and the magnetic compass indicates 110°. What action is required to correctly align the heading indicator with the magnetic compass? (See Figure 109.)

1—Select the slaved gyro mode and depress the counter-clockwise heading drive button.
2—Select the free gyro mode and depress the counter-clockwise heading drive button.
3—Select the slaved gyro mode and depress the clockwise heading drive button.
4—Select the free gyro mode and depress the clockwise heading drive button.

8030. What are the three fundamental skills involved in attitude instrument flying?

1—Instrument interpretation, trim application, and aircraft control.
2—Cross-check, instrument interpretation, and aircraft control.
3—Cross-check, emphasis, and aircraft control.
4—Fixation, omission, and emphasis.

8031. What is the third fundamental skill in attitude instrument flying?

1—Instrument interpretation.
2—Instrument cross-check.
3—Power control.
4—Aircraft control.

8032. What is the first fundamental skill in attitude instrument flying?

1—Aircraft control.
2—Instrument cross-check.
3—Instrument interpretation.
4—Pitch, bank, and power.

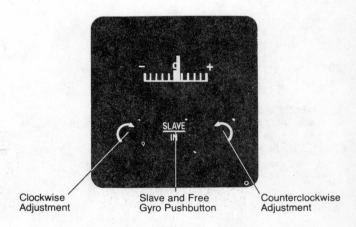

Figure 109

8033. What information does a Mach meter present?

1—The ratio of aircraft true airspeed to the speed of sound.
2—The ratio of aircraft indicated airspeed to the speed of sound.
3—The ratio of aircraft equivalent airspeed, corrected for installation error, to the speed of sound.
4—The ratio of aircraft calibrated airspeed to the speed of sound.

8034. During normal operation of a vacuum–driven attitude indicator, what attitude indication should you see when rolling out from a 180° skidding turn to straight–and–level coordinated flight?

1—A straight–and–level coordinated flight indication.
2—A nose–high indication relative to level flight.
3—The miniature aircraft shows a turn in the direction opposite the skid.
4—The miniature aircraft shows a turn in the original direction of the turn.

8035. During normal coordinated turns, what error due to precession would you see when rolling out to straight–and–level flight from a 180° steep turn to the right?

1—A straight–and–level coordinated flight indication.
2—The miniature aircraft would show a slight turn indication to the left.
3—The miniature aircraft would show a slight descent and wings–level attitude.
4—The miniature aircraft would show a slight turn to the right.

8036. During coordinated turns, which force moves the pendulous vanes of a vacuum–driven attitude indicator resulting in precession of the gyro toward the inside of the turn?

1—Acceleration.
2—Deceleration.
3—Coriolis.
4—Centrifugal.

8037. What indication is presented by the miniature aircraft of the turn coordinator?

1—Indirect indication of the bank attitude.
2—Direct indication of the bank attitude and the quality of the turn.
3—Quality of the turn.
4—Direct indication of both pitch and bank.

8038. As power is reduced to change airspeed from high to low cruise, which instruments are primary for pitch, bank, and power, respectively?

1—Attitude indicator, heading indicator, annd manifold pressure guage or tachometer.
2—Altimeter, attitude inndicator, and airspeed indicator.
3—Altimeter, heading indicator, and manifold pressure guage or tachometer.
4—Attitude indicator, turn coordinator, and airspeed indicator.

8039. The glide slope and localizer are centered but the airspeed is too fast. What should be adjusted?

1—Pitch and power.
2—Power only.
3—Pitch only.
4—Trim only.

8040. What is the primary bank instrument while transitioning from straight–and–level flight to a standard rate turn to the left?

1—Attitude indicator.
2—Heading indicator.
3—Turn coordinator (miniature aircraft).
4—Airspeed indicator.

8041. Identify the system that has failed and determine a corrective action to return the airplane to straight and level flight. (See Figure 110.)

1—Static system is clogged; lower the nose and level the wings to level flight attitude by use of attitude indicator.
2—Vacuum system has failed; reduce power, roll left to level wings, and pitch up to reduce airspeed.
3—Pitot is clogged; level the wings, and lower the nose to level attitude using attitude indicator.
4—Electrical system has failed; reduce power, roll left to level wings, and raise the nose to reduce airspeed.

8042. Which is the correct sequence for recovery from the unusual attitude indicated by Figure 111?

1—Level wings; add power; lower nose; descend to original altitude and heading.
2—Add power; lower nose; level wings; return to original altitude and heading.
3—Stop turn by raising right wing and add power at the same time; lower the nose and return to original altitude and heading.
4—Lower nose until descent is started; turn left to return to original heading. Upon reaching original altitude, level off and use power as necessary.

Figure 110

Figure 111

Figure 112

8043. What is the correct sequence for recovery from the unusual attitude indicated in Figure 112?

1—Level the wings, raise the nose of the aircraft to level flight, and reduce power until the desired airspeed is obtained.
2—Reduce power, increase back elevator pressure, and level the wings.
3—Reduce power, level the wings, bring pitch attitude to level flight.
4—Level the wings, raise the nose of the aircraft to level flight attitude, and obtain desired airspeed.

8044. Uncontrolled airspace is that airspace where

1—ATC does not control air traffic.
2—ATC controls only IFR flights which originate in controlled airspace and terminate in controlled airspace.
3—the minimum visibility for flight is 1 mi.
4—only VFR rules apply.

8045. What are the vertical limits of a transition area that is designated in conjunction with an airport having a prescribed instrument approach procedure?

1—Surface to 700 ft. AGL.
2—Surface to 1,200 ft. AGL.
3—1,200 ft. AGL to the base of the overlying controlled airspace.
4—700 ft. AGL or more to the base of the overlying controlled airspace.

8046. Which of the following statements on controlled airspace is correct?

1—A control zone will always contain a control tower.
2—Federal airways include airspace normally within 4 nautical miles each side of the centerline of the airway.
3—An airport traffic area may or may not have a control tower in operation.
4—An ATC clearance is always required while operating in a control zone, regardless of weather conditions.

8047. Which airspace is defined as a transition area when designated in conjunction with an airport which has a prescribed instrument approach procedure?

1—The airspace extending upward from 700 ft. or more above the surface and terminating at the base of the overlying controlled airspace.
2—That airspace extending from the surface and terminating at the base of the continental control area.
3—The airspace extending from the surface to 700 or 1,200 ft. AGL, where designated.
4—The airspace within a 5–statute mile radius of the airport and extending from the surface to 3,000 ft. AGL.

8048. The vertical extent of the positive control area throughout the conterminous U.S. is from

1—14,500 ft. to and including FL450.
2—18,000 ft. to and including FL450.
3—18,000 ft. to and including FL600.
4—12,500 ft. to and including FL600.

180

8049. How can you obtain the pressure altitude on flights below 18,000 ft.?

1—Set your altimeter to 29.92.
2—Use your computer to change the indicated altitude to pressure altitude.
3—Contact an FSS and ask for the pressure altitude.
4—Use the altitude shown on your altimeter.

8050. How can you determine the pressure altitude at an airport without a tower or FSS?

1—Set the altimeter to 29.92 and read the altitude indicated.
2—Set the altimeter to the current altimeter setting of a station within 100 mi. and correct this indicated altitude with local temperature.
3—Use your computer and correct the field elevation for temperature.
4—Set the altimeter to 29.92 and use indicated altitude and standard temperature to correct.

8051. Which altitude is indicated when the altimeter is set to 29.92?

1—Density.
2—Pressure.
3—Standard.
4—Calibrated.

8052. Why is hypoxia particularly dangerous during flights with one pilot?

1—Night vision may be so impaired that the pilot cannot see other aircraft.
2—Symptoms of hypoxia may be difficult to recognize before the pilot's reactions are affected.
3—The pilot may not be able to control the aircraft even if using oxygen.
4—Hypoxia can cause panic and eventual loss of control.

INTENTIONALLY LEFT BLANK

NOTE: The following information is used for questions 8053 through 8057.

Excerpt from L–3 chart (Figure 113): Variation 14°E; Cruising Altitude 7000 on V137 from IPL (g) to TRM (h); 9000 on V208 from TRM to JLI (i); TAS 150 knots. PA for 9,000 ft. is 9500.

```
WINDS AND TEMPERATURES ALOFT FORECAST
FT     ...       6000      9000     ...
                 0737-04   1043-10
```

8053. What is the estimated time en route between Imperial VORTAC (g) and Julian VORTAC (i) via V137 TRM (h), V208 JLI? (See NOTE.)

1—36 min.
2—39 min.
3—42 min.
4—45 min.

8054. What is the density altitude on the 9,000-foot leg? (See NOTE.)

1—9,100 ft.
2—8,800 ft.
3—8,500 ft.
4—8,000 ft.

8055. What is the calibrated airspeed for the 9,000-foot leg? (See NOTE.)

1—132.
2—135.
3—138.
4—141.

8056. Compute the true altitude when on V208 at 9,000 ft. indicated. (See NOTE.)

1—8,400.
2—8,800.
3—9,000.
4—9,200.

8057. How much colder is the forecast temperature at 9,000 ft. than standard temperature? (See NOTE.)

1—3°.
2—10°.
3—1°.
4—7°.

8058. What is the VHF ARTCC sector discrete frequency when flying on V458 eastbound to IPL (g)? (See Figure 113.)

1—123.65.
2—122.6.
3—133.4.
4—123.65 or 122.6.

8059. While proceeding from Thermal VORTAC (h) to Julian VORTAC (i) via V208, what is your position relative to V208 and WARNE Intersection if your instruments indicate as shown in the following illustration? (See Figure 113.)

1—Left of course, approaching WARNE Intersection.
2—Left of course, past WARNE Intersection.
3—Right of course, approaching WARNE Intersection.
4—Right of course, past WARNE Intersection.

8060. A pilot passes over Mission Bay VORTAC (k) at 1353Z and arrives at the VOR changeover point on V66 at 1408Z. Determine the wind direction and velocity. (See Figure 113.)

Route of flight..V66 IPL (g)
True airspeed...190 knots
Magnetic heading to maintain course........................067°
Magnetic variation...14°E

1—019° true at 44 knots.
2—001° true at 34 knots.
3—029° true at 34 knots.
4—047° true at 44 knots.

8061. What is the minimum crossing altitude at BOSUM Intersection (n) when flying outbound from Mission Bay VORTAC (k) on V66? (See Figure 113.)

1—5,200 ft.
2—5,500 ft.
3—4,000 ft.
4—8,000 ft.

8062. What does the symbol just to the left of the airport symbol for San Diego International–Lindbergh indicate? (See Figure 113, symbol I.)

1—In addition to providing ILS course guidance, the localizer has an ATC function.
2—The airport is served by a Category II ILS approach.
3—A published SDF (simplified direction finding) procedure is available.
4—A published ILS and/or localizer procedure is available.

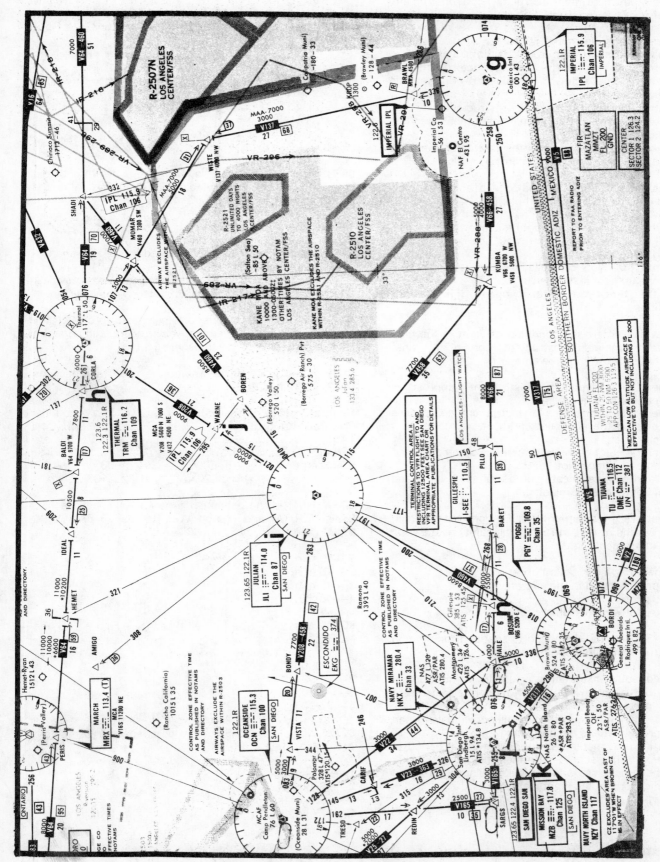

Figure 113

183

8063. What portion of dual instruction time may a certificated instrument flight instructor log as instrument flight time?

1—All time during which the instructor acts as pilot in command during an instrument training flight.
2—All time during which the instructor acts as instrument instructor, regardless of weather conditions.
3—All time during which the instructor acts as instrument instructor in actual instrument weather conditions.
4—Only the time during which the instructor flies the aircraft by reference to instruments.

8064. Which flight time may be logged as instrument time when on an instrument flight plan?

1—All of the time from lift-off until touchdown.
2—All of the time the aircraft was not controlled by ground references.
3—Only the time you controlled the aircraft solely by reference to flight instruments.
4—Only the time you were flying in IFR weather conditions.

8065. If a pilot enters the condition of flight in the pilot logbook as simulated instrument conditions, what additional information must be entered?

1—Number and type of instrument approaches completed and route of flight.
2—Number, type, and place of instrument approaches completed; name and pilot certificate number of an instructor pilot.
3—Place and type of each instrument aproach completed and name of safety pilot.
4—Name and pilot certificate number of safety pilot and type of approaches completed.

8066. What are the minimum qualifications for a person who occupies the other control seat as safety pilot during simulated instrument flight?

1—Designated as a competent observer.
2—Appropriately rated in the aircraft.
3—Private pilot.
4—Private pilot with instrument rating.

8067. The sensations which lead to spatial disorientation during instrument flight conditions

1—are frequently encountered by beginning instrument pilots, but never by pilots with moderate instrument experience.
2—may be minimized in susceptible individuals by an appropriate diet and health regime.
3—occur, in most instances, during the initial period of transition from visual to instrument flight.
4—must be suppressed and complete reliance placed on the indications of the flight instruments.

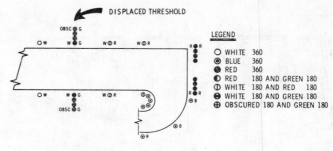

Figure 114

8068. What night operations, if any, are authorized between the approach end of the runway and the threshold lights? (See Figure 114.)

1—No aircraft operations are permitted short of the threshold lights.
2—Only taxi operations are permitted in the area short of the threshold lights.
3—Taxi and takeoff operations are permitted, providing the takeoff operations are toward the visible green threshold lights.
4—All aircraft operations are permitted provided the aircraft do not exceed the weight bearing limitation in the area short of the threshold lights.

NOTE: The following information is used for questions 8069, 8070, and 8071.

Flight altitude (VFR On Top)		7,500 ft.
Pressure altitude		7,000 ft.
TAS		165 knots
Variation		3°E
FD Excerpt	6000	9000
	2620–04	3234–08 ...

8069. What is the estimated time en route between St. Louis VOR (A) and Marion VOR (B) via V9 FAM V190 MWA? (See Figure 115 and NOTE.)

1—40 min.
2—43 min.
3—45 min.
4—48 min.

8070. What is the density altitude? (See Figure 115 and NOTE.)

1—6,000 ft.
2—6,500 ft.
3—7,000 ft.
4—7,500 ft.

8071. What is the CAS (calibrated airspeed)? (See Figure 115 and NOTE.)

1—151 knots.
2—153 knots.
3—155 knots.
4—165 knots.

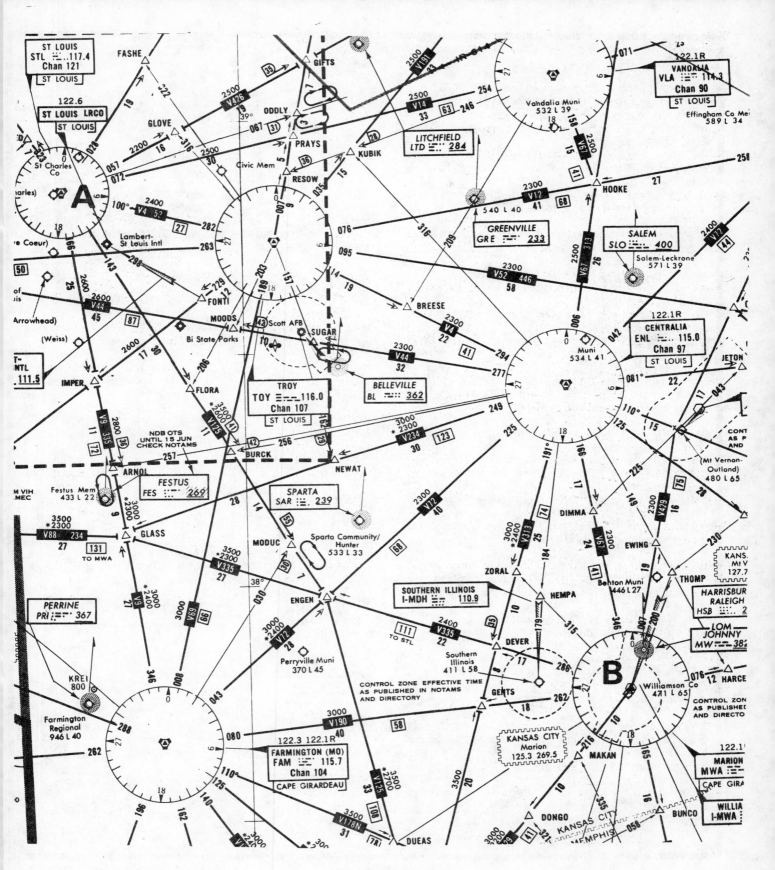

Figure 115

185

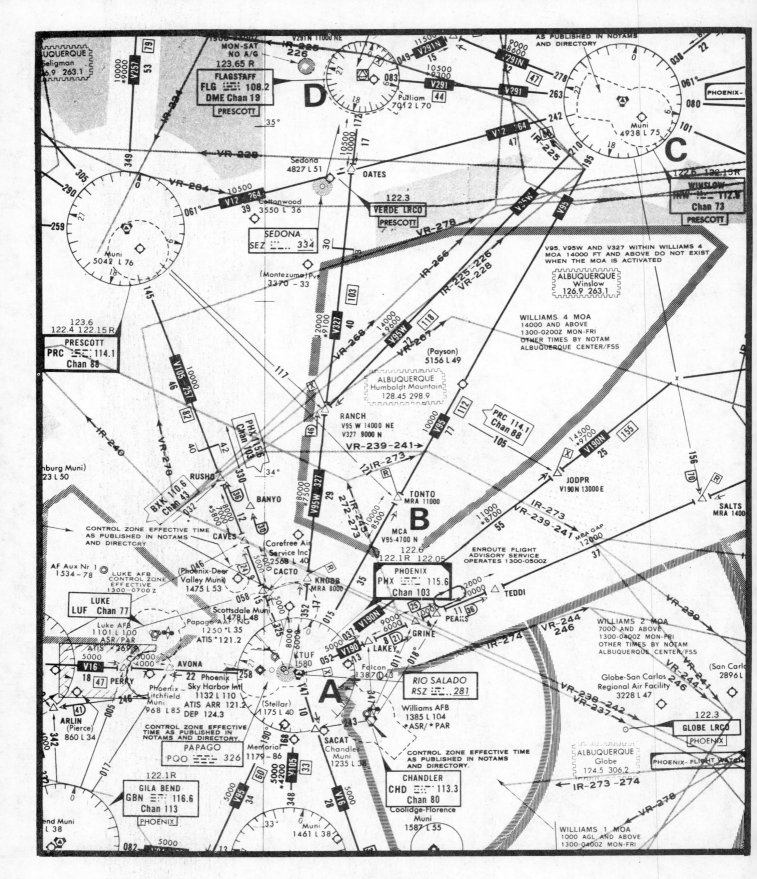

Figure 116

186

8072. What action should be taken if hyperventilation is suspected?

1—Breathe at a slower rate by taking very deep breaths.
2—Consciously breathe at a slower rate than normal.
3—Consciously force yourself to take deep breaths and breathe at a faster rate than normal.
4—If oxygen is available go on 100 percent oxygen.

8073. Which use of cockpit lighting is correct for night flight?

1—Reducing the lighting intensity to a minimum level will eliminate blind spots.
2—The use of regular white light, such as a flashlight, will impair night adaptation.
3—Coloration shown on maps is least affected by the use of direct red lighting.
4—When flying near thunderstorms having numerous lightning flashes, instrument lighting intensity should be reduced.

8074. How can an instrument pilot best overcome spatial disorientation?

1—Rely on kinesthetic sense.
2—Use a very rapid cross–check.
3—Read and interpret the flight instruments, and act accordingly.
4—Avoid banking in excess of 30°.

8075. A pilot is more subject to spatial disorientation if

1—ignoring or overcoming the sensations of muscles and inner ear.
2—kinesthetic senses are ignored.
3—eyes are moved often in the process of cross–checking the flight instruments.
4—body signals are used to interpret flight attitude.

8076. Which procedure is recommended to prevent or overcome spatial disorientation?

1—Reduce head and eye movements to the extent possible.
2—Rely on the kinesthetic sense.
3—Avoid steep turns and rough control movements.
4—Rely entirely on the indications of the flight instruments.

8077. If a pilot enters the condition of flight in the pilot logbook as simulated instrument conditions, what qualifying information must also be entered?

1—Place and type of each instrument approach completed and name of safety pilot.
2—Number and type of instrument approaches completed and route of flight.
3—Name and pilot certificate number of safety pilot and type of approaches completed.
4—Number, type, and place of instrument approaches completed; name and pilot certificate number of an instructor pilot.

8078. While en route along V95 between PHX (A) and INW (C), ATC requests a position report over TONTO Intersection (B). Which procedure is correct for the situation given? (See Figure 116.)

1—If southbound at 10,000 ft., you must climb to 11,000 ft. and confirm TONTO using PRC VOR, even if DME equipped.
2—If northbound at 10,000 ft. and cleared to remain at 10,000 ft., you may use PRC VOR to identify TONTO without climbing.
3—If northbound at 10,000 ft. and cleared to remain at 10,000 ft., you may use DME to identify TONTO at that altitude.
4—The fix cannot be legally identified by DME; therefore, 11,000 ft. is required to identify TONTO using PRC VOR.

8079. Where is the VOR changeover point between PHX VOR (A) and FLG VOR (D) along V327? (See Figure 116.)

1—The COP is located midway between the navigational facilities.
2—The COP is located at RANCH Intersection.
3—The COP is located 30 mi. south of FLG VOR.
4—The COP is not specified.

8080. What is your position relative to V95 and TONTO Intersection (B)? (See Figure 116 and the VOR indications shown in Figure 117.)

1—West of V95 and north of TONTO.
2—East of V95 and north of TONTO.
3—West of V95 and south of TONTO.
4—East of V95 and south of TONTO.

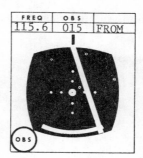 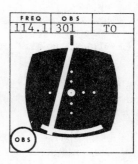

Figure 117

8081. What can a pilot expect if an airspeed indicator ram air input and drain hole are blocked?

1—The airspeed indicator will react as an altimeter.
2—The airspeed indicator will show a decrease with an increase in altitude.
3—No airspeed indicator change will occur during climbs or descents.
4—As speed increases in level flight, the airspeed indicator will show a decrease.

8082. What effect will a change in wind direction have upon maintaining a 3° glide slope at a constant true airspeed?

1—When groundspeed decreases, rate of descent must increase.
2—When groundspeed increases, rate of descent must increase.
3—Rate of descent must be constant to remain on the glide slope.
4—When groundspeed increases, rate of descent must decrease.

8083. If you are departing from an airport where you cannot obtain an altimeter setting, you should set your altimeter

1—on 29.92" Hg.
2—on zero ft.
3—on the current airport barometric pressure, if known.
4—to the airport elevation.

8084. Which action should you take if the ATC controller advises "Stop Altitude Squawk"?

1—Switch the transponder to standby.
2—Switch the transponder code to your assigned altitude.
3—Deactivate Mode C capability.
4—Switch transponder to OFF.

8085. Which action should you take if the ATC controller advises "Squawk Altitude"?

1—Switch the transponder to Mode B.
2—Switch the transponder code to your assigned altitude.
3—Activate Mode C for automatic altitude reporting, if so equipped.
4—Advise the controller of current altitude and press IDENT.

8086. Which range facility associated with the ILS is identified by the last two letters of the localizer identification group?

1—Inner marker.
2—Outer marker.
3—Outer compass locator.
4—Middle compass locator.

8087. Which range facility associated with the ILS can be identified by a two–letter coded signal?

1—IM (inner marker).
2—MM (middle marker).
3—OM (outer marker).
4—Compass Locator.

8088. FAA Deletion.

8089. What is a difference between an SDF and an LDA facility?

1—The SDF course is either 6° or 12° while the LDA is approximately 5°.
2—The SDF course has no glide slope guidance while the LDA does.
3—The SDF has no marker beacons while the LDA has at least an OM.
4—The SDF transmits on VHF frequencies while the LDA transmits on UHF frequencies.

8090. What is the difference between an LDA (localizer type directional aid) and the ILS localizer?

1—The LDA is not aligned with the runway.
2—The LDA uses a course width of 6° or 12°, while an ILS uses only 5°.
3—The LDA does not use OM's or LOM's for the FAF.
4—The LDA signal is generated from a VOR type facility and has no glide slope.

8091. How wide is an SDF course?

1—Either 3° or 6°.
2—Either 6° or 12°.
3—Varies from 5° to 10°.
4—10°.

8092. What are the main differences between the SDF (simplified directional facility) and the localizer of an ILS?

1—The usable off–course indications are limited to 35° for the localizer and up to 90° for the SDF.
2—The SDF transmits signals within a different frequency range.
3—The SDF course may not be aligned with the runway and the course may be wider.
4—The course width for the localizer will always be 5° while the SDF course will be between 6° and 12°.

8093. A pilot is making an ILS approach to a runway which has a VASI. What is the responsibility of the pilot if an electronic glide slope malfunction occurs and the pilot has the VASI in sight?

1—The pilot should inform ATC of the malfunction and then descend immediately to the localizer MDA and make a localizer approach.
2—The pilot must make a missed approach, inform ATC of the malfunction, and may request another type approach.
3—The pilot may continue the approach and use the VASI glide slope in place of the electronic glide slope.
4—The pilot must notify ATC immediately of the malfunction, may request the localizer approach, but must stay at or above the VASI glide slope until a lower altitude is necessary for a safe landing.

INTENTIONALLY LEFT BLANK

8094. Which of the following indications would a pilot see while approaching to land on a runway served by a 2–bar VASI (visual approach slope indicator)?

1—If below the glidepath, the near bars will be red and the far bars white.
2—If on the glidepath, the near bars will appear red, and the far bars will appear white.
3—If departing to the high side of the glidepath, the far bars will change from red to white.
4—If on the glidepath, both near bars and far bars will appear white.

8095. Which is a feature of the tricolor VASI?

1—Three light bars on each side of the runway.
2—One light projector with three colors: red, green, and amber.
3—Two visual glidepaths for the runway.
4—Three glidepaths, with the center path indicated by a white light.

8096. Which approach and landing objective is assured when the pilot remains on the proper glidepath of the VASI?

1—Touchdown at the runway threshold.
2—Continuation of course guidance after transition to VFR.
3—Safe obstruction clearance in the approach area.
4—Course guidance from the visual descent point to touchdown.

8097. What indications are correct for the glidepath positions on a tricolor VASI?

1—Red below glidepath; pink on glidepath; white above glidepath.
2—Red below glidepath; white on glidepath; amber above glidepath.
3—Red below glidepath; green on glidepath; amber above glidepath.
4—Red below glidepath; green on glidepath; white above glidepath.

8098. Where are the MAP's for the ILS and localizer RWY 10R approaches, respectively, at Boise, Idaho? (See Figure 118.)

1—Middle marker, middle marker.
2—Upon reaching 3,031 ft. MSL, middle marker.
3—Middle marker, 3.5 nautical miles from LOM.
4—Upon reaching 3,031 ft. MSL, 3.5 nautical miles from LOM.

8099. Upon reaching PARMO Intersection at 5,000 ft., you are cleared for the LOC RWY 10R approach (glide slope inoperative). What are your minimum altitudes until you have the proper landing requirements or have reached the MAP? (See Figure 118.)

1—4200 to LOM then 3031.
2—4200 to LOM then 3120.
3—4200 until within 10 nautical miles of LOM, 4100 to LOM, then 3031.
4—4200 until within 10 nautical miles of LOM, 4100 to LOM, then 3120.

8100. If a multiengine reciprocating engine–powered airplane has a V_{SO} of 62 knots and a maximum certificated gross weight of 5,700 lb., what should be the steady rate–of–climb with one engine inoperative at 5,000 ft.? (See Appendix 2.)

1—104 ft./min.
2—228 ft./min.
3—255 ft./min.
4—300 ft./min.

8101. A certain reciprocating engine–powered airplane has a certificated maximum gross weight of 9,500 lb. What should be the steady rate–of–climb with one engine inoperative? (See Appendix 2.)

1—At least 550 ft./min.
2—.027 multiplied by the V_{SO} squared (.027 x V_{SO}^2).
3—At least 300 ft./min.
4—At least 250 ft./min.

8102. A certain reciprocating engine–powered multi–engine airplane weighs 6,300 lb. at maximum gross weight and has a V_{SO} of 63 knots. What should be the steady rate–of–climb with one engine inoperative at 5,000 ft.? (See Appendix 2.)

1—The steady rate–of–climb must only be determined.
2—107 ft./min.
3—195 ft./min.
4—227 ft./min.

8103. A certain reciprocating engine–powered multi–engine airplane has a maximum gross weight of 5,200 lb. and a V_{SO} of 55 knots. What should be the steady rate–of–climb with one engine inoperative at 5,000 ft.? (See Appendix 2.)

1—82 ft./min.
2—164 ft./min.
3—225 ft./min.
4—The steady rate–of–climb must only be determined.

8104. A certain reciprocating engine–powered airplane has V_{SO} of 60 knots at a maximum certificated gross weight of 5,200 lb. What should be the steady rate of climb with one engine inoperative at an altitude of 5,000 ft.? (See Appendix 2.)

1—The rate–of–climb may be a negative value but must be determined.
2—68 ft./min.
3—186 ft./min.
4—300 ft./min.

8105. What guidance information is provided to the pilot during a MLS (Microwave Landing System) approach?

1—Approach azimuth angle and back azimuth angle (when installed), approach elevation angle, and range (DME).
2—Azimuth angle and approach elevation on both front and back courses and range (DME).
3—Azimuth angle and approach elevation on both front and back courses but no range (DME).
4—Approach azimuth angle only, approach elevation angle, and range (DME) for front course only.

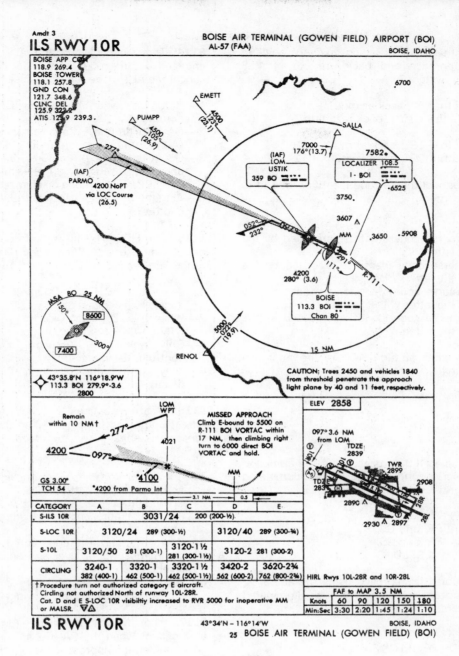

Figure 118

8106. What are the lateral approach azimuth angle limits, referenced to either side of the landing runway, of a MLS (Microwave Landing System)?

1—At least 10°.
2—At least 15°.
3—20°.
4—At least 40°.

8107. What are the respective range limits for the front and back guidance of a MLS (Microwave Landing System)?

1—10 NMI and 10 NMI.
2—15 NMI and 10 NMI.
3—20 NMI and 7 NMI.
4—30 NMI and 15 NMI.

8108. What is the maximum elevation guidance angle in degrees for the approach and back azimuth of MLS (Microwave Landing System)?

1—Approach azimuth +5°; back azimuth +5°.
2—Approach azimuth +15°; back azimuth +15° (if installed).
3—Approach azimuth +18°; back azimuth +10°.
4—Approach azimuth +20°; back azimuth +12°.

8109. What international morse code identifier is used to identify a specific interim standard microwave landing system?

1—A three letter morse code identifier preceded by the morse code for letter "I".
2—A two letter morse code identifier preceded by the morse code for the letters "IM".
3—A three letter morse code identifier preceded by the morse code for the letter "M".
4—A three letter morse code identifier preceded by the morse code for the letters "ML".

8110. To at least what altitude AGL is the approach azimuth guidance angle coverage?

1—20,000 ft.
2—10,000 ft.
3—8,000 ft.
4—5,000 ft.

8111. During a coupled ILS aproach using the autopilot, which mode annunciator indications will be illuminated prior to glide slope interception? (See Figure 119.)

1—FD, ALT, AP, APPR, and CPLD.
2—FD, ALT, ARM, APPR, and GS.
3—ALT, AP, HDG, APPR, and GS.
4—AP, HDG, APPR, and CPLD.

8112. During a coupled ILS aproach using the autopilot, which mode annunciator indications will be illuminated after glide slope interception? (See Figure 119.)

1—NAV, ARM, APPR, and GS.
2—FD, AP, APPR, CPLD, and GS.
3—AP, APPR, CPLD, GS, and GA.
4—FD, NAV, ALT, HDG, and CPLD.

8113. What indications are shcwn on the FCI (Flight Command Indicator) when using the GA (Go–around) mode? (See Figure 119.)

1—The command V–bar remains wings–level and indicates a level flight pitch attitude.
2—The command V–bar indicates a half–standard rate turn to a preselected heading and a pitch–up command.
3—The command V–bar disappears from view.
4—The command V–bar commands wings–level and indicates a pitch up.

8114. The autopilot and the ALT (Altitude) mode are engaged on the mode controller. What occurrences will cancel the ALT mode function? (See Figure 119.)

1—Autopilot switch to OFF or GA (Go–around) mode actuated.
2—GA (Go–around) mode actuated, disengaging ALT (Altitude) function, or autopilot switch to OFF.
3—GS (Glide Slope) capture, GA (Go–around) mode actuated, disengaging ALT (Altitude) function, or FD (Flight Director) mode disengaged.
4—Actuation vertical trim control and GS (Glide Slope) capture.

8115. The HDG (Heading) mode on the mode controller has been selected. What occurrences will cancel this function? (See Figure 119.)

1—When the BC (Back Course) function of the mode controller is engaged.
2—When the FD (Flight Director) mode is disengaged or NAV or APPR coupling occurs.
3—Only when the autopilot function of the mode controller is engaged.
4—Only when the FD (Flight Director) mode is disengaged.

8116. What indications will be presented by the FCI (Flight Command Indicator) when the FD (Flight Director) function is engaged on the mode controller? (See Figure 119.)

1—Command V–bar appears and commands wings level and aircraft pitch attitude.
2—Command V–bar does not appear but the delta (aircraft representation) adjusts to wings–level attitude.
3—If in a climb attitude, command V–bar appears, commands wings level and adjusts pitch attitude to level flight.
4—Command V–bar appears and, if in a bank, will indicate a banked attitude and level pitch attitude.

8117. What indications will be illuminated on the mode annunciator when the GA (Go–around) is used at the DH on a coupled ILS approach? (See Figure 119.)

1—FD and GA.
2—FD, HDG, and GA.
3—FD, HDG, NAV, and GA.
4—HDG and GA.

8118. Which functions of the mode controller must be used for radial interception and automatic tracking information to a VOR/VORTAC? (See Figure 119.)

1—HDG, NAV, and APPR.
2—FD and NAV.
3—HDG and NAV.
4—HDG, FD, and NAV.

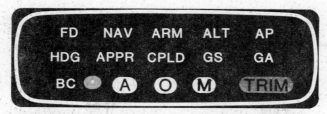

MODE
ANNUNCIATOR

FLIGHT
COMMAND
INDICATOR

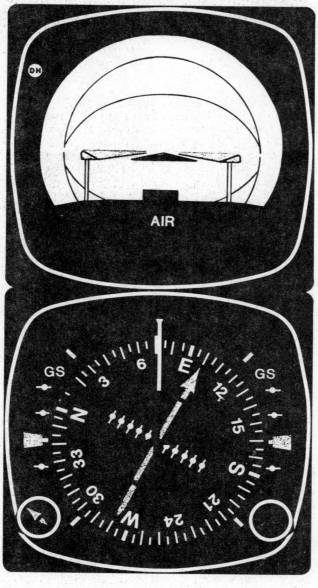

PICTORIAL
NAVIGATION
INDICATOR

MODE
CONTROLLER

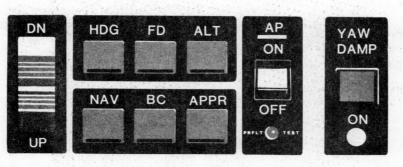

YAW MODE
CONTROLLER

Figure 119

APPENDIX 2

UNITED STATES GOVERNMENT FLIGHT INFORMATION PUBLICATION

AIRPORT/FACILITY DIRECTORY

DIRECTORY LEGEND
TABLE OF CONTENTS

ABBREVIATIONS

The following abbreviations are those commonly used within this Directory. Other abbreviations may be found in the Legend and are not duplicated below.

acft	aircraft	med	medium
apch	approach	NFCT	non-federal control tower
arpt	airport		
avbl	available	ngt	night
bcn	beacon	ntc	notice
blo	below	opr	operate
byd	beyond	ops	operates operation
ctc	contact	ovrn	overrun
dalgt	daylight	p-line	power line
dsplc	displace	req	request
dsplcd	displaced	rqr	requires
emerg	emergency	rgt tfc	right traffic
fld	field	rwy	runway
ints	intensity	svc	service
lgtd	lighted	tkf	take off
lgts	lights	tfc	traffic
ldg	landing	thld	threshold

1

DIRECTORY LEGEND

LEGEND

This Directory is an alphabetical listing of data on record with the FAA on all airports that are open to the public, associated terminal control facilities, air route traffic control centers and radio aids to navigation within the conterminous United States, Puerto Rico and the Virgin Islands. Airports are listed alphabetically by associated city name and cross referenced by airport name. Facilities associated with an airport, but with a different name, are listed individually under their own name, as well as under the airport with which they are associated.

The listing of an airport in this directory merely indicates the airport operator's willingness to accommodate transient aircraft, and does not represent that the facility conforms with any Federal or local standards, or that it has been approved for use on the part of the general public.

The information on obstructions is taken from reports submitted to the FAA. It has not been verified in all cases. Pilots are cautioned that objects not indicated in this tabulation (or on charts) may exist which can create a hazard to flight operation.

Detailed specifics concerning services and facilities tabulated within this directory are contained in Airman's Information Manual, Basic Flight Information and ATC Procedures.

The legend items that follow explain in detail the contents of this Directory and are keyed to the circled numbers on the sample on the preceding page.

① CITY/AIRPORT NAME
Airports and facilities in this directory are listed alphabetically by associated city and state. Where the city name is different from the airport name the city name will appear on the line above the airport name. Airports with the same associated city name will be listed alphabetically by airport name and will be separated by a dashed rule line. All others will be separated by a solid rule line.

② § NOTAM SERVICE
§—NOTAM "D" (Distant teletype dissemination) and NOTAM "L" (Local dissemination) service is provided for airport. Absence of annotation § indicates NOTAM "L" (Local dissemination) only is provided for airport. See AIM, Basic Flight Information and ATC Procedures for detailed description of NOTAM.

③ LOCATION IDENTIFIER
A three or four character code assigned to airports. These identifiers are used by ATC in lieu of the airport name in flight plans, flight strips and other written records and computer operations.

④ AIRPORT LOCATION
Airport location is expressed as distance and direction from the center of the associated city in nautical miles and cardinal points, i.e., 4 NE.

⑤ TIME CONVERSION
Hours of operation of all facilities are expressed in Greenwich Mean Time (GMT) and shown as "Z" time. The directory indicates the number of hours to be subtracted from GMT to obtain local standard time and local daylight saving time GMT—5(—4DT). The symbol ‡ indicates that during periods of Daylight Saving Time effective hours will be one hour earlier than shown. In those areas where daylight saving time is not observed that (—4DT) and ‡ will not be shown. All states observe daylight savings time except Arizona and that portion of Indiana in the Eastern Time Zone and Puerto Rico and the Virgin Islands.

⑥ GEOGRAPHIC POSITION OF AIRPORT

⑦ CHARTS
The Sectional Chart and Low and High Altitude Enroute Chart and panel on which the airport or facility is located.

⑧ INSTRUMENT APPROACH PROCEDURES
IAP indicates an airport for which a prescribed (Public Use) FAA instrument Approach Procedure has been published.

⑨ ELEVATION
Elevation is given in feet above mean sea level and is the highest point on the landing surface. When elevation is sea level it will be indicated as (00). When elevation is below sea level a minus (—) sign will precede the figure.

⑩ ROTATING LIGHT BEACON
B indicates rotating beacon is available. Rotating beacons operate dusk to dawn unless otherwise indicated in AIRPORT REMARKS.

⑪ SERVICING
S1: Minor airframe repairs.
S2: Minor airframe and minor powerplant repairs.
S3: Major airframe and minor powerplant repairs.
S4: Major airframe and major powerplant repairs.

DIRECTORY LEGEND

SAMPLE

CITY NAME
§ AIRPORT NAME (ORL) 4 E GMT—5(—4DT) 28°32'43"N 81°20'10"W JACKSONVILLE H-4G, L-19C
200 B S4 FUEL 100, JET A OX 1, 2, 3 TPA—1000(800) AOE CFR Index A Not insp. IAP

RWY 07-25: H6000X150 (ASPH-PFC) S-90, D-160, DT-300 HIRL CL
RWY 07: ALSF1. Trees.   RWY 25: REIL. Rgt tfc.
RWY 13-31: H4620X100 (ASPH) HIRL
RWY 13: VASI—GA 3.3° TCH 89'. Pole.   RWY 31: VASI—GA 3.1° TCH 36': Tree. Rgt tfc.
AIRPORT REMARKS: Special Air Traffic Rules—Part 93, see Regulatory Notices. Attended 1200-0300‡. LLWSAS. Parachute Jumping. CAUTION cattle and deer on arpt. Acft 100,000 lbs or over ctc Director of Aviation for approval (305) 894-9831. Fee for all airline charters, travel clubs and certain revenue producing acft. Flight Notification Service (ADCUS) available. Control Zone effective 1500-0700‡.
COMMUNICATIONS: ATIS 127.25   UNICOM 122.95
® NAME APP/DEP CON 128.35 (1200-0400Z‡)
NAME FSS (ORL) on fld. 123.65 122.65 122.2 122.1R 112.2T   (305) 894-0861
TOWER 118.7   GND CON 121.7   CLNC DEL 125.55   PRE TAXI CLNC 125.5
TCA GROUP II: See VFR Terminal Area Chart.
RADIO AIDS TO NAVIGATION: VHF/DF ctc FSS
NAME (H) ABVORTAC 112.2 ■ORL Chan 59 28°33'N 81°20'07"W   at fld.   1110/8E
TWEB avbl 1300-0100Z‡.
VOR unusable 050-060° beyond 15 NM below 5000'
HERNY NDB (LOM) 221   OR 28°30'24"N 81°26'03"W   067° 5.4 NM to fld.
ILS 109.9 I-ORL Rwy 07. LOM HERNY NDB
ASR/PAR
COMM/NAVAID REMARKS: Emerg frequency 121.5 not available at tower.

AIRPORT NAME (X30) 7 W GMT—5(—4DT) 28°31'50"N 81°32'26"W   JACKSONVILLE
130 S4 FUEL 100 OX 2
RWY 18-36: 2430X150 (TURF) LIRL   RWY 36: Thld dsplcd 270': Road.
RWY 18: Thld dsplcd 215': Trees.
AIRPORT REMARKS: Attended dawn-0300‡.
COMMUNICATIONS: UNICOM 122.8
NAME FSS (ORL)

§ D AIRPORT NAME (MCO) 6.1 SE GMT—5(—4DT) 28°25'53"N 81°19'29"W   JACKSONVILLE H-4G, L-19C
96 B FUEL 100, JET A LRA CFR Index D   IAP
RWY 18R-36L: H12004X300 (CONC-GRVD) S-100, D-200, DT-400 HIRL
RWY 18R: ALSF1. REIL. Rgt tfc.   RWY 36L: REIL.
RWY 18L-36R: H12004X200 (ASPH) S-165, D-200, DT-400 HIRL
RWY 18L: LDIN. ALSF1. TDZ. REIL. VASI—GA 3° TCH 36': Thld dsplcd 300': Trees. Rgt tfc.
AIRPORT REMARKS: Attended 1200-0300‡.
COMMUNICATIONS: UNICOM 123.0
NAME FSS (ORL) NOTAM FILE MCO
® APP CON 124.8 (337°-179°)   120.1 (180°-336°)   DEP CON 120.15
TOWER 124.3 Opr 1200-0400Z‡   GND CON 121.85   CLNC DEL 134.7
STAGE III SVC ctc APP CON
RADIO AIDS TO NAVIGATION:
(H) VORTAC 112.2 ORL   Chan 59 28°32'33"N 81°20'07"W   173° 5.7 NM to fld. 1110/8E
VOR unusable 050-060° beyond 15 NM below 5000'
ILS 109.3 I-MCO Rwy 36 BC unusable. Unmonitored.
ASR

E AIRPORT NAME (See PLYMOUTH)

All Bearings and Radials are Magnetic unless otherwise specified.
All mileages are nautical unless otherwise noted.
All times are GMT except as noted.

DIRECTORY LEGEND

(12) FUEL

CODE	FUEL
80	Grade 80 gasoline (Red)
100	Grade 100 gasoline (Green)
100LL	Grade 100LL gasoline (low lead) (Blue)
115	Grade 115 gasoline
A	Jet A—Kerosene freeze point—40° C.
A1	Jet A-1—Kerosene, freeze point—50° C.
A1+	Jet A-1—Kerosene with icing inhibitor, freeze point—50° C.
B	Jet B—Wide-cut turbine fuel, freeze point—50° C.
B+	Jet B—Wide-cut turbine fuel with icing inhibitor, freeze point—50° C.

(13) OXYGEN

OX 1 High Pressure
OX 2 Low Pressure
OX 3 High Pressure—Replacement Bottles
OX 4 Low Pressure—Replacement Bottles

(14) TRAFFIC PATTERN ALTITUDE

Traffic Pattern Altitude (TPA)—The first figure shown is TPA above mean sea level. The second figure in parentheses is TPA above airport elevation.

(15) AIRPORT OF ENTRY AND LANDING RIGHTS AIRPORTS

AOE—Airport of Entry—A customs Airport of Entry where permission from U.S. Customs is not required, however, at least one hour advance notice of arrival must be furnished.

LRA—Landing Rights Airport—Application for permission to land must be submitted in advance from U.S. Customs. At least one hour advance notice of arrival must be furnished.

NOTE: Advance notice of arrival at both an AOE and LRA airport may be included in the flight plan when filed in Canada or Mexico, where Flight Notification Service (ADCUS) is available and the airport remark will indicate this service. This notice will also be treated as an application for permission to land in the case of an LRA. Although advance notice of arrival may be relayed to Customs through Mexico, Canadian, and U.S. Communications facilities by flight plan, the aircraft operator is solely responsible for insuring that Customs receives the notification. (See Customs, Immigration and Naturalization, Public Health and Agriculture Department requirements in the International Flight Information Manual for further details.)

(16) CERTIFICATED AIRPORT (FAR 139)

Airports serving Civil Aeronautics Board certified carriers and certified under FAR, Part 139, are indicated by the CFR index; i.e., CFR Index A, which relates to the availability of crash, fire, rescue equipment.

FAR—PART 139 CERTIFICATED AIRPORTS

INDICES AND FIRE FIGHTING AND RESCUE EQUIPMENT REQUIREMENTS

Airport Index	Required No. Vehicles	Aircraft Length	Scheduled Departures	Agent + Water for Foam
A	1	≤90'	≥1	500 # DC or 450 # DC + 50 gal H₂O
AA	1	>90', ≤126'	<5	300 # DC + 500 gal H₂O
B	2	>90', ≤126'	≥5	Index A + 1500 gal H₂O
		>126', ≤160'	<5	
C	3	>126', ≤160'	≥5	Index A + 3000 gal H₂O
		>160', ≤200'	<5	
D	3	>160', ≤200'	≥5	Index A + 4000 gal H₂O
		>200'	<5	
E	3	>200'	≥5	Index A + 6000 gal H₂O

> Greater Than; < Less Than; ≥ Equal or Greater Than; ≤ Equal or Less Than; H₂O—Water; DC—Dry Chemical.

NOTE: If AFFF (Aqueous Film Forming Foam) is used in lieu of Protein Foam, the water quantities listed for Indices AA thru E can be reduced 33 ⅓%. See FAR Part 139.49 for full details. The listing of CFR index does not necessarily assure coverage for non-air carrier operations or at other than prescribed times for air carrier. CFR index Ltd.-indicates vehicle and capacity requirements for airports holding limited operating certificates and are determined on a case by case basis.

DIRECTORY LEGEND

(17) FAA INSPECTION

All airports not inspected by FAA will be identified by the note: Not insp. This indicates that the airport information has been provided by the owner or operator of the field.

(18) RUNWAY DATA

Runway information is shown on two lines. That information common to the entire runway is shown on the first line while information concerning the runway ends are shown on the second or following line. Lengthy information will be placed in the Airport Remarks.

Runway direction, surface, length, width, weight bearing capacity, lighting, gradient (when gradient exceeds 0.3 percent) and appropriate remarks are shown for each runway. Direction, length, width, lighting and remarks are shown for sealanes. The full dimensions of helipads are shown, i.e., 50X150.

RUNWAY SURFACE AND LENGTH

Runway lengths prefixed by the letter "H" indicate that the runways are hard surfaced (concrete, asphalt). If the runway length is not prefixed, the surface is sod, clay, etc. The runway surface composition is indicated in parentheses after runway length as follows;

(AFSC)—Aggregate friction seal coat   (GRVD)—Grooved   (TURF)—Turf
(ASPH)—Asphalt   (GRVL)—Gravel, or cinders   (TRTD)—Treated
(CONC)—Concrete   (PFC)—Porous friction courses   (WC)—Wire combed
(DIRT)—Dirt   (RFSC)—Rubberized friction seal coat

RUNWAY WEIGHT BEARING CAPACITY

Runway strength data shown in this publication is derived from available information and is a realistic estimate of capability at an average level of activity. It is not intended as a maximum allowable weight or as an operating limitation. Many airport pavements are capable of supporting limited operations with gross weights of 25-50% in excess of the published figures. Permissible operating weights, insofar as runway strengths are concerned, are a matter of agreement between the owner and user. When desiring to operate into any airport at weights in excess of those published in the publication, users should contact the airport management for permission. Add 000 to figure following S, D, DT, DDT and MAX for gross weight capacity.

S—Runway weight bearing capacity for aircraft with single-wheel type landing gear, (DC-3), etc.
D—Runway weight bearing capacity for aircraft with dual-wheel type landing gear, (DC-6), etc.
DT—Runway weight bearing capacity for aircraft with dual-tandem type landing gear, (707), etc.
DDT—Runway weight bearing capacity for aircraft with double dual-tandem type landing gear, (747), etc.
Quadricycle and dual-tandem are considered virtually equal for runway weight bearing consideration, as are single-tandem and dual-wheel.
Omission of weight bearing capacity indicates information unknown.

RUNWAY LIGHTING

Lights are in operation sunset to sunrise. Lighting available by prior arrangement only or operating part of the night only and/or pilot controlled and with specific operating hours are indicated under airport remarks. Since obstructions are usually lighted, obstruction lighting is not included in this code. Unlighted obstructions on or surrounding an airport will be noted in airport remarks.

Temporary, emergency or limited runway edge lighting such as flares, smudge pots, lanterns or portable runway lights will also be shown in airport remarks.

Types of lighting are shown with the runway or runway end they serve.

LIRL—Low Intensity Runway Lights
MIRL—Medium Intensity Runway Lights
HIRL—High Intensity Runway Lights
REIL—Runway End Identifier Lights
CL—Centerline Lights
TDZ—Touchdown Zone Lights
ODALS—Omni Directional Approach Lighting System.
AF OVRN—Air Force Overrun 1000' Standard Approach Lighting System.
LDIN—Lead-In Lighting System.
MALS—Medium Intensity Approach Lighting System.
MALSF—Medium Intensity Approach Lighting System with Sequenced Flashing Lights.
MALSR—Medium Intensity Approach Lighting System with Runway Alignment Indicator Lights.
SALS—Short Approach Lighting System.
SALSF—Short Approach Lighting System with Sequenced Flashing Lights.
SSALS—Simplified Short Approach Lighting System.
SSALF—Simplified Short Approach Lighting System with Sequenced Flashing Lights.
SSALR—Simplified Short Approach Lighting System with Runway Alignment Indicator Lights.
ALSF—High Intensity Approach Lighting System with Sequenced Flashing Lights.
ALSF1—High Intensity Approach Lighting System with Sequenced Flashing Lights, Category I, Configuration.
ALSF2—High Intensity Approach Lighting System with Sequenced Flashing Lights, Category II, Configuration.
VASI—Visual Approach Slope Indicator System.

VISUAL APPROACH SLOPE INDICATOR SYSTEMS

VASI—Visual Approach Slope Indicator
SAVASI—Simplified Abbreviated Visual Approach Slope Indicator

Aviation weather briefing service is provided by FSS's and CS/T's; however, CS/T personnel are not certified weather briefers and therefore provide only factual data from weather reports and forecasts. Flight and weather briefing services are also available by calling the telephone numbers listed.

Limited Remote Communications Outlet (LRCO)—Unmanned air/ground communications facility, which may be associated with a VOR. These outlets have receive-only capability and rely on a VOR or a remote transmitter for full capability.

Remote Communications Outlet (RCO)—An unmanned air/ground communications facility, remotely controlled and providing UHF or VHF communications capability to extend the service range of an FSS or C/ST.

Civil Communications Frequencies—Civil communications frequencies used in the FSS air/ground system are now operated simplex on 122.0, 122.2, 122.3, 122.4, 122.6, 123.6; emergency 121.5; plus receive-only on 122.05, 122.1, 122.15, and 123.6.

   a. 122.0 is assigned as the Enroute Flight Advisory Service channel at selected FSS's.

   b. 122.2 is assigned to all FSS's as a common enroute simplex service.

   c. 123.6 is assigned as the airport advisory channel at non-tower FSS locations, however, it is still in commission at some FSS's collocated with towers to provide part time Airport Advisory Service.

   d. 122.1 is the primary receive-only frequency at VOR's. 122.05, 122.15 and 123.6 are assigned at selected VOR's meeting certain criteria.

   e. Some FSS's are assigned 50 kHz channels for simplex operation in the 122-123 MHz band (e.g. 122.35). Pilots using the FSS A/G system should refer to this directory or appropriate charts to determine frequencies available at the FSS or remoted facility through which they wish to communicate.

Part time FSS hours of operation are shown in remarks under facility name.

Emergency frequency 121.5 is available at all Flight Service Stations, Towers, Approach Control and RADAR facilities, unless indicated as not available.

Frequencies published followed by the letter "T" or "R", indicate that the facility will only transmit or receive respectively on that frequency. All radio aids to navigation frequencies are transmit only.

TERMINAL SERVICES

ATIS—A continuous broadcast of recorded non-control information in selected areas of high activity.

UNICOM—A non-government air/ground radio communications facility utilized to provide general airport advisory service.

APP CON—Approach Control. The symbol ® indicates radar approach control.

TOWER—Control tower

GND CON—Ground Control

DEP CON—Departure Control. The symbol ® indicates radar departure control.

CLNC DEL—Clearance Delivery.

PRE TAXI CLNC—Pre taxi clearance

VFR ADVSY SVC—VFR Advisory Service. Service provided by Non-Radar Approach Control.

Advisory Service for VFR aircraft (upon a workload basis) ctc APP CON.

STAGE II SVC—Radar Advisory and Sequencing Service for VFR aircraft

STAGE III SVC—Radar Sequencing and Separation Service for participating VFR Aircraft within a Terminal Radar Service Area (TRSA)

TCA—Radar Sequencing and Separation Service for all aircraft in a Terminal Control Area (TCA)

TOWER, APP CON and DEP CON RADIO CALL will be the same as the airport name unless indicated otherwise.

㉑ RADIO AIDS TO NAVIGATION

The Airport Facility Directory lists by facility name all Radio Aids to Navigation, except Military TACANS, that appear on National Ocean Survey Visual or IFR Aeronautical Charts and those upon which the FAA has approved an Instrument Approach Procedure. All VOR, VORTAC, and ILS equipment in the National Airspace System has an automatic monitoring and shutdown feature in the event of malfunction. Unmonitored, as used in this publication for any navigational aid, means that FSS or tower personnel cannot observe the malfunction or shutdown signal.

NAVAID information is tabulated as indicated in the following sample:

	TWEB	TACAN/DME Channel		Geographical Position		Site Elevation
NAME (L) ABVORTAC 117.5	■ ABE	Chan 122	40°43′36″N 75°27′18″W	180°4.1 NM to fld.		1110/8E

     Class   Frequency   Identifier   Bearing and distance   Magnetic Variation
                                         facility to airport

                                  VOR unusable 020°-060° beyond 26 NM below 3500'

         Restriction within the normal altitude/range of the navigational aid (See primary alphabetical listing for restrictions on VORTAC and VOR/DME).

ASR/PAR—Indicates that Surveillance (ASR) or Precision (PAR) radar instrument approach minimums are published in U.S. Government Instrument Approach Procedures.

DIRECTORY LEGEND

S2L	2-box SAVASI on left side of runway	
S2R	2-box SAVASI on right side of runway	
V2R	2-box VASI on right side of runway	
V2L	2-box VASI on left side of runway	
V4R	4-box VASI on right side of runway	
V4L	4-box VASI on left side of runway	
V6R	6-box VASI on right side of runway	
V6L	6-box VASI on left side of runway	
V12	12-box VASI on both sides of runway	
V16	16-box VASI on both sides of runway	
*NSTD	Nonstandard VASI, VAPI, or any other system not listed above	

VASI approach slope angle and threshold crossing height will be shown when available, i.e., GA 3.5° TCH 37.0'.

PILOT CONTROL OF AIRPORT LIGHTING

Key Mike	Function
7 times within 5 seconds	Highest intensity available
5 times within 5 seconds	Medium or lower intensity available (Lower REIL or REIL-Off)
3 times within 5 seconds	Lowest intensity available (Lower REIL or REIL-Off)

Available systems will be indicated in the Airport Remarks, as follows:

    ACTIVATE MALSR Rwy 7, HIRL Rwy 7/25-122.8.

    or

    ACTIVATE MIRL Rwy 18/36-122.8.

    or

    ACTIVATE VASI and REIL, Rwy 7-122.8.

Where the airport is not served by an instrument approach procedure and/or has an independent type system of different specification installed by the airport sponsor, descriptions of the type lights, method of control, and operating frequency will be explained in clear text. See AIM, "Basic Flight Information and ATC Procedures," for detailed description of pilot control of airport lighting.

RUNWAY GRADIENT

Runway gradient will be shown only when it is 0.3 percent or more. When available the direction of slope upward will be indicated, i.e., 0.5% up NW.

RUNWAY END DATA

Lighting systems such as VASI, MALSR, REIL; obstructions; displaced thresholds will be shown on the specific runway end. "Rgt tfc" indicates right turns should be made on landing and takeoff for specified runway end.

⑲ AIRPORT REMARKS

LLWSAS—Indicates a Low Level Wind Shear Alert System consisting of a centerfield and several field perimeter anemometers is installed.

Landing Fee indicates landing charges for private or non-revenue producing aircraft, in addition, fees may be charged for planes that remain over a couple of hours and buy no services, or at major airline terminals for all aircraft.

Remarks—Data is confined to operational items affecting the status and usability of the airport.

⑳ COMMUNICATIONS

Communications will be listed in sequence in the order shown below:

Automatic Terminal Information Service (ATIS) and Private Aeronautical Stations (UNICOM), along with their frequency is shown, where available, on the line following the heading "COMMUNICATIONS" Whenever a second UNICOM frequency is shown in parentheses, it represents a proposed change to the current frequency with an uncertain date of change. If unable to contact the ground station on the regularly published UNICOM frequency, attempt to establish communications on the frequency shown in parenthesis.

Flight Service Station (FSS) information. The associated FSS will be shown followed by the identifier and information concerning availability of telephone service, e.g. "NOTAM FILE IAD." Where the FSS is located on the field it will be indicated as "on arpt" following the identifier. Frequencies available will follow. The FSS telephone number will follow along with any significant operational information. FSS's whose name is not the same as the airport on which located will also be listed in the normal alphabetical name listing for the state in which located. Limited Remote Communication Outlet: (LRCO) or Remote Communications Outlet (RCO) providing service to the airport followed by the frequency and name of the Controlling FSS.

FSS's and CS/T's provide information on airport conditions, radio aids and other facilities, and process flight plans. Airport Advisory Service is provided at the pilot's request on 123.6 or 123.65 by FSS's located at non-tower airports or when the tower is not in operation. (See AIM, ADVISORIES AT NON TOWER AIRPORTS.)

RADIO CLASS DESIGNATIONS

Identification of VOR/VORTAC/TACAN Stations by Class (Operational Limitations):

Normal Usable Altitudes and Radius Distances

Class	Altitudes	Distance (miles)
(T)	12,000' and below	25
(L)	Below 18,000'	40
(H)	Below 18,000'	40
(H)	Within the Conterminous 48 States only, between 14,500' and 17,999'	100
(H)	18,000' FL 450	130
(H)	Above FL 450	100

(H) = High   (L) = Low   (T) = Terminal

NOTE: An (H) facility is capable of providing (L) and (T) service volume and an (L) facility additionally provides (T) service volume.

The term VOR is, operationally, a general term covering the VHF omnidirectional bearing type of facility without regard to the fact that the power, the frequency protected service volume, the equipment configuration, and operational requirements may vary between facilities at different locations.

AB — Automatic Weather Broadcast (also shown with ■ following frequency.)
DF — Direction Finding Service.
DME — UHF standard (TACAN compatible) distance measuring equipment.
H — Non-directional radio beacon (homing), power 50 watts to less than 2,000 watts (50 NM at all altitudes).
HH — Non-directional radio beacon (homing), power 2,000 watts or more (75 NM at all altitudes).
H-SAB — Non-directional radio beacons providing automatic transcribed weather service.
ILS — Instrument Landing System (voice, where available, on localizer channel).
ISMLS — Interim Standard Microwave Landing System.
LDA — Localizer Directional Aid.
LMM — Compass locator station when installed at middle marker site (15 NM at all altitudes).
LOM — Compass locator station when installed at outer marker site (15 NM at all altitudes).
MH — Non-directional radio beacon (homing) power less than 50 watts (25 NM at all altitudes).
S — Simultaneous range homing signal and/or voice.
SABH — Non-directional radio beacon not authorized for IFR or ATC. Provides automatic weather broadcasts.
SDF — Simplified Direction Facility.
TACAN — UHF navigational facility-omnidirectional course and distance information.
VOR — VHF navigational facility-omnidirectional course only.
VOR/DME — Collocated VOR navigational facility and UHF standard distance measuring equipment.
VORTAC — Collocated VOR and TACAN navigational facilities.
W — Without voice on radio facility frequency.
Z — VHF station location marker at a LF radio facility.

DIRECTORY LEGEND

FREQUENCY PAIRING PLAN

The following is a list of paired VOR/ILS VHF frequencies with TACAN Channels:

Frequency MHz	Channel	Frequency MHz	Channel	Frequency MHz	Channel	Frequency MHz	Channel
108.0	17	110.5	42	113.0	77	115.5	102
108.1	18	110.6	43	113.1	78	115.6	103
108.2	19	110.7	44	113.2	79	115.7	104
108.3	20	110.8	45	113.3	80	115.8	105
108.4	21	110.9	46	113.4	81	115.9	106
108.5	22	111.0	47	113.5	82	116.0	107
108.6	23	111.1	48	113.6	83	116.1	108
108.7	24	111.2	49	113.7	84	116.2	109
108.8	25	111.3	50	113.8	85	116.3	110
108.9	26	111.4	51	113.9	86	116.4	111
109.0	27	111.5	52	114.0	87	116.5	112
109.1	28	111.6	53	114.1	88	116.6	113
109.2	29	111.7	54	114.2	89	116.7	114
109.3	30	111.8	55	114.3	90	116.8	115
109.4	31	111.9	56	114.4	91	116.9	116
109.5	32	112.0	57	114.5	92	117.0	117
109.6	33	112.1	58	114.6	93	117.1	118
109.7	34	112.2	59	114.7	94	117.2	119
109.8	35	112.3	70	114.8	95	117.3	120
109.9	36	112.4	71	114.9	96	117.4	121
110.0	37	112.5	72	115.0	97	117.5	122
110.1	38	112.6	73	115.1	98	117.6	123
110.2	39	112.7	74	115.2	99	117.7	124
110.3	40	112.8	75	115.3	100	117.8	125
110.4	41	112.9	76	115.4	101	117.9	126

(22) COMM/NAVAID REMARKS:
Pertinent remarks concerning communications and NAVAIDS.

PREFERRED IFR ROUTES

A system of preferred routes has been established to guide pilots in planning their route of flight, to minimize route changes during the operational phase of flight, and to aid in the efficient orderly management of the air traffic, using federal airways. The preferred IFR routes which follow are designed to serve the needs of airspace users and to provide for a systematic flow of air traffic in the major terminal and en route flight environments. Cooperation by all pilots in filing preferred routes will result in fewer traffic delays and will better provide for efficient departure, en route and arrival air traffic service.

The following lists contain preferred IFR routes for the low altitude stratum and the high altitude stratum. The high altitude list is in two sections; the first section showing terminal to terminal routes and the second section showing single direction route segments. Also, on some high altitude routes low altitude airways are included as transition routes.

The following will explain the terms/abbreviations used in the listing:

1. Preferred routes beginning/ending with an airway number indicate that the airway essentially overlies the airport and flight are normally cleared directly on the airway.

2. Preferred IFR routes beginning/ending with a fix indicate that aircraft may be routed to/from these fixes via a Standard Instrument Departure (SID) route, radar vectors (RV), or a Standard Terminal Arrival Route (STAR).

3. Preferred IFR routes for major terminals selected are listed alphabetically under the name of the departure airport. Where several airports are in proximity they are listed under the principal airport and categorized as a metropolitan area; e.g. New York Metro Area.

4. Preferred IFR routes used in one direction only for selected segments, irrespective of point of departure or destination, are listed numerically showing the segment fixes and the direction and times effective.

5. Where more than one route is listed the routes have equal priority for use.

6. Official location identifiers are used in the route description for VOR/VORTAC navaids.

7. Intersection names are spelled out.

8. Navaid radial and distance fixes (e.g., ARD201113) have been used in the route description in an expediency and intersection names will be assigned as soon as routine processing can be accomplished. Navaid radial (no distance stated) may be used to describe a route to intercept a specified airway (e.g., MIV MIV101 V39); another navaid radial (e.g. UIM UIM255 GSW081); or an intersection (e.g., GSW081 FITCH).

9. Where two navaids, an intersection and a navaid, a navaid and a navaid radial and distance point, or any navigable combination of these route descriptions follow in succession, the route is direct.

10. The effective times for the routes are in GMT. Pilots planning flight between the terminals or route segments listed should file for the appropriate preferred IFR route.

11. (90-170 incl) altitude flight level assignment in hundreds of feet.

12. The notations "pressurized" and "unpressurized" for certain low altitude preferred routes to Kennedy Airport indicate the preferred route based on aircraft performance.

LOW ALTITUDE

Terminals	Route	Effective Times (GMT)
ALBANY		
Boston	(60-170 incl) V2 GDM V431	1100-0300
Kennedy	(150-170 incl) V489 V157 ELLIS	1000-0300
	or	
	(90-100, unpressurized acft only) V91 V487 CMK	
La Guardia	(60-170 incl) V91 V487 V123	1000-0300
Newark	(80-170 incl) ALB205 SAX034 MOBBS	1000-0300
Philadelphia	(70-170 incl) V72 DNY 051 DNY V449	1100-1300
	LHY V149 MAZIE	
BALTIMORE—See Washington/Baltimore Metro		
BOSTON METRO AREA		
Buffalo	(60-170 incl) MHT V490 UCA V2 ROC	1000-0300
	V2N EHMAN.	
Cleveland	(60-170 incl) MHT V490 UCA V2 SYR V84	1000-0300
	GEE V464 V115 TDT V72 V232 CXR	
	CXR246 NOELS.	
Kennedy	(80-170 incl) V292 PUT V308 ORW V16	1000-0300
	MICKE	
La Guardia	(60-170 incl) HFD V3 CMK V123.	1000-0300
Martha's Vineyard	(60-170 incl) WACKY INT via ORW 134R V46	0000-2359
	CLAMY INT MVY	
Newark	(80-170 incl) V205 MOBBS.	1000-0300
Philadelphia	(80-170 incl) PUT V308 HTO V139 DRIFT	1000-0300
	V312 OOD	
Rochester	(60-170 incl) MHT V490 UCA V2	1000-0300
Syracuse	(60-170 incl) MHT V490 UCA V2	1000-0300

PREFERRED IFR ROUTES

Terminals	Route	Effective Times (GMT)
Baltimore	(90-140 incl) CYN V16 ENO V379 GRACO.	1100-0300
Boston	(130-170 incl, Turbojets and Heavy Turbo props) BELLE V229 MAD V475 PVD V139 HTM.	1100-0300
Boston	(70-170 incl, All other Types) BELLE V229 MAD V475 ORW V16.	1100-0300
Bradley	(60-170 incl) BELLE 197 BDR BDR014 JUDDS CMK058 BRISS	1100-0300
Dulles	(140-160 incl) RBV RBV289 MXE056 MXE V474 V143 SCOBY AML	1200-0300
	or	
	(80-100 incl) SBJ V30 V39 LRP V143S EMI FDK AML	1200-0300
Norfolk Metro Area	(60-170 incl) MANTA V139 CCV	1100-0300
Providence	(60-170 incl) HTO V139	1100-0300
Rochester	(110-170 incl) HUO V252 BGM V423 V34	1100-0300
Utica	(90-170 incl) HUO V252 V273 HNK HNK035 MILID V249.	1100-0300
Washington	(90-140 incl) CYN V16 ENO V379 DEALE	1100-0300
From LA GUARDIA only		
Albany	(60-170 incl) MARES V467 SEAMO V91 PWL V487 CANAN V130.	1100-0300
Baltimore	(90-170 incl) SBJ V3 V93 JARET.	1000-0300
Boston	(130-170 incl, Turbojets and Heavy props) MARES V475 PVD V139 HTM.	1100-0300
Boston	(60-170 incl, all other types) MARES V475 ORW V16	1100-0300
Bradley	(60-170 incl) MARES V467 BDR014 JUDDS CMK058 BRISS.	1100-0300
Cleveland	(90-170 incl) SBJ V30 SEG V6 YNG V6N NOELS.	1100-0300
Dulles	(80-100 incl) SBJ V30 V39 LRP V143S EMI FDK AML	1100-0300
Dulles	(110-170 incl) SBJ V30 V39 LRP V143 SCOBY AML	1100-0300
Norfolk Metro Area	(120-170 incl) VCN VCN226 SBY011 SBY V29 SWL V139 CCV	1200-0300
Pittsburgh	(90-170 incl) SBJ V30 PSB V58 GRACE.	1100-0300
Providence	(60-170 incl) MARES V475 ORW ORW112 LAFAY V139.	1100-0300
Rochester	(90-170 incl) SBJ V30 V39 LRP V143 SCOBY AML	1100-0300
Utica	(90-170 incl) SLOAT HUO V252 V273 HNK HNK035 MILID V249.	1100-0300
Washington	(90-170 incl) SBJ V3 MXE V378 BAL.	1200-0300
From WESTCHESTER COUNTY only		
Baltimore	(90-170 incl) SBJ V3 V93 JARET.	1100-0300
Cleveland	(90-170 incl) HUO V126 LHY V58 PSB V6 YNG V6N NOELS	1100-0300
Dulles	(80-100 incl) SBJ V30 V39 LRP V143 EMI FDK AML	1100-0300
Dulles	(110-170 incl) SBJ V30 V39 LRP V143 SCOBY AML	1100-0300
Norfolk Metro Area	(120-170 incl) VCN VCN226 SBY011 SBY V29 SWL V139 CCV	1200-0300
Pittsburgh	(90-170 incl) HUO V126 LHY V58 GRACE	1100-0300
Utica	(90-170 incl) HUO V252 V273 HNK HNK035 MILID V249.	1100-0300
Washington	(90-170 incl) SBJ V3 MXE V378 BAL.	1100-0300
NORFOLK METRO AREA		
Dulles	HPW RIC V38 V223 FLUKY.	1100-0300

6

Facility Name (Airport Name)	Freq.	Type VOT Facility	Remarks
Santa Ana (John Wayne/Orange Co)	113.9	G	Runup area rwy 19L.
	113.9	G	Taxiway A in front of Martin Aviation.
Santa Monica Muni	113.9	G	Taxiway 1 in front of Tower.
	113.9	G	Taxiway 4 in front of Wings West hangar.
Torrance Muni	113.9	G	Runup area rwy 29R.
	113.9	G	Runup area rwy 29L.
	113.9	G	Runup area rwy 11R.
	113.9	G	Runup area rwy 11L.

COLORADO

VOR RECEIVER CHECK POINTS

Facility Name (Arpt Name)	Freq/Ident	Type Check Pt. Gnd. AB/ALT	Azimuth from Fac. Mag	Dist. from Fac. N.M.	Check Point Description
Akron	114.4/AKO	A/6000	179	7	Over lgtd twr.
Colorado Springs	112.5/COS	A/9000	321	6.8	Over microwave twr.
Cortez (Cortez-Montezuma County)	108.4/CEZ	A/7000	196	0.5	Over apch end rwy 21.
Durango (Durango-La Plata County)	108.2/DRO	G	010		At turnout apch end rwy 20.
Gill (Weld County Muni)	122.8/GLL	A/6500	214	8.0	Over Great Western Sugar Beet Factory.
Grand Junction (Walker Field)	112.4/GJT	A/6500	059		Over intersection rwy 04-22 and 11-29.
Hayden (Craig-Moffat)	115.4/CHE	A/7200	248	9.6	Over apch end rwy 25.
Hayden (Yampa Valley)	115.4/CHE	G	104	4.5	On ramp at front of terminal.
Pueblo (Pueblo Memorial)	116.7/PUB	G	249	4.0	On painted circle with arrow on runup pad S side apch end rwy 08L.
	116.7/PUB	A/7300	294	7.8	Over KOA TV twr. 5.4 NM NW of arpt.

VOR TEST FACILITIES (VOT)

Facility Name (Airport Name)	Freq.	Type VOT Facility	Remarks
Stapleton Intl	110.0	G	

NEVADA

VOR RECEIVER CHECK POINTS

Facility Name (Arpt Name)	Freq/Ident	Type Check Pt. Gnd. AB/ALT	Azimuth from Fac. Mag	Dist. from Fac. N.M.	Check Point Description
Elko (Elko Muni-J.C. Harris Fld)	114.5/EKO	A/6100	324	4.1	Over the center field taxiway intersection.
Ely (Ely Arpt/Yelland Fld)	110.6/ELY	G	060		On southside twy leading to passenger terminal area.
Las Vegas (McCarran Intl)	116.9/LAS	G	351	9	On taxiway W between rwy 19L and taxiway D.
Reno (Cannon Intl)	117.9/RNO	G	229	5.8	On A.S.I. ramp at taxiway Northwest end taxiway A
Reno (Reno/Stead)	117.9/RNO	A/7000	291	5.5	Over atct.
Wells (Harriet Field)	114.2/LWL	A/6300	112	14.0	Over approach end rwy 08.

VOR RECEIVER CHECK
VOR RECEIVER CHECK POINTS
AND
VOR TEST FACILITIES (VOT)

The use of VOR airborne and ground check points is explained in Airman's Information Manual, Basic Flight Information and ATC Procedures.

NOTE: Under columns headed "Type of Check Point" & "Type of VOT Facility" G stands for ground. A/ stands for airborne followed by figures (2300) or (1000-3000) indicating the altitudes above mean sea level at which the check should be conducted. Facilities are listed in alphabetical order, in the state where the check points or VOTs are located.

ARIZONA

VOR RECEIVER CHECK POINTS

Facility Name (Arpt Name)	Freq/Ident	Type Check Pt. Gnd. AB/ALT	Azimuth from Fac. Mag	Dist. from Fac. N.M.	Check Point Description
Bard	116.8/BZA	A/2000	242	5.9	Over interstate 8 freeway crossing canal.
Douglas (Bisbee Douglas Intl)	108.8/DUG	G	169		At int rwy 30 and taxiway T-2.
Flagstaff (Pulliam)	108.2/FLG	G	158	0.5	At twy entrance to T-hangars midfield.
Fort Huachuca (Libby AAF/Sierra Vista Muni)	111.6/FHU	G	111		On compass rose rwy 11-29.
	111.6/FHU	G	164		On maltese cross on main rwy.
	111.6/FHU	G	210		On runup area rwy 02.
Gila Bend (Gila Bend AF Aux)	116.6/GBN	A/2000	191	5.5	Over apch end rwy 35.
Kingman (Mohave County)	108.8/GM	G	222		At center of runup area E of apch end rwy 03.
Prescott (Prescott Muni)	114.1/PRC	A/7000	124	5.0	Over apch end rwy 29.
Scottsdale Muni	115.6/PHX	A/1000	341	11.5	Over rwy 21 thld.
Tucson (Tucson Intl)	117.1/TUS	A/4000	258	6.0	Over main rwy intersection.
Winslow (Winslow Muni)	112.6/INW	A/6000	107	5.0	Over apch end rwy 29.

VOR TEST FACILITIES (VOT)

Facility Name (Airport Name)	Freq.	Type VOT Facility	Remarks
Phoenix (Sky Harbor Intl)	109.0	G	

Key to Aviation Weather Observations

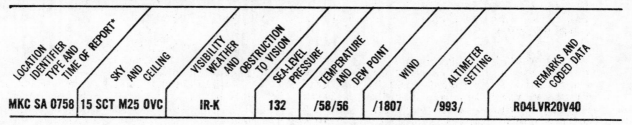

LOCATION IDENTIFIER	TYPE AND TIME OF REPORT*	SKY AND CEILING	VISIBILITY WEATHER AND OBSTRUCTION TO VISION	SEA-LEVEL PRESSURE	TEMPERATURE AND DEW POINT	WIND	ALTIMETER SETTING	REMARKS AND CODED DATA
MKC	SA 0758	15 SCT M25 OVC	IR-K	132	/58/56	/1807	/993/	R04LVR20V40

SKY AND CEILING
Sky cover contractions are in ascending order. Figures preceding contractions are heights in hundreds of feet above station.

Sky cover contractions are:

CLR Clear: Less than 0.1 sky cover.
SCT Scattered: 0.1 to 0.5 sky cover.
BKN Broken: 0.6 to 0.9 sky cover.
OVC Overcast: More than 0.9 sky cover.
— Thin (When prefixed to SCT, BKN, OVC)
—X Partial obscuration: 0.1 to less than 1.0 sky hidden by precipitation or obstruction to vision (bases at surface).
X Obscuration: 1.0 sky hidden by precipitation or obstruction to vision (bases at surface).

Letter preceding height of layer identifies ceiling layer and indicates how ceiling height was obtained. Thus:

E Estimated height **M** Measured **W** Indefinite
V Immediately following height, indicates a variable ceiling

VISIBILITY
Reported in statute miles and fractions. (V=Variable)

WEATHER AND OBSTRUCTION TO VISION SYMBOLS

A	Hail	SG	Snow grains
BD	Blowing dust	SP	Snow pellets
BN	Blowing sand	SW	Snow showers
BS	Blowing snow	T+	Severe thunderstorm
D	Dust	T	Thunderstorm
F	Fog	ZL	Freezing drizzle
GF	Ground fog	ZR	Freezing rain
H	Haze	K	Smoke
IC	Ice crystals	L	Drizzle
IF	Ice fog	R	Rain
IP	Ice pellets	RW	Rain showers
IPW	Ice pellet showers	S	Snow

Precipitation intensities: —Light; (no sign) Moderate; + Heavy.

WIND
Direction in tens of degrees from true north, speed in knots. 0000 indicates calm. G indicates gusty. Peak speed of gusts follows G or Q when gusts or squall are reported. The contraction WSHFT followed by GMT time group in remarks indicates windshift and its time of occurrence.

EXAMPLES: 3627 = 360 Degrees; 27 knots; 3627G40 = 360 Degrees, 27 knots, peak speed in gusts 40 knots.

ALTIMETER SETTING
The first figure of the actual altimeter setting is always omitted from the report.

RUNWAY VISUAL RANGE (RVR)
RVR is reported from some stations. Extreme values during 10 minutes prior to observation are given in hundreds of feet. Runway identification precedes RVR report.

DECODED REPORT
Kansas City: Record observation taken at 0758GMT, 1500 feet scattered clouds, measured ceiling 2500 feet overcast, visibility 1 mile, light rain, smoke, sea-level pressure 1013.2 millibars, temperature 58 F. dewpoint 56°F, wind 180°, 7 knots, altimeter setting 29.93 inches. Runway 04 left, visual range 2000 feet variable to 4000 feet.

*TYPE OF REPORT
SA—a scheduled record observation
SP—an unscheduled special observation indicating a significant change in one or more elements
RS—a scheduled record observation that also qualifies as a special observation.
All three types of observations (SA, SP, RS) are followed by a 24 hour-clock-time-group in GMT.

TERMINAL FORECASTS (FT)
East of Rockies: 0940Z, 1440Z, 2140Z
Rockies westward: 0940Z, 1540Z, 2240Z
24-hour fcst with last 6 hours in categorical form
(LIFR, IFR, MVFR, VFR)

TERMINAL FORECASTS contain information for specific airports on expected ceiling, cloud heights, cloud amounts, visibility, weather and obstructions to vision and surface wind. They are issued 3 times/day and are valid for 24 hours. The last six hours of each forecast are covered by a categorical statement indicating whether VFR, MVFR, IFR or LIFR conditions are expected. Terminal forecasts will be written in the following forms:

CEILING: Identified by the letter "C"

CLOUD HEIGHTS: In hundreds of feet above the station (ground)

CLOUD LAYERS: Stated in ascending order of height

VISIBILITY: In statute miles

but omitted if over 6 miles
WEATHER AND OBSTRUCTION TO VISION: Standard weather and obstruction to vision symbols are used

SURFACE WIND: In tens of degrees and knots; omitted when less than 10.

EXAMPLE OF TERMINAL FORECASTS

DCA 221010: DCA Forecast 22nd day of month—valid time 10Z-10Z

10 SCT C18 BKN 5SW — 3415G25 OCNL C8 X 1/2 SW. Scattered clouds at 1000 feet, ceiling 1800 feet broken, visibility 5 miles, light snow showers, surface wind 340 degrees 15 knots gusts to 25 knots, occasional ceiling 8 hundred feet sky obscured, visibility 1/2 mile in moderate snow showers.

12Z C50 BKN 3312G22: At 12Z becoming ceiling 5000 feet broken, surface wind 330 degrees 12 knots gusts to 22 knots.

04Z MVFR CIG: last 6 hours of FT after 04Z marginal VFR conditions due to ceiling.

CATEGORIES	CEILING		VISIBILITY
LIFR	<500	and/or	<1
IFR	≧ 500—<1000	and/or	≧1—<3
MVFR	≧1000—≦3000	and/or	≧3—≦5
VFR	>3000	and	>5

L in LIFR and M in MVFR indicate "LOW" and "MARGINAL".

AREA FORECASTS (FA)
—at 0040Z and 1240Z
18-hour fcst + 12-hour outlook in categorical form
(LIFR, IFR, MVFR, VFR)

AREA FORECASTS are 18-hour aviation forecasts plus a 12-hour categorical outlook prepared 2 times/day giving general descriptions of cloud cover, weather and frontal conditions for an area the size of several states. Heights of cloud tops, and icing are referenced ABOVE SEA LEVEL (ASL); ceiling heights, ABOVE GROUND LEVEL (AGL); bases of cloud layers are ASL unless indicated. Each SIGMET or AIRMET affecting an FA area will also serve to amend the Area Forecast.

WIND/TEMPERATURE ALOFT FORECASTS (FD)
Prepared by National Meteorological Center (call letters, WBC) contains upper air temperature forecasts issued for 100 locations in 48 states. Winds for in-between points can be obtained by interpolation.

WIND (AND TEMPERATURE) ALOFT FORECASTS are 12-hour forecasts of wind direction (nearest 10° true N) and speed (knots) for selected flight levels. Temperatures aloft (°C) are included for all but the 3000-foot level.

FORMAT OF WIND ALOFT FORECAST
FT	3000	6000	9000	etc.
DCA	2925	2833+00	2930—03	etc.

At 6000 feet ASL wind from 280° at 33 knots with temperature 0° Celsius

IN-FLIGHT ADVISORIES (WS, WST, WA)—as required
SIGMET (WS)—for all aircraft
CONVECTIVE SIGMET (WST)—for all aircraft
AIRMET (WA)—for small aircraft

SIGMET or AIRMET messages broadcast by FAA on NAVAID voice channels warn pilots of potentially hazardous weather, SIGMET concerns severe and extreme conditions of importance to all aircraft, (i.e. icing, turbulence, and duststorms/sandstorms). Convective SIGMETS are issued for thunderstorms by the National Severe Storms Forecast Center at Kansas City for the conterminous United States. AIRMETs concern less severe conditions which may be hazardous to some aircraft or to relatively inexperienced pilots.

TWEB Route Configuration Map

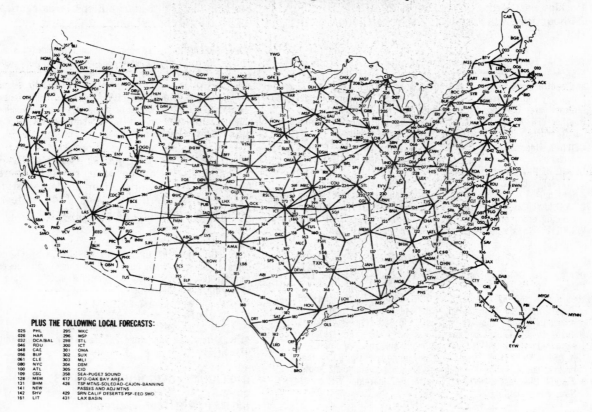

PLUS THE FOLLOWING LOCAL FORECASTS:

025	PHL	295	MKC
026	HAR	296	MSP
032	DCA/BAL	298	STL
046	RDU	300	ICT
048	CAE	301	OMA
056	BUF	302	SUX
061	CLE	303	MLI
080	NYC	304	DSM
100	ATL	305	CID
109	CSG	358	SEA-PUGET SOUND
128	MEM	417	SFO-OAK BAY AREA
131	BHM	426	TSP MTNS-SOLEDAD-CAJON-BANNING
141	NEW		PASSES AND ADJ MTNS
142	SHV	429	SRN CALIF DESERTS PSP-EED SWD
151	LIT	431	LAX BASIN

TRANSCRIBED WEATHER BROADCASTS (TWEBs) plus a SYNOPSIS (SYNS)

East of Rockies: 1040Z, 1740Z, 2240Z
Rockies westward: 1140Z, 1840Z, 2340Z

TWEB (Continuous Transcribed Weather Broadcast)—Individual route forecasts cover a 25-nautical-mile zone either side of a course line for the route. By requesting a specific route number, detailed en route weather for a 12- or 18-hour (depending on forecast issuance) period plus a synopsis can be obtained.

Forecast texts are prepared and furnished to FAA for dissemination via the continuous **Transcribed Weather Broadcasts (TWEBs)** over specified low/medium frequency (L/MF) (200-415 KHz) and very high frequency (VOR) (108.0-117.95 MHz) and the **Pilots Automatic Telephone Weather Answering Service (PATWAS)**. These texts serve as weather briefings for local or limited cross-country flights. Telephone numbers for PATWAS outlets are in the Airport/Facility Directory.

TRANSCRIBED WEATHER BROADCAST SERVICE (TWEB) provides:

Continuous weather information useable within receiving range (about 75 miles) of the broadcast outlet; Identification; Synopsis; Flight Precautions; TWEB Route Forecasts; Winds Aloft Forecasts; RAREPs; PIREPs; Surface Weather Reports; NOTAMs.

VOR Frequencies in MHz have line-of-sight range
NDB Frequencies in KHz have 75-mile range (GLS and GNI have 300-mile range)

WEATHER CHART SYMBOLS

THE WEATHER DEPICTION CHART

TOTAL SKY COVER

○ Clear

◐ Scattered

● Broken, or thin broken

◑ Overcast, with breaks

● Overcast

⊗ Obscured

OTHER

⚑ Clouds Topping Ridges

WEATHER AND OBSTRUCTIONS TO VISION

△ — Hail
R — Thunderstorm
•• — Rain
✳ — Snow
, — Drizzle
∞ — Haze
= — Fog
/∿ — Smoke

∿ — Freezing Rain
∿ — Freezing Drizzle
▽ — Rain Shower
▽ — Snow Shower
△ — Ice Pellets
-S(— Blowing Dust
-S(— Blowing Sand
-+ — Blowing Snow

Figures below the circle are cloud heights in hundreds of feet--either the ceiling; or, if there is no ceiling, the height of the lowest scattered. Figures and symbols to left of circle are visibility and weather or obstructions to vision.

LOW LEVEL PROG CHART

IFR — CEILING LESS THAN 1000 FT AND/OR VISIBILITY LESS THAN 3 MILES

MVFR — CEILING 1000-3000 FT INCLUSIVE AND/OR VISIBILITY 3-5 MILES

VFR — AREAS NOT OUTLINED INDICATE CEILING ABOVE 3000 FEET AND VISIBILITY MORE THAN 5 MILES.

MODERATE OR GREATER TURBULENCE

MODERATE TURBULENCE

SEVERE TURBULENCE

•••••••• FREEZING LEVEL SURFACE

------- FREEZING LEVEL ABOVE MSL

CONTINUOUS OR INTERMITTENT PRECIPITATION

LESS THAN .5 AREA COVERAGE

.5 OR MORE AREA COVERAGE

• INTERMITTENT RAIN

•• CONTINUOUS RAIN

✳ INTERMITTENT SNOW

✳ ✳ CONTINUOUS SNOW

∿ FREEZING PRECIP

,', DRIZZLE

SHOWERS

LESS THAN .5 AREA COVERAGE

.5 OR MORE AREA COVERAGE

▽ RAIN SHOWERS

✳▽ SNOW SHOWERS

R̲ THUNDERSTORMS

140------TOP IN 100ft

60------BASE IN 100ft

RADAR CHART LEGEND

SYMBOLS COMMON TO ALL PLOTTED RADAR WEATHER REPORTS

WEATHER SYMBOLS

A	Hail	IP	Ice Pellets
R	Rain	L	Drizzle
RW	Rain Showers	ZL	Freezing Drizzle
S	Snow	ZR	Freezing Rain
SW	Snow Showers	T	Thunderstorm

ECHO INTENSITY

-	Weak	X	Intense
(No symbol)	Moderate	XX	Extreme
+	Strong	U	Unknown
++	Very Strong		
Solidus (/)	Separates intensity from intensity trend		

TREND

+	Increasing	NC	No Change
-	Decreasing	NEW	New

Examples of Precipitation Types, Intensity, and Trend

TRW+/- — Thunderstorm, heavy rainshower, decreasing in intensity.

R-/NC — Light rain, no change in intensity.

TRW-/NEW — Thunderstorm, light rain shower, newly developed.

S — Snow (No intensity or characteristic is shown for frozen precipitation.)

MOVEMENT OF ECHOES
(Examples)

↗15 Northeast at 15 knots. (Individual Echo)

⊔⊔→ East at 25 knots. (Line or area movement)

HEIGHTS OF ECHO BASES AND TOPS

Heights in hundreds of feet MSL are entered above and/or below a line to denote echo tops and bases respectively. Examples are:

450̲ Average tops are 45,000 feet.

200̲/80 Tops 20,000 feet; bases 8,000 feet.

350̲ Top of individual cell, 35,000 feet.

620̲ Maximum tops, 62,000 feet.

A250̲ Tops 25,000 feet, reported by aircraft. Absence of a figure below the line indicates that echo base was not reported. Radar detects tops more readily than bases, since precipitation usually reaches the ground. Also, curvature of the earth prohibits the detection of bases of distant precipitation. Information from ATC radar shows tops only when reported by aircraft.

"Boxes" enclosed by dash lines indicate severe weather watch in effect. Refer to latest "WW" for specifics.

SYMBOLS INDICATING NO ECHOES

NE — No echo (equipment operating but no echoes observed).

NA — Observation not available.

OM — Equipment out for maintenance.

SYMBOLS USED WITH WEATHER SURVEILLANCE RADAR

▱ A line of echoes

☁ An area of echoes

○ Isolated cell

✳ Strong cell detected by two or more radars

⊕ Over 9/10 coverage

⊕ 6/10 thru 9/10 coverage

⊕ 1/10 thru 5/10 coverage

⊙ Less than 1/10 coverage

SYMBOLS USED WITH ARTCC ECHO REPORTS

▱ (Solid line) Echo boundary from ARTCC scopes.

▱ Line of echoes--possible squall line.

11

Contractions

NATIONAL WEATHER SERVICE FORECAST TERMS

ACFT	aircraft	LWR	lower
ACTV	active	LYR	layer
AFDK	after dark	MDT	moderate
AGL	above ground level	MRTM	maritime
		MSL	mean sea level
ALF	aloft		
AMS	air mass	MXD	mixed
ARND	around	NMI	nautical mile(s)
ASL	above sea level	NMRS	numerous
BFDK	before dark	NOTAM	notice to airmen
BKN	broken	OBSC	obscure
BLZD	blizzard	OCLN	occlusion
BRF	brief	OCNL	occasional, occasionally
BTN	between	OCR	occur
BTR	better	OTLK	outlook
BYD	beyond	OTRW	otherwise
CAT	clear air turbulence	OVC	overcast
CAVOK	cloud and visibility OK	PCPN	precipitation
		PIREP	pilot report
CHG	change	PRST	persist
CIG	ceiling	PBL	probable
CONT	continue	PSBL	possible
CSDRBL	considerable	PSG	passing
CVR	cover	PTLY	partly
DCR	decrease	PVL	prevail
DMSH	diminish	RAREP	radar report
DNS	dense	RESTR	restrict
DRZL	drizzle	RDG	ridge
DSIPT	dissipate	RGD	ragged
DVLP	develop	RMN	remain
EMBDD	embedded	RPD	rapid
EXTRM	extreme	RTE	route
EXTSV	extensive	RUF	rough
FCST	forecast	SCT	scattered
FLRY	flurry	SCTR	sector
FORNN	forenoon	SHFT	shift
FQT	frequent	SHWR	shower
FROPA	frontal passage	SKC	sky clear
FROSFC	frontal surface	SLGT	slight
GNDFG	ground fog	SMK	smoke
GRDL	gradual	SNW	snow
HGT	height	SQLN	squall line
HLSTO	hailstones	STBL	stable
HND	hundred	STG	strong
HURCN	hurricane	SVR	severe
HVY	heavy	THN	thin
ICGIC	icing in clouds	TSHWR	thundershower
ICGIP	icing in precipitation	TSTM	thunderstorm
IMDT	immediate	TURBC	turbulence
INCR	increase	TWD	toward
INDEF	indefinite	UPSLP	up slope
INTSFY	intensify	VRBL	variable
ISOLD	isolated	VSBY	visibility
JTSTR	jet stream	WDLY	widely
KT	knot(s)	WEA	weather
LGT	light	WK	weak
LMT	limit	WV	wave
LVL	level	WX	weather

NOAA/PA 71005
(Rev. 1979)

Conversion Tables

TIME

STANDARD TO GMT

Eastern	+5 hr	= GMT
Central	+6 hr	= GMT
Mountain	+7 hr	= GMT
Pacific	+8 hr	= GMT
Yukon	+9 hr	= GMT
Alaskan	+10 hr	= GMT
Bering	+11 hr	= GMT

Add one less hour for Daylight Time.

WINDSPEED

MPH	Knots
1–2	1–2
3–8	3–7
9–14	8–12
15–20	13–17
21–25	18–22
26–31	23–27
32–37	28–32
38–43	33–37
44–49	38–42
50–54	43–47
55–60	48–52
61–66	53–57
67–71	58–62
72–77	63–67
78–83	68–72
84–89	73–77
119–123	103–107

Knots x 1.15 =
Miles Per Hour
Miles Per Hour x
0.869 = Knots

PIREP FORM

(U)UA /OV				FL
MSG TYPE	LOCATION OF PHENOMENA	3-LTR IDENT	RADIAL DISTANCE	TIME (Z) FLT LVL

/TP	/SK		
TYPE AIRCRAFT	SKY COVER	BASE AMOUNT TOP	

/TA	/WV
TEMPERATURE-CELSIUS	WIND-DIRECTION SPEED

/TB	/IC
TURBULENCE-INTENSITY TYPE✫ ALTITIDE✫✫	ICING-INTENSITY TYPE ALTITUDE✫✫

/RM

REMARKS (MOST HAZARDOUS ELEMENT REPORTED FIRST)

LEGEND: ➤ = SPACE SYMBOL   ✫=ONLY FOR CAT   ✫✫=ONLY IF DIFFERENT FROM FL

FAA Form 7110-2 (9-76) SUPERSEDES FAA FORM 7110-2 TEST

PILOT WEATHER REPORTS (PIREP)

a. Whenever ceilings are at or below 5,000 feet, visibility at or below five miles, or thunderstorms are reported or forecast, facilities are required to solicit and collect PIREP's which describe conditions aloft. Pilots are urged to cooperate and volunteer reports of cloud tops, upper cloud layers, thunderstorms, ice, turbulence, strong winds, and other significant flight condition information. Such conditions observed between weather reporting stations are vitally needed. The PIREP's should be given to the FAA ground facility with which communication is established, i.e., FSS, Air Route Traffic Control Center or terminal ATC facility. In addition to complete PIREP's, pilots can materially help round out the in-flight weather picture by adding to routine position reports, both VFR and IFR, the type of aircraft and the following phrases as appropriate:

ON TOP

BELOW OVERCAST

WEATHER CLEAR

MODERATE (or HEAVY) ICING

LIGHT, MODERATE, SEVERE, EXTREME TURBULENCE

FREEZING RAIN (or DRIZZLE)

THUNDERSTORM (location)

BETWEEN LAYERS

ON INSTRUMENTS

ON AND OFF INSTRUMENTS

b. If pilots are not able to make PIREP's by radio, reporting upon landing of the in-flight conditions encountered to the nearest Flight Service Station or Weather Service Office will be helpful. Some of the uses made of the reports are:

(1) The Airport Traffic Control Tower uses the reports to expedite the flow of air traffic in the vicinity of the field and also forwards reports to other interested offices.

(2) The Flight Service Station uses the reports to brief other pilots.

(3) The Air Route Traffic Control Center uses the reports to expedite the flow of enroute traffic and determine most favorable altitudes.

(4) The Weather Service Forecast Office finds pilot reports very helpful in issuing advisories of hazardous weather conditions. This office also uses the reports to brief other pilots, and in forecasting.

Reporting Turbulence

INTENSITY	AIRCRAFT REACTION	REACTION INSIDE AIRCRAFT	REPORTING TERM-DEFINITION
Light	Turbulence that momentarily causes slight erratic changes in altitude and/or attitude (pitch, roll, yaw). Report as Light Turbulence.* or Turbulence that causes slight, rapid and somewhat rhythmic bumpiness without appreciable changes in altitude or attitude. Report as Light Chop.	Occupants may feel a slight strain against seat belts or shoulder straps. Unsecured objects may be displaced slightly. Food service may be conducted and little or no difficulty is encountered in walking.	Occasional—Less than ⅓ of the time. Intermittent—⅓ to ⅔. Continuous—More than ⅔.
Moderate	Turbulence that is similar to Light Turbulence but of greater intensity. Changes in altitude and/or attitude occur but the aircraft remains in positive control at all times. It usually causes variations in indicated airspeed. Report as Moderate Turbulence.* or Turbulence that is similar to Light Chop but of greater intensity. It causes rapid bumps or jolts without appreciable changes in aircraft altitude or attitude. Report as Moderate Chop.	Occupants feel definite strains against seat belts or shoulder straps. Unsecured objects are dislodged. Food service and walking are difficult.	**NOTE** 1. Pilots should report location(s), time (GMT), intensity, whether in or near clouds, altitude, type of aircraft and, when applicable, duration of turbulence. 2. Duration may be based on time between two locations or over a single location. All locations should be readily identifiable. EXAMPLES: a. Over Omaha, 1232Z, Moderate Turbulence, in cloud, Flight Level 310, B707. b. From 50 miles south of Albuquerque to 30 miles north of Phoenix, 1210Z to 1250Z, occasional Moderate Chop, Flight Level 330, DC8.
Severe	Turbulence that causes large, abrupt changes in altitude and/or attitude. It usually causes large variations in indicated airspeed. Aircraft may be momentarily out of control. Report as Severe Turbulence.*	Occupants are forced violently against seat belts or shoulder straps. Unsecured objects are tossed about. Food service and walking are impossible.	
Extreme	Turbulence in which the aircraft is violently tossed about and is practically impossible to control. It may cause structural damage. Report as Extreme Turbulence.*		

* High level turbulence (normally above 15,000 feet ASL) not associated with cumuliform cloudiness, including thunderstorms, should be reported as CAT (Clear Air Turbulence) preceded by the appropriate intensity, or light or moderate chop.
SC/AMS Meeting 7/67

14

Reporting Airframe Icing

INTENSITY	ICE ACCUMULATION
Trace	Ice becomes perceptible. Rate of accumulation slightly greater than rate of sublimation. It is not hazardous even though deicing / anti-icing equipment is not utilized, unless encountered for an extended period of time (over 1 hour).
Light	The rate of accumulation may create a problem if flight is prolonged in this environment (over 1 hour). Occasional use of deicing/anti-icing equipment removes/prevents accumulation. It does not present a problem if the deicing/anti-icing equipment is used.
Moderate	The rate of accumulation is such that even short encounters become potentially hazardous and use of deicing/anti-icing equipment or diversion is necessary.
Severe	The rate of accumulation is such that deicing/anti-icing equipment fails to reduce or control the hazard. Immediate diversion is necessary. APPROVED SC/AMS Meeting 4/68

Pilot Report: Aircraft Identification, Location, Time (GMT), Intensity of Type,* Altitude/FL, Aircraft Type, IAS.

*Rime Ice: Rough, milky, opaque ice formed by the instantaneous freezing of small supercooled water droplets.

Clear Ice: A glossy, clear, or translucent ice formed by the relatively slow freezing of large supercooled water droplets.

Icing Conditions

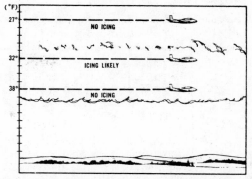

Ice forms when temperature is below freezing and there is visible moisture.

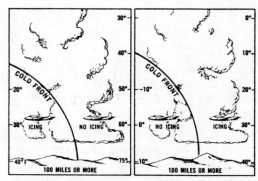

Probable icing conditions in these two examples of cold fronts are dissimilar because of different air mass temperatures.

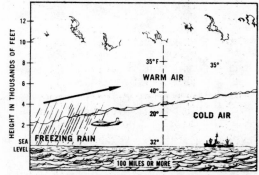

Example of freezing rain under a warm front.

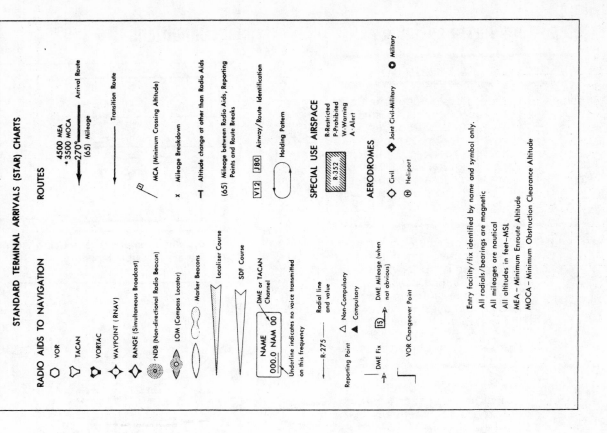

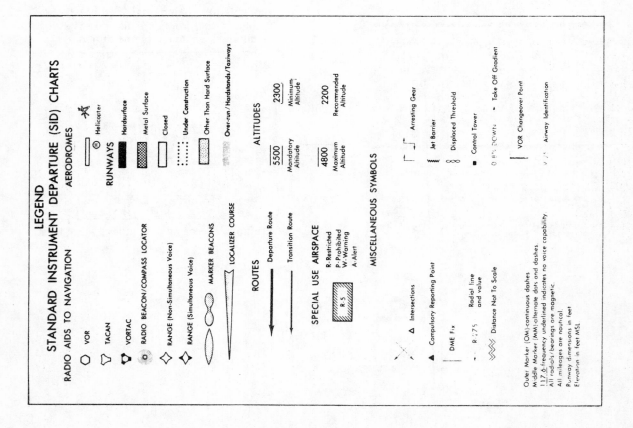

ENROUTE LOW ALTITUDE – U.S.
For use up to but not including 18,000' MSL

LEGEND

AERODROMES

Aerodromes/Seadromes shown in BLUE have an approved Low Altitude Instrument Approach Procedure published. Those shown in DARK BLUE have an approved DOD Low Altitude Instrument Approach Procedure and/or approved DOD RADAR MINIMA published in DOD FLIPS. Aerodromes/Seadromes shown in BROWN do not have a published Instrument Approach Procedure.

	LAND	SEA
Civil	◇	◇
Joint Civil-Military	◇	◇
Military	◎	◎
Heliport	Ⓗ	Ⓗ

RELATED FACILITIES
Pilot to Metro Service (PMSV)

- Continuous Operation
- Less Than Continuous
- Weather Radar (WXR)
- PMSV and WXR Combined

Published ILS and/or Localizer Procedure available

Published SDF Procedure available

1. Parentheses around aerodrome name indicate military landing rights not available.
2. Aerodrome elevation given in feet above or below mean sea level.
3. Length of longest runway given to nearest 100 feet with 70 feet as the dividing point (Add 00).
4. Aerodrome symbol may be off-set for enroute navigation aids.
5. Pvt-Private use, not available to general public.

Aerodrome Elevation — 349 ·180
*ASR/PAR
ATIS ·108.5

Automatic Terminal Information Service and Frequency. Star indicates operation less than continuous or part time.

No Runway Lighting Capability — 185 – 35₅ — Longest Landing Runway Length

Indicates Soft Surface

Night Landing Capability. Asterisk indicates lighting on request or operating part of night only. Circle indicates Pilot Controlled Lighting (PCL). For information consult Directory or FLIP IFR Supplement.

Radar Services Availability Star indicates prior request only

RADIO AIDS TO NAVIGATION AND COMMUNICATION BOXES

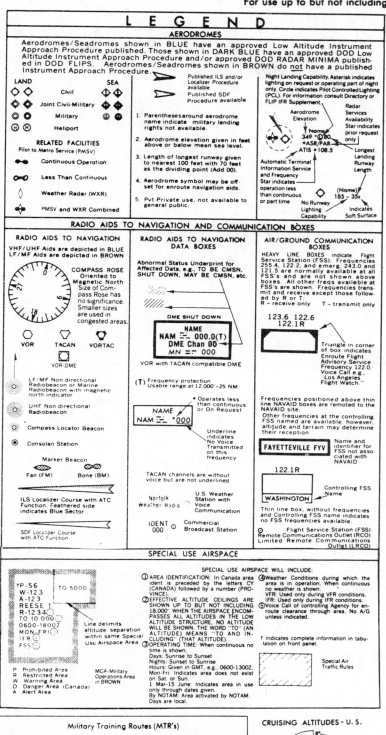

RADIO AIDS TO NAVIGATION

VHF/UHF Aids are depicted in BLUE
LF/MF Aids are depicted in BROWN

COMPASS ROSE Oriented to Magnetic North. Size of Compass Rose has no significance. Smaller sizes are used in congested areas.

VOR   TACAN   VORTAC

VOR-DME

LF/MF Non directional Radiobeacon or Marine Radiobeacon with magnetic north indicator

UHF Non directional Radiobeacon

Compass Locator Beacon

Consolan Station

Marker Beacon
Fan (FM)   Bone (BM)

ILS Localizer Course with ATC Function. Feathered side indicates Blue Sector.

SDF Localizer Course with ATC Function

RADIO AIDS TO NAVIGATION DATA BOXES

Abnormal Status Underprint for Affected Data, e.g., TO BE CMSN, SHUT DOWN, MAY BE CMSN, etc.

DME SHUT DOWN

NAME
NAM ⋯ 000.0(T)
DME Chan 80
MN ⋯ 000

VOR with TACAN compatible DME

(T) Frequency protection Usable range at 12,000'–25 NM

NAME
NAM ⋯ *000

* Operates less than continuous or On Request

Underline indicates No Voice Transmitted on this frequency

TACAN channels are without voice but are not underlined.

Norfolk Weather Radio — U.S. Weather Station with Voice Communication

IDENT 000 ⊙ Commercial Broadcast Station

AIR/GROUND COMMUNICATION BOXES

HEAVY LINE BOXES indicate Flight Service Station (FSS). Frequencies 255.4, 122.2, and emerg. 243.0 and 121.5 are normally available at all FSS's and are not shown above boxes. All other freqs available at FSS's are shown. Frequencies transmit and receive except those followed by R or T:
R – receive only   T – transmit only

123.6 122.6
122.1R

Triangle in corner of box indicates Enroute Flight Advisory Service Frequency 122.0. Voice Call e.g. "Los Angeles Flight Watch."

Frequencies positioned above thin line NAVAID boxes are remoted to the NAVAID site.

Other frequencies at the controlling FSS named are available, however, altitude and terrain may determine their reception.

FAYETTEVILLE FYV — Name and identifier for FSS not associated with NAVAID

122.1R
WASHINGTON — Controlling FSS Name

Thin line box, without frequencies and Controlling FSS name indicates no FSS frequencies available.

Ⓕ Flight Service Station (FSS)
Remote Communications Outlet (RCO)
Limited Remote Communications Outlet (LRCO)

SPECIAL USE AIRSPACE

†P-56
W-123
A-123
REESE 1
R-1234
TO 10 000
0600-1800‡
IFR⊙
FSS⊙
TO 5000

Line delimits altitude separation within same Special Use Airspace Area

P   Prohibited Area
R   Restricted Area
W   Warning Area
D   Danger Area (Canada)
A   Alert Area

MCA-Military Operations Area in BROWN

SPECIAL USE AIRSPACE WILL INCLUDE:

① AREA IDENTIFICATION: In Canada area ident is preceded by the letters CY (CANADA) followed by a number (PROVINCE).

② EFFECTIVE ALTITUDE CEILINGS ARE SHOWN UP TO BUT NOT INCLUDING 18,000'. WHEN THE CEILING ENCOMPASSES ALL ALTITUDES IN THE LOW ALTITUDE STRUCTURE, NO ALTITUDE WILL BE SHOWN. THE WORD "TO" (AN ALTITUDE) MEANS "TO AND INCLUDING" (THAT ALTITUDE).

③ OPERATING TIME: When continuous no time is shown.
Days: Sunrise to Sunset
Nights: Sunset to Sunrise
Hours: Given in GMT, e.g., 0600-1300Z.
Mon-Fri: Indicates area does not exist on Sat. or Sun.
1 Mar-15 June: Indicates area in use only through dates given.
By NOTAM: Area activated by NOTAM. Days are local.

④ Weather Conditions during which the area is in operation. When continuous no weather is shown.
VFR: Used only during VFR conditions.
IFR: Used only during IFR conditions.

⑤ Voice Call of controlling Agency for enroute clearance through area. No A/G unless indicated.

† Indicates complete information in tabulation on front panel.

Special Air Traffic Rules

Military Training Routes (MTR's)

Military Training Routes (MTR's) 5 NM or less
IR107 →   VR134 →

Military Training Routes (MTR's) greater than 5 NM
IR113 →   VR133 →

Arrow indicates Single Direction Route

All MTR's may extend from the surface upwards.
All MTR's (IR and VR) except those VR's at or below 1500' AGL are shown.
CAUTION: Inset charts do not depict Military Training Routes (MTR's).

CRUISING ALTITUDES – U.S.

IFR EVEN Thousands / IFR ODD Thousands
VFR or ON TOP EVEN Thousands Plus 500' / VFR or ON TOP ODD Thousands Plus 500'

VFR above 3000' AGL unless otherwise authorized by ATC
IFR Outside controlled airspace
IFR within controlled airspace as assigned by ATC
All courses are magnetic

AIR TRAFFIC SERVICES AND AIRSPACE INFORMATION

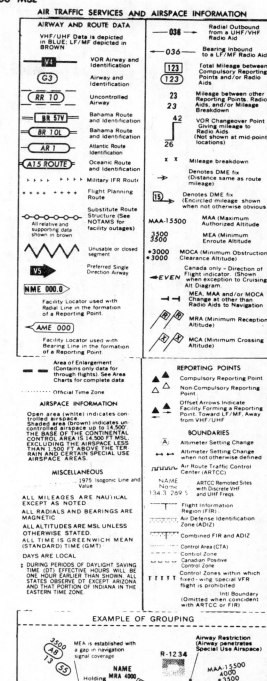

AIRWAY AND ROUTE DATA

VHF/UHF Data is depicted in BLUE; LF/MF depicted in BROWN

─036→ Radial Outbound from a UHF/VHF Radio Aid
─036→ Bearing Inbound to a LF/MF Radio Aid

V4   VOR Airway and Identification
G3   Airway and Identification
RR 10   Uncontrolled Airway
BR 57V   Bahama Route and Identification
BR 1OL   Bahama Route and Identification
AR 1   Atlantic Route Identification
A15 ROUTE   Oceanic Route and Identification

Military IFR Route
Flight Planning Route
Substitute Route Structure (See NOTAMS for facility outages)
All relative and supporting data shown in brown

Unusable or closed segment

V5   Preferred Single Direction Airway

NME 000.0   Facility Locator used with Radial Line in the formation of a Reporting Point.

AME 000.0   Facility Locator used with Bearing Line in the formation of a Reporting Point.

Area of Enlargement (Contains only data for through flights. See Area Charts for complete data)
········ Official Time Zone

123   Total Mileage between Compulsory Reporting Points and/or Radio Aids
123
23   Mileage between other Reporting Points, Radio Aids, and/or Mileage Breakdown
42   VOR Changeover Point Giving mileage to Radio Aids (Not shown at mid-point locations)
26
x   x   Mileage breakdown
→   Denotes DME fix (Distance same as route mileage)
15   Denotes DME fix (Encircled mileage shown when not otherwise obvious)
MAA-15500   MAA (Maximum Authorized Altitude)
3500   MEA (Minimum Enroute Altitude)
*3000   MOCA (Minimum Obstruction Clearance Altitude)
EVEN   Canada only – Direction of Flight indicator. (Shown when exception to Cruising Alt Diagram.)
   MEA, MAA and/or MOCA Change at other than Radio Aids to Navigation
R   MRA (Minimum Reception Altitude)
X   MCA (Minimum Crossing Altitude)

AIRSPACE INFORMATION

Open area (white) indicates controlled airspace.
Shaded area (brown) indicates uncontrolled airspace up to 14,500'. THE BASE OF THE CONTINENTAL CONTROL AREA IS 14,500 FT MSL, EXCLUDING THE AIRSPACE LESS THAN 1,500 FT ABOVE THE TERRAIN AND CERTAIN SPECIAL USE AIRSPACE AREAS.

MISCELLANEOUS

—— 1975 Isogonic Line and Value

ALL MILEAGES ARE NAUTICAL EXCEPT AS NOTED
ALL RADIALS AND BEARINGS ARE MAGNETIC
ALL ALTITUDES ARE MSL UNLESS OTHERWISE STATED.
ALL TIME IS GREENWICH MEAN (STANDARD) TIME (GMT).
DAYS ARE LOCAL

‡ DURING PERIODS OF DAYLIGHT SAVING TIME (DT) EFFECTIVE HOURS WILL BE ONE HOUR EARLIER THAN SHOWN. ALL STATES OBSERVE DT EXCEPT ARIZONA AND THAT PORTION OF INDIANA IN THE EASTERN TIME ZONE.

REPORTING POINTS

▲ ▲ Compulsory Reporting Point
△ △ Non-Compulsory Reporting Point
▲ ▲ Offset Arrows Indicate Facility Forming a Reporting Point. Toward VHF/UHF, Away from LF/MF

BOUNDARIES

Ⓐ Altimeter Setting Change
Altimeter Setting Change when not otherwise defined
Air Route Traffic Control Center (ARTCC)

NAME Name 134.3 269.5   ARTCC Remoted Sites with Discrete VHF and UHF Freqs

Flight Information Region (FIR)
Air Defense Identification Zone (ADIZ)
Combined FIR and ADIZ
Control Area (CTA)
Control Zone
Canadian Positive Control Zone
Control Zones within which fixed-wing special VFR flight is prohibited
Int'l Boundary (Omitted when coincident with ARTCC or FIR)

EXAMPLE OF GROUPING

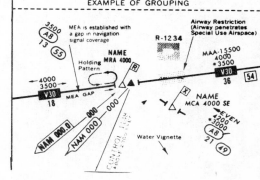

MEA is established with a gap in navigation signal coverage

Airway Restriction (Airway penetrates Special Use Airspace)

Holding Pattern

NAME MRA 4000
NAME MCA 4000 SE

Water Vignette

17

★ Indicates control tower or ATIS operates non-continuously.
Distances in nautical miles (except visibility in statute miles and Runway Visual Range in hundreds of feet).
Runway Dimensions in feet.
Elevations in feet Mean Sea Level (MSL).
Ceilings in feet above airport elevation.
Radials/bearings/headings/courses are magnetic.

ADF	Automatic Direction Finder
ALS	Approach Light System
APP CON	Approach Control
ARR	Arrival
ASR/PAR	Published Radar Minimums at this Airport
ATIS	Automatic Terminal Information Service
BC	Back Course
C	Circling
CAT	Category
Chan	Channel
CLNC DEL	clearance delivery
DH	Decision Height
DME	Distance Measuring Equipment
DR	Dead Reckoning
ELEV	elevation
FAF	Final Approach Fix
FM	Fan Marker
GPI	Ground Point of Intercept (ion)
GS	Glide Slope
HAA	Height Above Airport
HAL	Height Above Landing
HAT	Height Above Touchdown
HIRL	High Intensity Runway Lights
IAF	Initial Approach Fix
ICAO	International Civil Aviation Organization
Intcp	Intercept
INT, INTXN	Intersection
LDA	Localizer Type Directional Aid
Ldg	Landing
LDIN	Lead in Light System
LIRL	Low Intensity Runway Lights
LOC	Localizer
LR	Lead Radial. Provides at least 2 NM (Copter 1 NM) of lead to assist in turning onto the intermediate/final course
MALS	Medium Intensity Approach Light System
MALSR	Medium Intensity Approach Light Systems with RAIL
MAP	Missed Approach Point
MDA	Minimum Descent Altitude
MIRL	Medium Intensity Runway Lights
MLS	Microwave Landing System
NA	Not Authorized
NDB	Non-directional Radio Beacon
NoPT	No Procedure Turn Required (Procedure Turn shall not be executed without ATC clearance)
ODALS	Omnidirectional Approach Light System
RA	Radio Altimeter setting height
Radar Required	Radar vectoring required for this approach
RAIL	Runway Alignment Indicator Lights
RBn	Radio Beacon
REIL	Runway End Identifier Lights
RCLS	Runway Centerline Light System
RNAV	Area Navigation
RRL	Runway Remaining Lights
RVR	Runway Touchdown Zone. First 3000' of Runway Runway Visual Range
S	Straight-in
SALS	Short Approach Light System
SSALR	Simplified Short Approach Light System with RAIL
SDF	Simplified Directional Facility
TA	Transition Altitude
TAC	TACAN
TCH	Threshold Crossing Height (height in feet Above Ground Level)
TDZ	Touchdown Zone
TDZE	Touchdown Zone Elevation
TDZL	Touchdown Zone Lights
TLv	Transition Level
VDP	Visual Descent Point
WPT	Waypoint (RNAV)

RADIO CONTROL
AIRPORT LIGHTING SYSTEM

KEY MIKE	FUNCTION
7 times within 5 seconds	Highest intensity available
5 times within 5 seconds	Medium or lower intensity (Lower REIL or REIL-off)
3 times within 5 seconds	Lower intensity available (Lower REIL or REIL-off)

Available systems will be indicated on Instrument Approach Procedure (IAP) Charts, below the Minimums Data, as follows:

ACTIVATE MIRL Rwy 36-122.8, ACTIVATE MALSR Rwy 7-122.8
ACTIVATE VASI and REIL Rwy 7-122.8, ACTIVATE HIRL Rwy 7-25 - 122.8

INSTRUMENT APPROACH PROCEDURES EXPLANATION OF TERMS

The United States Standard for Terminal Instrument Procedures (TERPS) is the approved criteria for formulating instrument approach procedures.

AIRCRAFT APPROACH CATEGORIES

Speeds are based on 1.3 times the stall speed in the landing configuration at maximum gross landing weight. An aircraft shall fit in only one category. If it is necessary to maneuver at speeds in excess of the upper limit of a speed range for a category, the minimums for the next higher category should be used. For example, an aircraft which falls in Category A, but is circling to land at a speed in excess of 91 knots, should use the approach Category B minimums when circling to land. See following category limits:

Approach Category | Speed

A. Speed less than 91 knots.
B. Speed 91 knots or more but less than 121 knots.
C. Speed 121 knots or more but less than 141 knots.
D. Speed 141 knots or more but less than 166 knots.
E. Speed 166 knots or more.

RVR/Meteorological Visibility Comparable Values

The following table shall be used for converting RVR to meteorological visibility when RVR is inoperative.

RVR (feet)	Visibility (statute miles)
1600	1/4
2000	3/8
2400	1/2
3200	5/8
4000	3/4
4500	7/8
5000	1
6000	1 1/4

LANDING MINIMA FORMAT

In this example airport elevation is 1179, and runway touchdown zone elevation is 1152.

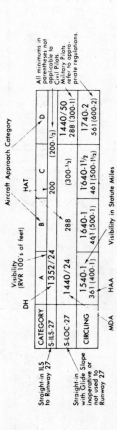

Straight-in ILS to Runway 27 → DH / Visibility (RVR 100's of feet) / HAT

Straight-in with Glide Slope inoperative or not used to Runway 27 → MDA / HAA / Visibility in Statute Miles

Aircraft Approach Category

All minimums in parentheses not applicable to Civil Pilots. Military Pilots, refer to appropriate regulations.

CATEGORY	A	B	C	D
S-ILS-27	1352/24			
		200	(200-½)	
S-LOC-27	1440/24		288	1440/50
				288 (300-1)
CIRCLING	1540-1 361 (400-1)	1640-1 461 (500-1)	1640-1½ 461 (500-1½)	1740-2 561 (600-2)

CORRECTIONS, COMMENTS AND/OR PROCUREMENT

Forward CORRECTIONS to and PROCURE from:

NATIONAL OCEAN SURVEY
DISTRIBUTION DIVISION, C44
RIVERDALE, MD. 20840

LEGEND

INSTRUMENT APPROACH PROCEDURES (CHARTS)

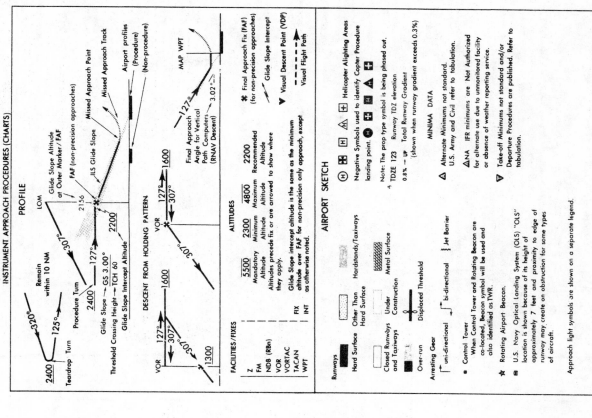

PROFILE

ALTITUDES

5500	Mandatory Altitude
2300	Minimum Altitude
4800	Maximum Altitude
2200	Recommended Altitude

Altitudes precede fix or are arrowed to show where they apply.

Glide Slope intercept altitude is the same as the minimum altitude over FAF for non-precision only approach, except as otherwise noted.

FACILITIES/FIXES

Z	
FM	
NDB (RBn)	
VOR	
VORTAC	
TACAN	
WPT	
FIX	
INT	

AIRPORT SKETCH

Runways

Hard Surface
Other Than Hard Surface
Closed Runways and Taxiways
Over-run
Hardstands/Taxiways
Metal Surface
Under Construction
Displaced Threshold

Arresting Gear

uni-directional
bi-directional
Jet Barrier

- Control Tower — When Control Tower and Rotating Beacon are co-located, Beacon symbol will be used and also identified as TWR.

★ Rotating Airport Beacon.

⊚ U.S. Navy Optical Landing System (OLS) "OLS" location is shown because of its height of approximately 7 feet and proximity to edge of runway may create an obstruction for some types of aircraft.

Helicopter Alighting Areas

Negative Symbols used to identify Copter Procedure landing point.

Note: The prop type symbol is being phased out.
TDZE 123   Runway TDZ elevation
0.8% — UP   Total Runway Gradient (shown when runway gradient exceeds 0.3%)

MINIMA DATA

△ Alternate Minimums not standard. U.S. Army and Civil refer to tabulation.

△NA IFR minimums are Not Authorized for alternate use due to unmonitored facility or absence of weather reporting service.

▽ Take-off Minimums not standard and/or Departure Procedures are published. Refer to tabulation.

Approach light symbols are shown on a separate legend.

LEGEND

INSTRUMENT APPROACH PROCEDURES (CHARTS)

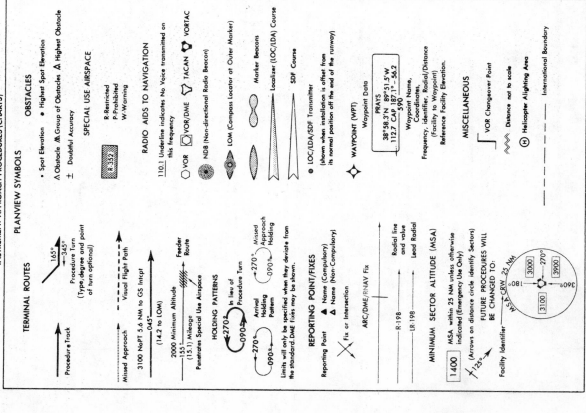

PLANVIEW SYMBOLS

TERMINAL ROUTES

Procedure Track

Procedure Turn (Type, degree and point of turn optional)

Missed Approach   Visual Flight Path

Feeder Route

Penetrates Special Use Airspace

HOLDING PATTERNS

Arrival Holding Pattern

In lieu of Procedure Turn

Missed Approach Holding

Limits will only be specified when they deviate from the standard. DME fixes may be shown.

REPORTING POINT/FIXES

▲ Name (Compulsory)
△ Name (Non-Compulsory)

✕ Fix or Intersection

ARC/DME/RNAV Fix

Radial line and value

Lead Radial

MINIMUM SECTOR ALTITUDE (MSA)

1400 MSA within 25 NM unless otherwise indicated (Emergency Use Only)

(Arrows on distance circle identify Sectors)

FUTURE PROCEDURES WILL BE CHANGED TO:

Facility Identifier

OBSTACLES

• Spot Elevation
● Highest Spot Elevation
⋀ Obstacle
⋀⋀ Group of Obstacles
⋀ Highest Obstacle
⊥ Doubtful Accuracy

SPECIAL USE AIRSPACE

R-Restricted
P-Prohibited
W-Warning

RADIO AIDS TO NAVIGATION

110.1 Underline indicates No Voice transmitted on this frequency

VOR   VOR/DME   TACAN   VORTAC

NDB (Non-directional Radio Beacon)

LOM (Compass Locator at Outer Marker)

Marker Beacons

Localizer (LOC/LDA) Course

SDF Course

LOC/LDA/SDF Transmitter (shown when installation is offset from its normal position at the end of the runway)

WAYPOINT (WPT)

Waypoint Data

PRAYS
38°58.3'N 89°51.5'W
112.7 CAP 187.1° — 56.2
590

Waypoint Name, Coordinates, Frequency, identifier, Radial/Distance (Facility to Waypoint) Reference Facility Elevation.

MISCELLANEOUS

VOR Changeover Point

Ⓗ Helicopter Alighting Area

Distance not to scale

International Boundary

▲ IFR ALTERNATE MINIMUMS
(Not applicable to USAF/USN)

Standard alternate minimums for nonprecision approaches are 800-2 (NDB, VOR, LOC, TACAN, LDA, VORTAC, VOR/DME or ASR); for precision approaches 600-2 (ILS or PAR). Airports within this geographical area that require alternate minimums other than standard or alternate minimums with restrictions are listed below. NA - means IFR minimums are not authorized for alternate use due to unmonitored facility or absence of weather reporting service. U. S. Army pilots refer to Army Reg. 95-1 for additional application. Civil pilots see FAR 91.83. USAF/USN pilots refer to appropriate regulations.

AIRPORT NAME	ALTERNATE MINIMUMS	AIRPORT NAME	ALTERNATE MINIMUMS
BISHOP .... VOR Rwy 27 Flint, Michigan Category D, 800-2¼		GOGEBIC COUNTY .... VOR Rwy 9 Ironwood, Michigan Cat A, B, 900-2; Cat C, 900-2½; Cat D, 1000-3 NA when control zone not effective.	VOR/DME Rwy 27
CHERRY CAPITAL .... VOR-A (TAC)* Traverse City, Michigan *Category C, 800-2¼ †Category C, 800-2¼; Category D, 800-2½. ‡ILS, Categories A, B, 800-2, Category C, 800-2¼, Category D, 800-2½; LOC, Category C, 800-2¼; Category D, 800-2¾.	NDB Rwy 28† ILS Rwy 28‡	HOUGHTON COUNTY MEM .... ILS Rwy 31 Hancock, Michigan *ILS, Category D, 700-2	
CHIPPEWA COUNTY INTL .... VOR-A Sault Ste. Marie, Michigan ILS, NA when control zone not effective, except for operators with approved weather reporting service.	ILS Rwy 15	JACKSON COUNTY-REYNOLDS FIELD .... ILS Rwy 23 Jackson, Michigan *ILS, Category D, 700-2	
DELTA COUNTY .... VOR Rwy 9 Escanaba, Michigan NA when control zone not effective, except for operators with approved weather reporting service.	VOR Rwy 18 VOR BC Rwy 27 LOC/DME Rwy 27	MANISTEE COUNTY-BLACKER .... VOR Rwy 9* Manistee, Michigan NA when control zone not effective, except for operators with approved weather reporting service. *Category D, 800-2¾	VOR Rwy 27*
EMMET COUNTY .... VOR Rwy 23* Pellston, Michigan *Category D, 800-2¾. **Category C, 800-2¼, Category D, 800-2½. †Category A, B, 900-2; Category C, 900-2½; Category D, 900-2¾. ‡ILS, Category D, 700-2¾; LOC, Category D, 800-2½.	VOR/DME Rwy 5† NDB Rwy 32** ILS Rwy 32‡	MARQUETTE COUNTY .... VOR Rwy 8* Marquette, Michigan **ILS, 700-2 *Category D, 800-2¾	ILS Rwy 8**
FORD .... ILS Rwy 1* Iron Mountain-Kingsford, Michigan *Authorized for DME equipped aircraft when control zone is effective. Alternate minimums NA. **NA when control zone not effective, except for operators with approved weather reporting service. †Category A, B, 900-2, Category C, D, 900-2¾.	VOR Rwy 19† VOR Rwy 31* LOC/DME BC Rwy 19**	MENOMINEE-MARINETTE TWIN COUNTY .... VOR Rwy 18 Menominee, Michigan NA when control zone not in effect, except for operators with approved weather reporting service.	
		OAKLAND-PONTIAC .... ILS Rwy 9R* Pontiac, Michigan	LOC BC Rwy 27L* VOR Rwy 9R* VOR Rwy 27L* RNAV Rwy 27L*
		REYNOLDS MUNI .... ILS Rwy 23* Jackson, Michigan *Category D, 700-2	
		*NA when control zone not effective.	

▼ IFR TAKE-OFF MINIMUMS AND DEPARTURE PROCEDURES

FAR 91.116(c) prescribes take-off rules and establishes standard take-off minimums as follows:

(1) Aircraft having two engines or less – one statute mile.

(2) Aircraft having more than two engines – one-half statute mile.

Airports within this geographical area with IFR take-off minimums other than standard are listed below alphabetically by airport name. Departure procedures and/or ceiling visibility minimums are established to assist pilots conducting IFR flight in avoiding obstacles during climb to the minimum enroute altitude.

Take-off minimums and departure procedures apply to all runways unless otherwise specified. Altitudes, unless otherwise indicated, are minimum altitudes in feet MSL.

AIRPORT NAME	TAKE-OFF MINIMUMS	AIRPORT NAME	TAKE-OFF MINIMUMS
AL MEYERS .... Rwys 18L, 18R, 27, 36L, 36R, 300-1 Tecumseh, Michigan		CASS COUNTY MEMORIAL .... Rwys 4, 9, 22, Dowagiac, Michigan IFR DEPARTURE PROCEDURE: Rwys 4, 9, 22 climb runway heading to 1500 before turning.	27, 400-1
ANN ARBOR MUNI .... Rwys 30, 300-1 Ann Arbor, Michigan IFR DEPARTURE PROCEDURE: Rwy 6 and 24, climb runway heading to 1200 before turning Northwest.		CHARLEVOIX MUNI .... Rwy 31, 400-1 Charlevoix, Michigan IFR DEPARTURE PROCEDURES: Rwys 4, 8, 13, 22, 26, climb runway heading to 1200 before turning.	
ANTRIM COUNTY .... Rwys 2, 20, 300-1 Bellaire, Michigan IFR DEPARTURE PROCEDURE: Rwy 2, climb runway heading to 2000 before turning.		CHEBOYGAN CITY-COUNTY .... Rwy 16, 400-1 Cheboygan, Michigan	
BERZ-MACOMB .... Rwys 4, 22, 200-1 Utica, Michigan		CHERRY CAPITAL .... Rwy 28, ½ mile* Traverse City, Michigan *with minimum climb of 300' per NM to 2000. (FAR 135) (750 ft per minute at 150k, 1000 ft per minute at 200k) Rwy 10, 400-1 or standard with minimum climb of 300' per NM to 1200. (750 ft per minute at 150k, 1000 ft per minute at 200k). Rwy 28, 1200-2, or standard with minimum climb of 300' per NM to 2000. (750 ft per minute at 150k, 1000 ft per minute at 200k). IFR DEPARTURE PROCEDURE: Rwys 5, 18, 23, 36, climb runway heading to 2000 before turning west.	Rwy 23, 400-1
BISHOP .... Rwy 9, RVR/24* Flint, Michigan *(FAR 135)		CHIPPEWA COUNTY INTL Sault Ste. Marie, Michigan Rwy 15, ½ mile (FAR 135) when control zone in effect. Rwy 15, ¾ mile (FAR 135) when control zone not in effect.	
BOYNE MOUNTAIN .... Rwy 17, 1000-1 Boyne Falls, Michigan IFR DEPARTURE PROCEDURE: Rwy 35 and 17 climb runway heading to 2000 before turning.	Rwys 35, 500-1	CUSTER .... Rwy 2, 300-1 Monroe, Michigan IFR DEPARTURE PROCEDURE: Rwys 2, 20 climb runway heading to 1400 before turning East.	
BRANCH COUNTY MEMORIAL .... Rwy 3, 300-1 Coldwater, Michigan		DAVISON-GENOVA .... Rwys 8, 26, 300-1 Davison, Michigan	
BROOKS FIELD .... Rwys 91/9R, ½ mile* Marshall, Michigan IFR DEPARTURE PROCEDURE: Rwys 10, 28, climb runway heading to 1100 before turning.			
CAPITAL CITY .... Rwy 27L, RVR/24* Lansing, Michigan Rwy 9R, ½ mile* Rwys 6, 32, 300-1 Rwy 14, 700-2** *(FAR 135) ** or standard with minimum climb of 240' per NM to 1600'. IFR DEPARTURE PROCEDURE: Rwys 91/9R, climb runway heading to 2000 before turning South. Rwys 6, 24, 27L, 27R, 32 climb runway heading to 1300 before turning southeast.			

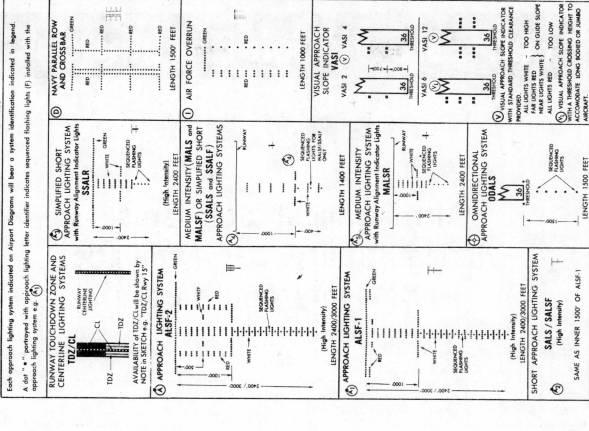

LEGEND
INSTRUMENT APPROACH PROCEDURES (CHARTS)
APPROACH LIGHTING SYSTEMS – UNITED STATES

Each approach lighting system indicated on Airport Diagrams will bear a system identification indicated in legend.

A dot " • " portrayed with approach lighting letter identifier indicates sequenced flashing lights (F) installed with the approach lighting system e.g. ⒶF

RUNWAY TOUCHDOWN ZONE AND CENTERLINE LIGHTING SYSTEMS
TDZ/CL

AVAILABILITY of TDZ/CL will be shown by NOTE in SKETCH e.g. "TDZ/CL Rwy 15"

Ⓐ APPROACH LIGHTING SYSTEM ALSF-2
(High Intensity)
LENGTH 2400'/3000 FEET

Ⓐ₁ APPROACH LIGHTING SYSTEM ALSF-1
(High Intensity)
LENGTH 2400'/3000 FEET

Ⓐ₂ SHORT APPROACH LIGHTING SYSTEM SALS / SALSF
(High Intensity)
SAME AS INNER 1500' of ALSF-1

Ⓐ₃ SIMPLIFIED SHORT APPROACH LIGHTING SYSTEM with Runway Alignment Indicator Lights SSALR
(High Intensity)
LENGTH 2400 FEET

Ⓐ₄ MEDIUM INTENSITY (MALSF and MALSR) OR SIMPLIFIED SHORT (SSALS and SSALF) APPROACH LIGHTING SYSTEMS
LENGTH 1400 FEET

Ⓐ₅ MEDIUM INTENSITY APPROACH LIGHTING SYSTEM with Runway Alignment Indicator Lights MALSR
LENGTH 2400 FEET

Ⓐ₆ OMNIDIRECTIONAL APPROACH LIGHTING SYSTEM ODALS
LENGTH 1500 FEET

Ⓓ NAVY PARALLEL ROW AND CROSS BAR
LENGTH 1500' FEET

Ⓘ AIR FORCE OVERRUN
LENGTH 1000 FEET

VISUAL APPROACH SLOPE INDICATOR VASI
Ⓥ VASI 4
Ⓥ VASI 2   VASI 6   VASI 12

Ⓥ VISUAL APPROACH SLOPE INDICATOR WITH STANDARD THRESHOLD CLEARANCE PROVIDED.
ALL LIGHTS WHITE – TOO HIGH
FAR LIGHTS RED – ON GLIDE SLOPE
NEAR LIGHTS WHITE
ALL LIGHTS RED – TOO LOW

Ⓥₗ VISUAL APPROACH SLOPE INDICATOR WITH A THRESHOLD CROSSING HEIGHT TO ACCOMODATE LONG BODIED OR JUMBO AIRCRAFT.

Instrument Approach Procedures (Charts)
INOPERATIVE COMPONENTS OR VISUAL AIDS TABLE

Landing minimums published on instrument approach procedure charts are based upon full operation of all components and visual aids associated with the particular instrument approach chart being used. Higher minimums are required with inoperative components or visual aids as indicated below. If more than one component is inoperative, each minimum is raised to the highest minimum required by any single component that is inoperative. ILS glide slope inoperative minimums are published on instrument approach charts as localizer minimums. This table may be amended by notes on the approach chart. Such notes apply only to the particular approach category(ies) as stated. See legend page for description of components indicated below.

(1) ILS, MLS, and PAR

Inoperative Component or Aid	Approach Category	Increase DH	Increase Visibility
MM*	ABC	50 feet	None
MM*	D	50 feet	¼ mile
ALSF 1 & 2, MALSR, & SSALR	ABCD	None	¼ mile

*Not applicable to PAR

(2) ILS with visibility minimum of 1,800 or 2,000 RVR.

Inoperative Component or Aid	Approach Category	Increase DH	Increase Visibility
MM	ABC	50 feet	To 2400 RVR
MM	D	50 feet	To 4000 RVR
ALSF 1 & 2, MALSR, & SSALR	ABCD	None	To 4000 RVR
TDZL, RCLS	ABCD	None	To 2400 RVR
RVR	ABCD	None	To ½ mile

(3) VOR, VOR/DME, VORTAC, VOR (TAC), VOR/DME (TAC), LOC, LOC/DME, LDA, LDA/DME, SDF, SDF/DME, RNAV, and ASR

Inoperative Visual Aid	Approach Category	Increase MDA	Increase Visibility
ALSF 1 & 2, MALSR, & SSALR	ABCD	None	½ mile
SSALS, MALS & ODALS	ABC	None	¼ mile

(4) NDB

Inoperative Visual Aid	Approach Category	Increase MDA	Increase Visibility
ALSF 1 & 2, MALSR, & SSALR	C	None	½ mile
	ABD	None	¼ mile
MALS, SSALS, ODALS	ABC	None	¼ mile

Federal Aviation Regulations

PART 23

Airworthiness Standards: Normal, Utility, and Acrobatic Category Airplanes

[§ 23.65   Climb: all engines operating.

[(a) Each airplane must have a steady rate of climb at sea level of at least 300 feet per minute and a steady angle of climb of at least 1:12 for landplanes or 1:15 for seaplanes and amphibians with—

[(1) Not more than maximum continuous power on each engine;

[(2) The landing gear retracted;

[(3) The wing flaps in the takeoff position; and

[(4) The cowl flaps or other means for controlling the engine cooling air supply in the position used in the cooling tests required by §§ 23.1041 through 23.1047.

[(b) Each airplane with engines for which the takeoff and maximum continuous power ratings are identical and that has fixed-pitch, two-position, or similar propellers, may use a lower propeller pitch setting than that allowed by § 23.33 to obtain rated engine r.p.m. at V_x, if—

[(1) The airplane shows marginal performance (such as when it can meet the rate of climb requirements of paragraph (a) of this section but has difficulty in meeting the angle of climb requirements of paragraph (a) of this section or of § 23.77); and

[(2) Acceptable engine cooling is shown at the lower speed associated with the best angle of climb.

[(c) Each turbine engine-powered airplane must be able to maintain a steady gradient of climb of at least 4 percent at a pressure altitude of 5,000 feet and a temperature of 81 degrees F (standard temperature plus 40 degree F) with the airplane in the configuration prescribed in paragraph (a) of this section.]

EXCERPT

§ 23.67   Climb: one engine inoperative.

(a) Each [reciprocating engine-powered] multiengine airplane of more than 6,000 pounds maximum weight must be able to maintain a steady rate of climb of at least $0.027 V_{s_0}^2$ (that is, the number of feet per minute is obtained by multiplying the square of the number of knots by 0.027 at an altitude of 5,000 feet with the—

(1) Critical engine inoperative, and its propeller in the minimum drag position;

(2) Remaining engines at not more than maximum continuous power;

(3) Landing gear retracted;

(4) Wing flaps in the most favorable position; and

(5) Cowl flaps in the position used in the cooling tests required by §§ 23.1041 through 23.1047.

(b) For [reciprocating engine-powered] multiengine airplanes of 6,000 pounds or less maximum weight, the following apply:

(1) Each airplane with a V_{s_0} of more than 61 knots must be able to maintain a steady rate of climb of at least $0.027 V_{s_0}^2$ (that is, the number of feet per minute is obtained by multiplying the square of the number of knots by 0.027), at an altitude of 5,000 feet with the—

(i) Critical engine inoperative and its propeller in the minimum drag position;

(ii) Remaining engines at not more than maximum continuous power;

(iii) Landing gear retracted;

(iv) Wing flaps in the most favorable position; and

(v) Cowl flaps in the position used in the cooling tests required by §§ 23.1041 through 23.1047.

(2) For each airplane with a stalling speed of 61 knots or less, the steady rate of climb at 5,000 feet must be determined with the—

(i) Critical engine inoperative and its propeller in the minimum drag position;

(ii) Remaining engines at not more than maximum continuous power;

(iii) Landing gear retracted;

(iv) Wing flaps in the most favorable position; and

(v) Cowl flaps in the position used in the cooling tests required by §§ 23.1041 through 23.1047.

[(c) For turbine-powered multiengine airplanes the following apply:

[(1) The steady gradient of climb must be determined at each weight, altitude, and ambient temperature within the operational limits established by the applicant, with the—

[(i) Critical engine inoperative, and its propeller in the minimum drag position;

[(ii) Remaining engines at not more than maximum continuous power or thrust;

[(iii) Landing gear retracted;

[(iv) Wing flaps in the most favorable position; and

[(v) The means for controlling the engine cooling air supply in the position used in the engine cooling tests required by §§ 23.1041 through 23.1047.

[(2) Each airplane must be able to maintain the following climb gradients with the airplane in the configuration prescribed in paragraph (c)(1) of this section:

[(i) 1.2 percent (or, if greater, a gradient equivalent to a rate of climb of 0.027 $V_{s_0}^2$) at a pressure altitude of 5,000 feet and standard temperature (41 degrees F).

[(ii) 0.6 percent (or, if greater, a gradient equivalent to a rate of climb of 0.014 $V_{s_0}^2$) at a pressure altitude of 5,000 feet and 81 degrees F (standard temperature plus 40 degrees F).

[(3) The minimum climb gradient specified in paragraphs (c)(2)(i) and (ii) of this section must vary linearly between 41 degrees F and 81 degrees F and must change at the same rate up to the maximum operating temperature approved for the airplane.

[(4) In paragraphs (c)(2)(i) and (ii) of this section, rate of climb is expressed in feet per minute and V_{s_0} is expressed in knots.

[(d) For all multiengine airplanes, the speed for best rate of climb with one engine inoperative must be determined.

MICROWAVE LANDING SYSTEM (MLS)

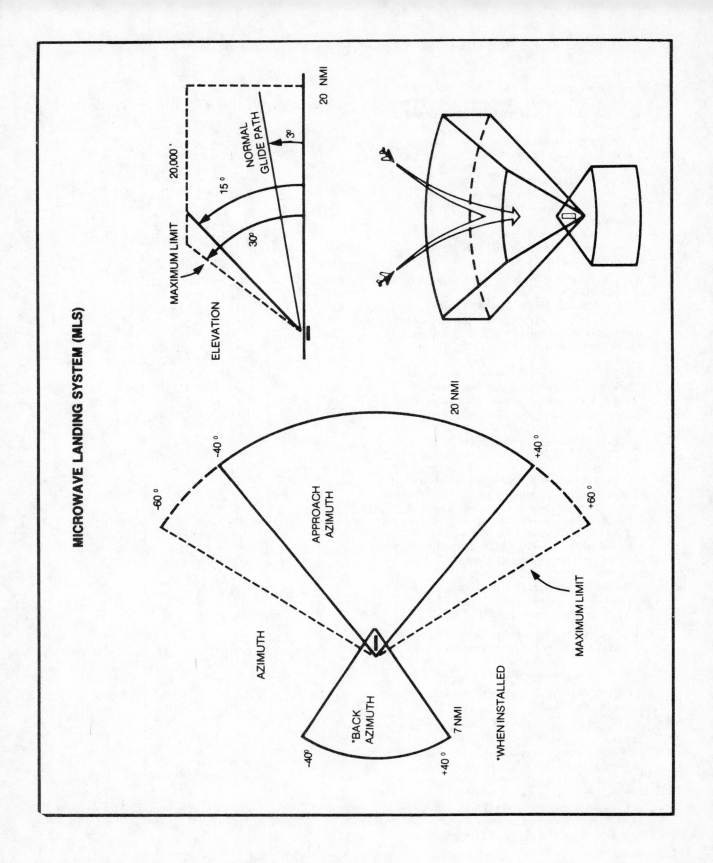

APPENDIX 3

QUESTION CATEGORIES AND REFERENCES

ABBREVIATIONS

The abbreviations listed below are used to identify the aircraft and reference associated with each test question listed in Appendix 1.

AIRCRAFT ABBREVIATIONS

AIR — Airplane
HLC — Helicopter
* HLC applies to helicopters only.

REFERENCE ABBREVIATIONS

AC — Advisory Circular
ACL — Aeronautical Chart Legend
AFD — Airport/Facility Directory
AIM — Airman's Information Manual
COMP — Computation
FAR — Federal Aviation Regulations
IAP — Instrument Approach Procedures
IEOG — IFR Exam–O–Gram
NOTAM — Notices to Airmen
SID — Standard Instrument Departure
B206 — Manufacturer's Manual
C310 — Manufacturer's Manual

AIRCRAFT CATEGORY AND REFERENCES

To determine the applicable category and reference for each question, refer to the question number in the following list.

For example, question 7003 contains subject matter appropriate to helicopter category aircraft (HLC) only and the reference is FAR 61. The correct response to question 7003 may be found in FAR 61. Since this question pertains to helicopter category aircraft only, the airplane applicant may wish to study subject matter appropriate to airplanes only.

Item	Aircraft	Reference	Item	Aircraft	Reference
7001.	AIR	FAR 61	7011.	AIR	FAR 61
7002.	AIR	FAR 61	7012.	HLC	FAR 61
7003.	HLC	FAR 61	7013.	AIR	FAR 61
7004.	AIR	FAR 61	7014.	HLC	FAR 61
7005.	HLC	FAR 61	7015.	HLC	FAR 61
7006.	AIR	FAR 61	7016.	HLC	FAR 61
7007.	AIR	FAR 61	7017.	HLC	FAR 61
7008.	AIR	FAR 61	7018.	HLC	FAR 61
7009.	AIR	FAR 61	7019.	HLC	FAR 61
7010.	AIR	FAR 61	7020.	HLC	FAR 61

Item	Aircraft	Reference	Item	Aircraft	Reference
7021.	HLC	FAR 61	7064.	HLC	FAR 91
7022.	HLC	FAR 61	7065.	AIR	FAR 91
7023.	HLC	FAR 61	7066.	AIR	FAR 91
7024.	HLC	FAR 61	7067.	AIR	FAR 91
7025.	HLC	FAR 61	7068.	AIR	FAR 91
7026.	HLC	FAR 61	7069.	AIR	FAR 91
7027.	HLC	FAR 61	7070.	AIR	FAR 91
7028.	HLC	FAR 61	7071.	AIR	FAR 91
7029.	HLC	FAR 61	7072.	AIR	FAR 91
7030.	HLC	FAR 61	7073.	AIR	FAR 91
7031.	AIR	FAR 61	7074.	AIR	FAR 91
7032.	AIR	FAR 61	7075.	AIR	FAR 91
7033.			7076.	AIR	FAR 91
7034.	AIR	FAR 61	7077.	HLC	FAR 91
7035.	AIR	FAR 91	7078.	AIR	FAR 91
7036.	HLC	FAR 61	7079.	AIR	FAR 91
7037.	AIR	FAR 61	7080.	AIR	FAR 91
7038.	AIR	FAR 61	7081.	AIR	FAR 91
7039.	AIR	FAR 61	7082.	AIR	FAR 91
7040.	AIR	FAR 61	7083.	AIR	AIM
7041.	HLC	FAR 61	7084.	AIR	AIM
7042.	HLC	FAR 61	7085.	AIR	AIM
7043.	AIR	FAR 91	7086.	AIR	AIM
7044.	AIR	FAR 91	7087.	AIR	AIM
7045.	AIR	FAR 91	7088.		
7046.	HLC	FAR 91	7089.	AIR	AIM
7047.	AIR	FAR 91	7090.	AIR	AIM
7048.	AIR	FAR 91	7091.	AIR	AIM
7049.	AIR	FAR 91	7092.	AIR	AIM
7050.	AIR	FAR 91	7093.	AIR	AFD
7051.	AIR	FAR 91	7094.	AIR	AIM
7052.	AIR	FAR 91	7095.	AIR	AIM
7053.	AIR	FAR 91	7096.	AIR	AIM
7054.	AIR	FAR 91	7097.	AIR	ACL
7055.	AIR	FAR 91	7098.	AIR	AFD
7056.	AIR	FAR 91	7099.	AIR	AFD
7057.	AIR	FAR 91	7100.	AIR	AFD
7058.	AIR	FAR 91	7101.	AIR	AFD
7059.	HLC	AC 61–23B	7102.	AIR	AFD
7060.	AIR	AC 61–23B	7103.	AIR	AFD
7061.	AIR	FAR 91	7104.	AIR	AFD
7062.	HLC	FAR 91	7105.	AIR	AFD
7063.	HLC	FAR 91	7106.	AIR	AFD

Item	Aircraft	Reference	Item	Aircraft	Reference
7107.			7150.	HLC	AC 91–23A
7108.	AIR	FAR 91	7151.	HLC	AC 91–23A
7109.	AIR	AFD	7152.	HLC	AC 91–23A
7110.	AIR	AFD	7153.	HLC	AC 91–23A
7111.	AIR	AFD	7154.	HLC	AC 91–23A
7112.	AIR	AFD	7155.	AIR	AC 61–27C
7113.	AIR	AFD	7156.	AIR	COMP
7114.	AIR	AFD	7157.	AIR	COMP
7115.	AIR	AIM	7158.	AIR	AC 61–21A
7116.	AIR	AIM	7159.		
7117.	AIR	AFD	7160.	AIR	C310
7118.	AIR	AFD	7161.	AIR	C310
7119.	AIR	AFD	7162.	AIR	C310
7120.	AIR	AFD	7163.	AIR	C310
7121.	AIR	AFD	7164.	AIR	C310
7122.	AIR	AFD	7165.	AIR	C310
7123.	AIR	AFD	7166.	AIR	C310
7124.	AIR	AFD	7167.	AIR	C310
7125.	HLC	B206	7168.		
7126.	HLC	B206	7169.	AIR	C310
7127.	HLC	B206	7170.		
7128.	HLC	B206	7171.	AIR	C310
7129.	HLC	B206	7172.	AIR	C310
7130.	HLC	B206	7173.	AIR	C310
7131.	HLC	B206	7174.	AIR	C310
7132.	HLC	B206	7175.	AIR	C310
7133.	HLC	B206	7176.	AIR	C310
7134.	HLC	B206	7177.	AIR	C310
7135.	HLC	B206	7178.	AIR	C310
7136.	AIR	AC 61–21A	7179.	AIR	C310
7137.	HLC	B206	7180.	AIR	C310
7138.	HLC	B206	7181.	AIR	C310
7139.	HLC	B206	7182.	AIR	C310
7140.	HLC	B206	7183.		
7141.	HLC	B206	7184.		
7142.	HLC	B206	7185.		
7143.	HLC	B206	7186.		
7144.	HLC	B206	7187.		
7145.	HLC	B206	7188.		
7146.	HLC	B206	7189.	AIR	C310
7147.	HLC	B206	7190.	AIR	C310
7148.	HLC	B206	7191.	AIR	C310
7149.	HLC	B206	7192.	AIR	C310

Item	Aircraft	Reference	Item	Aircraft	Reference
7193.	AIR	C310	7236.	AIR	C310
7194.	AIR	C310	7237.		
7195.	AIR	C310	7238.		
7196.	AIR	C310	7239.		
7197.	AIR	C310	7240.		
7198.	AIR	C310	7241.		
7199.	AIR	C310	7242.		
7200.	AIR	C310	7243.		
7201.	AIR	C310	7244.		
7202.	AIR	C310	7245.		
7203.	AIR	C310	7246.		
7204.			7247.		
7205.	AIR	C310	7248.		
7206.	AIR	C310	7249.	AIR	C310
7207.			7250.	AIR	C310
7208.	AIR	C310	7251.	AIR	C310
7209.			7252.	AIR	C310
7210.	AIR	C310	7253.	AIR	C310
7211.	AIR	C310	7254.	AIR	C310
7212.	AIR	C310	7255.	AIR	C310
7213.	AIR	C310	7256.	AIR	C310
7214.	AIR	C310	7257.	AIR	C310
7215.	AIR	C310	7258.	AIR	C310
7216.	AIR	C310	7259.	AIR	C310
7217.	AIR	C310	7260.	AIR	C310
7218.	AIR	C310	7261.	AIR	C310
7219.	AIR	C310	7262.		
7220.	AIR	C310	7263.		
7221.	AIR	C310	7264.	AIR	C310
7222.	AIR	C310	7265.	AIR	C310
7223.	AIR	C310	7266.	AIR	C310
7224.	AIR	C310	7267.	AIR	C310
7225.	AIR	C310	7268.	AIR	C310
7226.	AIR	C310	7269.	AIR	C310
7227.	AIR	C310	7270.	AIR	C310
7228.	AIR	C310	7271.	AIR	C310
7229.	AIR	C310	7272.	AIR	C310
7230.	AIR	C310	7273.	AIR	C310
7231.	AIR	C310	7274.	AIR	C310
7232.	AIR	C310	7275.	AIR	C310
7233.	AIR	C310	7276.	AIR	C310
7234.	AIR	C310	7277.	AIR	C310
7235.	AIR	C310	7278.	AIR	C310

Item	Aircraft	Reference	Item	Aircraft	Reference
7279.	AIR	C310	**7322.**	AIR	AC 00–6A
7280.	AIR	C310	**7323.**	AIR	AC 00–6A
7281.	AIR	C310	**7324.**	AIR	AC 00–6A
7282.	AIR	C310	**7325.**	AIR	AC 00–6A
7283.	AIR	C310	**7326.**	AIR	AC 00–6A
7284.	AIR	C310	**7327.**	AIR	AC 00–6A
7285.	AIR	C310	**7328.**	AIR	AC 00–6A
7286.			**7329.**	AIR	AC 00–6A
7287.			**7330.**	AIR	AC 00–6A
7288.			**7331.**	AIR	AC 00–6A
7289.	AIR	C310	**7332.**	AIR	AC 00–6A
7290.	AIR	C310	**7333.**	AIR	AC 00–6A
7291.	AIR	C310	**7334.**	AIR	AC 00–6A
7292.	AIR	C310	**7335.**	AIR	AC 00–6A
7293.			**7336.**	AIR	AC 00–6A
7294.			**7337.**	AIR	AC 00–6A
7295.			**7338.**	AIR	AC 00–6A
7296.	AIR	C310	**7339.**	AIR	AC 00–6A
7297.	AIR	AC 00–6A	**7340.**	AIR	AC 00–6A
7298.	AIR	AC 00–6A	**7341.**	AIR	AC 00–6A
7299.	AIR	AC 00–6A	**7342.**	AIR	AC 00–6A
7300.	AIR	AC 00–6A	**7343.**	AIR	AC 00–6A
7301.	AIR	AC 00–6A	**7344.**	AIR	AC 00–6A
7302.	AIR	AC 00–6A	**7345.**	AIR	AC 00–6A
7303.	AIR	AC 00–6A	**7346.**	AIR	AC 00–6A
7304.	AIR	AC 00–6A	**7347.**	AIR	AC 00–6A
7305.	AIR	FAR 91	**7448.**	AIR	AC 00–6A
7306.	AIR	AC 00–6A	**7349.**	AIR	AC 00–6A
7307.	AIR	AC 00–6A	**7350.**	AIR	AC 00–6A
7308.	AIR	AC 00–6A	**7351.**	AIR	AC 00–6A
7309.	AIR	AC 00–6A	**7352.**	AIR	AC 00–6A
7310.	AIR	AC 00–6A	**7353.**	AIR	AC 00–6A
7311.	AIR	AC 00–6A	**7354.**	AIR	AC 00–6A
7312.	AIR	AC 00–6A	**7355.**	AIR	AC 00–6A
7313.	AIR	AC 00–6A	**7356.**	AIR	AC 00–6A
7314.	AIR	AC 00–6A	**7357.**	AIR	AC 00–6A
7315.	AIR	AC 00–6A	**7358.**	AIR	AC 00–6A
7316.	AIR	AC 00–6A	**7359.**	AIR	AC 00–6A
7317.	AIR	AC 00–6A	**7360.**	AIR	AC 00–6A
7318.	AIR	AC 00–6A	**7361.**	AIR	AC 00–6A
7319.	AIR	AC 00–6A	**7362.**	AIR	AC 00–6A
7320.	AIR	AC 00–6A	**7363.**	AIR	AC 00–6A
7321.	AIR	AC 00–6A	**7364.**	AIR	AC 00–6A

Item	Aircraft	Reference	Item	Aircraft	Reference
7365.	AIR	AC 00–6A	7408.	AIR	AC 00–45B
7366.	AIR	AC 00–6A	7409.	AIR	AC 00–45B
7367.	AIR	AC 00–6A	7410.	AIR	AC 00–45B
7368.	AIR	AC 00–6A	7411.	AIR	AC 00–45B
7369.	AIR	AC 00–6A	7412.	AIR	AIM
7370.	AIR	AC 00–6A	7413.	AIR	AC 00–45B
7371.	AIR	AC 00–6A	7414.	AIR	AC 00–45B
7372.	AIR	AC 00–6A	7415.	AIR	AC 00–45B
7373.	AIR	AC 00–6A	7416.	AIR	AC 00–45B
7374.	AIR	AC 00–45B	7417.	AIR	AC 00–45B
7375.	AIR	AC 00–45B	7418.	AIR	AC 00–45B
7376.	AIR	AC 00–45B	7419.	AIR	AC 00–45B
7377.	AIR	AC 00–45B	7420.	AIR	AC 00–45B
7378.	AIR	AC 00–45B	7421.	AIR	AC 00–45B
7379.	AIR	AC 00–45B	7422.	AIR	AC 00–45B
7380.	AIR	AC 00–45B	7423.	AIR	AC 00–45B
7381.	AIR	AC 00–45B	7424.	AIR	AC 00–45B
7382.	AIR	AC 00–45B	7425.	AIR	AC 00–45B
7383.	AIR	AC 00–45B	7426.	AIR	AC 00–45B
7384.	AIR	AC 00–45B	7427.	AIR	AC 00–45B
7385.	AIR	AC 00–45B	7428.	AIR	AC 00–45B
7386.			7429.	AIR	AC 61–27C
7387.	AIR	AC 00–45B	7430.	AIR	AC 61–27C
7388.	AIR	AC 00–45B	7431.	AIR	AC 61–27C
7389.	AIR	AC 00–45B	7432.	AIR	AC 61–27C
7390.	AIR	AC 00–45B	7433.	AIR	AC 61–27C
7391.	AIR	AC 00–45B	7434.	AIR	AC 61–27C
7392.	AIR	AC 00–45B	7435.	AIR	AC 61–27C
7393.	AIR	AC 00–45B	7436.	AIR	AC 61–27C
7394.	AIR	AC 00–45B	7437.	AIR	AC 61–27C
7395.			7438.	AIR	AC 61–27C
7396.	AIR	AC 00–45B	7439.	AIR	AC 61–27C
7397.	AIR	AC 00–45B	7440.	AIR	FAR 91
7398.	AIR	AC 00–45B	7441.	AIR	AIM
7399.	AIR	AC 00–45B	7442.	AIR	AIM
7400.	AIR	AC 00–45B	7443.	AIR	AIM
7401.	AIR	AC 00–45B	7444.	AIR	AIM
7402.	AIR	AC 00–45B	7445.	AIR	AIM
7403.	AIR	AC 00–45B	7446.	AIR	IEOG
7404.	AIR	AC 00–45B	7447.	AIR	IEOG
7405.	AIR	AC 00–45B	7448.	AIR	AIM
7406.	AIR	AC 00–45B	7449.	AIR	AIM
7407.	AIR	AC 00–45B	7450.	AIR	AIM

Item	Aircraft	Reference	Item	Aircraft	Reference
7451.	AIR	IEOG	7494.	AIR	AIM
7452.	AIR	AIM	7495.	AIR	AIM
7453.	AIR	AIM	7496.	AIR	AIM
7454.	AIR	AIM	7497.	AIR	AIM
7455.	AIR	AIM	7498.	AIR	AIM
7456.	AIR	AIM	7499.	AIR	AIM
7457.	AIR	AIM	7500.	AIR	AIM
7458.	AIR	AIM	7501.	AIR	AIM
7459.	AIR	AIM	7502.	AIR	AIM
7460.	AIR	AIM	7503.	AIR	AC 61–27C
7461.	AIR	AC 61–27C	7504.	AIR	AC 61–27C
7462.	AIR	AC 61–27C	7505.	AIR	AC 61–27C
7463.	AIR	AIM	7506.	AIR	AC 61–27C
7464.	AIR	AIM	7507.	AIR	AC 61–27C
7465.	AIR	AIM	7508.	AIR	AC 61–27C
7466.	AIR	IAP	7509.	AIR	AC 61–27C
7467.	AIR	AIM	7510.	AIR	AC 61–27C
7468.	AIR	AC 61–27C	7511.	AIR	AC 61–27C
7469.	AIR	AC 91–46	7512.		
7470.	AIR	AC 91–46	7513.		
7471.	AIR	AC 61–27C	7514.		
7472.	AIR	FAR 91	7515.		
7473.	AIR	FAR 91	7516.	AIR	AC 61–27C
7474.	AIR	FAR 91	7517.	AIR	AC 61–27C
7475.	AIR	FAR 91	7518.	AIR	AFD
7476.	AIR	FAR 91	7519.	AIR	FAR 91
7477.	AIR	FAR 91	7520.	AIR	FAR 91
7478.	AIR	FAR 91	7521.	AIR	FAR 91
7479.	AIR	FAR 91	7522.	AIR	SID
7480.	AIR	FAR 91	7523.	AIR	SID
7481.	AIR	AFD	7524.	AIR	SID
7482.	AIR	FAR 91	7525.	AIR	AIM
7483.	AIR	AIM	7526.	AIR	IEOG
7484.	AIR	AIM	7527.	AIR	AIM
7485.	AIR	AC 61–27C	7528.	AIR	COMP
7486.	AIR	AC 61–27C	7529.	AIR	AIM
7487.	AIR	AC 61–27C	7530.	AIR	IEOG
7488.	AIR	AC 61–27C	7531.	AIR	IEOG
7489.	AIR	AIM	7532.	AIR	COMP
7490.	AIR	AIM	7533.	AIR	COMP
7491.	AIR	AIM	7534.	AIR	COMP
7492.	AIR	AIM	7535.	AIR	COMP
7493.	AIR	AIM	7536.	AIR	FAR 91

Item	Aircraft	Reference	Item	Aircraft	Reference
7537.	AIR	IEOG	7580.	AIR	AIM
7538.	AIR	AIM	7581.	AIR	AIM
7539.	AIR	FAR 91	7582.	AIR	AIM
7540.	AIR	EOG	7583.	HLC	FAR 91
7541.	AIR	AC 61–27C	7584.	AIR	AIM
7542.	AIR	AC 61–27C	7585.	AIR	FAR 91
7543.	AIR	AC 61–27C	7586.	AIR	FAR 91
7544.	AIR	AC 61–27C	7587.	AIR	ACL
7545.	AIR	AC 61–27C	7588.	AIR	AIM
7546.	AIR	FAR 91	7589.	AIR	FAR 91
7547.	AIR	AIM	7590.	AIR	ACL
7548.	AIR	ACL	7591.	HLC	FAR 91
7549.	AIR	ACL	7592.	AIR	FAR 91
7550.	AIR	AIM	7593.	AIR	AIM
7551.	AIR	AC 61–27C	7594.	AIR	ACL
7552.	AIR	AIM	7595.	AIR	FAR 91
7553.	AIR	FAR 91	7596.	AIR	AIM
7554.	AIR	ACL	7597.	AIR	FAR 91
7555.	AIR	ACL	7598.	AIR	AIM
7556.	AIR	AIM	7599.	AIR	AIM
7557.	AIR	FAR 91	7600.	AIR	AC 61–27C
7558.	AIR	AIM	7601.	AIR	AIM
7559.	AIR	AIM	7602.	AIR	AIM
7560.	AIR	AIM	7603.	AIR	AIM
7561.			7604.	AIR	AIM
7562.	AIR	AC 61–27C	7605.	AIR	ACL
7563.	AIR	AC 61–27C	7606.	AIR	AIM
7564.	AIR	AC 61–27C	7607.	AIR	AIM
7565.	AIR	AC 61–27C	7608.	AIR	IEOG
7566.	AIR	AIM	7609.	AIR	AIM
7567.	AIR	AIM	7610.	AIR	IEOG
7568.	AIR	FAR 91	7611.	AIR	IEOG
7569.	AIR	AIM	7612.	AIR	AIM
7570.	AIR	AIM	7613.	AIR	ACL
7571.	AIR	ACL	7614.	AIR	AIM
7572.	AIR	FAR 91	7615.		
7573.	AIR	AIM	7616.	AIR	FAR 91
7574.	AIR	ACL	7617.	AIR	AIM
7575.	AIR	AIM	7618.	AIR	IEOG
7576.	AIR	ACL	7619.	AIR	IEOG
7577.	AIR	ACL	7620.	AIR	IEOG
7578.	AIR	ACL	7621.	AIR	COMP
7579.	AIR	AIM	7622.	AIR	ACL

Item	Aircraft	Reference	Item	Aircraft	Reference
7623.	AIR	AIM	7666.	AIR	IEOG
7624.	AIR	IEOG	7667.	AIR	IEOG
7625.	AIR	IEOG	7668.	AIR	COMP
7626.	AIR	AIM	7669.	AIR	IEOG
7627.	AIR	FAR 91	7670.	AIR	AIM
7628.	AIR	COMP	7671.	AIR	AIM
7629.	AIR	AIM	7672.	AIR	AIM
7630.	HLC	FAR 91	7673.	AIR	AIM
7631.			7674.	AIR	FAR 91
7632.	AIR	FAR 91	7675.	AIR	FAR 91
7633.	AIR	IEOG	7676.	AIR	AC 61–27C
7634.	AIR	ACL	7677.	AIR	ACL
7635.	AIR	AC 61–27C	7678.	AIR	COMP
7636.	AIR	ACL	7679.	AIR	ACL
7637.	AIR	AIM	7680.	AIR	AIM
7638.	AIR	IEOG	7681.	AIR	FAR 91
7639.	AIR	AIM	7682.	AIR	FAR 91
7640.	AIR	FAR 91	7683.	AIR	FAR 91
7641.	AIR	AIM	7684.	AIR	FAR 91
7642.	AIR	AIM	7685.	AIR	AC 61–27C
7643.	AIR	AIM	7686.	AIR	AIM
7644.	AIR	AIM	7687.	AIR	FAR 91
7645.	AIR	AIM	7688.	AIR	AIM
7646.	AIR	AIM	7689.	AIR	ACL
7647.	AIR	AC 00–50A	7690.	AIR	ACL
7648.	AIR	AIM	7691.	AIR	ACL
7649.	AIR	AC 61–27C	7692.	AIR	AIM
7650.	AIR	AIM	7693.	AIR	COMP
7651.	AIR	AC 61–27C	7694.	AIR	AIM
7652.	AIR	AC 61–27C	7695.	AIR	AIM
7653.	AIR	AIM	7696.	AIR	AC 61–27C
7654.	AIR	AC 61–27C	7697.	AIR	ACL
7655.	AIR	AC 61–27C	7698.	AIR	ACL
7656.	AIR	FAR 91	7699.	AIR	COMP
7657.	AIR	IEOG	7700.	AIR	COMP
7658.			7701.	AIR	AIM
7659.	AIR	IEOG	7702.	AIR	IEOG
7660.	AIR	ACL	7703.	AIR	AIM
7661.	AIR	FAR 91	7704.	AIR	IEOG
7662.	AIR	AIM	7705.	AIR	ACL
7663.	AIR	AIM	7706.	AIR	AIM
7664.	AIR	AIM	7707.	AIR	AIM
7665.	AIR	ACL	7708.	AIR	ACL

Item	Aircraft	Reference	Item	Aircraft	Reference
7709.	AIR	COMP	7752.	AIR	AIM
7710.	AIR	AIM	7753.	AIR	AIM
7711.	AIR	ACL	7754.	AIR	COMP
7712.	AIR	COMP	7755.	AIR	AIM
7713.	AIR	COMP	7756.	AIR	ACL
7714.	AIR	FAR 91	7757.	AIR	AIM
7715.	AIR	FAR 91	7758.	AIR	IEOG
7716.	AIR	AIM	7759.	AIR	AIM
7717.	AIR	FAR 91	7760.	AIR	FAR 91
7718.	AIR	ACL	7761.	AIR	FAR 91
7719.	AIR	AIM	7762.	AIR	AFD
7720.	AIR	ACL	7763.	AIR	COMP
7721.	AIR	COMP	7764.	AIR	AIM
7722.	AIR	AIM	7765.	AIR	FAR 91
7723.	AIR	ACL	7766.	AIR	AIM
7724.	AIR	FAR 91	7767.	AIR	ACL
7725.	AIR	FAR 91	7768.	AIR	ACL
7726.	AIR	AFD	7769.	AIR	ACL
7727.	AIR	ACL	7770.	AIR	ACL
7728.	AIR	AIM	7771.	AIR	FAR 91
7729.	AIR	ACL	7772.	AIR	ACL
7730.	AIR	AIM	7773.	AIR	ACL
7731.	AIR	AIM	7774.	AIR	IEOG
7732.	AIR	AIM	7775.	AIR	AIM
7733.	AIR	ACL	7776.	AIR	FAR 91
7734.	AIR	COMP	7777.	AIR	IEOG
7735.	AIR	FAR 91	7778.		
7736.	AIR	FAR 91	7779.	AIR	AIM
7737.	AIR	FAR 91	7780.	AIR	AIM
7738.			7781.	AIR	FAR 91
7739.	AIR	ACL	7782.	AIR	FAR 91
7740.	AIR	AIM	7783.	AIR	AC 61–27C
7741.			7784.	AIR	IAP
7742.			7785.	AIR	AIM
7743.			7786.	AIR	AC 61–27C
7744.			7787.	AIR	AFD
7745.			7788.	AIR	AC 61–27C
7746.			7789.	AIR	AIM
7747.	AIR	AIM	7790.	AIR	AIM
7748.	AIR	AIM	7791.	AIR	AIM
7749.	AIR	AIM	7792.	AIR	AIM
7750.	AIR	AIM	7793.	AIR	AC 61–27C
7751.	AIR	ACL	7794.	AIR	AC 61–27C

Item	Aircraft	Reference	Item	Aircraft	Reference
7795.	AIR	AC 61–27C	7838.	AIR	AIM
7796.	AIR	AIM	7839.	AIR	IAP
7797.	AIR	AC 61–27C	7840.	AIR	IAP
7798.	AIR	IAP	7841.	HLC	FAR 97
7799.	HLC	FAR 97	7842.	AIR	IAP
7800.	HLC	FAR 97	7843.	AIR	IAP
7801.	AIR	IEOG	7844.	AIR	AC 00–50A
7802.	HLC	IAP	7845.	AIR	AC 91–43
7803.	HLC	FAR 97	7846.	AIR	AIM
7804.			7847.	AIR	AIM
7805.	AIR	IAP	7848.	AIR	AC 61–27C
7806.	AIR	AC 61–27C	7849.	AIR	AIM
7807.	HLC	FAR 97	7850.	AIR	AC 61–27C
7808.	AIR	AIM	7851.	AIR	AC 61–27C
7809.	AIR	AC 61–27C	7852.	AIR	AIM
7810.	AIR	FAR 91	7853.	AIR	AIM
7811.	AIR	AIM	7854.	AIR	AC 61–27C
7812.	AIR	AC 61–27C	7855.		
7813.	HLC	FAR 97	7856.	AIR	AIM
7814.	AIR	AC 61–27C	7857.	AIR	IAP
7815.	AIR	IEOG	7858.	AIR	AIM
7816.	AIR	AFD	7859.	AIR	AC 61–27C
7817.	AIR	AC 61–27C	7860.	AIR	AC 90–45A
7818.	AIR	AC 61–27C	7861.	HLC	FAR 97
7819.	AIR	AFD	7862.	AIR	AIM
7820.	AIR	IAP	7863.	HLC	FAR 97
7821.	AIR	AC 61–27C	7864.	AIR	AIM
7822.	AIR	FAR 91	7865.	AIR	COMP
7823.	AIR	AC 91–43	7866.	AIR	AIM
7824.	AIR	AIM	7867.	AIR	AC 61–27C
7825.	AIR	FAR 91	7868.	AIR	IAP
7826.	AIR	IAP	7869.	AIR	IAP
7827.	AIR	IEOG	7870.	AIR	IEOG
7828.	AIR	IAP	7871.	AIR	IEOG
7829.	AIR	IAP	7872.	AIR	IEOG
7830.	AIR	FAR 91	7873.	AIR	IAP
7831.	AIR	AC 61–27C	7874.	HLC	FAR 97
7832.	AIR	FAR 91	7875.	AIR	AC 61–27C
7833.	AIR	FAR 91	7876.	AIR	IAP
7834.	AIR	IAP	7877.	AIR	IAP
7835.	HLC	FAR 97	7878.	AIR	IAP
7836.	AIR	IAP	7879.	AIR	IAP
7837.	AIR	IAP	7880.	AIR	FAR 91

Item	Aircraft	Reference	Item	Aircraft	Reference
7881.	AIR	AIM	**7924.**	AIR	IEOG
7882.	AIR	AIM	**7925.**	AIR	AFD
7883.	AIR	FAR 91	**7926.**	AIR	IAP
7884.	AIR	AC 61–27C	**7927.**	AIR	IEOG
7885.	HLC	IAP	**7928.**	AIR	AFD
7886.	AIR	AIM	**7929.**	AIR	AIM
7887.	AIR	FAR 91	**7930.**	AIR	AIM
7888.	AIR	AIM	**7931.**	AIR	AC 91–24
7889.	HLC	FAR 97	**7932.**	AIR	IAP
7890.	AIR	IAP	**7933.**	AIR	IAP
7891.	AIR	AC 61–27C	**7934.**	AIR	IAP
7892.	AIR	AC 00–50A	**7935.**	AIR	IAP
7893.	AIR	FAR 91	**7936.**	AIR	IAP
7894.	HLC	FAR 97	**7937.**	AIR	IAP
7895.	HLC	FAR 97	**7938.**	AIR	AFD
7896.	AIR	AIM	**7939.**	AIR	AFD
7897.	AIR	AIM	**7940.**	HLC	AIM
7898.	AIR	IAP	**7941.**	HLC	FAR 91
7899.			**7942.**	AIR	AC 61–27C
7900.	AIR	AIM	**7943.**	AIR	AC 00–50A
7901.	AIR	AC 61–27C	**7944.**	AIR	IAP
7902.	AIR	AC 61–27C	**7945.**	AIR	IAP
7903.	AIR	FAR 91	**7946.**	AIR	AFD
7904.	AIR	AIM	**7947.**	AIR	AIM
7905.	AIR	AIM	**7948.**	AIR	AIM
7906.	AIR	IAP	**7949.**	AIR	IAP
7907.			**7950.**		
7908.	AIR	AIM	**7951.**	AIR	FAR 91
7909.	AIR	IAP	**7952.**	AIR	AC 61–27C
7910.	AIR	IAP	**7953.**	AIR	AIM
7911.	AIR	IAP	**7954.**	AIR	AIM
7912.	AIR	AFD	**7955.**	AIR	AC 61–27C
7913.	AIR	IEOG	**7956.**	AIR	AIM
7914.	AIR	IAP	**7957.**	AIR	AIM
7915.	AIR	IAP	**7958.**	AIR	FAR 91
7916.	AIR	AFD	**7959.**	AIR	FAR 91
7917.	AIR	AIM	**7960.**	AIR	FAR 91
7918.	AIR	AIM	**7961.**	AIR	AIM
7919.	AIR	AFD	**7962.**	AIR	AIM
7920.	AIR	AIM	**7963.**	AIR	AC 61–21A
7921.	AIR	AIM	**7964.**	AIR	AC 61–27C
7922.	AIR	AIM	**7965.**	AIR	AC 61–27C
7923.	AIR	AIM	**7966.**		

Item	Aircraft	Reference	Item	Aircraft	Reference
7967.	AIR	AC 61–27C	8010.	AIR	AC 61–27C
7968.	AIR	AC 61–27C	8011.	AIR	AC 61–27C
7969.	AIR	AC 61–27C	8012.	AIR	AC 61–27C
7970.	AIR	AC 61–27C	8013.	AIR	AC 61–27C
7971.	AIR	AC 61–27C	8014.	AIR	AC 61–27C
7972.	AIR	AC 61–27C	8015.	AIR	AC 61–27C
7973.	AIR	AC 61–27C	8016.	AIR	AC 61–27C
7974.	AIR	AC 61–27C	8017.	AIR	AC 61–27C
7975.	AIR	AC 61–27C	8018.	AIR	AC 61–27C
7976.	AIR	AC 61–27C	8019.	AIR	AC 61–27C
7977.	AIR	AC 61–27C	8020.	AIR	AC 61–27C
7978.	AIR	AC 61–27C	8021.	AIR	AC 61–27C
7979.	AIR	AC 61–27C	8022.	AIR	AC 61–27C
7980.	AIR	AC 61–27C	8023.	AIR	AC 61–27C
7981.	AIR	AC 61–27C	8024.	AIR	AC 61–27C
7982.	AIR	AC 61–27C	8025.	AIR	AC 61–27C
7983.	AIR	AC 61–27C	8026.	AIR	AC 61–27C
7984.	AIR	AC 61–27C	8027.	AIR	AC 61–27C
7985.	AIR	AC 61–27C	8028.	AIR	AC 61–27C
7986.	AIR	AC 61–27C	8029.	AIR	AC 61–27C
7987.	AIR	AC 61–27C	8030.	AIR	AC 61–27C
7988.	HLC	AC 61–27C	8031.	AIR	AC 61–27C
7989.	HLC	AC 61–27C	8032.	AIR	AC 61–27C
7990.	HLC	AC 61–27C	8033.	AIR	AC 61–27C
7991.	HLC	AC 61–27C	8034.	AIR	AC 61–27C
7992.	HLC	IEOG	8035.	AIR	AC 61–27C
7993.	HLC	IEOG	8036.	AIR	AC 61–27C
7994.	HLC	IEOG	8037.	AIR	AC 61–27C
7995.	AIR	IAP	8038.	AIR	AC 61–27C
7996.	AIR	AC 61–27C	8039.	AIR	AC 61–27C
7997.	AIR	AC 61–21A	8040.	AIR	AC 61–27C
7998.	AIR	AC 61–13B	8041.	AIR	AC 61–27C
7999.	AIR	AC 61–13B	8042.	AIR	AC 61–27C
8000.	AIR	AC 61–13B	8043.	AIR	AC 61–27C
8001.	HLC	AC 61–13B	8044.	AIR	AIM
8002.	HLC	AC 61–13B	8045.	AIR	AIM
8003.	HLC	AC 61–13B	8046.	AIR	AIM
8004.	HLC	AC 61–13B	8047.	AIR	AIM
8005.	HLC	AC 61–13B	8048.	AIR	AIM
8006.	HLC	AC 61–13B	8049.	AIR	AC 00–6A
8007.	AIR	AC 61–27C	8050.	AIR	AC 00–6A
8008.	AIR	AC 61–27C	8051.	AIR	AC 00–6A
8009.	AIR	AC 61–27C	8052.	AIR	AIM

Item	Aircraft	Reference	Item	Aircraft	Reference
8053.	AIR	COMP	8096.	AIR	AIM
8054.	AIR	COMP	8097.	AIR	AIM
8055.	AIR	COMP	8098.	AIR	IAP
8056.	AIR	COMP	8099.	AIR	IAP
8057.	AIR	COMP	8100.	AIR	FAR 23
8058.	AIR	ACL	8101.	AIR	FAR 23
8059.	AIR	AC 61–27C	8102.	AIR	FAR 23
8060.	AIR	COMP	8103.	AIR	FAR 23
8061.	AIR	IEOG	8104.	AIR	FAR 23
8062.	AIR	ACL	8105.	AIR	AIM
8063.	AIR	FAR 61	8106.	AIR	AIM
8064.	AIR	FAR 61	8107.	AIR	AIM
8065.	AIR	FAR 61	8108.	AIR	AIM
8066.	AIR	FAR 91	8109.	AIR	AIM
8067.	AIR	AC 61–27C	8110.	AIR	AIM
8068.	AIR	IEOG	8111.	AIR	AC 61–27C
8069.	AIR	COMP	8112.	AIR	AC 61–27C
8070.	AIR	COMP	8113.	AIR	AC 61–27C
8071.	AIR	COMP	8114.	AIR	AC 61–27C
8072.	AIR	AIM	8115.	AIR	AC 61–27C
8073.	AIR	AIM	8116.	AIR	AC 61–27C
8074.	AIR	AC 61–27C	8117.	AIR	AC 61–27C
8075.	AIR	AIM	8118.	AIR	AC 61–27C
8076.	AIR	AC 61–27C			
8077.	AIR	FAR 61			
8078.	AIR	ACL			
8079.	AIR	AIM			
8080.	AIR	IEOG			
8081.	AIR	AC 91–43			
8082.	AIR	AC 61–27C			
8083.	AIR	AIM			
8084.	AIR	AIM			
8085.	AIR	AIM			
8086.	AIR	AIM			
8087.	AIR	AIM			
8088.					
8089.	AIR	AIM			
8090.	AIR	AIM			
8091.	AIR	AIM			
8092.	AIR	AIM			
8093.	AIR	FAR 91			
8094.	AIR	AIM			
8095.	AIR	AIM			

☆ U.S. GOVERNMENT PRINTING OFFICE: 1983–426–069/178

INSTRUMENT PILOT
TEST BOOK
Answers & Explanations

7001. (2) FAR 61.57. To act as PIC under IFR, a pilot must have logged at least 6 hours of actual or simulated instrument time. At least 3 of the six hours must be flight time in the category of aircraft involved (airplanes or helicopter). There is no requirement for actual instrument time nor is there any requirement for time in class (for airplanes) or in type. The three hours not required in category can be logged in an approved ground trainer.

7002. (1) FAR 61.57. In addition to the hour requirements, a pilot must have made 6 instrument approaches within the last 6 months. There is no requirement that any of the approaches be done in any particular category, class or type aircraft. Any or all of the approaches may be accomplished in an approved ground trainer.

7003. (2) FAR 61.57. In addition to the hour requirements, a pilot must have made 6 instrument approaches within the last 6 months. There is no requirement that any of the approaches be done in any particular category, class or type aircraft. Any or all of the approaches may be accomplished in an approved ground trainer.

7004. (1) FAR 61.57. A pilot has a 6 month "grace" period after letting his IFR currency lapse. During this six months he can either accumulate the required hours and approaches for currency or he can take an instrument competency check. If a pilot has not been current for more than six months he must take an instrument competency check.

7005. (1) FAR 61.57. In addition to the hour requirements, a pilot must have made 6 instrument approaches within the last 6 months. There is no requirement that any of the approaches be done in any particular category, class or type aircraft. Any or all of the approaches may be accomplished in an approved ground trainer.

7006. (3) FAR 61.57. A pilot who has not been current for instruments for more than six months must take an instrument competency check in the category of aircraft involved. This check may be given by an FAA inspector, an FAA approved check pilot, an Armed Forces check pilot or by a certified instrument flight instructor.

7007. (3) FAR 61.57. A pilot is current for IFR flight if he has passed an instrument competency check within the last six months. The competency check removes the requirement for instrument time or approaches.

7008. (2) FAR 61.57. In addition to the hour requirements, a pilot must have made 6 instrument approaches within the last 6 months. There is no requirement that any of the approaches be done in any particular category, class or type aircraft. Any or all of the approaches may be accomplished in an approved ground trainer.

7009. (1) FAR 61.57. A pilot has a 6 month "grace" period after letting his IFR currency lapse. During this six months he can either accumulate the required hours and approaches for currency or he can take an instrument competency check. If a pilot has not been current for more than six months he must take an instrument competency check.

7010. (1) FAR 61.57. In addition to the hour requirements, a pilot must have made 6 instrument approaches within the last 6 months. There is no requirement that any of the approaches be done in any particular category, class or type aircraft. Any or all of the approaches may be accomplished in an approved ground trainer.

To act as PIC under IFR, a pilot must have logged at least 6 hours of actual or simulated instrument time. At least 3 of the six hours must be flight time in the category of aircraft involved (airplanes or helicopter). There is no requirement for actual instrument time nor is there any requirement for time in class (for airplanes) or in type. The three hours not required in category can be logged in an approved ground trainer.

7011. (1) FAR 61.57. To act as PIC under IFR, a pilot must have logged at least 6 hours of actual or simulated instrument time. At least 3 of the six hours must be flight time in the category of aircraft involved (airplanes or helicopter). There is no requirement for actual instrument time nor is there any requirement for time in class (for airplanes) or in type. The three hours not required in category can be logged in an approved ground trainer.

7012. (1) FAR 61.57. In addition to the hour requirements, a pilot must have made 6 instrument approaches within the last 6 months. There is no requirement that any of the approaches be done in any particular category, class or type aircraft. Any or all of the approaches may be accomplished in an approved ground trainer.

7013. (1) FAR 61.57. To act as PIC under IFR, a pilot must have logged at least 6 hours of actual or simulated instrument time. At least 3 of the six hours must be flight time in the category of aircraft involved (airplanes or helicopter). There is no requirement for actual instrument time nor is there any requirement for time in class (for airplanes) or in type. The three hours not required in category can be logged in an approved ground trainer.

In addition to the hour requirements, a pilot must have made 6 instrument approaches within the last 6 months. There is no requirement that any of the approaches be done in any particular category, class or type aircraft. Any or all of the approaches may be accomplished in an approved ground trainer.

7014. (2) FAR 61.57. To act as PIC under IFR, a pilot must have logged at least 6 hours of actual or simulated instrument time. At least 3 of the six hours must be flight time in the category of aircraft involved (airplanes or helicopter). There is no requirement for actual instrument time nor is there any requirement for time in class (for airplanes) or in type. The three hours not required in category can be logged in an approved ground trainer.

7015. (1) FAR 61.57. To act as PIC under IFR, a pilot must have logged at least 6 hours of actual or simulated instrument time. At least 3 of the six hours must be flight time in the category of aircraft involved (airplanes or helicopter). There is no requirement for actual instrument time nor is there any requirement for time in class (for airplanes) or in type. The three hours not required in category can be logged in an approved ground trainer.

In addition to the hour requirements, a pilot must have made 6 instrument approaches within the last 6 months. There is no requirement that any of the approaches be done in any particular category, class or type aircraft. Any or all of the approaches may be accomplished in an approved ground trainer.

7016. (1) FAR 61.57. To act as PIC under IFR, a pilot must have logged at least 6 hours of actual or simulated instrument time. At least 3 of the six hours must be flight time in the category of aircraft involved (airplanes or helicopter). There is no requirement for actual instrument time nor is there any requirement for time in class (for airplanes) or in type. The three hours not required in category can be logged in an approved ground trainer.

In addition to the hour requirements, a pilot must have made 6 instrument approaches within the last 6 months. There is no requirement that any of the approaches be done in any particular category, class or type aircraft. Any or all of the approaches may be accomplished in an approved ground trainer.

7017. (2) FAR 61.57. In addition to the hour requirements, a pilot must have made 6 instrument approaches within the last 6 months. There is no requirement that any of the approaches be done in any particular category, class or type aircraft. Any or all of the approaches may be accomplished in an approved ground trainer.

7018. (1) FAR 61.57. To act as PIC under IFR, a pilot must have logged at least 6 hours of actual or simulated instrument time. At least 3 of the six hours must be flight time in the category of aircraft involved (airplanes or helicopter). There is no requirement for actual instrument time nor is there any requirement for time in class (for airplanes) or in type. The three hours not required in category can be logged in an approved ground trainer.

In addition to the hour requirements, a pilot must have made 6 instrument approaches within the last 6 months. There is no requirement that any of the approaches be done in any particular category, class or type aircraft. Any or all of the approaches may be accomplished in an approved ground trainer.

7019. (3) FAR 61.57. To act as PIC under IFR, a pilot must have logged at least 6 hours of actual or simulated instrument time. At least 3 of the six hours must be flight time in the category of aircraft involved (airplanes or helicopter). There is no requirement for actual instrument time nor is there any requirement for time in class (for airplanes) or in type. The three hours not required in category can be logged in an approved ground trainer.

In addition to the hour requirements, a pilot must have made 6 instrument approaches within the last 6 months. There is no requirement that any of the approaches be done in any particular category, class or type aircraft. Any or all of the approaches may be accomplished in an approved ground trainer.

7020. (3) FAR 61.57. To act as PIC under IFR, a pilot must have logged at least 6 hours of actual or simulated instrument time. At least 3 of the six hours must be flight time in the category of aircraft involved (airplanes or helicopter). There is no requirement for actual instrument time nor is there any requirement for time in class (for airplanes) or in type. The three hours not required in category can be logged in an approved ground trainer.

7021. (2) FAR 61.57. To act as PIC under IFR, a pilot must have logged at least 6 hours of actual or simulated instrument time. At least 3 of the six hours must be flight time in the category of aircraft involved (airplanes or helicopter). There is no requirement for actual instrument time nor is there any requirement for time in class (for airplanes) or in type. The three hours not required in category can be logged in an approved ground trainer.

In addition to the hour requirements, a pilot must have made 6 instrument approaches within the last 6 months. There is no requirement that any of the approaches be done in any particular category, class or type aircraft. Any or all of the approaches may be accomplished in an approved ground trainer.

7022. (2) FAR 61.57. To act as PIC under IFR, a pilot must have logged at least 6 hours of actual or simulated instrument time. At least 3 of the six hours must be flight time in the category of aircraft involved (airplanes or helicopter). There is no requirement for actual instrument time nor is there any requirement for time in class (for airplanes) or in type. The three hours not required in category can be logged in an approved ground trainer.

7023. (2) FAR 61.57. To act as PIC under IFR, a pilot must have logged at least 6 hours of actual or simulated instrument time. At least 3 of the six hours must be flight time in the category of aircraft involved (airplanes or helicopter). There is no requirement for actual instrument time nor is there any requirement for time in class (for airplanes) or in type. The three hours not required in category can be logged in an approved ground trainer.

In addition to the hour requirements, a pilot must have made 6 instrument approaches within the last 6 months. There is no requirement that any of the approaches be done in any particular category, class or type aircraft. Any or all of the approaches may be accomplished in an approved ground trainer.

7024. (4) FAR 61.57. To act as PIC under IFR, a pilot must have logged at least 6 hours of actual or simulated instrument time. At least 3 of the six hours must be flight time in the category of aircraft involved (airplanes or helicopter). There is no requirement for actual instrument time nor is there any requirement for time in class (for airplanes) or in type. The three hours not required in category can be logged in an approved ground trainer.

In addition to the hour requirements, a pilot must have made 6 instrument approaches within the last 6 months. There is no requirement that any of the approaches be done in any particular category, class or type aircraft. Any or all of the approaches may be accomplished in an approved ground trainer.

7025. (3) FAR 61.57. To act as PIC under IFR, a pilot must have logged at least 6 hours of actual or simulated instrument time. At least 3 of the six hours must be flight time in the category of aircraft involved (airplanes or helicopter). There is no requirement for actual instrument time nor is there any requirement for time in class (for airplanes) or in type. The three hours not required in category can be logged in an approved ground trainer.

In addition to the hour requirements, a pilot must have made 6 instrument approaches within the last 6 months. There is no requirement that any of the approaches be done in any particular category, class or type aircraft. Any or all of the approaches may be accomplished in an approved ground trainer.

7026. (2) FAR 61.57. To act as PIC under IFR, a pilot must have logged at least 6 hours of actual or simulated instrument time. At least 3 of the six hours must be flight time in the category of aircraft involved (airplanes or helicopter). There is no requirement for actual instrument time nor is there any requirement for time in class (for airplanes) or in type. The three hours not required in category can be logged in an approved ground trainer.

7027. (3) FAR 61.57. To act as PIC under IFR, a pilot must have logged at least 6 hours of actual or simulated instrument time. At least 3 of the six hours must be flight time in the category of aircraft involved (airplanes or helicopter). There is no requirement for actual instrument time nor is there any requirement for time in class (for airplanes) or in type. The three hours not required in category can be logged in an approved ground trainer.

7028. (4) FAR 61.57. In addition to the hour requirements, a pilot must have made 6 instrument approaches within the last 6 months. There is no requirement that any of the approaches be done in any particular category, class or type aircraft. Any or all of the approaches may be accomplished in an approved ground trainer.

7029. (3) FAR 61.57. A pilot is current for IFR flight if he has passed an instrument competency check within the last six months. The competency check removes the requirement for instrument time or approaches.

7030. (2) FAR 61.57. A pilot has a 6 month "grace" period after letting his IFR currency lapse. During this six months he can either accumulate the required hours and approaches for currency or he can take an instrument competency check. If a pilot has not been current for more than six months he must take an instrument competency check.

7031. (3) FAR 61.3 and Pilot/Controller Glossary. A pilot must hold an instrument rating (airplane or helicopter as appropriate) for operations under instrument flight rules or in weather conditions less than those minimums prescribed for VFR flight. "VFR-ON-TOP" is a type of altitude assignment on an IFR clearance.

7032. (2) FAR 61.3. A pilot must hold an instrument rating (airplane or helicopter as appropriate) for operations under instrument flight rules or in weather conditions less than those minimums prescribed for VFR flight.

7033. (X) FAA Deletion.

7034. (3) FAR 61.3 and Pilot/Controller Glossary. A pilot must hold an instrument rating (airplane or helicopter as appropriate) for operations under instrument flight rules or in weather conditions less than those minimums prescribed for VFR flight. Normal operations in positive control airspace require that the aircraft be on an IFR clearance.

7035. (4) FAR 61.3 and Pilot/Controller Glossary. A pilot must hold an instrument rating (airplane or helicopter as appropriate) for operations under instrument flight rules or in weather conditions less than those minimums prescribed for VFR flight. Normal operations in positive control airspace require that the aircraft be on an IFR clearance.

7036. (3) FAR 61.3 and FAR 61.57. No person may act as pilot in command of a helicopter unless he has a valid pilot certificate with rotorcraft category and helicopter class ratings. In addition, to operate IFR, the PIC must have either an instrument-helicopter rating or an ATP with rotorcraft category, helicopter class and not limited to VFR. In addition to having the appropriate ratings, a pilot must have the required recent experience set forth in FAR 61.57.

7037. (4) FAR 61.129. A commercial pilot (airplane) must hold an instrument rating to be able to carry passengers for hire:
   (1) At night, or
   (2) In the daytime on cross-country flights of more than 50 nautical miles.

7038. (3) FAR 61.129. A commercial pilot (airplane) must hold an instrument rating to be able to carry passengers for hire:
   (1) At night, or
   (2) In the daytime on cross-country flights of more than 50 nautical miles.

7039. (3) FAR 61.129. A commercial pilot (airplane) must hold an instrument rating to be able to carry passengers for hire:
(1) At night, or
(2) In the daytime on cross-country flights of more than 50 nautical miles.
A pilot must hold a commercial pilot certificate with airplane category and appropriate class rating to carry persons or property for hire.

7040. (4) FAR 61.129. A commercial pilot (airplane) must hold an instrument rating to be able to carry passengers for hire:
(1) At night, or
(2) In the daytime on cross-country flights of more than 50 nautical miles.

7041. (4) FAR 61.3 and FAR 61.57. No person may act as pilot in command of a helicopter unless he has a valid pilot certificate with rotorcraft category and helicopter class ratings. In addition, to operate IFR, the PIC must have either an instrument-helicopter rating or an ATP with rotorcraft category, helicopter class and not limited to VFR. In addition to having the appropriate ratings, a pilot must have the required recent experience set forth in FAR 61.57.

7042. (2) FAR 61.3 and FAR 61.57. No person may act as pilot in command of a helicopter unless he has a valid pilot certificate with rotorcraft category and helicopter class ratings. In addition, to operate IFR, the PIC must have either an instrument-helicopter rating or an ATP with rotorcraft category, helicopter class and not limited to VFR. In addition to having the appropriate ratings, a pilot must have the required recent experience set forth in FAR 61.57.

7043. (4) FAR 91.5. Prior to any flight under IFR, a pilot must familiarize himself with all available information concerning that flight. This must include:
(1) Weather reports and forecasts
(2) Fuel requirements
(3) Alternatives available if the flight cannot be completed as planned.

NOTE: This does not mean an alternate must be filed.

(4) Any known traffic delays of which he has been advised by ATC.
(5) Runway lengths at airports of intended use and takeoff and landing distances required.

7044. (3) FAR 91.23. An Aircraft beginning an IFR flight must have enough fuel (considering weather reports and forecasts) to —
(1) Complete the flight to the first airport of intended landing;
(2) Fly from that airport to the alternate (if one is required; then
(3) Fly for 45 minutes at normal cruising speed.
NOTE: The 45 minute reserve is required even when an alternate airport is not.

An alternate airport is required if reports or forecasts indicate destination weather is or will be below a 2,000 foot ceiling or 3 miles visibility anytime from one hour prior to ETA to one hour after.

7045. (3) FAR 91.23. An aircraft beginning an IFR flight must have enough fuel (considering weather reports and forecasts) to —
(1) Complete the flight to the first airport of intended landing;
(2) Fly from that airport to the alternate (if one is required; then
(3) Fly for 45 minutes at normal cruising speed.
NOTE: The 45 minute reserve is required even when an alternate airport is not.

An alternate airport is required if reports or forecasts indicate destination weather is or will be below a 2,000 foot ceiling or 3 miles visibility anytime from one hour prior to ETA to one hour after.

7046. (3) FAR 91.23. An aircraft beginning an IFR flight must have enough fuel (considering weather reports and forecasts) to —
(1) Complete the flight to the first airport of intended landing;
(2) Fly from that airport to the alternate (if one is required; then
(3) Fly for 45 minutes at normal cruising speed.
NOTE: The 45 minute reserve is required even when an alternate airport is not.

An alternate airport is required if reports or forecasts indicate destination weather is or will be below a 2,000 foot ceiling or 3 miles visibility anytime from one hour prior to ETA to one hour after.

7047. (4) FAR 91.3, FAR 91.171. No person may "operate" an aircraft in controlled airspace under IFR unless it has had a static system check within the previous 24 calendar months. The pilot in command is the final authority as to the operation of the aircraft.

7048. (2) FAR 91.24. A coded transponder with altitude reporting (Mode C) is required for all operations within the 48 contiguous states and the District of Columbia above an altitude of 12,500 feet MSL. Operations in airspace below 2,500 feet AGL are excluded from this rule.

7049. (1) FAR 91.24. A coded transponder with altitude reporting (Mode C) is required for all operations within the 48 contiguous states and the District of Columbia above an altitude of 12,500 feet MSL. Operations in airspace below 2,500 feet AGL are excluded from this rule.

7050. (1) FAR 91.25. Prior to IFR operations, a VOR system must have been checked within the preceding 30 days and found to be within limits. There is no flight hour requirement.

7051. (2) FAR 91.25. The person making a VOR operational check must record the date, place, bearing error, and sign the aircraft log or other permanent record.

7052. (4) FAR 91.25. The person making a VOR operational check must record the date, place, bearing error, and sign the aircraft log or other permanent record.

7053. (2) FAR 91.25. The person making a VOR operational check must record the date, place, bearing error, and sign the aircraft log or other permanent record.

7054. (1) FAR 91.25. When making a "Dual VOR Check," the VOR's are tuned to the same station and the person making the check will note the indicated bearings to the VOR facility. The maximum allowable variation is 4°.

7055. (3) FAR 91.32. No oxygen is required for anyone on flights with cabin pressure altitudes as high as 12,500' MSL. The required minimum flight crew must use oxygen after 30 minutes at altitudes above 12,500' through 14,000' MSL. The required crew must use oxygen at all times above 14,000'. Passengers must be *PROVIDED* oxygen anytime the cabin pressure altitude exceeds 15,000' MSL.

7056. (4) FAR 91.32. No oxygen is required for anyone on flights with cabin pressure altitudes as high as 12,500' MSL. The required minimum flight crew must use oxygen after 30 minutes at altitudes above 12,500' through 14,000' MSL. The required crew must use oxygen at all times above 14,000'. Passengers must be *PROVIDED* oxygen anytime the cabin pressure altitude exceeds 15,000' MSL.

7057. (3) FAR 91.32. No oxygen is required for anyone on flights with cabin pressure altitudes as high as 12,500' MSL. The required minimum flight crew must use oxygen after 30 minutes at altitudes above 12,500' through 14,000' MSL. The required crew must use oxygen at all times above 14,000'. Passengers must be *PROVIDED* oxygen anytime the cabin pressure altitude exceeds 15,000' MSL.

7058. (3) FAR 91.32. No oxygen is required for anyone on flights with cabin pressure altitudes as high as 12,500' MSL. The required minimum flight crew must use oxygen after 30 minutes at altitudes above 12,500' through 14,000' MSL. The required crew must use oxygen at all times above 14,000'. Passengers must be *PROVIDED* oxygen anytime the cabin pressure altitude exceeds 15,000' MSL.

7059. (2) IFH. In a constant rate turn, the only instrument which confirms the correct bank angle is the rate-of-turn indicator. In a constant rate climb, proper pitch attitude is reflected in vertical speed or in airspeed indications. The FAA says vertical speed is the more appropriate of the two.

7060. (2) IFH. Errors in the VSI are usually constant. If a VSI shows 100' per minute descent while on the ground, it will read 100' per minute "low" in all flight conditions. Since the VSI is not a required instrument, there are no FAR requirements concerning calibration.

7061. (4) FAR 91.33. Regulations require that there be a two-way communications system and navigation appropriate to the ground facilities to be used. This requirement applies to departure and arrival facilities as well as those enroute.

7062. (2) FAR 91.33. An aircraft operated under IFR *MUST* have:
(1) All required VFR instruments and equipment including night equipment if appropriate;
(2) Two-way communications and NAV equipment appropriate for the ground facilities to be used;
(3) A rate-of-turn indicator (with certain exceptions);
(4) A slip-skid indicator;
(5) A sensitive altimeter adjustable for barometric pressure;
(6) A clock with a sweep-second pointer or digital presentation;
(7) A generator of adequate capacity;
(8) A gyroscopic bank and pitch indicator (artificial horizon); and
(9) Gyroscopic direction indicator (directional gyro).

Any other equipment is either not required or is required only for certain IFR operations.

7063. (4) FAR 91.33. An aircraft operated under IFR *MUST* have:
(1) All required VFR instruments and equipment including night equipment if appropriate;
(2) Two-way communications and NAV equipment appropriate for the ground facilities to be used;
(3) A rate-of-turn indicator (with certain exceptions);
(4) A slip-skid indicator;
(5) A sensitive altimeter adjustable for barometric pressure;
(6) A clock with a sweep-second pointer or digital presentation;
(7) A generator of adequate capacity;
(8) A gyroscopic bank and pitch indicator (artificial horizon); and
(9) Gyroscopic direction indicator (directional gyro).

Any other equipment is either not required or is required only for certain IFR operations.

7064. (3) FAR 91.33. An aircraft operated under IFR *MUST* have:
(1) All required VFR instruments and equipment including night equipment if appropriate;
(2) Two-way communications and NAV equipment appropriate for the ground facilities to be used;
(3) A rate-of-turn indicator (with certain exceptions);
(4) A slip-skid indicator;
(5) A sensitive altimeter adjustable for barometric pressure;
(6) A clock with a sweep-second pointer or digital presentation;
(7) A generator of adequate capacity;
(8) A gyroscopic bank and pitch indicator (artificial horizon); and
(9) Gyroscopic direction indicator (directional gyro).

Any other equipment is either not required or is required only for certain IFR operations.

7065. (1) FAR 91.33. DME is required if VOR is used for navigation on flights above 24,000 feet MSL.

7066. (3) FAR 91.171. No person may operate an aircraft in controlled airspace under IFR unless it has had a static system check within the previous 24 calendar months.

7067. (1) FAR 91.25. FAR 91.171. Prior to IFR operations, a VOR system must have been checked within the preceding 30 days and found to be within limits. There is no flight hour requirement.

No person may operate an aircraft in controlled airspace under IFR unless it has had a static system check within the previous 24 calendar months.

If a transponder has an altitude reporting feature (Mode C), it must have been tested, inspected and found to be within limits within the previous 24 calendar months.

7068. (3) FAR 91.171. No person may operate an aircraft in controlled airspace under IFR unless it has had a static system check within the previous 24 calendar months.

7069. (3) FAR 91.115. A pilot may not operate an aircraft under instrument flight in controlled airspace unless he has filed an IFR flight plan AND received an appropriate ATC clearance. IFR operations in uncontrolled airspace don't require either a flight plan or a clearance.

7070. (3) FAR 91.105, FAR 91.115, Pilot/Controller Glossary. A pilot must operate under IFR if the weather is less than that prescribed for VFR flight. An IFR flight plan must be filed and a clearance received prior to IFR flight in controlled airspace.

Most operations in positive controlled airspace require that the flight be on an IFR clearance regardless of weather conditions.

7071. (2) FAR 91.105, FAR 91.115, Pilot/Controller Glossary. A pilot must operate under IFR if the weather is less than that prescribed for VFR flight. An IFR flight plan must be filed and a clearance received prior to IFR flight in controlled airspace.

Most operations in positive controlled airspace require that the flight be on an IFR clearance regardless of weather conditions.

7072. (4) FAR 91.115. A pilot may not operate an aircraft under instrument flight in controlled airspace unless he has filed an IFR flight plan AND received an appropriate ATC clearance. IFR operations in uncontrolled airspace don't require either a flight plan or a clearance.

7073. (1) FAR 91.115. A pilot may not operate an aircraft under instrument flight in controlled airspace unless he has filed an IFR flight plan AND received an appropriate ATC clearance. IFR operations in uncontrolled airspace don't require either a flight plan or a clearance.

7074. (2) FAR 91.115. A pilot may not operate an aircraft under instrument flight in controlled airspace unless he has filed an IFR flight plan AND received an appropriate ATC clearance. IFR operations in uncontrolled airspace don't require either a flight plan or a clearance.

7075. (4) FAR 91.105, FAR 91.115, Pilot/Controller Glossary. A pilot must operate under IFR if the weather is less than that prescribed for VFR flight. An IFR flight plan must be filed and a clearance received prior to IFR flight in controlled airspace.

Most operations in positive controlled airspace require that the flight be on an IFR clearance regardless of weather conditions.

7076. (4) FAR 91.23. An alternate airport is required on an IFR flight plan unless from one hour before to one hour after the ETA at the destination aircraft weather reports and forecasts indicate that at the destination:
(1) The ceiling will be at least 2,000 feet above the airport elevation, and
(2) The visibility will be at least 3 miles.

7077. (2) FAR 91.23. An alternate airport is required on an IFR flight plan unless from one hour before to one hour after the ETA at the destination aircraft weather reports and forecasts indicate that at the destination:
(1) The ceiling will be at least 2,000 feet above the airport elevation, and
(2) The visibility will be at least 3 miles.

7078. (4) FAR 91.23, AWS. An alternate airport is required on an IFR flight plan unless from one hour before to one hour after the ETA at the destination aircraft weather reports and forecasts indicate that at the destination:
(1) The ceiling will be at least 2,000 feet above the airport elevation, and
(2) The visibility will be at least 3 miles.

The worst forecast weather for the period from 1830Z to 2030Z is "occasionally ceilings of 2,000 feet broken, 6 miles visibility in light rain showers."

7079. (2) FAR 91.83. To use an airport as an alternate on an IFR flight, current weather forecasts must indicate the ceiling and visibility will be at "alternate airport" minimums at the ETA. "Standard alternate minimums" are a 600 foot ceiling and 2 miles visibility for precision approaches or a ceiling of 800 feet and 2 miles visibility for non-precision approaches. Higher alternate minimums may be specified for particular approaches.

7080. (1) FAR 91.83. To use an airport as an alternate on an IFR flight, current weather forecasts must indicate the ceiling and visibility will be at "alternate airport" minimums at the ETA. "Standard alternate minimums" are a 600 foot ceiling and 2 miles visibility for precision approaches or a ceiling of 800 feet and 2 miles visibility for non-precision approaches. Higher alternate minimums may be specified for particular approaches.

7081. (4) FAR 91.83. An airport may be listed as an alternate even if it does not have an instrument approach procedure. In this case, weather forecasts for the ETA must indicate that a flight will be able to descend from the MEA and land at the alternate under basic VFR.

7082. (1) FAR 91.83. To use an airport as an alternate on an IFR flight, current weather forecasts must indicate the ceiling and visibility will be at "alternate airport" minimums at the ETA. "Standard alternate minimums" are a 600 foot ceiling and 2 miles visibility for precision approaches or a ceiling of 800 feet and 2 miles visibility for non-precision approaches. Higher alternate minimums may be specified for particular approaches.

7083. (1) AIM, Para. 297. When VFR flight is conducted for the first part of a flight, close the VFR portion *AND* request ATC clearance from the FSS nearest the point at which the change from VFR to IFR is proposed.

7084. (1) AIM, Para. 298. The flight plan should define the proposed route of flight by using airway designations, transition points between airways and fixes defining off airway routes. A composite flight should also indicate the point at which the transition from IFR to VFR is proposed.

7085. (2) AIM, Para. 297. ATC will accept a composite flight plan whenever one is filed.

7086. (4) AIM. When a flight plan has been filed, the pilot in command, upon canceling or completing the flight, shall notify the nearest FSS or ATC facility.

7087. (4) AIM, Para. 304. An IFR flight plan may be cancelled anytime the flight is in VFR weather and outside of positive control airspace.

7088. (X) FAA Deletion.

7089. (1) AIM, Para. 305. The requested altitude in Block 7 of the flight plan form should be the desired initial cruise altitude. Requests for changes in altitude assignment should be made in flight directly to ATC.

7090. (2) AIM, Para. 305. Total usable fuel on board should be entered in the flight plan.

7091. (4) AIM, Para. 305. Check both IFR and VFR boxes.

7092. (3) AIM, Para. 342. The pilot of an IFR flight should report changes in true airspeed of 10 knots or 5 percent, whichever is greater.

7093. (2) AFD. Preferred IFR routes beginning or ending with a fix indicate that aircraft will be routed to or from the fix by radar vectors, SIDs or STARs (as appropriate) or by direct routing. See AFD legend in Appendix.

7094. (4) AIM, Para. 298. The recommended method for filing an IFR flight plan while airborne is to do so through the nearest FSS facility. That FSS will also issue the IFR clearance.

7095. (3) AIM, Para. 294. The Airport/Facility Directory provides basic information on airports. Distant (D) Notams and Local (L) Notams provide information on changes to the status of facilities.

7096. (4) AIM, Para. 294. FDC Notams are issued to advise pilots of changes in flight data which affect instrument approach procedures, aeronautical charts, and flight restrictions prior to normal publication.

7097. (1) Chart Legend. All control zones, victor airways and special use airspace (e.g., restricted area, prohibited areas, etc.) are shown on low altitude enroute charts. Airport traffic areas and positive control airspace are not shown. See the chart legend in Appendix.

7098. (3) AFD. The radio aids section of the El Paso International listing notes the DME is unusable between the 260° and 290° radials below 12,500' MSL. A pilot could expect normal DME reception at and above 12,500'.

7099. (1) AFD. The Paine VOR is the TWEB (Transcribed Weather Broadcast) facility. That fact is designated by the "■" symbol preceding the 3-letter identifier. The next line in the listing notes that a general outlook is available from 0600Z to 1300Z (2200 to 0500 local). The complete TWEB is available at other times.

7100. (3) AFD. The airport remarks note that the field is attended from 1200Z to 0400Z and that outside that time the approach lights (MALSR) must be turned on by radio. However, the first line of Hot Springs listing gives the local time as GMT −6 hours. This means that the field is attended from 0600 to 2200 local time.

7101. (4) AFD. The upper right corner of the airport information lists all charts on which the airport is found. The notation "IAP" means that there is one or more instrument approach procedure published for that airport. See the AFD Legend in Appendix.

7102. (1) AFD, AIM Para 304. An IFR flight plan must be closed by the pilot if the flight lands at a "non-tower" airport. This can be done over the radio with ATC or a FSS or by telephone. At Orange County, there is a toll-free number for this purpose. A pilot cannot close an IFR plan on approach unless he is in VFR weather conditions.

7103. (4) AFD, AIM Para. 298. At tower controlled airports, an IFR clearance is issued by ground control (or clearance delivery). At Paine Field the ground control frequency is 121.8 MHz.

7104. (2) AFD, AIM Para. 294. Notams can be obtained from Hay FSS. Little Rock FSS is the proper such facility for Hot Springs.

7105. (4) AFD. VALTR NDB is designated as the TWEB facility. See AFD Legend.

7106. (1) AFD. The communication section says to contact approach control for Stage III services. The appropriate approach control frequency when north of V-16 is 118.7 MHz.

7107. (X) FAA Deletion.

7108. (4) FAR 91.23, AFD. If an airport has an instrument procedure the letters "IAP" will appear in the upper right corner of the listing along with the charts. Nampa can be assumed to have no instrument procedure published. An airport may be listed as an alternate even if it does not have an instrument approach procedure. In this case weather forecasts for the ETA must indicate that a flight will be able to descend from the MEA and land at the alternate under basic VFR.

7109. (4) AFD. The upper right corner of the airport information lists all charts on which the airport is found. The notation "IAP" means that there is one or more instrument approach procedure published for that airport. See the AFD Legend in Appendix.

7110. (2) AFD, AIM Para. 294. Notams can be obtained through any FSS. At Pocatello, it is a local call to the Burley FSS.

7111. (2) AFD, AIM Para. 294. Notams can be obtained through any FSS. At Rexburg-Madison, it is a toll-free call to Idaho Falls FSS.

7112. (3) AFD. BOI VORTAC (113.3 MHz) and USTIK NDB (359 KHz) are both designated as TWEB facilities.

7113. (2) AFD, FAR 91.25. The designated VOR checkpoint at Pocatello is on the parking ramp south of the terminal. The check is performed by tuning 112.6 MHz and ensuring the indication is ±4° of the 035° radial.

7114. (2) AFD, FAR 91.25. The designated ground checkpoint at Boise is on the north-south taxiway between 28L-10R and 28R-10L. The indication should be the 084° radial ±4°.

7115. (1) AIM Para. 341. When flying direct routes, the fixes used to define the route are considered compulsory reporting points.

7116. (1) Pilot/Controller Glossary. A waypoint is defined as "a predetermined geographical position used for route or instrument approach definition or progress reporting . . .".

7117. (2) AFD. At Will Rogers World Airport GALLY NDB is listed as a TWEB facility.

7118. (3) AIM, Para. 298, AFD. The OKC FSS serves Will Rogers Airport. The OKC FSS is located on Wiley Post Airport.

7119. (3) AFD. Low altitude charts are the L-6 and L-13. High altitude charts are H-2 and H-4. The letters refer to the chart panels.

7120. (4) AFD. The symbol "§" indicates Notam D information is disseminated for the airport. See AFD Legend.

7121. (2) AFD. Tower is closed between 0400Z and 1200Z but OKC FSS provides airport advisory service on 119.7.

7122. (4) AIM Para. 304, AFD. At non-tower airports a pilot must close his own IFR flight plan.

7123. (1) AFD. Runway 35R has ALSF2 approach lighting, which is defined in the Legend as "high intensity approach lighting system with sequenced flashing lights, Category II configuration."

7124. (4) AFD, FAR 91.25. Will Rogers airport has a VOT facility. A valid test on a VOT is the 360° radial ±4°.

7125. (4) B-206 Manual. Draw a vertical line from 150'/ Min. climb to the curved line labeled "hot day." From that point of intersection, draw a horizontal line to the left. The altitude should be between 6,000' and 7,000'.

7126. (2) B-206 Manual. Draw a vertical line from 400'/Min. to the curved line labeled "standard day." From that point of intersection draw a horizontal line to the left.

7127. (1) B-206 Manual. Draw a vertical line from 300'/Min. to the diagonal line labeled "–5°C." From that point of intersection, draw a horizontal line to the left.

7128. (1) B-206 Manual. Draw a horizontal line from 6,200 to a position where line intersects with a diagonal line representing 22°C. From that point of intersection, draw a vertical line down to the rate of climb.

NOTE: Extreme care must be taken on interpolations.

7129. (3) B-206 Manual. Draw a horizontal line from 7,500' altitude to the diagonal line labeled "5°C." From that point of intersection, draw a line vertically down to the rate of climb.

7130. (1) B-206 Manual. Draw a horizontal line from 7,500' altitude to the diagonal line labeled "–5°C." From that point of intersection, draw a line vertically down to the rate of climb.

7131. (4) B-206 Manual. Draw a horizontal line from 9,000' altitude to the curved line labeled "standard day." From that point of intersection, draw a vertical line down to the rate of climb.

7132. (4) B-206 Manual.
STEP 1:
Draw a horizontal line from 1,000' altitude to the point where it would intersect a diagonal line representing 0°C. From that point of intersection, draw a line vertically to the bottom of the graph. Rate of climb is about 880' per minute.
STEP 2:
Repeat the process using 8,000' altitude and – –15°C. Rate of climb is about 550' per minute.
STEP 3:
Determine the average rate of climb by adding 880 and 550 and dividing by 2.

NOTE: It is more accurate to calculate rates of climb every thousand feet or so, but it is unnecessary in this case because it won't significantly change the average.

7133. (3) B-206 Manual.
STEP 1:
Draw a horizontal line from 3,000' altitude to the diagonal line labeled "standard day." From that point of intersection, draw a line vertically down to the rate of climb. In this case 500' per minute.
STEP 2:
Repeat the procedure using 10,000' altitude. Rate of climb is 150' per minute.

STEP 3:
Determine average rate of climb by adding 500 and 150 and dividing by 2.

NOTE: Calculation of rates of climb at intermediate altitudes does not yield a significantly different answer.

7134. (2) B-206 Manual. Draw horizontal line from 3,000' altitude to the diagonal labeled "5°C." From that point of intersection, draw a vertical line down to the rate of climb, about 595' minute. Repeat the procedure using 9,000' and −25°C. The rate of climb should be about 620' per minute. Only one answer choice (610' per minute) falls between these extremes.

7135. (2) B-206 Manual.
STEP 1:
Draw a horizontal line from 2,000' altitude to the diagonal line labeled "−5°C." From that point of intersection, draw a vertical line down to the rate of climb, 900' per minute.
STEP 2:
Repeat Step 1 using 6,000' altitude and +7°C. Rate of climb is 300' per minute.
STEP 3:
Determine average rate of climb by adding 900' and 300' and then dividing by 2.

NOTE: Calculation of rates of climb at intermediate altitudes yields the same answer.

7136. (2) AC 61-21A. The performance of an aircraft in almost all flight conditions is determined in large part by density altitude.

7137. (2) B-206 Manual. Draw a line horizontally from 6,500' altitude to 23°C. From that point of intersection, draw a line vertically to the maximum weight.

7138. (2) B-206 Manual. Draw a line horizontally from 8,000' altitude to +14°C. From that point of intersection, draw a line vertically to the maximum weight.

7139. (1) B-206 Manual. Draw a line horizontally from 9,500' altitude to +13°C. From that point of intersection, draw a line vertically to the maximum weight.

7140. (3) B-206 Manual. Draw a line horizontally from 3,000' altitude to +35°C. From that point of intersection, draw a line vertically to the maximum weight.

7141. (1) B-206 Manual. Draw a line horizontally from 10,500' altitude to +20°C. From that point of intersection, draw a line vertically to the maximum weight.

7142. (2) B-206 Manual. Draw a line horizontally from 4,500' altitude to +40°C. From that point of intersection, draw a line vertically to the maximum weight.

7143. (2) B-206 Manual. Draw a line horizontally from 5,500' altitude to +28°C. From that point of intersection, draw a line vertically to the maximum weight.

7144. (2) B-206 Manual. At any allowable gross weight, the forward CG limit is 106.0".

7145. (2) B-206 Manual. Draw a line horizontally from 2,450 pounds to the diagonal line representing the aft CG limit. From that point of intersection, draw a line vertically to the bottom of the graph.

7146. (4) B-206 Manual. At any gross weight less than 2,350 pounds, the aft CG limit is 114.2".

7147. (3) B-206 Manual. Draw a line horizontally from 2,400 pounds to the diagonal line representing the aft CG limit. From that point of intersection, draw a line vertically to the bottom of the graph.

7148. (3) B-206 Manual. Draw a line horizontally from 2,600 pounds to the diagonal line representing the aft CG limit. From that point of intersection, draw a line vertically to the bottom of the graph.

7149. (2) B-206 Manual. Draw a line horizontally from 2,850 pounds to the diagonal line representing the aft CG limit. From that point of intersection, draw a line vertically to the bottom of the graph.

7150. (1) PWBH.
STEP 1:
Determine the original moment

$$2,400 \text{ lbs} \times 107.5" = 258,000" \text{ lbs}$$

STEP 2:
Determine the change in aircraft weight

$$1.2 \text{ hrs} \times 110 \text{ lb/hr} = 132 \text{ pound reduction}$$

STEP 3:
Determine the change in moment due to fuel burn

$$-132 \text{ lbs} \times 86.9" = -11,470.8" \text{ pounds}$$

STEP 4:
Determine the new weight and new moment

2,400 lbs.	258,000" pounds
−132 lbs	−11,470.8" pounds
= 2,268 lbs	246,529.2" pounds

STEP 5:
Determine the new center of gravity by dividing moment by weight.

$$\frac{246,529.2" \text{ Pounds}}{2,268 \text{ Pounds}} = 108.7"$$

STEP 6:
Determine the difference between the original CG and new CG. If the new CG is a larger number, it is aft of its original position.

7151. (1) PWBH. The solution follows the same steps as Question 7150, with the exception that **STEP 1** is already complete.
STEP 2:

Reduction in weight
$$= 1.3 \text{ hrs} \times 180 \text{ lbs/hr} = 234 \text{ lbs}$$

STEP 3:
Change in moment

$$= -234 \text{ lbs.} \times 149.2" = -34,912.8" \text{ lbs}$$

STEP 4:
New weight and moment

2,350 lbs	277,680.0
−234 lbs	−34,912.8
= 2,116 lbs	= 242,767.2

STEP 5:
New CG

$$\frac{242,767.2" \text{ lbs}}{2,116 \text{ lbs}} = 114.7"$$

STEP 6:
Original CG

$$\frac{277,680" \text{ lbs}}{2,350 \text{ lbs}} = 118.2"$$

STEP 7:
CG Change

$$= 118.2" - 114.7" = 3.4" \text{ forward}$$

7152. (2) PWBH. The solution follows the same steps as Question 7150.
STEP 1:
Original moment

$$= 2,450 \text{ lbs} \times 112.5" = 275,625" \text{ lbs}$$

STEP 2:
Reduction in weight

$$= 1.5 \text{ hrs} \times 180 \text{ lbs/hr} = 270 \text{ lbs}$$

STEP 3:
Change in moment

$$= -270 \text{ lbs} \times 122.3" = -33,021" \text{ lbs}$$

STEP 4:
New weight and moment

2,450 lbs	275,625 lbs
−270 lbs	−33,021 lbs
= 2,180 lbs	242,604 lbs

STEP 5:
New CG

$$\frac{242,604" \text{ lbs}}{2,180 \text{ lbs}} = 111.3"$$

STEP 6:
Change in CG

$$= 112.5" - 111.3" = 1.2" \text{ forward}$$

7153. (4) PWBH. The solution follows the same steps as Question 7150, except that **STEP 1** is already done.

STEP 2:
Reduction in weight

$$= 1.2 \text{ hrs} \times 155 \text{ lbs/hr} = 186 \text{ lbs}$$

STEP 3:
Change in moment

$$= -186 \text{ lbs} \times 148.0" = -27,528" \text{ lbs}$$

STEP 4:
New weight and moment

2,420 lbs	278,720" lbs
−186 lbs	−27,528" lbs
= 2,234 lbs	= 251,19?" lbs

STEP 5:
New CG

$$\frac{251,192" \text{ lbs}}{2,234 \text{ lbs}} = 112.4"$$

STEP 6:
Original CG

$$\frac{278,720" \text{ lbs}}{2,420 \text{ lbs}} = 115.1"$$

STEP 7:
Change in CG

$$= 115.1 - 112.4 = 2.7" \text{ forward}$$

7154. (4) PWBH. The solution follows the same steps as Question 7150, except that **STEP 1** is already done.
STEP 2:
Reduction in weight

$$= 1.5 \text{ hr} \times 170 \text{ lbs/hr} = 255 \text{ lbs}$$

STEP 3:
Change in moment

$$= -255 \text{ lb} \times 142.0" = -36,210" \text{ lbs}$$

STEP 4:
New weight and moment

2,450 lbs	275,650" lbs
− 255 lbs	− 36,210" lbs
= 2,195 lbs	= 239,440" lbs

STEP 5:
New CG

$$\frac{239,440" \text{ lbs}}{2,195 \text{ lbs}} = 109.1"$$

STEP 6:
Original CG

$$\frac{275,650" \text{ lbs}}{2,450 \text{ lbs}} = 112.4"$$

STEP 7:
Change in CG

$$= 112.4" - 109.1 = 3.4" \text{ forward}$$

7155. (1) PHAK. True airspeed is calibrated airspeed corrected for air density. The primary determinates of air density are pressure altitude and temperature.

7156. (3) Flight Computer. Set computer as shown.

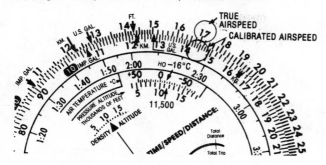

7157. (2) Flight Computer. Set computer as shown.

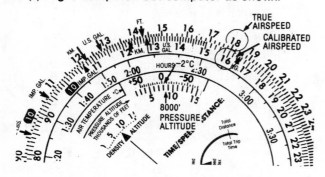

7158. (1) PHAK. A forward CG requires greater elevator input. At low airspeeds there might not be enough elevator force available to maintain a high nose attitude. This could preclude a full stall, short field landing because higher than normal approach and landing speeds could be required for adequate pitch control.

7159. (X) FAA Deletion.

7160. (3) C-310 Manual. The first step is to compute the total weight and total moment of the loaded aircraft. The weight and moment tables (Table 2) can be used for this. Note that all moments are in fact Moment/100.

Be careful on fuel computations. Table 1 lists fuel quantity in gallons. This must be converted to pounds.

ITEM	WEIGHT	MOMENT/100
Basic Empty Weight.	3,472	1,220
Seat 1	170	63
Seat 2	160	59
Seat 3 (68" Arm).	100	68
Seat 4 (68" Arm).	120	82
Wing Locker.	50	32
Bags — 126" Arm	65	82
Main Wing Tanks (100 Gal)	600	210
Aux. Wing Tanks (63 Gal).	378	178
Wing Locker (20 Gal)	120	59
	5,235	2,053

$$CG = \frac{Moment/100}{Weight} \times 100$$

OR

$$CG = \frac{2053}{5235} \times 100 = 39.22"$$

7161. (3) C-310 Manual. See Explanation #7160 for complete answer.

ITEM	WEIGHT	MOMENT/100
Basic Empty Weight	3472	1220
Seat 1	160	59
Seat 2	175	65
Seat 3 (71" Arm).	80	57
Seat 4 (71" Arm).	90	64
Nose Compartment	50	−16
		(Note the negative moment)
Wing Locker.	50	32
Bags — 96" Arm	50	48
Bags — 124" Arm	50	62
Main Wing Tank (100 Gal.).	600	210
Aux. Wing Tank (63 Gal.)	378	178
Wing Locker Tank (40 Gal.)	240	118
TOTALS	5395	2097

$$CG = \frac{2097}{5395} \times 100 = 38.87"$$

7162. (2) C-310 Manual. See Explanation #7160 for complete answer.

ITEM	WEIGHT	MOMENT/100
Basic Empty Weight	3472	1220
Seat 1	165	61
Seat 2	175	65
Seat 3 (68" Arm)	170	116
Seat 4 (68" Arm)	160	109
Seat 5	85	87
Seat 6	90	92
Nose Compartment	155	−48
		(Note the negative moment)
Bags — 126" Arm	50	63
Main Wing Tank (100 Gals.)	600	210
Aux. Wing Tank (63 Gals.)	378	178
TOTALS	5500	2153

$$CG = \frac{2153}{5500} \quad X\ 100 = 39.14"$$

7163. (4) C-310 Manual. See Explanation #7160 for complete answer.

ITEM	WEIGHT	MOMENT/100
Basic Empty Weight	3472	1220
Seat 1	160	59
Seat 2	150	56
Seat 4 (71" Arm)	200	142
Nose Compartment	150	−46
		(Note the negative moment)
Bags — 96"	100	96
Bags — 124"	105	130
Main Wing Tank (100 Gals.)	600	210
Aux. Wing Tank (63 Gals.)	378	178
Wing Locker Tanks (20 Gals.)	120	59
TOTALS	5435	2104

$$CG = \frac{2104}{5435} \quad X\ 100 = 38.71"$$

64. (1) C-310 Manual. See Explanation #7160 for complete answer.

ITEM	WEIGHT	MOMENT/100
Basic Empty Weight	3472	1220
Seat 1	200	74
Seat 2	205	76
Seat 3 (68" Arm)	175	119
Seat 4 (68" Arm)	30	20
Seat 5	65	66
Seat 6	105	107
Nose Compartment	155	−48
		(Note the negative moment)
Wing Locker	50	32
Bags — 126" Arm	65	82
Main Wing Tank (100 Gals.)	600	210
Aux. Wing Tank (63 Gals.)	378	178
TOTALS	5500	2136

$$CG = \frac{2136}{5500} \quad X\ 100 = 38.84"$$

7165. (2) C-310 Manual. See Explanation #7160 for complete answer.

ITEM	WEIGHT	MOMENT/100
Basic Empty Weight	3472	1220
Seat 1	170	63
Seat 2	160	59
Nose Compartment	110	−34
		(Note the negative moment)
Main Wing Tank (100 Gals.)	600	210
Aux. Wing Tank (63 Gals.)	378	178
TOTALS	4890	1696

$$\frac{1696}{4890} \quad X\ 100 = 34.68"$$

7166. (2) C-310 Manual. See Explanation #7160 for complete answer.

ITEM	WEIGHT	MOMENT/100
Basic Empty Weight	3472	1220
Seat 1	180	67
Seat 2	130	48
Seat 3 (68" Arm)	50	34
Seat 4 (68" Arm)	30	20
Seat 5	40	41
Seat 6	30	31
Nose Compartment	50	−16
		(Note the negative moment)
Wing Locker	30	19
Main Wing Tank (100 Gals.)	600	210
Aux. Wing Tank (63 Gals.)	378	178
Wing Locker Tank (40 Gals.)	240	118
TOTALS	5230	1970

$$\frac{1970}{5230} \quad X\ 100 = 37.67"$$

7167. (1) C-310 Manual. See Explanation #7160 for complete answer.

ITEM	WEIGHT	MOMENT/100
Basic Empty Weight	3472	1220
Seat 1	165	61
Seat 2	150	56
Seat 3 (68" Arm)	170	116
Seat 4 (68" Arm)	180	122
Nose Compartment	50	−16
Wing Locker	60	38
Bag — 126" Arm	30	38
Main Wing Tanks (100 Gals.)	600	210
Aux. Wing Tank (63 Gals.)	378	178
Wing locker Tank (20 Gals.)	120	59
TOTALS	5375	2082

$$\frac{2082}{5375} \quad X\ 100 = 38.73"$$

7168. (X) FAA Deletion.

7171. (2) C-310 Manual. See Explanation #7160 for complete answer.

ITEM	WEIGHT	MOMENT/100
Basic Empty Weight	3472	1220
Seat 1	160	59
Seat 2	170	63
Seat 3 (71" Arm)	80	57
Seat 4 (71" Arm)	60	43
Nose Compartment	130	−40
Bags — 96" Arm	40	38
Bags — 126" Arm	40	50
Main Wing Tanks (90 Gals.)	540	189
Aux. Wing Tanks (63 Gals.)	378	178
Wing Locker Tanks (40 Gals.)	240	118
TOTALS	5310	1975

$$\frac{1975}{5310} \times 100 = 37.19$$

7169. (1) C-310 Manual. See Explanation #7160 for complete answer.

ITEM	WEIGHT	MOMENT/100
Basic Empty Weight	3472	1220
Seat 1	175	65
Seat 2	170	63
Bags — 126" Arm	60	76
Main Wing Tank (85 Gals.)	510	178
Aux. Wing Tank (50 Gals.)	300	141
TOTALS	4687	1743

$$\frac{1743}{4687} \times 100" = 37.19$$

7170. (X) FAA Deletion.

7172. (4) C-310 Manual. See Explanation #7160 for complete answer.

ITEM	WEIGHT	MOMENT/100
Basic Empty Weight	3472	1220
Seat 1	130	48
Seat 2	180	67
Seat 3 (Arm — 68")	150	102
Seat 4 (Arm — 68")	150	102
Seat 5	130	133
Seat 6	140	143
Bags — 126" Arm	50	63
Main Wing Tank (100 Gals.)	600	210
Aux. Wing Tank (63 Gals.)	378	178
Wing Locker (20 Gals.)	120	59
TOTALS	5500	2325

$$\frac{2325}{5500} \times 100 = 42.27"$$

7173. (4) C-310 Manual. See Explanation #7160 for complete answer.

ITEM	WEIGHT	MOMENT/100
Basic Empty Weight	3472	1220
Seat 1	150	56
Seat 2	165	61
Seat 3 (71" Arm)	80	57
Seat 4 (71" Arm)	90	64
Nose Compartment	80	−25
		(Note the negative moment)
Bags — 96" Arm	30	29
Bags — 124" Arm	60	74
Main Wing Tanks (85 Gals.)	510	178
Aux. Wing Tanks (63 Gals.)	378	178
Wing Locker Tanks (20 Gals.)	120	59
TOTALS	5135	1951

$$\frac{1951}{5135} \times 100 = 37.99"$$

7174. (3) C-310 Manual. See Explanation #7160 for complete answer.

ITEM	WEIGHT	MOMENT/100
Basic Empty Weight	3472	1220
Seat 1	165	61
Seat 2	150	56
Seat 3 (68" Arm)	75	51
Seat 4 (68" Arm)	190	129
Seat 5	120	122
Seat 6	15	15
Nose Compartment	120	−37
		(Note the negative moment)
Wing Locker	40	25
Bags — 126" Arm	60	76
Main Wing Tank (100 Gals.)	600	210
Aux. Wing Tank (63 Gals.)	378	178
TOTALS	5385	2106

$$\frac{2106}{5385} \times 100 = 39.11"$$

7175. (4) C-310 Manual. See Explanation #7160 for complete answer.

ITEM	WEIGHT	MOMENT/100
Basic Empty Weight	3472	1220
Seat 1	180	67
Seat 2	205	76
Seat 3 (71" Arm)	155	110
Seat 4 (71" Arm)	160	114
Bags — 96" Arm	70	67
Bags — 124" Arm	70	87
Main Wing Tanks (100 Gals.)	600	210
Aux. Wing Tanks (63 Gals.)	378	178
TOTALS	5290	2129

$$\frac{2129}{5290} \times 100" = 40.25"$$

7176. (3) C-310 Manual. See Explanation #7160 for complete answer.

ITEM	WEIGHT	MOMENT/100
Basic Empty Weight	3472	1220
Seat 1	170	63
Seat 2	170	63
Seat 3 (68" Arm)	170	116
Seat 4 (68" Arm)	175	119
Seat 6	170	173
Nose Compartment	70	−22
		(Note the negative moment)
Bags — 126" Arm	60	76
Main Wing Tanks (90 Gals.)	540	199
Aux. Wing Tanks (63 Gals.)	378	178
Wing Locker Tanks (20 Gals.)	120	59
TOTALS	5495	2234

$$\frac{2234}{5495} \times 100 = 40.66"$$

7177. (3) C-310 Manual.

NOTE: Computations use "50 foot" distance because no answer is correct for ground roll.

Enter the table at the appropriate gross weight (5500 lbs). Then find the row appropriate for the pressure altitude (3000 feet). There is no takeoff distance listed for a temperature of 23°F so it is necessary to calculate the distance by interpolation. 23°F is exactly half way between 14°F and 32°F. The easiest way to calculate the distance is to add the distance for 14°F (2360) and the distance for 32°F (2540), then divide by 2:

$$\frac{2360 + 2540}{2} = 2450$$

This is the takeoff distance in calm wind conditions. This distance must be reduced by 7% for each 10 knots of headwind.

To calculate the headwind/tailwind component, enter the angular difference between the wind and runway (55°). Find the intersection with 18 knots winds from that point of intersection and go horizontally to the left.

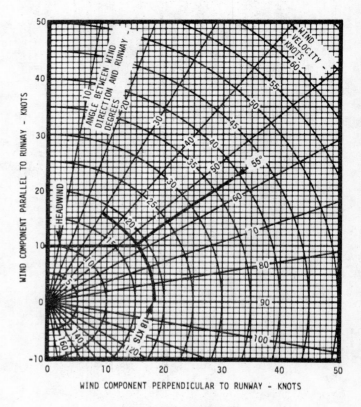

WIND COMPONENTS

7178. (3) C-310 Manual.

NOTE: Answer is distance to clear 50 feet because no answer choice is correct for ground roll distance.

Enter Table 6 at 5500 pounds and 50°F. There is no distance listed for 1500' altitude. So add the takeoff distances for 1000' and 2000' and then divide by 2:

$$\frac{2240 + 2470}{2} = 2355 \text{ feet}$$

Repeat the process for 5100 pounds:

$$\frac{1860 + 2040}{2} = 1950 \text{ feet}$$

To calculate the takeoff distance at a weight of 5300 pounds, add the distances for 5500 lbs. and 5100 lbs., then divide by 2:

$$\frac{2355 + 1950}{2} = 2153 \text{ feet}$$

This is the takeoff distance in calm wind conditions. The distance must be increased by 5% (108 feet) because of a 2-knot tailwind component.

To calculate the headwind/tailwind component, enter the angular difference between the wind and runway (100°). Find the intersection with 10 knots winds from that point of intersection and go horizontally to the left.

7179. (1) C-310 Manual.

NOTE: Answer is distance to clear 50 feet because no answer choice is correct for ground roll distance.

Enter Table 6 at 5100 pounds and 10°C (50°F). The takeoff distance at 6000 feet is 3160. Repeat the process for 4700 pounds. The takeoff distance is 2480. Calculate the takeoff distance at 4900 pounds by adding the distances for 5100 lbs. and 4700 lbs. and then divide by 2:

$$\frac{3160 + 2480}{2} = 2820 \text{ feet}$$

There is no wind correction since the entire wind vector is crosswind.

The sod runway requires that the takeoff distance be increased by 7.9% (223 feet):

$$2820 + 223 = 3043.$$

7180. (4) C-310 Manual.

NOTE: Answer is the distance to clear 50 feet. No answer choice is correct for ground roll distance.

This problem requires a 2-way interpolation. Find the takeoff distance at 4700 pounds for 32°F and 50°F and then repeat the process for 4300

pounds. The distances are 1430, 1530, 1160 and 1240 respectively. To calculate the takeoff distance at 4500 pounds and 41°F, add those numbers and divide by 4:

$$\frac{1430 + 1530 + 1160 + 1240}{4} = 1340$$

The tailwind component is 2 knots.

To calculate the headwind/tailwind component, enter the angular difference between the wind and runway (100°). Find the intersection with 10 knots wind from that point of intersection and go horizontally to the left.

The tailwind requires a 5% increase in takeoff distance (67') which raises the distance to 1407. The sod runway requires that distance to be increased by another 7.9% (111') for a total of 1518.

7181. (3) C-310 Manual. Enter Table 6 at 4300 pounds and determine the ground roll distance at −10°C for 8000' and 9000' (1720, 1910). The distance for 8500' is 1815'

$$(\frac{1720 + 1910}{2} = 1815)$$

To calculate the headwind/tailwind component, enter the angular difference between the wind and runway (75°). Find the intersection with 20 knots wind and from that point of intersection go horizontally to the left.

The takeoff distance can be reduced by 3.5% (64') because of the 5 KT headwind.

7182. (1) C-310 Manual. Determine the ground roll at 5100 pounds and 6000 feet for both −4°F and 14°F (1990, 2150). Determine the takeoff distance for 5°F by adding these distances and dividing by 2:

$$\frac{1990 + 2150}{2} = 2070'$$

To calculate the headwind/tailwind component, enter the angular difference between the wind and runway (100°). Find the intersection with 10 knots wind and from that point of intersection go horizontally to the left.

The tailwind component of 2 knots requires an increase of 5% (104').

7187. (X) FAA Deletion.

7183. (X) FAA Deletion.

7184. (X) FAA Deletion.

7188. (X) FAA Deletion.

7185. (X) FAA Deletion.

7189. (4) C-310 Manual Determine distance at 5500 pounds and +10°C for 5000' P.A. and 6000' P.A. (5090, 5490). Add these two numbers and divide by 2:

$$\frac{5090 + 5490}{2} = 5290$$

Increase this distance by 10% (529') for the 4 KT tailwind.

7190. (3) C-310 Manual. Determine distance at 5500 pounds and 2000' P.A. for both 50°F and 68°F (4050, 4340). Repeat the process for 5100 pounds (3390, 3580). Add these distances and divide by 4:

$$\frac{4050 + 4340 + 3390 + 3580}{4} = 3840'$$

7186. (X) FAA Deletion.

7191. (2) C-310 Manual. Determine the distance at 5100 pounds, 40°C, and 8000' P.A. (6420). Since there is a 16 KT headwind, reduce the distance by 12% (770').

7192. (2) C-310 Manual. Determine the distance at 4700 pounds and sea level for temperatures of −4°F and 14°F (2110, 2230). Add these two distances and divide by 2 to determine the distance at 5°F:

$$\frac{2110 + 2230}{2} = 2170'$$

The 20 KT headwind requires a reduction of 15% (326').

7193. (3) C-310 Manual. Determine the distance at 5500 pounds and 9000' P.A. for temperatures of 30°C and 40°C (8020, 8560). Add these distances and divide by two to get the distance at 35°C:

$$\frac{8020 + 8560}{2} = 8290'$$

The 2 KT tailwind requires that the distance be increased by 5% (415').

7194. (4) C-310 Manual. Determine the distance at 4700 pounds, 6000' P.A. and 68°F (3910'). Repeat the process for 4300 pounds (3160'). To determine the distance at 4500 pounds, add those two distances and divide by 2:

$$\frac{3910 + 3160}{2} = 3535"$$

There is no wind correction.

7195. (1) C-310 Manual. Determine the distance for 4300 pounds and 104°F for both 7000' and 8000' P.A. (3880, 4200). To determine the distance at 7500' P.A., add those two distances and divide by 2:

$$\frac{3880 + 4200}{2} = 4040$$

The 8 KT headwind requires the distance be reduced by 6% (242').

7196. (4) C-310 Manual. Determine the distance for 4700 pounds, 4000' P.A. and 86°F (3580'). Repeat the process for 4300 pounds (2900'). To determine the distance at 4500 pounds, add the two distances and divide by 2:

$$\frac{3580 + 2900}{2} = 3240'$$

The 2 KT tailwind requires the distance to be increased 5% (162').

7197. (1) C-310 Manual. Determine the distance at 4700 pounds and 3000' P.A. for both 50°F and 68°F (3000', 3160). To determine the distance at 59°F, add the distances and divide by two:

$$\frac{3000 + 3160}{2} = 3080'$$

The 4 KT headwind requires the distance to be reduced by 3% (92').

7198. (4) C-310 Manual. Determine the distance at 5100 pounds and 1000' P.A. for 32°F and 50°F (3020, 3180). Repeat the process for 4700 pounds (2500, 2640). To determine the distance for 4900 pounds and 41°F, add the distances and divide by 4:

$$\frac{3020 + 3180 + 2500 + 2640}{4} = 2835'$$

The 4 KT tailwind requires that the distance be increased 10% (284').

7199. (1) C-310 Manual. Determine the distance at 5100 pounds and 2000' P.A. for both −4°F and 14°F (2880, 3050). Repeat the process for 3000' P.A. (3070, 3250). To determine the distance at 2500' P.A. and 5°F, add these four distances and divide by 4:

$$\frac{2880 + 3050 + 3070 + 3250}{4} = 3063$$

There is no wind correction.

7200. (1) C-310 Manual. Determine the distance at 5500 pounds and 40°C for 8000' P.A. and 9000' P.A. (7780, 8560). Add those distances and divide by 2 to determine distance at 8500' P.A.:

$$\frac{7780 + 8560}{2} = 8170'$$

This distance must be reduced by 6% (490') because of the 8 KT headwind.

7201. (4) C-310 Manual. Pressure altitude is 4500 feet, which is half way between two values. Add 7020 to 13010 feet in the −10°C column and then divide by 2 to get accelerate-go distance in calm wind.

$$13,010 + 7,020 = 20,030$$
$$20,030 \div 2 = 10,015$$

There is a tailwind of 5 KTS, so Note #3 applies; 5 KTS = 10% increase in distance:

$$10,015 \times .10 = 1,001.5 \text{ feet}$$

Now add 1,001.5 + 10,015 = 11,016.5 feet and round to next higher number for 11,017 feet.

7202. (2) C-310 Manual. Aircraft weight is 5100 lbs, pressure altitude 4,000 feet, outside air temperature is 104°F. The accelerate-go distance is 10,430 feet because the wind is calm.

7203. (1) C-310. Find 2,460 feet in the 4,700 lb. gross weight, sea level line under 104°F. Note #2 applies. 30 KTS headwind equals 18% decrease in distance. Subtract 18% of 2,460 to find accelerate-go distance.

$$2,460 \times .18 = 442.8$$
$$2,460 - 443 = 2,017$$

7204. (X) FAA Deletion.

7205. (3) C-310 Manual. The 5,300 lbs. gross weight is half way between 5,500 lbs. and 5,100 lbs., so interpolate between the two weights for 5,300 lbs. The accelerate-go distance will be halfway between 4,160 and 2,940 feet: add 4,160 + 2,940, then divide the answer by 2 to get 3,550 feet. The wind is calm. The accelerate-go distance is 3,550.

$$4,160 + 2,940 = 7,100$$
$$7,100 \div 2 = 3,550$$

7206. (1) C-310 Manual. The accelerate-stop distance in calm wind is found halfway between 1,820 feet and 1,960 feet and is 1,890 feet:

$$1,820 + 1,960 = 3,780; \quad 3,780 \div 2 = 1,890$$

Note #2 applies. Subtract 9% of 1,890 for the 15 KT headwind (15 ÷ 10 = 1.5: 1.5 X 6% = 9%).

$$1,890 \times .09 = 170$$
$$1,890 - 170 = 1,720$$

The accelerate-go distance is 1,720 feet.

7207. (X) FAA Deletion.

7208. (4) C-310 Manual. Interpolate the values at –4°F and 5,000 feet PA between 4,700 lbs. and 4,300 lbs. Calm wind accelerate-go distance will be 2,480 feet.

$$
\begin{array}{r}
4,700 \text{ lbs} - 2,860 \\
4,300 \text{ lbs} - \underline{2,100} \\
4,960
\end{array}
$$

$$4,960 \div 2 = 2,480 \text{ feet}$$

Note #3 applies. 2% X 4 = 8%. Add 8% of 2,480 to 2,480 for accelerate-go distance with 4 KT tailwind.

$$2,480 \times .08 = 198.4 \text{ feet (198')}$$
$$2,480 + 198 = 2,678 \text{ feet}$$

Accelerate-go distance is 2,678 feet.

7209. (X) FAA Deletion.

7210. (3) C-310 Manual. Interpolate distances for 2,000' and 3,000' for aircraft weights 5,100 lbs. and 4,710 lbs.

5,100 lbs.

2,000'	3,090
2,500'	3,360
3,000'	3,630

$$3,090 + 3,630 = 6,720$$
$$6,720 \div 2 = 3,360$$

4,700 lbs.

2,000'	2,300
2,500'	2,450
3,000'	2,600

$$2,300 + 2,600 = 4,900$$
$$4,900 \div 2 = 2,450$$

The aircraft weight is 4,900 lbs., so interpolate between 5,100 lbs. and 4,700 lbs. The distances for 2,500 feet.

WT.	PA 2,500'
5,100'	3,360'
4,900'	2,905'
4,700'	2,450'

$$3,360 + 2,450 = 5,810$$
$$5,810 \div 2 = 2,905$$

The accelerate-go distance in calm wind: 2,905 feet.

7211. (3) C-310 Manual. Interpolate the temperatures 32°F and 50°F to find that 41°F is halfway between.

Now interpolate the distances for 32°F and 50°F at 6,000 PA, to get accelerate-go distance for 41°F at 6,000' PA.

PA	6,000'
50°	12,550
41°	10,515
32°	8,480

$$12,550 \div 8,480 = 21,030$$
$$21,030 \div 2 = 10,515$$

There is a 6 KT tailwind, so Note #3 applies.

$$2\% \times 6 = 12\%$$

Add 12% of 10,515 to 10,515 for accelerate-go distance with a 6-KT tailwind (11,777').

$$10,515 \times .12 = 1,261.8' \ (1,262)$$
$$10,515 + 1,262 = 11,777 \text{ feet}$$

7212. (2) C-310 Manual. Interpolate aircraft weight to find that 5300 lbs. is halfway between 5,500 lbs. and 5,100 lbs.

Now, interpolate temperature the same way. Twenty-three degrees is halfway between the two temperatures.

Interpolate distances for 14°F and 32°F.

5,500 lbs.

	PA 1,000'
32°	3,700'
23°	3,515'
14°	3,330'

$$3,700 + 3,330 = 7,030$$
$$7,030 \div 2 = 3,515$$

5,100 lbs.

	PA 1,000'
32°	2,690'
23°	2,580'
14°	2,470'

$$2,690 + 2,470 = 5,160$$
$$5,160 \div 2 = 2,580$$

Interpolate for 5,300 lbs. and 23°F.

23°F	PA 1,000'
5,500	3,515.0
5,300	3,047.5
5,100	2,580.0

$$3,515 + 2,580 = 6,095$$
$$6,095 \div 2 = 3,047.5$$

Note #2 applies.

$$30 \text{ KT} \div 10 \text{ KT} = 3$$
$$3 \times 6\% = 18\%$$

Subtract 18% of 3,047.5 (3,048) for the 30 KT headwind.

$$3,048 \times .18 = 548.64 \ (549)$$
$$3,048 - 549 = 2,499$$

7213. (3) C-310 Manual. Thirty-two degrees Fahrenheit equals zero degrees Celcius. Draw a vertical line from 0°C through 4,000 feet pressure altitude line. As accurately as possible, determine where the 5,000 feet pressure altitude line should be between 4,000 feet and 6,000 feet (approximately halfway between 4,000 feet and 6,000 feet). Where the 0°C line and the 5,000 foot pressure altitude lines meet, draw a horizontal line to the right until it intersects the heavy vertical reference line marked "5,500." Draw from this point a line parallel to the heavy curved lines until it intersects the vertical line representing the gross weight. Where these two lines intersect, draw a horizontal line to the right edge and read rate of climb.

7214. (1) C-310 Manual. Draw a vertical line from –10°C through 4,000 feet pressure altitude line. As accurately as possible, determine where the 5,000 feet pressure altitude line should be between 4,000 feet and 6,000 feet (approximately halfway between 4,000 feet and 6,000 feet).

Where the −10°C line and the 5,000 foot pressure altitude lines meet, draw a horizontal line to the right until it intersects the heavy vertical reference line marked "5,500." Draw from this point a line parallel to the heavy curved lines until it intersects the vertical line representing the gross weight. Where these two lines intersect, draw a horizontal line to the right edge and read rate of climb.

7215. (2) C-310 Manual Draw a vertical line from 0°F through 8,000 feet pressure altitude line. As accurately as possible, determine where the 7,500 feet pressure altitude line should be betwenn 6,000 feet and 8,000 feet (approximately three-fourths between 6,000 feet and 8,000 feet). Where the 0°C line and the 7,500 foot pressure altitude lines meet, draw a horizontal line to the right until it intersects the heavy vertical reference line marked "5,500." Draw from this point a line parallel to the heavy curved lines until it intersects the vertical line representing the gross weight. Where these two lines intersect, draw a horizontal line to the right edge and read rate of climb.

7216. (3) C-310 Manual. Fifty degrees Fahrenheit equals ten degrees Celcius. Draw a vertical line from 10°C through 14,000 feet pressure altitude line. As accurately as possible, determine where the 12,500 feet pressure altitude line should be between 12,000 feet and 14,000 feet (approximately one-fourth of the way between 12,000 feet and 14,000 feet). Where the 10°C line and the 12,500 foot pressure altitude lines meet, draw a horizontal line to the right until it intersects the heavy vertical reference line marked "5,500." Draw from this point a line parallel to the heavy curved lines until it intersects the vertical line representing the gross weight. Where these two lines intersect, draw a horizontal line to the right edge and read rate of climb.

7217. (1) C-310 Manual. Draw a vertical line from 80°F to sea level. Draw a horizontal line from the intersection of 80°F and sea level to the right until it intersects the heavy reference line marked "5,500." Because this reference line is also the 5,500 lb. gross weight line, it is not necessary to draw a parallel curved line. Just continue straight across to read rate of climb.

7218. (2) C-310 Manual. "ISA" means International Standard Atmosphere, and represents the temperature with standard lapse rate. So the standard temperature (or ISA temperature) for 10,000 feet is −5°C. (Temperature lapse rate is 2°C per 1,000 feet; standard sea level temperature is 15°C). ISA + 5°C is 0°C (+5°C − 5°C = 0°C).

Draw a vertical line from 0°C until it intersects 10,000 feet pressure altitude. Draw a horizontal line from this intersection to the right until it intersects the heavy vertical reference line. Draw a line parallel to the curved lines until it intersects the vertical representing 4,900 lbs. gross weight. From this point draw a horizontal line to the right and read rate of climb.

7219. (3) C-310 Manual. ISA (See Explanation #7218) at sea level is 15°C. Go to the sea level pressure altitude and ISA point. Draw a horizontal line to the right until it intersects the vertical reference line. Because gross weight (5,500 lbs.) is the reference line top, continue the horizontal line across to the edge and read rate-of-climb.

7220. (2) C-310 Manual. Draw a vertical line from 80°F through sea level. As accurately as possible, determine 1,000 feet pressure altitude. Where the 80°F line and 1,000 pressure altitude lines cross, draw a horizontal line to the right to the heavy vertical reference line. From this point, draw a line parallel to the heavy diagonal lines until it intersects the vertical line representing 5,300 lbs. From this point, draw a horizontal line to the right and read rate of climb.

7221. (3) C-310 Manual. For "ISA −5°C" see Explanation #7218. Temperature equals +5°C. The procedure is the same as problem #7220. Just substitute +5°C, 2,500 feet and 4,700 lbs. for the appropriate values.

7222. (4) C-310 Manual. The procedure is the same as problem #7220. The difficulty with this problem is accurately determining 90°F.

7223. (1) C-310 Manual. The procedure is the same as problem #7220.

7224. (1) C-310 Manual. The procedure is the same as problem #7220.

7225. (3) C-310 Manual. Two graphs will have to be plotted. The difference between the two will give the answers.

First, draw a vertical line from 20°F to 2,000 feet pressure altitude. Now draw a horizontal line from this point until it intersects the gross weight curved line 5,500 lbs. From this point, draw a vertical line down through the "Distance to Climb" line.

Plot the cruise altitude data the same way. For an explanation of ISA see Explanation #7218. (HINT: There is an "ISA" line drawn on the graph, just find 8,500 feet on the ISA line.)

Draw the horizontal AND vertical lines as was done for the takeoff data. The vertical lines cross the "Time-to-Climb," "Fuel-to-Climb," and "Distance-to-Climb" lines. Subtract the values on each line to get the answers.

TIME-TO-CLIMB:
Airport line . . . . 1 minute
Cruise line . . . . 7 minutes
Time to climb . . . . 6 minutes (7 − 1 = 6)

FUEL-TO-CLIMB:
Airport line. . . . . 4 lbs.
Cruise line. . . . . 28 lbs.
Fuel to climb . . . . 24 lbs. (28 − 4 = 24)

DISTANCE-TO-CLIMB:
Airport line . . . . 2 NM
Cruise line. . . . . 12 NM
Distance to climb. . . . . 10 NM
          (12 NM − 2 NM = 10 NM)

7226. (3) C-310 Manual. The procedure is the same as Explanation #7225. Remember to be as accurate as possible when plotting the 11,000 foot pressure altitude.

7227. (1) C-310 Manual. The procedure is the same as Explanation #7225, except that since the aircraft is departing from sea level, there is only one graph to plot. For an explanation of "ISA" see Explanation #7218.

Temperature at cruise is 0°C (–10°C + 10°C = 0°C).

Answer #1 is the best although it is not very accurate.

7228. (1) C-310 Manual. Use the same procedure as outlined in Explanation #7218. For aircraft weight, be sure to be as accurate as possible when graphing 4,900 lbs.

7229. (1) C-310 Manual. Use the same procedure as explained in Explanation #7218. Remember, 32°F equals 0°C, and accurately graph the aircraft weight.

7230. (3) C-310 Manual. Use the same procedure as in Explanation #7218.

7231. (1) C-310 Manual. Use procedure outlined in Explanation #7225.

7232. (1) C-310 Manual. Use procedure outlined in Explanation #7225.

7233. (2) C-310 Manual. Use procedure outlined in Explanation #7225.

7234. (4) C-310 Manual. Use procedure outlined in Explanation #7225.

7235. (1) C-310 Manual. Use procedure outlined in Explanation #7225.

7236. (4) C-310 Manual. Use procedure outlined in Explanation #7225.

7237. (X) FAA Deletion.

7238. (X) FAA Deletion.

7239. (X) FAA Deletion.

7240. (X) FAA Deletion.

7241. (X) FAA Deletion.

7242. (X) FAA Deletion.

7243. (X) FAA Deletion.

7244. (X) FAA Deletion.

7245. (X) FAA Deletion.

7246. (X) FAA Deletion.

7247. (X) FAA Deletion.

7248. (X) FAA Deletion.

7249. (2) C-310 Manual. Be sure to use the correct temperature scale. Draw a vertical line from the outside air temperature through the curved line representing the gross weight. From the point where they intersect, draw a horizontal line to the left and read service ceiling. Each horizontal line represents 200 feet. Note #2 applies. There is a difference of +.10 Hg, so ADD 100 FEET to the service ceiling.

7250. (1) C-310 Manual. Be sure to plot the gross weight as accurately as possible. Use the same procedure as in Explanation #7249. Note #3 applies. There is a difference of –.10 Hg, so subtract 100 feet from the service ceiling.

7251. (1) C-310 Manual. Plot the temperature and aircraft weight as accurately as possible. Then use the procedure in Explanation #7249, except subtract 50 feet because Note #3 applies. There is –.05 Hg difference which equals 50 feet.

7252. (3) C-310 Manual. One hundred four degrees fahrenheit (104°F) equals 40°C. It is easier to use the 40°C. Note #3 applies. There is –.05 Hg difference, so subtract 50 feet from the ceiling obtained. (See Explanation #7249 for procedure.)

7253. (2) C-310 Manual. Use the same procedure as Explanation #7249. Be sure to accurately plot +6°C. Note #2 applies, so add 50 feet to ceiling obtained.

7254. (3) C-310 Manual. Use the same procedure as Explanation #7249. A correction factor does not apply since the altimeter setting is 29.92" Hg.

7255. (4) C-310 Manual. Use procedure in Explanation #7249. Be very accurate when determining aircraft weight. Note #2 applies. There is a difference of +.20" Hg, so add 200 feet to ceiling obtained.

7256. (3) C-310 Manual. Use procedure in Explanation #7249. Note #2 applies. There is +.15" Hg difference, so add 150 feet to ceiling obtained.

7257. (1) C-310 Manual. Use procedure in Explanation #7249. Note #3 applies. There is a difference of –.15" Hg, so subtract 150 feet from ceiling obtained.

7258. (2) C-310 Manual. Be extremely accurate in plotting the aircraft weight. The weight of 4,900 is halfway between 4,700 Lbs. and 5,100. The halfway point between these two lines at 80°F will give you a service ceiling of 8,800. Note #2 applies, so add 20 feet to 8,800 for a corrected service ceiling of 8,820.

7259. (3) C-310 Manual. Use procedure in Explanation #7249. Note #3 applies. There is a –.02" Hg difference (29.90 – 29.92 = –.02). This is 20% of 100 feet which equals 20 feet, so subtract 20 feet from altitude obtained.

7260. (3) C-310 Manual. Use procedure in Explanation #7249. Note #3 applies. There is a difference of –.19" Hg which equals –190 feet. Subtract the 190 feet from the altitude obtained.

7261. (3) C-310 Manual. For ISA see Explanation #7218. Standard temperature (5°C) equals ISA at 5,000 feet. Note #2 applies. In the column marked 5°C (Standard Temperature), go down to the figure that is opposite 2,300 RPM and 24.5 MP. TAS is found in the middle figure (182). Since Note #2 applies, add 2 KTS to 182 (182 + 2 = 184 KTS TAS).

7262. (X) FAA Deletion.

7263. (X) FAA Deletion.

7264. (4) C-310 Manual. Use the 77°F column and 2,100 RPM/20 MP line for 2,500 feet.

% BHP = 43.1 : LB/HR = 114 : TAS = 145

Gross weight as given is 4,900 lbs. so Note #2 applies.

5,500 lbs. – 4,900 lbs. = 600 lbs.

Divide 600 lbs. by 400 lbs. to get a percentage value to increase TAS:

$$600 \div 400 = 1.5 \ (150\%); \ 1.5 \times 2 \ KTS = 3 \ KTS$$

TAS then is 3 + 145 = 148 KTS.

7265. (3) C-310 Manual. Use 2,500 feet chart. Interpolate the temperatures to find that ISA −10°C is halfway between −10°C and +10°C (ISA = +10°C; +10° − −10°C = 0°C). Interpolate the performance values, too.

	PA 2,500	% BHP	TAS	LB/HR
Gr. Wt.	−10°C	50.6	152	131
	0°C	49.7	152	129
5,500 lbs.	+10°C	48.8	152	127

INTERPOLATIONS FOR 0°C:

% BHP:
50.6 + 48.8 = 99.4
99.4 ÷ 2 = 49.7

TAS = 152

LB/HR:
131 + 127 = 258
258 ÷ 2 = 129

Gross weight is 4,700 lbs., so Note #1 applies.

$$5,500 \ lbs. - 4,700 \ lbs. = 800 \ lbs.$$
$$800 \ lbs. \div 400 \ lbs. = 2$$
$$2 \times 2 \ KTS = 4 \ KTS$$

Increase TAS by 4 KTS: 4 + 152 = 156 KTS.

The correct values are:

% BHP: 49.7
TAS: 156
LB/HR: 129

7266. (1) C-310 Manual. Interpolate the temperature. It falls halfway between +10°C and +30°C (ISA for 2,500' is +10°C; ISA +10°C is +10°C + 10°C = +20°C.) Interpolate the performance chart similarly.

% BHP	PA 2,500'
10°C	45.5
20°C	44.7
30°C	43.9

$$45.5 + 43.9 = 89.4$$
$$89.4 \div 2 = 44.7$$

TAS	PA 2,500'
10°C	146
20°C	145
30°C	144

LB/HR	PA 2,500'
10°C	119
20°C	117
30°C	115

Gross weight is 4,900 lbs., so Note #1 applies.

$$5,500 \ lbs. - 4,900 \ lbs. = 600 \ lbs.$$
$$600 \ lbs. \div 400 \ lbs. = 1.50\%$$
$$1.5 \times 2 = 3 \ KTS$$

Subtract actual gross weight from chart gross weight. Then divide the answer by 400 to get the percentage increase of 2 KTS.

Multiply the percentage by 2 KTS and add the product to the TAS:

$$3 \ KTS + 145 = 148 \ KTS$$

The correct values are:

% BHP: 44.7
TAS: 148
LB/HR: 117

7267. (3) C-310 Manual. Interpolate the temperature:

$$32°F + 68°F = 100°F$$
$$100°F \div 2 = 50°F$$

50°F is halfway between the two columns. Interpolate the performance figures similarly:

% BHP	
32°	50.90
50°	49.95
68°	49.00

$$50.9 + 49.0 = 99.9$$
$$99.9 \div 2 = 49.95$$

TAS	
32°C	161
50°C	160
60°C	159

LB/HR	
32°	132
50°	130
68°	128

Gross weight is 4,700 lbs, so Note #1 applies. Subtract 5,500 lbs. from 4,700 lbs; 5,500 − 4,700 = 800 lbs. Divide 800 lbs. by 400 lbs. to get a percentage increase:

$$800 \div 400 = 2.0$$
$$2 \times 3 \ KTS = 6 \ KTS$$
$$6 \ KTS + 160 \ KTS = 166 \ KTS$$

Multiply the result by 3 KTS and add the product to the TAS.

7268. (3) C-310 Manual. Interpolate the temperature:

$$23°F + (-13°F) = +10°F$$
$$10°F \div 2 = 5°F$$

The performance values must also be interpolated.

% BHP

–13°	56.8
5°	55.8
23°	54.8

$$56.8 + 54.8 = 111.6$$
$$111.6 \div 2 = 55.8$$

TAS

–13°	170
5°	170
23°	170

LB/HR

–13°	146
5°	144
23°	142

The gross weight is 5,300 lbs., so Note #2 applies. Subtract 5,300 from 5,500:

$$5,500 - 5,300 = 200 \text{ lbs.}$$

Divide 200 by 400 to get percentage increase of 4 KTS.

$$200 \div 400 = .5$$

Multiply this answer by 4 KTS:

$$.5 \times 4 \text{ KTS} = 2 \text{ KTS}$$

Now add 2 KTS to the TAS for the correct TAS at 5,300 lbs.:

$$170 \text{ KTS} + 2 \text{ KTS} = 172 \text{ KTS}$$

7269. (3) C-310 Manual. Interpolate the temperature:

$$0°C + (-20°C) = -20°C$$
$$-20°C \div 2 = -10°C$$

–10°C is halfway between the two temperatures. Interpolate the performance figures similarly.

% BHP

–20°	72.20
–10°	70.95
0°	69.70

$$72.2 + 69.7 = 141.9$$
$$141.9 \div 2 = 70.95$$

TAS

–20°	185
–10°	186
0°	187

LB/HR

–20°	181
–10°	178
0°	175

The gross weight is 5,100 lbs., so Note #1 applies. Subtract 5,100 from 5,500:

$$5,500 - 5,100 = 400 \text{ lbs.}$$

Add 3 KTS to the TAS:

$$3 \text{ KTS} + 186 \text{ KTS} = 189 \text{ KTS}$$

The correct answers are:

% BHP: 70.95
TAS: 189
LB/HR: 178

Answer #3 is best.

7270. (3) C-310 Manual. Interpolate the temperatures to find that 50°F is ¾ the distance from 23°F to 59°F.

The total difference between 23° and 59° is 36° (59 – 23 = 36).

When divided, this gives .75 or ¾. Fifty degrees is three-fourths the distance from 23° to 59°. The performance values will have to be interpolated this way too.

% BHP

23°	50.50
50°	49.15
59°	48.70

$$50.5 - 48.7 = 1.8$$
$$1.8 \times 75\% = 1.35$$
$$50.5 - 1.35 = 49.15$$

TAS

23°	163.0
50°	161.5
59°	161.0

$$163 - 161 = 2$$
$$2 \times 75\% = 1.5$$
$$163 - 1.5 = 161.5$$

LB/HR

23°	131
50°	128
59°	127

$$131 - 127 = 4$$
$$4 \times .75 = 3$$
$$131 - 3 = 128$$

The gross weight is 5,300 lbs. Subtract 5,300 from 5,500:

$$5,500 - 5,300 = 200 \text{ lbs.}$$

Note #4 applies, so divide 200 by 400:

$$200 \div 400 = .5$$

Multiply 4 KTS by .5 and add the product to the TAS:

$$4 \text{ KTS} \times .5 = 2 \text{ KTS}$$

$$2 \text{ KTS} + 161.5 \text{ KTS} = 163.5 \text{ KTS}$$

The correct values are:

% BHP: 49.1
TAS: 163
LB/HR: 128

7271. (2) C-310 Manual. Interpolation is not necessary for this problem. The only calculation necessary is for TAS. Percent of BHP and total LB/HR are read directly off the chart because ISA is "STD TEMP." To calculate TAS, first subtract 5,490 from 5,500 and find that Note #1 applies.

$$5,500 - 5,490 = 10$$

Divide 10 by 400 to get percentage of TAS increase of 3 KTS:

$$10 \div 400 = .025 \ (2.5\%)$$

Multiply 3 KTS by .025 and add the product to the TAS: .025 X 3 = .075. The increase is less than ¼ of one knot, so TAS remains 138 KTS.

7272. (2) C-310 Manual. Interpolate the temperatures to find that 41°F is halfway between the 23°F and 59°F temperatures:

The same thing must be done to the performance values:

% BHP

23°	49.3
41°	48.4
59°	47.5

$$49.3 + 47.5 = 96.8$$

$$96.8 \div 2 = 48.4$$

TAS

23°	160
41°	159
59°	158

LB/HR

23°	128
41°	126
59°	124

The gross weight is 4,800 lbs., so Note #2 applies. Subtract 4,800 from 5,500:

$$5,500 - 4,800 = 700 \text{ lbs.}$$

Now divide 700 lbs. by 400:

$$700 \div 400 = 1.75$$

Multiply 4 KTS by 1.75:

$$1.75 \times 4 = 7 \text{ KTS}$$

Add 7 KTS to the TAS for the correct TAS:

$$7 \text{ KTS} + 159 \text{ KTS} = 166 \text{ KTS}$$

The correct values are:

% BHP: 48.4
TAS: 166
LB/HR: 126

Answer #2 is best.

7273. (1) C-310 Manual. Be as accurate as possible when reading the graph. First, find 8,500 feet on the left margin, then draw a horizontal line until it intersects the heavy diagonal line. From this point, draw a vertical line down through the "Distance to Descend" scale. Do exactly the same for 2,000 feet. The answers will be the difference between the two vertical lines, read on the appropriate scales.

	2,000'	8,500'	Value
Time to Descend	3.9	17	13.1
Fuel Used to Descend	9.6	43	33.4
Distance to Descend	11	50.9	39.9

7274. (3) C-310 Manual. Be as accurate as possible when reading the graph. First, find 11,000 feet on the left margin, then draw a horizontal line until it intersects the heavy diagonal line. From this point, draw a vertical line down through the "Distance to Descend" scale. Do exactly the same for 3,000 feet. The answers will be the difference between the two vertical lines, read on the appropriate scales.

	11,000	3,000'	Value
Time to Descend	21	5.9	15.1
Fuel Used to Descend	53	14.8	38.2
Distance to Descend	63.3	16.9	46.4

7275. (2) C-310 Manual. Be as accurate as possible when reading the graph. First, find 12,500 feet on the left margin, then draw a horizontal line until it intersects the heavy diagonal line. From this point, draw a vertical line down through the "Distance to Descend" scale. Do exactly the same for Sea Level feet. The answers will be the difference between the two vertical lines, read on the appropriate scales.

	12,500'	Sea Lvl	Value
Time	22.5	0	22.5
Fuel	57	0	57
Distance	68	0	68

7276. (1) C-310 Manual. Be as accurate as possible when reading the graph. First, find 14,000 feet on the left margin, then draw a horizontal line until it intersects the heavy diagonal line. From this point, draw a vertical line down through the "Distance to Descend" scale. Do exactly the same for 6,000 feet. The answers will be the difference between the two vertical lines, read on the appropriate scales.

	14,000	6,000	Value
Time	24.1	12.0	12.1
Fuel	60.3	30.4	29.9
Distance	73.8	35.0	38.9

7277. (4) C-310 Manual. Be as accurate as possible when reading the graph. First, find 11.500 feet on the left margin, then draw a horizontal line until it intersects the heavy diagonal line. From this point, draw a vertical line down through the "Distance to Descend" scale. Do exactly the same for 1,500 feet. The answers will be the difference between the two vertical lines, read on the appropriate scales.

	11,500	1,500	Value
Time	20.5	2.9	17.6
Fuel	54.5	7.2	47.3
Distance	65.0	8.0	57.0

Answer #4 is best.

7278. (1) C-310 Manual. Be as accurate as possible when reading the graph. First, find 9,500 feet on the left margin, then draw a horizontal line until it intersects the heavy diagonal line. From this point, draw a vertical line down through the "Distance to Descend" scale. Do exactly the same for 3,250 feet. The answers will be the difference between the two vertical lines, read on the appropriate scales.

	9,500	3,250	Value
Time	19.0	6.5	12.5
Fuel	48.3	16.1	32.2
Distance	57.0	18.3	38.7

7279. (1) C-310 Manual. Be as accurate as possible when reading the graph. First, find 9,000 feet on the left margin, then draw a horizontal line until it intersects the heavy diagonal line. From this point, draw a vertical line down through the "Distance to Descend" scale. Do exactly the same for 1,000 feet. The answers will be the difference between the two vertical lines, read on the appropriate scales.

	9,000	1,000	Value
Time	18.0	1.75	16.25
Fuel	45.7	4.50	41.20
Distance	53.7	5.00	48.70

7280. (3) C-310 Manual. Be as accurate as possible when reading the graph. First, find 10,500 feet on the left margin, then draw a horizontal line until it intersects the heavy diagonal line. From this point, draw a vertical line down through the "Distance to Descend" scale. Do exactly the same for 1,500 feet. The answers will be the difference between the two vertical lines, read on the appropriate scales.

	10,500	1,500	Value
Time	20.5	2.9	17.6
Fuel	52.3	7.2	45.1
Distance	61.6	8.0	63.6

7281. (4) C-310 Manual. Be as accurate as possible when reading the graph. First, find 8,000 feet on the left margin, then draw a horizontal line until it intersects the heavy diagonal line. From this point, draw a vertical line down through the "Distance to Descend" scale. Do exactly the same for 2,000 feet. The answers will be the difference between the two vertical lines, read on the appropriate scales.

	8,000	2,000	Value
Time	16.0	3.9	12.1
Fuel	40.7	9.6	31.1
Distance	47.7	11.0	36.7

7282. (1) C-310 Manual. Be as accurate as possible when reading the graph. First, find 9,000 feet on the left margin, then draw a horizontal line until it intersects the heavy diagonal line. From this point, draw a vertical line down through the "Distance to Descend" scale. Do exactly the same for 3,000 feet. The answers will be the difference between the two vertical lines, read on the appropriate scales.

	9,000	3,000	Value
Time	18.0	5.8	12.2
Fuel	45.8	14.5	31.3
Distance	53.7	16.8	36.9

7283. (2) C-310 Manual. Be as accurate as possible when reading the graph. First, find 12,000 feet on the left margin, then draw a horizontal line until it intersects the heavy diagonal line. From this point, draw a vertical line down through the "Distance to Descend" scale. Do exactly the same for 4,000 feet. The answers will be the difference between the two vertical lines, read on the appropriate scales.

	12,000	4,000	Value
Time	22.0	7.8	14.2
Fuel	55.4	19.8	35.6
Distance	66.7	22.8	48.9

7284. (1) C-310 Manual. Be as accurate as possible when reading the graph. First, find 7,000 feet on the left margin, then draw a horizontal line until it intersects the heavy diagonal line. From this point, draw a vertical line down through the "Distance to Descend" scale. Do exactly the same for 500 feet. The answers will be the difference between the two vertical lines, read on the appropriate scales.

	7,000	500	Value
Time....................	14.0	.9	13.1
Fuel.....................	35.4	2.1	33.3
Distance.................	41.2	2.4	38.8

7285. (4) C-310 Manual.

1. Interpolate the ground roll distance.
2. Compute the headwind component on Figure 17:

   STEP 1:
   Determine the angle of the wind to the runway.

   NOTE Assume that wind direction is magnetic when landing.

   STEP 2:
   Find the angle on the graph and draw a line toward zero.

   STEP 3:
   Accurately plot the wind speed on the left edge vertical line. Draw an arc from this point until it intersects the wind angle line.

   STEP 4:
   Draw a horizontal line to the left edge and read headwind component. Draw a vertical line to the bottom edge and read crosswind component.

   GROUND ROLL INTERPOLATION:

	PA	Ground Roll
	1,000	450
4,600 lbs.	1,500	455
	2,000	460

   HEADWIND COMPONENT:

   RWY 36 = 360' or 0°
   WIND = 030°
   ANGLE = 30°
   HEADWIND = 20 KTS

3. Note #3 applies. Divide the headwind by 4 KTS:

$$20 \div 4 = 5$$

   Multiply 5 by 3%:

$$5 \times 3\% = 15\%$$

Multiply the calm wind ground roll by 15%:

$$455' \times .15 = 68.25 \ (68)$$

Now subtract the result from the ground run (this is a headwind):

$$455 - 68 = 387'$$

This is the ground run with a 20-KT headwind.

7286. (X) FAA Deletion.

7287. (X) FAA Deletion.

7288. (X) FAA Deletion.

7289. (4) C-310 Manual. See Explanation #7285. Interpolate the aircraft weight to find that it is halfway between 4,600 lbs. and 4,200 lbs.:

Also interpolate the distances for total to clear 50-foot obstacle figures:

Total to Clear 50-Foot Obstacle

4,600 lbs.	1,710
4,400 lbs.	1,660
4,200 lbs.	1,610

Find headwind component. Calm wind has zero headwind. Note #2 applies. Multiply total to clear 50-foot obstacle figure by 35%:

$$.35 \times 1,660 = 581$$

Add this to the obstacle figure:

$$1,660 + 581 = 2,241$$

7290. (3) C-310 Manual. See Explanation #7285. Interpolate the temperatures.

5°F is halfway between the two temperatures. Interpolate the distances similarly.

$$1,560 + 1,570 = 3,130$$
$$3,130 \div 2 = 1,565$$

	5°F
4,200 lbs.	1,565

Determine headwind component and apply Note #3. Tailwind = 2 KTS. Because this is a tailwind, add 5% of 1,565 to 1,565:

$$1,565 \times .05 = 78.25 \ (78)$$
$$1,565 + 78 = 1,643$$

7291. (4) C-310 Manual. See Explanation #7285. Interpolate the temperature. It is halfway between 20°C and 30°C, so interpolate the total to clear 50-foot obstacle figures the same way.

$$1,910 + 1,930 = 3,840 : 3,840 \div 2 = 1,920$$

Determine headwind component and apply Note #3. This is a direct headwind of 20 KTS. Divide 20 by 4:

$$20 \div 4 = 5$$

Multiply 3% by 5: 3% X 5 = 15%.

Multiply 1,920 by 15% (.15): .15 X 1,920 = 288.

Note #2 also applies. Multiply 1,920 by 35% (.35):

$$1,920 \times .35 = 672$$

Because there is a headwind, subtract Note #3 from Note #2:

$$672 - 288 = 384$$

Now add 384 and 1,920: 1,920 + 384 = 2,340.

What the FAA did to get their answer is this:

$$1,920 - 288 = 1,632$$

Subtract headwind:

$$1,632 \times .35 = 571.2 \ (571)$$

Find no-flap landing increase.

$$571 + 1,632 = 2,203$$

Add Note #2 to landing distance with Note #3.

7292. (3) C-310 Manual. See Explanation #7285. Interpolate the weight to find that 4,800 lbs. is halfway between 5,000 and 4,600. Interpolate the ground roll distance similarly.

	40°C
5,000	660
4,800	605
4,600	550

$$660 + 550 = 1,210$$
$$1,210 \div 2 = 605$$

Determine headwind component and apply Note #3. Because this is a direct crosswind, the headwind component is zero.

No notes apply, so the correct answer is 605 feet.

7293. (X) FAA Deletion.

7294. (X) FAA Deletion.

7295. (X) FAA Deletion.

7296. (2) C-310 Manual.

1. Figure headwind component angle between RWY 26 and wind of 340 @ 23 KTS.

$$340° \text{ (wind)} - 260° \text{ (runway)} = 80°$$

Angle between runway and airplane is 80°. Headwind equals 4 KTS.

2. Temperature is 77°F, which is halfway between 68°F and 86°F. Therefore, all of the calculated distances will also be halfway between those distances in the table.

3. Flap setting in Table 31 is not listed so an assumption will be made that flaps are in the DOWN position, because the answers are too small for a flaps up landing.

4. Note #3 applies. Therefore, subtract 3% from ground roll distance. By interpolation, no wind ground roll is 385'.

$$385 \times .03\% = 11.55'$$

$$385 - 11.5 = 373.5 \text{ w/FLAPS}$$

WITHOUT FLAPS: Answers are too large for choices given.

5. Because distance arrived at is halfway between two choices, take the answer that gives more distance than required. A landing cannot be made on a too-short runway.

7297. (1) AW, AC 00-06A. "The amount of solar energy received by any region of the earth varies with time of day, with seasons, and with latitude. These differences in solar energy create temperature variations. Temperatures also vary with differences in topographical surface and with altitude. These temperature variations create forces that drive the atmosphere in its endless motions."

7298. (4) AC 00-6A, AW. The "decrease of temperature with altitude is defined as lapse rate. The average lapse rate in the troposphere is 2°C per 1,000 feet." According to the winds and temperatures aloft forecast at 9,000 feet, the temperature is negative 10°C (–10°C). Using the average lapse rate of 2°C per 1,000 feet, the temperature change from sea level to 9,000 feet is 18°C. Standard sea level temperature is 15°C. Subtract 18°C (the average lapse rate) from 15°C to get –3°C. Compare this with the winds and temperatures aloft forecast at 9,000 feet. The difference is 7°C.

7299. (4) AC 00-06A, AW. "An inversion often develops near the ground on clear, cool nights when wind is light. The ground radiates and cools much faster than the overlying air. Air in contact with the ground becomes cold while the temperature a few hundred feet above changes very little. Thus, temperature increases with height."

7300. (3) AC 00-06A, AW. "Within the lower few thousand feet of the troposphere, pressure decreases roughly one inch for each 1,000 feet increase in altitude." Since pressure decreases at one inch for each 1,000 feet of altitude increase, then by

subtracting the two altimeter setting we get a difference of .15 inches of mercury. This equals 150 feet of altitude change (.15 X 1,000). When pressure decreases and the true altitude remains the same, the altimeter will show a decrease in altitude. So the altimeter will show 150 feet lower.

7301. (4) AC-00-06A, AW Chap. 3. ". . . as you fly from warm to cold air, your altimeter reads too high — you are lower than your altimeter indicates." Conversely, when flying from standard or lower than standard air temperatures to a warmer temperature the altimeter reads lower than the actual (true) altitude.

7302. (3) AC-00-06A, AW Chap. 3. Standard atmospheric conditions exist when sea level temperature is 59°F and air pressure is 29.92 inches of mercury and standard lapse rates for temperature (2°C per 1000 feet) and pressure (one inch of mercury per 1000 feet) also exist. By definition, pressure altitude equals true altitude for altitude chosen.

EXAMPLE: At sea level, temperature and pressure are standard. At Denver, standard pressure altitude would be 5000 feet. True altitude is also 5000 feet.

If either temperature or pressure are other than standard, then pressure altitude will not equal true altitude. Answer #1 does not consider non-standard pressure. Answer #2 does not consider non-standard temperature. Answer #4, the altimeter only considers air pressure and not both air pressure and temperature.

7303. (1) AC-00-06A, AW. "Pressure, temperature and humidity determine air density. On a hot day, the air becomes 'thinner' or lighter. This is equivalent to a higher altitude in the standard atmosphere — thus the term "high density altitude." On a cold day, the air becomes heavy; its density is the same as that at an altitude in the standard atmosphere lower than your altitude — 'low density altitude'." The only requirement for density altitude to equal a given pressure altitude is standard temperature for that pressure altitude.

7304. (1) AC-00-06A, AW. "Since the altitude scale is adjustable, you can set the altimeter to read true altitude at some specified height. Takeoff and landing are the most critical phases of flight; therefore, airport elevation is the most desirable altitude for a true reading of the altimeter." "Altimeter setting is the value to which the scale of the pressure altimeter is set so the altimeter indicates true altitude at the field elevation."

7305. (2) FAR 91.81, AC-00-06A, AW. "At or above 18,000 feet MSL, the altimeter is set to 29.92" Hg." "You can always determine pressure altitude from your altimeter whether inflight or on the ground. Simply set the altimeter to the standard altimeter setting of 29.92 inches, and the altimeter indicates pressure altitude."

7306. (2) AC-00-06A, AW. "Indicated altitude depends on air temperature below the aircraft. Since pressure is equal at the bases and equal at the tops of each column, indicated altitude is the same at the top of each column. When air is colder than average (right), the altimeter reads higher than true altitude. When air is warmer than standard (left), the altimeter reads lower than true altitude."

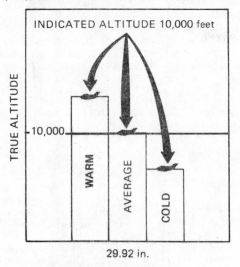

INDICATED ALTITUDES

7307. (3) AC-00-06A, AW. ". . . The pressure gradient force drives the wind and is perpendicular to isobars. When a pressure gradient force is first established, wind begins to blow from higher to lower pressure directly across the isobars. However, the instant air begins moving, Coriolis force deflects it to the right. Soon the wind is deflected a full 90° and is parallel to the isobars or contours. At this time, Coriolis force exactly balances pressure gradient force."

7308. (3) AC-00-06A, AW Chap. 4. ". . . Pressure gradient force drives the wind and is perpendicular to isobars. When a pressure gradient force is first established, wind begins to blow from higher to lower pressure directly across the isobars. However, the instant air begins moving, Coriolis force deflects it to the right. Soon the wind is deflected a full 90° and is parallel to the isobars or contours. At this time, Coriolis force exactly balances pressure gradient force."

"As frictional force slows the wind speed, Coriolis force decreases. However, friction does not affect pressure gradient force. Pressure gradient and Coriolis forces are no longer in balance. The stronger pressure gradient force turns the wind at an angle across the isobars toward lower pressure until the three forces are in balance."

7309. (2) AC-00-06A, AW Chap. 4. Friction between the wind and the terrain surface slows the wind. The rougher the terrain, the greater is the frictional effect. Also, the stronger the wind speed, the greater is the friction.

As frictional force slows the windspeed, Coriolis force decreases. However, friction does not affect pressure gradient force. Pressure gradient and Coriolis forces are no longer in balance. The stronger pressure gradient force turns the wind at an angle across the isobars toward lower pressure until the three forces balance.

Frictional and Coriolis forces combine to just balance pressure gradient force.

The angle of surface wind to isobars is about 10° over water, increasing with roughness of terrain.

7310. (2) AC-00-06A, AW. Friction between the wind and the terrain surface slows the wind. The rougher the terrain, the greater is the frictional effect.

As frictional force slows the windspeed, Coriolis force decreases. However, friction does not affect pressure gradient force. Pressure gradient and Coriolis forces are no longer in balance. The stronger pressure gradient force turns the wind at an angle across the isobars toward lower pressure until the three forces balance.

Frictional and Coriolis forces combine to just balance pressure gradient force.

The angle of surface wind to isobars is about 10° over water, increasing with roughness of terrain.

7311. (1) AC-00-06A, AW Chap. 5. Water vapor is always present in air. There are three states in which water may exist: solid, liquid or gaseous. Water vapor is the gaseous or invisible state. Clouds, fog and dew are visible forms of water in the liquid state. In order for any of these three types of visible water to occur, water vapor must condense from the gaseous state.

Answer #2 is incorrect because water vapor is present even on clear cloudless days.

Answer #3 is incorrect because ". . . some condensation nuclei have an affinity for water and can induce condensation . . . even when air is almost but not completely saturated."

Answer #4 is incorrect for the same reason as #3 above. When temperature and dewpoint are equal, 100% humidity exists.

7312. (2) AC-00-06A, AW Chap. 5. Temperature largely determines the maximum amount of water vapor air can hold. Warm air can hold more water vapor than cool air.

If a given volume of air is cooled to some specific temperature, it can hold no more water vapor than is actually present, relative humidity becomes 100%, and saturation occurs.

7313. (1) AC-00-06A, AW Chap. 5. Wet snow at your altitude means that the temperature at your altitude is above freezing because the snow has begun to melt.

For snow to form, water vapor must go from the vapor state to the solid state (known as sublimation) with the temperature below freezing.

Since melting snow has been encountered, the freezing level must be at a higher altitude.

7314. (1) AC-00-06A, AW Chap. 5. Dewpoint is the temperature to which air must be cooled to become saturated by the water vapor already present in the air. Aviation weather reports normally include the air temperature and dewpoint temperature. Dewpoint when related to air temperature reveals qualitatively how close the air is to saturation.

7315. (3) AC-00-06A, AW Chap. 5. Frost forms in much the same way as dew. The difference is that the dewpoint of surrounding air must be colder than freezing. Water vapor then sublimates directly as ice crystals or frost rather than condensing as dew. Sometimes dew forms and later freezes; however, frozen dew is easily distinguished from frost. Frozen dew is hard and transparent while frost is white and opaque.

7316. (3) AW Chap. 5. "Rain falling through colder air may become supercooled, freezing on impact as freezing rain; or it may freeze during its descent, falling as ice pellets. Ice pellets always indicate freezing rain at higher altitude."

7317. (2) AW Chap. 5. "Rain falling through colder air may become supercooled, freezing on impact as freezing rain; or it may freeze during its descent, falling as ice pellets. Ice pellets always indicate freezing rain at higher altitude."

7318. (3) AW Chap. 6. If a sample of air is forced upward into the atmosphere, there are two possibilities:

(1) The air may become colder than the surrounding air, or
(2) Even though it cools, the air may remain warmer than the surrounding air.

If the upward moving air becomes colder than surrounding air, it sinks; but if it remains warmer, it is accelerated upward as a convective current. Whether it sinks or rises depends on the ambient or existing temperature lapse rate.

Do not confuse existing lapse rate with adiabatic rates of cooling in the vertically moving air. The difference between the existing lapse rate of a given mass of air and the adiabatic rates of cooling in upward moving air determines if the air is stable or unstable.

7319. (2) AW Chap. 6. Cumuliform cloud base heights can be estimated using surface temperature — dewpoint spread. Unsaturated air in a convective current cools at about 5.4°F (3.0°C) per 1000 feet; dewpoint decreases at about 1°F (5/9°C). Thus, in a convective current, temperature and dewpoint converge at about 4.4°F (2.5°C) per 1000 feet. We can estimate the height of a convective cloud base in thousands of feet by dividing 4.4 into the dewpoint spread.

EXAMPLE:

$$\begin{array}{rl} 82° & \text{Temperature} \\ -55° & \text{Dewpoint} \\ \hline 27° & \text{Dewpoint spread} \end{array}$$

$$27 \div 4.4 = 6.136$$

$$6.136 \times 1000 = 6136 \text{ feet}$$

"This method of estimating is reliable only with unstable type clouds and during the warmer part of the day."

7320. (1) AW Chap. 2. An inversion is defined as "an increase in temperature with altitude." That is, the lapse rate is inverted. Instead of the temperature decreasing with altitude it increases. When warm air overlies cold air it is said to be stable. It is this condition which produces an inversion.

7321. (1) AW Chap. 6. "Unsaturated air moving upward and downward cools and warms at about 3.0°C (5.4°F) per 1000 feet."

7322. (4) AW Chap. 6. "Unstable air favors convection. A 'cumulus' cloud . . . forms in a convective updraft and builds upward."

Initial lifting to trigger a cumuliform cloud can be either orographic (topographical, i.e. mountains) or by surface heating.

For convective cumuliform clouds to develop, the air must be unstable after saturation.

7323. (3) AW Chap. 6. "Whether the air is stable or unstable within a layer largely determines cloud structure." Stratiform clouds (stable conditions) and cumuliform clouds (unstable conditions) can both be forced to ascend by the same factors. Answer #1 therefore does not address the question.

Answer #2 addresses whether or not clouds would form due to sufficient moisture being present and not to the types of clouds that would be seen.

Answer #4, again, does not address the types of clouds that form, but whether clouds would form at all.

7324. (2) AW Chap. 6. If a sample of air is forced upward into the atmosphere, there are two possibilities:
(1) The air may become colder than the surrounding air, or
(2) Even though it cools, the air may remain warmer than the surrounding air.

If the upward moving air becomes colder than surrounding air, it sinks; but if it remains warmer, it is accelerated upward as a convective current. Whether it sinks or rises depends on the ambient or existing temperature lapse rate.

Do not confuse existing lapse rate with adiabatic rates of cooling in vertically moving air. The difference between the existing lapse rate of a given mass of air and the adiabatic rates of cooling in upward moving air determines if the air is stable or unstable.

7325. (4) AW Chaps. 6,7. Unstable air characteristically mixes the pollutants in the air so that they do not have opportunity to settle down to the lower layers. This results in good visibility. This same mixing, however, also causes turbulence. Also see explanation #7331

7326. (1) AW Chaps. 2,6. A stable layer of air is characterized by warmer air lying above colder air. By definition an inversion is characterized by an inverted lapse rate. That is, the temperature gets warmer with altitude.

7327. (4) AW Chaps. 6,7. "Stratiform clouds indicate stable air. Flight generally will be smooth, but low ceiling and visibility might require IFR." Also see explanation #7331.

7328. (1) AW Chap. 6. "Since stable air resists convection, either from heating or orographic, clouds in stable air form in horizontal layers called stratus type clouds.

7329. (4) AW Chap. 6. When stable air (left) is forced upward, the air tends to retain horizontal flow, and any cloudiness is flat and stratified. When unstable air is forced upward, the disturbance grows, and any resulting cloudiness shows extensive vertical development.

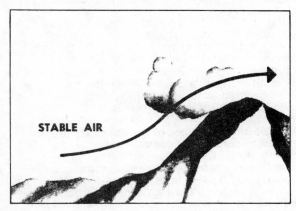

STABLE AIR

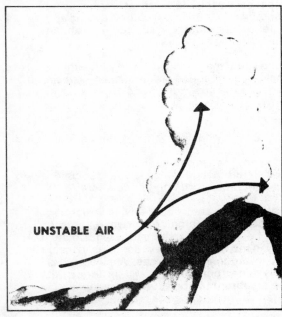

UNSTABLE AIR

7330. (2) AW Chaps. 6,7. "Since stable air resists convection, clouds in stable air form in horizontal, sheet-like layers or "strata." Thus, within a stable layer, clouds are stratiform."

7331. (1) AW Chaps. 6,7. Stability of air mass determines its typical weather characteristics. When one type of air mass overlies another, conditions change with height. Characteristics typical of an unstable and a stable air mass are as follows:

Unstable Air	Stable Air
Cumuliform clouds	Stratiform clouds and fog
Showery precipitation	Continuous precipitation
Rough air (turbulence)	Smooth air
Good visibility, except in blowing obstructions	Fair to poor visibility in haze and smoke

7332. (4) AW Chap. 6. When stable air is forced upward, the air tends to retain horizontal flow, and any cloudiness is flat and stratified. When unstable air is forced upward, the disturbance grows, and any resulting cloudiness shows extensive vertical development. See Explanation #7329.

7333. (4) AW Chap. 7. For identification purposes, cloud types are divided into four "families." The families are: high clouds, middle clouds, low clouds, and clouds with extensive vertical development.

7334. (3) AW Chaps. 7,10. "The high cloud family is cirriform and includes cirrus, cirrocumulus and cirrostratus. They are composed almost entirely of ice crystals."

"Two conditions are necessary for structural icing in flight:

(1) The aircraft must be flying through visible water such as rain or cloud droplets, and
(2) The temperature at the point where the moisture strikes the aircraft must be 0°C or colder."

As stated above, the high cloud family is composed almost entirely of ice crystals.

Because ice crystals are already frozen, they most likely won't stick to an aircraft.

7335. (2) AW Chaps. 7,9. Standing lenticular altocumulus clouds are formed on the crests of waves created by barriers to the wind flow. The clouds show little movement, hence the name STANDING. Wind, however, can be quite strong blowing through such clouds. They are characterized by their smooth, polished edges. The presence of these clouds is a good indication of very strong turbulence and should be avoided.

7336. (2) AW Chap. 7. " . . . The prefix NIMBO or the suffix NIMBUS means raincloud. Thus, stratified clouds from which rain is falling are NIMBO-STRATUS. A heavy, swelling cumulus type cloud which produces precipitation is a CUMULO-NIMBUS."

7337. (3) AW Chaps. 7,9. Standing lenticular altocumulus clouds are formed on the crests of waves created by barriers to the wind flow. The clouds show little movement, hence the name STANDING. Wind, however, can be quite strong blowing through such clouds. They are characterized by their smooth, polished edges. The presence of these clouds is a good indication of very strong turbulence and should be avoided. Always anticipate possible mountain wave turbulence when strong winds of 40 knots or greater blow across a mountain or ridge and the air is stable.

"Standing lenticular . . . clouds suggest a mountain wave; expect turbulence many miles to the lee of mountains and relative smooth flight on the windward side." See also Explanation #7336.

7338. (2) AW Chap. 9. "When convection extends to great heights, it develops large towering cumulus clouds and cumulonimbus with anvil-like tops. The cumulonimbus gives visual warning of violent convective turbulence." Answers #1 and #3 would also have turbulence but not downdrafts. Therefore, greater turbulence would be encountered in a cumulonimbus.

7339. (2) AW Chap. 8. Cool air moving over a warm surface is heated from below, generating instability and increasing the possibility of showers.

Stability of an air mass determines its typical weather characteristics. When one type of air mass overlies another, conditions change with height. Characteristics typical of an unstable and a stable air mass are as follows:

Unstable Air	Stable Air
Cumuliform clouds	Stratiform clouds and fog
Showery precipitation	Continuous precipitation
Rough air (turbulence)	Smooth air
Good visibility, except in blowing obstructions	Fair to poor visibility in haze and smoke

7340. (1) AW Chap. 8. "Frontal waves and cyclones (areas of low pressure) usually form on slow-moving cold fronts or stationary fronts."

7341. (1) AW Chap. 8. "Wind always changes across a front. Wind discontinuity may be in direction, in speed or in both."

Answer #2 is incorrect because pressure will abruptly increase when flying into colder air. When flying into warmer air, pressure will gradually decrease and then remain steady or decrease further.

Answer #3 is incorrect because there may be insufficient moisture to produce clouds.

Answer #4 is incorrect because temperature may increase when the front passes.

7342. (2) AC-00-50A. Wind shear occurs with a cold front just after the front passes the airport and for a short period thereafter. If the front is moving 30 knots or more, the frontal surface will usually be 5,000 feet above the airport about three hours after the frontal passage.

With a warm front, the most critical period is before the front passes the airport. Warm front shear may exist below 5,000 feet for approximately six hours. The problem ceases to exist after the front passes the airport. Data compiled on wind shear indicates that the amount of shear in warm fronts is much greater than that found in cold fronts.

7343. (4) AW, AC-00-50A. Wind shear may develop at any altitude if the conditions are right. Low level wind shear may result from a frontal passage. Thunderstorm activity or low level temperature inversion.

Wind shear may also be found at higher altitudes in association with a frontal passage due to wind shift through the frontal zone. "Wind changes abruptly in the frontal zone and can induce wind shear turbulence." "An inversion aloft will develop when conditions are favorable. For example, a current of warm air aloft overrunning cold air near the surface produces an inversion aloft."

7344. (4) AW, AC-00-50A. The "strongest turbulence within the cloud occurs with shear between updrafts and downdrafts. Outside the cloud, shear turbulence has been encountered several thousand feet above and 20 miles laterally from a severe storm. A low level turbulent area is the shear zone between the plow wind (the sudden rush of air that preceeds the thunderstorm at low level) and surrounding air. The first gust causes a rapid and sometimes drastic change in surface wind ahead of an approaching storm."

7345. (4) AW. "Wind shear may be associated with either a wind shift or a wind speed gradient at any level in the atmosphere. Three conditions are of special interest:

(1) Wind shear with a low level temperature inversion,
(2) Wind shear in a frontal zone, and
(3) Clear air turbulence at high levels associated with a jetstream or strong circulation."

As is stated in the above quote, wind shear can and does occur at any altitude. Answer #1 can be ruled out because wind shear does not occur "primarily in the lower altitude," nor does it occur primarily in mountainous areas. Answer #2 is obviously incorrect. Answer #3 is incorrect because an abrupt temperature decrease is not associated with a shear zone.

7346. (4) AW. "In stratiform clouds, you can likely alleviate icing by changing to a flight level with above-freezing temperatures or to one colder than −10°C. An altitude change also may take you out of clouds."

Answer #2 would be correct if the question had been referring to cumulus type clouds.

Answers #1 and #3 do not apply.

7347. (2) AW. "Rain falling through colder air may become supercooled, freezing on impact as freezing rain; or it may freeze during its descent, falling as ice pellets. Ice pellets always indicate freezing rain at a higher altitude."

As the rain falls through air that is below freezing its temperature begins to fall below freezing yet without freezing solid. This is freezing rain. The process requires that the temperature of the rain must be above freezing before it becomes supercooled. Therefore, when freezing rain is encountered it indicates that warmer temperatures are above.

7348. (4) AW. "A condition favorable for rapid accumulation of clear ice is freezing rain below a frontal surface. It may occur with either a warm front or a cold front. The icing can be critical because of the large amount of supercooled water."

Clear ice can be found in cumulonimbus clouds, sometimes with high rates of accumulation. However, the water droplets are still in suspension and so are not as large as freezing rain that is already falling.

7349. (4) AW. "Frost does not change the basic aerodynamic shape of the wing, but the roughness of its surface spoils the smooth flow of air, thus causing a slowing of the airflow. This slowing of the air causes early air flow separation over the affected airfoil, resulting in a loss of lift."

7350. (2) AW, AWS. Answer #1 is incorrect by definition:

LIGHT ICING

The rate of accumulation may create a problem if flight is prolonged in this environment (over one hour). OCCASIONAL use of deicing/anti-icing equipment removes/prevents accumulation. It does not present a problem if the deicing/anti-icing equipment is used."

The definition says that occasional use of the deicing equipment is sufficient for a light accumulation.

Answer #3 is incorrect because anti-icing is "the protection of aircraft against icing by PREVENTING ice formation (e.g., by continuous heating)."

De-icing, on the other hand, is "the protection of aircraft against icing by allowing ice to build up and causing it to be removed by mechanical, chemical or thermal means."

Answer #4 is incorrect because what is recommended to be done is the opposite of what should be done to reduce ice accumulation.

7351. (3) AW. "Tornadoes occur with isolated thunderstorms at times, but much more frequently, they form with steady state thunderstorms associated with cold fronts or squall lines."

7352. (4) AW. "For a thunderstorm to form, the air must have:
(1) Sufficient water vapor,
(2) An unstable lapse rate, and
(3) An initial upward boost (lifting) to start the storm process in motion."

Answer #1 is only partially correct, an unstable lapse rate is also needed.

Answers #2 and #3 both have "cumulus cloud." The cumulus cloud is not one of the three necessary elements. Sufficient moisture is correct. An inverted lapse rate does not apply to thunderstorm formation.

7353. (2) AW. "Precipitation beginning to fall from the cloud base is an indication that a downdraft has developed and a cell has entered the mature stage."

Answer #1: The anvil top will complete its development at the end of the mature stage.

Answer #3: The gust front is the result of the downdrafts but may not be visible.

Also, the gust front is not as early an indication as falling precipitation because the gust front forms as a result of the precipitation and downdrafts.

7354. (3) AW. Following are some Do's and Don'ts DURING thunderstorm penetration:
(1) Do keep your eyes on your instruments. Looking outside the cockpit can increase the danger of temporary blindness from lightning.
(2) Don't change power settings; maintain settings for reduced airspeed.
(3) Do maintain a constant ATTITUDE; let the aircraft "ride the waves." Maneuvers in trying to maintain constant altitude increase stresses on the aircraft.
(4) Don't turn back once you are in the thunderstorm. A straight course through the storm most likely will get you out of the hazards most quickly. In addition, turning maneuvers increase stresses on the aircraft.

7355. (2) AW. A SQUALL LINE is a non-frontal, narrow band of active thunderstorms. Often it develops ahead of a cold front in moist, unstable air, but it may develop in unstable air far removed from any front. The line may be too long to easily detour and too wide and severe to penetrate. It often contains severe steady-state thunderstorms and presents the single most intense weather hazard to aircraft. It usually forms rapidly, generally reaching maximum intensity during the late afternoon and the first few hours of darkness.

7356. (1) AC 00-24B. A thunderstorm is always accompanied by lightning and thunder.

7357. (2) AW. The key feature of the cumulus stage is the updraft. The key feature of the mature stage is precipitation beginning to fall from the cloud base. Downdrafts characterize the dissipating stage.

7358. (4) AW. "For a thunderstorm to form, the air must have:
(1) Sufficient water vapor,
(2) An unstable lapse rate, and
(3) An initial upward lifting to start the storm process in motion."

7359. (4) AW. Usually, thunderstorms are quite visible to the pilot. However, when a thunderstorm is present but not visible to the pilot due to other clouds, such as a thick stratus layer, the thunderstorm is said to be "embedded."

7360. (3) AW, AWS. When flying in severe turbulence, maintaining positive aircraft control may be nearly impossible to do. Severe turbulence is defined as, "Turbulence that causes large, abrupt changes in altitude and/or attitude. It usually causes large variations in indicated airspeed. Aircraft may be momentarily out of control."

In attempting to maintain a constant altitude, the stresses applies to the aircraft are greatly increased." Stresses will be least if the aircraft is held in a constant ATTITUDE and allowed to "ride the waves."

Wide fluctuations in airspeed will probably have to be tolerated in order to reduce aircraft stresses.

7361. (4) AW. When flight into a thunderstorm is imminent, disengage the altitude hold mode on the autopilot. The altitude hold mode will increase maneuvers of the aircraft thus increasing structural stresses.

Although Answer #3 has everything Answer #4 has, the FAA says nothing about deicing or anti-icing equipment during thunderstorm penetration. This equipment will be used during icing conditions whether or not an aircraft is in a thunderstorm.

7362. (2) AW. Answer #2 is the most complete.

Answer #1 and #4 contains items that should not be done while in a thunderstorm. Answer #1 says to maintain altitude and Answer #4 says to turn 180° as soon a possible. Both maneuvers create greater stresses on the aircraft than there would otherwise be. Wide fluctuations of airspeed are the norm while flying in thunderstorms. Set the power to a safe setting and leave it. Trying to maintain a constant airspeed only puts greater stresses on the aircraft.

7363. (2) AW. The greatest hazard from lightning is temporary blindness rendering the pilot momentarily unable to navigate either by instrument or by visual reference. "Lightning has been suspected of igniting fuel vapors causing explosion; however serious accidents due to lightning strikes are extremely rare."

7364. (1) AW. Answer #1 is a quote from "Aviation Weather."

Answer #2 would be correct for radiation fog.

Answers #3 and #4 are conditions which would not cause advection fog to form because this fog requires a moist air mass to move over a colder surface.

7365. (2) AW. Radiation fog is restricted to land because water surfaces cool little from nighttime radiation.

Advection fog forms when moist air moves over colder ground or water. It is most common along coastal areas but often develops deep in continental areas. At sea it is called "sea fog." Advection fog deepens as wind speed increases up to about 15 knots. Wind much stronger than 15 knots lifts the fog into a layer of low stratus or stratocumulus.

Steam fog, often called "sea smoke," forms in winter when cold, dry air passes from land areas over comparatively warm ocean waters. Moisture evaporates rapidly from the water surface; but since the cold air can hold only a small amount of water vapor, condensation takes place just above the surface of the water and appears as "steam" rising from the ocean. This fog is composed entirely of water droplets that often freeze quickly and fall back into the water as ice particles. Low level turbulence can occur and icing can become hazardous.

7366. (4) AW. Conditions favorable for radiation fog are clear sky, little or no wind, and small temperature-dewpoint spread (high relative humidity). The fog forms almost exclusively at night or near daybreak. Terrestrial radiation cools the ground; in turn, the cool ground cools the air in contact with it. When the air is cooled to its dewpoint, fog forms.

Answer #1 describes precipitation fog.

Answer #2 describes advection fog.

Answer #3 does not describe conditions favorable for fog formation.

7367. (1) AW. Conditions favorable for radiation fog are clear sky, little or no wind, and small temperature-dewpoint spread (high relative humidity). The fog forms almost exclusively at night or near daybreak. Terrestrial radiation cools the ground; in turn, the cool ground cools the air in contact with it. When the air is cooled to its dewpoint, fog forms.

7368. (4) AW. "Advection fog forms when moist air moves over colder ground or water." Upslope fog forms as a result of moist, stable air being cooled adiabatically as it moves up sloping terrain. Once the upslope wind ceases, the fog dissipates.

7369. (1) AW. Advection fog "is most common along coastal areas but often develops deep in continental areas."

7370. (2) AW. During the winter, advection fog over the central and eastern United States results when moist air from the Gulf of Mexico spreads northward over cold ground. The fog may extend as far north as the Great Lakes.

Answer #1 describes upslope fog.

Answer #3 describes steam fog.

Answer #4 does not describe a fog condition.

7371. (2) AW. Abundant condensation nuclei enhance the formation of fog. Thus, fog is prevalent in industrial areas where byproducts of combustion provide a high concentration of these nuclei.

7372. (4) AW. Fog may form (1) by cooling air to its dewpoint, or (2) by adding moisture to air near the ground. The colder surface cools the moist air to its dewpoint. At this point, fog begins to form.

7373. (2) AW. In midlatitudes, wind speed in the jetstream averages considerably stronger in winter than in summer. Also the jet shifts farther south in winter than in summer.

7374. (1) AC 00-45B, AWS. "A hatched area indicates severe thunderstorms . . ."

7375. (4) AC 00-45B. "When obscuring phenomena is surface based and partially obscures the sky, a remark reports tenths of sky hidden. For example, K6 which means 6/10 of the sky is hidden by smoke." Now go back and look at BOI. Note the remark RF2 which means 2/10 of the sky is hidden by rain and fog. The rest of the remark, "RB12," is translated thus, "R" refers to rain; the "B" refers to began and "12" refers to the number of minutes after the previous hour (relative to the time of the present observation) that the rain was observed to have begun to fall.

7376. (3) AC 00-45B. The remarks section will state how much of the sky is being obscured by partial obstruction of vision. The notation "F2" in the remarks section means fog is obscuring 2/10 of the sky. See also Explanation #7375.

7377. (1) AWS, AC 00-45B. Pilot reports of cloud base precedes the sky cover symbol, and top follows the symbol. For example,

38 BKN 70

means base of a broken layer at 3,800 feet and top 7,000 feet (all MSL).

After decoding the top of the pilot reported overcast (6,500 feet MSL), it is important to remember that ceilings are reported as height ABOVE GROUND LEVEL. To find the base of the overcast in MSL, add the station altitude to the base of the overcast.

        Station Altitude. . . . . 1,000 MSL
        Base of Overcast. . . . . +700 AGL
        Base of Overcast. . . . . 1,750 MSL

The pilot reported cloud tops at 6,500 feet MSL, as read off of his altimeter. To find how thick the overcast is, subtract the base of the overcast (in MSL) from the top of the overcast.

        6,500   Top
        −1,700 Base
        4,800   Thickness of Overcast

7378. (4) AC 00-45B. Ceiling is defined as:
  (1) Height of the lowest layer of clouds or obscuring phenomena aloft that is reported as broken or overcast and not classified as thin, or
  (2) Vertical visibility into a surface-based obscuring phenomena that hides all the sky.

7379. (4) AC 61-23B, PHAK. Scheduled Terminal Forecasts are issued three times daily by WSFOs, and are valid for a total validity period of 24 hours. This validity period includes expected weather for the following 18 hours with an additional 6-hour categorical outlook.

7380. (1) AC 00-45B, AWS, Appendix.

Turbulence Reporting Criteria

INTEN-SITY	AIRCRAFT REACTION	REACTION INSIDE AIRCRAFT	REPORTING TERM DEFINITION
LIGHT	Turbulence that momentarily causes slight, erratic changes in altitude and/or attitude (pitch, roll, yaw). Report as LIGHT TURBULENCE;* OR Turbulence that causes slight, rapid and somewhat rhythmic bumpiness without appreciable changes in altitude or attitude. Report as LIGHT CHOP.	Occupants may feel a slight strain against seat belts or shoulder straps. Unsecured objects may be displaced slightly. Food service may be conducted and little or no difficulty is encountered in walking.	Occasional—Less than 1/3 of the time. Intermittent—1/3 to 2/3. Continuous—More than 2/3.

7381. (3) AC 00-45B. "The surface analysis chart provides a ready means of locating pressure systems and fronts and also gives an overview of winds, temperatures and dewpoints AS OF MAP TIME." The chart also shows weather and obstruction to vision symbols. It does not show cloud heights or tops or the expected movement of any item depicted. Expected movement would be contained in a forecast.

7382. (4) AC 00-45B, IFR EOG #15. "Cloud height is entered under the station circle in hundreds of feet — the same as coded in a surface aviation weather report (SA). If total sky cover is few or scattered, the height is the base of the lowest layer."

The symbol ◐ means sky coverage is from 1/10 to 5/10 inclusive and is read "scattered." Visibility is not reported unless it is less than 7 miles. When it is reported, it will be put on the left side of the sky coverage symbol.

7383. (3) AC 00-45B, IFR EOG #15, Chart Legends. The frontal-area in Illinois is characterized by the symbols ℞ thunderstorms, ● intermittent rain slight at time of observation, ●● continuous rain slight at time of observation, ●•● continuous rain moderate at time of observation. The symbols in the other states indicate no rain, or rain of lesser intensities.

TOTAL SKY COVER

- ◯ Clear
- ◔ Scattered
- ◕ Broken, or thin broken
- ◑ Overcast, with breaks
- ● Overcast
- ⊗ Obscured

OTHER

- ⬧ Clouds Topping Ridges

WEATHER AND OBSTRUCTIONS TO VISION

- △ – Hail
- ℞ – Thunderstorm
- •• – Rain
- ✳ – Snow
- ● – Drizzle
- ∞ – Haze
- ☰ – Fog
- ∿ – Smoke
- ⌒ – Freezing Rain
- ⌒ – Freezing Drizzle
- ▽ – Rain Shower
- ▽ – Snow Shower
- △ – Ice Pellets
- ⌖ – Blowing Dust
- ⌖ – Blowing Sand
- ⌖ – Blowing Snow

Figures below the circle are cloud heights in hundreds of feet--either the ceiling; or, if there is no ceiling, the height of the lowest scattered.
Figures and symbols to left of circle are visibility and weather or obstructions to vision.

WEATHER CHART SYMBOLS

450 — Highest precipitation tops in area in hundreds of feet.

LEVEL	ECHO INTENSITY	PRECIPITATION INTENSITY	POSSIBLE TURBULENCE	WIND GUSTS	HAIL	LIGHTNING
1	WEAK	LIGHT	LGT/MDT			
2	MODERATE	MODERATE	LGT/MDT			
3	STRONG	HEAVY	SEVERE			
4	VERY STRONG	VERY HEAVY	SEVERE	POSSIBLE	POSSIBLE	YES
5	INTENSE	INTENSE	SEVERE	ORGANIZED	LIKELY	YES
6	EXTREME	EXTREME	SEVERE	EXTENSIVE	LARGE	YES

* The numbers representing the intensity level do not appear on the chart. Beginning from the first contour line, bordering the area, the intensity level is 1-2; second contour is 3-4; and third contour is 5-6.

— SYMBOLS USED ON CHART —

SYMBOL	MEANING
R	RAIN
RW	RAIN SHOWERS
A	HAIL
S	SNOW
IP	ICE PELLETS
SW	SNOW SHOWERS
L	DRIZZLE
T	THUNDERSTORM
ZR, ZL	FREEZING PRECIPITATION
NE	NO ECHOES OBSERVED
NA	OBSERVATIONS UNAVAILABLE
OM	OUT FOR MAINTENANCE
STC	STC ON -- all precipitation may not be seen

SYMBOL	MEANING
+	INTENSITY INCREASING OR NEW ECHO
-	INTENSITY DECREASING
NO SYMBOL	NO CHANGE
35 ↗	CELL MOVEMENT TO NE AT 35 KNOTS
↘	LINE OR AREA MOVEMENT TO EAST AT 20 KNOTS
MA	ECHOES MOSTLY ALOFT
PA	ECHOES PARTLY ALOFT

SYMBOL	MEANING
▬	LINE OF ECHOES
SLD	OVER 9/10 COVERAGE IN A LINE
WS999	THUNDERSTORM WATCH
WT999	TORNADO WATCH
LEWP	LINE ECHO WAVE PATTERN

KEY TO RADAR SUMMARY CHART

7384. (3) AC 00-45B, IFR EOG #15, Chart Legends. The legend to Figure 18 says that shaded areas indicate IFR with ceilings less than 1,000 feet and/or visibilities less than 3 miles. The solid black sky coverage symbols indicate overcast skies. The symbol "●●" means continuous rain slight at time of observation, ▽ means slight rain showers. The number to the left of the sky coverage symbol is visibility; the number underneath is cloud height or ceiling AGL.

7385. (4) AC 00-45B, IFR EOG #17, Chart Legend. The Radar Chart Legend contained in Appendix 2 of the question book is only partially valid for the new computer generated charts. At left is a reproduction of the correct chart legend.

Memorize the "echo intensity" levels (weak, Level 1; to extreme, Level 6). Also read the radar chart legend contained on the map.

Area "A" indicates an intensity level of 3 to 4, strong to very strong. Echo tops for a single cell is indicated by " 300".

The height is abbreviated just as in surface weather reports. Thunderstorms and rain showers are indicated by "TRW."

7386. (X) FAA Deletion.

7387. (3) AC 00-45B, IFR EOG #17. See Explanation #7385. Area movement is shown by \⟶, an arrow with speed "feathers" or "pennants." A whole feather is 10 KTS and half a feather is 5 KTS. Two whole feathers is 20 KTS. The arrow points the direction the area is moving. Echo intensity is 3 to 4, strong to very strong. Echo tops are 28,000 feet. See the example of cell tops in problem #7385.

7388. (3) AC 00-45B, IFR EOG #17. See Explanation #7385. Individual cell movement is shown by an arrow pointing in the direction of travel and a number showing cell speed 50. The smallest contour shows intensity level 5 to 6, intense to extreme. Tops of cells are 29,000 feet.

7389. (1) AC 00-45B, IFR EOG #17. See Explanation #7385. Storm intensity that is increasing will have a "+" after the weather symbol, i.e., "TRW+." Storm intensity that is decreasing will show a "–", i.e., "TRW–." Storm intensity that is not changing will show just the weather symbol, i.e., "TRW."

7390. (2) AC 00-45B. The solid black line means "line of echoes." If they were solid, there would be the symbol " SLD " WHICH MEANS "over 9/10 coverage in a line." Echo intensity is never described as "severe." Severe, in reference to this chart, refers to turbulence. "TRW" means thunderstorms and rain showers. Highest echo tops are listed as 460/ which is 46,000 feet (southwest of the line of thunderstorms). The only movement in the area indicated is of single cells

as evidenced by the numbers near the arrow heads.

7391. (1) AC 00-45B, Map Legend. The map legend shows that tops are shown 999 and bases are shown 999. This is a misprint. They should show tops — 999 and bases — 999. In area "G" the bases are 100 or 10,000 feet. There is a single cell moving northeasterly at 15 KTS ⟋15 and echo intensity in the area is level 1 to 2, weak to moderate. Rain is also in the area as evidenced by the "R" under the cloud bases figure.

7392. (2) AC 00-45B. The radar summary chart aids in preflight planning by identifying general areas and movement of precipitation and/or thunderstorms. Radar detects only drops or ice particles of precipitation size; it does not detect clouds and fog. Therefore, the absence of echoes does not guarantee clear weather. Furthermore, cloud tops may be higher than precipitation tops detected by radar. The chart must be used in conjunction with other charts, reports and forecasts.

The weather depiction chart shows general weather conditions more readily than from any other source. It gives a "bird's eye" view at map time of areas of favorable and adverse weather and pictures frontal and pressure systems associated with the weather.

7393. (1) AC 00-45B. The radar summary chart does not show cloud cover. Radar can only detect moisture that is of precipitation size. Furthermore, cloud tops may be higher than precipitation tops detected by radar. Radar does show lines of thunderstorms and thunderstorm cells, all of which are hazardous.

7394. (3) AC 00-45B. From the charts you can approximate the observed temperature, wind, and temperature-dewpoint spread along your proposed route. Usually you can select a constant pressure chart close to your planned altitude. For altitudes about midway between two charted surfaces, interpolate between the two charts.

"To readily delineate areas of high moisture content, station circles are shaded indicating temperature-dewpoint spreads of 5°C or less." "Wind direction parallels the contours."

7395. (X) FAA Deletion.

7396. (2) AC 00-45B. "Absence of a visibility entry specifically implies visibility more than 6 miles." "Omission of a wind entry specifically implies wind less than 10 knots." This applies to the first 18 hours of the forecast. The last 6 hours are the categorical outlook portion.

7397. (2) AC 00-45B. "Absence of a visibility entry specifically implies visibility more than 6 miles."

7398. (1) AC 00-45B. In the U.S., the body of the FT is for an area within a 5-mile radius of the runway complex while the remarks section is for a 10-mile radius.

7399. (3) AC 00-45B. "Omission of a wind entry specifically implies wind less than 10 KTS."

7400. (4) AC 00-45B. 6-HOUR CATEGORICAL OUTLOOK. The last 6 hours of the forecast is a categorical outlook. "04Z VFR WIND . ." means that from 0400Z until 1000Z — the end of the forecast period — weather will be ceiling more than 3,000 and visibility greater than 5 (VFR); wind will be 25 knots or stronger. The double period (. .) signifies the end of the forecast for the specific terminal.

7401. (3) AC 00-45B. "Absence of a visibility entry specifically implies visibility more than 6 miles."

7402. (4) AC 00-45B. "Omission of a wind entry specifically implies wind less than 10 knots."

7403. (4) AC 00-45B, AC 61-23B. TERMINAL FORECASTS. A Terminal Forecast (FT) differs from an Area Forecast in that the FT is a prediction of weather conditions to be expected for a specific airport rather than a larger area. The size of area covered in a Terminal Forecast is within a 5-mile radius of the center of the runway complex.

Generally, the Terminal Forecast includes expected ceiling and clouds, visibility, weather and obstructions to vision, and surface wind conditions at each terminal. Also included are remarks that more completely describe expected weather. If a change is expected during the forecast period, this change and expected time of change are included.

Answers #2 and #3 are not forecasts but are observed reports. They are "old" weather. A forecast is weather that has yet to occur.

7404. (2) AC 00-45B. "Absence of a visibility entry specifically implies visibility more than 6 miles."

7405. (1) AC 00-45B. The significant clouds and weather section, identified by the contraction,

SIG CLDS AND WX

forecasts, in broad terms, cloudiness and weather significant to flight operations.

The SIG CLDS AND WX section usually is several paragraphs. The breakdown may be by States, by well known geographical areas, or in reference to location and movement of a pressure system or front.

7406. (1) AC 00-45B. FLIGHT PRECAUTION. Covers hazardous weather expected to occur during the first 12 hours of the forecast period, including low level wind shear. If no hazards expected a negative statement is inserted, i.e., "No hazus wx expct."

7407. (3) AC 00-45B. The TWEB Route Forecast is similar to the Area Forecast (FA) except more specific information is contained in a route format. Forecast sky cover (height and amount of cloud bases), cloud tops, visibility (including vertical visibility), weather and obstructions to vision are described for a corridor 25 miles either side of the route.

7408. (4) AC 00-45B. Almost all of the listed reports and forecasts will contain information about icing hazards. SIGMETS and AIRMETS are issued when there is an icing hazard. PIREPS (pilot reports) contain information from pilots actually flying in the area forecast to have icing conditions.

7409. (1) AC 00-45B, AIM Para. 504. Answers #2, #3, #4 are conditions that would be reported in an AIRMET (WA).

A SIGMET advises of weather potentially hazardous to all aircraft and not covered in a Convective SIGMET. In the conterminous U.S. items covered are:
1. Severe icing
2. Severe or extreme turbulence
3. Widespread sand or dust storms lowering visibilities to less than 3 miles.

In Alaska and Hawaii there are no Convective SIGMETS. In these states additional items covered are:
4. Tornadoes
5. Lines of thunderstorms
6. Embedded thunderstorms
7. Hail of ¾ in. or greater in diameter

An AIRMET is for weather that may be hazardous to single engine and other light aircraft. The items covered
1. Moderate icing
2. Moderate turbulence
3. Sustained winds of 30 knots or greater at the surface
4. Widespread areas of visibility below 3 miles and/or ceilings less than 1,000 feet
5. Extensive mountain obscurement

7410. (3) AC 00-45B. "Height of cloud base precedes the sky cover symbol, and top follows the symbol.

FOR EXAMPLE:

38 BKN 70,

means base of a broken layer at 3,800 feet and top 7,000 feet (all MSL)."

The following example appended to an aviation weather report,

DSM SA 1755 M8 OVC 3R-F 132/45/44/3213/992/UA /OV DSM 320012 1735/SK OVC 065/080 OVC 140.

is decoded "…. pilot reports at 1735 GMT 12 (nautical miles) northwest of Des Moines, top of the lower overcast 6,500 MSL; base of a second layer (overcast) at 8,000 and top, 14,000 feet MSL."

7411. (2) AC 00-45B, AIM Para. 504. "A SIGMET advises of weather potentially hazardous to all aircraft and not covered in a Convective SIGMET."

"An AIRMET is for weather that may be hazardous to single-engine and other light aircraft."

7412. (3) AIM Para. 508. "AIRMETs are broadcast upon receipt and then at 30 minute intervals H + 15 (hour plus 15 minutes) and H + 45 during the first hour after issuance."

7413. (4) AC 00-45B. "No winds are forecast within 1,500 feet of station elevation. No temperatures are forecast for the 3,000-foot level or for a level within 2,500 feet of station elevation."

7414. (2) AC 00-45B. "No temperatures are forecast for the 3,000-foot level or for a level within 2,500 feet of station elevation."

7415. (2) AC 00-45B. "When forecast windspeed is less than 5 knots, the coded group is "9900" and read, LIGHT AND VARIABLE." The "+00" is the outside air temperature for that altitude in degrees Celcius.

7416. (3) AC 00-45B. Encoded windspeed 100 to 199 knots have 50 added to the direction code and 100 subtracted from the speed. The STL forecast for 39,000 feet is "731960." Wind is 230° at 119 knots, temperature –60.

A coded direction of more than "36" indicates winds 100 knots or more; the coded direction will range from 51 through 86.

If windspeed is forecast at 200 knots or greater, the wind group is coded as 199 knots; i.e., "7799" is decoded 270° at 199 knots or greater.

So 830558 would be done thus, wind direction 83 –50 = 230°; wind speed 05 + 100 = 105 KTS; temperatures are negative above 24,000 feet so 58 becomes –58°C.

7417. (3) AC 00-45B. The wind direction for all reports and forecasts are always given in relation to TRUE NORTH. The windspeed is always reported and forecast in KNOTS.

7418. (2) AC 00-45B. "A convective outlook (AC) describes prospects of both severe and general thunderstorms during the following 24 hours. Use the outlook primarily for planning flights later in the day."

7419. (3) AC 00-45B. "A convective outlook (AC) describes prospects of both severe and general thunderstorms during the following 24 hours. Use the outlook primarily for planning flights later in the day."

7420. (3) AC 00-45B. The low level prog is a four-panel chart. The two lower panels are 12- and 24-hour surface progs. The two upper panels are 12- and 24-hour progs of significant weather from the surface to 400 millibars (24,000 feet). The charts show conditions as they are forecast to be AT the valid time of the chart.

The U.S. high level significant weather prog encompasses airspace from 400 to 70 millibars (24,000 feet to 63,000 feet pressure altitude).

7421. (1) AC 00-45B, Table 8-3. "The U.S. high level significant weather prog outlines areas of forecast turbulence, continuous dense cirriform clouds and cumulonimbus clouds."

"Large-scalloped lines enclose areas of dense, continuous cirriform clouds of broken or overcast coverage. Expected base and top are given with the notation "LYR" meaning either single or multiple layers. A single digit preceding the notation "LYR" is coverage in "octas" or eighths, eight-eighths being overcast.

7422. (3) AC 00-45B. The low level prog is a four-panel chart. The two lower panels are 12- and 24-hour surface progs. The two upper panels are 12- and 24-hour progs of significant weather from the surface to 400 millibars (24,000 feet).

The U.S. high level significant weather prog encompasses airspace from 400 to 70 millibars (24,000 feet to 63,000 feet pressure altitude).

"The charts show conditions as they are forecast to be AT the valid time of the chart."

7423. (1) AC 00-45B. The low level prog is a four-panel chart. The two lower panels are 12- and 24-hour surface progs. The two upper panels are 12- and 24-hour progs of significant weather from the surface to 400 millibars (24,000 feet).

The U.S. high level significant weather prog encompasses airspace from 400 to 70 millibars (24,000 feet to 63,000 feet pressure altitude).

"The charts show conditions as they are forecast to be AT the valid time of the chart."

7424. (3) AC 00-45B. A pilot reported over (OV) MRB at 6,000 feet (FL060), sky conditions (SK) intermittently between layers (BL), turbulence (TB) of moderate (MDT) intensity, remarks (RM) rain (R) and turbulence (TURBC) increasing (incrs) westward (WWD).

7425. (1) AC 00-45B. On the low level and high level significant weather prog charts, only turbulence that is forecasted to be moderate or greater is shown on these charts. The symbol " —⋏— " indicates moderate turbulence. The altitudes at which turbulence is expected to occur are shown both with the highest altitude over the line and the lowest altitude below the line. If the altitude is not shown below the line on the low level prog it means turbulence begins at the surface. If it is missing on the high altitude prog it means that the turbulence begins below the lower limit of the chart (below 24,000 feet). In this case, look at the low level prog. If the altitude is missing above the line on the low level prog the turbulence extends above the upper limit of the chart (above 24,000 feet).

7426. (2) AC 00-45B, Chart Legend. The upper panels depict ceiling, visibility, turbulence, and freezing level. Note the legend near the center of the chart which explains methods of depiction.

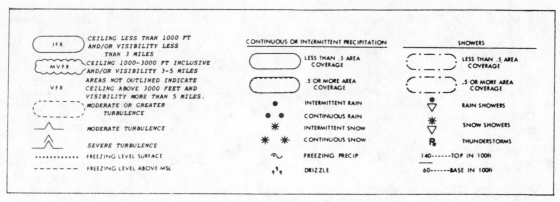

LOW LEVEL PROG CHART

Smooth lines enclose areas of forecast IFR weather; scalloped lines enclose areas of marginal weather (MVFR); VFR areas are not outlined. Recall that this is the same manner of depiction used on the weather depiction chart to portray ceiling and visibility.

Long-dashed lines enclose general areas of forecast moderate or greater turbulence.

Note that the left panel is for 12 hours and the right panel for 24 hours.

7427. (2) AC 00-45B, Tables 8-1 and 8-2. Shaded areas indicate half or more coverage. Answers #1 and #4 are now excluded. Thunderstorms are shown by the symbol " ℟ ." This is not on the chart so Answer #3 is now excluded. Answer #2 is correct because West Virginia is covered by a shaded area indicating more than half the area is covered; the "●●" pair of dots means continuous rain while the symbol " ▽ " means rain shower. The shaded area is bounded by a line with intermittent dots. This means showery precipitation.

7428. (3) AC 00-45B, Figure 21, Chart Legend. Make sure that panels C and D are used. These are valid at 1200Z. Continuous rain is shown by the two dots "●●," showery precipitation is shown by the border of the shaded area. The shaded area means half or more of the area is covered with the type of weather shown on the chart. The freezing level is found on Chart C. The freezing level above the surface is shown by dashed lines with the altitude shown in hundreds of feet. The freezing level for the route of flight is beween 8,000 and 12,000 feet at approximately the 10,000-foot level.

7429. (4) AC 61-23B, 61-27C. When on an east or west heading, no error is apparent while entering a turn to north or south.

If on a northerly heading and a turn is made toward east or west, the initial indication of the compass lags or indicates a turn in the opposite direction. This lag diminishes as the turn progresses toward east or west where there is no turn error.

If on a southerly heading and a turn is made toward the east or west, the initial indication of the compass needle will indicate a greater amount of turn than is actually made. This lead also diminishes as the turn progresses toward east or west where there is no turn error.

7430. (2) AC 61-23B. If on a northerly heading and a turn is made toward east or west, the initial indication of the compass lags or indicates a turn in the opposite direction. This lag diminishes as the turn progresses toward east or west where there is no turn error.

7431. (4) AC 61-23B, 61-27C. When on an east or west heading, no error is apparent while entering a turn to north or south.

If on a northerly heading and a turn is made toward east or west, the initial indication of the compass lags or indicates a turn in the opposite direction. This lag diminishes as the turn progresses toward east or west where there is no turn error.

If on a southerly heading and a turn is made toward the east or west, the initial indication of the compass needle will indicate a greater amount of turn than is actually made. This lead also diminishes as the turn progresses toward east or west where there is no turn error.

7432. (4) AC 61-23B, 61-27C. When on an east or west heading, no error is apparent while entering a turn to north or south.

If on a northerly heading and a turn is made toward east or west, the initial indication of the compass lags or indicates a turn in the opposite direction. This lag diminishes as the turn progresses toward east or west where there is no turn error.

If on a southerly heading and a turn is made toward the east or west, the initial indication of the compass needle will indicate a greater amount of turn than is actually made. This lead also diminishes as the turn progresses toward east or west where there is no turn error.

7433. (2) AC 61-23B. If on a northerly heading and a turn is made toward east or west, the initial indication of the compass lags or indicates a turn in the opposite direction. This lag diminishes as the turn progresses toward east or west where there is no turn error.

7434. (4) AC 61-23B, 61-27C. When on an east or west heading, no error is apparent while entering a turn to north or south.

If on a northerly heading and a turn is made toward east or west, the initial indication of the compass lags or indicates a turn in the opposite direction. This lag diminishes as the turn progresses toward east or west where there is no turn error.

If on a southerly heading and a turn is made toward the east or west, the initial indication of the compass needle will indicate a greater amount of turn than is actually made. This lead also diminishes as the turn progresses toward east or west where there is no turn error.

7435. (1) AC 61-23B. If on a southerly heading and a turn is made toward the east or west, the initial indication of the compass needle will indicate a greater amount of turn than is actually made. This lead diminishes as the turn progresses toward east or west where there is no turn error.

7436. (3) AC 61-23B. A 15° bank is approximately a standard rate turn for most general aviation aircraft. When the aircraft heading approaches 090° and 270°, there isn't any turning error. When the heading progresses past 090° and 270°, the turning errors become apparent again.

7437. (4) AC 61-27C. A number of compass errors are caused by the deflection of the aircraft compass needles as they seek alignment with the earth's magnetic lines of force. This is known as magnetic dip.

7438. (1) AC 61-23B. If on a southerly heading and a turn is made toward the east or west, the initial indication of the compass needle will indicate a greater amount of turn than is actually made. This lead diminishes as the turn progresses toward east or west where there is no turn error.

7439. (1) AC 61-27B. The postural sense derives its sensations from the expansion and contraction of muscles and tendons, touch and pressure, and the shifting of abdominal muscles. Without visual aid, postural sense during flight often interprets centrifugal force as a sensation of rising or falling which may be contrary to fact.

7440. (1) FAR 91.75. Each pilot in command who (though not deviating from a rule of this subpart) is given priority by ATC in an emergency, shall, if requested by ATC, submit a detailed report of that emergency within 48 hours to the chief of that ATC facility.

7441. (2) AIM Para. 290. Briefing service may be obtained from an FSS either by telephone or interphone, by radio when airborne or by a personal visit to the station. The objective is to communicate a "picture" of meteorological and aeronautical information necessary for the conduct of a safe and efficient flight. Briefers use all available weather and aeronautical information to summarize data applicable to the proposed flight.

7442. (1) AIM Paras. 290, 294. NOTAMS which are known in sufficient time for publication and are of 7 days duration or longer are normally incorporated into the Notices to Airmen (Class II) publication and carried there until cancellation time. FDC NOTAMs, which apply to instrument flight procedures, are also included in the Notices to Airmen publication up to and including the number indicated in the FDC NOTAM legend.

7443. (3) AFD. FAST FILE FLIGHT PLAN SYSTEM. Some Flight Service Stations have inaugurated this system for pilots who desire to file IFR/VFR flight plans. Pilots may call the discrete telephone numbers listed and file flight plans in accordance with prerecorded taped instructions. IFR flight plans will be extracted from the recorder and subsequently entered in the appropriate ARTCC computer. VFR flight plans will be transcribed; and both IFR/VFR flight plans will be filed in the FSS. This equipment is designed to automatically disconnect after 8 seconds of no transmission, so pilots are instructed to speak at a normal speech rate without lengthy pauses between flight plan elements. Pilots are urged to file flight plans into this system at least 30 minutes in advance of proposed departure. The system may be used to close and cancel flight plans.

7444. (3) AIM. Airport Advisory Service (AAS) is a service provided by an FSS physically located on an airport which does not have a control tower or where the tower is temporarily closed or operated on a part-time basis.

7445. (2) AIM Paras. 157, 304. "Airport Advisory Service (AAS) is a service provided by an FSS physically located on an airport which does not have a control tower or where the tower is temporarily closed or operated on a part-time basis."

An FSS that is located on an airport where there is no tower will provide airport advisory services to all aircraft; both VFR and IFR. They do not, however, automatically cancel or close an IFR flight plan.

"If operating on an IFR flight plan to an airport where there is no functioning control tower, the pilot must initiate cancellation fo the IFR flight plan. This can be done after landing if there is a functioning FSS or other means of direct communications with ATC."

7446. (4) IFR EOG #28. "Category II holding lines are used only when Category II operations are in progress. Otherwise, conventional holding lines should be used."

7447. (2) IFR EOG #28. "To prevent interference with ILS guidance signals, and to keep the touchdown area clear during Category II approaches, three "critical areas" must be protected. They are the localizer critical area, the glide slope critical area, and the obstacle critical area."

7448. (3) AIM Para. 60.

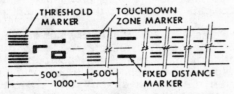

PRECISION INSTRUMENT RUNWAY

7449. (3) AIM Para. 60.

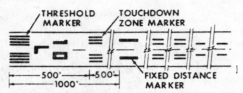

PRECISION INSTRUMENT RUNWAY

7450. (4) AIM Para. 60.

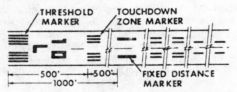

PRECISION INSTRUMENT RUNWAY

7451. (2) IFR EOG #33. At night, "no aircraft operations are permitted short of displaced threshold lights, if edge-of-runway lights (white or colored) are absent."

7452. (2) AIM Para. 60. Displaced thresholds are marked by arrows pointing to the displaced threshold, on instrument and non-instrument runways.

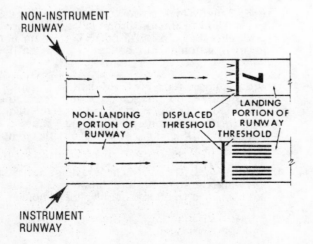

7453. (4) AIM Para. 227. Low Level Wind Shear Alert System (LLWAS):

This computerized system detects the presence of a possible hazardous low-level wind shear by continuously comparing the winds measured by sensors installed around the periphery of an airport with the wind measured at the centerfield location. If the difference between the centerfield wind sensor and a peripheral wind sensor becomes excessive, a thunderstorm or thunderstorm gust front wind shear is probable. When this condition exists, the tower controller will provide arrival and departure aircraft with an advisory of the situation which includes the centerfield wind plus the remote site location and wind.

7454. (3) AIM Para. 43. REILs are installed at many airfields to provide rapid and positive identification of the approach end of a particular runway. The system consists of a pair of synchronized flashing lights, one of which is located laterally on each side of the runway threshold facing the approach area. REILs may be located longitudinally 200 feet either upwind or downwind from the runway threshold. They are effective for:
1. Identification of a runway surrounded by a preponderance of other lighting.
2. Identification of a runway which lacks contrast with surrounding terrain.
3. Identification of a runway during reduced visibility.

7455. (2) AIM Para. 43. REILs are installed at many airfields to provide rapid and positive identification of the approach end of a particular runway. The system consists of a pair of synchronized flashing lights, one of which is located laterally on each side of the runway threshold facing the approach area. REILs may be located longitudinally 200 feet either upwind or downwind from the runway threshold. They are effective for:
1. Identification of a runway surrounded by a preponderance of other lighting.
2. Identification of a runway which lacks contrast with surrounding terrain.
3. Identification of a runway during reduced visibility.

7456. (2) AIM Para. 48. "In control zones, operation of the airport beacon during the hours of daylight often indicates that the ground visibility is less than 3 miles and/or the ceiling is less than 1,000 feet. Pilots should not rely solely on the operation of the airport beacon to indicate weather conditions, IFR versus VFR."

7457. (1) AIM Para. 161. ATIS broadcasts shall be updated upon the receipt of any official weather, regardless of content change and reported values. A new recording will also be made when there is a change in other pertinent data such as runway change, instrument approach in use, etc.

7458. (2) AIM Para. 161. ATIS broadcasts shall be updated upon the receipt of any official weather, regardless of content change and reported values. A new recording will also be made when there is a change in other pertinent data such as runway change, instrument approach in use, etc.

7459. (1) AIM Para. 161. ATIS information includes the time of the latest weather sequence, ceiling, visibility (if the weather is above a ceiling/sky condition of 5,000 feet and the visibility is 5 miles or more, inclusion of the ceiling/sky condition, visibility, and obstructions to vision in the ATIS message is optional), obstructions to visibility, temperature, dewpoint (if available), wind direction (magnetic) and velocity, altimeter, other pertinent remarks, instrument approach and runways in use is continuously broadcast on the voice feature of a TVOR/VOR/VORTAC located on or near the airport, or in a discrete VHF/UHF frequency.

7460. (3) AIM Para. 161. "Pilots should notify controllers that they have received the ATIS broadcast by repeating the alphabetical code word appended to the broadcast.

EXAMPLE:

"INFORMATION SIERRA RECEIVED."

7461. (4) AC 61-23B. The ball is a balance indicator, and is used as a visual aid to determine coordinated use of the aileron and rudder control. During a turn it indicates the relationship between the angle of bank and rate of turn. It indicates the "quality" of the turn or whether the aircraft has the correct angle of bank for the rate of turn.

7462. (2) AC 61-27C. If the airspeed is increased in a turn, the angle of attack must be decreased and/or the angle of bank increased in order to maintain level flight.

As airspeed is increased in a constant-rate level turn, both the radius of turn and centrifugal force increase. This increase in centrifugal force must be balanced by an increase in the horizontal lift component, which can be accomplished only by increasing the angle of bank. Thus, to maintain a turn at a constant rate, the angle of bank must be varied with changes in airspeed.

7463. (4) AIM Para. 235. "A pilot who has just landed should not change from the tower frequency to the ground frequency until he is directed to do so by the controller."

7464. (3) AIM Para. 235. "A pilot who has just landed should not change from the tower frequency to the ground frequency until he is directed to do so by the controller."

7465. (2) AIM Glossary, AC 00-45B. RUNWAY VISUAL RANGE is the maximum horizontal distance down a specified instrument runway at which a pilot can see and identify standard high intensity runway lights. It is always determined using a transmissometer and is reported in hundreds of feet."

7466. (3) Instrument Approach Procedures.

RVR/Meteorological Visibility Comparable Values Table

The following table shall be used for converting RVR to meteorological visibility when RVR is inoperative.

RVR (feet)	Visibility (SM)
1600	¼
2000	⅜
2400	½
3200	⅝
4000	¾
4500	⅞
5000	1
6000	1¼

7467. (2) AIM Glossary, AC 00-45B. RUNWAY VISUAL RANGE is the maximum horizontal distance down a specified instrument runway at which a pilot can see and identify standard high intensity runway lights. It is always determined using a transmissometer and is reported in hundreds of feet."

7468. (4) AC 61-27C. With the altimeter set to the current reported altimeter setting, note any variation between the known field elevation and the altimeter indication. If the variation is in the order of plus or minus 75 feet, the accuracy of the altimeter is questionable and the problem should be referred to an appropriately rated repair station for evaluation and possible correction.

7469. (3) AC 91-4B. The following are items that should be checked before starting the engine(s).

If instruments are electrical, turn on and listen for any unusual or irregular mechanical noise.

Check instruments for poor condition, mounting, marking, broken or loose knobs. Also check the power-off indications of the instrument pointers and warning flags.

Check heading and attitude indicators to ascertain that they are uncaged. Check turn and slip indicator and magnetic compass for fluid level (should be full).

Check condition and security of outside mounted venturi if aircraft is so equipped.

7470. (2) AC 91-4B. The following are items that should be checked before starting the engine(s).

If instruments are electrical, turn on and listen for any unusual or irregular mechanical noise.

Check instruments for poor condition, mounting, marking, broken or loose knobs. Also check the power-off indications of the instrument pointers and warning flags.

Check heading and attitude indicators to ascertain that they are uncaged. Check turn and slip indicator and magnetic compass for fluid level (should be full).

Check condition and security of outside mounted venturi if aircraft is so equipped.

7471. (2) AC 61-27C, 91-46. The ball will move with the centrifugal force so that while the aircraft is turning on the ground the ball will move to the outside of the turn (opposite the direction of turn). The needle is designed to indicate the direction and rate of turn so that when the aircraft turns on the ground (or in the air), the needle points in the same direction as the turn.

7472. (3) FAR 91.25. The maximum bearing error permitted when using a VOT test signal is plus or minus 4°. The VOT is primarily a ground based test facility but may be used while airborne if the station is listed in the Airport/Facility Directory and the AFD says that airborne use is permitted. In either case, the bearing error is plus or minus 4°.

7473. (2) FAR 91.25, AIM Para. 4. The allowable bearing error is plus or minus 4°. To test for VOR accuracy center the CDI (Course Deviation Indicator needle) on 0° or 360°. The flag should show "from," or center the CDI on course 180° with the flag showing "to." With the 360° course setting, the allowable range is 356° to 004°. With the 180° course, the allowable range is 176° to 184°.

7474. (2) FAR 91.25, AIM Para. 4. The allowable bearing error is plus or minus 4°. To test for VOR accuracy center the CDI (Course Deviation Indicator needle) on 0° or 360°. The flag should show "from," or center the CDI on course 180° with the flag showing "to." With the 360° course setting, the allowable range is 356° to 004°. With the 180° course, the allowable range is 176° to 184°.

7475. (1) FAR 91.25, AIM Para. 4. The allowable bearing error is plus or minus 4°. To test for VOR accuracy center the CDI (Course Deviation Indicator needle) on 0° or 360°. The flag should show "from," or center the CDI on course 180° with the flag showing "to." With the 360° course setting, the allowable range is 356° to 004°. With the 180° course, the allowable range is 176° to 184°.

7476. (3) FAR 91.25, AIM Para. 4. The procedure to use a ground VOR check is to center the needle on the designated radial with a "FROM" flag indication (all radials proceed from the station). The tolerance is plus or minus 4° of the selected radial.

7477. (2) FAR 91.25. If dual system VOR (units independent of each other except for the antenna) is installed in the aircraft, the person checking the equipment may check one system against the other.

He shall tune both systems to the same VOR ground facility and note the indicated bearings to that station. The maximum permissible variation between the two indicated bearings is 4 degrees.

7478. (1) FAR 91.25. If dual system VOR (units independent of each other except for the antenna) is installed in the aircraft, the person checking the equip-

ment may check one system against the other. He shall tune both systems to the same VOR ground facility and NOTE THE INDICATED BEARINGS TO THAT STATION. The maximum permissible variation between the two indicated bearings is 4 degrees.

7479. (4) FAR 91.25, AIM Para. 4. The allowable bearing error is plus or minus 4°. To test for VOR accuracy center the CDI (Course Deviation Indicator needle) on 0° or 360°. The flag should show "from," or center the CDI on course 180° with the flag showing "to." With the 360° course setting, the allowable range is 356° to 004°. With the 180° course, the allowable range is 176° to 184°.

176° TO is for one of the VORs and 003° FROM is for the second VOR.

7480. (1) FAR 91.25, AIM Para. 4. The allowable bearing error is plus or minus 4°. To test for VOR accuracy center the CDI (Course Deviation Indicator needle) on 0° or 360°. The flag should show "from," or center the CDI on course 180° with the flag showing "to." With the 360° course setting, the allowable range is 356° to 004°. With the 180° course, the allowable range is 176° to 184°.

7481. (3) AFD. The Airman's Information Manual describes how to make a VOT test. Graphic Notices and Supplemental Data books are no longer published.

7482. (1) FAR 91.25. The indicated VOR bearing when over the ground check point cannot be more than plus or minus 6° of the designated radial. The flag will have a "FROM" indication.

7483. (2) AIM Para. 170. "When making routine code changes, pilots should avoid inadvertent selection of codes 7500, 7600 or 7700 thereby causing momentary false alarms at automated ground facilities."

7484. (2) AIM Para. 170. Adjust transponder to reply on the MODE A/3 code specified by ATC and, if equipped, to reply on MODE C with altitude reporting CAPABILITY ACTIVATED unless deactivation is directed by ATC or unless the installed aircraft equipment has not been tested and calibrated as required by FAR 91.36. If deactivation is required by ATC, turn off the altitude reporting feature of the transponder.

7485. (1) AC 61-27C. If the horizon bar erects to the horizontal position and remains at the correct position for the attitude of the airplane, or if it begins to vibrate after this attitude is reached and then slowly stops vibrating altogether, the instrument is operating properly. If the horizon bar fails to remain in the horizontal position during straight taxiing, or tips in excess of 5° during taxi turns, the instrument is unreliable.

7486. (4) AC 61-27C. Allow 5 minutes after starting engines for the gyro rotor of the vacuum operated attitude indicator to attain normal operating speed.

7487. (2) AC 61-27C. Allow 5 minutes after starting engines for the gyro rotor of the vacuum-operated heading indicator to attain normal operating speed. Before taxiing, or while taxiing straight, set the heading indicator to correspond with the magnetic compass heading. Be sure the instrument is fully uncaged if it has a caging feature. Before takeoff, recheck the heading indicator. If the magnetic compass and deviation card are accurate, the heading indicator should show the known taxiway or runway direction when the airplane is aligned with them (within 5°).

7488. (4) AC 61-27C. Check the card for freedom of movement and be sure that the bowl is full of fluid. Determine compass accuracy by comparing the indicated heading against a known heading while the airplane is stopped or taxiing straight.

7489. (4) AIM Para. 270. When ATC has not used the term "AT PILOT'S DISCRETION" nor imposed any climb or descent restrictions, pilots should initiate climb or descent promptly on acknowledgment of the clearance. Descend or climb at an optimum rate consistent with the operating characteristics of the aircraft to 1,000 feet above or below the assigned altitude, and then attempt to descend or climb at a rate of 500 feet per minute until the assigned altitude is reached. If at anytime the pilot is unable to climb or descend at a rate of at least 500 feet a minute, advise ATC. If it is necessary to level off at an intermediate altitude during climb or descent, advise ATC, except for level off at 10,000 feet MSL on descent or 3,000 feet above airport elevation (prior to entering an airport traffic area), when required for speed reduction. (FAR 91.70).

7490. (4) AIM Para. 165. The purpose of this service is to provide separation between all PARTICPIATING VFR aircraft and all IFR aircraft operating within the airspace defined as the Terminal Radar Service Area (TRSA)."

7491. (1) AIM Para. 3. "The only positive method of identifying a VOR is by its Morse Code identification or by the recorded automatic voice identification which is always indicated by use of the word "VOR" following the range's name. During periods of maintenance, the coded facility identification is removed."

If a navigational signal is being received without the corresponding Morse Code identification, the VOR is out for maintenance.

7492. (3) AIM Para. 3. "The only positive method of identifying a VOR is by its Morse Code identification or by the recorded automatic voice identification which is always indicated by use of the word "VOR" following the range's name. During periods of maintenance, the coded facility identification is removed."

If a navigational signal is being received without the corresponding Morse Code identification, the VOR is out for maintenance.

7493. (4) AIM Para. 7. VOR/DME, VORTAC, ILS/DME, and LOC/DME facilities are identified by synchronized identifications which are transmitted on a time share basis. The VOR or localizer portion of the facility is identified by a coded tone modulated at 1020 Hz or a combination of code and voice. The TACAN or DME is identified by a coded

tone modulated at 1350 Hz. The DME or TACAN coded identification is transmitted one time for each three or four times that the VOR or localizer coded identification is transmitted. When either the VOR or the DME is inoperative, it is important to recognize which identifier is retained for the operative facility. A single coded identification with a repetition interval of approximately 30 seconds indicates that the DME is operative.

7494. (2) AIM Para. 7. "Distance information received from DME equipment is SLANT RANGE distance and not actual horizontal distance." It is measured in nautical miles, and since 6,000 feet equals one nautical mile, the DME will show 1.0 NM above the VORTAC.

7495. (3) AIM Paras. 322 & 262. In order for a pilot to fly a given clearance (abbreviated or otherwise), he must have a clearance limit, either to the destination airport or an intermediate fix. Not all airports have SIDs or transitions so an abbreviated clearance could be received that does not contain a SID.

7496. (3) AIM Para. 322. "Cleared to (destination) airport as filed" does NOT include the enroute altitude filed in a flight plan. An enroute altitude will be stated in the clearance or the pilot will be advised to expect an assigned or filed altitude within a given time frame or at a certain point after departure. This may be done verbally in the departure instructions or stated in the SID.

7497. (2) AIM Para. 323. If operating from an airport not served by a control tower, the pilot may receive a clearance containing a provision that if the flight has not departed by a specific time, the clearance is void. In this situation, the pilot who does not depart prior to the void time must advise ATC as soon as possible, but no later than 30 minutes, of his intentions.

7498. (2) AIM Para. 265. Pilots of airborne aircraft should read back THOSE PARTS of ATC clearances and instructions containing altitude assignments or vectors, as a means of mutual verification. The readback of the "numbers" serves as a double check between pilots and controllers and reduces the kinds of communications errors that occur when a number is either "misheard" or is incorrect.

7499. (2) AIM Para. 322. The clearance as issued will include the destination airport filed in the flight plan.

"Cleared to (destination) airport as filed" does NOT include enroute altitude filed in a flight plan. An enroute altitude will be stated in the clearance or the pilot will be advised to expect an assigned or filed altitude within a given time frame or at a certain point after departure. This may be done verbally in the departure instructions or stated in the SID.

ATC procedures now require the controller to state the SID name, the current number and the SID Transition name after the phrase "Cleared to (destination) airport" and prior to the phrase, "then as filed," for ALL departure clearances when the SID or SID Transition is to be flown. The procedures apply whether or not the SID is filed in the flight plan.

7500. (1) IFH. The DME indicator displays slant range distance in nautical miles.

7501. (2) IFH. The greatest slant-range error occurs when flying directly over the DME facility (VORTAC, VOR/DME), when the displayed distance is the height above the facility in nautical miles. IFH states: "Slant-range error is neglible if the aircraft is one mile or more from the ground facility for each 1,000 feet of altitude above the elevation of the facility."

7502. (4) AC 61-27C, AIM. Using the A/FD Legend in Appendix 2 of the test book (page 5), note the maximum distance allowed from a high altitude VOR at altitudes between 14,500 and 17,999 is 100 NM. Therefore, the H class VORs could be no more than 200 NM from each other.

7503. (2) IFR EOG #7. A "FROM" indication and the CDI pointing left of center would indicate that the selected radial (360°) is to the left of the aircraft's spot position and is not related whatsoever to it's heading.

7504. (2) IFH. MH + RB = MB "TO" the station, MB "FROM" the station = MB "TO" ± 180°. 215° + 140° = 355° "TO" the station, 355° – 180° = 175° "FROM" the station.

7505. (4) IFH. MH + RB = MB "TO" the station. 215° + 140° = magnetic bearing of 355° "TO" the station.

7506. (2) MH + RB = MB "TO" the station. 330° + 270° = 600° "TO", = 600° – 360° = 240° "TO". 240° ("TO") – 180° = 060° "FROM."

7507. (3) IFH. MH + RB = MB "TO" the station. 330° + 270° = 600° "TO" = 600° – 360° = 240° "TO" the station.

7508. (4) IFH. VOR radials are "FROM" the station indicated on a radio magnetic indicator (RMI) by the tail of the bearing indicator, which is 335° in illustration D of Fig. 25. The head of the arrow would be the bearing "TO" the station.

7509. (1) IFH. The tail of the indicator points at 115° in illustration A of Fig. 25.

7510. (2) IFH. The tail of the indicator points at 315° in illustration B of Fig. 25.

7511. (3) IFH. The tail of the indicator points at 010° in illustration C of Fig. 25.

7512. (X) FAA Deletion.

7513. (X) FAA Deletion.

7514. (X) FAA Deletion.

7515. (X) FAA Deletion.

7516. (1) IFH. A VOT provides tolerances of ±4° with a "TO" indication for the 180° radial and a "FROM" indication for the 360° radial. Illustration A shows a "TO" indication with the head of the needles.

7517. (1) IFH. With a VOT tuned into the nav receiver, the TO/FROM flag will indicate "TO" with the OBS selector set on 180° and a "FROM" indication with a 360° setting.

7518. (3) AIM Para. 4. Locations of airborne checkpoints, ground checkpoints and VOTs are published in the Airport/Facility Directory.

7519. (4) AIM Para. 4. For a dual VOR check using one system against the other, the CDI needles must be within 4° of each other as shown in Fig. 29(d).

7520. (2) AIM Para. 4. The VORs must be within 4° of each other.

7521. (2) AIM Para. 4. For checking VORs with a designated checkpoint on an airport surface, the aircraft is placed at this position facing any direction — VOR senses spot position only. Tolerance is ±4°.

7522. (2) SID. The note on the Reno Six departure plate (Fig. 30) states minimum climb rate of 350' per NM to 9,000' required.

7523. (4) SID. The SID requires a climb gradient of 350' per nautical mile. An aircraft with a groundspeed of 150 knots is covering 2.5 nautical miles per minute (150 KTS ÷ 60 Min. = 2.5 NM/Min.). 2.5 NM/Min. X 350 ft/NM = 875 ft. per minute.

7524. (2) SID. The departure route description states the procedure to be followed if lost communications before reaching 9,000 ft.

7525. (1) AIM Para. 325. The departure route description states: climb via Reno localizer south course to Wagge Int. for radar vector to assigned route. Since V6N is the assigned route in the question, that is the route the pilot will be vectored to.

7526. (1) IFR EOG #7. Illustration (b) shows the aircraft is to the left of the LOC centerline on departure and (d) shows having already passed Wagge intersection.

7527. (3) IFH. ATC will assign a SID if it is felt necessary. If pilot does not have at least the text portion of a SID it must be stated so in the remarks section of the IFR Flight Plan.

7528. (4) COMP. The question when broken down asks for the information given in feet per nautical mile to be converted to feet per minute, using the given climb rate (210 feet/nautical mile) and a groundspeed of 140 knots.

First, 140 knots (NM/hour):

$$\frac{140 \text{ NM/HR}}{60 \text{ Min.}} = 2.33 \text{ NM/Min.}$$

Then it's the climb rate multiplied by groundspeed which has just been converted into nautical miles per minute:

$$= 490 \text{ Ft/Min.}$$

7529. (3) AIM Para. 325, IFH. IFH states: "The use of a SID requires pilot possession of at least the textual description of the approved effective SID."

7530. (2) IFH, IFR EOG #34. The pilot should contact departure control on the assigned frequency upon release from the control tower.

7531. (4) IFH, IFR EOG #34. The pilot should contact departure control on the assigned frequency upon release from the control tower.

7532. (3) COMP. The distances and groundspeeds are measured and computed for each leg. Then times are calculated and summed up including the extra six minutes allowed for climbing to 12,000 feet.

LEG	TAS	WIND	GS	DISTANCE	TIME
V23 — MCKEN.................. 180		3230	195	36	:11
V204 — WHYTE.................. 180		3230	206	42	:12
V204 — YKM 180		3230	198	50	:15
V25 — ELN 180		3230	156	27	:10
V25 — EAT 180		3230	165	25	:09
V2N — SEA 180		3230	159	86	:33
Climb from 425' MSL to 12000' MSL					:06
					1:36

7533. (4) Computation:

LEG	TIME	FUEL (180 Lb/Hr)
ETE..................	1:40	300
Alternate..................	:24	72
Reserve..................	:45	135
Taxi/Takeoff/Climb..................		+ 22
	TOTAL	529

7534. (1) Reference Flight Computer setup.

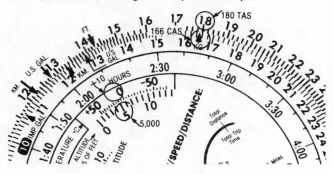

7535. (2) Reference Flight Computer Setup.

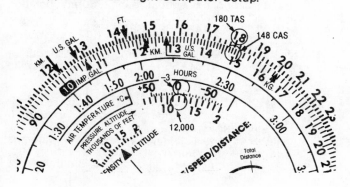

7536. (4) FAR 91.127. If the failure occurs in IFR conditions, or if paragraph (b) of this section cannot be complied with, each pilot shall continue the flight according to the following:

ALTITUDE. At the highest of the following altitudes or flight levels for the route segment being flown:
1. The altitude or flight level assigned in the last ATC clearance received;
2. The minimum altitude (converted, if appropriate, to minimum flight level as prescribed in § 91.81(c)) for IFR operations; or
3. The altitude or flight level ATC has advised may be expected in a further clearance

NOTE: Follow the route of flight closely, watching for changes in MEAs for a given airway for different directions.

7537. (4) IFR EOG #8. The MEA to Blako is 6,000 feet but the MCA is 7,500 feet on V2S-4 eastbound. V25 does not start at Gleed, but at YKM continuing up to ELN and EAT.

7538. (3) AIM Para. 345. The COP is located midway between the navigation facilities for straight route segments, or at the intersection of radials or courses forming a dogleg in the case of dogleg route segments. When the COP is NOT located at the midway point, aeronautical charts will depict the COP location and give the mileage to the radio aids.

7539. (1) FAR 91.121. A pilot with a "VFR ON TOP" clearance must not only continue to fly by instrument flight rules but must also fly by VFR cruising altitudes. On V25 from YKM to ELN, fly even altitudes plus 500 feet and V25 from ELN to EAT is for odd altitudes plus 500 feet, and maintain VFR cloud clearance requirements.

7540. (4) IFR EOG #16. Full-scale deflection of the CDI needle indicates an error of approximately 1,000 feet per nautical mile from the station. With a constant ½ scale needle deflection as in the question, the distance from the radial is increasing with time. The ½ scale deflection to the right indicates the relative position of the radial from the aircraft.

7541. (4) IFH. The illustration indicates that the aircraft is on the 050° bearing inbound which places it right of course.

7542. (2) IFH. When homing to a beacon or flying inbound with a 0° relative bearing with a crosswind, the aircraft will curve to the downside due to wind drift.

7543. (3) IFH. The compass card shows a heading of 195° indicating the aircraft is inbound for the NDB RWY 19 approach. The ADF needle pointing rearward shows that the beacon has been passed.

7544. (3) IFH. Because of the change of the value of full scale deflection with a change in the distance from the station, flying inbound to the VOR the aircraft must be coming closer to radial in order to maintain the constant ¼ scale deflections.

7545. (4) IFH. Answers #1 and #2 are obviously incorrect since the VOR is not dependent whatsoever on the heading of the aircraft, only on the aircraft's geographical position. If a FROM indication is used, the aircraft will always be on the same side of the facility as the selected radial on the OBS, and in this case it is on the radial. With a TO flag, the aircraft is always geographically on the opposite side of the selected radial.

7546. (4) FAR 91.109. The MEA is 5,000 feet, however a pilot on a VFR ON TOP clearance must maintain VFR cruising altitudes which for a heading of 198° would be even plus 500 feet.

7547. (4) AIM Para. 346. If the restricted area is not active and has been released to the controlling agency (FAA), ATC will allow the aircraft to operate in the restricted airspace without issuing specific clearance for it to do so.

If the restricted area is active and has not been released to the controlling agency (FAA), ATC will issue a clearance which will ensure the aircraft avoids the restricted airspace unless it is on an approved altitude reservation mission or has obtained its own permission to operate in the airspace and so informs the controlling facility.

7548. (4) ACL. The MCA (Minimum Crossing Altitude) flag ✍ at Alder indicates in the note under the intersection's name that it pertains only to eastbound aircraft and Answers #1 and #2 pertain to MCAs at McKEN intersection. For northbound aircraft, there is no MCA so only the MEA of 9,000 feet applies in this direction.

7549. (2) ACL. At Cetra intersection, the MEA changes from 4,000 feet southbound to 5,000 feet as indicated by the MEA, MAA and/or MOCA change mark (⊣).

7550. (3) AIM Para. 345. The COP is located midway between the navigation facilities for straight route segments, or at the intersection of radials or courses forming a dogleg in the case of dogleg route segments. When the COP is NOT located at the midway point, aeronautical charts will depict the COP location and give the mileage to the radio aids.

7551. (4) IFH. MH + RB = MB; 345° + 195° = 540° − 360° = 180°. The aircraft is outbound on course with a magnetic bearing of 180° for the NDB RWY 18 approach.

7552. (2) AIM Pilot/Controller Glossary. An RNAV waypoint is a predetermined geographical position used for route or instrument approach definition or progress reporting purposes that is defined relative to a VORTAC station position.

7553. (4) FAR 91.90. To enter a Group I TCA such as San Francisco, a pilot is required to have an appropriate clearance from ATC prior to operation in that area, a private pilot certificate, a VOR or TACAN, a two-way radio, and an altitude reporting Mode C transponder. DME is not a required piece of equipment.

7554. (1) ACL. There is no FSS at San Francisco Intl. which would be indicated by a heavy lined VOR box.

7555. (2) ACL. The OLYMM intersection may not be identified with the SFO localizer 281° course, but can be identified with the SFO R-281 and the SAV R-204, or the SFO R-281 and DME only.

7556. (4) AIM Para. 503. All flight watch facilities (enroute flight advisory services) operate on 122.0 MHz and is indicated on enroute charts in the VOR box with triangles in the upper corners.

7557. (2) FAR 91.70. No person may operate an aircraft below 10,000 feet MSL and inside a TCA at an IAS of more than 250 knots (288 MPH). Aircraft operations in airspace underlying a TCA or in a VFR corridor at an IAS of more than 200 KTS (230 MPH), in airport traffic areas an IAS of 156 KTS (180 MPH) for reciprocating engine aircraft and 200 KTS (230 MPH) for turbine engine powered aircraft may not be exceeded.

7558. (2) AIM Para. 503. "To contact a flight watch facility on 122.0 MHz use the name of the controlling FSS and the words FLIGHT WATCH or, if the controlling FSS is unknown, simply call "FLIGHT WATCH" and give the aircraft position."

EXAMPLE:

OAKLAND FLIGHT WATCH, LEAR TWO THREE FOUR FIVE KILO OVER.

7559. (2) AIM Para. 341. "When informed by ATC that their aircraft are in 'radar contact,' pilots should discontinue position reports over designated reporting points. They should resume normal position reporting when ATC advises — RADAR CONTACT LOST or RADAR SERVICE TERMINATED."

7560. (2) AIM Para. 342. The following reports should be made to ATC or FSS facilities without a specific ATC request:

WHEN NOT IN RADAR CONTACT:
1. When leaving final approach fix inbound on final approach.
2. A corrected estimate at anytime it becomes apparent that an estimate as previously submitted is in error in excess of 3 minutes.

7561. (X) FAA Deletion.

or 10 knots (whichever is greater) from that filed in the flight plan.

6. The time and altitude or flight level upon reaching a holding fix or point to which cleared.

7. When leaving any assigned holding fix or point.

NOTE: The reports in subparagraphs 6 and 7 may be omitted by pilots of aircraft involved in instrument training at military terminal area facilities when radar service is being provided.

8. Any loss, in controlled airspace, of VOR, TACAN, ADF, low frequency navigation receiver capability, complete or partial loss of ILS receiver capability or impairment of air/ground communications capability.

9. Any information relating to the safety of flight.

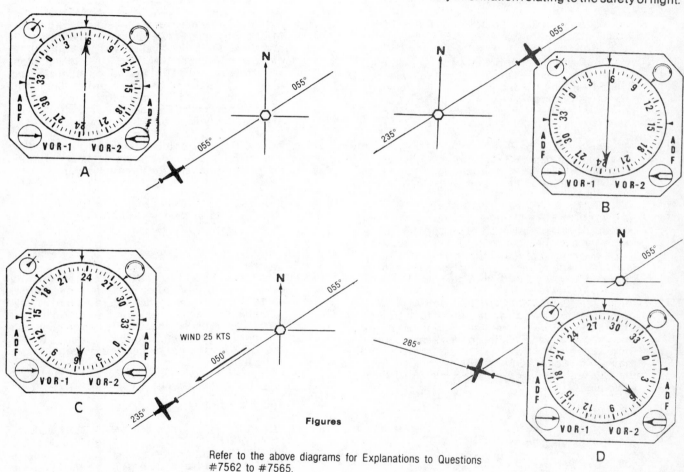

Figures

Refer to the above diagrams for Explanations to Questions #7562 to #7565.

7562. (2) IFH. The RMI needle points "TO" the inbound course to a station. The tail end of the needle shows the outbound course on radial. Heading is displayed under the lubber line.

7563. (1) IFH. The RMI needle points "TO" the inbound course to a station. The tail end of the needle shows the outbound course on radial. Heading is displayed under the lubber line.

7564. (3) IFH. The RMI needle points "TO" the inbound course to a station. The tail end of the needle shows the outbound course or radial. Heading is displayed under the lubber line.

7565. (2) IFH. The RMI needle points "TO" the inbound course to a station. The tail end of the needle shows the outbound course or radial. Heading is displayed under the lubber line.

7566. (3) AIM Para. 192. The term initial contact or initial callup means the first radio call made to a given facility, or the first call to a different controller or FSS specialist within a facility. USE THE FOLLOWING FORMAT:
1. name of facility being called,
2. the FULL aircraft identification as filed in the flight plan or as discussed under Aircraft Call Signs below,
3. type of message to follow or your request if it is short, and
4. the word "Over."

EXAMPLES:

"NEW YORK RADIO, MOONEY THREE ONE ONE ECHO, OVER."

"COLUMBIA GROUND, CESSNA THREE ONE SIX ZERO FOXTROT, IFR MEMPHIS, OVER."

"MIAMI CENTER BARON FIVE SIX THREE HOTEL, REQUEST VFR TRAFFIC ADVISORIES, OVER."

7567. (4) ACL. VOR changeover points (⌐) are indicated on enroute charts ONLY when they are not located at the midpoint, otherwise obvious changes in course. On V199 there is a course change at MOLEN intersection, thus making it the changeover point.

7568. (4) AIM Para. 266. On a "VFR ON TOP CLEARANCE" the pilot must use VFR cruising altitudes, which for V87 northbound with a magnetic course of 347 would be even thousand plus 500 feet.

7569. (2) FAR 95.1. The MRA (Minimum Reception Altitude) indicated by the flag with an "R" in it applies to the operation of an aircraft over an intersection used in the nagivation of that aircraft. The MRA is the lowest altitude at which the intersection can be determined using a radial not part of the airway.

7570. (2) AIM Para. 345. The COP is located midway between the navigation facilities for straight route segments, or at the intersection of radials or courses forming a dogleg in the case of dogleg route segments. When the COP is NOT located at the midway point, aeronautical charts will depict the COP location and give the mileage to the radio aids.

7571. (2) ACL.

Frequencies positioned above thin line NAVAID boxes are remoted to the NAVAID site.
Other frequencies at the controlling FSS named are available, however altitude and terrain may determine their reception

122.1R

Controlling FSS Name

WASHINGTON

Thin line box, without frequencies and Controlling FSS name indicates no FSS frequencies available.

Frequencies are transmitted and received by the FSS except those followed by "R" or "T":

R — FSS Receives only.

T — FSS transmits only.

7572. (3) FAR 91.127. Fly the highest of the following altitudes or flight levels for the route segment being flown:
1. The altitude or flight level assigned in the last ATC clearance received;
2. The minimum altitude (converted, if appropriate, to minimum flight level as prescribed in § 91.81(c)) for IFR operations; or
3. The altitude or flight level ATC has advised may be expected in a further clearance.

7573. (4) AIM Para. 132. Nonparticipating aircraft are not prohibited from flying within an MTR; however, extreme vigilance should be exercised when conducting fight through or near these routes. Pilots should contact FSSs within 100 NM of a particular MTR to obtain current information or route usage in their vicinity. Information available includes times of scheduled activity, altitudes in use on each route segment, and actual route width. Route width varies for each MTR and can extend several miles on either side of the charted MTR centerline. Route width information for IR and VR MTRs is also available in the FLIP AP/1B along with additional MTR (SR/AR) information. When requesting MTR information, pilots should give the FSS their position, route of flight, and destination in order to reduce frequency congestion and permit the FSS specialist to identify the MTR routes which could be a factor.

7574. (4) ACL. ARTCC Remoted Sites with Discrete VHF and UHF frequencies are indicated on low altitude enroute charts for the area covered.

7575. (3) AIM Para. 345. The COP is located midway between the navigation facilities for straight route segments, or at the intersection of radials or courses forming a dogleg in the case of dogleg route segments. When the COP is NOT located at the midway point, aeronautical charts will depict the COP location and give the mileage to the radio aids.

7576. (2) ACL. PECOS is a "VOR" ⬡ with "DME" ▢ and is a "compulsory reporting point" ▲ .

7577. (3) ACL. AIR/GROUND COMMUNICATION BOXES. HEAVY LINE BOXES indicate Flight Service Station (FSS). Frequencies 255.4, 122.2, and emerg. 243.0 and 121.5 and are not shown above boxes. All other frequencies available at FSSs are shown.

7578. (4) ACL. ARTCC Remoted Sites with Discrete VHF and UHF Frequencies are indicated on low altitude enroute charts for the area covered.

7579. (1) AIM Para. 162. Radar traffic information is given by the controller which includes: The azimuth from the aircraft's GROUND TRACK in terms of a 12-hour clock, distance in nautical miles, direction that the target is preceding and type of aircraft and altitude if known.

7580. (1) AIM Pilot/Controller Glossary. RESUME OWN NAVIGATION — Used by ATC to advise a pilot to resume his own navigational responsibility. It is issued after completion of a radar vector or when radar contact is lost while the aircraft is being radar vectored.

7581. (2) AIM Pilot/Controller Glossary. RADAR CONTACT — Used by ATC to inform an aircraft that it is identified on the radar display and radar flight following will be provided until radar identification is terminated. Radar service may also be provided within the limits of necessity and capability. When a pilot is informed of "radar contact" he automatically discontinues reporting over compulsory reporting points.

7582. (4) AIM Pilot/Controller Glossary. RESUME OWN NAVIGATION — Used by ATC to advise a pilot to resume his own navigational responsibility. It is issued after completion of a radar vector or when radar contact is lost while the aircraft is being radar vectored.

7583. (4) FAR 91.119. Except when necessary for takeoff or landing, or unless otherwise authorized by the Administrator, no person may operate an aircraft under IFR below —
1. The applicable minimum altitudes prescribed in Parts 95 and 97; or
2. If no applicable minimum altitude is prescribed in those parts —

In the case of operations over an area designated as a mountainous area in Part 95 an altitude of 2,000 feet above the highest obstacle within a horizontal distance of five statute miles from the course to be flown; or

In any other case, an altitude of 1,000 feet above the highest obstacle within a horizontal distance of five statute miles from the course to be flown.

7584. (2) AIM Pilot/Controller Glossary. MINIMUM EN ROUTE IFR ALTITUDE/MEA — The lowest published altitude between radio fixes which assures acceptable navigational signal coverage and meets obstacle clearance requirements between those fixes. The MEA prescribed for a Federal airway or segment thereof, area navigation low or high route or other direct route applies to the entire width of the airway, segment or route between the radio fixes defining the airway, segment, or route.

7585. (4) FAR 91.129. OPERATION UNDER IFR IN CONTROLLED AIRSPACE: MALFUNCTION REPORTS — The pilot in command of each aircraft operated in controlled airspace under IFR, shall report immediately to ATC any of the following malfunctions of equipment occurring in flight:
1. Loss of VOR, TACAN, ADF, or low frequency navigation receiver capability.

2. Complete or partial loss of ILS receiver capability.
3. Impairment of air/ground communications capability.

In each report required by preceding paragraph, the pilot in command shall include the —
1. Aircraft identification;
2. Equipment affected;
3. Degree to which the capability of the pilot to operate under IFR in the ATC system is impaired; and
4. Nature and extent of assistant he desires from ATC.

NOTE: The word "aircraft" is used and not airplane or helicopter.

7586. (4) FAR 91.90. No person may operate inside a Group I terminal control area without a two-way radio, a VOR, a Mode C transponder, a private pilot license to takeoff or land, and an appropriate clearance from ATC.

7587. (4) ACL. A "MEA GAP" is established where there is a gap in the navigation signal coverage. However, obstacle clearance is still provided.

7588. (4) FAR 91.109. When operating below 18,000 feet MSL and —
1. On a magnetic course of zero degrees through 179 degrees, any odd thousand foot MSL altitude plus 500 feet (such as 3,500, 5,500, or 7,500); or
2. On a magnetic course of 180 degrees through 359 degrees, any even thousand foot MSL altitude plus 500 feet (such as 4,500, 6,500, or 8,500).

7589. (3) FAR 91.115. No person may operate an aircraft in controlled airspace under IFR unless —
1. He has filed and IFR flight plan; and
2. He has received an appropriate ATC clearance.

7590. (3) ACL. ARTCC Remoted Sites with Discrete VHF and UHF Frequencies are indicated on low altitude charts for the area covered.

7591. (1) FAR 91.119. Except when necessary for takeoff or landing, or unless otherwise authorized by the Administrator, no person may operate an aircraft under IFR below —
1. The applicable minimum altitudes prescribed in Parts 95 and 97; or
2. If no applicable minimum altitude is prescribed in those parts —

In the case of operations over an area designated as a mountainous area in Part 95 an altitude of 2,000 feet above the highest obstacle within a horizontal distance of five statute miles from the course to be flown; or

In any other case, an altitude of 1,000 feet above the highest obstacle within a horizontal distance of five statute miles from the course to be flown.

NOTE: The word "aircraft" is used and not airplane or helicopter.

7592. (2) FAR 91.109. When operating below 18,000 feet MSL and —
1. On a magnetic course of zero degrees through 179 degrees, any odd thousand foot MSL altitude plus 500 feet (such as 3,500, 5,500, or 7,500); or
2. On a magnetic course of 180 degrees through 359 degrees, any even thousand foot MSL altitude plus 500 feet (such as 4,500, 6,500, or 8,500).

7593. (3) AIM Pilot/Controller Glossary. The MCA is the lowest altitude at certain fixes at which an aircraft must cross when proceeding in the direction of a higher minimum enroute IFR altitude (MEA). The MCA southbound on V21E is 11,400 feet and 12,000 feet eastbound on V293. 12,000' eastbound must be reached by the Cedar City VOR.

7594. (2) ACL. HEAVY LINE BOXES Indicate Flight Service Stations (FSS). Frequencies 255.4, 122.2, and emerg. 243.0 and 121.5 are available and are not shown above boxes. All other frequencies available at FSSs are shown.

| Fayetteville FYV |

7595. (3) FAR 91.32 states that no person may operate a civil aircraft of U.S. registry —
1. At cabin pressure altitudes above 12,500 feet (MSL) up to and including 14,000 feet (MSL), unless the required minimum flight crew is provided with and uses supplemental oxygen for that part of the flight at those altitudes that is of more than 30 minutes duration;
2. At cabin pressure altitudes above 14,000 feet (MSL), unless the required minimum flight crew is provided with and uses supplemental oxygen during the entire flight time at those altitudes; and
3. At cabin pressure altitudes above 15,000 feet (MSL), unless each occupant of the aircraft is provided with supplemental oxygen.

7596. (4) AIM Para. 503. All "FLIGHT WATCH" (enroute flight advisory service (EFAS)) facilities may be contacted on 122.0 MHz.

7597. (2) FAR 91.129. If a two-way radio communications failure occurs in VFR conditions, or if VFR conditions are encountered after the failure each pilot shall continue the flight under VFR and land as soon as practicable.

7598. (4) AIM Para. 80. Uncontrolled airspace is that portion of the airspace that has not been designated as continental control area, control area, control zone, terminal area, or transition area. Since transition areas are the lowest reaching controlled airspace, which is 700 feet AGL with uncontrolled airspace underlying it.

7599. (3) AIM Pilot/Controller Glossary. DISCRETE FREQUENCY — A separate radio frequency for use in direct pilot-controller communications in air traffic control which reduces frequency congestion by controlling the number of aircraft operating on a particular frequency at one time. Discrete frequencies are normally designated for each control sector in enroute/terminal ATC facilities.

Air Route Traffic Control Center (ARTCC)
NAME
Name   ARTCC Remoted Sites
134.3 269.5 with Discrete VHF and UHF Freqs.

7600. (1) AC 67-27C. The first VOR is tuned in to the "BCE" VORTAC with "FROM" indication on V85 (060°) and the second VOR is tuned into the HVE VORTAC with a "TO" indication for the section of V85 which is past the mileage breakdown point. The two VORs indicate that the aircraft is to the right of V85 (060°) from the "BCE" VORTAC and to the left of V85 extending from the "HVE" VORTAC as illustrated below.

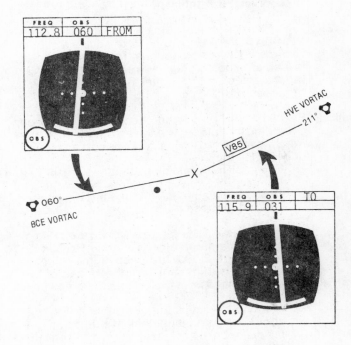

7601. (2) AIM Para. 266. When operating in VFR conditions with an ATC authorization to "MAINTAIN VFR ON TOP/MAINTAIN VFR CONDITIONS" pilots on IFR flight plans must:
1. Fly at the appropriate VFR altitude as prescribed in FAR 91.109.
2. Comply with the VFR visibility and distance from cloud criteria in FAR 91.105 (BASIC VFR WEATHER MINIMUMS.)
3. Comply with instrument flight rules that are applicable to this flight (i.e., *minimum IFR altitudes*, position reporting, radio communications, course to be flown, adherence to ATC clearance, etc.).

NOTE: Pilots should advise ATC prior to any altitude change to insure the exchange of accurate traffic information.

7602. (3) AIM Para. 266 states that a pilot operating in VFR conditions with an ATC authorization to "maintain VFR ON TOP/maintain VFR conditions," pilots on IFR flight plans must fly at appropriate VFR altitude as prescribed in FAR 91.109. FAR 91.109 describes VFR cardinal altitudes plus 500 feet.

7603. (4) AIM Pilot/Controller Glossary states that the MEA (Minimum Enroute Altitude) is the lowest published altitude between radio fixes which assures acceptable navigational signal coverage and meets obstacle clearance requirements between those fixes. The MEA prescribed for a Federal airway or segment thereof, area navigation low or high route or other direct route applies to the entire width of the airway, segment or route between the radio fixes defining the airway, segment, or route.

7604. (4) AIM Para. 266 states that a pilot operating in VFR conditions with an ATC authorization to "maintain VFR ON TOP/maintain VFR conditions," pilots on IFR flight plans must fly at appropriate VFR altitude as prescribed in FAR 91.109. FAR 91.109 describes VFR cardinal altitudes plus 500 feet.

7605. (2) ACL. A star (★) next to a frequency indicates that the operation is less than continuous or is part time.

7606. (4) AIM Para. 266 states that a pilot operating in VFR conditions with an ATC authorization to "maintain VFR ON TOP/maintain VFR conditions," pilots on IFR flight plans must fly at appropriate VFR altitude as prescribed in FAR 91.109. FAR 91.109 describes VFR cardinal altitudes plus 500 feet.

7607. (2) AIM Para. 114. "MOAs consist of airspace of defined vertical and lateral limits established for the purpose of separating certain military training activities from IFR traffic. Whenever a MOA is being used, nonparticipating IFR traffic may be cleared through a MOA if IFR separation can be provided by ATC. Otherwise, ATC will reroute or restrict nonparticipating IFR traffic."

7608. (2) IFR EOG #8, AIM Para. 262. A flight altitude at the MOCA may be requested by a pilot, or assigned by ATC for traffic control purposes, for use within 22 nautical miles of the VOR. The MOCA may be assigned beyond 22 nautical miles provided certain special conditions exist. Beyond 22 nautical miles, the MOCA assures only obstruction clearance.

The term "CRUISE" may be used instead of "MAINTAIN" to assign a block of airspace, to a pilot, from the minimum IFR altitude up to and including the altitude specified in the cruise clearance. The pilot may level off at any intermediate altitude within this block of airspace. Climb/descent within the block is to be made at the discretion of the pilot. However, once the pilot starts descent and verbally reports leaving an altitude in the block, he may not return to that altitude without additional ATC clearance.

7609. (4) AIM Para. 345. The COP is located midway between the navigation facilities for straight route segments, or at the intersection of radials or courses forming a dogleg in the case of dogleg route segments. When the COP is NOT located at the midway point, aeronautical charts will depict the COP location and give the mileage to the radio aids.

7610. (2) IFR EOG #23. LOBOE Intersection is defined by the 010° radial of the ADM VORTAC and by the 089° radial of OKC VORTAC. Indicator "A" is set appropriately for flying a 269° course for the inbound leg and indicator "C" designates ADM's 010° radial.

7611. (1) IFR EOG #8. At the Reno VORTAC there is a MCA (Minimum Crossing Altitude) specified which does not affect the first lag northeast bound on V6. However, there is a MCA specified for flight southbound on V165 which 10,000 feet. The MCA altitudes are noted above Reno VOR box.

MCA is the minimum altitude at which certain radio facilities or intersections must be crossed in specified directions of flight. If a normal climb, commenced immediately after passing a fix beyond which a higher MEA applies, would NOT assure adequate obstruction clearance, an MCA is specified.

7612. (4) FAR 91.109. Each person operating an aircraft under VFR in level cruising flight more than 3,000 feet above the surface shall maintain the appropriate altitude or flight level prescribed below, unless otherwise authorized by ATC:

When operating below 18,000 feet MSL and —
1. On a magnetic course of zero degrees through 179 degrees, any odd thousand foot MSL altitude plus 500 feet (such as 3,500, 5,500, or 7,500); or
2. On a magnetic course of 180 degrees through 359 degrees, any even thousand foot MSL altitude plus 500 feet (such as 4,500, 6,500, or 8,500).

7613. (3) ACL. A "MEA GAP" is established where there is a gap in the navigation signal coverage. However, obstacle clearance is still provided.

7614. (2) AIM Para. 114. MOAs consist of airspace of defined vertical and lateral limits established for the purpose of separating certain military training activities from IFR traffic. Whenever a MOA is being used, nonparticipating IFR traffic may be cleared through a MOA if IFR separation can be provided by ATC. Otherwise, ATC will reroute or restrict nonparticipating IFR traffic.

7615. (X) FAA Deletion.

7616. (4) AIM Par. 347. The heading upon entry will be approximately 137°. There is a 5° zone either side of this heading where either a parallel or direct entry would be considered equally correct.

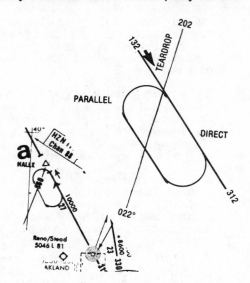

7617. (2) AIM Para. 347. The clearance instructed the pilot to hold with 10 mile legs south of Halle Int. The DME distance to Halle intersection is 27 NM. 27 NM − 10 NM = 17 DME from the Reno (RNO 117.9) VORTAC.

7618. (4) IFR EOG #8. Obstruction clearance is normally at least 1,000 feet in non-mountainous areas above the highest terrain or obstruction 4 miles either side of centerline of the airway or route.

7619. (1) IFR EOG #1. If a normal climb, commenced immediately after passing a fix beyond which a higher MEA applies, would NOT assure adequate obstruction clearance, then a MCA is specified. Otherwise the radio fix is crossed at the MEA at which it is approached, and then a climb is commenced to the next higher MEA.

7620. (1) IFR EOG #8. MRA (Minimum Reception Altitude) is the lowest altitude required to receive adequate signals to determine specific fixes. Reception of signals from a radio facility located off the airway being flown may be inadequate at the designated MEA, in which case, an MRA is designated for the fix.

7621. (4) Computation:
Dist = 111 NM; GS = 171 KTS;
Course = 186° (203°T);
Time = 39 Mins.

7622. (3) ACL. Circle around "Ⓛ" indicates pilot controlled lighting (PCL).

"*" Asterisk indicates lighting on request or operating part of night only.

7623. (2) AIM Pilot/Controller Glossary. REMOTE COMMUNICATIONS OUTLET/RCO AND REMOTE TRANSMITTER/RECEIVER/RTR — An unmanned communications facility remotely controlled by air traffic personnel. RCOs serve FSSs. RTRs serve terminal ATC facilities. An RCO or RTR may be UHF or VHF and will extend the communication range of the air traffic facility.

7624. (3) IFR EOG #8. MCA (Minimum Crossing Altitude) is the minimum altitude at which certain radio facilities or intersections must be crossed in specified directions of flight. If a normal climb, commenced immediately after passing a fix beyond which a higher MEA applies, would NOT assure adequate obstruction clearance, an MCA is specified.

7625. (2) IFR EOG #8. MCA (Minimum Crossing Altitude) is the minimum altitude at which certain radio facilities or intersections must be crossed in specified directions of flight. If a normal climb, commenced immediately after passing a fix beyond which a higher MEA applies, would NOT assure adequate obstruction clearance, an MCA is specified.

7626. (4) AIM 266. VFR ON TOP flights may be conducted up to, but not including F180, wich eliminates Answers #1 through #3.

7627. (3) FAR 91.32 states that no person may operate a civil aircraft of U.S. registry:
1. At cabin pressure altitudes above 12,500 feet (MSL) up to and including 14,000 feet (MSL), unless the required minimum flight crew is provided with and uses supplemental oxygen for that part of the flight at those altitudes that is of more than 30 minutes duration;
2. At cabin pressure altitudes above 14,000 feet (MSL), unless the required minimum flight crew is provided with and uses supplemental oxygen during the entire flight time at those altitudes; and
3. At cabin pressure altitudes above 15,000 feet (MSL), unless each occupant of the aircraft is provided with supplemental oxygen.

7628. (2) Computation:

	Time / NM	
Butte VORTAC	08:50	0
Divid Intersection	08:54	9
DBS VORTAC	09:43	110

2.25 NM/Min.

$$\frac{110 \text{ NM}}{2.25 \text{ NM/Min.}} = 49 \text{ Mins.}$$

08:54 + 49 Mins. = 09:43

7629. (3) ACL. VOR changeover point(s) (⌐) are indicated on enroute charts ONLY when they are not located at the mid-point, otherwise the changeover point is half the distance between the two VORs. In this case, the changeover point is just west of QUIRT intersection. Note the changeover point is 15 miles from Jackson VORTAC and QUIRT is 12 miles from Jackson.

7630. (2) FAR 91.24. Persons operating helicopters in terminal control areas at or below 1,000 feet AGL under the terms of a letter of agreement are relieved from the requirement to have an operating transponder.

7631. (X) FAA Deletion.

7632. (3) FAR 91.90. Equipment requirements for flight in a Group II TCA include a 2-way radio with appropriate frequencies, a 4096 transponder (Mode C NOT required) and a VOR or TACAN.

7633. (3) IFR EOG #7. The CDI needle points toward the selected course.

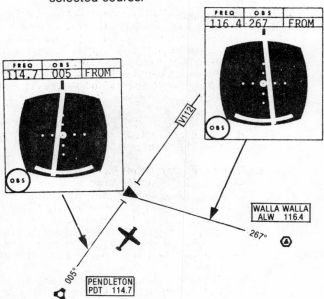

7634. (3) ACL. Borders indicate the divisions between various ARTCC and area (i) is next to the Pendleton remote site for Seattle ARTCC.

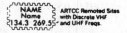

7635. (1) Computation:

Mag. Wind = 250° (270 – 20°E variation)

The wind correction angle is 9° right (see computer solution).

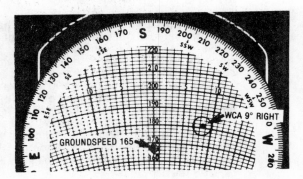

7636. (4) ACL. Open area (white) indicates controlled airspace. Shaded area (brown) indicates uncontrolled airspace up to 14,500 feet.

7637. (3) AIM Para. 347. The heading to the fix 014° which falls into the teardrop entry area.

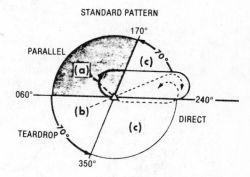

7638. (3) IFR EOG #8. MRA (Minimum Reception Altitude) is the lowest altitude required to receive adequate signals to determine specific fixes. Reception of signals from a radio facility located off the airway being flown may be inadequate at the designated MEA, in which case, an MRA is designated for the fix.

7639. (3) AIM Para. 347. Outbound leg timing begins over/abeam the fix, whichever occurs later.

7640. (1) FAR 91.123. COURSE TO BE FLOWN. Unless otherwise authorized by ATC, no person may operate an aircraft within controlled airspace, under IFR, except as follows:
1. On a Federal airway, along the centerline of that airway.
2. On any other route, along the direct course between the navigational aids or fixes defining that route.

However, this section does not prohibit maneuvering the aircraft to pass well clear of other air traffic or the maneuvering of the aircraft, in VFR conditions to clear the intended flight path both before and during climb or descent.

7641. (3) AIM Pilot/Controller Glossary. Pilots are expected to maintain a speed of plus or minus 10 knots IAS or a Mach number of 0.02 of the specified speed.

7642. (3) AIM Para. 362. Aircraft will normally be informed when it is necessary to vector across the final approach course for spacing and other reasons. If approach course crossing is imminent and the pilot has not been informed that he will be vectored across the final approach course, he should query the controller.

7643. (4) AIM Para. 362. Where radar is approved for approach control service, it is used not only for radar approaches (ASR and PAR) but is also used to provide vectors in conjunction with published nonradar approaches based on radio navaids (ILS, VOR, NDB, TACAN). Radar vectors can provide course guidance and expedite traffic to the final approach course of any establshed IAP or the traffic pattern for a visual approach.

7644. (4) AIM. Contact approaches will only be authorized when requested by the pilot and the reported ground visibility at the destination airport is at least 1 statute mile.

SIDS and STARS are assigned as determined necessary by ATC.

7645. (3) AIM Pilot/Controller Glossary. A CRUISE CLEAR-ANCE is used in an ATC clearance to authorize a pilot to conduct flight at any altitude from the minimum IFR altitude up to and including the altitude specified in the clearance. The pilot may level off at any intermediate altitude within this block of airspace. Climb/descent within the block is to be made at the discretion of the pilot. However, once the pilot starts descent and verbally reports leaving an altitude in the block he may not return to that altitude without additional ATC clearance.

7646. (1) FAR 91.123. Unless otherwise authorized by ATC, no person may operate an aircraft within controlled airspace, under IFR, except as follows:
1. On a Federal airway, along the centerline of tha airway.
2. On any other route, along the direct course between the navigational aids or fixes defining that route.

However, this section does not prohibit maneuvering the aircraft to pass well clear of other air traffic or the maneuvering of the aircraft, in VFR conditions to clear the intended flight path both before and during climb or descent.

FAR 91.123 states that the pilot MUST maintain the centerline of that airway, however, he should also maintain a continuous scan for other aircraft.

7647. (3) AC 00-50A. Assume that the aircraft encounters an instantaneous wind shear where the 20-knot headwind shears away completely. At that instant, several things will happen; the airspeed will drop from 140 to 120 knots, the nose will begin to pitch down, and the aircraft will begin to drop below the glide slope. The aircraft will then be both slow and low in a "power deficient" state. The pilot may then pull the nose up to a point even higher than before the shear in an effort to recapture the glide slope. This will aggravate the airspeed situation even further until the pilot advances the throttles and sufficient time elapses at the higher power setting for the engines to replenish the power deficiency. If the aircraft reaches the ground before the power deficiency is corrected, the landing will be short, slow, and hard. However, if there is sufficient time to regain the proper airspeed and glide slope before reaching the ground, then the "double reverse" problem arises. This is because the throttles are set too high for a stabilized approach in a no-wind condition. So, as soon as the power deficiency is replenished, the throttles should be pulled back even further than they were before the shear

(because power required for a 3° ILS in no wind is less than for a 20-knot headwind). If the pilot does not quickly retard the throttles, the aircraft will soon have an excess of power; i.e., it will be high and fast and may not be able to stop in the available runway length.

7648. (3) AIM Para. 380. Aircraft that execute a side-step maneuver will be cleared for a specified approach and landing on the adjacent parallel runway. Example, "cleared for ILS runway 07 left approach, side-step to runway 07 right." Pilots are expected to commence the side-step maneuver as soon as possible after the runway or runway environment is in sight.

7649. (4) IFH. The small hand indicates thousands of feet. The long, thin hand indicates hundreds of feet. The very thin hand with the triangular tip indicates tens of thousands of feet.

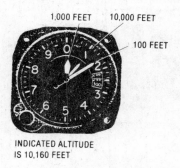

INDICATED ALTITUDE
IS 10,160 FEET

7650. (4) AIM Para. 531. For flight below 18,000 MSL, set altimeter to the current reported altimeter setting of a station along the route and within 100 NM of the aircraft, or if there is no station within this area, the current reported altimeter setting of an appropriate available station. When an aircraft is enroute on an instrument flight plan, the ATC controller will furnish this information to the pilot at least once while the aircraft is in his area of jurisdiction. In the case of an aircraft not equipped with a radio, set to the elevation of the departure airport or use an appropriate altimeter setting available prior to departure.

7651. (3) IFH. Enroute at FL290 the pilot would have his altimeter set to 29.92 inches since his altitude is above FL180, and remains at this setting since he failed to reset it to the local altimeter setting of 30.26 during descent. Since 30.26 − 29.92 = 0.34 and 1 inch per 1,000 feet equals 0.1 inch per 100 feet and 0.01 inch per 10 feet., The altimeter will then indicate an error of 340 feet. Because the flight went from a low pressure area to a high pressure area, the altimeter error is subtracted from the field elevation of 134 feet (134' − 340' = −206') to find the indicated altitude of −206 feet.

7652. (2) IFH. The small hand indicates thousands of feet. The long, thin hand indicates hundreds of feet. The very thin hand with the triangular tip indicates tens of thousands of feet.

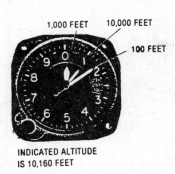

INDICATED ALTITUDE
IS 10,160 FEET

7653. (4) AIM Para. 531. The cruising altitude or flight level of aircraft shall be maintained by reference to an altimeter which shall be set, when operating at or above 18,000 feet MSL, to 29.92 inches of mercury (standard setting).

7654. (4) IFH. Enroute at FL290, the pilot would have his altimeter set to 29.92 inches since his altitude is at or above FL180, and remains at this setting since he failed to reset it to the local altimeter setting of 30.57 during descent. Since 30.57 − 29.92 = 0.65 and 1 inch per 1,000 feet equals 0.1 inch per 100 feet and 0.01 inch per 10 feet, the altimeter will then indicate an error of 650 feet. Because the flight went from a low pressure area to a high pressure area, the altimeter error is subtracted from field elevation of 650 feet:

$$650 - 650 = 0' \text{ MSL}$$

7655. (2) IFH. Pressure altitude is the altitude indicated when the altimeter setting window is adjusted to 29.92. This is the standard datum plane, a theoretical plane where air pressure (corrected to 15°C.) is equal to 29.92 inches of mercury. Because the pilot is flying at FL250 his altimeter will be set at 29.92 inches Hg since he is above FL180.

7656. (2) AIM Para. 98. Pilots operating IFR within controlled airspace will fly at an altitude or flight level assigned by ATC. When operating IFR within controlled airspace with an altitude assignment of VFR ON TOP, flight is to be conducted at an appropriate VFR altitude which is not below the minimum IFR altitude for the route. VFR ON TOP is not permitted in certain airspace areas, such as positive control airspace, certain Restricted Areas, etc. Consequently, IFR flights operating VFR ON TOP will avoid such airspace.

7657. (3) IFR EOG #7. The CDI needle points towards the selected course. The aircraft is in the area NE of the intersection.

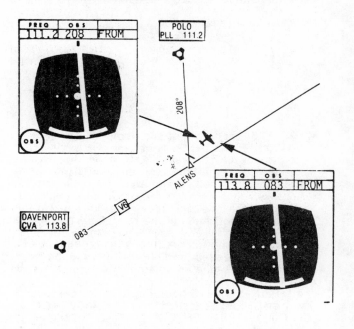

7658. (X) FAA Deletion.

7659. (4) ACL. Since Wapel intersection is beyond the halfway point from the Ottumway (OTM 111.6) VORTAC (Note: No VOR COP charted), the pilot should have already switched his VOR receiver to the Moline (MZV 114.4) VORTAC. The same is true for the Burlington (BRL 111.4) VORTAC which is 35 miles from the intersection with the halfway point being 28.5. The only two remaining radials are the R-142 from Iowa City (IOW) and the R-253 from Moline (MZV), both of which are less than halfway from Wapel intersection.

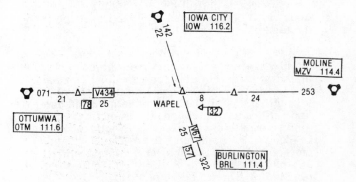

7660. (1) ACL. Borders indicate the divisions between various ARTCC and area (h) is next to the Bradford remote site for Chicago ARTCC.

Air Route Traffic Control Center (ARTCC)

NAME Name 134.3 269.55 ARTCC Remoted Sites with Discrete VHF and UHF Freqs.

7661. (4) FAR 91.33. For flight at and above 24,000 feet MSL, if VOR navigational equipment is required, no person may operate a U.S. registered civil aircraft within the 50 states, and the District of Columbia, unless that aircraft is equipped with approved distance measuring equipment (DME). When DME fails at and above 24,000 feet MSL, the pilot in command of the aircraft shall notify ATC immediately, and may then continue operations at and above 24,000 feet MSL to the next airport of intended landing at which repairs or replacement of the equipment can be made.

7662. (3) AIM Para. 266. When operating in VFR conditions with an ATC authorization to "MAINTAIN VFR ON TOP/MAINTAIN VFR CONDITIONS" pilots on IFR flight plans must:

1. Fly at the appropriate VFR altitude as prescribed in FAR 91.109.
2. Comply with the VFR visibility and distance from cloud criteria in FAR 91.105 (BASIC VFR WEATHER MINIMUMS.)
3. Comply with instrument flight rules that are applicable to this flight (i.e., *minimum IFR altitudes*, position reporting, radio communications, course to be flown, adherence to ATC clearance, etc.).

NOTE: Pilots should advise ATC prior to any change to insure the exchange of accurate traffic information.

7663. (2) AIM Para. 266. A pilot on an IFR flight plan operating in VFR weather conditions, may request VFR ON TOP in lieu of an assigned altitude. This would permit the pilot to select an altitude or flight level of his choice (subject to any ATC restrictions).

ATC may not authorize VFR ON TOP/VFR CONDITIONS operations unless the pilot requests the VFR operation or a clearance to operate in VFR CONDITIONS will result in noise abatement benefits where part of the IFR departure route does not conform to an FAA approved noise abatement route or altitude.

7664. (2) AIM Para. 266. Pilots desiring to climb through a cloud, haze, smoke, or other meteorological formation and then either cancel their IFR flight plan or operate VFR ON TOP may request a climb to VFR ON TOP. The ATC authorization shall contain either a top report or a statement that no top report is available, and a request to report reaching VFR ON TOP. Additionally, the ATC authorization may contain a clearance limit, routing and an alternative clearance if VFR ON TOP is not reached by a specified altitude.

7665. (4) IFR EOG #7.

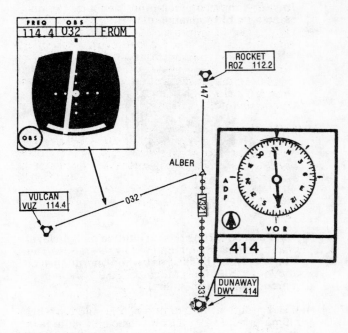

7666. (1) ACL.

Air Route Traffic Control Center (ARTCC)

NAME Name 134.3 269.55 ARTCC Remoted Sites with Discrete VHF and UHF Freqs.

7667. (3) ACL. Look at the note to the left of the GADSDEN VOR. V325E is a substitute airway using the 136 merging to DUNAWAY NDB. Note the arrow to the east of ARBEE intersection pointing to the NDB, and the arrow to the west of the intersection pointing to ARBEE. These are the only nav aid that may be used to identify that intersection.

7668. (2) Computation:

Hokes Intersection at 18:43
GAD VORTAC at 18:45

　　　　　　　　　　　　　　　　2:00

　　　　　　　　　　　　　　　　5 NM

5 NM/2 Min. = 2.5 NM/1 Min.

Distance from GAD VORTAC to MSL VORTAC = 83 NM:

$$\frac{83 \text{ NM}}{2.5 \text{ NM/Min.}} = 33 \text{ Min.}$$

18:45 + 33 Min. = 19:18

7669. (1) IFR EOG #8. MRA (Minimum Reception Altitude) is the lowest altitude required to receive adequate reception of the signals from a radio facility located off the airway. A DME fix arrow (→ or ⑲ ⟶) at a fix where an MRA is given, indicates that the fix may also be identified with DME. *If DME is used* to identify the fix, *the MRA does not apply* since it is not necessary to receive the facility off the airway. Note that BOUNT intersection is 22 NM from VULCAN, allowing adequate reception of the VOR at the MOCA.

7670. (4) AIM Para. 345. The COP is located midway between the navigation facilities for straight route segments, or at the intersection of radials or courses forming a dogleg in the case of dogleg route segments. When the COP is NOT located at the midway point, aeronautical charts will depict the COP location and give the mileage to the radio aids.

7671. (3) AIM Para. 347.

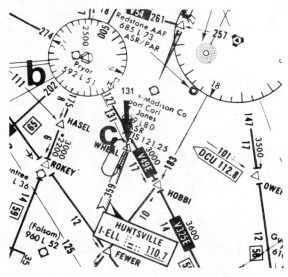

The depicted holding pattern is approached from the parallel quadrant.

7672. (1) AIM Para. 271. Separation will be provided between all aircraft operating on IFR flight plans except during that part of the flight (outside of a TCA or TRSA) being conducted on a VFR ON TOP/VFR CONDITIONS clearance. Under these conditions, ATC may issue traffic advisories but it is the sole responsibility of the pilot to be vigilant so as to see and avoid other aircraft.

7673. (1) AIM Para. 266. A pilot on an IFR flight plan operating in VFR weather conditions, may request VFR ON TOP in lieu of an assigned altitude. This would permit the pilot to select an altitude or flight level of his choice (subject to any ATC restrictions).

7674. (2) FAR 91.105.

Basic VFR Weather Minimums Table

ALTITUDE	FLIGHT VISIBILITY	DISTANCE FROM CLOUDS
1,200 feet or less above the surface (regardless of MSL altitude) Within controlled airspace	3 statute miles	500 feet below. 1,000 feet above. 2,000 feet horizontal.
Outside controlled airspace	1 statute mile except as provided in § 91.105(b)	Clear of clouds.
More than 1,200 feet above the surface but less than 10,000 feet MSL— Within controlled airspace	3 statute miles	500 feet below. 1,000 feet above. 2,000 feet horizontal.
Outside controlled airspace	1 statute mile	500 feet below. 1,000 feet above. 2,000 feet horizontal.
More than 1,200 feet above the surface and at or above 10,000 feet MSL	5 statute miles	1,000 feet below. 1,000 feet above. 1 mile horizontal.

NOTE: The change in both flight visibility and in cloud distances at or above 10,000 feet MSL.

7675. (1) FAR 91.105.

More than 1,200 feet above the surface but less than 10,000 feet MSL— Within controlled airspace	3 statute miles	500 feet below. 1,000 feet above. 2,000 feet horizontal.

7676. (2) ACL.

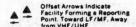

Offset Arrows Indicate
Facility Forming a Reporting
Point. Toward LF/MF. Away
from VHF/UHF

All the instruments indicate a western heading, and the only two NDBs are the TL 379 (006) and Egmont KEY 310 (101°). Figure (b) shows an NDW to the west which is not the case for the 310 FQ, and Figure (c) shows an NDB to the south where there is none for the 379 FQ.

7677. (4) ACL.

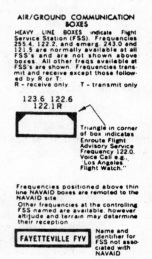

AIR/GROUND COMMUNICATION BOXES

HEAVY LINE BOXES indicate Flight Service Station (FSS). Frequencies 255.4, 122.2, and emerg. 243.0 and 121.5 are normally available at all FSS's and are not shown above boxes. All other freqs available at FSS's are shown. Frequencies transmit and receive except those followed by R or T:
R - receive only   T - transmit only

123.6 122.6
122.1 R

Triangle in corner of box indicates Enroute Flight Advisory Service Frequency 122.0. Voice Call e.g., "Los Angeles Flight Watch."

Frequencies positioned above thin line NAVAID boxes are remoted to the NAVAID site

Other frequencies at the controlling FSS named are available, however altitude and terrain may determine their reception

FAYETTEVILLE FYV

Name and identifier for FSS not associated with NAVAID

7678. (1) COMP.

Leg	HDG	GS
GNI VORTAC to Magee Int......	098°	193 KTS
Magee Int. to Mlg. Brkg. Pt......	101°	191.5 KTS
Mileage Brkg Pt. to Crabi Int....	099°	192 KTS
Crabi Int. to Egmont Key NDB....	101°	192 KTS

Leg	Distance	Time
GNI VORTAC to Magee Int....	122 NM	38.0 Min.
Magee Int. to Mlg. Brkg. Pt....	54.0 NM	17.0 Min.
Mlg. Brkg Pt. to Crabi Int. ...	115 NM	36.0 Min.
Crabi Int. to Egmont Key NDB...	107	33.5 Min.

124.5 Min
= 2:04:30

7679. (4) AIR ROUTE TRAFFIC CONTROL CENTER (ARTCC) Borders indicate the divisions between various ATCC and Crabi Intersection falls within the MIAMI boundaries.

7680. (1) AIM Para. 266. When operating in VFR conditions with an ATC authorization to "MAINTAIN VFR ON TOP/MAINTAIN VFR CONDITIONS" pilots on IFR flight plans must:
1. Fly at the appropriate VFR altitude as prescribed in FAR 91.109.

2. Comply with the VFR visibility and distance from cloud criteria in FAR 91.105 (BASIC VFR WEATHER MINIMUMS).
3. Comply with instrument flight rules that are applicable to this flight (i.e., minimum IFR altitudes, position reporting, radio communications, course to be flown, adherence to ATC clearance, etc.).

NOTE: Pilots should advise ATC prior to any altitude change to insure the exchange of accurate traffic information.

7681. (3) FAR 91.105.

More than 1,200 feet above the surface and more than 10,000 feet MSL —
Within controlled airspace ...... 5 statute miles.... 1,000 feet below.
1,000 feet above.
1 mile horizontal.

NOTE: The change in both flight visibility and in cloud distances at or above 10,000 feet MSL

7682. (3) FAR 91.105, 91.109. VFR ON TOP flight must be conducted at or above the minimum IFR altitude and in basic VFR weather conditions.

7683. (3) FAR 91.109. When a pilot is operating on a "VFR ON TOP" clearance, he must fly VFR cruising altitudes which are based on MAGNETIC COURSE.

7684. (3) FAR 91.109. A pilot operating on a "VFR ON TOP" clearance must fly VFR cruising altitudes which are effective below 18,000 feet MSL, the floor of the positive control area, above which VFR flight is not allowed.

7685. (1) IFR EOG #7. The CDI needle points towards the selected course.

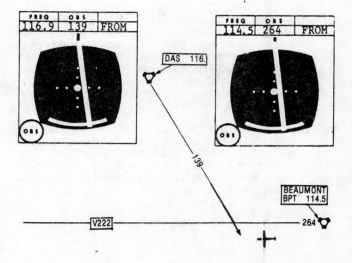

7686. (1) AIM Para. 347.

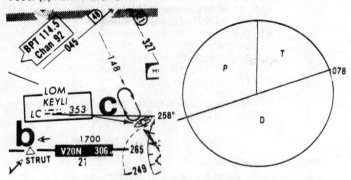

A heading of about 070° requires a parallel entry.

7687. (4) FAR 91.127. If holding instructions have been received, leave the holding fix at the expect-further-clearance time received, or, if an expected approach clearance time has been received, leave the holding fix in order to arrive over the fix from which the approach begins as close as possible to the expected approach clearance time.

7688. (4) AIM Para. 345. The COP is located midway between the navigation facilities for straight route segments, or at the intersection of radials or courses forming a dogleg in the case of dogleg route segments. When the COP is NOT located at the midway point, aeronautical charts will depict the COP location and give the mileage to the radio aids.

7689. (3) ACL.

The Scholes airport (j) has the above localizer course symbol indicated.

7690. (3) ACL. HEAVY LINE BOXES indicate Flight Service Station (FSS). Frequencies 255.4, 122.2, and emerg. 243.0 and 121.5 are available and are not shown above boxes. All other frequencies available at FSSs are shown. Frequencies transmit and receive except those followed by R or T:

R — receive only

T — transmit only

7691. (3) ACL.

The Jefferson Co. airport (e) has two of the above symbols depicted at the airport, one of which is for the back course.

7692. (1) AIM Para. 345. The COP is located midway between the navigation facilities for straight route segments, or at the intersection of radials or courses forming a dogleg in the case of dogleg route segments. When the COP is NOT located at the midway point, aeronautical charts will depict the COP location and give the mileage to the radio aids.

7693. (2)

LOCATION	TIME AT LOCATION	TOTAL ELAPSED TIME	ACTUAL TIME	DISTANCE FOR LEG
SCHOLES VORTAC	08:32:20	0.0 MIN.	08:32:20	0 NM
BOLDS INTERSECTION	08:39:02	6.7 MIN.	08:39:02	15 NM
LAKE CHARLES VORTAC	09:21:28	42.4 MIN.	09:21:28	95 NM

08:39:02 − 08-32:20 = 00:06:42 = 6 + (42 ÷ 6) = 6.7 MIN.

15 NM ÷ 6.7 = 2.2 NM/MIN.

95 NM ÷ 2.2 NM/MIN. = 42.4 MIN. = 42 + (0.4)(60) = 00:42:26

08:39:02 + 00:42:26 = 9:21:28

7694. (1) AIM Para. 372. TIMED APPROACHES may be conducted when the *following conditions are* met:

1. A control tower is in operation at the airport where the approaches are conducted.
2. Direct communications are maintained between the pilot and the center or approach controller until the pilot is instructed to contact the tower.
3. If more than one missed approach procedure is available, none require a course reversal.
4. If only one missed approach procedure is available, the following conditions are met:

   Course reversal is not required; and,

   Reported ceiling and visibility are equal to or greater than the highest prescribed circling minimums for the IAP.
5. When cleared for the approach, pilots should not execute a procedure turn. (FAR 91.116(h)

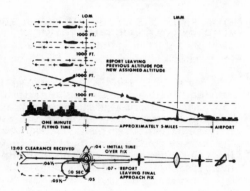

7695. (1) AIM Pilot/Controller Glossary. A cruise clearance used in an ATC clearance is to authorize a pilot to conduct flight at any altitude from the minimum IFR altitude up to and including the altitude specified in the clearance. The pilot may level off at any intermediate altitude within this block of airspace. Climb/descent within the block is to be made at the discretion of the pilot. However, once the pilot starts descent and verbally reports leaving an altitude in the block he may not return to that altitude without additional ATC clearance.

7696. (1) ACL. Fraud intersection may be identified by the Macon VORTAC (MCN 114.2) only, and its assigned DME. The Albany VORTAC (ABY 116.1) is past the VOR "COP". It should not be used. The DME off the Vienna VORTAC can legally be used to identify Fraud intersection as indicated by the DME fix arrow (➡). However, this is not one of the VORTACs to choose from for the answer, so a radial is not available to be used together with the DME arc. Both of which must be available in order to properly identify the fix.

7697. (4) ACL. If a SDF procedure was available it would have the same symbol with just the outline.

Published ILS and/or
Localizer Procedure
available

7698. (2) ACL. ARTCC Remoted sites with Discrete VHF and UHF Frequencies are located on enroute charts showing the area served by the remoted site.

NAME
Name
134.3 269.55
ARTCC Remoted Sites
with Discrete VHF
and UHF Freqs.

7699. (1) Computation:
MC = 259°; TAS = 144.5 KTS; GS = 140 KTS; WCA = +8°.

MH = MC (±) WCA = 259° + 8° = 267°

7700. (4) Computation:
Distance = 85 NM; MC = 077°; GS = 166.5 KTS; Time = 30.5 Mins.

TOTAL FUEL	(0.51 HRS) (78 LB/HR)	= 39.78 (cruise)
	(0.75 HRS) (78 LB/HR)	=20.0 (taxi, climb & app)
		+ 58.5 (45 Min. reserve)
		= 118.28

7701. (2) AIM Para. 346. ATC facilities apply the following procedures when aircraft are operating on an IFR clearance (including those cleared by ATC to maintain VFR ON TOP) via a route which lies within joint-use restricted airspace.

If the restricted area is not active and has been released to the controlling agency (FAA), the ATC facility will allow the aircraft to operate in the restricted airspace without issuing specific clearance for it to do so.

If the restricted area is active and has not be released to the controlling agency (FAA), the ATC facility will issue a clearance which will ensure the aircraft avoids the restricted airspace unless it is on an approved altitude reservation mission or has obtained its own permission to operate in the airspace and so informs the controlling facility.

7702. (4) IFR EOG #8. There is a MRA listed under Shant and a (⟋) flag at the intersection indicating that this altitude is the lowest altitude required to receive adequate signals to determine specific fixes. Reception of signals from a radio facility located off the airway being flown may be inadequate at the designated MEA, in which case, an MRA is designated for the fix.

7703. (3) AIM Para. 503. To contact a flight watch facility on 122.0 MHz, use the name of the controlling FSS and the words "FLIGHT WATCH" or, if the controlling FSS is unknown, simply call "FLIGHT WATCH" and give the aircraft position.

Triangle in corner of box indicates Enroute Flight Advisory Service Frequency 122.0. Voice Call e.g., "Los Angeles Flight Watch."

7704. (1) IFR EOG #8. MRA (Minimum Reception Altitude) is the lowest altitude required to receive adequate signals to determine specific fixes. Reception of signals from a radio facility located off the airway being flown may be inadequate at the designated MEA, in which case, an MRA is designated for the fix. A DME fix arrow (→ or ) at a fix where an MRA is given, indicates that the fix may also be identified with DME. If DME is used to identify the fix, the MRA does not apply since it is not necessary to receive the facility off the airway.

7705. (2) ACL. The Palm Beach Intl. airport has the symbol shown below located at it.

ILS Localizer Course with ATC Function. Feathered side indicates Blue Sector

7706. (4) AIM. Notice that the question stated that the aircraft is equipped with only ONE VOR and ONE DME. Having just one VOR, it is not possible to identify more than one radial, eliminating Answers #2 and #3.

7707. (3) AIM Para. 114. MOAs consist of airspace of defined vertical and lateral limits established for the purpose of separating certain military training activities from IFR traffic. Whenever a MOA is being used, nonparticipating IFR traffic may be cleared through a MOA if IFR separation can be provided by ATC. Otherwise, ATC will reroute or restrict nonparticipating IFR traffic.

7708. (2) ACL.

122.1R

Controlling FSS Name

WASHINGTON

Thin line box, without frequencies and Controlling FSS name indicates no FSS frequencies available.

The question asks what should be used for COMMUNICATION with the FSS. The "R" indicates that the FSS can only receive on that frequency and a "T" would indicate that the FSS can only transmit on that frequency. The ONLY freqencies that are remoted to a navaid site are indicated above the thin line navaid box.

7709. (1) Computation:

	Time / Distance
LaBelle	13:30 / 00
Miami	13:54 / 72

GS = 179 KTS; Course = 135°; Time = 24.2 Mins.; MH = 129°.

13:30 + 24 = 13:54

7710. (1) AIM Para. 114. MOAs consist of airspace of defined vertical and lateral limits established for the purpose of separating certain military training activities from IFR traffic. Whenever a MOA is being used, nonparticipating IFR traffic may be cleared through a MOA if IFR separation can be provided by ATC. Otherwise, ATC will reroute or restrict nonparticipating IFR traffic.

7711. (4) ACL. ARTCC Remoted Sites with Discrete VHF and UHF Freqencies are indicated on low altitude enroute charts for the area covered.

NAME Name 134.3 269.55 — ARTCC Remoted Sites with Discrete VHF and UHF Freqs.

7712. (4) COMP. FIND: TAS at 7,000 ft (PA); GIVEN: +15°C, 150 KTS CAS.

TAS = 171 KTS

7713. (4) COMP. FIND: CAS for 180 KTS TAS at 8,000 ft.; GIVEN: PA is 7,500 ft, Temp. is 15°C.

CAS = 157.5 KTS

7714. (4) FAR 91.33. For flight at and above 24,000 feet MSL if VOR navigational equipment is required, no person may operate a U.S. registered civil aircraft within the 50 states, and the District of Columbia, unless that aircraft is equipped with approved distance measuring equipment (DME). When DME fails at and above 24,000 feet MSL, the pilot in command of the aircraft shall notify ATC immediately, and may then continue operations at and above 24,000 feet MSL to the next airport of intended landing at which repairs or replacement of the equipment can be made.

7715. (1) FAR 91.129. The pilot in command of each aircraft operated in controlled airspace under IFR, shall report immediately to ATC any of the following malfunctions of equipment occurring in flight:
1. Loss of VOR, TACAN, ADF, or low frequency navigation receiver capability.
2. Complete or partial loss of ILS receiver capability.
3. Impairment of air/ground communications capability.

In each report required by the preceding paragraph of this section, the pilot in command shall include the —
1. Aircraft identification;
2. Equipment affected;
3. Degree of which the capability of the pilot to operate under IFR in the ATC system is impaired; and
4. Nature and extent of assistance he desires from ATC.

7716. (2) AIM Paras. 91, 95. The Continental Control Area consists of the airspace of the 48 contiguous States, the District of Columbia and Alaska, excluding the Alaska peninsula west of longitude 160 degrees 00 minutes 00 seconds W, at and above 14,500 feet MSL, but does not include:
1. The airspace less than 1,500 feet above the surface of the earth; or

2. Prohibited and Restricted areas, other than the Restricted areas listed in FAR 71, Subpart D.

Control Zones are controlled airspace which extend upward from the surface and terminate at the base of the Continental Control Area. Control Zones that do not underlie the Continental Control Area have no upper limit. A Control Zone may include one or more airports and is normally a circular area within a radius of 5 statute miles and any extensions necessary to include instrument departure and arrival paths.

7717. (4) FAR 91.127. The altitude to be flown if two-way radio communications failure occurs is the highest of the following altitudes or flight levels for the route being flown:
1. The altitude or flight level assigned in the last ATC clearance received;
2. The minimum altitude (converted, if appropriate, to minimum flight level as prescribed in § 91.81(c)) for IFR operations; or
3. The altitude or flight level ATC has advised may be expected in a further clearance.

7718. (2) ACL.

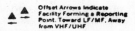

▲ ▲ Offset Arrows Indicate Facility Forming a Reporting Point. Toward LF/MF. Away from VHF/UHF

→ Denotes DME fix (Distance same as route mileage)

⑲ Denotes DME fix (Encircled mileage shown when not otherwise obvious)

7719. (4) AIM Para. 341. FARs require pilots to maintain a listening watch on the appropriate frequency and, unless in radar contact, to furnish position reports passing certain reporting points. Reporting points are indicated by symbols on enroute charts. The designated compulsory reporting point symbol is a solid triangle and the "on request" reporting point symbol is the open triangle. Reports passing an "on request" reporting point are only necessary when requested by ATC.

7720. (4) IFR EOG #8. MRA (Minimum Reception Altitude) is the lowest altitude required to receive adequate signals to determine specific fixes. Reception of signals from a radio facility located off the airway being flown may be inadequate at the designated MEA, in which case, an MRA is designated for the fix. A DME fix arrow (→ or ⑲→) at a fix where an MRA is given, indicates that the fix may also be identified with DME. If DME is used to identify the fix, the MRA does not apply since it is not necessary to receive the facility off the airway.

Note that the question states that two VORS, DME, and a transponder are on board the airplane.

7721. (1) COMP. Fuel Burn: 144 lb./hr; TAS = 190 KTS.

	DISTANCE	COURSE	TIME	FUEL BURN	GS
ATL — MADDI	51 NM	089°	17.7 MINS.	42.5 LB.	173 KTS
MADDI — GRD	73 NM	061°	26.4 MINS.	63.4 LB.	167 KTS
GRD — ALTERNATE	—	—	30 MIN.	72 LBS.	—
TAXI, RUN-UP & CLIMB	—	—	—	8 LBS.	—
RESERVE	—	—	45 MINS.	108.0 LBS.	—
TOTAL				293.9 LBS.	

7722. (4) AIM Para. 347. The outbound heading is 279° which is within 5° of a parallel entry in the teardrop entry area, so it is the pilot's choice as to which entry to use.

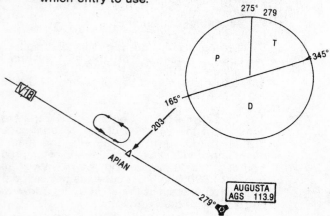

7723. (1) ACL. ALL TIME IS GREENWICH MEAN (STANDARD) TIME (GMT) — DAYS ARE LOCAL. During periods of daylight saving time (DT) effective hours will be one hour earlier than shown. All states observe DT except Arizona and that portion of Indiana in the eastern time zone.

The question states Anderson FSS is in the eastern standard time zone (EST), which is GMT minus five hours. The enroute chart says the FSS is open from 1100-0300Z = (1100-0500) — (0300-0500) = 0600-2200EST.

7724. (3) FAR 91.129. The pilot in command of each aircraft operated in controlled airspace under IFR, shall report immediately to ATC any of the following malfunctions of equipment occurring in flight:
1. Loss of VOR, TACAN, ADF, or low frequency navigation receiver capability.
2. Complete or partial loss of ILS receiver capability.

3. Impairment of air/ground communications capability.

7725. (3) FAR 91.33. FLIGHT AT AND ABOVE 24,000 FEET MSL. If VOR navigational equipment is required no person may operate a U.S. registered civil aircraft within the 50 states, and the District of Columbia, at or above 24,000 feet MSL unless that aircraft is equipped with approved distance measuring equipment (DME). When DME fails at and above 24,000 feet MSL, the pilot in command of the aircraft shall notify ATC immediately, and may then continue operations at and above 24,000 feet MSL to the next airport of intended landing at which repairs or replacement of the equipment can be made.

7726. (3) AFD (SE U.S.). The enroute chart depicts that runway lights are available on a part-time basis with an (*). The excerpt below explains the exact hours of operation of the Barkley airport runway lights:

PADUCAH		ST. LOUIS
FSS	(PAH) on Barkley Regional. 122.5 122.2 122.1R 119.6 502-442-6828	L-21C

PADUCAH

§ **BARKLEY REGIONAL** (PAH) 7.8 W GMT −6(−5DT) 37°03′39″N 88°46′25″W   ST. LOUIS
   410 B S4 FUEL 100LL, JET A OX 2, 4 CFR Index A   H-3B, L-21C
   RWY 04-22: H6499X150 (ASPH) S-65, D-93, DT-170 HIRL 46% up SW   IAP
     RWY 04: MALSR. Tree.   RWY 22: REIL. VASI(V4L) — GA 3.0° TCH 59.4′. Tree.
   RWY 14-32: H4001X150 (ASPH) S-54, D-60, DT-125 MIRL
     RWY 14: Tree.   RWY 32: Road.
   AIRPORT REMARKS: Attended 1200-0300Z‡. Fuel avbl 1200-0300Z‡ Mon-Fri, 1230-0230Z‡ Sat. 1230-0300Z‡
     Sun. Arpt closed Part 121 air carrier opr 0500-1200Z‡ except by prior call 502-442-0521. For HIRL Rwy
     04/22 and MIRL Rwy 14/32 after 0500Z‡ ctc PADUCAH FSS. Control Zone effective continuously.
   COMMUNICATIONS: CTAF 119.6   UNICOM 123.0
     PADUCAH FSS (PAH) on arpt 122.5 122.2 122.1R 119.6 (502) 442-6828 Toll free call dial 1-800-592-5415
     CUNNINGHAM RCO 122.1R 113.6T (PADUCAH FSS)
   Ⓡ MEMPHIS CENTER APP/DEP CON 128.05
     PADUCAH TOWER 119.6 (Tmpry closed for extd durn.)   GND CON 121.7
   RADIO AIDS TO NAVIGATION:
     CUNNINGHAM (L) VORTAC 113.6   CNG   Chan 83   37°00′31″N 88°50′13″W   040° 3.8 NM to fld
     480/03E
     BELLGRADE NDB (MHW) 254   BDD   37°08′46″N 88°40′19″W   220° 6.6 NM to fld.
     ILS 108.5 I-PAH Rwy 04

7727. (2) ACL.

AIR/GROUND COMMUNICATION BOXES

HEAVY LINE BOXES indicate Flight Service Station (FSS). Frequencies 255.4, 122.2, and emerg. 243.0 and 121.5 are normally available at all FSS's and are not shown above boxes. All other freqs available at FSS's are shown. Frequencies transmit and receive except those followed by R or T.
R - receive only   T - transmit only

123.6 122.6
122.1R

Triangle in corner of box indicates Enroute Flight Advisory Service Frequency 122.0. Voice Call e.g. ''Los Angeles Flight Watch.''

Frequencies positioned above thin line NAVAID boxes are remoted to the NAVAID site
Other frequencies at the controlling FSS named are available, however, altitude and terrain may determine their reception

FAYETTEVILLE FYV   Name and identifier for FSS not associated with NAVAID

7728. (1) AIM Para. 340. When radio contact cannot be made, the pilot should, if workload and equipment capability permit, maintain a listening watch on the affected frequency while attempting to comply with the following recommended communications procedures:

1. If two-way communications cannot be established with the ARTCC after changing frequencies, a pilot should attempt to recontact the transferring controller for the assignment of an alternative frequency or other instructions.

2. When an ARTCC radio frequency failure occurs after two-way communications have been established, the pilot should attempt to reestablish contact with the center on any other known ARTCC frequency, preferable that of the next responsible sector when practicable, and ask for instructions. However, when the next normal frequency change along the route is known to involve another ATC facility, the pilot should contact that facility, if feasible, for instructions. If communications cannot be reestablished by either method, the pilot is expected to request communications instructions from the FSS appropriate to the route of flight.

7729. (2) ACL. Published ILS and/or Localizer Procedure is available at the Barkley regional airport as indicated on the enroute chart by the symbol

Published ILS and/or
Localizer Procedure
available

7730. (4) AIM Para. 347. The outbound heading is 166° which falls inside the parallel entry area and is also within 5° of the teardrop entry area, so the pilot can choose either entry procedure he wishes.

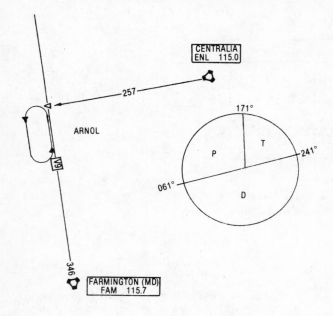

7731. (3) AIM Para. 345. The COP is located midway between the navigation facilities for straight route segments, or at the intersection of radials or courses forming a dogleg in the case of dogleg route segments. When the COP is NOT located at the midway point, aeronautical charts will depict the COP location and give the mileage to the radio aids.

7732. (2) AIM Para. 345. The COP is located midway between the navigation facilities for straight route segments, or at the intersection of radials or courses forming a dogleg in the case of dogleg route segments. When the COP is NOT located at the midway point, aeronautical charts will depict the COP location and give the mileage to the radio aids.

7733. (3) ACL. Aerodromes/Seadromes shown in BLUE have an approved Low Altitude Instrument Approach Procedure published. Those shown in DARK BLUE have an approved DOD Low Altitude Instrument Approach Procedure and/or approved DOD RADAR MINIMA published in DOD FLIPS. Aerodromes/Seadromes shown in BROWN do NOT have a published Instrument Approach Procedure.

7734. (3) Computation:

Note the question states to assume a constant groundspeed.

	TIME	DISTANCE (LEG)	GS	LAPSE TIME	
ENL VORTAC	10:32:25	0 NM	—	0.00 HR.	
ZORAL INTERSECTION	10:43:07	25 NM	140 NM	0.18 HR.	
MAW VORTAC	11:23:00	92 NM	140 NM	0.65 HR.	= 40.8 MIN.

7735. (3) FAR 91.129. The pilot in command of each aircraft operated in controlled airspace under IFR, shall report immediately to ATC any of the following malfunctions of equipment occurring in flight:
1. Loss of VOR, TACAN, ADF, or low frequency navigation receiver capability.
2. Complete or partial loss of ILS receiver capability.
3. Impairment of air/ground communications capability.

7736. (2) FAR 91.129. The pilot in command of each aircraft operated in controlled airspace under IFR, shall report immediately to ATC any of the following malfunctions of equipment occurring in flight:
1. Loss of VOR, TACAN, ADF, or low frequency navigation receiver capability.
2. Complete or partial loss of ILS receiver capability.
3. Impairment of air/ground communications capability.

7737. (2) FAR 91.75. Each pilot in command who deviates, in an emergency, from an ATC clearance or instruction shall notify ATC of that deviation as soon as possible.

7738. (X) FAA Deletion.

7739. (1) ACL.

FAYETTEVILLE FYV — Name and identifier for FSS not associated with NAVAID

AIR/GROUND COMMUNICATION BOXES
HEAVY LINE BOXES indicate Flight Service Station (FSS). Frequencies 255.4, 122.2, and emerg. 243.0 and 121.5 are normally available at all FSS's and are not shown above boxes. All other freqs available at FSS's are shown. Frequencies transmit and receive except those followed by R or T:
R - receive only   T - transmit only

7740. (4) AIM Para. 192. If you are attempting to establish contact with a ground station and you are receiving on a different frequency than that transmitted, indicate the VOR name or the frequency on which you expect a reply. Most FSSs and control facilities can transmit on several VOR stations in the area. Use the appropriate FSS call sign as indicated on charts.

7741. (X) FAA Deletion.

7742. (X) FAA Deletion.

7743. (X) FAA Deletion.

7744. (X) FAA Deletion.

7745. (X) FAA Deletion.

7746. (X) FAA Deletion.

7747. (4) AIM Para. 471. TRANSPONDER OPERATION DURING TWO-WAY COMMUNICATIONS FAILURE — If a pilot of an aircraft with a coded radar beacon transponder experiences a loss of two-way radio capability he should:
1. Adjust his transponder to reply on MODE A/3, Code 7700 for a period of 1 minute.
2. Then change to Code 7600 and remain on 7600 for a period of 15 minutes or the remainder of the flight, whichever comes first.
3. Repeat steps 1 and 2 as practicable.

The pilot should understand that he may not be in an area of radar coverage.

7748. (3) AIM Para. 471. TRANSPONDER OPERATION DURING TWO-WAY COMMUNICATIONS FAILURE — If a pilot of an aircraft with a coded radar beacon transponder experiences a loss of two-way radio capability he should:
1. Adjust his transponder to reply on MODE A/3, Code 7700 for a period of 1 minute.
2. Then change to Code 7600 and remain on 7600 for a period of 15 minutes or the remainder of the flight, whichever comes first.
3. Repeat steps 1 and 2 as practicable.

The pilot should understand that he may not be in an area of radar coverage.

7749. (3) AIM Para. 471. TRANSPONDER OPERATION DURING TWO-WAY COMMUNICATIONS FAILURE — If a pilot of an aircraft with a coded radar beacon transponder experiences a loss of two-way radio capability he should:
1. Adjust his transponder to reply on MODE A/3, Code 7700 for a period of 1 minute.
2. Then change to Code 7600 and remain on 7600 for a period of 15 minutes or the remainder of the flight, whichever comes first.
3. Repeat steps 1 and 2 as practicable.

The pilot should understand that he may not be in an area of radar coverage.

7750. (3) AIM/ACL. EFAS is a service specifically designed to provide enroute aircraft with timely and meaningful weather advisories pertinent to the type of flight intended, route of flight and altitude. EFAS is not intended to be used for filing or closing flight plans, position reporting, to get a complete pre-flight briefing, or to obtain random weather reports and forecasts. In such instances, the flight watch specialist will provide the name and radio frequency of the FSS to contact for such services.

7751. (2) ACL. ARTCC Remoted Sites with Discrete VHF and UHF Frequencies are located on enroute charts showing the area served by the remoted site.

7752. (2) AIM Para. 345. The COP is located midway between the navigation facilities for straight route segments, or at the intersection of radials or courses forming a dogleg in the case of dogleg route segments. When the COP is NOT located at the midway point, aeronautical charts will depict the COP location and give the mileage to the radio aids.

7753. (3) AIM Para. 345, ACL. VOR changeover points ( ) are indicated on enroute charts ONLY when they are not located at the midpoint, or otherwise obvious changes in course. There is a course change at the mileage breakdown point just to the east of RASAK intersection.

7754. (2) Computation:

	DISTANCE	TIME	LAPSE TIME	COURSE	GS
FINDLAY VORTAC . . . . —		1021	0.0	—	—
GAREN INTERSECTION . . . . 63 NM		1050	29 Min.	291°	180 KTS
			= 0.48		
LPD VORTAC. . . . . 48 NM		1112	21.5 Min.	016°	131 KTS
			= 0.36		
JXN . . . . 18 NM		1120	7.6 Min.	050°	143 KTS

7755. (4) AIM Para. 345. The COP is located midway between the navigation facilities for straight route segments, or at the intersection of radials or courses forming a dogleg in the case of dogleg route segments. When the COP is NOT located at the midway point, aeronautical charts will depict the COP location and give the mileage to the radio aids.

7756. (4) ACL, AIM Para. 341. FARs require pilots to maintain a listening watch on the appropriate frequency and, unless operating under radar contact, to furnish position reports passing certain reporting points. Reporting points are indicated by symbols on enroute charts. The designated compulsory reporting point symbol is a solid triangle and the "on request" reporting point symbol is the open triangle. Reports passing an "on request" reporting point are only necessary when requested by ATC.

REPORTING POINTS
Compulsory Reporting Point
Non-Compulsory Reporting Point

7757. (2) FAR 91.129. The pilot in command of each aircraft operated in controlled airspace under IFR, shall report immediately to ATC any of the following malfunctions of equipment occurring in flight:
1. Loss of VOR, TACAN, ADF, or low frequency navigation receiver capability.
2. Complete or partial loss of ILS receiver capability.
3. Impairment of air/ground communications capability.

7758. (2) IFR EOG #8. MRA (Minimum Reception Altitude) is the lowest altitude required to receive adequate signals to determine specific fixes. Reception of signals from a radio facility located off the airway being flown may be inadequate at the designated MEA, in which case, an MRA is designated for the fix. A DME fix arrow (→ or 🔲→) at a fix where an MRA is given, indicates that the fix

may also be identified with DME. If DME is used to identify the fix, the MRA does not apply since it is not necessary to receive the facility off the airway.

7759. (1) AIM Para. 347. The outbound heading is 274° which falls in the direct pattern entry area for Irish intersection.

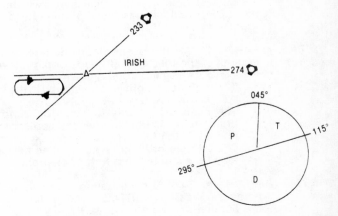

7760. (1) AIM Para. 471. If a pilot of an aircraft with a coded radar beacon transponder experiences a loss of two-way radio capability he should:
1. Adjust his transponder to reply on MODE A/3, Code 7700 for a period of 1 minute.
2. Then change to Code 7600 and remain on 7600 for a period of 15 minutes or the remainder of the flight, whichever comes first.
3. Repeat steps 1 and 2 as practicable.

7761. (1) FAR 91.127. LEAVE HOLDING FIX. If holding instructions have been received, leave the holding fix at the expect-further-clearance time received, or, if an expected approach clearance time has been received, leave the holding fix in order to arrive over the fix from which the approach begins as close as possible to the expected approach clearance time.

7762. (1) AFD, Appendix 2. The preferred IFR routes are listed in the back of the AFD, and in the Appendix of this book.

7763. (2) ELAPSE

ROUTE	COURSE	ELAPSE TIME	TIME AT DESTINATION 0840	GS	DISTANCE
LGA — HFD	061°	37 MIN.	0917	127	79 NM
HFD — MOLDS	333°	20 MIN.	0937	122	40 NM

CAS = 133; TAS = 147 KTS

Temperature standard = 2°C/1,000
at 7,000 ft:

(−14°C) + 15°C = +1°C

7764. (4) AIM Para. 345. The COP is located midway between the navigation facilities for straight route segments, or at the intersection of radials or courses forming a dogleg in the case of dogleg route segments. When the COP is NOT located at the midway point, aeronautical charts will depict the COP location and give the mileage to the radio aids.

7765. (4) FAR 91.127. In the event of radio failure, fly the highest of the following altitudes or flight levels for the route segment being flown:
1. The altitude or flight level assigned in the last ATC clearance received;
2. The minimum altitude (converted, if appropriate, to minimum flight level as prescribed in § 91.81(c)) for IFR operations; or
3. The altitude or flight level ATC has advised may be expected in a further clearance.

7766. (2) AIM Para. 347. The outbound heading while holding at the CMK VORTAC is 016° which falls in the parallel pattern entry area.

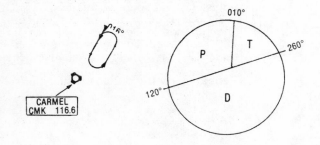

7767. (3) ACL.

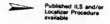

The Westchester Co. airport (j) has two of the above symbols located by it.

7768. (4) ACL.

ARTCC Remoted Sites with Discrete VHF and UHF Frequencies are located on enroute charts showing the area served by the remoted sites.

7769. (3) ACL. Note the small ⚓ located with the effective times. Look at the enroute legend in the appendix and find that during periods of daylight saving time (DT) effective hours will be one hour earlier than shown.

1100 — 0400 to 0300 — 0400

0700 GMT to 2300 GMT

7770. (4) ACL.

Three ILS/Localizer symbols are shown at the Bradley Intl airport (c), with one of the symbols indicating that it serves an ATC function.

7771. (1) FAR 91.127. If the failure occurs in VFR conditions, or if VFR conditions are encountered, the flight shall be continued under VFR and land as soon as practicable.

7772. (2) ACL. The DME symbol is a square, and encloses the appropriate facility that it is colocated with.

7773. (3) ACL.

Triangle in corner of box indicates Enroute Flight Advisory Service Frequency 122.0. Voice Call e.g., "Los Angeles Flight Watch."

7774. (4) IFR EOG #8. MAA (Maximum Authorized Altitude) is the highest altitude authorized for instrument flight for a particular segment of an airway or route for which a MAA has been designated in FAR Part 95. For example, a segment of a Jet Route on a High Altitude Enroute Chart might have an MAA designated due to interference from VOR navigation signals on the same frequency at altitudes above the MAA. MAAs are designated on some Low Altitude Enroute Charts due to military requirements above that altitude.

7775. (3) AIM Para. 347. 1810 – 1803 = 0007.

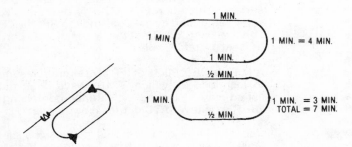

7776. (2) FAR 91.90. Note that towards the bottom of the chart that Washington National is labeled as Terminal Control Area I.

7777. (2) IFR EOG #8. MEA (Minimum Enroute Altitude) is the minimum altitude in effect between radio fixes which
1. meets obstruction clearance requirements;
2. assures acceptable navigational signal coverage for accurate navigation; and
3. assures two-way radio communication.

7778. (X) FAA Deletion.

7779. (3) AIM Para. 504. AIRMETS are broadcast at H + 15 and H + 45.

7780. (1) AIM Para. 511. The controller's primary function is to provide safe separation between aircraft. Any additional service, such as weather avoidance assistance, can only be provided to the extent that it does not derogate the primary function. The separation workload is generally greater than normal when weather disrupts the usual flow of traffic. ATC radar limitations and frequency congestion may also be a factor in limiting the controller's capability to provide additional service.

7781. (3) FAR 91.87. An airport traffic area has radius of 5 miles.

7782. (1) FAR 91.127. Route to be flown in the event of radio failure:
1. By the route assigned in the last ATC clearance received;
2. If being radar vectored, by the direct route from the point of radio failure to the fix, route, or airway specified in the vector clearance;
3. In the absence of an assigned route, by the route that ATC has advised may be expected in a further clearance; or
4. In the absence of an assigned route or a route that ATC has advised may be expected in a further clearance, by the route filed in the flight plan.

At the highest of the following altitudes or flight levels for the route segment being flown:

1. The altitude or flight level assigned in the last ATC clearance received;
2. The minimum altitude (converted, if appropriate, to minimum flight level as prescribed in § 91.81(c)) for IFR operations; or
3. The altitude or flight level ATC has advised may be expected in a further clearance.

7783. (1) IFH.

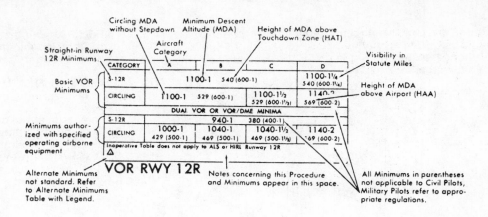

494

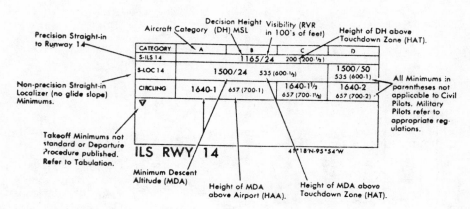

7785. (2) AIM Pilot/Controller Glossary. VISUAL DESCENT POINT/VDP is a defined point on the final approach course of a nonprecision straight-in approach procedure from which normal descent from the MDA to the runway touchdown point may be commenced, provided the approach threshold of that runway, or approach lights, or other markings identifiable with the approach end of that runway are clearly visible to the pilot.

7786. (1) IFH. The mandatory altitude is shown with both an under and over scored line for the appropriate altitude.

Altitudes (Profile view only)

5500	2300	4800	2200
Mandatory Altitude	Minimum Altitude	Maximum Altitude	Recommended Altitude

7787. (3) AFD. 09R-27L has HIRL. 09R has VASI and a displaced threshold. The remarks section states the landing restrictions for 09R.

7788. (1) IFH. MISSED APPROACH POINT (MAP). The missed approach points are different for the complete ILS (with glide slope) and for the localizer only approach. The MAP for the ILS is at the decision height (DH) while the "localizer only" MAP is usually over the (straight-in) runway threshold. In some non-precision procedures, the MAP may be prior to reaching the runway threshold in order to clear obstructions in the missed approach climb-out area. In non-precision procedures, the pilot determines when he is at the missed approach point (MAP) by timing from the final approach fix (FAF). The FAF has been clearly identified by use of the maltese cross symbol in the profile section. The distance from FAF to MAP and time and speed table, for easy calculation, are found below the aerodrome sketches (figures 15 and 16). This does not apply to VOR/DME procedures, or when the facility is on the airport and the facility is the MAP.

7789. (2) AIM Pilot/Controller Glossary. A CONTACT APPROACH is an approach wherein an aircraft on an IFR flight plan, having an air traffic control authorization, operating clear of clouds with at least 1 mile flight visibility and a reasonable expectation of continuing to the destination airport in those conditions, may deviate from the instrument approach procedure and proceed to the destination airport by visual reference to the surface. This approach will only be authorized when requested by the pilot and the REPORTED GROUND VISIBILITY at the destination airport is at least 1 statute mile.

7790. (4) AIM Para. 360. Pilots of IFR civil aircraft destined to locations for which STARs have been published may be issued a clearance containing a STAR whenever ATC deems it appropriate.

Use of STARs requires pilot possession of at least the approved textual description. As with any ATC clearance or portion thereof, it is the responsibility of each pilot to accept or refuse an issued STAR. A pilot should notify ATC if he does not wish to use a STAR by placing "NO STAR" in the remarks section of the flight plan or by the less desirable method of verbally stating the same to ATC.

7791. (1) AIM Para. 347. Outbound leg timing begins OVER/ABEAM the fix, whichever occurs later. If the ABEAM position cannot be determined, start timing when turn to outbound is completed.

7792. (4) AIM Para. 581. NTSB Part 830 deals with reporting aircraft accidents and incidents.

7793. (1) IFH, AC 90-1A. Since a glideslope is provided on this approach, it is a precision approach. The missed approach then is the DH, or in this case, 1,540 ft.

7794. (1) IFH, AC 90-1A. The procedure turn must be made within 10 NM of CLAMM intersection. The note also says the turn may be *STARTED* at Callahan NDB.

7795. (1) IFH, AC 90-1A. The procedure turn is made at 5,000 ft. Upon established inbound, you may descend to 4,200 to reach the intersection.

7796. (3) AIM Para. 12. The Localizer-type Directional Aid (LDA) is of comparable utility and accuracy to a localizer but is not part of a complete ILS. The LDA course usually provides a more precise approach course than the similar Simplified Directional Facility (SDF) installation, which may have a course width of 6 or 12 degrees. The LDA is not aligned with the runway. Straight-in minima may be published where alignment does not exceed 30 degrees between the course and runway. Circling minima only are published where this alignment exceeds 30 degrees.

7797. (3) IFH, AC 90-1A. A stepdown fix may be provided on the final, i.e., between the final approach fix and the airport for the purpose of authorizing a lower MDA after passing an obstruction. This stepdown fix may be made by an NDB bearing, fan marker, radar fix, radial from another VOR, or by a DME. If the fix cannot be established, due to equipment failure or the like, the higher minimum applies.

7798. (2) IFH, AC 90-1A. Minimums are specified for the various aircraft speed/weight combinations. Speeds are based upon a value 1.3 times the stalling speed of the aircraft in the landing configuration at maximum certificated gross landing weight.

7799. (1) FAR 97. Helicopters may use airplane approach procedures using the Category A minimum descent altitude (MDA) or decision height (DH). The required visibility minimum may be reduced to one-half the published visibility minimum for Category A aircraft, but in no case may it be reduced to less than one-quarter mile or 1,200 feet RVR.

7800. (2) FAR 97. Helicopters may use airplane approach procedures using the Category A minimum descent altitude (MDA) or decision height (DH). The required visibility minimum may be reduced to one-half the published visibility minimum for Category A aircraft, but in no case may it be reduced to less than one-quarter mile or 1,200 feet RVR.

The published visibility minimum for the LDA RWY 5 approach is 1 mile for Category A, half of which is ½ mile which is the visibility minimum for helicopters.

7801. (1) IFR EOG #42. "Helicopter only" approach procedures are not approved for use by fixed wing aircraft.

7802. (3) IFR EOG #42. The normal 10-mile procedure turn area is usually reduced to 5 nautical miles where only helicopters are to be operated.

7803. (3) IFR EOG #42. When using instrument approach procedures for fixed wing aircraft, the same navigational equipment requirements or restrictions apply to helicopters. The approach criteria for helicopters are based on airspeeds not exceeding 90 knots, regardless of weight. Thus, all helicopters are considered to be in approach Category "A."

7804. (X) FAA Deletion.

7805. (2) AIM Pilot/Controller Glossary. MINIMUM SECTOR ALTITUDES — Altitudes depicted on approach charts which provide at least 1,000 feet of obstacle clearance within a 25-mile radius of the navigation facility upon which the procedure is predicated. Sectors depicted on approach charts must be at least 90 degrees in scope. These altitudes are for emergency use only and do not necessarily assure acceptable navigational signal coverage. Note that the question asked for radials and the approach chart gives the sectors in "bearings," so take the reciprocal.

7806. (2) IFH, AC 90-1A. The HAT (Height Above Touchdown Zone) is shown in the minimums sections to the right of the MDA/DHs and visibility requirements.

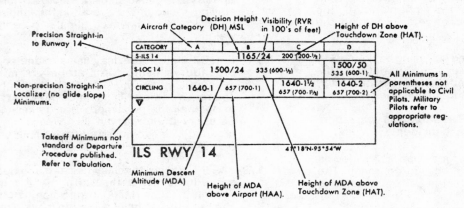

CATEGORY	A	B	C	D
S-ILS 14		1165/24	200 (200-½)	
S-LOC 14		1500/24	535 (600-½)	1500/50 535 (600-1)
CIRCLING	1640-1 657 (700-1)		1640-1½ 657 (700-1½)	1640-2 657 (700-2) -

Labels:
- Precision Straight-in to Runway 14
- Aircraft Category
- Decision Height (DH) MSL
- Visibility (RVR in 100's of feet)
- Height of DH above Touchdown Zone (HAT).
- Non-precision Straight-in Localizer (no glide slope) Minimums.
- All Minimums in parentheses not applicable to Civil Pilots. Military Pilots refer to appropriate regulations.
- Takeoff Minimums not standard or Departure Procedure published. Refer to Tabulation.
- Minimum Descent Altitude (MDA)
- Height of MDA above Airport (HAA).
- Height of MDA above Touchdown Zone (HAT).

ILS RWY 14   41°18'N-95°54'W

7807. (4) FAR 97. Helicopters may use fixed airplane approach procedures using the Category A minimum descent altitude (MDA) or decision height (DH). The required visibility minimum may be reduced to one-half the published visibility minimum for Category A aircraft, but in no case may it be reduced to less than one-quarter mile or 1,200 feet RVR.

The published visibility minimum for the VOR/DME RWY 10R approach an RVR of 24 for Category "A," half of which is 12 RVR which is the visibility minimum for helicopters.

7808. (1) AIM Para. 347. The outbound heading will be 111° which falls inside the direct pattern entry area.

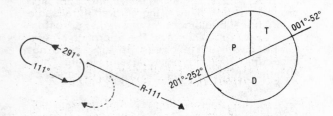

7809. (1) IFH, AC 90-1A. MISS APPROACH POINT (MAP). The missed approach points are different for the complete ILS (with glide slope) and for the localizer only approach. The MAP for the ILS is at the decision height (DH) while the "localizer only" MAP is usually over the (straight-in) runway threshold. In some non-precision procedures, the MAP may be prior to reaching the runway threshold in order to clear obstructions in the missed approach climb-out area. In non-precision procedures, the pilot determines when he is at the missed approach point (MAP) by timing from the final approach fix (FAF). The FAF has been clearly identified by use of the maltese cross symbol in the profile section. The distance from FAF to MAP and time and speed table, for easy calculation, are found below the aerodrome sketches (figures 15 and 16). This does not apply to VOR/DME procedures, or when the facility is on the airport and the facility is the MAP.

7810. (2) FAR 91.83. If an instrument approach procedure has been published in Part 97 of this chapter for that airport, the alternate airport minimums specified in that procedure or, if none are so specified, the following minimums:
1. Precision approach procedure: Ceiling 600 feet and visibility 2 statute miles.
2. Nonprecision approach procedure: Ceiling 800 feet and visibility 2 statute miles.

7811. (3) AIM Pilot/Controller Glossary. RADAR SERVICE TERMINATED — Used by ATC to inform a pilot that he will no longer be provided any of the services that could be received while under radar contact. Radar service is automatically terminated and the pilot is not advised in the following cases:
1. When the aircraft cancels its IFR flight plan, except within a TCA, TRSA, or where Stage II service is provided.
2. At the completion of a radar approach.
3. When an arriving VFR aircraft receiving radar services, is advised to contact the tower.
4. When an aircraft conducting a visual approach or contact approach is advised to contact the tower.
5. When an aircraft making an instrument approach has landed or the tower has the aircraft in sight, whichever occurs first.

7812. (4) FAR 91.116. A pilot shall maintain the last altitude assigned until the aircraft is established on a segment of a published route or instrument approach procedure unless a different altitude is assigned by ATC. After the aircraft is so establshed, published altitudes apply to descent within each succeeding route or approach segment unless a different altitude is assigned by ATC.

7813. (1) Helicopters may use airplane approach procedures using the Category A minimum descent altitude (MDA) or decision height (DH). The required visibility minimum may be reduced to one-half the published visibility minimum for Category A aircraft, but in no case may it be reduced to less than one-quarter mile or 1,200 feet RVR.

7814. (3) IFH, AC 90-1A. For the LOC/DME BC RWY 27 the MAP is determined upon reaching the proper DME distance as given in the profile section of the approach plate.

7815. (2) IFR EOG #7. The CDI needle tuned to 110.9 shows that the selected course is to left (the aircraft is north of the LOC BC course). The CDI needle tuned to 114.0 shows that the selected course is also to right (the aircraft is east of JLI R-200).

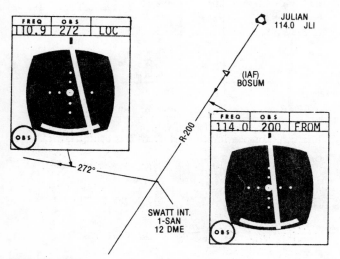

7816. (2) AFD.

NEVADA

VOR RECEIVER CHECK POINTS

Facility Name (Arpt Name)	Freq/Ident	Type Check Pt. Gnd. AB/ALT	Azimuth from Fac. Mag	Dist. from Fac. N.M.	Check Point Description
Elko (Elko Muni-J.C. Harris Fld)	114.5/EKO	A/6100	324	4.1	Over the center field taxiway intersection.
Ely (Ely Arpt/Yelland Fld)	110.6/ELY	G	060		On southside twy leading to passenger terminal area.
Las Vegas (McCarran Intl)	116.9/LAS	G	351	9	On taxiway W between rwy 19L and taxiway D.
Reno (Cannon Intl)	117.9/RNO	G	229	5.8	On A.S.I. ramp at taxiway
	117.9/RNO	G	239	5.5	Northwest end of taxiway A
Reno (Reno/Stead)	117.9/RNO	A/7000	291	14.0	Over stct.
Wells (Harriet Field)	114.2/LWL	A/6300	112		Over approach end rwy 08.

A VOR check is conducted with an azimuth set to a "FROM" indication which on an RMI is shown with the TAIL of needle on the radial as shown in Fig. b with the correct radial selected as listed above under Reno (Cannon International) for VOR receiver checks.

7817. (1) IFH. The ADF needle indicates that the aircraft is to the left of course with the NDB ahead of the aircraft. The glide slope needle is pointing down-ward indicating that the aircraft is above the glideslope.

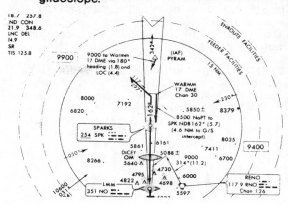

7818. (4) IFH, AC 90-1A. The procedure turn minimum altitude is 9,000 feet until established on the inbound course. The glideslope intercept altitude is 8,500 feet and the MDA is 5,400 feet for circling category aircraft.

7819. (3) AFD.

RADIO AIDS TO NAVIGATION:
RENO (H) ABVORTAC 117.9 ▪ RNO Chan 126 39°31'53"N 119°39'18"W 237° 5.5 NM to fld.
5940/18E. Route forecast only 0600-1300Z‡.
SPARKS NDB (H-SAB) 254 ▪ SPK 39°41'48"N 119°46'06"W 162° 11.2 NM to fld
Route forecast only 0600-1300Z‡.

The solid square box in front of the "RNO" VOR identifier and the "SPK" NDB identifier indicate that TWEBs is available on both 117.9 MHz and 254 KHz.

7820. (1) IAP. The note on the profile section states that the missed approach procedure starts at the middle compass locator (LMM).

7821. (3) IFH, AC 90-1A. The transition route from PYAAM to WARMM Int. is 180°. The note NoPT at WARMM indicates the flight should not make a course reversal. The MAP is at the LMM.

7822. (2) IFH, AC 90-1A. STRAIGHT-IN MINIMUMS are shown on instrument approach procedure charts when the final approach course of the instrument approach procedure is within 30° of the runway alignment and a normal descent can be made from the IFR altitude shown on the instrument approach procedures to the runway surface. When either the normal rate of descent or the runway alignment factor of 30° is exceeded, a straight-in minimum is not published and a circling minimum applies. The fact that a straight-in minimum is not published does not preclude the pilot from landing straight-in if he has the active runway in sight in sufficient time to make a normal landing. Under such conditions and when Air Traffic Control has cleared him for landing on that runway, he is not expected to circle even though only circling minimums are published. If he desires to circle at a controlled Airport, he should advise ATC.

The question states that a descent to landing can be made at a normal rate of descent. The reason that straight-in minimum are "not authorized" is because of the note listed toward the bottom of the plate stating that the glideslope is unusable below 4,570 feet MSL.

7823. (3) AC 91-43. If both the ram air input and drain hole are completely blocked by ice, the trapped pressure in the system and the airspeed indicator may react as an altimeter:
1. During level flight — airspeed indication will not change even when actual airspeed is varied by large power changes.
2. During climb — airspeed indication will increase.
3. During descent — airspeed indication will decrease.

7824. (1) IFH, AC 90-1A. If RVR minimums for takeoff or landing are published in an instrument approach procedure, but RVR is inoperative and cannot be reported for the runway at that time, it is necessary that the RVR minimums which are specified in the procedure be converted and applied as ground visibility in accordance with the table below.

RVR	Visibility (statue miles)
1,600 feet	¼ mile
2,400 feet	½ mile
3,200 feet	⅝ mile
4,000 feet	¾ mile
4,500 feet	⅞ mile
5,000 feet	1 mile
6,000 feet	1¼ mile

7825. (2) FAR 91.116. A pilot shall maintain the last altitude assigned until the aircraft is established on a segment of a published route or instrument approach procedure unless a different altitude is assigned by ATC. After the aircraft is so established,

published altitudes apply to descent within each succeeding route or approach segment unless a different altitude is assigned by ATC.

7826. (4) IFH, AC 90-1A, ACL. APPROACH LIGHT SYSTEM.

INOPERATIVE COMPONENTS OR VISUAL AIDS TABLE

1 ILS and PAR with visibility of ½ mile (RVR 2400) or greater.

Inoperative Component or Aid	Increase DH	Increase Visibility	Approach Category
OM*, MM*	50 feet	By None	ABC
OM*, MM*	50 feet	By ¼ mile	D
ALS	50 feet	By ¼ mile	ABCD
SALS	50 feet	By ¼ mile	ABC

*Not applicable to PAR

2 ILS and PAR with visibility minimum of 1,800 or 2,000 feet RVR.

Inoperative Component or Aid	Increase DH	Increase Visibility	Approach Category
OM*, MM*	50 feet	To ½ mile	ABC
OM*, MM*	50 feet	To ¾ mile	D
ALS	50 feet	To ¾ mile	ABCD
HIRL, TDZL, RCLS	None	To ½ mile	ABCD
RVR	None	To ½ mile	ABCD

*Not applicable to PAR

3 VOR, VOR/DME, LOC, LDA, and ASR.

Inoperative Visual Aid	Increase MDA	Increase Visibility	Approach Category
ALS, SALS	None	By ½ mile	ABC
HIRL, MALS, REILS	None	By ½ mile	ABC

4 NDB (ADF) and RNG.

Inoperative Visual Aid	Increase MDA	Increase Visibility	Approach Category
ALS	None	By ¼ mile	ABC

5 LOC Approaches

Inoperative Component or Aid	Increase MDA	Increase Visibility	Approach Category
ALS, MM	None	By ¼ mile	D

Note that the approach light system is listed under all instrument approaches.

7827. (2) IFR EOG #7. The DME display indicates a distance of 12.0 DME. The SPO localizer is at 0.8 DME and 1.0 NM from the threshold of the runway as shown in the profile view, so the runway threshold is 0.2 NM away at 0.0 DME. Then at 12.0 DME the edge is (12.0 + 0.2) 12.2 NM from the threshold.

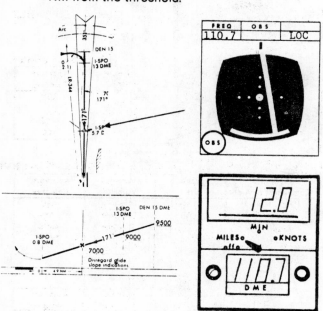

7828. (3) IFH, AC 90-1A. The minimum altitudes are indicated by being underlined on the approach plate with each segment of the DME arc being labeled its particular minimum altitude. 9,000 feet is the minimum altitude from LR-344 until 13 DME. From 13 DME until 5.7 DME, the minimum altitude is reduced down to 7,000 feet. The MDA for a straight-in approach for runway 17R is 5,580 feet.

7829. (4) IAP. The plan view indicates the navigation and communication frequencies that are available at Stapleton International.

7830. (1) IFH, AC 90-1A. Note that the RVR for the straight-in approach on runway 17 Right is 5,000 feet (located to the right of the decision height).

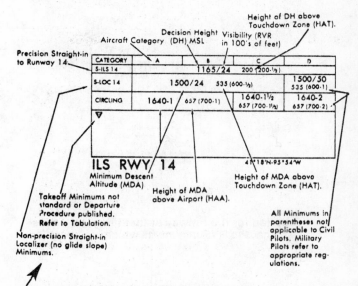

7831. (3) IFH, AC 90-1A. The HAA (Height Above Airport) is located in the circling to land minimums section to the right of the MDA and the visibility requirement.

7832. (1) FAR 91.83. If an instrument approach procedure has been published in Part 97 of this chapter for that airport, the alternate airport minimums specified in that procedure or, if none are so specified, the following minimums:
1. Precision approach procedure: Ceiling 600 feet and visibility 2 statute miles.
2. Nonprecision approach procedure: Ceiling 800 feet and visibility 2 statute miles.

7833. (1) FAR 91.90. TERMINAL CONTROL AREA GROUP II EQUIPMENT REQUIREMENTS. Unless otherwise authorized by ATC in the case of in-flight VOR, TACAN, or two-way radio failure; or unless otherwise authorized by ATC in the case of a transponder failure occurring at any time, no person may operate an aircraft within a Group II terminal control area unless that aircraft is equipped with —
1. An operable VOR or TACAN receiver (except in the case of helicopters);
2. An operable two-way radio capable of communicating with ATC on the appropriate frequencies for that terminal control area; and
3. The applicable equipment specified in § 91.24, except that automatic pressure altitude reporting equipment is not required for any operation within the terminal control area, and a transponder is not required for IFR flights operating to or from an airport outside of but in close proximity to the terminal control area, when the commonly used transition, approach, or departure procedures to such airport require flight within the terminal control area.

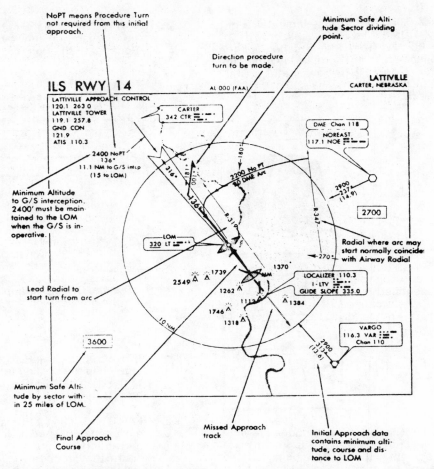

NoPT means Procedure Turn not required from this initial approach.

Direction procedure turn to be made.

Minimum Safe Altitude Sector dividing point.

ILS RWY 14

AL 000 (FAA)

LATTIVILLE
CARTER, NEBRASKA

LATTIVILLE APPROACH CONTROL
120.1 263.0
LATTIVILLE TOWER
119.1 257.8
GND CON
121.9
ATIS 110.3

CARTER
342 CTR

DME Chan 118
NOREAST
117.1 NOE

2400 NoPT
136°
11.1 NM to G/S intcp
(15 to LOM)

2200 No PT
10 DME Arc

2900
237°
(14.9)

Minimum Altitude to G/S interception. 2400' must be maintained to the LOM when the G/S is inoperative.

R-347

2700

LOM
320 LT

Radial where arc may start normally coincide with Airway Radial

270°

1370

1739

Lead Radial to start turn from arc

2549

1262

1112

1384

LOCALIZER 110.3
I-LTV
GLIDE SLOPE 335.0

1746

1318

VARGO
116.3 VAR
Chan 110

2900
(13.6)

3600

Minimum Safe Altitude by sector within 25 miles of LOM.

Final Approach Course

Missed Approach track

Initial Approach data contains minimum altitude, course and distance to LOM

7834. (2) IFH, AC 90-1A. The R-290 and R-330 are not lead radials, but are used to establish MEA changes on the DME arc.

7835. (2) FAR 97. Helicopters may use airplane approach procedures using the Category A minimum descent altitude (MDA) or decision height (DH). The required visibility minimum may be reduced to one-half the published visibility minimum for Category A aircraft, but in no case may it be reduced to less than one-quarter mile or 1,200 feet RVR.

7836. (2) IFH, AC 90-1A. MISSED APPROACH POINT (MAP). Missed approach points are different for the complete ILS (with glideslope) and for the localizer only approach. The MAP for the ILS is at the decision height (DH) while the "localizer only" MAP is usually over the (straight-in) runway threshold. In some non-precision procedures, the MAP may be prior to reaching the runway threshold in order to clear obstructions in the missed approach climb-out area. In non-precision procedures, the pilot determines when he is at the missed approach point (MAP) by timing from the final approach fix (FAF). The FAF has been clearly identified by use of the maltese cross

symbol in the profile section. The distance from FAF to MAP and time and speed table, for easy calculation, are found below the aerodrome sketches (figures 15 and 16). This does not apply to VOR/DME procedures, or when the facility is on the airport and the facility is the MAP.

7837. (1) IFH, AC 90-1A. Touchdown Zone (TDZ) elevation is noted on the aerodrome data sketch on each approach plate.

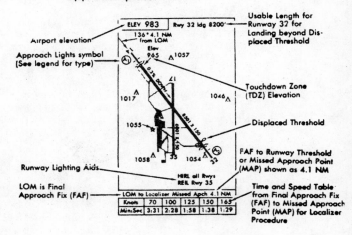

ELEV 983   Rwy 32 ldg 8200'

Usable Length for Runway 32 for Landing beyond Displaced Threshold

Airport elevation

136°4.1 NM from LOM

Approach Lights symbol (See legend for type)

Elev 965

1057

1017

1046

Touchdown Zone (TDZ) Elevation

1055

Displaced Threshold

1058

1054

FAF to Runway Threshold or Missed Approach Point (MAP) shown as 4.1 NM

Runway Lighting Aids

HIRL all Rwys
REIL Rwy 35

LOM is Final Approach Fix (FAF)

LOM to Localizer Missed Apch 4.1 NM					
Knots	70	100	125	150	165
Min:Sec	3:31	2:28	1:58	1:38	1:29

Time and Speed Table from Final Approach Fix (FAF) to Missed Approach Point (MAP) for Localizer Procedure

7838. (4) AIM Para. 404. Following a missed approach, the pilot will request clearance for specific action; i.e., another approach, hold for improved conditions, proceed to an alternate airport, etc. The controller will, in response to the pilot's intentions, issue a clearance to an alternate airport, to a holding fix, or for reentry into the approach sequence, as traffic conditions permit.

7839. (1) IFH, AC 90-1A. MISSED APPROACH POINT (MAP). Missed approach points are different for the complete ILS (with glide slope) and for the localizer only approach. The MAP for the ILS is at the decision height (DH) while the "localizer only" MAP is usually over the (straight-in) runway threshold. In some non-precision procedures, the MAP may be prior to reaching the runway threshold in order to clear obstructions in the missed approach climb-out area. In non-precision procedures, the pilot determines when he is at the missed approach point (MAP) by timing from the final approach fix (FAF). The FAF has been clearly identified by use of the maltese cross symbol in the profile section. The distance from FAF to MAP and time and speed table, for easy

calculation, are found below the aerodrome sketches (figures 15 and 16). This does not apply to VOR/DME procedures, or when the facility is on the airport and the facility is the MAP.

7840. (3) IFH, AC 90-1A. The note towards the bottom plate which applies when the control zone is not in effect as stated in the question is marked with an asterisk (*). In the minimums section for ILS RWY 31 only the straight in for localizer 31 is noted with an asterisk and NOT the straight in for the ILS 31. However, in the note itself it states the "all DH/MDAs increased 260 feet" when the control zone is not effective. Since only ILS approaches have DHs, it is suggested that the note also applies to the S-ILS 31. It appears that this has caused some confusion since (as of this writing) the current approach plate for Dubuque Muni, Dubuque, Iowa now has eliminated the asterisk symbol all together. So now the note definitely applies to both straight in approaches. After having researched this we feel that the increase in the DH/MDAs applies to both approaches and the answer with the raised minimums.

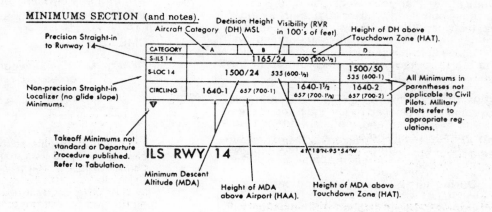

7841. (3) FAR 97. Helicopters may use fixed airplane approach procedures using the Category A minimum descent altitude (MDA) or decision height (DH). The required visibility minimum may be reduced to one-half the published visibility minimum for Category A aircraft, but in no case may it be reduced to less than one-quarter mile or 1,200 feet RVR.

7842. (3) TERPS. None of the answers are very good, yet #3 best describes the limits of the procedure turn area. The P.T. must be made within 10 NM of ZWINGLE intersection and to the east side of the course.

7843. (1) IFH, AC 90-1A. Note that the 10 NM inner ring is the boundary of the procedure that is charted to scale. The aircraft outbound will be on a heading of 322° as shown in Figs. W and X. The VOR needle will be pointing "TO" the station on the 142° radial as shown in Fig. W, and the ADF needle will be pointing to the 093° bearing. The

question is asking for indicates at the proper position to start the turn outbound from "CASSY" intersection in the missed approach holding pattern.

7844. (1) AC 00-50A. Consider an aircraft flying a 3° ILS On a stabilized approach at 140 nots indicated airspeed (IAS) with a 20-knot headwind. Assume that the aircraft encounters an instantaneous wind shear where the 20-knot headwind shears away completely. At that instant, several things will happen; the airspeed will drop from 140 to 120 knots, the nose will begin to pitch down, and the aircraft will begin to drop below the glide slope. The aircraft will then be both slow and low in a "power deficient" state. The pilot may then pull the nose up to a point even higher than before the shear in an effort to recapture the glide slope. This will aggravate the airspeed situation even further until the pilot advances the throttles and sufficient time elapses at the higher power setting for the engines to replenish the power deficiency. If the aircraft reaches the ground before the power deficiency is corrected, the landing will be short, slow, and hard. However,

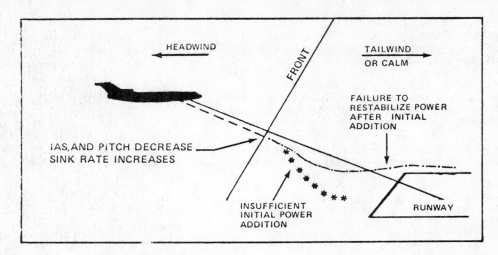

HEADWIND

TAILWIND OR CALM

FRONT

FAILURE TO RESTABILIZE POWER AFTER INITIAL ADDITION

IAS, AND PITCH DECREASE SINK RATE INCREASES

INSUFFICIENT INITIAL POWER ADDITION

RUNWAY

if there is sufficient time to regain the proper airspeed and glide slope before reaching the ground, then the "double reverse" problem arises. This is because the throttles are set too high for a stabilized approach in a no-wind situation. So, as soon as the power deficiency is replenished, the throttles should be pulled back even further than they were before the shear (because power required for a 3° ILS in no wind is less than for a 20-knot headwind). If the pilot does not quickly retard the throttles, the aircraft will soon have an excess of power; i.e., it will be high and fast and may not be able to stop in the available runway length.

7845. (1) AC 91.43. If both the ram air input and drain hole are completely blocked by ice, the trapped pressure in the system and the airspeed indicator may react as an altimeter:
1. During level flight — airspeed indication will not change even when actual airspeed is varied by large power changes.
2. During climb — airspeed indication will increase.
3. During descent — airspeed indication will decrease.

7846. (3) AIM Para. 543. A crosswind will decrease the lateral movement of the upwind VORTEX and increase the movement of the downwind VORTEX. Thus a light wind of 3 to 7 knots could result in the upwind VORTEX remaining in the touchdown zone for a period of time and hasten the drift of the downwind VORTEX toward another runway. Similarly, a tailwind condition can move the vortices of the preceding aircraft forward into the touchdown zone. THE LIGHT QUARTERING TAILWIND REQUIRES MAXIMUM CAUTION. Pilots should be alert to large aircraft upwind from their approach and takeoff flight paths.

7847. (4) AIM Para. 542. The strength of the VORTEX is governed by the weight, speed, and shape of the wing of the generating aircraft. The VORTEX characteristics of any given aircraft can also be changed by extension of flaps or other wing configuring devices as well as by change in speed. However, as the BASIC FACTOR IS WEIGHT, the VORTEX strength increases proportionately. The greatest VORTEX strength occurs when the generating aircraft is HEAVY, CLEAN, and SLOW.

In Answer #4 the aircraft is at a high gross weight which is the number one basic factor, and the jet transport is at a high angle of attack that indicates it is at a slow airspeed which is one of three items that causes the greatest VORTEX strength as mentioned above.

7848. (3) IFH. Degrees of bearing change = 5°. Minutes between bearing change = 1.5 Min. TAS = 95 KTS.

TIME TO STATION:

$$\frac{(60) \ (\text{Minutes between bearing change})}{\text{Degrees of Bearing Change}}$$

$$= \frac{(60) \ (1.5 \ \text{Mins})}{5°} = 18 \ \text{Minutes}$$

DISTANCE TO STATION:

$$\frac{(\text{TAS}) \ (\text{Minutes Flown})}{\text{Degrees of Bearing Change}}$$

$$= \frac{(95 \ \text{KTS}) \ (1.5 \ \text{Minutes})}{(5°)} = \frac{142.5}{5} = 28.5 \ \text{NM}$$

7849. (2) FAR 91.67. When weather conditions permit, regardless of whether an operation is conducted under Instrument Flight Rules or Visual Flight Rules, vigilance shall be maintained by each person operating an aircraft so as to see and avoid other aircraft in compliance with this section. When a rule of this section gives another aircraft the right of way, he shall give way to that aircraft and may not pass over, under, or ahead of it, unless well clear.

7850. (1) IFH. The small hand indicates thousands of feet.

The long, thin hand indicates hundreds of feet.

The very thin hand with the triangular tip indicates tens of thousands of feet.

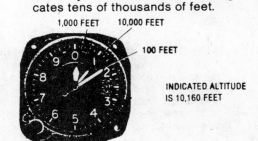

1,000 FEET   10,000 FEET

100 FEET

INDICATED ALTITUDE IS 10,160 FEET

7851. (2) IFH. The VOR needle points to the station on a RMI, in this case 195°. The RMI indicates a 06° wind correction angle (WCA).

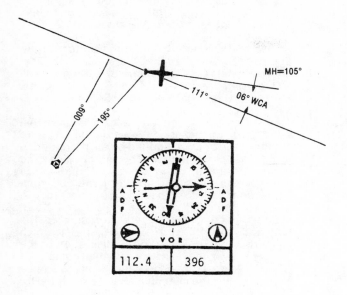

7852. (1) AIM Para. 383. When it will be operationally beneficial, ATC may authorize an aircraft to conduct a visual approach to an airport or to follow another aircraft when flight to, and landing at, the airport can be accomplished in VFR weather. The aircraft must have the airport or the identified preceding aircraft in sight before the clearance is issued. If the pilot has the airport in sight but cannot see the aircraft he is following, ATC may still clear the aircraft for a visual approach; however, ATC retains both separation and wake VORTEX separation responsibility. When visually following a preceding aircraft, acceptance of the visual approach clearance, constitutes acceptance of pilot responsibility for maintaining a safe approach interval and adequate wake turbulence separation.

7853. (3) IFH, AC 90-1A. A stepdown fix may be provided on final, i.e., between the final approach fix and the airport for the purpose of authorizing a lower MDA after passing an obstruction. This stepdown fix may be made by an NDB bearing, fan marker, radar fix, radial from another VOR, or by a DME.

7854. (3) IFH. The GJT LR-330 is a lead radial represented to indicate when to start a turn from the arcs.

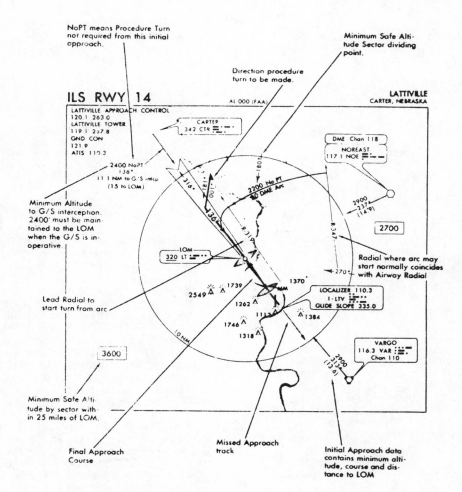

7855. (X) FAA Deletion.

7856. (4) FAR 91.67. When weather conditions permit, regardless of whether an operation is conducted under Instrument Flight Rules or Visual Flight Rules, vigilance shall be maintained by each person operating an aircraft so as to see and avoid other aircraft in compliance with this section. When a rule of this section gives another aircraft the right of way, he shall give way to that aircraft and may not pass over, under, or ahead of it, unless well clear.

7857. (4) IAP Legend.

WAYPOINT (WPT)
Waypoint Data

PRAYS
38°58.3'N 89°51.5'W
112.7 CAP 187.1° – 56.2
590

Waypoint Name,
Coordinates,
Frequency, identifier, Radial/Distance
(Facility to Waypoint)
Reference Facility Elevation.

7858. (3) AIM Para. 347. The outbound heading for the holding pattern is 042°. A heading of 050° requires the teardrop pattern area.

7859. (2) AC 90-45A. The MAP is a waypoint and the TO/FROM indicator will show passage of the "phantom station."

7860. (4) AC 90-45A. An approved RNAV receiver is required for this approach.

BENDY
34°49.7'N 92°06.2'W
113.9 LIT 018.0° – 9.8
240

7861. (2) FAR 97. Helicopters may use airplane approach procedures using the Category A minimum descent altitude (MDA) or decision height (DH). The required visibility minimum may be reduced to one-half the published visibility minimum for Category A aircraft, but in no case may it be reduced to less than one-quarter mile or 1,200 feet RVR.

7862. (2) AIM Para. 347. DME holding is subject to the same entry and holding procedures except that distances (nautical miles) are used in lieu of time values. The OUTBOUND COURSE of a DME holding pattern is called the outbound leg of the pattern. The length of the outbound leg will be specified by the controller. The end of the outbound leg is determined by the odometer reading.

7863. (4) Helicopters may use airplane approach procedures using the Category A minimum descent altitude (MDA) or decision height (DH). The required visibility minimum may be reduced to one-half the published visibility minimum for Category A aircraft, but in no case may it be reduced to less than one-quarter mile or 1,200 feet RVR.

Notice that the note towards the bottom of the approach plate states that when using the Sieynour Johnson AFB, NC altimeter setting that all MDAs are increased 140 feet. For S-19 normal MDA is 400 feet (400 + 140 = 540 ft.).

7864. (4) AIM Para. 371. A procedure turn is specified when it is necessary to reverse direction to establish the aircraft inbound on an intermediate or final approach course. The IAP specifies the outbound and inbound courses, the distance within which the procedure turn shall be completed and the side of the inbound course (by the magnetic compass direction) on which the turn shall be made. Unless otherwise restricted, the type and rate of the turn and the point at which the turn is begun is left to the discretion of the pilot. However, the maneuver must be completed within the prescribed procedure turn distance and not below the minimum altitude specified for its completion.

7865. (2) COMP. Distance from the FAF to the MAP is 4.4 NM as shown in the profile view.

FAF to MAP — 4.4 NM

Knots	60	90	120	150	180
Min:Sec	4:24	2:56	2:12	1:46	1:28

The time and speed table from the final approach fix (FAF) to the missed approach point (MAP) for the SDF RWY 19 approach is shown above. The pilot must interpolate the 75 knot groundspeed given in the question from the chart.

$$\frac{60}{75} \quad X\ 4.4 = 3.52\ Min. = 3:31$$

7866. (3) AIM Para. 304. If operating on an IFR flight plan to an airport where there is no functioning control tower, the pilot must initiate cancellation of the IFR flight plan. This can be done after landing if there is a functioning FSS or other means of direct communications with ATC. In the event there is no FSS and air/ground communications with ATC is not possible below a certain altitude, the pilot should, weather conditions permitting, cancel his IFR flight plan while still airborne and able to communicate with ATC by radio. This will not only save the time and expense of cancelling the flight plan by telephone but will quickly release the airspace for use by other aircraft.

7867. (4) TERPS. The angle of intersection between the initial approach course and the intermediate course shall not exceed 120 degrees. When the angle exceeds 90 degrees, a radial or bearing which provides at least 2 miles of lead shall be identified to assist in leading the turn onto the intermediate course.

7868. (4) The MDA for a circling approach in Category C at Pitt-Greenville is 540 feet. However, there is a note located towards the bottom of the approach plate when the local altimeter setting is not available that all MDAs are increased 140 feet (540 + 140 = 680 feet).

7869. (3) IFH, AC 90-A. In non-precision procedures, the pilot determines when he is at the missed approach point (MAP) by timing from the final approach fix (FAF). The FAF has been clearly identified by use of the maltese cross symbol in the profile section. The time from the final approach fix (FAF) to the missed approach (MAP) can be easily calculated by reference to the time-speed table for a given groundspeed, located towards the bottom of the approach plate.

7870. (1) IFR EOG #7. Note that the localizer needle will give "reverse sensing" since the aircraft heading is almost opposite to that of the runway heading.

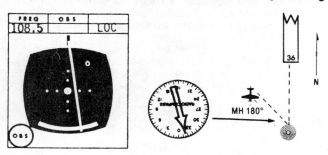

7871. (4) IFR EOG #7. Note that the localizer needle will give "reverse sensing" since the aircraft heading is almost opposite to that of the runway heading.

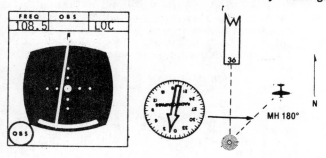

7872. (1) IFR EOG #7. Note that the localizer needle will give "reverse sensing" since the aircraft heading is almost opposite to that of the runway heading.

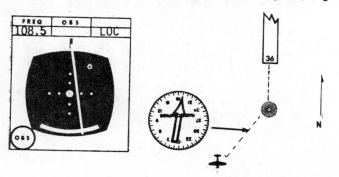

7873. (4) IFR EOG #7. Note that the localizer needle will give "reverse sensing" since the aircraft heading is almost opposite to that of the runway heading.

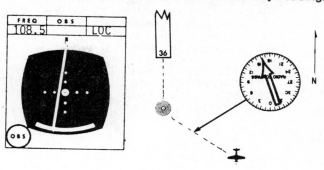

7874. (2) FAR 97. Helicopters may use airplane approach procedures using the Category A minimum descent altitude (MDA) or decision height (DH). The required visibility minimum may be reduced to one-half the published visibility minimum for Category A aircraft, but in no case may it be reduced to less than one-quarter mile or 1,200 feet RVR.

7875. (3) IFH, AC 90-1A. In non-precision procedures, the pilot determines when he is at the missed approach point (MAP) by timing from the final approach fix (FAF). The FAF has been clearly identified by use of the maltese cross symbol in the profile section. The time from the final approach fix (FAF) to the missed approach (MAP) can be easily calculated by reference to the time-speed table for a given groundspeed, located towards the bottom of the approach plate.

7876. (2) IAP. The R-351 from the Holston Mountain (HMV) VORTAC intercepts the localizer from Tri-City forming KEIPY Intersection.

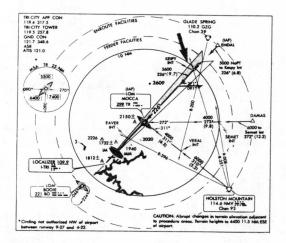

7877. (3) IAP. The minimum sector altitude (MSA) is indicated on the Tri-City ILS RWY 22 approach plate with a circle encompassing the facility showing the various altitudes for each individual sector divided by magnetic headings. The procedure turn at Tri-City falls inside the sector with an MSA of 5,500 feet.

7878. (3) IAP. The runway lights for a given runway will be listed along the bottom of the airport diagram. They will be listed along the bottom. The approach lights are coded and are located next to the runway they service. The key to these lights is in the back of the exam booklet.

AVAILABILITY of TDZ/CL will be shown by NOTE in SKETCH e.g. "TDZ/CL Rwy 15"

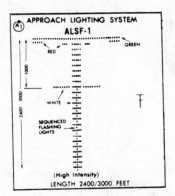

7879. (1) IFH, AC 90-1A. If RVR minimums for takeoff or landing are published in an instrument approach procedure, but RVR is inoperative and cannot be reported for the runway at that time, it is necessary that the RVR minimums which are specified in the procedure be converted and applied as ground visibility in accordance with the table below.

RVR	Visibility (statute miles)
1,600 feet	¼ mile
2,400 feet	½ mile
3,200 feet	⅝ mile
4,000 feet	¾ mile
4,500 feet	⅞ mile
5,000 feet	1 mile
6,000 feet	1¼ mile

7880. (4) FAR 91.83. An alternate does not need to be filed for any airport that has forecasted at least one hour before and one hour after the ETA, a ceiling of at least 2,000 feet AGL, and a visibility of at least 3 miles.

7881. (1) AIM Para. 12. When the glideslope fails, the ILS reverts to a nonprecision localizer approach.

7882. (1) FAR 91.116. A compass locator or precision radar may be substituted for the outer or middle marker of an ILS.

7883. (3) FAR 91.116, AC 90-1A. DME, VOR, or nondirectional beacon fixes authorized in the standard instrument approach procedure or surveillance radar may be substituted for the outer marker. The inoperative components table for an ILS approach states that the DH is increased 50 feet for an inoperative middle marker.

7884. (4) IFH, AC 90-1A. A stepdown fix may be provided on the final, i.e., between the final approach fix and the airport for the purpose of authorizing a lower MDA after passing an obstruction. This stepdown fix may be made by an NDB bearing, fan marker, radar fix, radial from another VOR, or by DME.

7885. (2) Helicopters may use airplane approach procedures using the Category A minimum descent altitude (MDA) or decision height (DH). The required visibility minimum may be reduced to one-half the published visibility minimum for Category A aircraft, but in no case may it be reduced to less than one-quarter mile or 1,200 feet RVR.

Take care to read any notes that may appear on the approach plates. A note on the ILS RWY 9 for Riverside Muni indicates that when the control zone is not effective (as stated in the question) that all DH/MDAs are increased 40 feet.

7886. (1) AIM Para. 347. The outbound heading for the missed approach holding pattern at Riverside Muni is 078° which is inside direct entry area.

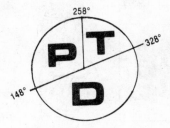

7887. (3) FAR 91.116. A pilot shall maintain the last altitude assigned to that pilot until the aircraft is established on a segment of a published route or instrument approach procedure unless a different altitude is assigned by ATC. After the aircraft is so established, published altitudes apply to descent within each succeeding route or approach segment unless a different altitude is assigned by ATC.

7888. (3) AIM Para. 371. Where a holding pattern is specified in lieu of a procedure turn, the holding maneuver must be executed within the 1 minute time limitation or published leg length. The maneuver is completed when the aircraft is established on the inbound course after executing the appropriate holding pattern entry. If cleared for the approach prior to returning to the holding fix, and the aircraft is at the prescribed altitude, additional circuits of the holding pattern are not necessary nor expected by ATC.

7889. (3) Helicopters may use airplane approach procedures using the Category A minimum descent altitude (MDA) or decision height (DH). The required visibility minimum may be reduced to one-half the published visibility minimum for Category A aircraft, but in no case may it be reduced to less than one-quarter mile or 1,200 feet RVR.

7890. (4) IAP. The plan view indicates the navigation and communication frequencies that are available at the Billy Mitchell airport.

7891. (1) IFH. The RMI indicates that the airplane is on course approaching the NDB (FAF) ahead, with a 10° WCA (wind correction angle).

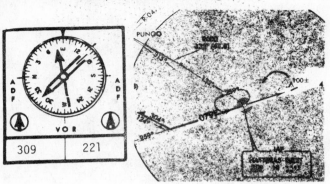

7892. (4) AC 00-50A. When on approach in a tailwind condition that shears into a calm wind or headwind, initially, the IAS and pitch will increase and the aircraft will balloon above the glide slope. Power should initially be reduced to correct this condition or the approach may be high and fast with a danger of overshooting. However, after the intial power reduction is made and the aircraft is back on speed and glide slope, the "double reverse" again comes into play. An appropriate power increase will be necessary to restabilize in the headwind. If this power increase is not accomplished promptly, a high sink rate can develop and the landing may be short and hard (see Fig. below). The double reverse problem arises primarily in downdraft and frontal passage shears. Other shears may require a consistent correction throughout the shear.

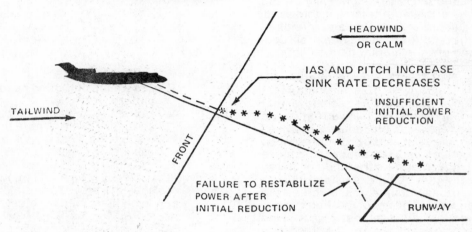

HEADWIND OR CALM

IAS AND PITCH INCREASE
SINK RATE DECREASES

INSUFFICIENT INITIAL POWER REDUCTION

TAILWIND

FRONT

FAILURE TO RESTABILIZE POWER AFTER INITIAL REDUCTION

RUNWAY

7893. (2) FAR 91.116. A compass locator or precision radar (PAR) may be substituted for the outer or middle marker.

7894. (4) Helicopters may use airplane approach procedures using the Category A minimum descent altitude (MDA) or decision height (DH). The required visibility minimum may be reduced to one-half the published visibility minimum for Category A aircraft, but in no case may it be reduced to less than one-quarter mile or 1,200 feet RVR.

7895. (4) Helicopters may use airplane approach procedures using the Category A minimum descent altitude (MDA) or decision height (DH). The required visibility minimum may be reduced to one-half the published visibility minimum for Category A aircraft, but in no case may it be reduced to less than one-quarter mile or 1,200 feet RVR.

7896. (4) AIM Para. 7. When either the VOR or the DME is inoperative, it is important to recognize which identifier is retained for the operative facility. A single coded identification with a repetition interval of approximately 30 seconds indicates that the DME is operative.

7897. (1) AIM Para. 347. The heading outbound for the missed approach holding pattern at Carbon is 182° which falls inside the direct entry area.

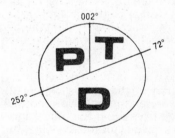

7898. (2) IFH, AC 90-1A. For the VOR RWY 36 approach the facility is on the airport and the facility is the MAP.

7899. (X) FAA Deletion.

7900. (2) AIM Para. 364. Minimum Safe Altitudes (MSA) are published for emergency use on approach procedure charts utilizing NDB or VOR type facilities. the altitude shown provides at least 1,000 feet of clearance above the highest obstacle in the defined sector to a distance of 25 NM from the facility. As many as four sectors may be depicted with different altitudes for each sector displayed in rectangular boxes in the plan view of the chart. A single altitude for the entire area may be shown in the lower right portion of the plan view. Navigational course guidance is not assured at the MSA within these sectors.

7901. (1) AC 61-27C. When an aircraft is established on the 10 DME arc between 026° radial and the 093° radial the minimum altitude is 11,000 feet. A descent may be commenced at or after crossing the 093° radial to 8,000 feet. An aircraft cannot descend below 8,000 feet until it is ESTABLISHED on the final approach course. After it is established on the final approach course, between 10 DME and 4 DME, the aircraft may descend to 6,500. At or after reaching the 4 DME fix the aircraft may descend to, but not below, the MDA of 6,220 feet. When landing requirements are met the aircraft may descend below the MDA for landing.

7902. (2) AIM Para. 12. The inner marker (IM), where installed, will indicate a point at which an aircraft is at a designated decision height (DH) on the glide path between the MM and landing threshold. the IM is modulated at 3000 Hz and identified with continuous dots keyed at the rate of six dots per second and a white marker beacon light.

7903. (3) AIM Para. 382, FAR 91.116. If visual reference is lost while circling to land from an instrument approach, the missed approach specified for that particular procedure must be followed (unless an alternate missed approach procedure is specified by ATC). To become established on the prescribed missed approach course, the pilot should make an initial climbing turn toward the landing runway and continue the turn until he is established on the missed approach course. Inasmuch as the circling maneuver may be accomplished in more than one direction, different patterns will be required to become established on the prescribed missed approach course, depending on the aircraft position at the time visual reference is lost. Adherence to the procedure will assure that an aircraft will remain within the circling and missed approach obstruction clearance areas.

7904. (3) AIM Para. 381. STRAIGHT-IN-MINIMUMS are shown on IAP charts when the final approach course of the IAP is within 30 degrees of the runway alignment and a normal descent can be made from the IFR altitude shown on the IAPs to the runway surface. When either the normal rate of descent or the runway alignment factor of 30 degrees is exceeded, a straight-in minimum is not published and a circling minimum applies. The fact that a straight-in minimum is not published does not preclude the pilot from landing straight-in if he has the active runway in sight and has sufficient time to make a normal approach for landing. Under such conditions and when ATC has cleared him for landing on that runway, he is not expected to circle even though only circling minimums are published. If he desires to circle he should advise ATC.

7905. (3) AIM Para. 347. The inbound course is always flown toward the fix. All answers with "B" are therefore incorrect (#2 and #4). Left hand patterns are entered exactly as right hand patterns. To determine aircraft entry do the following:
1. Get aircraft magnetic heading (350°).
2. FOR NON-STANDARD HOLDING PATTERNS (left turns) count 70° to the left of the aircraft heading (280°)

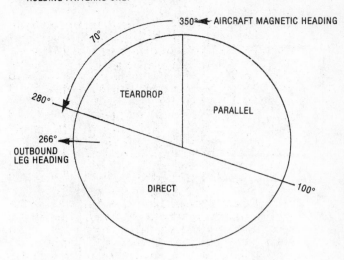

FOR NON-STANDARD HOLDING PATTERNS ONLY

350° ← AIRCRAFT MAGNETIC HEADING
70°
280°
TEARDROP
PARALLEL
266°
OUTBOUND LEG HEADING
DIRECT
100°

3. Determine outbound heading for the holding pattern (266°).
4. Now find where the outbound heading would be on the circle. Where this heading falls on the circle will show which pattern entry to use.

7906. (4) AC 61-27C. When a one minute holding pattern replaces the procedure turn, the standard entry and the holding pattern must be followed except when RADAR VECTORING is provided or when NoPT is shown on the approach course. As in the procedure turn, the descent from the minimum holding pattern altitude to the final approach fix altitude (when lower) may not commence until the aircraft is established on the inbound course.

7907. (X) FAA Deletion.

7908. (3) AC 61-27C. When the final approach fix is not located on the field, the missed approach procedure specifies the distance from the facility to the missed approach point. The "Aerodrome Data" on the approach chart shows the time from the facility to missed approach at various ground speeds, which you must determine from airspeed, wind, and distance values. At this time, you report and execute a missed approach if you do not have applicable minimums.

7909. (1) IAP. The circle to land minimums must be used because the aircraft is landing on a runway other than RWY 17. Without the local altimeter setting and using the Oklahoma City altimeter setting, the note says to increase all MDAs by 200 feet. So 1,440 becomes 1,640 and 1,540 becomes 1,740. Only 1,640 is given as an answer.

7910. (3) AC 90-1A. FAR 91.116 contains new rules applicable to landing minimums. Ceiling minimums are no longer prescribed in approach procedures as a landing limit. The published visibility is the required weather condition for landing as prescribed in FAR 91.116b. FAR 91 now allows approach down to the prescribed minimum descent altitude (MDA) or decision height (DH), as appropriate to the procedure being executed, without regard to reported ceiling.

7911. (3) AIM Para. 404, IAP. "Comply with the missed approach instructions for the instrument approach procedure (IAP) being executed unless other MISSED APPROACH instructions are specified by ATC."

"Advise ATC that a missed approach has been made. Include the reason for the missed approach unless the missed approach is initiated by ATC."

"Following the missed approach, request clearance for specific action; i.e., another approach, hold for improved conditions, proceed to an alternate airport, etc."

The missed approach instructions on the IAP say to climb to 2,400 feet BEFORE starting a left turn.

7912. (4) AIM Para. 304. If operating on an IFR flight plan to an airport where there is no functioning control tower, the pilot must initiate cancellation of the IFR flight plan. This can be done after landing if there is a functioning FSS or other means of direct communications with ATC. In the event there is no FSS and air/ground communications with ATC is not possible below a certain altitude, the pilot should, weather conditions permitting, cancel his IFR flight plan while still airborne and able to communicate with ATC by radio. This will not only save the time and expense of cancelling the flight plan by telephone but will quickly release the airspace for use by other aircraft.

7913. (1) IFR EOG #7. For Goshen VORTAC (Freq. 113.7) the following apply:
1. Set the frequency selector to the frequency of the VOR/VORTAC used to designate the intersection. Then identify the station.
2. Set the OBS to the published radial FROM the station.

With the receiver set up in this manner, the following statements will always be true:

1. The TO-FROM display will indicate "FROM."
2. Before passing the intersection, the CDI needle will be deflected in the direction of the station used for the intersection.
3. The CDI needle will begin movement toward the center when the aircraft is approximately 10° from the desired radial.
4. The CDI needle will center when the radial is crossed.
5. After passing the intersection, the CDI needle will move from the center to the side away from the station used for the intersection.

The SDF (Freq. 111.5) is interpreted the same as a localizer. On the front course when the aircraft is to the right of course the CDI will be to the left of center. When the aircraft is to the left of course the CDI will be to the right of center. This is a back-course SDF, therefore, inbound we will get reverse sensing.

7914. (4) IAP. The transition altitude from SBN to the SDF localizer course is 2,800 feet. The note shows the arrival time to be 0515Z. The Airport/Facility Directory shows under "Airport Remarks" that the control zone is not effective after 0430Z Sunday through Friday or after 0300Z on Saturday. Because of this the note on the instrument approach procedure applies, which says to "increase all MDAs 40 feet." The MDA then becomes 1,280 feet for Category A aircraft.

7915. (3)

	TRUE COURSE	VARIATION	MAG. COURSE
Aircraft	089°	1°W	090°
Wind	100°		
	15 KTS		
TAS	105 KTS		

CALCULATE GROUND SPEED = 90 KTS.

Time from FAF to MAP = 4:00 Minutes:Seconds

Time at COVEY Intersection 1015:25

Time at which missed approach should be started: 1019.25Z.

$$1015:25 + 4:00 = 1019:25$$

7916. (4) AFD Legend.

Types of lighting are shown with the runway or runway end they serve.

LIRL—Low Intensity Runway Lights
MIRL—Medium Intensity Runway Lights
HIRL—High Intensity Runway Lights
REIL—Runway End Identifier Lights
CL—Centerline Lights
TDZ—Touchdown Zone Lights
ODALS—Omni Directional Approach Lighting System.
AF OVRN—Air Force Overrun 1000' Standard Approach Lighting System.
LDIN—Lead-In Lighting System.
MALS—Medium Intensity Approach Lighting System.
MALSF—Medium Intensity Approach Lighting System with Sequenced Flashing Lights.
MALSR—Medium Intensity Approach Lighting System with Runway Alignment Indicator Lights.

SALS—Short Approach Lighting System.
SALSF—Short Approach Lighting System with Sequenced Flashing Lights.
SSALS—Simplified Short Approach Lighting System.
SSALF—Simplified Short Approach Lighting System with Sequenced Flashing Lights.
SSALR—Simplified Short Approach Lighting System with Runway Alignment Indicator Lights.
ALSAF—High Intensity Approach Lighting System with Sequenced Flashing Lights
ALSFI—High Intensity Approach Lighting System with Sequenced Flashing Lights, Category I, Configuration.
ALSF2—High Intensity Approach Lighting System with Sequenced Flashing Lights, Category II, Configuration.
VASI—Visual Approach Slope Indicator System.

VISUAL APPROACH SLOPE INDICATOR SYSTEMS

VASI—Visual Approach Slope Indicator
SAVASI—Simplified Abbreviated Visual Approach Slope Indicator

7917. (4) AIM Para. 347. Determine entry turn from aircraft heading upon arrival at the holding fix. Plus/minus 5 degrees in heading is considered to be within allowable good operating limits for determining entry.

The aircraft heading is 090° when it arrives over Poler intersection.

T = Teardrop
P = Parallel
D = Direct

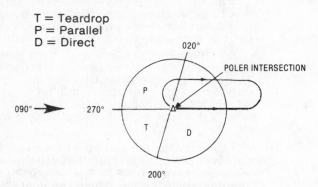

The aircraft heading falls between parallel and teardrop entries. It is the pilot's choice which one to use. If both are given in one answer, mark both.

7918. (2) AIM Para. 347. Outbound leg timing begins OVER/ABEAM the fix, whichever occurs later. If the ABEAM position cannot be determined, start timing when turn to outbound is completed.

7919. (3) AIM Para. 304. If operating on an IFR flight plan to an airport where there is no functioning control tower, the pilot must initiate cancellation of the IFR flight plan. This can be done after landing if there is a functioning FSS or other means of direct communications with ATC. In the event there is no FSS and air/ground communications with ATC is not possible below a certain altitude, the pilot should, weather conditions permitting, cancel his IFR flight plan while still airborne and able to communicate with ATC by radio.

7920. (1) AIM Para. 410. On a visual approach, radar service is automatically terminated without advising the pilot when the aircraft is instructed to contact the tower.

7921. (4) AIM Para. 385. "Pilots operating in accordance with an IFR flight plan, provided they are clear of clouds and have at least 1 mile flight visibility and can reasonably expect to continue to the destination airport in those conditions, may request ATC authorization for a contact approach."

7922. (4) AIM Para. 383. "When it will be operationally beneficial, ATC may authorize an aircraft to conduct a visual approach to an airport or to follow another aircraft when flight to, and landing at, the airport can be accomplished in VFR weather. The aircraft must have the airport or the identified aircraft in sight before the clearance is issued."

7923. (2) AIM Paras. 383, 385. A visual approach may be assigned by ATC anytime that it would be operationally beneficial, and the aircraft would be able to proceed to the airport in VFR conditions. (See Explanation #7922.) A contact approach

must be requested by the pilot; it will never be offered by ATC. (See Explanation #7921.)

7924. (3) IFR EOG #8. "MRA (Minimum Reception Altitude) is the lowest altitude required to receive adequate signals to determine specific fixes. Reception of signals from a radio facility located off the airway being flown may be inadequate at the designated MEA, in which case, an MRA is designated for the fix." Picks Intersection has an MRA of 3,500 feet.

7925. (4) AFD. In the exerpt of the Airport/Facility Directory for Middleton Field, the communications portion shows Atlanta Center approach/departure control 118.55. Also, the approach plate, on the plan view, in the upper left corner lists the frequencies that are used during the approach.

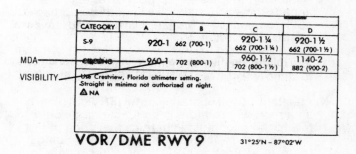

CATEGORY	A	B	C	D
S-9	920-1 662 (700-1)		920-1¼ 662 (700-1¼)	920-1½ 662 (700-1½)
CIRCLING	960-1 702 (800-1)		960-1½ 702 (800-1½)	1140-2 882 (900-2)

Use Crestview, Florida altimeter setting.
Straight in minima not authorized at night.
⚠ NA

VOR/DME RWY 9   31°25'N – 87°02'W

7926. (2) IAP, AC 90-1A. The aircraft is on a circle to land approach to RWY 18, therefore circle to land minima must be used. Remember, ceiling minimums are not prescribed in approach procedures as a landing limit. Visibility is the only required weather condition for landing.

7927. (4) IAP, AIM Para. 403. The MEA on V20 is 2,300 feet. This is the lowest altitude on V20 to MVC VORTAC. Upon reaching MVC, the lowest altitude becomes 2,000 feet while in the holding pattern and until crossing Belle (11 DME) FAF. From Belle to the 13 DME fix the minimum altitude is 1,300 feet. After the 13 DME fix the published MDA for Category B aircraft applies, which is 920 feet.

7928. (2) AIM Para. 304, AFD. If operating on an IFR flight plan to an airport where there is no functioning control tower, the pilot must initiate cancellation of the IFR flight plan. This can be done after landing if there is a functioning FSS or other means of direct communications with ATC. In the event there is no FSS and air/ground communications with ATC is not possible below a certain altitude, the pilot should, weather conditions permitting, cancel his IFR flight plan while still airborne and able to communicate with ATC by radio.

7929. (1) AIM Para. 347. Determine entry turn from aircraft heading upon arrival at the holding fix. Plus/minus 5 degrees in heading is considered to be within allowable good operating limits for determining entry.

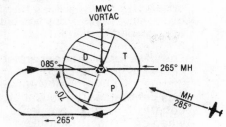

7930. (4) AIM Paras. 385, 402. Pilots operating in accordance with an IFR flight plan, provided they are clear of clouds and have at least 1 mile flight visibility and can reasonably expect to continue to the destination airport in those conditions, may request ATC authorization for a contact approach.

Controllers may authorize a contact approach if Contact Approach is specifically requested by the pilot. ATC cannot initiate this approach.

7931. (3) AC 91-24. Hydroplaning may occur as a result of aircraft speed and water on the runway. As the speed of the aircraft and the depth of the water increase, the water layer builds up an increasing resistance to displacement, resulting in the formation of a wedge of water beneath the tire. The vertical component of this resistance progressively lifts the tire decreasing the area in contact with the runway until, with certain aircraft configurations and depths, the tire is completely out of contact with the runway surface and starts hydroplaning on a film of water.

Dynamic hydroplaning occurs when there is standing water on the runway surface. Water about one-tenth of an inch deep acts to lift the tire off the runway as explained above.

Viscous hydroplaning is due to the viscous properties of water. In this type, a thin film of fluid not more than one-thousandth of an inch in depth cannot be penetrated by the tire and the tire rolls on top of the film. This can occur at a much lower speed than dynamic hydroplaning but requires a smooth or smooth-acting surface.

7932. (4) IAP. The MEA from NOCKS intersection to OKC VORTAC is 3,000 feet. Three thousand feet is also the minimum altitude for the one minute holding pattern procedure turn. After crossing OKC VORTAC inbound minimum altitude is 2,000 feet to SOONE INT (FAF). Passing SOONE Intersection the 1,700 foot MDA applies.

7933. (3) AC 90-1A. Answer #2 is incorrect because groundspeed is needed, not indicated airspeed. The missed approach can be determined by two means; timing from the FAF to the MAP or using the 7.9 DME fix. The DME feature of the VORTAC may be used but is not required for the approach.

7934. (2) IAP, AC 90-1A, AIM Para. 373. The upper left corner of the plan view contains information on frequencies and radar services. The notation "ASR" means that airport surveillance radar is available and that an ASR approach to Will Rogers World Airport could be accomplished.

7935. (4) IAP, AIM Para. 7, TERPS. The accuracy of the VOR radial becomes less the further from the VOR an aircraft proceeds. Because all stations have accuracy limitations, the geographical point which is identified is not precise, but may be anywhere within a quadrange which surrounds the plotted point of intersection. The accuracy limitations of a crossing VOR radial is plus or minus 3.6°. Thus the error allowable for a crossing radial would be (in problem #7935) approximately 1.7 NM (±.85 NM). The allowable error using a DME fix is .5 NM or 3% whichever is greater. At 5 NM the error would be plus or minus .5 NM.

7936. (4) IAP. "Ceiling minimums are no longer prescribed in approach procedures as a landing limit. The published visibility is the required weather condition for landing as prescribed in FAR 91.16b."

7937. (2) IAP, AIM Para. 364, AC 61-27C. The minimum safe altitude diagram on the plan view of the approach procedure shows magnetic courses to the VORTAC. All radials proceed from the VORTAC. The 165° magnetic course is the 345° radial and the 255° magnetic course is the 075° radial; both radials are magnetic courses from the VORTAC.

7938. (1) IAP, AFD Legend. There are two places to find this information. On the approach plate, the aerodrome data sketch has the symbol " Ⓥ " at the approach end of each runway that has a VASI system. In the Airport/Facility Directory each runway is listed with the type of runway lighting and visual approach aids available.

7939. (3) IAP Legend (Aerodrome Data). The Aerodrome Data sketch has the symbol " Ⓐ " which means approach lighting system ALSF-2. The "●" indicates sequenced flashing lights installed with the approach lighting system. (See runway information in AFD.)

7940. (1) IFR EOG #42, AIM Para. 385. When using instrument approach procedures for fixed wing aircraft, the same navigational equipment requirements or restrictions apply to helicopters.

Pilots operating in accordance with an IFR flight plan, provided they are clear of clouds and have at least 1 mile flight visibility and can reasonably expect to continue to the destination airport in those conditions, may request ATC authorization for a contact approach.

7941. (3) IFR EOG #42, FAR 91.116, 97.3. All MDA and DH requirements apply to helicopters, as published for fixed wing aircraft. However, all helicopters are considered to be Category A aircraft and may use one half the published visibility for fixed wing aircraft (never less than 1,200 RVR: see FAR 97.3).

7942. (1) AC 90-1A, AC 61-27C. "If it is necessary to maneuver at speeds in excess of the upper limit of the speed range for each category, the minimum for the next higher approach category should be used."

7943. (3) AC 00-50A. When an aircraft that is flying with a tailwind suddenly encounters calm air it is the same as encountering a headwind. "Initially, the IAS and pitch will increase and the aircraft will balloon above the glide slope."

7944. (3) AIM Para. 364, IAP. "As many as four sections may be depicted with different altitudes for each sector displayed in rectangular boxes in the plan view of the chart. A single altitude for the entire area may be shown in the lower right (left in the Fig.) portion of the plan view.

7945. (4) IAP. The altitude "5000" would be the lowest altitude unless ATC assigned the altitude that the asterisk refers to, which is 2,800 feet. See CHINN INT in profile view.

7946. (2) IAP. The symbol " ⊙ " refers to ALSF-1 with sequenced flashing lights ("●").

7947. (3) AIM Para. 235. "A pilot who has just landed should not change from the tower frequency to the ground control frequency until he is directed to do so by the controller."

7948. (4) AIM Para. 503. Flight Watch is also known as Enroute Flight Advisory Service or EFAS. "All communications are conducted on the designated EFAS frequency, 122.0 MHz."

7949. (3) IAP. The height above the ground at which the glide slope passes over the threshold is known as the threshold crossing height (TCH). This is found in the profile view as

$$\frac{\text{GS } 3.00°}{\text{TCH } 56}$$

7950. (X) FAA Deletion.

7951. (1) FAR 91.116. An ILS approach is a precision approach procedure, because it has an electronic glide slope. The missed approach point (MAP) on a precession approach is always the decision height (DH).

7952. (4) AC 61-27C. The vertical speed indicator (VSI) shows rate of change of altitude. The faster an aircraft descends the greater the rate of descent shown on the VSI. The slower an aircraft descends the slower the rate of descent shown on the VSI. An aircraft descending on a glideslope at 90 KIAS into a 90 KT headwind will have a groundspeed of zero and a vertical speed of zero (if it remains on the glide slope). As the wind speed decreases the ground speed of the aircraft begins to increase. At the same time, in order to stay on the glide slope, the vertical speed begins to increase as the aircraft proceeds over the ground. Thus the vertical speed required is dependent on the ground speed when flying on a fixed glide slope.

7953. (2) AIM Paras. 543, 544, 545. "Avoid flight below and behind a large aircraft's path. If a large aircraft is observed above on the same track (meeting or overtaking) adjust your position laterally, preferably upwind."

The wake turbulence generated by a large aircraft descends at about 500' per minute to approximately 1,000 feet below the altitude at which it was generated. To prevent an unintentional encounter fly above the large aircraft's altitude when crossing its flight path.

7954. (2) AIM Para. 543. "A crosswind will decrease the lateral movement of the upwind VORTEX and increase the movement of the downwind VORTEX. Thus a light wind of 3 to 7 knots could result in the upwind VORTEX remaining in the touchdown zone for a period of time and hasten the drift of the downwind VORTEX toward another runway."

7955. (3) AC 61-27C. The vertical speed indicator (VSI) shows rate of change of altitude. The faster an aircraft descends the greater the rate of descent shown on the VSI. The slower an aircraft descends the slower the rate of descent shown on the VSI. An aircraft descending on a glideslope at 90 KIAS into a 90 KT headwind will have a groundspeed of zero and a vertical speed of zero (if it remains on the glideslope). As the wind speed decreases the ground speed of the aircraft begins to increase. At the same time, in order to stay on the glideslope, the vertical speed begins to increase as the aircraft proceeds over the ground. Thus the vertical speed required is dependent on the groundspeed when flying on a fixed glideslope.

7956. (2) AIM Para. 12. "The MM indicates a position at which an aircraft is approximately 3,500 feet from the landing threshold. This will also be the position at which an aircraft on the glide path will at an altitude of approximately 200 feet above the elevation of the touchdown zone."

7957. (4) AIM Para. 545. "When landing behind a large aircraft, stay at or above the large aircraft's final approach flight path — note his touchdown point and land beyond it."

7958. (2) FAR 91.116. "A compass locator or precision radar may be substituted for the outer or middle marker. DME, VOR, or nondirectional beacon fixes authorized in the standard instrument approach procedure or surveillance radar may be substituted for the outer marker."

7959. (2) FAR 91.116. "A compass locator or precision radar may be substituted for the outer or middle marker. DME, VOR, or nondirectional beacon fixes authorized in the standard instrument approach procedure or surveillance radar may be substituted for the outer marker."

7960. (1) IAP. "If more than one component is inoperative, each minimum is raised to the highest minimum required by any single component that is inoperative."

7961. (3) AIM Para. 373. "... the pilot will be advised when to commence descent to the MDA ... in addition the pilot will be advised of the location of the missed approach point (MAP) prescribed for the procedure and his position each mile on final from the runway, airport or heliport or MAP, as appropriate."

7962. (3) IAP, IFR EOG #27. All instrument approach procedures have landing minimums to which pilots must adhere. Surveillance approaches also have published minimums which can be found in the regional instrument approach chart booklets, in the pages titled Civil Radar Instrument Approach Minimums.

7963. (3) AC 61-21A, Flying Light Twins Safely. An increase in altitude in a light, non-turbo charged twin will reduce engine horsepower resulting in a decreased operative engine moment, which decreases V_{MCA}. Moving the CG from aft to forward increases the effectiveness of the rudder moment, also decreasing V_{MCA}. The FAA states that "banking 5° INTO THE GOOD ENGINE ensures that the airplane will be controllable at any speed above the certificated V_{MC} ..." Answer #3 is the opposite of this and would cause an increase in the V_{MCA}.

7964. (2) AC 61-27C. "The true airspeed indicator combines computer operation and indicator in one instrument to provide both true and indicated airspeed (within the cruising range).

With the adjusting knob, pressure altitude is set opposite outside air temperature. The needle then shows indicated airspeed in both knots and miles per hour, and true airspeed in MPH."

7965. (2) AC 61-27C. When an aircraft makes a taxiing left turn the turn coordinator will show the same indications as a level, no bank left turn in flight. Those indications are, the miniature airplane will show a left turn (the direction of turn and rate) while the ball will show an uncoordinated turn (a skid), by moving to the right.

7966. (X) FAA Deletion.

7967. (4) AC 61-27C. The vertical speed indicator (VSI) shows rate of change of altitude. The faster an aircraft descends the greater the rate of descent shown on the VSI. The slower an aircraft descends the slower the rate of descent shown on the VSI. An aircraft descending on a glideslope at 90 KIAS into a 90 KT headwind will have a groundspeed of zero and a vertical speed of zero (if it remains on the glideslope). As the wind speed decreases the ground speed of the aircraft begins to increase. At the same time, in order to stay on the glideslope, the vertical speed begins to increase as the aircraft proceeds over the ground. Thus the vertical speed required is dependent on the groundspeed when flying on a fixed glideslope.

7968. (2) AC 61-27C. "On the roll-in, use the attitude indicator to establish the approximate angle of bank. Maintain the bank for this standard rate turn, using the miniature aircraft of the turn indicator as the primary bank reference and the attitude indicator as the supporting bank instrument."

7969. (2) AC 61-27C. "In place of the conventional turn needle indication of rate-of-turn, the turn coordinator displays the movement of the aircraft on the roll axis that is proportional to the roll rate. When the roll rate is reduced to zero, the instrument provides an indication of the rate-of-turn."

7970. (1) AC 61-27C. Both a narrower-than-usual runway and an upsloping runway, upsloping terrain or both, can create an illusion that the aircraft is at a higher altitude than it actually is.

7971. (3) AC 61-27C. "During attitude instrument training, a pilot must develop three fundamental skills involved in all instrument flight maneuvers: instrument cross-check, instrument interpretation and aircraft control."

7972. (1) AC 61-27C. "A narrower-than-usual runway can create an illusion that the aircraft is higher than it actually is, leading to a lower approach."

7973. (2) AC 61-27C. "The attitude indicator shows any change in bank attitude directly and instantly." "The miniature aircraft of the turn coordinator gives an indirect indication of bank..." The heading indicator and the magnetic compass show bank attitude indirectly. The inclinometer shows the quality of a turn, not direction.

7974. (1) AC 61-27C. "The rate of turn at any given airspeed depends on the amount of sideward force causing the turn; that is the horizontal lift component. The horizontal lift component varies directly in proportion to bank in a correctly executed turn."

7975. (2) AC 61-27C. "Slant-range error is negligible if the aircraft is one mile or more from the ground facility for each 1,000 feet of altitude above the elevation of the facility."

7976. (2) AC 61-27C. "A skidding turn results from excess centrifugal force over the horizontal lift component pulling the aircraft toward the outside of hte turn." As centrifugal force increases the load factor also increases.

7977. (1) AC 61-27C. As the power is increased for a constant rate climb, the airspeed indicator is primary for pitch control until the vertical speed approaches the desired value. The heading indicator is primary for bank and the tachometer or manifold pressure guage is primary for power.

7978. (1) AC 61-27C. The attitude indicator is primary only during transitions from one attitude to another. Once stabilized, the attitude indicator becomes a supporting instrument. The turn coordinator is a supporting instrument in straight flight.

7979. (1) AC 61-27C. Primary pitch information during the transition is attitude indicator for pitch, heading indicator for bank and tachometer or manifold pressure for power. When the airspeed has stabilized the airspeed indicator becomes primary for pitch.

7980. (2) AC 61-27C. To maintain a straight flight path, a pilot must keep the wings of the airplane level with the horizon. This is done by using the heading indicator as primary bank indication and by using the turn coordinator and attitude indicator as supporting bank instruments.

7981. (3) AC 61-27C. Pitch and power control techniques are the same as those used during changes in airspeed in straight and level flight. The altimeter is primary for pitch control, the vertical-speed indicator and attitude indicator will be supporting pitch instruments.

7982. (1) AC 61-27C. "As the airspeed approaches the desired airspeed, the manifold pressure is adjusted and becomes the supporting power instrument. The airspeed indicator again becomes primary for power."

7983. (2) AC 61-27C. "On the roll-in, use the attitude indicator to establish the approximate angle of bank (primary), then check the miniature aircraft of the turn coordinator for a standard rate turn indication (secondary)."

7984. (2) AC 61-27C. As an straight and level flight, the altimeter is the primary pitch instrument.

7985. (4) AC 61-27C. "On the roll-in, use the attitude indicator to establish the approximate angle of bank (primary), then check the miniature aircraft of the turn coordinator for a standard rate turn indication (secondary)."

7986. (1) AC 61-27C. "The miniature aircraft of the turn coordinator displays only rate of roll and rate of turn. It does not directly display the bank angle of the aircraft."

7987. (4) AC 61-27C. Once established in the climbing turn at a constant airspeed, the airspeed indicator is primary for pitch.

7988. (3) AC 61-27C. When making initial pitch attitude corrections to maintain altitude, the changes of attitude should be small and smoothly applied. The initial movement of the horizon bar should not exceed one bar high or low. If further change is required, an additional correction of one-half bar will normally correct any deviation from the desired altitude. This correction (one and one-half bars) is normally the maximum for pitch attitude corrections from level flight attitude.

7989. (1) AC 61-27C. To enter autorotation, reduce collective pitch smoothly to maintain a safe rotor RPM and apply pedal trim to keep the ball of the turn coordinator centered. The pitch attitude of the helicopter should be approximately level as shown by the attitude indicator. The airspeed indicator is the primary pitch instrument and should be adjusted to the recommended autorotation speed. The heading indicator is primary for bank in a straight-ahead autorotation. In a turning autorotation, a standard rate turn should be maintained by reference to the miniature aircraft of the turn coordinator.

7990. (4) AC 61-27C. "The pitch attitude of the helicopter should be approximately level as shown by the attitude indicator.

7991. (2) AC 61-27C. "During the initial acceleration, the pitch attitude of the helicopter, as read on the attitude indicator, should be one to two bar widths low."

7992. (3) IFR EOG #42. "The approach criteria for helicopters are based on airspeeds not exceeding 90 knots, regardless of weight. Thus, all helicopters are considered to be approach Category "A."

7993. (1) IFR EOG #42. "The approach criteria for helicopters are based on airspeeds not exceeding 90 knots, regardless of weight. Thus, all helicopters are considered to be approach Category "A."

7994. (4) IFR EOG #42. "The published approach Category "A" MDA and DH minimums apply; however, FAR Part 97 provides for a reduction of the fixed wing visibility requirements to one-half those published but in no case less than one-quarter mile or 1,200 RVR."

7995. (4) AIM Glossary. Initial Approach Fixes — The fixes depicted on the instrument approach procedure charts that identify the beginning of the initial approach segment(s).

7996. (4) AC 61-27C, FAR 91.116. "Unless otherwise authorized, each person operating an aircraft shall, when an instrument letdown to an airport is necessary, use a standard instrument approach procedure prescribed for that airport."

"Unless otherwise authorized by the administrator, no person operating an aircraft ... may land that aircraft using a standard instrument approach procedure unless the visibility is at or above the landing minimum prescribed ... for the procedure used."

7997. (3) AC 61-23B. "Lift acts upward and perpendicular to the relative wind and to the wing span."

7998. (3) AC 61-13B. LOW FREQUENCY VIBRATIONS. Abnormal vibrations in this category are always associated with the main rotor. The vibration will be some frequency related to the rotor RPM and the number of blades of the rotor, such as one vibration per revolution (1 per rev.), 2 per rev., or 3 per rev. Low-frequency vibrations are slow enough that they can be counted.

7999. (2) AC 61-13B. Each rotor blade is also attached to the hub by a vertical hinge, called a drag or lag hinge, that permits each blade, independently of the others, to move back and forth in the plane of the rotor disc. This movement is called dragging, lead-lag, or hunting. The location of this hinge is chosen primarily with regard to controlling vibration. Dampers are normally incorporated in the design of this type rotor system to prevent excessive motion about the drag hinge. The purpose of the drag hinge and dampers is to absorb the acceleration and deceleration of the rotor blades caused by coriolis effect.

8000. (1) AC 61-13B. In recovering from a settling-with-power condition, the tendency on the part of the pilot to first try to stop the descent by increasing collective pitch will result in increasing the stalled area of the rotor and increasing the rate of descent. Since inboard portions of the blades are stalled, cyclic control will be reduced. Recovery can be accomplished by increasing forward speed, and/or partially lowering collective pitch.

8001. (2) AC 61-13B. The major warnings or approaching retreating blade stall conditions in the order in which they will generally be experienced are:
1. Abnormal 2 per revolution vibration in two-bladed rotors or 3 per revolution vibration in three-bladed rotors.
2. Pitchup of the nose.
3. Tendency for the helicopter to roll.

8002. (2) AC 61-13B. THE STALL OF A ROTOR BLADE LIMITS THE HIGH AIRSPEED POTENTIAL OF A HELICOPTER. The airflow over the retreating blade of the helicopter slows down as forward airspeed of the helicopter increases; the airflow over the advancing blade speeds up as forward airspeed increases. The retreating blade must, however, produce the same amount of lift as the advancing blade. Therefore, as the airflow over the retreating blade decreases with forward airspeed, the blade angle of attack must be increased to help equalize lift throughout the rotor disc area. As this increase in angle of attack is continued, the retreating blade will stall at some high forward airspeed. The advancing blade has relatively low angles of attack and is not subject to blade stall. Blade stall occurs during powered flight at the tip of the retreating blade, spreading inboard as forward airspeed increases.

8003. (4) AC 61-13B. "As the altitude increases, the never exceed speed (red line) for most helicopters decreases."

8004. (4) AC 61-13B. When operating at HIGH FORWARD AIRSPEEDS, stalls are more likely to occur under conditions of:
1. High gross weight.
2. Low RPM.
3. High density altitude.
4. Steep or abrupt turns.
5. Turbulent air.

Since #4 (high rotor RPM) does not appear in the above list, it is the best answer.

8005. (2) AC 61-13B. When operating at HIGH FORWARD AIRSPEEDS, stalls are more likely to occur under conditions of:
1. High gross weight.
2. Low RPM.
3. High density altitude.
4. Steep or abrupt turns.
5. Turbulent air.

8006. (4) AC 61-13B. Helicopter performance will be decreased as the density altitude increases. An increased density altitude is caused by decreasing atmospheric pressure, increasing temperature, increasing relative humidity or any combination of the above.

8007. (2) AC 61-27C. The turn coordinator (showing a lack of turn) is not in agreement with the other instruments. This indicates an ELECTRICAL SYSTEM malfunction. The attitude indicator and directional gyro show a right turn. The airspeed indicator, altimeter, and VSI show respectively a constant speed climb at 500 feet per minute.

8008. (4) AC 61-27C. None of the three bank instruments agree. Since only ONE SYSTEM is malfunctioning it must be the vacuum causing both the DG and attitude indicator to give erroneous readings. Having eliminated these it can be seen that the aircraft is in straight-and-level flight.

8009. (1) AC 61-27C. Notice this question asks which instrument has malfunctioned and says nothing of systems. The attitude indicator disagrees with the turn coordinator and DG in its bank indication. It also disagrees with the altimeter, VSI, and airspeed indicator in its pitch indication. Elimination of the attitude indicator shows the airplane to be in a climbing turn to the right.

8010. (2) AC 61-27C. Notice the question asks about an instrument malfunction not a system malfunction. Although the airspeed indicator shows a decrease the other pitch instruments (attitude indicator, altimeter, and VSI) all agree and show the aircraft in level flight. The three bank instruments are in agreement showing a turn to the right.

8011. (3) AC 61-27C. Notice the question asks about an entire SYSTEM failure. The turn coordinator, DG, and attitude indicator show the aircraft to be turning right (based on the vacuum and electrical systems backing each other up). The attitude indicator also shows a descent. Since the pitot static instruments all appear frozen and show no indication of descending this system has failed. Upon elimination of the pitot/static instruments the panel can be interpreted to show a descending turn to the right.

8012. (3) AC 61-27C. All instruments show straight-and-level flight except the airspeed indicator. Since this is the only instrument which uses ram air from the pitot tube this is the system which has malfunctioned.

8013. (3) AC 61-27C. The Instrument Flying Handbook lists the altimeter as the primary pitch instrument during level flight. The attitude indicator, vertical speed indicator and airspeed indicator provide secondary attitude information.

8014. (3) AC 61-27C. The Instrument Flying Handbook lists the heading indicator as the primary bank instrument. The attitude indicator and turn coordinator provide secondary bank information.

8015. (4) AC 61-27C. The attitude indicator is the primary pitch instrument during changes in pitch. Altimeter and VSI show the direction and magnitude of the correction.

8016. (4) AC 61-27C. In addition to the attitude indicator, the altimeter, vertical speed indicator and airspeed indicator provide pitch information.

8017. (2) AC 61-27C. Reduce power to prevent excessive airspeed and loss of altitude, correct the bank attitude with coordinated aileron and rudder pressure and raise the nose to level flight attitude.

8018. (2) AC 61-27C. As soon as an unusual attitude is detected, recovery should be initiated primarily by reference to the airspeed indicator and altimeter.

8019. (1) AC 61-27C. When the rate of movement of altimeter and airspeed indicator needles decreases and the vertical speed indicator reverses its trend, the aircraft is approaching level pitch attitude.

8020. (2) AC 61-27C. The key is the notation of the instrument "4 MIN. TURN." On a 4-Min. Turn Indicator one needle width is a one-half standard rate turn, or 1.5° per second. Remember, a standard rate turn is 3° per second. To perform a coordinated standard rate turn, we must increase our rate of turn. In addition, we must correct the skid we are in by applying additional right rudder.

8021. (1) AC 61-27C. See Explanation #8020 and remember with a 4 Min. Turn indicator the needle must be on the "doghouse" to acquire a standard rate turn. This time the slip indicated must be corrected by applying additional left rudder.

8022. (3) AC 61-27C. All the figures show the aircraft in a left turn so simply identify those that are skidding. To skid means to allow centrifugal force to exceed the horizontal lift. This is indicated by the length of the force vectors on Figure C and by the ball being outside the turn on instrument F.

8023. (2) AC 61-27C. All figures show the aircraft in a left turn so simply identify those that are slipping. To slip means to allow horizontal lift to exceed centrifugal force. This is indicated by the length of the force vectors on Figure 8 and by the ball being inside the turn on instrument E.

8024. (4) AC 61-27C. In a coordinated turn horizontal lift equals centrifugal force and the ball on the turn and slip indicator should be centered.

8025. (3) AC 61-27C. An aircraft requires a sideward force to make it turn. In a normal turn this force is supplied by banking the aircraft so that lift is exerted inward as well as upward. The horizontal lift component is the sideward force that causes the aircraft to turn.

8026. (2) AC 61-27C. In a coordinated turn horizontal lift equals centrifugal force and the ball on the turn and slip indicator should be centered.

8027. (2) SLAVE AND FREE GYRO PUSHBUTTON — When depressed, the system is in the slaved gyro mode. When the button is in the outer position (not engaged), the system is in the free gyro mode.

CLOCKWISE ADJUSTMENT — When the system is in the free gyro mode, depressing the clockwise manual heading drive button will rotate the compass card to the right to eliminate left compass card error.

COUNTERCLOCKWISE ADJUSTMENT — When the system is in the free gyro mode, depressing the counterclockwise manual heading drive button will rotate the compass card to the left to eliminate right compass card error.

8028. (3) Reference Explanation #8027.

8029. (4) Reference Explanation #8027.

8030. (2) AC 61-27C. The three fundamental skills involved in all instrument flight maneuvers are: instrument cross-check, instrument interpretation, and aircraft control.

8031. (4) AC 61-27C. The three fundamental skills involved in all instrument flight maneuvers are: instrument cross-check, instrument interpretation, and aircraft control.

8032. (2) AC 61-27C. The three fundamental skills involved in all instrument flight maneuvers are: instrument cross-check, instrument interpretation, and aircraft control.

8033. (1) AC 61-27C. The mach meter "indicates the ratio of aircraft true airspeed to the speed of sound at flight altitude."

8034. (3) AC 61-27C. "A skidding turn moves the pendulous vanes from their vertical position, precessing the gyro toward the inside of the turn. After return of the aircraft to straight-and-level, coordinated flight, the miniature aircraft shows a turn in the direction opposite the skid."

8035. (2) AC 61-27C. "If a 180° steep turn is made to the right and the aircraft is rolled-out to straight-and-level flight by visual references, the miniature aircraft will show a slight climb and turn to the left."

8036. (4) AC 61-27C. "During a normal turn, movement of the vanes by centrifugal force causes precession of the gyro toward the inside of the turn."

8037. (1) AC 61-27C. "The turn needle (or miniature aircraft) indicates the rate at which the aircraft is turning about the vertical axis in number of degrees per second. Properly understood, the instrument provides bank as well as rate-of-turn information but it tells you nothing about bank attitude UNLESS you understand the relationship between airspeed, angle-of-bank and rate-of-turn."

8038. (3) AC 61-27C. "As the power is reduced, the altimeter is primary for pitch, the heading indicator for bank, and the manifold pressure gauge is momentarily primary for power."

8039. (2) AC 61-27C. In order to maintain the glideslope and reduce the airspeed, both power and pitch need to be adjusted. As power is reduced, the airspeed will slow, however, if no pitch adjustment is made the aircraft will descend below the glideslope. Therefore, a pitch adjustment must also be made.

8040. (1) AC 61-27C. "On the roll-in, use the attitude indicator to establish the approximate angle of bank, then check the miniature aircraft of the turn coordinator for a standard-rate turn indication."

8041. (1) AC 61-27C. When the static port is clogged, the airspeed indicator works as an altimeter; the higher the aircraft climbs, the higher the indicated airspeed becomes. Because the altimeter and vertical speed indicators are only connected to the static line, when it is clogged neither instrument will work until a new static source is supplied. The aircraft in Figure 110 is in a climbing, right turn.

8042. (2) AC 61-27C. "If the airspeed is decreasing or below the desired airspeed, increase power (as necessary in proportion to the observed deceleration), apply forward elevator pressure to lower the nose and prevent a stall, and correct the bank by applying coordinated aileron and rudder pressure to level the miniature aircraft and center the ball of the turn coordinator. The corrective control applications are made almost simultaneously but in the sequence given above."

8043. (3) AC 61-27C, IFH. Associated Conditions: Airspeed is high, nose is below horizon, vertical speed shows excesive rate of descent, compass indicates right turn, and turn coordinator shows uncoordinated greater than standard rate turn.

If the airspeed is increasing, or is above the desired airspeed, reduce power to prevent excessive airspeed and loss of altitude. Correct the bank attitude with coordinated aileron and rudder pressure to straight flight by referring to the turn coordinator. Raise the nose to level flight attitude by smooth back elevator pressure.

8044. (1) AIM. Uncontrolled airspace is that portion of the airspace that has not been designated as Continental Control Area, Control Area, Control Zone, TCA, or Transition Area. If flight is conducted outside of these areas, ATC does not exercise control over that flight.

8045. (4) AIM. Transition Areas are controlled airspace extending upward from 700 feet or more above the surface when designated in conjunction with an airport for which an instrument approach procedure has been prescribed; or from 1,200 feet or more above the surface when designated in conjunction with airway route structures or segments. Unless specified otherwise, Transition Areas terminate at the base of overlying controlled airspace.

This question specifies a prescribed instrument approach procedure, in which case the vertical limits of transition area are 700 feet AGL to the base of the overlying controlled airspace.

8046. (2) FAR 71.5. Each federal airway includes the airspace within parallel boundary lines 4 miles (nautical; ED.) each side of the centerline. Please see FAR 71.5 for complete explanation of airway boundaries under other specified conditions.

8047. (1) AIM. Transition Areas are controlled airspace extending upward from 700 feet or more above the surface when designated in conjunction with an airport for which an instrument approach procedure has been prescribed; or from 1,200 feet or more above the surface when designated in conjunction with airway route structures or segments. Unless specified otherwise, Transition Areas terminate at the base of overlying controlled airspace.

This question specifies a prescribed instrument approach procedure, in which case the vertical limits of transition area are 700 feet AGL to the base of the overlying controlled airspace.

8048. (3) AIM, FAR 71.193. The positive control area includes airspace within the conterminous U.S. from 18,000 feet to and including FL600.

8049. (1) AC 00-6A. You can always determine pressure altitude from your altimeter whether in flight or on the ground. Simply set your altimeter at the standard altimeter setting of 29.92 inches, and your altimeter indicates pressure altitude.

8050. (1) AC 00-6A, AW. You can always determine pressure altitude from your altimeter whether in flight or on the ground. Simply set your altimeter at the standard altimeter setting of 29.92 inches, and your altimeter indicates pressure altitude.

8051. (2) AC 00-6A, AW. You can always determine pressure altitude from your altimeter whether in flight or on the ground. Simply set your altimeter at the standard altimeter setting of 29.92 inches, and your altimeter indicates pressure altitude.

8052. (2) AIM. The effects of hypoxia are usually quite difficult to recognize, especially when they occur gradually.

8053. (2)

LEG	WIND	DIST.	G.S.	TIME
IPL — WISTE	080° @ 37 KTS	37	153	14:31
WISTE — TRM	080° @ 37 KTS	31	183	10:10
TRM — JLI	100° @ 43 KTS	36	156	14:13
		104		38:54

8054. (2) Pressure altitude 9,500', temperature –10°C, density altitude under these conditions is 8,757'. Set pressure altitude opposite temperature in degrees Celsius. Read density altitude at D.A. arrow.

8055. (1) Pressure altitude 9,500', temperature –10°C, TAS 150 KTS. Under these conditions CAS is 132 KTS. Set pressure altitude opposite temperature in degrees Celsius, read CAS under 150 knot TAS (outer scale).

8056. (2) Pressure altitude 9,500', temperature –10°C. Set pressure altitude opposite temperature in degrees Celsius. Read true altitude on outer scale opposite calibrated altitude of 9,000 on inner scale.

8057. (4) 2° Celsius (standard lapse rate) X 9,000 = 18° standard conditions temperature decrease. Standard sea level temperature (15°C) – 18° = – 3°. For standard atmosphere at 9,000'. Minus 10°C is 7° colder than standard.

8058. (3) IPL VORTAC is in Los Angeles Center Julian Sector, frequency 133.4.

8059. (1) VOR display indicates flight has not reached the IPL 295° radial southbound, and the tail of the RMI needle indicates the 025 radial. This position is left of course and approaching Warne intersection.

8060. (4) Distance covered is 39 NM in 15 minutes, groundspeed is 156 KTS. Set groundspeed under grommet, place wind dot at 190 (KTS TAS) and 9° left correction. Rotate ring until wind dot is under true index. Wind speed is determined by subtracting the groundspeed (156 KTS) from the number under the wind dot (199 KTS). Magnetic wind direction is read under true index. For true winds add 14° variation, true wind is 47°.

8061. (1) IFR EOG #8. The Minimum Crossing Altitude (MCA) is the minimum altitude at which certain radio facilities or intersections must be crossed in specified directions of flight. The ⬦ flag denotes a minimum crossing altitude on the low altitude enroute chart.

Bosun Intersection has an MCA flag. The crossing restriction is specified below the intersection as 5,200' V66 eastbound.

8062. (4) IFR EOG #39. This symbol ▷ indicates a localizer and or ILS Procedure is available. No additional ATC function is provided by the facility. In contrast, this symbol ▷ indicates that the localizer has an ATC function in addition to provide course guidance for an ILS or LOC approach.

8063. (3) FAR 61.51. An instrument flight instructor may log as instrument flight time that time during which he acts as instrument flight instructor in actual instrument weather conditions.

8064. (3) FAR 61.51. INSTRUMENT FLIGHT TIME. A pilot may log as instrument flight time only that time during which he operates the aircraft solely by reference to instruments, under actual or simulated instrument flight conditions. Each entry must include the place and type of each instrument approach completed, and the name of the safety pilot for each simulated instrument flight.

8065. (3) FAR 61.51. INSTRUMENT FLIGHT TIME. A pilot may log as instrument flight time only that time during which he operates the aircraft solely by reference to instruments, under actual or simulated instrument flight conditions. Each entry must include the place and type of each instrument approach completed, and the name of the safety pilot for each simulated instrument flight.

8066. (2) FAR 91.21. No person may operate a civil aircraft in simulated instrument flight unless an appropriately rated pilot occupies the other control seat as a safety pilot.

8067. (4) AC 61-27C. The sensations which lead to illusions during instrument flight conditions are normal perceptions experienced by normal individuals. These undesirable sensations cannot be completely prevented, but they can and must be ignored or sufficiently suppressed by developing absolute reliance upon what the fight instruments are telling us about the attitude of our aircraft.

8068. (3) IFR EOG #33. The information given in the illustrations and sample test items can be remembered as follows:

No landings permitted short of displaced threshold lights.

No aircraft operations permitted short of displaced threshold lights, if edge-of-runway lights (white or colored) are absent.

Takeoffs permitted in area short of displaced threshold lights if edge-of-runway lights appear as —
1. red, when takeoff is toward visible displaced threshold lights.
2. white (normal), and no displaced threshold is visible (due to 180° obscuration of lights).

TAXIING ONLY — permitted in area short of displaced threshold lights, if edge-of-runway lights appear as blue (taxiways and runway areas designated as taxiways are bounded by blue lights).

8069. (2)

LEG	WIND		DIST.	G.S.	TIME
STL — FAM	290	27	72	179	24:12
FAM — MWA	290	27	58	188	18:31
			130		42:43

8070. (1) Pressure altitude is 7,000', temperature –6°C. Density altitude under these conditions is 6,140'. Set pressure altitude opposite temperature in degree Celsius. Read density altitude at D.A. arrow. Six thousand is the closest answer choice.

8071. (1) Pressure altitude 7,000', temperature –6°C, TAS 165 KTS. Under these conditions, CAS is 151 KTS. Set pressure altitude opposite temperature in degrees Celsius, read CAS under 165 knot TAS (outer scale).

8072. (2) AIM. The symptoms of hyperventilation subside within a few minutes after the rate and depth of breathing are consciously brought back under control. The buildup of carbon dioxide in the body can be hastened by controlling breathing in and out of a paper bag held over the nose and mouth.

8073. (2) AIM. In darkness, vision becomes more sensitive to light, a process called dark adaptation. Although exposure to total darkness for at least 30 minutes is required for complete dark adaptation, the pilot can achieve a moderate degree of dark adaptation within 20 minutes under dim red cockpit lighting. Since red light severely distorts colors, especially on aeronautical charts, and can cause serious difficulty in focusing the eyes on objects inside the aircraft, its use is advisable only where optimum outside night vision capability is necessary. Any degree of dark adaptation is lost within a few seconds of viewing a bright light.

8074. (3) AC 61-27C. .... become proficient in the use of flight instruments and rely upon them. Sight is the only reliable sense during instrument flight.

8075. (4) AIM, AC 61-27C. Illusions that lead to spatial disorientation are created by information received from our motion sensing system, located in each inner ear. In flight, the system may be stimulated by motion of the aircraft alone, or in combination with head and body movement. Sight is the only reliable sense when flying solely by reference to flight instruments.

8076. (4) AC 61-27C. The sensations which lead to illusions during instrument flight conditions are normal perceptions experienced by normal individuals. These undesirable sensations cannot be completely prevented, but they can and must be ignored or sufficiently suppressed by developing absolute reliance upon what the flight instruments are telling us about the attitude of our aircraft.

8077. (1) FAR 61.51. INSTRUMENT FLIGHT TIME. A pilot may log as instrument flight time only that time during which he operates the aircraft solely by reference to instruments, under actual or simulated instrument flight conditions. Each entry must include the place and type of each instrument approach completed, and the name of the safety pilot for each simulated instrument flight.

8078. (3) ACL. The arrow ⟶▷ indicates that Tonto intersection is a DME fix off PHX VORTAC. If DME equipped and at an altitude sufficient to ensure adequate navigational signal coverage (the MEA), DME may be used to identify Tonto intersection.

8079. (3) AIM, ACL. ⌐ denotes a VOR changeover point. Mileage is given to radio aids.

8080. (1) IFR EOG. The left VOR display indicates that our position is left (west) of course. The right VOR display indicates that we have passed Tonto intersection northbound. Be careful to note the TO flag on the Prescott VOR. The right VOR display indicates that we are north of the 121 radial and have passed the intersection.

8081. (1) AC 91-43. If the ram air input plus the drain hole is blocked, the pressure is trapped in the system and the airspeed indicator may react as an altimeter.

8082. (2) AC 61-27C. For any increase in groundspeed, the rate of descent must also increase in order to maintain the same glideslope.

8083. (4) FAR 91.81. Where the current altimeter setting cannot be obtained, the altimeter should be set to field elevation.

8084. (3) AIM. "Stop Altitude Squawk" — turn off altitude reporting switch, or discontinue Mode C.

8085. (3) Activate Mode C automatic altitude reporting if so equipped.

8086. (4) AIM Para. 12. Compass locators transmit two letter identification groups. The outer locator transmits the first two letters of the localizer identification group, and the middle locator transmits the last two letters of the localizer identification group.

8087. (4) AIM Para. 12. Compass locators transmit two letter identification groups. The outer locator transmits the first two letters of the localizer identification group, and the middle locator transmits the last two letters of the localizer identification group.

8088. (X) FAA Deletion.

8089. (1) AIM Paras. 12, 13. An LDA is of comparable utility and accuracy to a localizer but is not part of a complete ILS. The LDA usually provides a more precise approach course than the SDF, which may have a course width of 6 or 12 degrees. The LDA is not aligned with the runway.

8090. (1) AIM Paras. 12, 13. An LDA is of comparable utility and accuracy to a localizer but is not part of a complete ILS. The LDA usually provides a more precise approach course than the SDF, which may have a course width of 6 or 12 degrees. The LDA is not aligned with the runway.

8091. (2) AIM, AC 61-27C. The SDF signal emitted from the transmitter is either 6° or 12° wide as necessary to provide maximum flyability and optimum course quality.

8092. (3) AIM, AC 61-27C. The SDF course may not be aligned with the runway and the course may be wider.

8093. (4) FAR 91.87. "An airplane approaching to land on a runway served by a visual approach slope indicator, shall maintain an altitude at or above the glideslope until a lower altitude is necessary for a safe landing." This includes an airplane that is making an ILS approach when the glideslope fails and the pilot has the VASI system in sight. See also FAR 91.116, visual references for the intended runway.

8094. (3) AIM Para. 41. 2-bar VASI (4 light units shown).

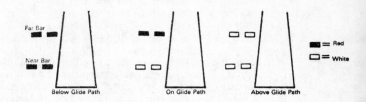

When on the glide path the pilot will see red-over-white. As the airplane levels off and departs the airport, it flys through the transition zone for the far bars. The far bars will turn from red to white, and the airplane will be above the glide path.

8095. (2) AIM Para. 42. Tri-color visual approach slope indicators normally consist of a single light unit projecting a three-color visual approach path into the final approach area of the runway upon which the indicator is installed. The below glide path indication is red, the above glide path indication is amber, and the on glide path indication is green. These types of indicators have a useful range of approximately one-half to one mile during the day and up to five miles at night depending upon the visibility conditions.

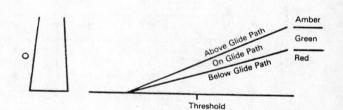

8096. (3) AIM Para. 41. The VASI is a system of lights so arranged to provide visual descent guidance information during the approach to a runway. These lights are visible from 3-5 miles during the day and up to 20 miles or more at night. The visual glide path of the VASI provides safe obstruction clearance within plus or minus 10 degrees of the extended runway centerline and to 4 NM from the runway threshold. Descent, using the VASI, should not be initiated until the aircraft is visually aligned with the runway. Lateral course guidance is provided by the runway or runway lights.

8097. (3) AIM Para. 42. Tri-color visual approach slope indicators normally consist of a single light unit projecting a three-color visual approach path into the final approach area of the runway upon which the indicator is installed. The below glide path indication is red, the above glide path indication is amber, and the on glide path indication is green. These types of indicators have a useful range of approximately one-half to one mile during the day and up to five miles at night depending upon the visibility conditions.

8098. (4) AC 90-1A. "The MAPs are different for the complete ILS and for the localizer only approach. The MAP for the ILS is at the decision height (DH) while the "localizer only" MAP is over the (straight-in) runway threshold. In some non-precision procedures, the pilot determines when he is at the MAP by timing from the final approach fix. The distance from the FAF to MAP and time and speed table are found below the aerodrome sketch."

8099. (2) IAP. The note in the profile sketch indicates that at the LOM the minimum altitude from Parmo Int. is 4,200 feet. The MDA for the S-LOC IOR localizer only approach is 3,120 feet.

8100. (1) Appendix 2 Excerpt Part 23. "The number feet per minute is obtained by multiplying the square of the number of knots by .027."

$$62 \times 62 = 3,844$$

$$3844 \times .027 = 103.788$$

Round 103.788 to 104.

8101. (2) Appendix 2 Excerpt Part 23. "The number feet per minute is obtained by multiplying the square of the number of knots by .027."

8102. (2) Appendix 2 Excerpt Part 23. "The number feet per minute is obtained by multiplying the square of the number of knots by .027."

$$63 \times 63 = 3,969$$

$$3,969 \times .027 = 107.163$$

Round 107.163 to 107.

8103. (4) Appendix 2, FAR Part 23. Using the excerpt from Part 23 in the appendix, note 23.67(a) is for reciprocating engines more than 6,000 Lbs. 23.67(b) is for reciprocating engines less than 6,000 Lbs. 23.67(b)(2) defines our airplane which has a V_{SO} of 61 KTS or less and must only be able to determine the steady-rate-of-climb.

8104. (1) Appendix 2 Excerpt Part 23. "For each airplane with a stalling speed of 61 knots of less, the steady rate of climb speed at 5,000 feet must be determined ..." There is no minimum rate of climb that must be maintained, only that the rate of climb be determined.

8105. (1) AIM Para. 14. The MLS provides precision navigation guidance for exact alignment and descent of aircraft on approach to and landing on a runway. It provides azimuth and elevation angle guidance and range information — all of which is interpreted by the aircraft receiver to determine the aircraft's position.

The system may be divided functionally into five parts:

1. Approach azimuth angle guidance.
2. Back azimuth angle guidance.
3. Approach elevation angle guidance.
4. Range guidance.
5. Data communications.

8106. (4) AIM Para. 14. The azimuth coverage extends:
1. Laterally, at least 40 degrees on either side of the runway.
2. In elevation, up to an angle of 15 degrees — and to at least 20,000 feet.
3. In range, to a distance of at least 20 NM.

8107. (3) AIM Para. 14. The front azimuth provides coverage as follows:
1. Laterally, at least 40 degrees on either side of the runway.
2. In elevation, up to an angle of 15 degrees — and to at least 20,000 feet.
3. In range, to a distance of at least 20 NM.

The back azimuth provides coverage as follows:
1. Laterally, at least 40 degrees on either side of the runway.
2. In elevation, up to an angle of 15 degrees.
3. In range, to a distance of at least 7 NM from the runway stop end.

8108. (2) AIM Para. 14. Elevation coverage is provided in the approach region throughout the same volume of airspace as the azimuth guidance signals:
1. In elevation, to at least +15 degrees.
2. Laterally, 40 degrees on either side of the runway.
3. In range, to a distance of at least 20 NM.

For the back azimuth, the actual coverage will normally be the same as for the approach azimuth.

8109. (3) AIM Para. 15. The identification consists of a three letter Morse Code identifier preceded by the Morse Code for "M" (- -) (e.g., M—STP). The "M" will distinguish this system from ILS which is preceded by the Morse Code for "I" (..) (e.g., I-STP).

8110. (1) AIM Para. 14. This question is most likely refering to the microwave landing system. The maximum height AGL for azimuth angle coverage is 20,000 feet.

8111. (1) KFC 200 Pilot's Guide. "FD" indicates the flight director is in use. "ALT" is altitude hold which will be effective until glideslope intercept. "AP" means the autopilot is engaged. "APPR" and "CPLD" indicate that the localizer has been captured.

8112. (2) KFC 200 Pilot's Guide. "FD" and "AP" indicate that the flight director and autopilot are engaged. "APPR," "CPLD" and "GS" indicate that the localizer and glideslope have been captured.

8113. (4) KFC 200 Pilot's Guide. Depression of the go-around switch during an approach cancels the existing flight director modes and engages the go-around (GA) mode. A wings-level and pitch-up command is displayed by the FCI. "FD" and "GA" will be illuminated on the annunciator panel.

8114. (3) KFC 200 Pilot's Guide. The altitude hold mode is cancelled by automatic glideslope capture, selection of go-around mode, disengaging ALT function, or selection of FD to "OFF."

8115. (2) KFC 200 Pilot's Guide. The HDG mode is cancelled when NAV or APPR coupling occurs or when FD mode is selected to off.

8116. (1) KFC 200 Pilot's Guide. When the flight director mode is activated the FCI command V-bar will appear and provide the pilot with steering commands to maintain wings level and the pitch attitude that existed.

8117. (1) KFC 200 Pilot's Guide. Depression of the go-around switch during an approach cancels the existing flight director modes and engages the go-around (GA) mode. A wings-level and pitch-up command is displayed by the FCI. "FD" and "GA" will be illuminated on the annunciator panel.

8118. (4) KFC 200 Pilot's Guide. The "FD" and "HDG" modes will track the heading selected with the "BUG" on the panel. The "NAV" mode instructs the system to capture and track the course selected on the course pointer.